DORDT INFORMATION SERVICES

3 6520 0055824 /

D1029468

# THE GEOPHYSIOLOGY
# OF AMAZONIA

# WILEY SERIES IN CLIMATE AND THE BIOSPHERE

**Edited by Michael H. Glantz**

THE GEOPHYSIOLOGY OF AMAZONIA: VEGETATION AND CLIMATE
INTERACTIONS
Robert E. Dickinson   Editor

# THE GEOPHYSIOLOGY OF AMAZONIA
## VEGETATION AND CLIMATE INTERACTIONS

Robert E. Dickinson, Editor

A Wiley-Interscience Publication
JOHN WILEY & SONS
New York   Chichester   Brisbane   Toronto   Singapore

for THE UNITED NATIONS UNIVERSITY

Copyright © 1987 by The United Nations University
Published by John Wiley & Sons, Inc.

All rights reserved. Published simultaneously in Canada.

Reproduction or translation of any part of this work
beyond that permitted by Section 107 or 108 of the
1976 United States Copyright Act without the permission
of the copyright owner is unlawful. Requests for
permission or further information should be addressed to
the Permissions Department, John Wiley & Sons, Inc.

*Library of Congress Cataloging-in-Publication Data:*
The Geophysiology of Amazonia.

(Wiley series in climate and biosphere)
Results of the International Conference on Climatic,
Biotic, and Human Interactions in the Humid Tropics with
Emphasis on the Vegetation and Climate Interactions in
Amazonia, convened by the United Nations University at
The Instituto de Pesquisas Espaciais in São José dos
Campos, Brazil, Feb. 25–Mar. 1, 1985.
Includes bibliographies and index.
1. Amazon River Region—Climate—Congresses.
2. Vegetation and climate—Amazon River Region—
Congresses. 3. Biogeochemical cycles—Amazon River
Region—Congresses. I. Dickinson, Robert E. (Robert
Earl) 1940–     . II. United Nations University.
III. International Conference on Climatic, Biotic, and
Human Interactions in the Humid Tropics with Emphasis
on the Vegetation and Climatic Interactions in Amazonia
(1985: Instituto de Pesquisas Espaciais, São José dos
Campos, São Paulo, Brazil) IV. Series.
QC988.A66G46  1986      551.6981'1      86-11015
ISBN 0-471-84511-6

Printed in the United States of America

10  9  8  7  6  5  4  3  2  1

# Contributors

Peter Bunyard
The Ecologist
Camelford, United Kingdom

Ralf Conrad
Max-Planck Institute for Chemistry
Mainz, Federal Republic of
   Germany

Paul J. Crutzen
Max-Planck Institute for Chemistry
Mainz, Federal Republic of
   Germany

Robert E. Dickinson
National Center for Atmospheric
   Research
Boulder, Colorado

Philip M. Fearnside
National Institute for Research in
   the Amazon
Manaus, Amazonia, Brazil

B. S. Ghuman
International Institute of Tropical
   Agriculture
Ibadan, Nigeria

Ann Henderson-Sellers
University of Liverpool
Liverpool, United Kingdom

Robert C. Harriss
NASA Langley Research Center
Hampton, Virginia

Rattan Lal
International Institute of Tropical
   Agriculture
Ibadan, Nigeria

Patrick Lavelle
Laboratoire de Zoologie
Ecole Normale Supérieure
Paris, France

James E. Lovelock
Coombe Mill
Cornwall, United Kingdom

Luiz C. B. Molion
Institute for Space Research
São José dos Campos, Brazil

Scott A. Mori
New York Botanical Garden
Bronx, New York

JAN PAEGLE
University of Utah
Salt Lake City, Utah

GHILLEAN T. PRANCE
New York Botanical Garden
Bronx, New York

MARIA DE NAZARÉ GOÉS RIBEIRO
National Institute for Research in
    the Amazon
Manaus, Amazonia, Brazil

JEFFREY E. RICHEY
University of Washington
Seattle, Washington

ENEAS SALATI
Center for Nuclear Energy and
    Agriculture
University of São Paulo
São Paulo, Brazil

JESUS MARDEN DOS SANTOS
Institute for Space Research
São José dos Campos, Brazil

WOLFGANG SEILER
Max-Planck Institute for Chemistry
Mainz, Federal Republic of
    Germany

PIERS J. SELLERS
University of Maryland
College Park, Maryland

JAGADISH SHUKLA
University of Maryland
College Park, Maryland

HASSAN VIRJI
National Science Foundation
Washington, District of Columbia

# Foreword

This volume is the result of a collective effort by a diverse group of scientists to better comprehend the current knowledge of the natural environment of an ecological zone—Amazonia—from the viewpoint of the science of *geophysiology*. Geophysiology, as James Lovelock has conceived it, deals with the functions, processes, and phenomena of a planetary-scale system composed of the biosphere and its support elements, principally the hydrosphere, upper lithosphere, and atmosphere, or any of its regional components. Of particular importance are the processes and mechanisms of interaction among the many elements of the system.

Improved understanding of the interactions between the climate, biota, and hydrological and soil substrates in the humid tropics on one hand and the impacts of human activity on the natural systems on the other is the focus of a project of the United Nations University (UNU). This Project on Climatic, Biotic, and Human Interactions in the Humid Tropics is a part of the University's efforts to tackle the complex problem of reducing environmental degradation while simultaneously satisfying the development needs and aspirations of populations in the humid tropics. The humid tropics was selected as the project's area of emphasis for several reasons:

- The suspected critical importance of the tropics to the global climate
- The paucity of knowledge about this zone, relative to knowledge about other ecological zones
- The extreme complexity of the tropics as a natural ecological system
- The alarmingly high rate of conversion currently taking place in an ecological zone that is so poorly known but has such potential importance

- The poor rate of success in converting tropical forest for sustainable agricultural utilization, and
- The food, raw material, and space needs of an expanding population aspiring to an increased standard of living on the fringes of the tropical forests

A major activity of the UNU project is to assemble leading scientists from a broad range of relevant disciplines in meetings, each focused on a topic of current interest relating to these interactions in the humid tropics. This book is the result of the first of these meetings, the International Conference on Climatic, Biotic and Human Interactions in the Humid Tropics with Emphasis on the Vegetation and Climate Interactions in Amazonia, convened by the United Nations University at the Instituto de Pesquisas Espaciais in São José dos Campos, Brazil, from February 25 to March 1, 1985.

This meeting was organized with expert guidance of the Conference Steering Committee composed of the following members:

Edward S. Ayensu, Smithsonian Institution, United States

William C. Clark, International Institute for Applied Systems Analysis, Austria

Paul J. Crutzen, Max-Planck-Institut für Chemie, Federal Republic of Germany

Robert E. Dickinson, National Center for Atmospheric Research, United States

James E. Lovelock, Coombe Mill Experimental Station, United Kingdom

Antonio Divino Moura, Instituto de Pesquisas Espaciais, Brazil

Sanga Sabhasri, Ministry of Science and Technology, Thailand

The UNU gratefully acknowledges the valuable assistance of the Committee and particularly of Robert E. Dickinson, who so competently undertook the task of editing this volume, Antonio Divino Moura, who so graciously organized and was host to the Conference in Brazil, and James E. Lovelock, who has so kindly guided the UNU Project from its inception.

The University is grateful to Nelson A. Parada, the Director of the Instituto de Pesquisas Espaciais, and the Instituto staff for their valuable contributions to the Conference, and to the U.S. National Science Foundation, which through the good offices of Hassan Virji provided financial support for many Conference participants.

WALTER SHEARER
*Senior Program Officer*
*United Nations University*

*Tokyo, Japan*
*July 1986*

# Preface to the Series

The Climate and the Biosphere series focuses on the interaction of atmospheric processes and the biosphere. In recent years there has been a growing awareness of the extent to which atmospheric processes affect ecological systems and society. Human activities, such as deforestation and the burning of fossil fuels, have likewise directly or indirectly modified the atmosphere. Changes in the atmospheric processes, in turn, affect ecological processes and societal activities.

Several scientific issues involving the atmosphere have been identified in the past as being crucial to society. Each of these has become a major concern to a set of scientists and policymakers not only in the United States but in other developed as well as developing countries. They include:

- Nuclear winter
- El Niño-Southern Oscillation phenomenon
- Carbon dioxide increases, trace gas production and their effects on global atmospheric temperatures and ultimately on rainfall regimes
- Stratospheric ozone depletion
- The effects of different land-use practices (overgrazing, irrigation, deforestation, groundwater depletion) on atmospheric processes (especially on climatic elements such as temperature and precipitation)
- Climate modification schemes in theory and in practice
- The causes of persistent and prolonged drought in Africa and other drought-prone regions

Scientific research continually discovers and confirms, modifies, or rejects theories about the interactive mechanisms between the climate and the biosphere. Climate and the Biosphere is an important area of concern not only to the scientific community but to policymakers as well, because only with a proper understanding of these interactions can human activities be modified to mitigate or avert adverse interactions while selectively reinforcing the positive ones.

The series is intended to encompass different methodologies and disciplines. It will focus on the interactions between the atmosphere and various other elements of the broadly defined biosphere, including societies.

MICHAEL H. GLANTZ

# Preface

The region of the Amazon has been one of intense popular interest and concern, both for the countries of South America and for the industrialized countries of the Northern Hemisphere. Many of us have enjoyed some of the television series on this region such as that by Jacques Cousteau. I am reminded every morning of the Amazon by my young son, who brings to breakfast three stuffed toy parrots for company.

In spite of their popular appeal, the Amazon region and moist tropical regions in general are scientifically poorly understood because they have received comparatively little attention. Some progress has been made in studying their meteorology, hydrology, climate, soils, biology, ecology, paleontology, biogeography, biogeochemistry, forestry, and agriculture. Yet the resources devoted to research in these areas are meager indeed compared to those devoted to the study of temperate-latitude problems such as the effects of acid rain on Europe and North America. Furthermore, interdisciplinary efforts to follow the linkages among these different subjects are almost nonexistent.

Many of the more accessible tropical forests have now largely disappeared under the pressures of human exploitation, but at least half of the world's tropical forests and much of the Amazon remain in a practically undisturbed state. With the current rapid development in the Amazon and other tropical forests, many of these primary forests may be replaced in the next few decades by other land uses, in many cases by impoverished secondary forests, since some of the forest species are effective successional pioneers. Many severe environmental consequences of deforestation and other environmental transformations in the humid tropics are already recognized.

These alone would justify immediate actions to control irreversible degradation. Even more severe or more widespread consequences may lurk in the future as a result of processes still virtually unstudied by scientists. Especially important may be the interactions between changing climate systems and tropical vegetation on space scales corresponding to regions and nations or larger. To address these interactions, the United Nations University Project on Climatic, Biotic, and Human Interactions in the Humid Tropics, through its Steering Committee, organized speakers and topics to treat subjects of potential relevance to such interactions, and convened an interdisciplinary group of some of the most knowledgeable scientists from the Amazonian countries and elsewhere.

The conference was held at the Brazilian Institute for Space Studies (INPE) at São José dos Campos, Brazil, and was organized and supported by the United Nations University. The papers presented at the conference and the accompanying discussion and workshop form the basis of this book: *The Geophysiology of Amazonia*. The workshop made a first attempt to confront the possibility of a dramatic level of development in the Amazon region over the next half century and to provide a menu of actions needed to minimize damage to regional and global systems and to make utilization of forested lands sustainable.

ROBERT E. DICKINSON

*Boulder, Colorado*
*October 1986*

# Acknowledgments

Many people contributed to this book. Nancy Mielinis edited several drafts and made numerous improvements. Jennifer Robinson's suggestions enhanced several chapters. Paul Alvim, Therezinha Bastos, Edith Brown-Weiss, Robert Chervin, William Clark, Paul Crutzen, Philip Fearnside, Enrique Forero, Ann Henderson-Sellers, Jeffrey Kiehl, Volker Kirchhoff, James Lovelock, J. Marden dos Santos, Scott Mori, Carlos Nobre, Francisca Pinheiro, Venkatachalam Ramaswamy, William Reifsnyder, Cynthia Rosenzweig, Walter Shearer, Starley Thompson, Michel Verstraete, and Maureen Wilson also reviewed parts of the manuscript and offered some major suggestions for improvements to various parts of the text.

Ann Modahl and other National Center for Atmospheric Research (NCAR) staff did an excellent job in typing several drafts of most of the manuscript and contributed helpful editing suggestions. Support was also provided by the NCAR Graphics Department.

R.E.D.

# Contents

## I. CLIMATE, VEGETATION, AND HUMAN INTERACTIONS IN THE AMAZON

1. **Introduction to Vegetation and Climate Interactions in the Humid Tropics**    3
   Robert E. Dickinson

2. **Geophysiology: A New Look at Earth Science**    11
   James E. Lovelock

3. **Climate, Natural Vegetation, and Soils in Amazonia: An Overview**    25
   Jesus Marden dos Santos
   *Comments by Robert E. Dickinson*

4. **Causes of Deforestation in the Brazilian Amazon**    37
   Philip M. Fearnside
   *Comments by Roger Revelle*
   *Reply to comments by Philip M. Fearnside*

5. **Dam Building in the Tropics: Some Environmental and Social Consequences**    63
   Peter Bunyard

6. **Species Diversity, Phenology, Plant–Animal Interactions, and Their Correlation with Climate, as Illustrated by the Brazil Nut Family (Lecythidaceae)**    69
   Scott A. Mori and Ghillean T. Prance

7. Climate Change in the Humid Tropics,
   Especially Amazonia, Over the Last Twenty
   Thousand Years                                          91
   Robert E. Dickinson and Hassan Virji

## II. BIOGEOCHEMICAL CYCLES IN THE TROPICS

8. Role of the Tropics in Atmospheric Chemistry          107
   Paul J. Crutzen
   *Comments by Steven C. Wofsy*

9. Contribution of Tropical Ecosystems to the
   Global Budgets of Trace Gases, Especially
   $CH_4$, $H_2$, CO, and $N_2O$                          133
   Wolfgang Seiler and Ralf Conrad
   *Comments by Ralph J. Cicerone*

10. Influence of a Tropical Forest on Air
    Chemistry                                             163
    Robert C. Harriss

11. Biological Processes and Productivity of Soils
    in the Humid Tropics                                  175
    Patrick Lavelle
    *Comments by Rattan Lal*

12. Effects of Deforestation on Soil Properties
    and Microclimate of a High Rain Forest in
    Southern Nigeria                                      225
    B. S. Ghuman and Rattan Lal

13. Element Cycling in the Amazon Basin:
    A Riverine Perspective                                245
    Jeffrey E. Richey and Maria de Nazaré Goés Ribeiro

## III. CLIMATE, MICROMETEOROLOGY, AND THE HYDROLOGICAL CYCLE IN THE MOIST TROPICS

14. Micrometeorology of an Amazonian Rain
    Forest                                                255
    Luiz C. B. Molion
    *Comments by William E. Reifsnyder*

15. The Forest and the Hydrological Cycle                273
    Eneas Salati
    *Comments by John C. Rodda*

16. Modeling Effects of Vegetation on Climate            297
    Piers J. Sellers
    *Comments by Keith G. McNaughton*
    *Reply to Comments by Piers J. Sellers*

## IV. TROPICAL CLIMATE AND GENERAL CIRCULATION: ITS SUSCEPTIBILITY TO HUMAN INTERVENTION

17. **Interactions Between Convective and Large-Scale Motions Over Amazonia** 347
   Jan Paegle
   *Comments by John M. Wallace*

18. **On the Dynamic Climatology of the Amazon Basin and Associated Rain-Producing Mechanisms** 391
   Luiz C. B. Molion

19. **General Circulation Modeling and the Tropics** 409
   Jagadish Shukla
   *Comments by James E. Hansen*

20. **Effects of Change in Land Use on Climate in the Humid Tropics** 463
   Ann Henderson-Sellers
   *Comments by John S. Perry*

## V. CONFERENCE DISCUSSIONS AND FUTURE DEVELOPMENT: SCENARIO WORKSHOP

**Foreword to the Conference** 499
Nelson de Jesus Parada

**The Conference** 501

**Scenario Workshop and Recommendations** 505

**Appendix** 517

**Index** 521

# PART I

# CLIMATE, VEGETATION, AND HUMAN INTERACTIONS IN THE AMAZON

Many of the problems that now confront us require a global and inter-disciplinary view of Earth's environmental systems. Current large changes occurring in the areas of tropical rain forests, in general, and the Amazon Basin, in particular, may threaten these systems, but our scientific framework is yet inadequate to make such judgments (Chapter 1). Lovelock (Chapter 2) suggests that development of the required framework may lead to a new discipline, "geophysiology," a science directed toward procedures for the diagnosis and prevention of plan-etary maladies. The Amazon region is vast, containing nearly half of Earth's tropical moist forest, and has great biological diversity. The dis-tribution of plant communities depends not only on rainfall but also on soil characteristics (Marden dos Santos, Chapter 3). Rainfall occurs largely in convective storms and is affected by many factors including reevaporation by the forests.

A complex network of immediate and indirect social and economic forces promotes the rapid deforestation of the Amazon in Brazil (Fearn-side, Chapter 4). Government and rampant inflation have provided many incentives to accelerate deforestation in Amazonia, including generous tax write-offs and negative real interest loans. Government policies for land tenure and reserve protection also affect deforestation. Increasing road networks and land speculation have encouraged forest removal in a positive-feedback relationship. Agriculture and grazing with the cur-rent use systems only temporarily give reasonable yields before the land reverts to savanna or impoverished secondary forest. Increasing indus-trialization of the Amazon is applying additional pressures on the forest, including the harvesting of trees for charcoal and timber and the flood-ing of the forest by dams to provide hydroelectric power, the process highlighted by Bunyard (Chapter 5). Fearnside argues that the long-term benefit of the Amazon's residents requires measures to slow and contain deforestation, using a sound understanding of the forces motivating deforestation and a clear definition of development goals. He suggests that, in view of the current pace of deforestation, such measures would have to be implemented quickly to be effective.

Tropical forest species are adapted to the current climate not only directly but also indirectly through the network of their interactions with

1

other plant and animal species. Mori and Prance (Chapter 6) discuss how species of the Brazil nut family depend on climate-linked processes of pollination and seed dispersal that could be disrupted by changes in the seasonality of rainfall or by changes in microclimatic conditions. Paleoclimatic evidence indicates more extended dry seasons in the Amazon during the last ice age and a concomitant near disappearance of the tropical forest (Dickinson and Virji, Chapter 7). Thus, if climate were to change into a regime of lesser and more seasonal rainfall, a widespread collapse of the tropical forest systems might occur. Without a better understanding of the geophysiology of Amazonia, we cannot judge whether or not some degree of deforestation or other human activities could lead to such a collapse. Subsequent sections of this book are intended to help begin the required framework.

# Chapter 1

# Introduction to Vegetation and Climate Interactions in the Humid Tropics

**Robert E. Dickinson**

Nations and peoples have for many centuries used, exploited, and often degraded their environment in their quests for food, fiber, energy, and sometimes amusement. Yet only in recent years have the *global* environmental systems that are fundamental to the habitability of the planet come under stress from the combination of advanced technologies and increases in the numbers and living standards of people.

Concern has been expressed that "We are moving beyond the acute, localized, and relatively simple environmental problems reversible at economically reasonable costs and on politically realistic time and space scales. We are moving into a period of chronic, global and extremely complex syndromes of ecological and economic interdependence. These emerging syndromes threaten to constrain and even reverse progress in human development. They will be manageable—if at all—only with a commitment of resources and a consistency of purpose that transcends normal cycles and boundaries of scientific research and political action" (Clark and Holling, 1985).

At the same time, scientists are recognizing that the physical, fluid dynamical, chemical, and biological processes of the oceans, atmosphere, and Earth's surface are coupled together in a closely linked system that requires "a global view, and a new effort to study the Earth and its living inhabitants as a tightly connected system of interacting parts—an endeavor in which scientific disciplines forsake their accustomed imperatives and serve as tools rather than ends in themselves. An effort so defined has no real precedent, for it would require not only the cooperation of nations but an intercourse and sharing between fields of study that are often seen as isolated and territorial . . . the need for action is so great as to warrant the mounting of a bold new program . . . to describe and understand the interactive physical, chemical, and biological processes that regulate the Earth's unique environment for life, the changes that are occurring in this system, and the manner in which they are influenced by human activities'' (NAS, 1986).

Various names are now being given to such proposed international programs for the study of these interlinked global systems, for example, *global habitability, geosphere–biosphere, global change,* or *Earth science system.* To recognize the strong connections with human systems and the need to focus on diagnosis and treatment of planetary ecological stresses, James Lovelock in Chapter 2 suggests the term *geophysiology.*

Having recognized the need for a holistic view of the global systems, we must, nevertheless, again revert to the reductionist approach of looking at individual pieces if we hope to make *scientific* progress. We must consider particular problems of global concern as, for example, the warming and resulting climate change and ecological stresses that are occurring as a result of increasing atmospheric concentrations of carbon dioxide and other trace gases (Dickinson and Cicerone, 1986) or the various threats to the ozone layer. In addition, we must consider individual geographical regions and their interactions with other parts of the global environment; this approach has been taken by the United Nations University (UNU) Project on Climatic, Biotic, and Human Interactions in the Humid Tropics.

## INTERACTIONS IN THE HUMID TROPICS

The UNU has been operating since 1975 to bring about a better understanding of the problems facing humankind and to contribute to the solution of these problems through the instruments of scholarship, research, advanced training, and the dissemination of knowledge. Its Project on the Climatic, Biotic, and Human Interactions in the Humid Tropics deals with the impact of large-scale human activities on the environment in such regions as the Amazon Basin, the central African tropical forests, and the rain forests of southeast Asia. The project was initially suggested to the UNU in 1982 by James Lovelock, who was and is concerned about the relationships between the degradation of regional ecosystems and global climatic conditions. He is disturbed by the possibility of degradation thresholds that, once exceeded, would lead to a catastrophic change in the climatic–biogeochemical systems. His current ideas on this subject are presented in Chapter 2 of this book. Some complex biological systems, such as the anchovy populations off the coast of Peru, have in the past collapsed in response to human pressures and climatic variations (e.g., Glantz and Thompson, 1981).

We are too ignorant of the relationships between the tropical biological systems and climate to anticipate such collapses or, for that matter, to anticipate any large-scale changes, detrimental or beneficial, that might occur as a result of human development in the tropics. The humid tropics, although

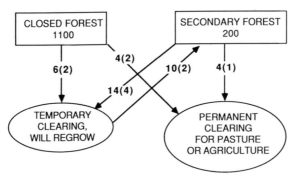

**FIGURE 1.** Tropical forests and their rates of conversion. The numbers in the boxes indicate cover in millions of hectares. About half of this forest is in Amazonia. The arrows indicate conversion processes, the numbers show the annual rates of conversion in million hectares (estimates for the Amazon are given in parentheses). The numbers are estimates for 1985, inferred from global data for the late 1970s (Melillo et al., 1985) and more recent information on Amazonia as given in various later chapters of this book. The numbers, although rather uncertain, illustrate the kinds of information needed to consider interactions between tropical forests and climate. Closed forest refers to either primary forests or those disturbed only by selective lumbering. Secondary forests are regrowth either for fallow or after being abandoned for pasture or agriculture.

largely neglected by the press and often given short shrift by research communities, encompasses as much biological activity and rainfall as the rest of the world combined. Our inattention to the tropics and to connections between biology and climate is such that drastic events can go almost unnoticed, as happened, for example, when 3 million hectares of tropical rain forest were damaged by fire in Kalimantan (Indonesian Borneo) in 1983 (Malingreau, Stephens, and Fellows, 1985).

Tropical forests have been disappearing rapidly or deteriorating biologically in the last several decades due to population pressures and nonsustainable resource utilization (Fig. 1). For example, much of the commercially valuable timber in the forests of southeast Asia has been harvested, and these forests have been made more accessible to human settlement and agriculture.

We have considerable evidence of the severe direct biological degradation that can result from careless use of forests, including the loss of countless species, many of potential commercial value (Myers, 1984). Severe erosion often follows forest removal, with drastic consequences both locally and in areas downstream, which suffer from the large increases in silt loads carried by rivers.

Most of the world's tropical forests are found in countries with many very poor people and rapidly growing populations. These countries are rightly concerned with providing their people with a decent standard of living and improving their quality of life. But the exploitation of natural resources must be made sustainable if their needs and aspirations and certainly those of

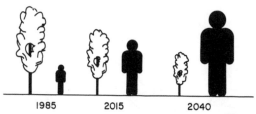

**FIGURE 2.** Comparison of possible growth of population and decrease of forests in the humid tropics. Population and forest cover are represented by the heights of the person and tree figures. Population in the humid tropics is indicated to grow at 2.3% per year to 2015 and at a rate of 1.6% per year from then to 2040. The forest cover is assumed to decline at a rate of 1% per year to 2015 and 1.6% per year to 2040. Sustainability requires both population and forest cover to stabilize at some level.

future generations are to be met (Fig. 2). Scientific research on tropical agriculture, agroforestry, and biological reserves has begun to give us some knowledge of how this can be done.

This book treats neither the problems of population growth in tropical countries nor the questions of utilization and degradation of biological resources, though such issues are always close at hand. Rather it attempts to bring together the current scientific knowledge that can contribute to a better understanding of the present and future interactions between the biological and climatic systems resulting from human activities; that is, it is concerned with the geophysiology of the tropics (see Fig. 3) and, in particular, the Amazon region.

## AMAZONIA

The Amazon Basin holds about half of the world's remaining tropical forest and, until recently, was little disturbed. Now there is a rapid thrust by the

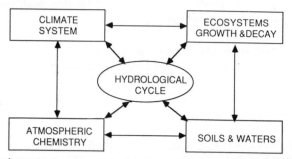

**FIGURE 3.** An important component of the geophysiology of the tropics is the hydrological cycle, which closely links the climate system, atmospheric chemistry, soils and waters, and ecosystem growth and decay. These systems are also closely coupled through energy exchange driven by solar radiation.

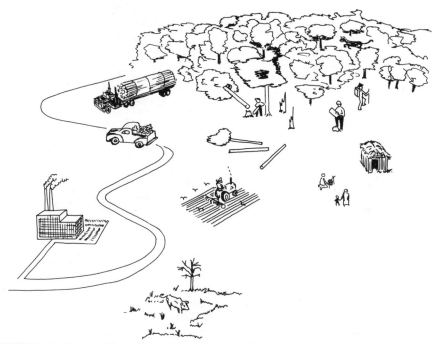

**FIGURE 4.** Tropical forests may either be utilized by mining the forest resources and converting them to other uses or through sustainable and nondestructive exploitation. Because of resource limits, only the latter approach will be available for inhabitants of the tropics a century from now.

countries of the Amazon Basin to exploit the natural resources in this region, as testified to by many recent scholarly and popular publications (e.g., Hecht, 1982; NAS, 1982; Moran, 1983; Kandell, 1984; Caufield, 1984; Sioli, 1984; Stone, 1985).

This book focuses on the Amazon region as the largest and perhaps the most important tropical forest region with regard to climatic and biotic interactions. The vegetation and climate systems of Amazonia are being modified by human activities (Fig. 4), particularly by cattle ranching, agriculture, and industrialization (large dams, mines, and mineral extraction). Such activities will continue and may accelerate. We must ask what are the possible future developmental paths of Amazonia and what might be their consequences for the geophysiology of Amazonia. The renewal and survival of the forest depend on a complex web of ecological processes such as pollination, seed ripening and dispersal, germination and seedling survival, competition, photosynthesis, and nutrient cycling. Which of these processes are especially vulnerable to disruption by forest removal and climate change? The current status of modeling forests has been reviewed by Shugart (1984).

The Amazon forests have many links to the atmosphere, soils, and rivers

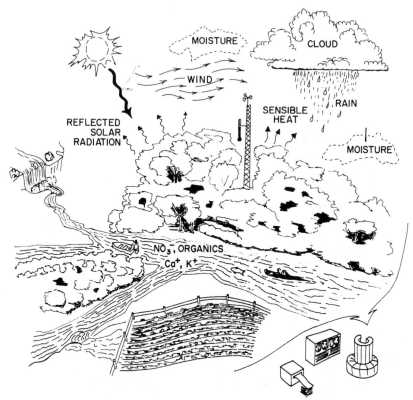

**FIGURE 5.** Scientific exploration of the linkages of tropical forests to atmosphere, soils, and rivers, as discussed in this book.

(Fig. 5). These links include the exchange of important trace gases, heat, and moisture with the atmosphere. Some trace gases, in particular methane and nitrous oxide, are products of biological processes and are already supplied in copious amounts from tropical forest environments. Others, such as ozone and nitric oxide, are products of industrial pollution and are found only in very low concentrations in the pristine tropical forests. Methane, nitrous oxide, and ozone all are important for global climate, and excess ozone along with acid rain could seriously stress forest vegetation in the future.

Some of the soils in Amazonia, for example, those along the flood plains of the white-water rivers, may have potential for agriculture. However, only by careful planning for their use is this potential likely to be realized fully and serious damage to other parts of the system avoided. Studies of the transfer of materials from the forest and soils to the rivers help to provide an integrated view of the impacts of human activities on the system.

The Amazon forests have a climate with a near constant temperature and heavy rainfall for most of the year. They may be more sensitive to changes in the length of the dry season than to changes in the annual rainfall amounts. Conversion of the forests to other uses changes soil moisture retention and fluxes of moisture and heat to the atmosphere. These flux changes modify regional climate and may also affect global climate. The scientific challenge is to relate forest conversion to climate changes using validated mathematical models. It is the task of national and international political processes to judge whether this climate change and the other environmental changes resulting from forest removal warrant actions, preemptive or remedial. This question is complicated by the possibility that the climate change—for example, lengthening of the dry season—may itself accelerate forest ecosystem declines and in doing so jeopardize attempts to preserve biological richness through establishment of reserves. The forest systems may, furthermore, be at risk because of global climate change associated with carbon dioxide and other trace gases, that is, they may experience in the next century a global warming up to several degrees, accompanied by intensification of evaporation and rainfall rates and possibly large shifts in regional and seasonal climate patterns (e.g., Dickinson and Cicerone, 1986).

The essays in this book address many aspects of the linkages between tropical forests and climate. They make clear that we cannot answer some of the most crucial questions. Will the forest climate system coevolve as plausibly suggested by Sioli (1984)? "The water cycles will be interrupted by lack of sufficient water vapor, when too much forest is destroyed. . . . The total annual rainfall will decrease and the seasonality of the rains will increase. . . . [This] will affect the structure and composition of the remaining forest. . . . Once a critical point has been reached an irreversible chain reaction will start." What role will deliberate and accidental fires play in such changes? Will disruptions of the Amazon and other tropical forests act through trace gases or the hydrological cycle to significantly modify global climate? What will be the effects of future global climate change on the tropical forests? The answers to such questions could have grave consequences for the inhabitants of tropical forests and perhaps of the globe.

The last two days of the conference were devoted to an attempt to treat such questions of future change in Amazonia. Several extreme scenarios were constructed for hypothetical future development, and the participants pondered the measures that would be needed to ameliorate the potential damage. The results of this workshop are summarized in Part V of this book.

## REFERENCES

Caufield, C., 1984. *In the Rainforest*, Knopf, New York.

Clark, W. C. and Holling, C. S., 1985. Sustainable development of the biosphere, human activities and global change, in T. F. Malone and J. G. Roederer, Eds., *Global Change*, Cambridge University Press, Cambridge, England.

Dickinson, R. E., and Cicerone, R. J., 1986. Future global warming from atmospheric trace gases. *Nature* **319**, 109–115.

Glantz, M. H. and Thompson, J. D., Eds., 1981. *Resource Management and Environmental Uncertainty: Lessons from Coastal Upwelling Fisheries*, Wiley, New York.

Hecht, S. B., Ed., 1982. *Amazonia: Agriculture and Land Use Research*, Proceedings of the CIAT Conference, 1980, Centro Internacional de Agricultura Tropical, Cali, Colombia.

Kandell, J., 1984. *Passage through Dorado*, Morrow, New York.

Malingreau, J. P., Stephens, G., and Fellows, L., 1985. Remote sensing of forest fires: Kalimantan and North Borneo in 1982–83. *Ambio* **14**, 314–321.

Melillo, J. M., Palm, C. A., Houghton, R. A., Woodwell, G. M., and Myers, N., 1985. A comparison of two recent estimates of disturbances in tropical forests, *Environ. Cons.* **12**, 37–40.

Moran, E. F., Ed., 1983. *The Dilemma of Amazonian Development*, Westview, Boulder, CO.

Myers, N., 1984. *The Primary Source: Tropical Forests and Our Future*, Norton, New York.

NAS, 1982. *Ecological Aspects of Development in the Humid Tropics*, Committee on Selected Biological Problems in the Humid Tropics, National Academy of Sciences, National Academy Press, Washington, DC.

NAS, 1986. *Global Change in the Geosphere-Biosphere*, U.S. Committee for an IGBP, National Academy of Sciences, National Academy Press, Washington, DC.

Shugart, H. H., 1984. *A Theory of Forest Dynamics. The Ecological Implications of Forest Succession Models*, Springer-Verlag, New York.

Sioli, H., 1984. Former and recent utilizations of Amazonia and their impact on the environment, in H. Sioli, Ed. *The Amazon: Limnology and Landscape Ecology of a Mighty Tropical River and Its Basin*, W. Junk, Dordrecht, The Netherlands.

Stone, R. D., 1985. *Dreams of Amazonia*, Viking Penguin, New York.

# Chapter 2

# Geophysiology: A New Look at Earth Science

**James E. Lovelock**

Few of us have avoided the experience of imagining at one time or another that we were the victims of some fatal but romantic disease. It usually happens after reading a medical textbook and identifying our minor symptoms with those described.

In the affluent parts of the world, society may be undergoing collectively the same experience. The difference is that the apparent hypochondria is about the world itself rather than about individual selves. The equivalent of the medical textbooks are the ubiquitous doom scenarios. There is no shortage of planetary ailments to identify with, from the psychosociological drama of Orwell's nightmare vision to nuclear winter, acid rain, and so on.

As in hypochondria, the problem is not that these global maladies are unreal but the uncertainty over whether the present symptoms are prodromal of disaster or whether they are no more than the growing pains of the world.

Intelligent hypochondriacs do not consult a biochemist or a molecular biologist about their worries; they go instead to a physician. A good physician knows that hypochondria often masks a real ailment quite different from the one imagined by the patient. Could it be that our very deep concern about the state of the world is a form of global hypochondria? If it is, then we might ask whether it is wise in such an event to seek only the advice of expert scientists like climatologists or biogeochemists. It could be that the real planetary malaise is beyond the understanding of their expertise. It may seem that we have no other options; the practice of planetary medicine does not yet exist.

Let us assume that there is some truth in the foregoing speculation and consider what then might be the next step to take. It might involve the establishment of the new profession of planetary medicine.

What would be the qualifications for such a profession? If the history of medicine is to be a guide, it will grow from guesses and empiricism. But early in the history of medicine, physiology—the systems science of individual humans—strongly influenced its further progress. The recognition by Paracelsus that "the poison is the dose" is a physiological enlightenment still to be discovered by those environmentalists who seek the unattainable and pointless zero for pollutants.

The discovery of the circulation by Harvey added further to the wisdom of medicine, as did meteorology to our understanding of Earth. The expert sciences of biochemistry and microbiology came much later, and it took a long time before the products of their new vision enhanced the practice of medicine.

The purpose of this chapter is to introduce geophysiology as a systems approach to Earth science. It is the essential theoretical basis for the putative profession of planetary medicine. In no way would geophysiology replace or lessen the importance of the established sciences; it is complementary to them.

This chapter will discuss the theoretical basis of geophysiology and conclude by considering how this approach might assist in the design of procedures for the diagnosis and prevention of the incipient maladies of the planet. The conclusions will be especially applicable to the humid tropics.

## THEORETICAL BASIS OF GEOPHYSIOLOGY

Notions that Earth was some kind of living system have a long history. In the last century Dumas and Boussingault described the cycling of elements like carbon and nitrogen between life and the environment and laid the foundations for the science of biogeochemistry. The first scientific expression of the idea that the sum of the biota might be more than just a catalog of species was that of Vernadsky (1945), who coined the term *biosphere* for the region of the planet where life could be found. This new science was extensively developed by Sillen (1966), Redfield (1958), and Hutchinson (1954) and most recently by Bolin and Cook (1983), McElroy (1983), Garrels, Lerman, and McKenzie (1976), Broecker (1980), and Whitfield (1981).

Geophysiology developed in the late 1960s as an unintentional by-product of the space exploration program of NASA. It arose during attempts to design experiments to detect life on other planets, particularly on Mars. For the most part, these experiments were geocentric and based on the notion of landing a miniaturized biological or biochemical laboratory on the planet and using it to recognize life by the well-known techniques available to life scientists on Earth. Hitchcock and Lovelock (1966) took the opposing view that not only were such experiments likely to fail because of their geocentricity but also that there was a more certain way of detecting planetary life, whatever its form might be. This alternative approach to life detection came from a systems view of planetary life. In particular, it suggests that if life can be taken to constitute a global entity, its presence would be revealed by a change in the chemical composition of the planet's atmosphere. The change in composition could be compared with that of the abiological steady state of a lifeless planet. The reasoning behind this idea was that the planetary biota would be obliged to use any mobile medium available to them as a source of essential nutrients and a sink for the disposal of the products of their metabolism. Such activity would render a planet with life as recognizably different from a lifeless one. At that time, there was a fairly detailed compositional analysis, from infrared astronomy, of the atmospheres of Mars and Venus, and it revealed both planets to have atmospheric compositions not far from chemical equilibrium. Therefore, they were probably lifeless. By contrast, Earth's atmosphere viewed in this way was seen to be far from equilibrium, with oxidizing and reducing gases coexisting in what was clearly an unstable state that was nevertheless maintained steady by life. In the infrared, Earth radiates its signature of life so clearly as to be recognizable from well outside the solar system. The success of this approach to life detection forced our attention back to Earth and to the nature of the system that could hold so unstable an atmosphere in a steady state that was even more remarkably just right for life.

In the early 1970s, Lynn Margulis and I (1974) introduced the Gaia hypothesis. It postulated Earth to be a self-regulating system comprising the biota and their environment and with the capacity to maintain the climate and chemical composition at a steady state favorable for life.

Most Earth scientists today would accept that the atmosphere is a biological product, and this is a tribute to the success of biogeochemistry. But most would disagree that the biota in any way "control" atmospheric composition or any of the important variables (such as global temperature and surface redox potential) that depend on the atmosphere. The principal objection to Gaia or the geophysiological approach is that it is teleological. That is, the regulation of climate or chemical composition on a planetary scale would require some kind of forecasting or clairvoyance on the part of the biota. I will now try to show that this objection is wrong and that geophysiological regulation requires neither foresight nor planning. It is in fact a simple consequence of Darwinian natural selection. The evolution of the species is not independent of the evolution of the environment. The two evolutionary processes are in fact tightly coupled. Life and its environment evolve together as a single system so that not only does the species that leaves the most progeny tend to inherit the environment but also the environment that favors the most progeny is itself sustained. What then is the mechanism of geophysiological regulation?

Let us accept for the moment that the biota can profoundly influence the environment. The converse is also self-evidently true; that is, organisms are affected by the environment. To take atmospheric composition as an example, plants and animals are obviously not only dependent on the oxygen,

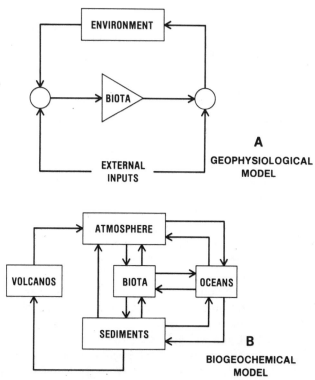

**FIGURE 1.** (*a*) Diagram drawn from control theory to illustrate as a single system the active feedback between the biota and its environment. The biota are represented as an amplifier connected to a sensor that recognizes any departure from the operating point of the system. Physical or chemical variables, such as temperature or oxygen concentration, coming from the environment or from external inputs, such as the sun or pollution, are summed and compared with the operating point of the system. If there is a difference, the biota respond by active feedback so as to oppose it and to keep the system in homeostasis. The system also has the capacity to evolve, thus moving the operating point to a new steady value. This form of systems evolution is called homeorhesis. (*b*) Diagram taken from biogeochemistry to illustrate the mass and energy transfer between the biota and its environment. In biogeochemistry, the system is treated as a set of linked but separate parts. A change in one part, say the atmosphere, can alter the conditions of another part, such as the biota or the oceans, but the feedback between them, whether negative or positive, is taken to be passive rather than active and responsive. In biogeochemical systems, the evolution of the biota and the evolution of the environment are usually considered as separate and uncoupled processes.

carbon dioxide, and nitrogen of the air but they also produce all three of these gases. In other words, life and its environment are two parts of a closely coupled system where these two components are arranged in a feedback loop (Fig. 1*a*). Perturbations of one will affect the other, and this in turn will feed back on the original change. The feedback may be negative and oppose the change or positive, that is, enhance it; but it will not in general

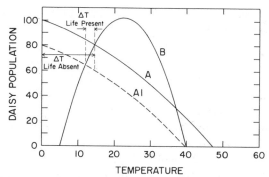

**FIGURE 2.** The effect of daisy cover on the mean temperature of Daisyworld (*A*) and the effect of temperature on the growth of daisies (*B*). In this example, the daisies are taken to be lighter in color than the bare planetary surface so that increasing daisy cover reflects more sunlight and so lowers the mean temperature. The left intersection of curves *A* and *B* is a stable equilibrium between daisies and temperature. The dashed curve ($A_1$) is drawn for a lower solar luminosity than with curve *A*. If the daisy cover did not respond to temperature, the difference in planetary temperature for the two solar luminosities would be *dT*, about 16°C. If, as is more normal, the daisies responded to the cooler sun by covering less of the planet, the temperature difference would be $dT_1$, about 2°C. This simple responsive coupling between life and its environment is the basis of geophysiological regulation.

be nonexistent. Geophysiological models are distinguished from the conventional models of biogeochemistry (Fig. 1*b*) by their amplified active feedback. As a consequence, they are more powerful and can adjust their operating points as the system evolves. Biogeochemical models are puny by comparison, and the operating point is commonly fixed by the chemical and physical constraints of the system.

What properties does this close coupling between life and its environment confer on the whole system? Does it explain the homeostasis that is observed? The difficulty is that the diagram (Fig. 1*a*) is much too simple; in reality, the biota and the environment are vastly complex entities, interconnected in multiple ways and there is hardly a single aspect of their interaction that can be confidently described by a mathematical equation. It occurred to me that a drastic simplification was needed; namely, reducing the environment to a single variable—temperature—and the biota to a single species—daisies. I first described Daisyworld in 1982, and I am indebted to my colleague Andrew Watson for the clear graphic way of expressing it (illustrated in Fig. 2).

## DAISYWORLD MODEL

Daisyworld is a cloudless planet with a negligible atmospheric greenhouse and bears life only in the form of daisies. To start with, let us assume that the daisies are white. Because they are lighter than the ground in which they grow, they tend to increase the albedo of their locality and as a consequence the surface is cooler than a comparable area of bare ground. Where the daisies cover a substantial proportion of the planetary surface, they will influence the mean surface temperature of the planet. The variation will be as illustrated by curve *A* in Fig. 2. The parallel dotted line shows how curve *A* might shift if there were a change in some external variable that influences planetary temperature. An example of such a variable is the output of radiant heat from Daisyworld's sun.

The daisies, like nearly all plant life, grow best over a restricted range of temperatures. The growth rate peaks near 20°C and falls to zero below 5 and above 40°C. As a function of temperature, the steady-state population of daisies will be as in curve *B* of Fig. 2. Curves *A* and *B* of Fig. 2 relate the temperature to the Daisyworld population at steady state, and the steady state of the whole system must be specified by the point of intersection of these two curves. In the example, it can be seen that there are two possible steady-state solutions. It turns out that the solution where the derivatives of the two curves have opposite signs is unconditionally stable, whereas the other solution is unstable. If the system is initialized at some arbitrary point, it will normally settle down at the stable solution.

What happens to this stable solution when some change of the external environment alters the planetary temperature? Suppose, for example, that the sun warms up, as our sun is said to be doing. If the Daisyworld population is artificially held constant, the planetary temperature will simply follow the change in heat output of the sun; there will be a much larger temperature change than if we allow the daisies to grow to their new natural steady state. In this new stable state, the Daisyworld population has changed so as to oppose the effects of a change in solar output.

Very few assumptions are made in this model. It is not necessary to invoke any sense of purpose or foresight on the part of the daisies. We have merely assumed that the growth of the daisies can affect the mean planetary temperature and vice versa. Note that the mechanism works equally well whatever direction the effect is. Black daisies would have done as well. As long as the Daisyworld albedo is different from that of the bare ground, some thermostasis will result. The assumption that growth is restricted to a narrow range of temperature is crucial to the working of the mechanism, but all mainstream life is observed to be limited within this same narrow range; indeed, the peaked growth curve *B* is common to other variables besides temperature, for example, pH and the abundance of many different nutrients.

In a recent paper (Watson and Lovelock, 1983), this model is discussed in depth; it is emphasized there that the exercise was conducted not because daisies or other colored plants are thought to regulate Earth's temperature by this mechanism but because it is easily understood as a model of the close coupling between the biota and the environment. The Daisyworld populations were modeled by differential equations borrowed directly from theoretical ecology (Carter and Prince, 1981).

Daisyworld models have a novel and wholly unexpected property. Their mathematical solution is not limited to two species only, as are conventional ecological models. Indeed, the number of species that can be accommodated appears to be limited only by the speed and size of the computer system and the patience of the user. The inclusion of feedback from the environment appears to stabilize the system of differential equations used to model the growth and competition of the species. Theoretical ecology models have nearly always ignored the environment of their imaginary species, just as geophysical and geochemical models of the environment have tended to ignore the biota. Daisyworld and similar models are admittedly primitive and as yet limited to a few species and a single environmental variable. But they are models of the evolution of an active system where the biota and the environment are closely coupled, and they do share with the real world the same strong tendency to homeostasis and stability.

The power of the Daisyworld model is perhaps best illustrated by the imaginary world depicted in Fig. 3. It illustrates the time history of a planet where thermostasis is maintained during the progressive increase of luminosity of its sun and in spite of disasters that destroy a substantial proportion of the daisies. In addition, this world is also populated by rabbits that graze the daisies and by foxes that feed on the rabbits. A good measure of the health of a self-regulating system is its capacity to resist perturbation and by the rapidity and smoothness of the return to normal. The system illustrated in Fig. 3a was perturbed four times during the course of its evolution by the abrupt but temporary deletion of 40% of the plant population.

These four perturbations were effectively resisted, and the system rapidly recovered its former state of homeostasis. Figure 3b illustrates the variation of the population of the species during the evolution of this imaginary world. Between the perturbations, both the environment and the population of the species are stable. At the disturbances, the changes in the population and in the properties of the environment take place in synchrony. The model is not concerned with the cause of the perturbations, and they could have been either internally or externally generated. This form of response resembles that described by S. J. Gould in his hypothesis of the punctuated evolution of the species.

Gaia models are limited neither to daisies nor to the regulation of temperature by albedo change. Other environmental variables such as the pH of the soil or sea or the abundance of oxygen and other essential elements can plausibly be shown to keep within a narrow range by the same homeostatic processes illustrated in Fig. 1.

The regulation of climate as a consequence of an evolutionary feedback system involving atmospheric $CO_2$ and the weathering of the rocks by the biota has already been described (Lovelock and Watson, 1982; Lovelock and Whitfield, 1982).

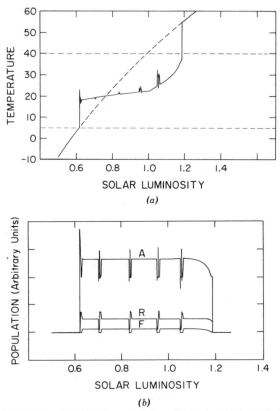

**FIGURE 3.** (a) Evolution of the temperature on an imaginary Daisyworld populated by daisies. The color of Daisyworld changes in response to temperature over the range 5–40°C. It is also populated by rabbits that graze on the daisies and by foxes that hunt the rabbits. In addition, at intervals, Daisyworld is perturbed by catastrophes that cause the death of 40% of the daisy population. It is assumed that Daisyworld is warmed by a star that increases its luminosity linearly with time. When the planetary temperature exceeds 5°C, the daisies grow rapidly and are dark colored in response to the initial low temperature. The mean temperature rises by positive feedback until the operating temperature for homeostasis is reached. Homeostasis is maintained and the four perturbations resisted. The capacity of the system to restore homeostasis after a disturbance is seen to decline as the increasing solar output carries the system nearer to its limit. The dashed line illustrates the planetary temperature expected in the absence of life. (b) The populations of daisies (A), rabbits (R), and foxes (F) during the evolution of Daisyworld. To be taken in conjunction with Fig. 3a.

The model is based on that of Walker, Hays, and Kasting (1981), who assumed that when life started, the climate was warm enough in spite of the cooler sun on account of a much higher concentration of carbon dioxide in the air. It was thought to make up between 10 and 30% of the atmosphere. As the sun evolves and increases its flux of radiation, the temperature is kept nearly constant by a progressive decrease of $CO_2$. The process of $CO_2$

removal is the weathering of calcium silicate rocks. The Gaian variant of Walker's model assumes that the biota are actively engaged in the process of weathering and that the rate of this process is directly related to the biomass of the planet. If conditions are too cold, the rate of weathering declines, and as a consequence of the constant input of $CO_2$ by degassing from Earth's interior, the $CO_2$ partial pressure rises.

Models of this kind about $CO_2$ and climate could add to the current interest in this most important environmental problem. They are based on an active feedback control system and predict the possible development of instability and oscillations enhanced by positive feedback; these are most likely when the system nears the limits of its capacity to regulate. It is interesting to compare the predictions of the model with the observations of a correlation between $CO_2$ and climate that characterize the last glaciation and with the sudden and apparently simultaneous rise of $CO_2$ and temperature at the end of the cold period that led to the present warmer state. The exact sequence of temperature and $CO_2$ increase at the end of the last glaciation still is uncertain, but few would doubt that the end was sudden and that both $CO_2$ and temperature increased substantially on a global scale. This rapid change some 12,000 y ago cannot be explained by geophysical or geochemical theory alone. It suggests a change in the biota, most probably the sudden death of a substantial proportion of the marine phytoplankton, an event that would reduce the rate of pumping of $CO_2$ from the atmosphere.

The geophysiological prediction of an oscillatory instability near the limits of regulation fits these observations. It is well known that the glaciations are in synchrony with the variations in solar luminosity consequent upon Earth's orbital position and inclination, the Milankovich effect. This effect alone cannot account for the rapid reversal of a glaciation. But the Milankovich effect could be the trigger that synchronizes an otherwise free-running biological oscillator.

## CONTEMPORARY GEOPHYSIOLOGY AND THE HUMID TROPICS

Gaia theory suggests that we inhabit and are part of a quasi-living entity that has the capacity for global homeostasis. This is the basis of geophysiology, and if this theory is correct, then we cannot model the consequences of perturbations, such as those caused by our own actions, as if the world were a passive system like the spaceship Earth.

It has been said by politically inclined critics that the Gaia hypothesis is a fabrication, an argument developed to allow industry to pollute at will, since mother Gaia will clean up the mess. It is true that a system in homeostasis is more forgiving about disturbances. But this is only when it is healthy and well within the bounds of its capacity to regulate. When such a system is stressed to near the limits of regulation, even a small disturbance may cause it to jump to a new stable state or even to fail entirely. In these circumstances, pollution and changes in land use or in the ecology of the continental shelves could be the recipes for global disaster.

It could be that regulation of Earth's climate is not far from one of these limits. Thus, if some part of climate regulation is connected with the natural level of $CO_2$, then clearly we are close to the limits of its regulation. Carbon dioxide cannot be reduced much below the level observed for the last glaciation, about 180 ppm, without seriously limiting the rate of growth of the more abundant C3-type plants. If we perturb Earth's radiation balance by adding more $CO_2$ and other greenhouse gases to the atmosphere, reduce Earth's capacity to regulate by decreasing the area of forests, or both of these together, then we could be surprised by a sudden jump of both $CO_2$ and temperature to a new and much warmer steady state or by the initiation of periodic fluctuations between that state and our present climate. A biogeochemist or a climatologist could argue that even if a geophysiological system, Gaia, exists, its responses to environmental change would be infinitesimally slow compared with practical human concerns. Reasonable though this criticism may seem, it begs the question, for we as animals are a part of Gaia and can respond to human concerns. Also, it is wrong to assume that a system that includes processes with slow response times cannot act quickly.

The anomalously low concentration of $CO_2$ on Earth compared with other terrestrial planets, and especially the fact that the mean temperature of Earth are on the cool side of optimum for regulation, suggests strongly that the biota is regulating the climate by pumping $CO_2$ from the air. The common feature of most of our pollutions and of our exploitation of the land surface seems to be unintentionally to thwart this natural process.

How then do questions of global regulation bear on our special interest in the humid tropics? It reinforces, in several ways, the general conviction from conventional modeling that large-scale changes of land use in the tropics will not be limited in their effects to those regions only (Dickinson, 1986); the climatic effects of forest clearance are likely at least to be additive to those of $CO_2$ and other greenhouse gases. Even the most intricate climate models of the present type cannot predict the consequences of these changes unless the biota are included in the model in a way that recognizes its very active presence and its preference for a narrow range of environmental variables. Putting the biota in a box with inputs and outputs, as in a biogeochemical model, does not do this. By analogy, the most detailed knowledge of the biochemistry of oxidative metabolism in humans says nothing about how we sustain our personal thermostasis in the hot or cold environments that we encounter.

Most climatologists agree that forests tend to increase the cloudiness of the atmosphere above them and that the clouds alter the climate of forest regions both in terms of temperature and rainfall (e.g., Salati, Chapter 15; Henderson-Sellers and Hughes, 1984). The geophysiologist would see, in addition, that the active process of evapotranspiration by the forest trees could be coupled with the climatology so as to maintain the region in a state of homeostasis within that climate range preferred by the trees.

There is as yet no answer to the question What is the area of land of a region of the humid tropics that can be developed as open farmland or as silviculture without significantly perturbing both the regional and the global environment? It is a question like What is the proportion of skin area that can be burned without suffering a significant systems failure? This second question has been answered by direct observations of the consequences of accidental burns; so far as I am aware, it has not been modeled. Perhaps, detailed geophysiological modeling can answer the environmental question. Certainly, the simple models illustrated here were very well behaved. But if human physiology is a guide, empirical conclusions drawn from a close study of the local climatic consequences of regional changes of land use are more likely to yield the information we seek.

In some ways, the ecosystem of, for example, a forest in the humid tropics is like a human colony in Antarctica or on the moon. It is only self-supporting to a limited extent, and its continued existence depends on the transport of nutrients and other essential ingredients from the world. At the same time, ecosystems and colonies try to minimize their losses by conserving water, heat, or essential nutrients; to this extent, they are self-regulating. The tropical rain forest likewise keeps wet by modifying its environment so as to favor rainfall. Traditional ecology has tended to consider ecosystems in isolation. Geophysiology reminds us that all ecosystems are interconnected. By analogy, in an animal the liver has some capacity for the regulation of its internal environment, and its liver cells can be grown in the isolation of a tissue culture. But neither the animal nor its liver can live alone; they depend on their interconnection.

We do not know if there are vital ecosystems on Earth, although it would be difficult to imagine life continuing without the anoxic ecosystems of the sediments. The forests of the humid tropics do not significantly add to the world's oxygen budget nor to the exchange of essential elements through the atmosphere. Their intensive biosynthesis is recycled inside their boundaries. Where they may be significant on a global scale is in their effects on climate through evapotranspiration and the effect of their presence on the regional albedo. The transfer of nutrients and the products of weathering down tropical rivers are obviously part of their interconnection and may also have a global significance.

If evapotranspiration or the movements of materials in rivers to the oceans from tropical forests are vital to the maintenance of the present homeostasis, then their replacement with agricultural or grassland surrogates would not only deny those regions to their surviving inhabitants but also might threaten the rest of the system as well. We do not yet know whether the tropical forest systems are vital to the present planetary ecology. They might be like the temperate forests, which seem to be expendable without serious harm to the system as a whole; temperate forests have suffered extensive destruction during glaciations as well as during the recent expansion of agriculture.

We are, so far as geophysiology is concerned, very much in the natural history phase of information gathering. It would seem, therefore, that the traditional ecological approach of examining the forest ecosystem in isolation is as important to our understanding as the consideration of its interdependence with the whole system. Insight into the potential value of physiology for the understanding of global problems can come from reading the book by Riggs (1970), particularly those sections concerned with temperature regulation and systems failure. The recent paper by Holling (1986) relates the physiological approach to contemporary problems.

If it turns out that Gaia theory provides a fair description of Earth's operating system, then most assuredly we have been visiting the wrong specialists for the diagnosis and cure of our global ills. We need answers to such questions as: How stable is the present system? What will perturb it? Can the effects of perturbation be reversed? Can the world maintain its present climate and composition without the humid tropics in their present form? These are all questions within the province of geophysiology.

## REFERENCES

Bolin, B. and Cook, R., Eds., 1983. *The Major Biogeochemical Cycles and Their Interactions*, *SCOPE*, Vol. 21, Wiley Chichester, London.

Broecker, W. S., Peng, T. H., and Engh, R., 1980. Modeling the carbon system, *Radiocarbon* **22**, 565–568.

Carter, R. N. and Prince, S. D., 1981. Epidemiological models used to explain biogeographical distribution limits, *Nature* **293**, 644–645.

Dickinson, R. E., 1986. Impact of human activities on climate, in W. C. Clark and R. E. Munn, Eds., *Sustainable Development of the Biosphere*, Cambridge University Press, London.

Garrels, R. M., Lerman, A., and McKenzie, F. T., 1976. Controls of atmospheric oxygen: Past, present, and future, *Amer. Sci.* **64**, 306–315.

Henderson-Sellers, A. and Hughes, N. A., 1984. in A. Henderson-Sellers, Ed., *Satellite Sensing of a Cloudy Atmosphere*, Taylor and Francis, London.

Hitchcock, D. R. and Lovelock, J. E., 1967. Life detection by atmospheric analysis, *Icarus* 7, 149–159, 1986.

Holling, C. S., 1986. Resilience of ecosystems; local surprise and global change, in W. C. Clark and R. E. Munn, Eds., *Sustainable Development of the Biosphere*, Cambridge University Press, London.

Hutchinson, G. E., 1954. Biochemistry of the terrestrial atmosphere, in Kuiper, Ed., *The Solar System*, The University of Chicago Press, Chicago, IL, Chapter 8.

Lovelock, J. E. and Margulis, M., 1974. Atmospheric homeostasis by and for the biosphere, *Tellus* **26**, 1–10.

Lovelock, J. E. and Watson, A. J., 1982. The regulation of carbon dioxide and climate, *Planet. Space Sci.* **30**, 795–802.

Lovelock, J. E. and Whitfield, M., 1982. Life span of the biosphere, *Nature* **296,** 561–563.

McElroy, M. B., 1983. *Global Change: A Biogeochemical Perspective*, JPL Publication 83-51, JPL, Pasadena, CA.

Redfield, A. C., 1958. The biological control of chemical factors in the environment, *Amer. Sci.* **46,** 205–221.

Riggs, D. S., 1970. *Control Theory and Physiological Feedback Mechanisms*, Williams and Wilkins, Baltimore, MD.

Sillen, L. G., 1966. Regulation of $O_2$, $N_2$ and $CO_2$ in the atmosphere: Thoughts of a laboratory chemist, *Tellus* **18,** 198–206.

Vernadsky, V., 1945. The biosphere and the noosphere, *Amer. Sci.* **33,** 1–12.

Walker, J. C. J., Hays, P. B., and Kasting, J. F., 1981. A negative feedback mechanism for the long term stabilization of the earth's surface temperature, *J. Geophys. Res.* **86,** 9776–9782.

Watson, A. J. and Lovelock, J. E., 1983. Biological homeostasis of the global environment: The parable of daisy world, *Tellus*, **35B,** 284–289.

Whitfield, M., 1981. The world ocean: mechanism or machination, *Interdisc. Sci. Rev.* **6,** 12–35.

# Chapter 3

# Climate, Natural Vegetation, and Soils in Amazonia: An Overview

**Jesus Marden dos Santos**

In the Amazon region is found almost half of the forested area of the Brazilian territory. According to UNESCO/UNEP/FAO (1978), the estimated area covered with tropical moist forest in the world is about $9.35 \times 10^6$ km$^2$, 39% of which is the Brazilian evergreen rain forest. From these simple statistics, we can infer the importance of this tall forest with aseasonal climate, warm temperatures, and high rainfall. The detailed distribution of vegetative cover, whether forest, open woodland, or scrub, is still poorly known.

The plants of this evergreen, humid, and warm forest show great diversity, with richness of species and ecological niches, the result of a macroclimate with rainfall varying from 1.8 to 3.5 m, sometimes with no dry season and in some regions with from 1 to 3 or 4 months of water deficit. The area is an important heat source for the general circulation of the atmosphere, since a large amount of solar radiation is absorbed by the surface and transformed into latent heat.

The water vapor from evapotranspiration and the diurnal warming make the atmosphere unstable. In the planetary boundary layer, water vapor is carried upward and, after condensation into cumulus clouds, warms up the large-scale environment, creating favorable conditions for water vapor convergence at lower levels over a broad area. This convergence reinforces deep convection by making water vapor available for individual cumulus clouds, driving interactions between large and small scales of motion (Nobre, 1983). Nobre has shown that localized and intense heat sources in the tropical atmosphere resulting from continental precipitation give rise to strong upward motion with associated convergence at lower levels and divergence at upper levels, promoting large-scale subsidence outside the source region.

The macroclimate of the forest is regulated by the regional atmospheric circulation. The whole Amazon Basin is situated in equatorial latitudes, far from the subtropical high-pressure centers. Its tropospheric circulation is frequently disturbed by the intertropical convergence zone and by squall lines of tropical instability, causing rain.

Although Amazonian climate would be considered highly homogeneous on the basis of temperature, the region actually has many distinct climates as a result of differences in rainfall, varying from no dry period to 4 months of water deficit. The rainfall variability is large and associated with the cloud cover, which controls the solar radiation fluxes in daily and yearly patterns. In some regions, periods of water deficit are seasonal. Where water storage of the rooting zone is less, the forest structure shows an adaptation to water stress, and in regions with ample water supply, the forest system shows an adaptation to maximum evapotranspiration.

## THE VEGETATION

In the Amazonian forest, there are more than 2500 tall tree species, compared with a few dozen or less in most temperate-latitude forests. The richness and heterogeneity of the Amazonian forest systems have been shown by various surveys. Surveys in the Manaus region found 50 species of trees among 180 individual plants, 12 species of palm among 82 trees, and 20 species of lianas among 40 individual plants in a 500 × 500-m quadrat (Aubré-ville, 1961). In a survey of a 5-ha *terra firme* (never flooded) forest in the Belém region, Murça Pires (1978) found 224 species representing 136 genera and 52 families among 2607 trees having girth at breast height (gbh) ≥30 cm. Certain species are represented by a large number of individuals, and a large number of species are represented by a small number of individuals.

Murça Pires (1978) gives a good overview of Amazon forest surveys. In particular, for an area of 3.5 ha in Amazonia, Murça Pires, Dobzhansky, and Black (in Cain et al., 1956) list 179 tree species with a diameter at breast height (dbh) ≥10 cm, of which 117 are identified, 46 identified to genus and 16 only to the family. In a study near Manaus, Aubréville (1961), from a total of 1652 woody and herbaceous plants, listed 100 plants that were entirely unknown (20 plants without even vernacular names); 45 species were identified to the family, 31 to the genus, and only 30 were completely identified. Heinsdijk (1960) made five large-scale inventories on the right bank of the Amazon River along a 1300-km stretch parallel to the equator. These inventories, commissioned by FAO, covered 15 million hectares containing 126,517 trees with a dbh ≥25 cm. Though identification was precise, of 374 species known by vernacular names, only 240 were identified. Heinsdijk and Bastos (1963) summarized the inventories made in the Amazon region (covering 20 million hectares by representative sampling); for 348 vernacular names (some of which are conventional), they provided a list of 260 identified species.

## Soils and Nutrients

In tropical moist forests most of the available nutrients are already bound into plant tissues. While binding the shallow topsoil, the tree root systems with their associated mycorrhizae are efficient recyclers of any organic matter falling to the earth. The crowns shade the soil from damaging sunlight and protect the soil from compacting and leaching by rain. The many trees and other plant species are the source of food for a large number of animals, including especially fish and invertebrates. Because these species interact in complex ways and because soil resources are so restricted, the whole system is fragile. Disruption by cutting collapses the intricate web of relationships. The level of productivity of the ecosystem is rapidly diminished; and, even more critical, the nutrients contained in the system are quickly exhausted, most of them simply lost or destroyed (Heltne, 1981).

A highly important property of tropical soils is the extent of alteration of their parent rock. Rocks are rapidly decomposed because of the high temperature and humidity. Thus, with the absence of Quaternary glaciations and the protection of the forest, the Amazonian soils have developed to great depth.

These soils have a low mineral content with kaolinite predominant within their clay fraction, giving a weak capacity for cation absorption. They are rich in silica and free iron oxides, and most contain equally large quantities of free alumina. They are generally acid and poor in macronutrients. Nevertheless, the presence of the forest modifies their fertility (discussed further by Lavelle, Chapter 11). Ranzani (1979) discusses 10 taxonomic soil units in the Amazon region.

## Distribution of Vegetation

The main aspects of the distribution of the vegetation in the Amazon presented here are based on the recent work of Braga (1979). The whole Amazon region is a phytogeographical unit with a tropical wet forest of high biomass and large heterogeneity. At present, 130 families of dicotyledonous and 31 of monocotyledonous plants have been described in the region. Of these, only the Dialypalanthaceae, Duckeodendraceae, and Rhabdodendraceae, small families with a few species, are confined to Amazonia. Thirteen families of dicotyledonous and five of monocotyledonous plants are neotropical, and a few have their center of distribution in Amazonia. According to Prance (1978), the Amazon vegetation is derived from other areas. Prance (1977) has proposed a phytogeographical subdivision of Amazonia: Atlantic coast, Jari/Trombetas, Xingu/Madeira, Roraima/Manaus, Northwest/High Rio Negro, Solimões/Western Amazon, and Southwest. If the forest in any of the regions were completely destroyed, a large number of species would become extinct.

An area of 3,303,000 km², about 90% of Brazilian Amazonia, is covered by forest. This forest is physiognomically highly uniform with constant variation in the botanic composition. Another characteristic is a great mixture of species without predominance of any one species.

Some of the characteristics of the Amazonian forest are the presence of exposed roots, trunks with irregular formation, and plants that flower just once and die. This tall vegetation grows on soils poor in nutrients. The forest can be subdivided into: *mata densa* or tall closed forest, 3,063,000 km²; *mata de cipó* or liana forest, 100,000 km²; *open mata of bamboo* or open bamboo forest, 85,000 km²; *campinarana* or white sandy soil forest, 30,000 km²; *várzea* or flooded land forest, 55,000 km²; and *igapó* or swamp forest, 15,000 km². The area not covered with forest can be divided into *campo de várzea*, 15,000 km²; *savanna*, 150,000 km²; and *campinas*, 34,000 km².

The tall forest (after Murça Pires, 1978) includes areas of flooded lowlands (*várzea alta*), such as occur in the southwest of Marajó Island. The distribution of tall dense forest is not continuous because the vegetation includes shorter or dwarf trees and shrubs, or *campos*. The species in the forest shade are generally medium-sized or small trees, but there are exceptions. Of the shade-tolerant species, there are a large number of young small individuals; the numbers diminish gradually as the diameter class increases. Of the light-demanding species, the greatest number of individuals are in the intermediate-size class. For example, the greatest number of *Bertholletia excelsa* (Brazil nut tree) in the forest of the Jari basin are in the class of dbh >1 m, whereas trees of very small diameters are completely absent in the dense shaded forest.

In the *várzea* bottomland forest areas, there is considerable variation caused chiefly by the extent of inundation. Wet-season flooding can last for months; the *várzeas* of the lower Amazon Basin, with twice daily tidal flooding, have robust grasses, while the *várzeas* of the Amazon estuary are forests, except on Marajó Island, where the grasslands are lower than those of the lower basin and of the littoral savanna type. The *igapó* forests are similar to the *várzeas*, the greatest difference being that the submerged state persists for a long period of the year, with the result that the floodwaters deposit their sediments.

The *matas de cipó* are low forests with many lianas and occupy all the Itacaiunas River basin. Besides the relatively low trees, there are scattered trees that may exceed 50 m. Definite species associations are common, such as the *Orbignya–Bertholletia* association of the Itacaiunas River basin.

The small height of the liana forest is probably not a result of the drier climate or soil impoverishment. Much of the area of the Transamazon highway between Marabá and Altamira is covered by liana forests on all types of soils, including the ones of high fertility.

Klinge, Medina, and Herrera (1977), studying the Amazon *campinarana*, report that their distribution is centered in the upper and middle portions of the Rio Negro basin. One disjunct area occurs at the upper Solimões (near São Paulo de Olivença). Both areas have many species of plants in common.

The *campinas* consist of poor deep sandy soils and various kinds of vegetation, arboreal or shrubby. During the wet season, excess moisture induces waterlogging. Soils are of the regosol or podzol type. There are many endemic species. The *campinas* occupy an enormous area in small disjunct patches throughout the Amazon and as large patches in some regions, such as in the Rio Branco basin or in the middle and upper Rio Negro.

## Tucuruí Survey

Recently, in studies performed in an area of 2500 km² that will be covered by the lake of the Tucuruí Dam, the biomass of 10 different forest plots was measured. This survey was made through a toposequence method including the following zones.

Zone 1 is characterized by flat hills of small area and short slopes with maximum inclination of 25% and a luxuriant *terra firme* forest. Zone 3, near Breu Branco, is covered with a well-developed forest, with trees of smaller size than in zone 1. In zone 4, the relief is flat with soil in the depressions. The vegetation consists of trees with an average height of 32 m and an underforest modified by the fall of large trees and invasion of *cipós* in the lowland areas. Zone 5 is similar to zone 1 with many specimens of Brazil nut trees. Zone 6 is formed of small hills with steep slopes and sandy soils in valleys with temporary rivers. The vegetation is well developed, but the trees do not surpass 25 m in height. Zone 7 shows a gentle relief with a maximum slope of 10%, hydromorphic lowlands with a few samples of babaçu (*Orbignya speciosa*). Zone 8 is similar to zone 7, but with predominance of babaçu. Tables 1 and 2 show the phytomass properties estimated by direct and indirect methods in different zones.

**TABLE 1. Phytomass Estimated by Direct Method in Different Zones**[a]

| Zones | 1 | 4 | 6 | 8 |
|---|---|---|---|---|
| Trunks | 533.8 | 190.2 | 158.6 | 117.5 |
| Branches | 355.5 | 116.3 | 148.5 | 104.7 |
| Leaves | 15.1 | 11.7 | 9.7 | 12.1 |
| Litter | 11.1 | 11.4 | 19.4 | 31.6 |
| Total biomass, tonne ha$^{-1}$ | 915.5 | 329.6 | 336.2 | 265.9 |
| Basal area, m² ha$^{-1}$ | 57.3 | 24.1 | 25.5 | 18.2 |

[a] Tonne ha$^{-1}$ = 0.1 kg m$^{-2}$. See text for description of zones.

**TABLE 2.  Interzonal Comparison of Vegetation Properties as Determined by Indirect Method**

| Zone | Basal Area $(m^2 \ ha^{-1})$ | Volume $(m^3 \ ha^{-1})$ | Basal Area of Trees With Diameter $>0.4$ m $(m^2 \ ha^{-1})$[a] |
|------|------|--------|--------|
| 5 | 39.7 | 631 | 28.4 (71.5) |
| 6 | 38.2 | 396 | 23.3 (61.1) |
| 1 | 35.1 | 416 | 19.7 (56.1) |
| 3 | 31.8 | 338 | 16.0 (50.4) |
| 4 | 30.8 | 321 | 13.9 (45.1) |
| 7 | 30.6 | 433 | 16.1 (52.8) |
| 8 | 26.6 | 263 | 12.9 (48.5) |

[a] Percentage of total tree area shown in parentheses.

## Phenology

Lately a few phenological studies and inventories have been made by groups of the Instituto Nacional de Pesquisas da Amazonia (INPA) at Manaus and Instituto Emilio Goeldi at Belém. In particular, Araujo (1970) started phenological and systematic studies in Ducke Reserve and observed that

a. anthesis (flowering) occurs mostly in dry seasons (June–November);
b. fruiting is distributed over the whole year;
c. for some species, leaf change occurs during development of fruit, but as a rule before anthesis (only few species show completely caducous leaves);
d. there are species with anthesis and fruiting every year, biannually, polyannually, or only once ("tachi group");
e. some species do not depend on the season for anthesis, fruiting, and leaf change;
f. some species flower and fruit in the rainy season;
g. some species flower and fruit in the dry season;
h. some species flower in the wet season and fruit in the dry season; and
i. some species flower in the dry season and fruit the following year, in the wet season.

In a continuation of his studies, Araujo (1984) selected three species for a study of the application of biometeorological units for determining the time of fruiting and flowering: *Scleronema micranthum* (Ducke) Ducke, *Goupia glabra* (Aubl.), and *Caryocar villosum* (Aubl.) Pers.

Four definitions were used for biometeorological units:

**a.** degree-days with base temperatures of 5, 10, and 15°C;
**b.** ratio of degree-days multiplied by ratio of hours of bright sunshine to duration of daylight;
**c.** photosynthetic irradiance; and
**d.** photosynthetic irradiance multiplied by ratio of solar radiation flux at surface to its value at the top of the atmosphere.

Rain distribution and occurrence of water stress periods were considered. The models were found to be suitable for the study of the chosen species, and it was possible to characterize good and bad years for flowering and fruiting. The hypothesis was established that flowering needs a water stress period (2 months) for its start. Setting of fruit would be prevented by either a longer water stress period or a year-round rainy season.

*Cardeiro* trees [*Scleronema micranthum* (Ducke) Ducke] have a rain threshold between 3.6 and 5.45 mm d$^{-1}$ in the periods July–October or August–November. In years when the rain is under or over these values, flowering is inhibited. The base temperature of 15°C was found to be appropriate for the three species. Good flowering was observed in years with a sharp drop in total precipitation during June or July.

## Factors Affecting Vegetation

Three main factors are likely responsible for the distribution of plant communities in Amazonia: relief, soil type, and precipitation regime. Since in Amazonia we find various plant systems under almost the same humid tropical climate, climatic conditions alone apparently cannot be decisive for determining their distribution. The differences in the geographical distribution of plants is correlated to the physical characteristics of soil, mainly the water balance, and to the water requirements of those plants. The drought resistance of plants is one of the factors responsible for plant distribution. For instance, lack of water availability, in combination with low nutrient status of the soil, governs the formation of Amazon *campinas*. Some species are more competitive than most of the mixed forest species under these conditions and form, together with other similarly adapted species, the particular flora of this forest type (Klinge et al., 1977).

The dependence of the flowering and fruiting phenology on the seasonality of rainfall is also important for the reproduction of many individual species (as discussed further by Mori and Prance, Chapter 6). Other aspects of microclimate, in particular the degree of shading and soil temperatures, affect the viability of young and mature forest species.

## CLIMATE

The study of the Amazonia climate must include macro-, meso-, and microclimate. The predominant vegetation system is important for the meso- and microclimates. Interest has increased in the climate of Amazonia during the past 10 y because of the significance of the region to global climate.

The region from Belém to Manaus is a large wet plain, almost at sea level. Temperatures change little, with means varying from 24 to 28°C, but as mentioned earlier, Amazonia has a wide range of rainfall regimes. Nobre (1984) discusses the mechanisms believed responsible for the observed distribution of precipitation in the Amazon. He suggests that present understanding of the large-scale atmospheric processes and of the interaction of the forested surface with the atmosphere is incomplete. Whereas the extremely high precipitation localized in narrow strips along the Andean eastern slopes results from the easterly winds being lifted when they flow over the Andes, other precipitation maxima are less well understood. The semicircle of maximum precipitation along the basin's southern and western border and roughly parallel to the Andes may also result from the low-level but large-scale convergence caused by mechanical deflection of the air by the Andes.

Kousky and Molion (1981) have suggested alternatively that these maxima are caused by westward-moving lines of instability, originating in the sea breeze along the Atlantic coast. As these lines of instability propagate westward, they cross the regions of low precipitation in the lower Amazon during nighttime, where they would generate less convection and thus less precipitation. When these lines of instability reach the western Amazon during the following day, they might intensify because of the strong surface heating by the sun, thus causing more rainfall and so contributing to the precipitation maximum in that region. Firm observational evidence for this hypothesis is still lacking both in terms of frequency of events (i.e., a large number of these lines would have to occur in a year to account for the observed distribution of rainfall) and also in terms of the rain-generating potential of these events.

Kousky (1980) has suggested that the coastal rainfall maximum is probably caused by nocturnal convergence between the trade winds and the nocturnal land breeze. The difference in surface friction of land and of the ocean surface could also contribute to convergence along the coast and hence the rainfall maximum. It is not known which physical mechanism is more important in determining that rainfall maximum.

Rainfall patterns are controlled by large-scale convergence or divergence and near the coast by local land–sea breeze circulation systems. Considerable convergence and rainfall occur along the coast (Soure) at night, while Belém remains dry, presumably because of sinking motion, which would have the effect of drying the air, thus producing the observed relatively low nighttime value of precipitable water, an average of 12% less precipitable water at 1200 GMT than during the day (Kousky and Kagano, 1981). Manaus has an opposite diurnal variation of precipitable water content with values at 0000 GMT during the day that are slightly less than at 1200 GMT at night.

Kousky (1980) suggests that a nocturnal maximum in precipitation, and presumably precipitable water, occurring about 500 km inland from the coast results from sea-breeze-induced convection continuing to propagate inland during the nighttime hours, as supported by a sequence of infrared satellite pictures that show the formation of convection along the coast and its subsequent inland propagation. For the sea breeze moisture to be advected inland 1000 km to Manaus in about 18–21 h would require a speed of 13–15 m s$^{-1}$, which is fairly close to the climatological mean wind speeds during the period June–September.

Kousky and Kagano (1981) have studied the tropospheric circulation over the Amazon region using monthly mean data for Manaus and Belém from 1968 to 1976. They find, at both stations, an annual oscillation at low levels and a semiannual oscillation at high levels. The maximum geopotential height for the upper troposphere occurs during April–May and a secondary maximum 6 months later. Surface pressure and low-level geopotential have a single maximum at low levels during July and a single broad minimum during the summer months.

The upper troposphere wind at Manaus is from the south or southeast during the period December–April. It abruptly shifts to the northwest in May and to the west in September. Near the surface, the winds are southeasterly from May to August and northeasterly the rest of the year, as the equatorial trough shifts from north to south of Manaus.

The upper troposphere winds at Belém are predominantly southwesterly during the period October–March, southeasterly in April, and westerly or northwesterly from May to September. Southeasterly winds prevail near the surface throughout the year. These reach a distinct maximum in July and a relative minimum from February through April.

The low-level, large-scale winds move water vapor from ocean to land, and the convergence or divergence of winds at all levels indicates upward or downward mean vertical motions that, respectively, enhance or suppress rainfall. These circulations interact with evapotranspiration determined by the forest microclimate (as observed by Molion, Chapter 14, and modeled by Sellers, Chapter 16) and help establish the fraction of rainfall coming from recycled water (an issue addressed further by Salati in Chapter 15). More extensive discussions of the physical mechanisms important for producing rainfall through the interactions of tropical convection and large-scale motions are given by Paegle, Chapter 17, and Molion, Chapter 18.

Consideration of possible changes in Amazonian forests or climate must start from a good understanding of the natural systems. This chapter has attempted to introduce these natural systems.

## REFERENCES

Araujo, V. C., 1970. Fenologia de esséncias florestais amazônicas, *Bol. Inst. Pesquisas Amazôn.* **4**, 1–25.

Araujo, V. C., 1984. Unidades bioclimáticas e essências florestais na Amazônia, M.S. thesis, Instituto de Pesquisas da Amazônia, Manaus.

Aubréville, A., 1961. Études écologiques des principales formations végétales du Brésil, Nogent-sur-Marne, Centre Tech. For. Tropical.

Braga, Pedro I. S., 1979. Subdivisão fitogeográfica, tipos de vegetação, conservação e inventário florístico da floresta amazônica, *Sup. Acta Amazôn.* **9**(4), 53–80.

Cain, S. A., Castro, G. M. O., Pires, J. M., and Silva, N. T., 1956. Application of some phytosociological techniques to Brazilian rain forest, *Amer. J. Bot.* **43**, 911–941.

Heinsdijk, D., 1960. Dryland forest on the Tertiary and Quaternary south of the Amazon river, *FAO Report* **1284**, Parts I–II, Rome.

Heinsdijk, D. and Miranda Bastos, A., 1963. Inventários florestais na Amazônia. *Bol. Setor Invent. Flor. (Brasília)* **6**, 1–100.

Heltne, P. G., 1981. Tropical forest ecosystem development, in J. Talbot and W. Swanson, Eds., *Woodpower: New Perspectives on Forest Usage*, Pergammon, New York.

Klinge, H., Medina, E., and Herrera, R., 1977. Studies on the ecology of Amazon caatinga forest in South Venezuela, *Acta Cient. Venezol.* **28**, 270–276.

Kousky, V. E., 1980. Diurnal rainfall variation in northeast Brazil, *Mon. Weather Rev.* **108**, 488–498.

Kousky, V. E. and Kagano, M. T., 1981. A climatological study of the tropospheric circulation over the Amazon region, *Acta Amazôn.* **11**, 743–756.

Kousky, V. E. and Molion, L. C. B., 1981. Uma contribuicão à climatologia dinâmica da troposfera sobre a Amazônia, INPE-2030-RPI/050 São José dos Campos, S. P., Brazil.

Murça Pires, J., 1978. The forest ecosystems of the Brazilian Amazon: Description, functioning and research needs, in *Tropical Forest Ecosystems*, Natural Resources Research Collection, Vol XIV, UNESCO/UNEP/FAO, Rome.

Nobre, C. A., 1983. Tropical heat sources and their associated large-scale atmospheric circulation, Ph. D. Thesis, Massachusetts Institute of Technology, Cambridge, MA.

Nobre, C. A., 1984. *The Amazon and Climate*, Proceedings of the Climate Conference for Latin American and the Caribbean, WMO, Geneva, No. 632, pp. 409–416.

Prance, G. T., 1977. The phytogeographic subdivisions of Amazonia and their influence on the selection of biological reserves, in G. T. Prance and T. S. Elias, Eds., *Extinction is Forever*, New York Botanical Garden, Bronx, NY.

Prance, G. T., 1978. The origin and evolution of Amazon flora, *Interciência* **3**, 207–222.

Ranzani, G., 1979. Reansos pedológicos da Amazônia, *Acta Amazôn.* **9** (December Suppl.), 23–36.

UNESCO/UNEP/FAO, 1978. *Tropical Forest Ecosystems*, Natural Resources Research Collection, Vol. XIV, UNESCO/UNEP/FAO, Rome.

# ☐ COMMENTS ON "CLIMATE, NATURAL VEGETATION, AND SOILS IN AMAZONIA: AN OVERVIEW"

**Robert E. Dickinson**

This essay introduces Amazonia by reminding us of its large size, both relative to Brazil and to tropical moist forests as a whole. The different types of vegetation, many known species, and their phenology are described. Climate is nearly uniform in temperature, but rainfall has large seasonal variations as well as significant spatial variations. Soils are mostly ancient, acidic, and poor in nutrients, with only a weak capacity for cation absorption. Consequently, most of the nutrients required for plant growth are stored in the vegetation itself, and litter fall is quickly reassimilated into the living biomass. Variations in vegetation under the same climate are associated with variations in soil types and degree of flooding. Some data on month-to-month variations in climatological means are available. Suggested links of spatial and diurnal variations in rainfall to orography and coastal sea breezes are mentioned.

Although a nice naturalist's view of the Amazonian vegetation and climate is provided, this essay does not address many of the questions important for understanding how Brazil and the other countries of Amazonia may most effectively manage and develop this region for improving the living standards of their population. These questions must be addressed in the context of the next 50–100 y, in part because large increases are expected before the South American countries will be able to achieve constant populations. Lack of careful attention to the optimum use of their tropical natural resources could not only condemn many millions of citizens to very marginal and impoverished lives but also increase social unrest and political instability.

Unfortunately, what is the best use of the Amazon forests is still not very well known, though many lessons have been learned in attempts to develop the resources of these forests over the past century and especially over the past few decades. The negative lessons are, perhaps, most widely publicized. For example, now quite well known are the disastrous consequences of large-scale attempted conversion of humid tropical forests to cattle ranching. The most common experience has been the rapid deterioration of the cattle-stocking capacity of the grassland followed by regrowth of an impoverished secondary forest. Perhaps more appropriate species of grass, addition of mineral supplements, and careful selection of soil types may provide practical procedures for sustainable and economically viable cattle ranching and perhaps the means to partially reverse the damage in degraded areas. However, more labor-intensive land use would still appear to be more desirable (Goodland, 1980; Fearnside, 1983; Hecht, 1983).

Many positive lessons have also been learned of the usefulness of tropical forests. Many valuable benefits have been gained from the wild plants of the Amazon, and many more are anticipated (e.g., Myers, 1984; Prance, 1984). For example, some wild peanuts of Amazonia have provided a needed resistance to leafspot disease estimated to be worth U.S. $500 million annually (NAS, 1982). Much is still to be learned by studying the cultures of the native Indians who have developed a thousand-year-old reservoir of knowledge of the benefits available from the Amazonia forest (Moran and Herrera, 1984, and accompanying articles).

It seems that much more knowledge is necessary before a large-scale development program can be viewed as anything but a dangerous gamble for the countries of Amazonia. Gaining such knowledge requires both small-scale practical experimentation and high-quality scientific research. For example, the Tucuruí Dam project may provide enough much needed energy to Amazonia to warrant the ecological havoc it is now wreaking. The answer will not be known for many years, and further such experiments are not warranted until then.

With regard to the climate system, it is unlikely that effects of human changes could be detected until large-scale and permanent changes are established. Thus, to avoid possibly disastrous gambling with the weather and climate of Amazonia and adjacent lands, which might perhaps result from large-scale land use changes, it will be necessary to apply the most advanced research techniques available over whatever time is required to achieve reliable solutions. We still have but a poor understanding of the details of climate and weather processes in Amazonia and the possible consequences of vegetation change. Both extensive and focused observational studies and much improved numerical simulation approaches will be needed.

## REFERENCES

Fearnside, P. M., 1983. Development alternatives in the Brazilian Amazon: An ecological evaluation, *Interciência* **8**, 65–78.

Goodland, R. J. A., 1980. Environmental ranking of Amazonian development projects in Brazil, *Environ. Conserv.* **1**, 9–25.

Hecht, S., 1983. Cattle ranching in the eastern Amazon: Environmental and social implications, in E. F. Moran, Ed., *The Dilemma of Amazonian Development*, Westview, Boulder, CO.

Moran, E. F. and Herrera, R., 1984. Human ecology in the Amazon Basin, *Interciencia*, **9**, 342–343.

Myers, N., 1984. *The Primary Source: Tropical Forests and Our Future*, Norton, New York.

NAS, 1982. *Ecological Aspects of Development in the Humid Tropics*, National Academy Press, Washington, D.C.

Prance, G. T., 1984. Introduction on knowledge and use of the Amazon forest. *Interciência* **9**, 275–279.

# Chapter 4

# Causes of Deforestation in the Brazilian Amazon

**Philip M. Fearnside**

The present rate and probable future course of forest clearing in Brazilian Amazonia are closely linked to the human use systems that replace the forest. These systems, including the social forces leading to particular land use transformations, are at the root of the present accelerated pattern of deforestation and must be a key focus of any set of policies designed to contain the clearing process.

The present extent and likely changes in the various agricultural systems found in the region are reviewed elsewhere (Fearnside, 1985a). Cattle pasture is by far the dominant land use in cleared portions of the *terra firme* (unflooded uplands), not only in areas of large cattle ranches, such as southern Pará and northern Mato Grosso, but also in areas initially felled by smallholders for slash-and-burn cultivation of annual crops, such as the Transamazon Highway colonization areas in Pará (Fig. 1). Pasture is even dominant in areas like Rondônia where government programs have intensively promoted and financed cacao and other perennial crops (Léna, 1981; Furley and Leite, 1985). The forces leading to continued increase in pasture area, despite the low productivity and poor prospects for sustainability of this use system, are those that most closely affect the present rate of deforestation.

The extent or rate of deforestation in Brazil's Amazon rain forest is a subject of profound disagreement among both scholars and policymakers in Brazil and elsewhere. Equally controversial is the question of whether or not potential future consequences of deforestation are sufficient to justify the immediate financial, social, and political costs of taking measures to contain the process. The lack of effective policies to control deforestation in the Amazon today speaks for both the preference among decision makers for minimizing such concerns and the strength of forces driving the defor-

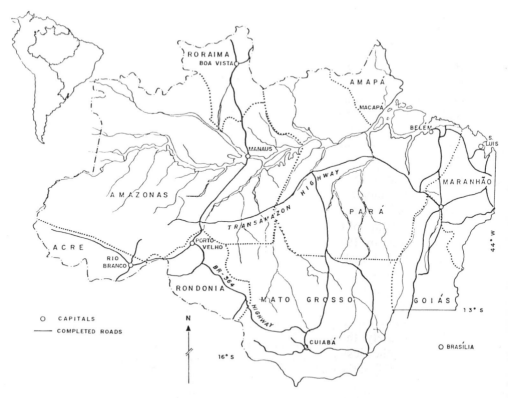

**FIGURE 1.** Brazil's Legal Amazonia.

estation process. Here it is argued that deforestation is rapid and its potential impact severe, amply justifying the substantial costs of speedy government action needed to slow, and at some point stop, forest clearing.

## EXTENT AND RATE OF DEFORESTATION

The vast areas of as yet undisturbed forest in the Brazilian Amazon frequently lead visitors, researchers, and government officials to the mistaken conclusion that deforestation is a minor concern unlikely to reach environmentally significant proportions within the "foreseeable" future. Such conclusions are unwarranted; they also have the dangerous effect of decreasing the likelihood that timely policy decisions will be made with a view to slowing and limiting the process of deforestation. Not only is better monitoring information needed for describing the process but also better understanding of underlying causes of deforestation. Such understanding would allow more realistic projections of future trends under present and alternative policy regimes and permit identification of effective measures to control the process.

The most recent available survey of deforestation covering the entire Brazilian Amazon was made by Brazil's National Institute for Space Research (INPE) based on LANDSAT satellite images taken in 1978 (Tardin et al., 1980). The same study also interpreted images from 1975. The survey's finding that only 1.55% of the area legally defined as Amazonia had been deforested up to 1978 contributed to the popular portrayal in Brazil of deforestation as an issue raised only by alarmists. The INPE figure underestimates clearing because of the inability of the technique to detect *very small* clearings and of the difficulty of distinguishing second growth from virgin forest. For example, the Zona Bragantina, a 30,000-km² region surrounding the town of Bragança in northeastern Pará that was completely deforested in the early years of this century (Egler, 1961; Sioli, 1973), is larger than the area indicated by 1975 images analyzed in the INPE study as deforested in Brazil's entire Legal Amazon and is almost four times the area indicated as cleared in the state of Pará (Fearnside, 1982). Regardless of any underestimation due to image interpretation limitations, the conclusion that the area cleared through 1978 was small in relation to the 4,975,527-km² Legal Amazon is quite correct.

Unfortunately, the small area cleared by 1978 is a far less important finding than another less publicized one apparent from the same data set (Carneiro et al., 1982): the explosive rate of clearing implied by comparing values for cleared areas at the two image dates analyzed, 1975 and 1978. If the growth pattern over the region as a whole was exponential during this period, as it may have been, the observed increase in cleared area from 28,595.25 to 77,171.75 km² implies a growth rate of 33.093% $y^{-1}$ and a doubling time of only 2.09 y. Deforestation rates vary widely in different parts of the region, being highest in southern Pará, northern Mato Grosso, and in Rondônia and Acre. An analysis of a longer time series of LANDSAT images from one of these areas, Rondônia, is presented elsewhere (Fearnside, 1982). Comparisons of cleared areas for 1973, 1975, 1976, and 1978 in two areas of government-sponsored colonization by farmers with 100-ha lots and in two areas dominated by 3000-ha cattle ranches indicate that deforestation in these areas may have been progressing in an exponential fashion during the period, although data are too few for firm conclusions (Fearnside, 1982).

LANDSAT image interpretation by the Brazilian government for the state of Rondônia as a whole (243,044 km²) indicates that cleared areas rose from 1,216.5 km² in 1975 (Tardin et al., 1980) to 4,184.5 km² in 1978 (Tardin et al., 1980) to 7,579.3 km² in 1980 (Carneiro et al., 1982), and to 13,955.2 km² in 1983 (Brazil, Ministério da Agricultura, 1985; Fearnside and Salati, 1985). The cleared area therefore increased from 0.50 to 3.12% of Rondônia's total area in only 5 y and jumped to 5.74% in the succeeding 3 y. It should be remembered that limitations of the image interpretation methodology mean that the true cleared areas were probably larger than these numbers imply.

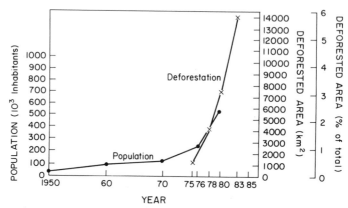

**FIGURE 2.** Growth of population and deforested area in the state of Rondônia. Deforested area is growing even more rapidly than population in this focus of rain forest clearing in Amazonia. Ten-year interval populations are from census data compiled by the Brazilian Institute for Geography and Statistics (IBGE) (Saunders, 1974; Brazil, Presidência da República, IBGE, 1982: 74); 1976 intercensal estimate is by IBGE (Mesquita and Egler, 1979: 73). Deforestation estimates for 1975 and 1978 are from Tardin et al. (1980); 1980 and 1983 estimates are from Brazil, Ministério da Agricultura, IBDF (1983, 1985).

Even with this limitation, the clearing estimates reveal not only that deforestation proceeded rapidly throughout the period but also that it showed no signs of slowing as of 1980 (Fig. 2) and continued through 1983 at a faster-than-linear pace.

LANDSAT data from 1980 images (Brazil, Ministério da Agricultura, IBDF, 1983) reveal that strong exponential growth in cleared areas over the 1975–1980 period also occurred in Mato Grosso and Acre, while increase was roughly linear in Pará, Maranhão, and Goiás (Fearnside, 1984a, 1985b). No 1980 data are yet available for Roraima, Amazonas, or Amapá.

Some of the forces behind deforestation are linked to positive-feedback processes, which can be expected to produce exponential changes. Road building, for example, is closely tied to the rate of arrival of new immigrants: More and better roads attract more immigrants, while the presence of a larger population justifies the construction of still more and better roads (Fig. 3). In Rondônia, the population has been growing even more rapidly than in other parts of the region because of the flood of new immigrants from southern Brazil (Fig. 2).

Projections of unchanging exponential rates for deforestation into the future, even in deforestation foci like Rondônia, are hazardous for anything but illustrations because there are many other factors affecting the process. As the relative importance of different factors shifts in future years, some of the changes will serve to increase deforestation rates while others will slow them. Within completely occupied blocks of colonist lots, for example, clearing of virgin forest proceeds roughly linearly for about 6 y, after which

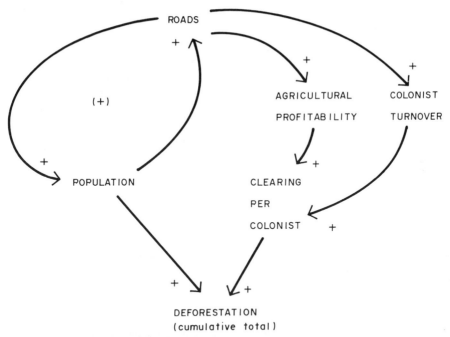

**FIGURE 3.** Causal loop diagram of the relationship between road building and deforestation. Signs by arrow heads indicate the direction of change that would result from an increase in the quantity at the tail of the arrow. Roads and population form a positive-feedback loop. Roads also increase land values, leading the original colonists to sell their land to newcomers who clear more rapidly. Improved transport for agricultural production makes farming more profitable, leading colonists to clear and plant larger areas.

a plateau is reached (Fearnside, 1984b). The rate at which an individual lot is cleared is increased by such events as the arrival of road access and turnover in the lot's occupants (Fearnside, 1980a, 1984b) (Fig. 3).

At present, regional scale clearing appears to be dominated by immigration, along with other forces that accelerate deforestation such as the positive effect of improved road access on market availability and land value appreciation. In the future, the behavior of the population already established in the region should gain in relative importance. Other reasons for an eventual slowing (but not halting) of clearing include poorer soil quality and inaccessibility of remaining unoccupied land, the finite capacity of source areas to supply immigrants at ever increasing rates, decreased relative attractiveness of Amazonia after this frontier of unclaimed land "closes," and limits to the available capital, petroleum, and other inputs that would be necessary if rates of felling should greatly increase (Fearnside, 1985c). However, nothing short of a comprehensive program of government actions based on conscious decisions can be expected to contain deforestation before the region's forests are lost (Fearnside, 1985b).

The accelerating course of deforestation cannot be adequately represented by any simple algebraic formula such as the exponential equation, nor can its eventual slowing be expected to follow a smooth and symmetrical trajectory such as a logistic growth path. The complex interacting factors bearing on the process are more appropriate for analysis with the aid of computer simulation (Fearnside, 1983a). An idea can be gained of the relationships of the factors involved by examining more closely some of the causes of deforestation in Amazonia.

## CAUSES OF DEFORESTATION

Present causes of deforestation can be divided, somewhat artificially, into proximal causes (Table 1) and underlying causes (Table 2). Proximal causes motivate land owners and claimants to direct their efforts to clearing forest as quickly as possible. The underlying causes link wider processes in Brazil's economy either to the proximal motivations of each individual deforester or to increases in numbers of deforesters present in the region.

Some of the principal motives for deforestation apply most forcefully to large landholders, especially those motives connected to government incentive programs. These represent forces relatively easily controlled by governmental actions, as has already occurred to a small degree (see footnote, Table 1). Deforestation is also linked to long-standing economic patterns in Brazil, such as high inflation rates, which have shown themselves to be particularly resistant to government control (Fig. 4).

Changes in agricultural patterns in southern Brazil have had heavy impacts. The rise of soybeans has displaced an estimated 11 agricultural workers for every one finding employment in the new production system (Zockun, 1980). Sugarcane plantations, encouraged by the government for alcohol production, have likewise expelled smallholders. Replacement of labor-intensive coffee plantations with mechanized farms raising wheat and other crops, a trend driven by killing frosts and relatively unfavorable coffee prices, has further swollen the ranks of Amazonian immigrants (Sawyer, 1984).

Within Amazonia, most evident are the forces of land speculation (Fearnside, 1979a; Mahar, 1979), the magnifying effect of cattle pasture on the impact of population (Fearnside, 1983b), and the positive-feedback relationship between road building and population increases (Fearnside, 1982).

Profits from sale of agricultural production are added to speculative gains, tax incentives, and other forms of government subsidy in making clearing financially attractive. Small farmers often come to the region intent on making their fortunes as commercial farmers, but they gradually see the higher profits to be made from speculation as their neighbors sell their plots of land for prices that dwarf the returns realized from years of hard labor. Agriculture then becomes a means for individuals to meet living expenses while

**TABLE 1. Proximal Causes of Deforestation**

| Principal Present Motives | Link to Deforestation | Relative Importance by Size of Holding | |
|---|---|---|---|
| | | Small Properties | Large Properties |
| Land speculation | Clearing establishes proprietary claims, raises resale value of land | Important in squatter areas and for tentatively documented colonists in official settlement areas | Important in areas held by *grileiros* (land grabbers) as well as in legally documented areas (difficult to defend from squatters) |
| Tax incentives | Businesses can avoid paying taxes owed on enterprises elsewhere in Brazil if money is invested in Amazonian ranches (Bunker, 1980; de Almeida, 1978; Fearnside, 1979a; Mahar, 1979) | Not a factor | Important in projects approved by Superintendency for the Development of Amazonia (SUDAM) (mostly in Pará) or by Superintendency for the Manaus Free Trade Zone (SUFRAMA) (in Amazonas)[a] |
| Tax penalties | Higher taxes on "unused" (i.e., uncleared) land (Brazil, Ministério da Agricultura, INCRA, 1980) | Not important | May become important |
| Negative interest loans and other subsidies | Financing of government-approved ranching projects at nominal interest rates lower than inflation | Not a factor | Important; as with tax incentives, most important in southern Pará |
| "Chronograms" for projects with incentives | Government-approved ranching projects must adhere to a schedule for clearing to qualify for continued incentives | Not a factor | Important in SUDAM and SUFRAMA project areas, but many ranches receive subsidies without full compliance |

**43**

**TABLE 1.** (*continued*)

| Principal Present Motives | Link to Deforestation | Relative Importance by Size of Holding | |
|---|---|---|---|
| | | Small Properties | Large Properties |
| Special crop loans | Cacao, coffee, rubber, black pepper, sugar cane, and annual crops financed in some areas; these crops would not be attractive without favorable loan terms | Important in official colonization areas | Important for relatively few large holdings, although medium-sized holdings (500–2000 ha) benefit in Rondônia |
| Exportable production | Beef, and to a lesser extent cacao, upland rice, and other crops, sold in other regions or countries | Important among small farmers who depend on cash crop sales for year-to-year survival; speculative benefits come as windfall for these, although significant number of lots owned by nonresident speculators for whom agricultural production is minor consideration | Important, although often larger holdings are integrated into more diversified investment portfolios. In the case of operations largely motivated by subsidies and speculative opportunities, sale of production, even if meager, adds to profit from clearing |
| Subsistence production | Relatively minor | Minor, especially in government colonization areas, where most clearing is for cash crop planting | Not significant |

*a* New incentives for cattle ranches from the Superintendency for Development of the Amazon (SUDAM) were suspended in 1979 for areas classified as "high forest," but new projects continue to be approved for "transition forest" areas, and the hundreds of previously approved projects in the high forest areas continue to receive incentives for clearing, most of which has yet to be done.

**TABLE 2. Underlying Causes of Deforestation**

| Cause | Link to Deforestation |
|---|---|
| Inflation | a. Speculation in real property, especially pasture land<br>b. Increased attractiveness of low-interest bank loans for clearing |
| Population growth | a. Increased demand for subsistence production (minor factor)<br>b. Increased capacity to clear and plant, both for subsistence and cash crops<br>c. Increased political pressure for road building (feeds back to road building) |
| Mechanization of agriculture in southern Brazil and absorption of small holdings by large estates in south and northeast | a. Immigration of landless laborers (increasing felling both as squatters and as workers on other properties)<br>b. Immigration of smallholders to purchase land (both augment population growth) |
| Road building and improvement | a. Immigration to Amazonia (feeds back to population growth)<br>b. Increased clearing by persons already present |
| Low land prices | a. Extensive land uses (e.g., pasture)<br>b. Little concern for sustainability of production<br>c. Attraction of smallholders to immigrate to Amazonia<br>d. Little motivation for landholders to defend uncleared areas from squatters<br>e. Greater potential speculative gains |
| National politics | a. Tendency of Amazonian interior residents to support incumbent governments provides incentive to increase political representation of these areas by creating new territories and states, justified by population growth achieved through colonization programs and highway construction<br>b. During specific periods of social tension in non-Amazonian portions of Brazil, as in 1970, road building and colonization programs in Amazonia have been seen as ways to alleviate pressure for land reform (e.g., Ianni, 1979); effect of publicity surrounding programs appears to be more important than actual population flow |

**TABLE 2.**  (*continued*)

| Cause | Link to Deforestation |
| --- | --- |
| International geopolitics | Government leaders frequently justify road building and colonization near international borders as protecting the country from invasion (Kleinpenning, 1975, 1977; Tambs, 1974); claims can be effective in rationalizing government programs desired for other reasons (Fearnside, 1984b; Kleinpenning, 1977, p. 310) |
| Concentration of land tenure in Amazonia | Displaces population when squatters' claims or small holdings are taken by large ranches; displaced persons move to clear new areas |
| Fear of forest | Deep-seated psychological aversion to forest and fear of dangerous animals impedes forested land uses; fear is especially powerful among recent arrivals from other regions (e.g., Moran, 1980, p. 99). |
| Status from cattle | Long-standing Iberian tradition of according higher social status to ranchers than farmers leads to preference for pasture independent of expected profit (Denevan, 1982; Smith, 1982, p. 84) |
| Availability of alternative investments elsewhere | Heavy discounting of expected future costs and returns for investments in the Amazon, leading to little concern for sustainability of production systems (see Clark 1973, 1976) |
| Distribution of environmental costs of deforestation over society at large | Increases relative economic attractiveness to individual investors of land uses requiring large deforested areas, as compared to intensive use of small clearings or sustained management of standing forest (see Hardin, 1968) |
| Unsustainable land use choices for cleared areas | Clearing more area to substitute for no-longer-productive land |
| Low labor requirement of predominant land use (i.e., pasture) | a. Small population can clear and exploit large area<br>b. Little contribution to solving problems of unemployment, underemployment, and landlessness, which encourage further deforestation |

**TABLE 2.** *(continued)*

| Cause | Link to Deforestation |
| --- | --- |
| Low agricultural yields | a. Increased area needed to supply subsistence demand (relatively minor)<br>b. Money from government subsidies spent on unproductive ranches and other projects fuels inflation by increasing purchasing power of beneficiaries, without contributing corresponding amounts of production to the economy (feeds back to item 1) |

awaiting the opportunity of a profitable land sale and a move to a more distant frontier. Although individual variability is high, most new farmers aspire to produce enough to live well by the standards of their own pasts while awaiting an eventual sale. Farmers usually see such sales as providing the reward for *improvements* made on the land during their tenure, rather than as speculation. Larger operators are more likely to begin their activities in the region with speculation in mind but are likewise always careful to describe themselves as *producers* rather than as speculators.

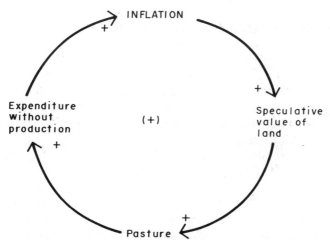

**FIGURE 4.** Causal loop diagram of the relationship of inflation to deforestation for cattle pasture. High inflation leads to land speculation as a means of preserving the value of money. Pasture is planted to secure these investments against squatters or other claimants. The low production of beef from pastures on these soils means that the money invested in ranching is increasing the demand for products in the marketplace without contributing anything that can be bought. The increase of demand over supply raises prices, contributing to still higher inflation.

Subsistence production is always a contributor to forest clearing, although it is not presently the major factor that it is in many other rain forest areas, as in Africa (Myers, 1980, 1982). The speculative and commercial motives for clearing in Amazonia mean that the relationship of commodity prices to clearing is positive for most of the farmers involved. In areas of the tropics where cash crops are grown primarily for supplying subsistence needs, the relationship can be the reverse: A positive-feedback loop exists whereby falling prices for a product mean that larger areas must be planted for the farmer to obtain the same subsistence level of cash income, while the resulting increased supply of the product further drives prices down (Gligo, 1980, p. 136; Plumwood and Routley, 1982). For most Amazonian farmers, however, desire for cash so greatly exceeds the income-producing capacity of the farms that only the restraints of available labor and capital limit the areas cleared and planted (Fearnside, 1980b).

Future deforestation trends will probably reflect changes in the balance of forces listed in Tables 1 and 2, resulting from declining impact of new arrivals relative to the resident population. Future trends can also be expected to show the effects of projected major developments (Table 3). As timber export, presently a negligible factor, becomes more important, outright deforestation will be supplemented by the often heavy disturbances following selective felling that presently characterize much of the forest conversion in Asia and Africa. Charcoal production, especially that derived from native forest, is foreseen as a major factor in the southeastern portion of the region in the coming decades.

Large firms such as lumber companies requiring marketable timber or steel manufacturing industries requiring charcoal, pose the additional problem of playing more active and forceful roles in seeing that environmental conflicts of interest are resolved in their favor. Chances are higher that governments will abandon previous commitments to reserves of untouched forest in order to benefit these interests than would be the case for the small investors. This neglect of previous commitments recently occurred in the case of timber concessions operating in the area now flooded by the Tucuruí Hydroelectric Dam: despite not having fulfilled its role in removing forest from areas to be flooded, the concessionnaire was reportedly granted logging rights to 93,000 ha in two nearby Amerindian reservations when commercially valuable tree species proved less common than anticipated in the reservoir area, according to the head of the firm involved (Pereira, 1982).

Future deforestation appears likely to proceed at a rapid rate. Although limited availability of fossil fuel, capital, and other resources should eventually force a slowdown, these constraints cannot be counted on to prevent loss of large areas of forest. Even at rates slower than those of the recent past, the forest could be reduced to remnants within a short span of years. The deforestation process is subject to control and influence at many points. Decisions affecting rates of clearing must be based on understanding of the

**TABLE 3.   Expected Additional Motives for Future Deforestation**

| Motive | Reason Expected |
|---|---|
| 1. Timber export | Expected to increase with coming end to southeast Asian rainforests now supplying world markets (Fearnside 1984a) |
| 2. Charcoal production | Expected to increase for steel production for the Grande Carajás Project, in southeastern Pará; both native forest harvest and plantations planned |
| 3. Support of mineral development sites | Expected to accompany developments at Carajás, Trombetas, Serra Pelada, and elsewhere |
| 4. Hydroelectric projects | Planned projects at Balbina (Rio Uatumã), Samuel (Rio Jamari), and Itapunara (Rio Jari) would total 4445 km² of reservoir area (Goodland, 1980), plus additional unknown areas from two dams on the Rio Xingu and up to four additional dams on the Rio Tocantins (Goodland, 1980);[a] existing dams in region at Curuá-Una (Rio Curuá-Una) and Paredão, also known as Coary Nunes (Rio Araguarí), and Tucuruí (Rio Tocantins) total 2539 km²; some new area will be cleared by persons displaced by dams, as well as by expected support communities; fluctuations in released water volume, as at Balbina, will also kill substantial forest areas downstream of dams; forest loss from hydroelectric projects, however, is small when compared with losses to ranching or other activities |

[a] Ultimate goals for Rio Tocantins and its tributaries reportedly call for construction of 8 large dams (including Tucuruí) plus 19 smaller ones, while the Rio Xingu would eventually have 9–10 large dams (Caufield, 1982).

causes of deforestation. Such decisions are made, either actively or by default. They define areas to undergo agricultural or other development and reserves where such development will be excluded. Making timely choices of this kind depends on decision makers' conception of the likely course of deforestation. Understanding the system of forces driving the process is also essential for evaluating the probable effectiveness of any changes contemplated.

## POLICY IMPLICATIONS

The negative consequences of deforestation (Fearnside, 1985c) should give pause to planners intent on promoting forms of development requiring large areas of cleared rainforest. Nevertheless, such plans continue to be proposed and realized. Part of the problem is a lack of awareness among decision makers of the magnitude of the eventual costs implied by these actions, but such lack of knowledge explains only a part of the reluctance to take effective actions to contain and slow deforestation. At least as important is the distribution of the costs and benefits, both in time and space. Most of the costs of deforestation will be paid only in the future, while the benefits are immediate. Many of the costs are also distributed over society at large, while the benefits accrue to a select few. In the many cases where land is controlled by absentee investors, there is even less reason for negative consequences within the region to enter individual decisions. In other cases, the costs are highly concentrated, as when indigenous groups are deprived of their resource base, while the perhaps meagre benefits of clearing are enjoyed by a constituency that is both wider and more influential.

Brazil's national government has the task of balancing the interests of different generations and interest groups. At the same time, the Amazon has long suffered from exploitation as a colony whose products serve mainly to benefit other parts of the globe, most recently and importantly the industrialized regions of Brazil's central south. The unsustainable land uses resulting from this kind of *endocolonialism*, as Sioli (1980) calls it, require that decision-making procedures guarantee the interests of the Amazon's residents when conflicts arise with more influential regions of the country.

Clear definitions of development objectives are essential as a prerequisite for any planning (Fearnside, 1983c). I suggest that development alternatives be evaluated on the basis of benefits to the residents of the Amazon region and their descendants. Coherent policies must include the maintenance of the human population below carrying capacity, the implantation of agronomically and socially sustainable agroecosystems, and limitations on total consumption and on the concentration of resources. The inclusion of future generations of local residents in any considerations means that greater weight must be accorded the delayed costs implied by such potential consequences of deforestation as hydrological changes, degradation of agricultural resources, and sacrifice of as yet untappable benefits from rain forests. The folly of present trends toward rapid conversion of rain forests to low-yielding and short-lived cattle pasture is evident, at least with respect to the long-term interests of Amazonia's residents (Fearnside, 1979b, 1980c; Goodland, 1980; Hecht, 1981).

## ACKNOWLEDGMENTS

I thank J. G. Gunn, D. H. Janzen, G. T. Prance, J. M. Rankin, and G. M. Woodwell for their valuable comments on earlier versions of the manuscript.

## REFERENCES

Brazil, Ministério da Agricultura, Instituto Brasileiro de Desenvolvimento Florestal (IBDF), 1983. Desenvolvimento Florestal no Brasil, Project PNUD/FAO/BRA-82-008, *Folha Inf.* **5.**

Brazil, Ministério da Agricultura, Instituto Brasileiro de Desenvolvimento Florestal (IBDF), 1985. Alteração da cobertura vegetal natural do Estado de Rondônia. Map scale: 1:1,000,000, IBDF, Brasília.

Brazil, Ministério da Agricultura, Instituto Nacional de Reforma Agrária (INCRA), 1980. *Imposto Territorial Rural: Manual de Orientação, 1980*, INCRA, Brasília.

Brazil, Presidência da República, Secretaria de Planejamento, Fundação Instituto Brasileiro de Geografia e Estatística (IBGE), 1982. *Anuário Estatístico do Brasil, 1981*, Vol. 42, IBGE, Rio de Janeiro.

Bunker, S. G., 1980. Forces of destruction in Amazonia, *Environment* **22,** 14–43.

Carneiro, C. M. R., Lorensi, C. J., dos Santos Barbosa, M. P., de O. Almeida, S. A., de Queiroz, E. C., Daros, L. L., Moreira, M. L., and Pereira. M. T., 1982. *Programa de Monitoramento da Cobertura Florestal do Brasil: Alteração da Cobertura Vegetal Natural do Estado de Rondônia*, Instituto Brasileiro de Desenvolvimento Florestal (IBDF), Brasília.

Caufield, C., 1982. Brazil, energy and the Amazon, *New Sci.* **96,** 240–243.

Clark, C. W., 1973. The economics of overexploitation, *Science* **181,** 630–634.

Clark, C. W., 1976. *Mathematical Bioeconomics: The Optimal Management of Renewable Resources*, Wiley-Interscience, New York.

de Almeida, H., 1978. *O desenvolvimento da Amazônia e a Política de Incentivos Fiscais*, Superintendência do Desenvolvimento da Amazônia (SUDAM), Belém.

Denevan, W. M., 1982. Causes of deforestation and forest and woodland degradation in tropical Latin America, Report to the Office of Technology Assessment (OTA), Congress of the United States, Washington, D.C.

Egler, E. G., 1961. A Zona Bragantina do Estado do Pará. *Rev. Brasil. Geogr.* **23,** 527–555.

Fearnside, P. M., 1979a. The development of the Amazon rain forest: Priority problems for the formulation of guidelines, *Interciência* **4,** 338–343.

Fearnside, P. M., 1979b. Cattle yield prediction for the Transamazon Highway of Brazil, *Interciência* **4,** 220–225.

Fearnside, P. M., 1980a. Desmatamento e roçagem de capoeira entre os colonos da Transamazônica e sua relação à capacidade de suporte humano, *Ciência Cult.* **32,**(Suppl.), 507 (Abstract).

Fearnside, P. M., 1980b. Land use allocation of the Transamazon Highway colonists of Brazil and its relation to human carrying capacity, in F. Barbira-Scazzocchio, Ed., *Land, People and Planning in Contemporary Amazonia*, Centre of Latin American Studies Occasional Paper No. 3, Cambridge University, Cambridge, England.

Fearnside, P. M., 1980c. The effects of cattle pasture on soil fertility in the Brazilian Amazon: Consequences for beef production sustainability, *Trop. Ecol.* **21,** 125–137.

Fearnside, P. M., 1982. Deforestation in the Brazilian Amazon: How fast is it occurring? *Interciência* **7**, 82–88.

Fearnside, P. M., 1983a. Stochastic modeling and human carrying capacity estimation: A tool for development planning in Amazonia, in E. F. Moran, Ed., *The Dilemma of Amazonian Development*, Westview Press, Boulder, CO.

Fearnside, P. M., 1983b. Land use trends in the Brazilian Amazon region as factors in accelerating deforestation, *Environ. Conserv.* **10**, 141–148.

Fearnside, P. M., 1983c. Development alternatives in the Brazilian Amazon: An ecological evaluation, *Interciência* **8**, 65–78.

Fearnside, P. M., 1984a. A floresta vai acabar? *Ciência Hoje* **2**(10), 42–52.

Fearnside, P. M., 1984b. Land clearing behaviour in small farmer settlement schemes in the Brazilian Amazon and its relation to human carrying capacity, In A. C. Chadwick and S. L. Sutton, Eds., *The Tropical Rain Forest: The Leeds Symposium*, Leeds Philosophical and Literary Society, Leeds, England.

Fearnside, P. M., 1984c. Brazil's Amazon settlement schemes: Conflicting objectives and human carrying capacity, *Habit. Int.* **8**, 45–61.

Fearnside, P. M., 1985a. Agriculture in Amazonia, in G. T. Prance and T. E. Lovejoy, Eds., *Amazonia*, Pergamon, Oxford, England.

Fearnside, P. M., 1985b. Deforestation and decision-making in the development of Brazilian Amazonia. *Interciência*. **10**, 243–247.

Fearnside, P. M., 1985c. Environmental change and deforestation in the Brazilian Amazon, in J. Hemming, Ed., *Change in the Amazon Basin: Man's Impact on Forests and Rivers*, University of Manchester Press, Manchester, England.

Fearnside, P. M. and Salati, E., 1985. Explosive deforestation in Rondônia, Brazil. *Environ. Conserv.* **12**, 344–356.

Furley, P. A. and Leite, L. L., 1985. Land development in the Brazilian Amazon with particular reference to Rondônia and the Ouro Preto Colonization Project, in J. Hemming, Ed., *Change in the Amazon Basin: The Frontier after a Decade of Colonization*, University of Manchester Press, Manchester, England.

Gligo, N., 1980. The environmental dimension in agricultural development in Latin America, *Comisión Economica para América Latina (CEPAL) Review*, December 1980, pp. 129–135.

Goodland, R. J. A., 1980. Environmental ranking of Amazonian development projects in Brazil, *Environ. Conserv.* **7**, 9–26.

Hardin, G., 1968. The tragedy of the commons, *Science* **162**, 1243–1248.

Hecht, S. B., 1981. Deforestation in the Amazon basin: Practice, theory and soil resource effects, *Studies in Third World Societies* **13**, 61–108.

Ianni, O., 1979. *Colonização e Contra-Reforma Agrária na Amazônia*, Editora Vozes, Petrópolis, Rio de Janeiro.

Kleinpenning, J. M. G., 1975. *The Integration and Colonisation of the Brazilian Portion of the Amazon Basin*, Katholieke Universiteit, Geografisch Planologisch Instituut, Nijmegen, Holland.

Kleinpenning, J. M. G., 1977. An evaluation of the Brazilian policy for the integration of the Amazon region (1964–1974), *Tijdschr. Econ. Soc. Geogr.* **68**, 297–311.

Léna, P. 1981. Dinâmica da estrutura agrária e o aproveitamento dos lotes em um projeto de colonização de Rondônia, in C. C. Mueller, Ed., *Expansão da Fronteira Agropecuária e Meio Ambiente na América Latina*, Departamento de Economia, Universidade de Brasília, Brasília, 2 vols.

Mahar, D. J., 1979. *Frontier Development Policy in Brazil: A Study of Amazonia*, Praeger, New York.

Mesquita, M. G. G. C. and Egler, E. G. 1979. Povoamento, in O. Valverde, Ed., *A Organização do Espaço na Faixa da Transamazônica*, Vol. 1, *Introdução, Sudeste Amazônico, Rondônia e Regiões Vizinhas*, Fundação Instituto Brasileiro de Geografia e Estatística (IBGE), Rio de Janeiro.

Moran, E. F. 1980. *Developing the Amazon*, Indiana University Press, Bloomington, IN.

Myers, N. 1980. *Conversion of Tropical Moist Forests*, National Academy of Sciences, Washington, DC.

Myers, N. 1982. Depletion of tropical moist forests: A comparative review of rates and causes in the three main regions, *Acta Amazôn.* **12**, 745–758.

Pereira, F. 1982. Tucuruí: Já retirados 15% da madeira, *Gazeta Mercantil* (Brasília), October 6, 1982, p. 11.

Plumwood, V. and Routley, R. 1982. World rainforest destruction: The social factors, *Ecologist* **11**(6), 4–22.

Saunders, J. 1974. The population of the Brazilian Amazon, in C. Wagley, Ed., *Man in the Amazon*, University Presses of Florida, Gainesville, FL, pp. 160–180.

Sawyer, D. 1984. Frontier expansion and retraction in Brazil, in M. Schmink and C. H. Wood, Eds., *Frontier Expansion in Amazonia*, University Press of Florida, Gainesville, FL.

Sioli, H., 1973. Recent human activities in the Brazilian Amazon Region and their ecological effects, in B. J. Meggers, E. S. Ayensu, and W. D. Duckworth, Eds., *The Tropical Forest Ecosystem in Africa and South America: A Comparative Review*, Smithsonian Institution, Washington, DC.

Sioli, H., 1980. Foreseeable consequences of actual development schemes and alternative ideas, in F. Barbira-Scazzocchio, Ed., *Land People and Planning in Contemporary Amazonia*, Centre of Latin American Studies Occasional Paper No. 3, Cambridge University, Cambridge, England.

Smith, N. J. H., 1982. *Rainforest Corridors: The Transamazon Colonization Scheme*, University of California Press, Berkeley, CA.

Tambs, L. A., 1974. Geopolitics of the Amazon, in C. Wagley, Ed., *Man in the Amazon*, University Presses of Florida, Gainesville, FL.

Tardin, A. T., Lee, D. C. L., Santos, R. J. R., de Assis, O. R., dos Santos Barbosa, M. P., de Lourdes Moreira, M., Pereira, M. T., Silva, D., and dos Santos Filho, C. P., 1980. *Sub projeto Desmatamento, Convênio IBDF/CNPq-INPE 1979*, Instituto Nacional de Pesquisas Espaciais-INPE, Relatorio INPE-1649-RPE/103, São Paulo, São José dos Campos.

Zockun, M. H. G. P., 1980. *A expansão da Soja no Brasil: Alguns Aspectos da Produção*, Instituto de Pesquisas Econômicas da Universidade de São Paulo, São Paulo.

## ☐ COMMENTS ON "CAUSES OF DEFORESTATION IN THE BRAZILIAN AMAZON"

**Roger Revelle**

This essay gives a valuable description of the proximal and underlying causes of deforestation in the Brazilian Amazon. It emphasizes the probable underestimate of the rate from LANDSAT satellite imagery. Although it is implied that deforestation has negative consequences and costs, the potential benefits of a properly managed conversion to agriculture, animal husbandry, agroforestry, and tree plantations are given rather short shrift.

Among the unfortunate consequences of deforestation in Amazonia are the destruction of large portions of habitats and resource base of the Amerindian population, the possible extinction of many native species of plants and animals, and undesirable changes in the hydrological regime. Other workers (Myers, 1980; NAS, 1982; Mori and Prance, Chapter 6) have emphasized the richness and diversity of the Amazonian flora and fauna, and our ignorance of even the existence of hundreds of thousands of species that live in the tropical rain forest. Various authors have speculated that forest removal would result in a lower rate of evapotranspiration and hence larger river runoff and lower rainfall, bringing about a gradual desiccation. Moreover, the present course of deforestation to make room for quickly exhausted cattle-grazing lands is clearly a wasteful use of resources. But many of the soils of the Amazon Basin, if properly managed and supplied with soil amendments and fertilizers, could support much more humanly useful biological production than can be harvested from the rain forests. Much research must be done to determine the ways in which a high level of sustainable agricultural and silvicultural production can be attained in the lands of Amazonia.

The problems of deforestation are not confined to the Legal Amazon of Brazil. Nine countries of tropical South America contain extensive tracts of tropical rain forest, including Bolivia, Colombia, Ecuador, French Guiana, Guyana, Peru, Suriname, and Venezuela, in addition to Brazil. The Brazilian Amazon, of course, possesses the largest area of these forests, covering 336 million hectares in the mid 1970s, while the Amazonian forest area for the other five countries that extend into the basin—Bolivia, Peru, Ecuador, Colombia, and Venezuela—was 144 million hectares (Myers, 1980). Fearnside cites the survey of deforestation in the Brazilian Amazon made by Brazil's National Institute for Space Research (INPE), which found that about 8 million hectares had been cleared up to 1978. He rightly points out that this is probably a marked underestimate. A very rough check can be made by examining the FAO statistics of land use between 1974–1976 and 1981 (FAO, 1982).

In 1974–1976, the total forested area in the six Amazonian countries covered 825 million hectares (FAO, 1982). During the next 6 y, according to FAO, 24 million hectares were cleared, or an average of 4 million hectares per year. The average rate of clearing was thus close to 0.5% per year. The average rate of deforestation in Brazil, with a total forested area in 1974–1976 of 573 million hectares, was 2.37 million hectares, or 0.4% per year, while in the other five countries, about 10 million hectares were cleared, an average rate of 1.67 million hectares or 0.66% per year. Less than one third of the total cleared area was converted to cattle pasture and about 60% to croplands. If the FAO statistics for 1974–1976, 1977, 1979, and 1981 can be trusted, the rate of clearing in Brazil varied between 2.25 and 2.45 million hectares per year, with no indication of an exponential increase in the rate of clearing.

Any consideration of the fate of the Amazonian rainforest must take into account Brazil's future population size and economic growth. The United Nations Population Division has projected (World Bank, 1984) that by the year 2050—only 65 y from now—Brazil will contain between 240 and 280 million people—115–155 million more than at present. This projection is based on the perhaps optimistic estimate that a net reproduction rate of 1.0 will be attained in Brazil during the next 25 y, by 2010. Because of the country's young age distribution, a stationary population will not be reached until the end of the twenty-first century, when Brazil is likely to contain slightly more than 300 million people. Arable land per person was 0.56 ha in 1975 and 0.585 ha in 1981 (FAO, 1982). Cultivated land per person will likely continue to increase slightly; but this tendency may be slowed by improving agricultural technology, which will provide higher crop yields per hectare.

For the future Brazilian population to attain a more satisfactory diet, in particular: a higher proportion of animal products, primary crop and forage production for human food and animal feed should be increased by at least 10% per person, to around 5500 kcal day$^{-1}$. At present, the average Brazilian consumes less total calories and less protein of either plant or animal origin than the world average (FAO, 1982). If the future arable land area is to be 0.6 ha per person, food and feed production should be raised to at least 1.5 tons of cereal grain equivalent per hectare, and the cultivated area must be increased by the year 2050 by 70–90 million hectares. An increase by 180 million hectares will be needed by the end of the twenty-first century. These numbers take account of the likelihood that much Brazilian agricultural land will continue to be used for coffee, cacao, soybeans, and other export crops. A large fraction of the needed new agricultural land could be obtained by forest clearing in the Amazon.

Another potential use of large areas now covered by tropical rain forest could be their conversion to managed plantations of fast-growing trees. Brazil has a severe shortage of known fossil fuel resources. During recent years, fuel imports made up more than 50% of its total imports (World Bank, 1984). This shortage is being partially alleviated by production of fuel alcohol for automobile and truck transportation from sugarcane. Plantations of fast-growing trees are an equally promising future source of commercial energy. In contrast to the natural rain forest, which can provide very little production for human use on a sustainable basis [at most only 2 or 3 tons ha$^{-1}$ y$^{-1}$ (Revelle, 1979)], about 40 tons of biomass per hectare can be harvested each year in modern tree plantations containing genetically improved stocks (Kulp, 1983).

Commercial energy use in Brazil increased by about 6% per year from 1974 to 1981, corresponding to a doubling in 11.5 y. Total energy use in 1981, including both commercial and noncommercial energy, amounted to 1.75 tons of coal equivalent per person, or a total of 219 million tons (World Bank, 1984). With continued economic growth, energy use could reach 4 tons of coal equivalent per person by 2050, or a total of 1.1 billion tons for the population of 280 million expected by that time. If the wood obtained from harvesting fast-growing trees on a regular cycle of 5 or 6 y were converted to charcoal for ease in transportation and use, it should be possible to produce about 12.5 tons of coal equivalent per hectare. Brazil's total energy requirement in 2050 could be obtained by replanting 90 million hectares of present tropical forest with fast-growing trees. The total area deforested for farmlands and tree plantations 65 y from now would then be 180 million hectares. This implies an average rate of clearing of 3 million hectares per year. The remaining forest area in Brazil as a whole would amount to 390 million hectares and presumably at least 156 million hectares in the Legal Amazon.

Tropical rain forests were estimated by Whittaker and Likens (1975) to contain 200 tons of carbon per hectare. Thus the clearing of 180 million hectares would add 36 billion tons of carbon to the atmosphere as carbon dioxide. This is equal to the amount of $CO_2$ now being added by fossil fuel combustion in 7 y (NAS, 1983). According to our previous estimate of the rate of clearing of all South American tropical forests—4.4 million hectares per year—about 0.9 billion tons of carbon are being added to the atmosphere as $CO_2$. This is 15% of the total annual influx of $CO_2$ to the atmosphere. The net flux may be less than this because $CO_2$ acts as a fertilizer for plants, and consequently the rate of growth of natural forests may now be greater than it was several decades ago, before the modern increase in atmospheric $CO_2$.

Fearnside emphasizes the soil degradation and erosion that occur when tropical rain forests are converted to pastureland. He is undoubtedly right, but in many areas, such soil destruction may not be inevitable. Development of agricultural technology for the humid tropics is one of the great challenges facing mankind. What is needed are both careful surveys and experimental research. The soils of the tropics are far from homogeneous, and surveys of the soil characteristics of different regions on both a micro- and a macro-scale could reveal large areas where sustainable agriculture or agroforestry might be profitably practiced. Many other regions should undoubtedly be left in their natural state. The existing forests cover such a vast area that more than half could remain untouched, even if all of Brazil's future food and energy needs were to be met in the Amazon. Recent advances in no-till agriculture, mixed cropping, animal husbandry, and the use of perennial tree crops instead of annual varieties offer promising opportunities for application and research. We must learn to think of the Amazon not as a frontier to be carelessly exploited for temporary gain but as a great laboratory in which long-lasting benefits can be obtained for future populations of tropical South America.

## REFERENCES

Food and Agriculture Organization of the United Nations (FAO), 1982. *FAO Production Yearbook*, Vol. 36, FAO, Rome.

Kulp, L. J., 1983. Integration of forestry and products research, *Svensk Papperstidning* **11**, 25–38.

Myers, N., 1980. *Conversion of Tropical Moist Forests*, National Research Council, NAS, Washington, DC.

NAS, Committee on Selected Biological Problems in the Humid Tropics, 1982. *Ecological Aspects of Development in the Humid Tropics*, National Academy of Sciences, National Academy Press, Washington, DC.

NAS, Carbon Dioxide Assessment Committee, 1983. *Changing Climate*, National Academy of Sciences, National Academy Press, Washington, DC.

Revelle, R., 1979. Energy sources for rural development, in *Energy*, Vol. 4, Pergamon, London.

Whittaker, R. H. and Likens, G. E., 1975. The biosphere and man, in H. Lieth and R. H. Whittaker, Eds., *Primary Productivity of the Biosphere*, Springer-Verlag, New York.

World Bank, 1984. *World Development Report*. Oxford University Press, New York.

## REPLY TO COMMENTS

### Philip M. Fearnside

The comments on my essay "Causes of Deforestation in the Brazilian Amazon" contribute a number of statistics that are important to consider in thinking about planning in the Amazon region. It is essential to realize, however, the distinction between what should ideally happen and what is actually happening or is likely to happen in the region. The "short shrift" that "properly managed conversion" is allegedly given is a reflection of the minor role such conversions play in the vast areas being felled in Brazil's Amazon region.

The commentator asserts that "most of the soils in the Amazon Basin, if properly managed and supplied with soil amendments and fertilizers, could support much more humanly useful biological production. . . ." The much higher production of fertilized agriculture is indisputable. However, large-scale conversion to such practices is unlikely to occur in Brazilian Amazonia. Impediments include extremely high costs (including transport), lack of phosphate deposits in the region, lack of cultural traditions for high-input agriculture, lack of capital for large-scale conversions, and speculative motives for opting for extensive rather than intensive use of land areas. Ultimately, both market limitations for many of the products produced by intensive agriculture and global supplies of needed nutrients (such as phosphorus) militate against conversion of very large areas to capital-intensive agriculture (Fearnside, 1985).

The rapid conversion of large areas to cattle pastures in the Brazilian Amazon is masked by the statistic Revelle chose to present: "less than one third of the total cleared area was converted to cattle pasture and about 60% to croplands" (FAO, 1982; see also FAO data in Lanly, 1982). This figure appears to apply to all of the Amazon Basin rather than to the Brazilian portion of the region. Cattle pastures are relatively much more important in Brazil than, for example, in the Peruvian Amazon (Fearnside, 1985). Even so, the figure cited for pasture appears low. I suspect that it does not recognize the fact that most of the croplands are subsequently converted to cattle pasture after only 1 or 2 y of use under annual crops.

The data on deforestation trends cited may likewise be overly conservative: "If the FAO statistics for 1974–1976, 1977, 1979, and 1981 can be trusted [there is] . . . no indication of an exponential increase in the rate of clearing." Perhaps the answer here is that they cannot be trusted, since the data in the report alluded to are based on statements by government officials rather than on measurements by independent techniques such as LANDSAT image analysis. For Brazil, the only existing LANDSAT interpretation covering the entire Legal Amazon is for images from the years 1975 and 1978, with 1980 data available for six of the nine states and territories of the region. Discussion of the observed trends is presented elsewhere (Fearnside, 1984a). The positive-feedback relationships among such factors as road building and population (Fearnside, 1982) could be expected to lead to deforestation at an accelerating pace provided the required inputs, for example, capital and petroleum, are available.

The yields ascribed to some of the alternative land uses envisioned by Revelle appear overly optimistic: "Another potential use of large areas now covered by tropical rain forest could be their conversion to managed plantations of fast-growing trees . . . about 40 tons of biomass per hectare can be harvested each year in modern tree plantations." Two questions arise: first are these high yields expected over *large areas* (which is very different from obtaining this rate of growth in small experimental plantations or in limited areas of good soil quality)? second, are these yields sustainable?

Reason for doubt can be found in the experience at Jari, where average yields have been much lower than the cited figure despite good soils in a part of the estate. The original anticipation was for the 40 tons $ha^{-1} y^{-1}$ production mentioned, but obtaining this production in practice proved to be quite another matter (Fearnside and Rankin, 1980, 1982a, 1985). The long-term sustainability of such plantations, especially if expanded to large areas, is also open to question (Fearnside and Rankin, 1982b).

Overly optimistic expectations for plantations would have significant impact were these to be translated into national energy policies: "If the wood obtained from harvesting fast-growing trees on a regular cycle of 5 or 6 y were converted to charcoal . . . it should be possible to produce about 12.5 tons of coal equivalent per hectare. Brazil's total energy requirement in 2050 could be obtained by replanting 90 million hectares of present tropical forest with fast-growing trees." There are two problems with these statements: first, the estimate appears to be based on converting the wood obtained from harvesting to coal equivalents, but what is most important is the *net* gain after deducting the inputs to production and the energy cost of transporting the product to the place where it will be used; second, the calculation of needed area depends on the expected high yields being obtained, especially since the required production inputs magnify the impact of any shortfall. If gross yields were half the expected amount, more than twice the area would be needed to produce the same net output.

In addition to counting on better yields than commercial-scale operations have obtained so far, Revelle makes some unlikely assumptions in the realm of physical resources: "Surveys of the soil characteristics of different regions . . . could reveal large areas where sustainable agriculture or agroforestry might be profitably practiced." Unfortunately, estimates of the area of best soil types in the Legal Amazon occurring in significant amounts (i.e., *terra roxa*: Alfisol) have declined in successive publications of Brazil's agriculture and cattle ranching research enterprise (EMBRAPA) as the region has become better known (see Fearnside, 1984b, 1986). Furthermore, the *terra roxa* areas are already occupied (e.g., in Rondônia, the Altamira area of the Transamazon Highway, the Tucumã Project in the upper Xingu, and Jari). While more such areas may be discovered, it is best not to base planning on them until they are actually found.

Amazonia is portrayed as a potential solution to Brazil's needs for food production to feed anticipated national population growth and to substitute fossil fuels through charcoal production in silvicultural plantations: "The existing forests cover such a vast area that more than half could remain untouched, even if all of Brazil's future food and energy needs were to be met in the Amazon." This statement assumes high yields, a radical transformation of behavior patterns among farmers, and halting of the growth of demand after the first half of Amazonia is converted to these uses. The very concept that Amazonia should solve the problems of other regions is questionable if the standard of long-term well-being of the region's residents and their descendants is applied (Fearnside, 1983, 1984c, 1986).

Focusing on research into agricultural techniques distracts attention from broader policy decisions that must be faced immediately: "Recent advances in no-till agriculture, mixed cropping, animal husbandry, and the use of perennial tree crops instead of annual varieties offer promising opportunities for application and research." While true that these avenues should be pursued, these promising opportunities have little likelihood of affecting any significant part of Brazil's $5 \times 10^6$-km$^2$ Legal Amazon before it is converted to cattle pasture. Conversion to cattle pasture is likely to continue to dominate because of market limits for perennial crops such as cacao, the nonagricultural motives for conversion of land to pasture as a means of securing land tenure, and the unrealistically high inputs required for many of the land uses. It is important not to be tranquilized by the existence of promising opportunities—with the result that immediate measures to attack the underlying causes of deforestation are given less priority. Research on better land use is indeed needed, but it is of lower urgency than actions directly affecting deforestation and the reorientation of overall development policy.

Once the fundamental decisions are made to redirect development toward sustainable support for the Amazon region's population and their descendants, at defined standards of consumption and environmental quality, then governments will make the needed efforts to develop the requisite components—such as mixed cropping agroecosystems, agroforestry, and the like. Without such a reorientation of development policy, advances like those listed will have no significant impact on the race to convert Amazonian forest to low-grade cattle pastures.

Understanding the consequences of deforestation, some of which are the focus of other contributions to this volume, is an essential first step toward governments' decisions to reorient development policy. Information on the causes of deforestation, outlined in my own contribution, is an equally essential part of the basis for making such a fundamental policy decision.

## REFERENCES

Fearnside, P. M., 1982. Deforestation in the Brazilian Amazon: How fast is it occurring? *Interciência* **7**, 82–88.

Fearnside, P. M., 1983. Development alternatives in the Brazilian Amazon: An ecological evaluation, *Interciência* **8**, 65–78.

Fearnside, P. M., 1984a. A floresta vai acabar? *Ciência Hoje* **2**(10), 42–52.

Fearnside, P. M., 1984b. Initial soil quality conditions on the Transamazon Highway of Brazil and their simulation in models for estimating human carrying capacity, *Trop. Ecol.* **25**, 1–21.

Fearnside, P. M., 1984c. Brazil's Amazon settlement schemes: Conflicting objectives and human carrying capacity, *Habit. Int.* **8**, 45–61.

Fearnside, P. M., 1985. Agriculture in Amazonia, in G. T. Prance, and T. E. Lovejoy, Eds., *Amazonia*, Pergamon, Oxford, England.

Fearnside, P. M., 1986. *Human Carrying Capacity of the Brazilian Rainforest*, Columbia University Press, New York.

Fearnside, P. M. and Rankin, J. M., 1980. Jari and development in the Brazilian Amazon, *Interciência* **5**, 146–156.

Fearnside, P. M. and Rankin, J. M., 1982a. The new Jari: Risks and prospects of a major Amazonian development, *Interciência* **7**, 329–339.

Fearnside, P. M. and Rankin, J. M., 1982b. Jari and Carajás: The uncertain future of large silvicultural plantations in the Amazon, *Interciência* **7**, 326–328.

Fearnside, P. M. and Rankin, J. M., 1985. Jari revisited: Changes and the outlook for sustainability in Amazonia's largest silvicultural estate, *Interciência* **10**, 121–129.

Food and Agriculture Organization (FAO) of the United Nations, *FAO Production Yearbook*, Vol. 36, FAO, Rome.

Lanly, J. P., 1982. *Tropical Forest Resources*, FAO Forestry Paper 30, Food and Agriculture Organization of the United Nations (FAO), Rome.

# Chapter 5

# Dam Building in the Tropics: Some Environmental and Social Consequences

Peter Bunyard

Man's desire to hold back water so that he can irrigate crops and extend the growing season goes back thousands of years; indeed, the ancient civilizations of Sumeria, Babylonia, Egypt, Ceylon, and Cambodia were all renowned for their irrigation works. Even the rare rains and resulting flash floods in desert regions were sometimes ingeniously controlled through a series of small dams and runoff channels built along the length of a wadi, as can be seen in the Negev Desert, south of Beersheba, where, several hundreds of years before Christ, the Nabateans built their beautiful desert cities, such as Avdat and Shivta, and managed to stock them with food grown in fields fed by runoff water.

The discovery in the nineteenth century that electricity could be generated by directing water through a turbine led to another use of dams besides that of providing water for irrigation projects, and the industrialized world, in particular the United States, began to embark increasingly on a spate of damming rivers in order to tap the flow of energy before it had all been dissipated downstream. Today advances in construction technology and design, together with the use of giant earth-moving machinery, have led to increasingly ambitious projects and the building of structures capable of containing enormous reservoirs of water. The largest to date, the Volta Dam in Ghana, impounds a reservoir covering 8500 km², about 5% of the total area of that country and an area the size of Lebanon. In Egypt, the Aswan High Dam is 17 times more massive than the Great Pyramid of Cheops (Goldsmith and Hildyard, 1984).

Meanwhile in Brazil, Eletronorte last year closed the Tucuruí Dam on the Tocantins River, the intention being to generate 4000 MW and at a cost of more than U.S. $4 billion. This dam is the first phase of the complete

Tocantins River Basin Hydroelectric Project, which would entail 8 large dams and 20 smaller ones on the river and its tributaries and would convert the Tocantins River into an almost continuous chain of lakes 1900 km long (Barham and Caufield, 1984). Since the project is not intended for any irrigation, the sole purpose of the dams is to generate electricity and thereby attract foreign investors and industry into the Amazon. Indeed, foreign companies including Shell, Rio Tinto Zinc, and Alcoa are already being enticed with promises of guaranteed cheap electricity. If all the energy contained in the rivers of the world were to be harnessed by dams (with their very high efficiency of conversion), then 73,000 TW-h ($10^{12}$ W-h) of electricity could be generated annually, the equivalent of some 12,000-GW-size nuclear power stations. At a recent World Energy Conference, experts suggested that a reasonable aim would be to exploit a quarter of the hydropower potential of the world's rivers, hence some 19,000 TW-h. About 1300 TW-h are produced worldwide today, much of it in the industrialized countries (Goldsmith and Hildyard, 1984). The 19,000 TW-h from hydropower would be equivalent to all the world's present population having available as much electricity as the average Briton now consumes. At first sight, this power development might seem a worthy aim, given such power is "clean," with none of the polluting connotations of thermal plants, whether fossil, fuel, or nuclear.

The Hoover Dam, built in 1936 on the Colorado River near Las Vegas, Nevada, was the first of the world's large dams. Since then, 175 have been built, most of them since the 1970s, and another 38 large dams are under construction. Superdam technology, and the use of thin concrete shells, is nonetheless still a relatively untried technology. With more than $10 \times 10^6$ m$^3$ of water held back by such dams, the consequences of dam failure would be catastrophic.

To date, most of the world's superdams have been built in the industrialized nations, particularly in the United States, the USSR, and Canada. Indeed, California alone has 9.5% of the world's total. But tropical countries, with their own dreams of development and often endowed with enormous catchment areas and large rivers, have set their sights on catching up. Whereas in 1980 the developing countries had altogether no more than 10 dams over 150 m high, by the end of the 1980s, they will have tripled that number to 30 such dams, aided in large measure by World Bank and other overseas loans. Brazil is no exception in its desire to get on the dam bandwagon. With a gigantic river system passing through $3.5 \times 10^6$ km$^2$ of tropical forest, Brazil intends to dam its rivers and exploit the energy. All told, the rivers could supply some 100 GW, equivalent to 100 nuclear power stations and more than double the projected future electricity demand in Brazil. The present aim is to develop some 22 GW of hydropower in the Amazon Basin by the year 2000, including the Tocantins River Basin Project (Barham and Caufield, 1984). Officials anticipate that by the end of the 1990s as much as one sixth of Brazil's Amazon region will have been transformed into an integrated industrial zone, with the development of mining, metal processing, forestry, agriculture, cattle ranching and human settlements. The main source of power would be hydroelectricity. Clearly, the total development of the area, if pursued with the zeal that has been shown to date, will have environmental impacts far beyond those caused by the damming of the rivers and the creation of enormous expanses of water. In addition, the Itaipu Dam on the Parana River, further to the south, is expected to generate 12.5 GW.

Even though the promoters of large dam projects have come to recognize in recent years that there are costs to offset the benefits of such ventures, the tendency is to underplay the negative aspects. Closer scrutiny of the environmental consequences of large dam projects reveals a far-from-satisfactory situation.

Apart from ensuring that the siting of the dam is in a geologically safe place, one of the first problems encountered by dam builders is that of having to resettle those whose land and livelihood will vanish beneath the floodwaters. Resettlement has rarely proved satisfactory even when compensation has been deemed adequate. The damming of the Volta in Ghana led to 78,000 people from over 700 towns and villages having to be resettled, while the Pa Mong project in Vietnam uprooted almost half a million. The Victoria Dam on the Mahaweli River in Sri Lanka has flooded 123 villages, some several thousands of years old, and uprooted at least 45,000 people (Goldsmith and Hildyard, 1984). Families that are displaced will receive just £90 in compensation. The Victoria Dam is being built by Great Britain.

The Tucuruí Dam has inundated some 17 towns and villages, requiring the resettlement of some 15,000 people. In addition, some 10,000 squatters in the area have no rights and are ineligible for compensation. Three Amerindian reservations will be seriously affected by the project; one will be almost completely flooded, another partially flooded and the third will be ''lacerated by the incursions of a power transmission line, an electrified iron ore railroad and by construction and maintenance roads'' (Goodland, 1977). Both groups of Indians involved, the Parakanan and Gavioes, have suffered considerably since their first contact with Europeans; today, however, they have received some compensation for the loss of their ancestral lands.

The damming of rivers inevitably leads to the loss of land, sometimes highly productive. Thus 400,000 ha vanished beneath the waters of Lake Nasser; 848,200 ha were lost with the Volta Dam, and 510,000 ha were flooded by the Kariba Dam. The Victoria Dam in Sri Lanka has destroyed 3000 acres of land cultivated with paddy rice, tobacco, vegetables, and other food crops and 4000 acres cultivated with mixed fruit, coffee, cocoa, coconut, spices, and soft wood. The use of irrigated water further downstream from the dam is supposed to more than compensate for the loss of any cultivated land, and one of the main rationalizations for proceeding with massive dam and water projects is to increase the amount of irrigated land in the world so as to match the demands of a rapidly growing world population. However, from time immemorial irrigation schemes have brought a host of problems in their wake (as reviewed by Worthington, 1977); the most serious such problems are the waterlogging of soils through the raising of the water table and salinization as salts are drawn up to the soil surface.

Since Brazil does not intend to use its reservoirs for anything other than electricity production, it should avoid the problems associated with irrigation. But the impounding of waters can, and often does, lead to major problems of disease (Goodland, 1977; Caufield, 1984). Malaria has become the single most important disease in Amazonia, and around Tucuruí as many as one out of five people are found to be infected. When in operation, the Tucuruí Dam will undoubtedly exacerbate the malaria problem insofar as the calculated 12-m drawdown will decrease the surface area of the lake from 2160 to 1260 km$^2$, thus exposing a 900-km$^2$ area ideal for mosquito breeding, particularly given the likely growth of water weeds in the many dendritic sidearms of the reservoir.

Schistosomiasis is also becoming a serious problem in Brazil with some 14 million Brazilians affected overall. The region immediately surrounding the Tucuruí is free of the vector snail at the present time, but poor hygiene combined with infection being brought in, plus the possibility that the snail may be introduced into the reservoir, could create problems in the future. The River Tocantins at Tucuruí has, in contrast to many rivers in the Amazon, a neutral or slightly alkaline pH, and given that limestone quarrying takes place a little upstream at Marabá, the snail could find the reservoir an ideal habitat. Goodland (1977) fears that once the area has been thoroughly opened up, with visitors carrying the schistosome coming in increasing numbers, the chances of the disease becoming endemic to the area are considerable.

Originally Eletronorte had no plans to clear the forest from the area to be flooded by the Tucuruí Dam, but experience in Surinam, the former Dutch colony to the north of Brazil, when 1500 km$^2$ of forest were inundated to create Lake Brokopondo, indicates that the decomposing forest can give rise to momentous pollution problems. Workers at the Brokopondo Dam had to wear gas masks for 2 y against the overpowering smell of hydrogen sulfide. Meanwhile the slightly acidic waters of the river (pH 6.5) became more strongly acidic (pH 5.3) through decomposition of the vegetation, causing the corrosion of the casings of both turbines and leading to the need for expensive repairs. By 1977, the decomposition over, the pH of the waters had risen to 7.3. Once the Brokopondo Dam was completed in 1964, a new problem came to light with the rapid spread of water hyacinth and other weeds, including a floating fern (Ceratopteris). Thus by the third year, water hyacinth covered more than 40% of the reservoir and the fern another 20%. The weeds were finally controlled by spraying the reservoir with the phenoxy herbicide 2,4-D at a cost of U.S. $2.5 million. Both the decomposition of the forest and the dense mat of vegetation on the surface of the reservoir brought the oxygen content of the water sharply down, the actual oxygen content decreasing with depth from some 5 to 7 mg $l^{-1}$ in the top meter to almost anoxic levels at depths below 15 m. For the first few years after closure, the anoxic water traveled all the way to the estuary, some 90 km away. Gradually the oxygen content of the river improved, and fish have returned to the entire stretch of river below the dam.

Similar problems of sulfurous smells and of invasion by water weeds were also encountered when the 20-MW Curúa-Una Dam was closed 70 km south of Santarem in Brazil. Again the forest drowned by the project was left intact.

The Tucuruí Dam will create a reservoir with an average depth of 20 m when at its normal maximum. When the water is drawn down, the average depth will be 16 m, and thus many tree trunks will be exposed. The retention time of water in the reservoir, on average some 2 months, will also be considerably less than is the case for Lake Brokopondo. Thus much of the decomposition at Tucuruí should proceed aerobically, with the avoidance of sulfurous gas production. Another advantage of leaving the forest intact prior to flooding is that the vegetation protects the reservoir bed, thereby reducing erosion.

In 1979, Eletronorte decided to institute selective clearing of the area to be inundated and brought in a company called CAPEMI. However, having cleared no more than one tenth of the area it was contracted to clear, CAPEMI went bankrupt, owing more than $4 million to its 3000 workers. It was then discovered that CAPEMI had used defoliants to clear the forest and had abandoned large quantities of sodium pentachlorophenol at the site, some of which may have washed into the water. One report suggests more than 300 drums of the defoliant were recovered by the liquidators (Barham and Caufield, 1984).

Eletronorte also intends to use herbicides to destroy more than 2000 $km^2$ of forest from the area destined to be flooded with the closing of the Balbina Dam near Manaus (del Quiaro, 1985).

This brief survey has barely touched on the full environmental and social consequences of the dam projects being undertaken in Brazil, particularly those now being carried out in the Amazon region. Without question, species of plants and animals that have never yet been recorded will be lost forever. The enormous quantities of hydroelectricity generated by the various projects will inevitably lead to a massive development of the Amazon region, accelerating the deforestation that is already taking place. Wide-scale deforestation is likely to lead to rapid erosion of the tropical soils in the Amazon Basin and to considerable runoff of rainwater. Both are detrimental to dam projects. Silt shortens the useful life of a dam, and the runoff, with its burden of silt, endangers the safety of the structure. The Santo Grande Dam on the Santo Antonio River receives silt at a rate exceeding 80,000 $m^3$ per month on occasions, while heavy runoff, exacerbated by intensive agriculture in the watershed, completely smashed two hydrodams on the Rio Alto Pardo in the 1970s, with a massive loss in investment.

## REFERENCES

Barham, J. and Caufield, C., 1984. The problems that plague a Brazilian dam, *New Sci.*, **11**, 10.

Caufield, C., 1984. *In the Rainforest*, Knopf, New York.

Goldsmith, E. and Hildyard, 1984. *The Social and Environmental Effects of Large Dams*, Vol. I: *Overview*, Wadebridge Ecological Centre, Cornwall, United Kingdom, summarized in *The Ecologist*, **14**, 1–16.

Goodland, R., 1977. *Environmental Reconnaissance of the Turcuruí Hydro Project*, Eletronorte, Brasília.

del Quiaro, R., 1985. Brazil to drown forest in herbicides, *New Sci.*, **14**, 9.

Worthington, E. B., Ed., 1977. *Arid Land Irrigation in Developing Countries: Environmental Problems and Effects*, Pergamon, New York.

# Chapter 6

# Species Diversity, Phenology, Plant–Animal Interactions, and Their Correlation With Climate, as Illustrated by the Brazil Nut Family (Lecythidaceae)

## Scott A. Mori and Ghillean T. Prance

Lowland, humid, neotropical (New World tropical) forests are characterized by high diversity of plant and animal species and a very high degree of plant–animal interactions. Counts of trees over 10 cm in diameter on 1-ha plots in Amazonian and Guianan forests have yielded values as low as 65 (Klinge and Rodrigues, 1968) and as high as 179 (Prance et al. 1976). In a recent study of a French Guianan forest, in an area of 17,600 ha proposed as a national park, we calculated that there are 546 species of trees capable of attaining diameters of at least 10 cm (Mori and Boom, in press). This figure is in sharp contrast to the 500 species of trees estimated by Thiel (1983) for all of French Guiana. Prance (1977) estimates that the flora of tropical America has 90,000 species of angiosperms, or 37.5% of the worldwide total. Consequently, it is increasingly apparent that high species diversity is common to all neotropical forests with sufficient rainfall and without limiting soil factors (see Gentry, 1982, for a review).

Animal diversity is even higher than plant diversity. Recent work by the entomologist Terry Erwin and his associates in Amazonian Peru shows that 1 ha of seasonal forest in lowland Panama may harbor 41,000 species of arthropods, and that there might be 30 million or more species of insects in tropical rainforests (Erwin, 1982). Such high numbers of both plants and animals reflect a long history of evolutionary interactions. Plants depend on animals for pollination and seed dispersal, and they have developed chemical and physical defense systems to protect themselves from predation by animals. Gilbert and Raven (1975) provide an excellent review of the kinds of coevolutionary systems found in the neotropics. Examples of coevolution for specific neotropical families are provided by Gentry (1974) for the Bignoniaceae family of plants, and for the Lecythidaceae family by Mori, Orchard, and Prance (1980), Mori, Prance, and Bolten (1978), Mori and Prance (1981a, 1981b), Prance (1976), Prance and Mori (1978, 1979, 1983), Prance et al. (1983).

Species diversity results from many factors. Gentry (1982) points out that wetter neotropical forests generally have more diverse plant communities than do drier ones. However, he has recently suggested (Gentry, in press) that rainfall beyond 4 m year$^{-1}$ is not accompanied by an increase in plant species diversity. Other exceptions occur where local edaphic conditions, such as periodically water-logged soils or soils with low water retention capacity, limit species diversity. For example, certain Amazonian species grow preferentially in periodically inundated flood plains (*várzea*) whereas others prefer noninundated forests (*terra firme*) (Spruce, 1908).

Pires and Prance (1977) have illustrated this habitat preference with a series of ecological maps of eastern Amazonian species, and Ducke (1948) clearly demonstrated differences in dispersal strategies of taxonomically related species of the two habitats. For a forest on the Rio Xingu in Brazil, Campbell et al. (unpublished) have shown that species diversity in *terra firme* (134 species per hectare) is nearly triple that of nutrient-poor, clear-water *várzea* forest (45 species per hectare). In a study of a Guyanan forest, Davis and Richards (1934) recognized five different vegetation types, which they attributed to differences in soil moisture and organic content. Their extreme cases, the "Mora" forest association, which occurs on highly organic soils that never dry out, and the "Wallaba" forest association, which is found on white sand soils that rapidly dry out in the dry season, showed least species diversity. Associations with intermediate moisture and organic matter ("Morabukea," Mixed, and "Greenheart") were more diverse.

Amount of rainfall and edaphic factors provide incomplete explanations for diversity patterns. Increased diversity may also come through longer evolutionary history, which gives more time for speciation; more dissected topography, which provides more niches for speciation; or lack of a dry season, which saves plants from having to adapt to drought stress. Effects are convolved, and the data often support multiple interpretations.

The complexity of controls on diversity may be illustrated by our findings on forest sites in southern Bahia, eastern Amazonia, and French Guiana. Summary statistics for the three sites are presented in Table 1. As expected, the wettest site (French Guiana) is most diverse. However, longer geological history and greater topographic relief may also contribute to its high diversity. The driest site (southern Bahia) is more diverse than the site with intermediate precipitation (eastern Amazonia). This difference could be explained by either the lack of dry season, and hence of seasonal stress, at the Bahia site or by its relatively great topographic relief—or by both.

Climatic changes throughout the Pleistocene (Chapter 7) have dramatically affected plant species diversity and composition throughout the lowland neotropics. Drier periods have brought about the expansion of savanna and the contraction of forests; wetter periods have caused the reverse

**TABLE 1. Factors Contributing to Diversity of Tree Species on Three Neotropical Sites**

| Location | Sample Size | Number of Species over 10 cm dbh | Trees Per Species | Annual Total Precipitation (m) | Dry Season | Time of Colonization by Forests | Relief |
|---|---|---|---|---|---|---|---|
| Eastern Amazonia | 1000[a] | 208[a] | 4.8[a] | 1.7–2.5[d] | September–December[d] | Pleistocene[f-i] | Lowest |
| Southern Bahia | 600[b] | 178[b] | 3.4[b] | 1.8[e] | No marked[e] | Pleistocene[k] | Intermediate[b] |
| French Guiana | 800[c] | 294[c] | 2.7[c] | 2.4[c] | August–November[c] | Tertiary[g,i,j] | Highest[c] |

Sources:
[a] Mori et al., unpublished data.
[b] Mori et al., 1983.
[c] Mori and Boom, in press.
[d] Fundação Instituto Brasileiro de Geografia e Estatística, 1977.
[e] Mori, Lisboa, and Kallunki, 1982.
[f] Haffer, 1969.
[g] Prance, 1978.
[h] Prance, 1983.
[i] Granville, 1982.
[j] Descimon, 1977.
[k] Bigarella and Andrade, 1964; Bigarella, 1975; Bigarella, Andrade-Lima, and Ries, 1975.

71

(Prance, 1973, 1982). Savannas, with less precipitation and a longer dry season, are generally less species rich, especially in trees, than are neotropical forests, and any climatic modifications that promote the formation of savannas will drastically reduce tree diversity.

We use the Lecythidaceae to illustrate what might happen to the diversity and biological interactions among trees of neotropical lowland moist forests if massive deforestation is continued and if climate is modified. We will describe the family in general terms and then discuss its phenology, pollination biology, and dispersal ecology.

## THE BRAZIL NUT FAMILY (LECYTHIDACEAE)

The Lecythidaceae, *sensu lato*, is a family of small to very large trees found in the tropics of both hemispheres (Fig. 1). The family includes four subfamilies: Planchonioideae with 55 species in 6 genera distributed throughout tropical Asia, Malaysia, northern Australia, and the Pacific Islands; Foetidioideae with 5 species in a single genus distributed in Madagascar, India, and Malaysia; Napoleonaeoideae with 12 species in 3 genera distributed in West Africa and the upper Rio Negro region of Amazonia; and the Lecythidoideae with about 212 species in 10 genera distributed throughout tropical South America from Veracruz, Mexico, to southern Brazil (Kowal et al., 1977; Prance and Mori, 1979). Our discussion will be limited to the Lecythidoideae, which includes all of the New World members of the family except *Asteranthos brasiliensis* Desfontaines, a member of the Napoleonaeoideae. Further references to the Lecythidaceae in this essay are restricted to the Lecythidoideae.

The Lecythidaceae grow mainly in lowland moist forests. Few species have entered savanna vegetations (e.g., *Cariniana rubra* Gardner ex Miers and *Eschweilera nana* (Berg) Miers of Central Brazil, *Lecythis miersiana* Mori and *L. schomburgkii* Berg of Roraima, Brazil), and only 14 species, all belonging to the genus *Eschweilera*, are known to occur at altitudes over 1000 m (Prance and Mori, 1979). In moist lowland forests, species diversity of the family is greatest on well-drained sites with relatively rich soils, but some species have successfully invaded the periodically inundated *várzea* habitat where they may be among the most conspicuous elements of the vegetation [e.g., *Allantoma lineata* (Mart. ex Berg) Miers, *Couratari oligantha* A. C. Smith, *C. tenuicarpa* A. C. Smith, *Eschweilera ovalifolia* (DC) Niedenzu, *E. parvifolia* Mart. ex DC, and *E. tenuifolia* (Berg) Miers]. In the forests bounded by the Amazon, Negro, and Orinoco rivers, the Lecythidaceae are often among the five leading families (Cain et al., 1956; Davis and Richards, 1934; Mori and Boom, in press; Prance et al., 1976; Schulz, 1960). They are ecologically less important in Atlantic coastal Brazil (Mori et al., 1983) and perhaps in extreme western Amazonia (Balslev et al., in

**FIGURE 1.**   The Brazil nut (*Bertholletia excelsa*) in Amapá, Brazil. This is the best-known member of the Lecythidaceae because of its importance in world commerce.

press). The family is also ecologically important in the lowland wet forests of Chocó, Colombia.

Where the forest has been burned after felling, species of Lecythidaceae are usually absent from the subsequent secondary vegetation. However, many species of the family can sprout from cut trunks. Therefore, if an area is not burned after being cleared, regrowth may include a relatively high number of Lecythidaceae (Prance, 1975).

In summary, the Lecythidaceae is a relatively small family of neotropical trees found, for the most part, in undisturbed tropical moist forests. Modification of this habitat will result in the loss of many individuals and perhaps the extinction of species of this family.

## PHENOLOGY

Botanical phenology is the study of the timing of vegetative activities, flowering, and fruiting and their relationship to environmental factors. The Lecythidaceae tend to flower in the dry season and fruit at the beginning of
the wet season. In areas where there is no dry season, other environmental
factors may influence phenological events.

For example, in the area surrounding Saül, French Guiana, where annual
precipitation averages 2.4 m, there is a distinct dry season from August
through November. There, Mori and Prance (in press) found that all 26
species of Lecythidaceae either flower entirely within the dry season or
initiate flowering during the transition from the dry to the wet season. Only
*Gustavia hexapetala* (Aubl.) Smith flowers predominantly in the wet season.
Seed drop of Lecythidaceae in this area is highly correlated with the onset
of the wet season. Even if fruit is set early in the dry season, it appears that
fruit development is arrested in order to ensure that seeds fall at the beginning
of the wet season. These data support the work of Sabatier (1983), who
found that all 10 species of Lecythidaceae at his study site near St. Elie,
French Guiana, flower in the dry season and fruit at the beginning of the
wet season. In a detailed study of a central Panamanian population of *Gustavia superba* (Kunth) Berg, Mori and Kallunki (1976) found that peak leaf
fall occurs in the first month of the wet season; leaf flush is bimodal, with
one peak in the late wet to early dry season and the other at the onset of
the wet season; flowering occurs in the dry season; and fruits become ripe
at the beginning of the wet season (Fig. 2).

Rainfall is an important environmental cue for phenological events (Alvim
and Alvim, 1978; Mori and Pipoly, 1984; Opler et al., 1976). Augspurger
(1979, 1981, 1982) has even induced flowering in the Panamanian shrub *Hybanthus prunifolius* (Schult.) Schulze by withholding water and then irri-
gating it.

In regions with no dependable dry season, species of Lecythidaceae may
respond to other environmental cues. In southern Bahia, where annual rainfall averages 1.8 m, there are no months with predictably less rainfall (Mori
et al., 1982). There, *Lecythis pisonis* Cambess. always flowers in the Southern Hemisphere's spring, apparently in response to the increasingly longer
photoperiods or to higher temperatures of that time of the year (Mori, Mattos
Silva, and dos Santos, 1980). Peak flowering of most other trees in southern
Bahia also occurs in the spring (Mori et al., 1982).

Abnormally dry or wet years may upset plant phenologies. For example,
the failure of the central Panamanian population of *G. superba* to produce
fruit in 1975 may be the result of an unusually severe dry season. Flowering
in 1974–1975 took place in two spurts: one, as normal for the species, in
the dry season, and the other at the onset of the wet season (Fig. 2). In that
year, rainfall was extremely low from January to April. Mori and Kallunki
(1976) have suggested that the early flowering did not result in fruit set

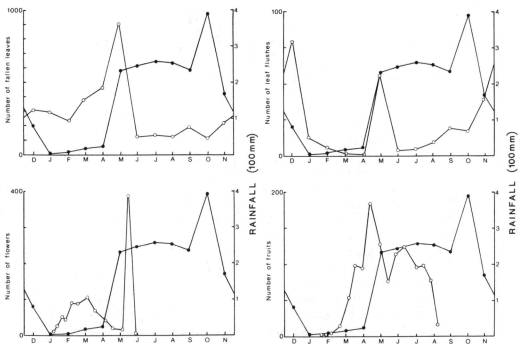

**FIGURE 2.** Graphs depicting phenological events of *Gustavia superba*. *Leaf fall*: The open circles represent the number of leaves that fell each month into an area of 77 square meters. *Leaf production*: The open circles represent the number of leaf flushes observed on the first of the month following the month in which they flushed. *Flower production*: The open circles represent the number of flowers observed on a given date. *Fruit production*: The open circles represent the number of fruits observed on a given date. However, few, if any, of these fruits reached maturity. In all graphs the rainfall for each month during the course of the study is represented by a closed circle and the tick marks on the abscissa represent the middle of the month. [Reprinted from Mori and Kallunki (1976) with permission of *Biotropica*, copyright 1976.]

because there was not enough water available for fruit development, and the later flowering was unsuccessful because the appropriate pollinators were not present.

For plants dependent on rainfall cues for their phenological events, climatic changes could adversely affect their vegetative and sexual reproduction. Plants at the margins of forests or in too-small plots left after human disturbance may not reproduce properly because of microclimatic modifications. Disturbance of their phenological cycles may be the first step in their extinction.

## POLLINATION

Some of the closest coevolutionary relationships between plants and animals in the lowland neotropics occur between flowering plants and their pollinators. The flowers of Lecythidaceae have evolved specialized structures to attract and accommodate their pollinators (Prance and Mori, 1979). These relationships make plants indirectly vulnerable to extinction if their pollinators are adversely affected and unavailable at the time of flowering. The relationships among Lecythidaceae, their bee pollinators (Prance and Mori, 1979), and orchids (Dressler, 1982) illustrate the intricacy and fragility of this web of species relationships.

The principal pollinators of neotropical Lecythidaceae are bees (Mori et al., 1978; Mori and Boeke, in press; Prance, 1976; Prance and Mori, 1979; Prance et al., 1983). The only confirmed exception is the bat-pollinated *Lecythis poiteaui* Berg (Mori et al., 1978). This species possesses nocturnal flowers, inflorescences projected above the crown, numerous stamens, abundant nectar, emission of a musty fruity odor from the flowers, and greenish-white, inrolled, relatively inconspicuous petals, features that are all part of the syndrome of bat pollination (Mori, 1981).

The two principal floral types of neotropical Lecythidaceae differ in the structure of the androecium (male part of flower). One type has a radially symmetrical flower (actinomorphic) (Figs. 3 and 4), and the other type has a bilaterally symmetrical flower (zygomorphic). The latter is prolonged on one side into a stamen-free area (ligule), terminated by an appendage-bearing hood (Figs. 3 and 5). The hood appendages may or may not bear anthers.

The actinomorphic Lecythidaceae offer only fertile pollen as a reward to pollinators. Bees can easily enter their flowers, and they are visited by numerous bees of all size. The specialized euglossine, or orchid bees, however, have never been captured and only infrequently observed at the flowers of actinomorphic species. In contrast, the zygomorphic species offer either nectar, or specialized "fodder" pollen—or both—to attract pollinators (Mori and Boeke, in press; Mori et al., 1978). The "fodder" pollen is probably sterile and may differ from fertile pollen in color, texture, and grain aggregation (separate grains versus grains organized into tetrads) (Mori and Orchard, 1979; Mori, Orchard, and Prance, 1980; Ormond et al., 1981).

Some zygomorphic species have completely antherless appendages in the hood and may offer fodder pollen in one to several rows of stamens on the ligular side of the staminal ring. The anthers of these stamens are usually yellow in contrast to the white ones of the remainder of the ring. More commonly, the zygomorphic species without hood anthers offer nectar, which is produced in the hood at the apex of an inwardly coiled flap (Figs. 3 and 5), as a pollinator reward.

The flower structures of zygomorphic Lecythidaceae tend to make their rewards accessible only to specialized pollinators. The androecial hood of many, but not all, of these species is tightly appressed to the summit of the ovary, which limits floral entry to those bees strong enough and endowed with the proper "psychology" or "intelligence" to force it open (Fig. 6). The coiled flap makes nectar available only to species with long enough tongues to reach it (Fig. 3).

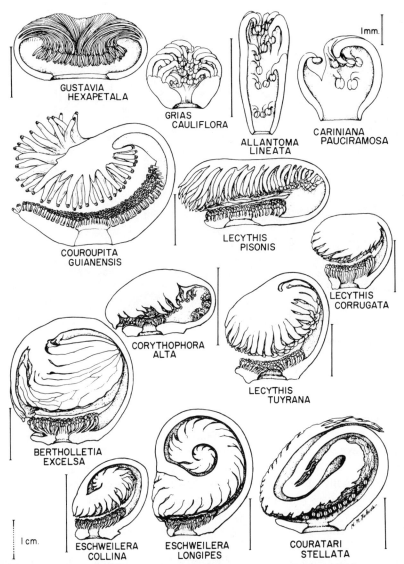

**FIGURE 3.** Medial sections of the androecia (male part of the flower) of selected species of New World Lecythidaceae. All of the other floral parts have been removed. Floral evolution in this family has involved the coevolution of the androecium with bees. The species represented in the top row have radially symmetrical androecia, whereas the remainder of the species have bilaterally symmetrical androecia. These have a prolongation on one side of the staminal ring, which is divided into a basal "ligule" and apical "hood." The radially symmetrical species offer fertile pollen as a pollinator reward, whereas the bilaterally symmetrical *Couroupita guianensis*, *Corythophora alta* R. Knuth, and *Lecythis pisonis* offer "fodder" pollen located in the hood. In *Lecythis corrugata*, dual rewards appear to be offered, "fodder" pollen in the innermost part of the staminal ring and nectar at the junction of the ligule with the hood. The remaining species attract bees with nectar produced within the coiled hood. [Reprinted from Prance and Mori (1979) with permission of the New York Botanical Garden, copyright 1979.]

77

**FIGURE 4.** *Gustavia superba* from Panama, a species with radially symmetrical flowers. (Reprinted with permission of *Flora Neotropica*, vol. 21, frontispiece, copyright 1979, Prance and Mori and The New York Botanical Garden.)

Flower parts are arranged in a fashion that favors pollination. Fodder pollen is usually located in the stamens of the hood but may also be found in one or several rows on the ligular side of the staminal ring (Fig. 3). Fertile pollen is always located in the staminal ring. Our studies of *L. pisonis* have shown that pollen from the hood does not germinate whereas that from the staminal ring does germinate *in vitro* (Mori and Orchard, 1979; Mori, Orchard, and Prance, 1980). Observations of this species in southern Bahia and eastern Amazonia reveal that the principal pollinators are females of the carpenter bee, *Xylocopa frontalis* (Olivier). When this bee enters the flower, it lands on the hood in a position that enables it to collect fodder pollen from the hood while fertile pollen from the staminal ring is deposited on its head and back (Fig. 6). The fodder pollen is placed in the bee's scopae for later feeding to its larvae whereas the fertile pollen from the staminal ring is in the correct position to be deposited on the stigma of the next flower visited.

Euglossine bees have both the strength needed to open the closed hood of zygomorphic Lecythidaceae and long enough tongues to reach the nectar at the end of the coil. They are implicated in the pollination of all zygomorphic, nectar-producing species studied, and on the basis of the geography and ecology of these two taxa (described below), as well as the apparent

**FIGURE 5.** *Eschweilera sagotiana* Miers from Surinam, a species with bilaterally symmetrical flowers. Note the flower mimic, the spider *Epicadus heterogaster*, waiting to attack an unsuspecting pollinator.

morphological adaptations of the Lecythidaceae flower to the long tongue of euglossines, we suggest that the zygomorphic, nectar-producing floral type has evolved in response to selective pressures exerted by this group of bees.

Species of *Bombus* and various Anthophorid bees do collect nectar from zygomorphic-flowered Lecythidaceae, but the euglossines are their principal visitors. The more coiled and complex the androecial hood, the greater the euglossine dominance. For example, the economically important Brazil nut (*Bertholletia excelsa* H.B.K.), which has a partially coiled androecial hood (Fig. 3), is visited by the bees *Bombus, Centris, Xylocopa* (Müller et al.,

**FIGURE 6.** The carpenter bee, *Xylocopa frontalis*, removing "fodder" pollen from the flower of the sapucaia, *Lecythis pisonis*. [Reprinted with permission of Mori et al. (1980), *Science*, vol. 209, pp. 400–403, copyright 1980.]

1980) and *Epicharis* (Moritz, 1984; Müller et al., 1980) as well as various species of euglossines (Müller et al., 1980).

The geographical distribution of zygomorphic, nectar-producing Lecythidaceae, including all species of *Bertholletia, Eschweilera, Couratari*, and some species of *Lecythis*, falls within the range of the euglossine bees (Moure, 1967). These kinds of Lecythidaceae are strictly neotropical, ranging from Mexico to southern Brazil, but they are absent from the Caribbean except for the South American island of Trinidad. Likewise, the euglossines are virtually limited to mainland tropical America; only *Euglossa jamaicensis* Moure from the Greater Antilles is known to be outside the area (Dressler, 1982). Even the ecological preferences of the euglossine bees are similar to those of neotropical Lecythidaceae; they are most diverse in moist forest, but a few range into savannas and gallery forests. They are found from sea level up to 1500 or 1600 m elevation but are rarely found above 2000 m even as transients (Dressler, 1982).

Research has shown that euglossine bees are also important in neotropical orchid pollination. Male bees visit orchid flowers to collect perfumelike substances, which are thought to aid them in the attraction of mates. The euglossines also depend on other plants for nectar, pollen, and resins as well as these perfumes (Dressler, 1982). The Lecythidaceae partially provide two of these resources, pollen and nectar.

The relationship among Lecythidaceae, bees (in particular euglossines), and orchids is only one example of the complex interactions that have evolved in the pollination systems of lowland neotropical forests. The continuation of these relationships depends on the maintenance of climatic and other environmental conditions that favor lowland moist forests. The difficulty in recreating the environmental conditions necessary for the reproduction of native species is illustrated by man's failure to successfully grow Brazil nuts in plantations. Under plantation cultivation, Brazil nut production is drastically reduced, probably because pollinators are not present in quantities necessary for adequate cross-pollination.

## SEED DISPERSAL

The fruits of neotropical Lecythidaceae have evolved a variety of forms in response to pressures exerted by different seed dispersal agents and fruit and seed predators. Major evolutionary differentiations caused by these selective pressures are (a) indehiscence (remaining closed and retaining seeds at maturity) versus dehiscence (opening and releasing seeds at maturity, Fig. 7); (b) fleshy versus woody pericarps (fruit walls); (c) seed fall from the fruit or with the fruit at maturity; (d) lateral versus basal fleshy arils (Fig. 7); (e) the loss of arils; and (f) the development of membranous, winglike arils. These trends have coevolved with animal or wind seed dispersors throughout a long coevolutionary history under rain forest conditions. The animal dispersors, in particular, are sensitive to climatic modifications, and therefore seed dispersal in the Brazil nut family will be reduced if the climate becomes drier.

Indehiscent fruits of the genera *Gustavia, Grias,* and *Couroupita* may have soft or hard fruit walls. Both have coevolved with animal dispersors. Soft pericarps are found in *Gustavia* and *Grias* and serve to attract mammals as dispersal agents. For example, the entire fruit walls of *Gustavia superba* and *G. grandibracteata* (Croat and Mori) attract mammals, which in turn scatter the seeds while in the act of eating the fruit walls. Fish may assist the dispersal of the principally riverine species (G. augusta L. (Prance and Mori, 1983). Humans consume the fruits of *G. superba, G. speciosa* (Kunth) DC, and *Grias neuberthii* J. F. MacBride in Panama, Colombia, and Peru,

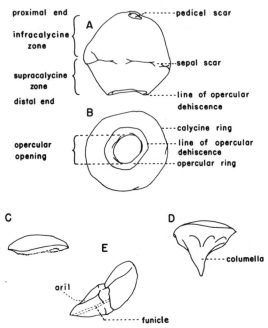

**FIGURE 7.** General fruit features of the New World dehiscent Lecythidaceae as illustrated by *Lecythis*. (*a*) Lateral view of the fruit. (*b*) Distal view of the fruit. (*c–d*) The lid or operculum which falls at maturity. (*e*) Seed with funicle surrounded by fleshy aril. Depending on the species, the fruit wall, seed, or aril may serve to attract dispersal agents. (Reprinted with permission of *Flora Neotropica*, vol. 21, pp. 1–270, copyright 1979, Prance and Mori and the New York Botanical Gardens.)

respectively. In the genus *Couroupita*, the pericarp is thin but hard. At maturity, the fruits fall to the ground and break open, exposing a bluish-green pulp in which the seeds are embedded. One observation of dispersal of *C. guianensis* Aublet indicates that wild pigs are the dispersal agent. A herd of pigs foraging under this tree ate all available fruit. They apparently seek the fruit for the pulp and pass the seeds, or at least some of them, unharmed through their digestive tracts (Prance and Mori, 1983).

Other species of Lecythidaceae possess woody pericarps that may have evolved in response to animal predation (Figs. 7, 8). The thick, tough walls of the fruit protect the developing seeds from most, but not all, predators. Moreover, we have noted the presence of viscous mucilage in the fruits of *Lecythis chartacea* Berg and *L. lurida* (Miers) Mori that oozes out of ducts in the sepals and pericarp. We feel that this mucilage may protect the seeds from predation by gumming up insect mouth parts, as hypothesized for *Hymenaea courbaril* L. (Janzen, 1975) and for *Stemmadenia donnell-smithii* Woodson (McDiarmid et al., 1977).

The fruits of *B. excelsa* (Brazil nut) and *L. pisonis* (sapucaia) illustrate

**FIGURE 8.** Fruits of the sapucaia, *Lecythis pisonis*. Note that the fruits have a large opening at maturity and that the seeds are subtended by a large white structure known botanically as an aril. Bats remove the seeds from the fruit in order to eat the aril, thereby dispersing the seeds away from the mother tree.

the role that dispersal agents may play in the evolution of fruit structures. At maturity the fruits of the Sapucaia open and the opercular lid falls to the ground. The seeds, which are attached by a slender funicle that is in turn surrounded by a large fleshy aril (Fig. 8), are removed by bats. The bats eat the aril, thereby scattering the seeds away from the mother tree (Greenhall, 1965; Mori and Prance, 1981a; Prance and Mori, 1983). In contrast, the entire fruit of the Brazil nut falls to the ground at maturity (Fig. 9). The seeds remain inside because the diameter of the opercular opening is smaller than that of the seeds. Brazil nut fruits are gnawed open by agoutis (Huber, 1910), a common rodent in neotropical forests, which eat a few and bury the remainder for subsequent use. Those seeds that are forgotten germinate up to a year later, at some distance from the mother tree. Although Smythe (1978), in a study of Panamanian agoutis, has shown that their home range is relatively small, the potential for dispersal is much greater because agoutis in adjacent ranges often remove originally cached seeds and rebury them even further from the parent tree. The seeds are either eaten and destroyed by the agouti (there is no aril) or left in a forgotten cache where they eventually germinate. The differences in dispersal mechanisms of these species have enabled economic exploitation of the Brazil nut on a large scale, whereas

**FIGURE 9.** Fruits of the Brazil nut. The seeds are retained within the fruit at maturity because the fruit opening is smaller in diameter than that of the seeds. The seeds are dispersed by agoutis (*Dasyprocta* spp.), which gnaw open the fruits to obtain them.

the sapucaia, equally delicious to eat, is so difficult to collect in quantities that commercial exploitation has not been possible.

In *Cariniana* and *Couratari*, the aril has been flattened into a membranous wing that facilitates wind dispersal. Most species of these genera are large trees, many emerging above the surrounding plant canopy. Therefore, when seeds are released, they are exposed to maximum wind velocities.

## SENSITIVITY TO DEFORESTATION AND CLIMATE CHANGE

Neotropical lowland moist forests are highly diverse and interdependent assemblages of plants and animals. This high diversity is dependent on the climate under which these forests have evolved. Any modification of the climate, especially in the direction of less and more-seasonal rainfall, will result in the extinction of countless species and thus reduce diversity. Many taxa, like the Brazil nut family and similar economically important families such as the Chrysobalanaceae, Lauraceae, and Sapotaceae, are largely restricted to primary, lowland, moist forests. These taxa are poorly represented in savanna and mostly absent from secondary vegetation. Consequently, deforestation of lowland moist forests can be expected to directly eliminate much of the species diversity. Moreover, climatic changes caused by extensive deforestation in other areas may result in savannization of much larger areas, thereby indirectly eliminating moist forest species.

The interaction of plants and animals in moist forests is so finely tuned that the disappearance of one species will have direct and indirect consequences on numerous other species. For example, the Brazil nut (*B. excelsa*) is pollinated, for the most part, by large-sized forest bees, and its seeds are dispersed by agoutis (*Dasyprocta* spp.). Similarly, the sapucaia (*L. pisonis*) is pollinated by the carpenter bee (*X. frontalis*), and its seeds are dispersed by bats. Any changes, such as climatic modification, that remove one of these organisms from the environment will have direct and adverse consequences on the others involved in the interaction.

The best strategy for the preservation of species diversity and the accompanying plant–animal interactions in the lowland moist forest of the Amazon is the continued acquisition and protection of large tracts of primary forest. Brazil has been concerned about the preservation of her Amazonian forest for some time and has taken many initiatives in that direction. A plan for development of the Amazon has been elaborated (Instituto Nacional de Pesquisas da Amazonia, 1979), and many national parks and reserves have been set aside in Amazonia and throughout Brazil (Jorge Pádua, 1983). Nevertheless, the Amazon is large, and sustained and effective effort by Brazil and all of the other Amazonian countries is needed to ensure preservation of a representative part of this amazing biotic diversity.

## ACKNOWLEDGMENTS

We are grateful to the United Nations University, INPE (the Brazilian Institute for Space Research), and the National Science Foundation of the United States for providing the senior author with the opportunity to participate in this conference. We thank João Murça Pires and Jennifer Robinson for reviewing the manuscript and Donald Black for help in assembling the illustrations.

## REFERENCES

Alvim, P. de T. and Alvim, R., 1978. Relation of climate to growth periodicity in tropical trees, in: *Tropical Trees as Living Systems*, P. B. Tomlinson and M. H. Zimmerman, Eds., Cambridge University Press, New York.

Augspurger, C. K., 1979. Irregular rain cues and the germination and seedling survival of a Panamanian shrub (*Hybanthus prunifolius*), *Oecologia* **44**, 53–59.

Augspurger, C. K., 1981. Reproductive synchrony of a tropical shrub: Experimental studies on effects of pollinators and seed predators on *Hybanthus prunifolius* (Violaceae), *Ecology* **62**, 775–788.

Augspurger, C. K., 1982. A cue for synchronous flowering, in E. G. Leigh, Jr., A. S. Rand, and D. M. Windsor, Eds., *The Ecology of a Tropical Forest: Seasonal Rhythms and Long-Term Changes*, Smithsonian Institution, Washington, DC.

Balslev, H., Luteyn, J., Øllgard, B., and L. Holm-Nielsen, in press. Composition and structure of adjacent unflooded and flood plain forest in Amazonian Ecuador, *Opera Bot.*

Bigarella, J. J., 1975. The Barreiras group in northeastern Brazil, *Anais Acad. Brasil. Ci.* **47** (Suppl.), 365–394.

Bigarella, J. J. and Andrade, G. O., 1964. Considerações sobre a estratigrafia dos sedimentos cenozoicos de Pernambuco (Grupo Barreiras), *Arg. Inst. Ci. Terra* **2**, 2–14.

Bigarella, J. J., Andrade-Lima, D. A., and Riehs, P. J., 1975. Considerações a respeito das mudanças paleoambientais na distribuiçoo de algumas espécies vegetais e animais no Brasil, *Anais Acad. Brasil. Ci.* **47** (Suppl.), 411–464.

Cain, S. A., de Oliveira Castro, G. M., Murça Pires, J., and Silva, N. T., 1956. Application of some phytosociological techniques to Brazilian rain forest, *Amer. J. Bot.* **43**, 911–941.

Campbell, D., Daly, D., and Prance, G. T., *unpublished.* Quantitative ecological inventory of terra firme and várzea tropical forest on the Rio Xingu, Brazilian Amazon.

Davis, T. A. W. and Richards, P. W., 1934. The vegetation of Moraballi Creek, British Guiana: An ecological study of a limited area of tropical rain forest. Part II, *J. Ecol.* **22**, 106–155.

Descimon, H., Ed., 1977. Biogéographie et evolution en Amérique Tropicale, *Publ. Lab. Ecole Supér.* **9** (Suppl.).

Dressler, R. L., 1982. Biology of the orchid bees (Euglossini), *Ann. Rev. Ecol. Syst.* **13**, 373–394.

Ducke, A., 1948. Arvores amazônicas e sua propagação, *Bol. Mus. Paraense Hist. Nat.* **10**, 81–92.

Erwin, T. L., 1982. Tropical forests: Their richness in Coleoptera and other insect species, *Coleopter. Bull.* **36**, 74–75.

Fundação Instituto Brasileiro de Geografia e Estatística, 1977. *Sinopse Estatística do Brasil*, Vol. 5., Diretoria de Divulgação.

Gentry, A., 1974. Coevolutionary patterns in Central American Bignoniaceae, *Ann. Missouri Bot. Gard.* **61**, 728–759.

Gentry, A., 1982. Patterns of neotropical plant species diversity in M. K. Hecht, B. Wallace, and G. T. Prance, Eds., *Evolutionary Biology*, Vol. 15, Plenum, New York.

Gentry, A., in press. Some preliminary results of botanical studies in Manu Park, in *Estudios Biologicos de Parque Nacional de Manu*, Ministerio de Agricultura, Lima.

Gilbert, E. and Raven, P. H., 1975. *Coevolution of Animals and Plants*, University of Texas Press, Austin.

Granville, J. J., 1982. Rain forest and xeric flora refuges in French Guiana, in G. T.

Prance, Ed., *Biological Diversification in the Tropics*, Columbia University Press, New York.

Greenhall, A. M., 1965. Sapucaia nut dispersal by greater spear-nosed bats in Trinidad, *Caribbean J. Sci.* **5**, 167–171.

Haffer, J., 1969. Speciation in Amazonian forest birds, *Science* **165**, 131–137.

Huber, J., 1910. Mattas e madeiras amazônicas, *Bol. Mus. Paraense Hist. Nat.* **6**, 91–225.

Instituto Nacional de Pesquisas da Amazonia, 1979. Estratégias para a política florestal na Amazônia Brasileira, *Acta Amazon.* **9**(4): (Suppl.), 1–216.

Janzen, D. H., 1975. Behavior of *Hymenaea courbaril* when its seed predator is absent, *Science* **189**, 145–147.

Jorge Pádua, M. T., 1983. Os parques nacionais e reservas biológicas do Brasil, Instituto Brasileiro de Desenvolvimento Florestal-IBDF, Brasília.

Klinge, H. and Rodrigues, W., 1968. Litter production in an area of Amazonian terra firme forest. Part I. Litter-fall, organic carbon and total nitrogen contents of litter, *Amazoniana* **1**, 287–302.

Kowal, R. R., Mori, S. A. and Kallunki, J. A., 1977. Chromosome numbers of Panamanian Lecythidaceae and their use in subfamilial classification, *Brittonia* **29**, 399–410.

McDiarmid, R. W., Ricklefs, R. E., and Foster, M. S., 1977. Dispersal of *Stemmadenia donnell-smithii* (Apocynaceae) by birds, *Biotropica* **9**, 9–25.

Mori, S. A., 1981. New species and combinations in neotropical Lecythidaceae, *Brittonia* **33**, 357–370.

Mori, S. A. and Boeke, J., in press. Pollination, in S. A. Mori, Ed., The Lecythidaceae of a Lowland Neotropical Forest, La Fumée Mountain, French Guiana, *Mem. New York Bot. Gard.*

Mori, S. A. and Boom, B. M., in press. The forest, in S. A. Mori, Ed., The Lecythidaceae of a Lowland Neotropical Forest, La Fumée Mountain, French Guiana, *Mem. New York Bot. Gard.*

Mori, S. A. and Kallunki, J. A., 1976. The phenology and floral biology of *Gustavia superba* (Lecythidaceae) in Central Panama, *Biotropica* **8**, 184–192.

Mori, S. A. and Orchard, J. E., 1979. Fenologia, biologia floral e evidência sobre dimorfismo fisiológico do pólen de *Lecythis pisonis* Cambess (Lecythidaceae), *Anais da Sociedade Botânica do Brasil* **30**, 109–116.

Mori, S. A. and Pipoly, J. J., 1984. Observations on the big bang flowering of *Miconia minutiflora* (Melastomataceae), *Brittonia* **36**, 337–341.

Mori, S. A. and Prance, G. T., 1981a. The "Sapucaia" group of *Lecythis* (Lecythidaceae), *Brittonia* **33**, 70–80.

Mori, S. A. and Prance, G. T., 1981b. Relações entre a classificação genérica de Lecythidaceae do Novo Mundo e seus polinizadores e dispersadores, *Revta. Brasil. Bot.* **4**, 31–37.

Mori, S. A. and Prance, G. T., in press. Phenology, in S. A. Mori, Ed., The Lecythidaceae of a Lowland Neotropical Forest, La Fumée Mountain, French Guiana, *Mem. New York Bot. Gard.*

Mori, S. A., Lisboa, G., and Kallunki, J. A., 1982. Fenologia de uma mata higrófila sul-baiana, *Revt. Theobr.* **12**, 217–230.

Mori, S. A., Mattos Silva, L. A., and dos Santos, T. S., 1980. Observações sobre a fenologia e biologia floral de *Lecythis pisonis* (Lecythidaceae), *Revt. Theobr.* **10**, 103–111.

Mori, S. A., Orchard, J. E., and Prance, G. T., 1980. Intrafloral pollen differentiation in the New World Lecythidaceae, subfamily Lecythidoideae, *Science* **209**, 400–403.

Mori, S. A., Prance, G. T., and Bolten, A. B., 1978. Additional notes on the floral biology of neotropical Lecythidaceae, *Brittonia* **30**, 113–130.

Mori, S. A., Boom, B. M., de Carvalho, A. M., and dos Santos, T. S., 1983. Southern Bahian moist forests, *Bot. Rev. (Lancaster)* **49**, 155–232.

Moritz, A., 1984. Estudos Biológicos da Floração e da Frutificação, *Castanha-do-Brasil, EMBRAPA, CPATU*, Belem, Brazil.

Moure, J. S., 1967. A check-list of the known euglossine bees, *Atas do Simpósio sôbre a biota Amazônica*, Vol. 5 (Zoologia) pp. 395–415. Consel ho Nacional de Pesquis, Rio de Janeiro.

Müller, H. C., Rodrigues, I. A., Müller, A. A., and Müller, N. R. M., 1980. *Castanha-do-Brasil, EMBRAPA, CPATU, Miscelânea* **2,**1–25.

Opler, P. A., Frankie, G. W., and Baker, H. G., 1976. Rainfall as a factor in the release, timing, and synchronization of anthesis by tropical trees and shrubs, *Biogeography* **3**, 231–236.

Ormond, W. T., Pinheiro, M. C. B., and Cortella de Castells, A. R., 1981. A contribution to the floral biology and reproductive system of *Couroupita guianensis* Aublet (Lecythidaceae), *Ann. Missouri Bot. Gard.* **68**, 514–523.

Pires, J. M. and Prance, G. T., 1977. The Amazon forest: a natural heritage to be preserved, in G. T. Prance and T. S. Elias, Eds., *Extinction is Forever*, New York Botanical Garden, New York.

Prance, G. T., 1973. Phytogeographic support for the theory of Pleistocene forest refuges in the Amazon Basin, based on evidence from distribution patterns in Caryocaraceae, Chrysobalanaceae, Dichapetalaceae and Lecythidaceae, *Acta Amazôn.* **3**, 5–28.

Prance, G. T., 1975. The history of the INPA capoeira based on ecological studies of Lecythidaceae, *Acta Amazôn.* **5**, 261–263.

Prance, G. T., 1976. The pollination and androphore structure of some Amazonian Lecythidaceae, *Biotropica* **8**, 235–241.

Prance, G. T., 1977. Floristic inventory of the tropics: Where do we stand, *Ann. Missouri Bot. Gard.* **64**, 659–684.

Prance, G. T., 1978. The origin and evolution of the Amazon flora, *Interciência* **3**, 207–222.

Prance, G. T., Ed., 1982. *Biological Diversification in the Tropics*, Columbia University Press, New York.

Prance, G. T., 1983, A review of phytogeographic evidences for Pleistocene climate change in the Neotropics, *Ann. Missouri Bot. Gard.* **69**, 594–624.

Prance, G. T., Idrobo, J. M., and Castaño M., O. V., 1983. Mecanismos de polinización de *Eschweilera garagarae* Pittier en el Chocó, Colombia, *Mutisia* **60**, 1–7.

Prance, G. T. and Mori, S. A., 1978. Observations on the fruits and seeds of neo-tropical Lecythidaceae, *Brittonia* **30**, 21–33.

Prance, G. T. and Mori, S. A., 1979. The actinomorphic-flowered New World Le-cythidaceae. Lecythidaceae—Part I, *Flora Neotrop.* **21**, 1–270.

Prance, G. T. and Mori, S. A., 1983. Dispersal and distribution of Lecythidaceae and Chrysobalanaceae, *Sonderbd. Naturwiss. Ver. Hamburg* **7**, 163–186.

Prance, G. T., Rodrigues, W. A., and da Silva, M. F., 1976. Inventário florestal de um hectare de mata de terra firme km 30 da estrada Manaus-Itacoatiara, *Acta Amazôn.* **6**, 9–35.

Sabatier, D., 1983. Saisonalité de la fructification en forêt guyanaise, *Office de la Recherche Scientifique et Technique Outre-Mer*, Centre ORSTOM de Cayenne, mimeograph.

Schulz, J. P., 1960. Ecological studies of rain forest in northern Suriname, *Meded. Bot. Mus. Herb. Rijks. Univ. Utrecht* **163**, 1–267.

Smythe, N., 1978. The natural history of the Central American agouti (*Dasyprocta punctata*), *Smithsonian Contr. Zool.* **257**, 1–51.

Spruce, R., 1908. In A. R. Wallace, Ed., Notes of a Botanist on the Amazon and Andes, 2 vols., Macmillan, London.

Thiel, J., 1983. Reconnaissance pratique des arbres sur pied de la forêt guyanaise, *Rev. Bois Forêts Trop.* **201**, 35–59.

# Chapter 7

# Climate Change in the Humid Tropics, Especially Amazonia, Over the Last Twenty Thousand Years

**Robert E. Dickinson and Hassan Virji**

The Amazon region is now rapidly changing because of human intervention. One strategy for more fully understanding climate and vegetation interactions in the humid tropics is to look not only at the present and future but also at the past climate record. The possible effects of human activities on tropical vegetation and climate should be considered in the context of large natural changes that have previously occurred. Instrumental records for South American tropical areas do not extend very far into the past, but various kinds of geological deposits and biological evidence can be examined as proxy indicators of climate. The Amazon rain forest has been a poor environment for preserving such proxy records, but some are being found, especially for the time since the peak of the last ice age, 20,000 y ago. The moist tropical forests in the Amazon may have largely disappeared during the last ice age as a result of increased aridity. Before summarizing the evidence for ice-age and post-ice-age climates in the Amazon, we briefly review the overall geological history of the tropical climate system.

## CLIMATE AND ATMOSPHERIC COMPOSITION OVER GEOLOGICAL HISTORY

Earth is about 4.5 billion years old, and geologists can find rocks tracing back to all but the first 700 million years or so. However, on these longest time scales, we learn mostly of the planet as a whole and little specific to the tropics. Evidence of primitive single-cell anaerobic life forms has been found in some of the earliest sedimentary rocks, and evidence for photosynthesis nearly as far back. Atmospheric carbon dioxide concentrations in the early atmosphere may have been many hundreds of times greater than at present (Walker, Hays, and Kasting, 1981), as required to compensate for a faint early sun (solar constant 70% of present, Newkirk, 1983). Atmospheric oxygen probably rose to near-present levels within the last 2 billion years as a consequence of photosynthesis and burial of organic carbon compounds within ocean sediments (Cloud, 1968).

Details of plate tectonics and of quantities of continental crust, hence dry land mass, during the first 2 billion years are obscure. At some point, crustal plates and continents, such as we have today, formed and acted to stir and recycle crustal material on the several-hundred-million-year time scale required for ocean basins to open and close. This crustal recycling has been important for determining the composition of the atmosphere and especially the concentrations of oxygen and carbon dioxide.

Large plants have been present on land for about the last 400 million years, but flowering plants only first evolved during the Cretaceous, beginning about 150 million years ago. During that time, the continents were drifting into their present positions; in particular, what is now the equatorial belt was somewhat south of the equator in the Early Cretaceous, and the continent of Gondwana was just beginning to drift apart into the continents of Africa and South America.

During much of the Cretaceous, continental areas were extensively covered by shallow seas. Carbon dioxide concentrations may have been 4–10 times the current values (Berner, Lasaga, and Garrels, 1983; Berner and Barron, 1984), and temperatures in tropical areas may have been as much as 5°C warmer than at present (e.g., Barron and Washington, 1984). Temperature and carbon dioxide are both crucial factors for the growth of vegetation; however, the significance of such drastic departures from current conditions for tropical forests in the Cretaceous has not yet been examined. Present tropical forests lose most of their gross photosynthesis to temperature–dependent plant respiration (Box, 1978). Thus, if the temperatures in tropical forests are increased by more than several degrees from present values, many species might be severely stressed by respiratory losses of carbohydrate and either die prematurely or not even be viable. On the other hand, increased concentrations of carbon dioxide may promote their survival.

How tropical forests evolved and fared during the extreme warmth of the Cretaceous is thus relevant in view of the climate changes projected to occur over the next hundred years as a result of increasing atmospheric carbon dioxide, which is mostly from fossil fuel burning. Concentrations have risen from about 275 to 340 ppm over the last hundred years and may reach 500–600 ppm late in the next century. Other trace gases important for global radiation balance are also increasing, so that tropical temperatures could rise 1–5°C in the next century (WMO/UNEP/ICSU, 1986).

Over the last 65 million years, global temperatures and presumably carbon dioxide concentrations decayed, most likely with many fluctuations, to their current levels. Likewise, tropical forests evolved into their current general form. Expansion of rain forest into East Africa occurred briefly about 3.3 million years ago (Williamson, 1985). About 2 million years ago, a sequence of glacial periods began (Crowley, 1983). For nearly the last million years, these ice ages have occurred about every hundred thousand years with relatively brief interruptions by interglacial periods of 10,000–20,000 y in length, such as we are in now (Imbrie et al., 1984). Global temperature has been further modulated by changes of Earth's orbital parameters with periods of about 20,000 and 40,000 y. Stable carbon isotope ratios also have been found to vary with these periodicities; these changes are interpreted in terms of large variations of tropical forest biomass (Keigwin and Boyle, 1985). Ice ages are characterized by continental ice sheets that have at times covered substantial parts of North America and Europe. Over the same periods, there has been extensive expansion of glaciers in the mountains of the Southern Hemisphere, as well as the Antarctic ice sheet and sea ice. The last such glaciation reached its maximum extent about 18,000 y ago (CLIMAP Project Members, 1976).

## VEGETATION AND CLIMATE IN THE HUMID TROPICS, ESPECIALLY AMAZONIA, DURING THE LAST ICE AGE

Until about 25 y ago, tropical climates and vegetation were considered to have been little affected by the glacial and interglacial periods of extratropical climates (Flenley, 1979). However, the last ice ages are now known to have been accompanied by climates that apparently had drastic effects on tropical vegetation (e.g., Peterson et al., 1979; Smith, 1982). During at least the latter parts of the last ice age, much of the humid tropics was colder and drier than at present, and rain forests on several continents shrank to an area much smaller than their current range. Concentrations of atmospheric carbon dioxide were considerably lower than at present, that is, about 200 ppm from 14,000 to 30,000 y ago (Oeschger et al., 1984) compared to twentieth-century values greater than 300 ppm. Extensive sand dunes occurred in central America (Ward, 1973) and generally on half of the land from 30° S to 30° N (Sarnthein, 1978). Tropical lake levels on all continents, especially in the Northern Hemisphere, were mostly very low 14,000–21,000 y ago, but on the average were high for at least the preceding 10,000 y (Street and Grove, 1979; Street-Perrott and Harrison, 1984).

Tropical climates for southeast Asia during the last ice age have been reviewed by Webster and Streten (1978) and Verstappen (1980) and for Africa by Livingstone (1982). Cooling is inferred from the depression of the altitudes of vegetation limits in mountain areas and downward extensions of mountain glaciers. However, ocean temperatures inferred from sediments indicate much less tropical cooling than the land evidence does (e.g., Rind and Peteet,

1985). The most detailed information for tropical South America has been provided by palynological (pollen core) studies in the northern Andes (e.g., Van der Hammen et al., 1981), showing a wet period from about 50,000 to 25,000 y ago and a dry period from 21,000 to about 13,000 y ago near the end of the last ice age. A similar dry period is inferred from a pollen core from the Rupununi savanna in Guyana (Van der Hammen, 1982). From variations between Andean forest and tundra in the high plains of Bogota, Colombia, a descent of the altitudinal limit of forests by 1200–1500 m is inferred (Van der Hammen, 1982). Likewise, a pollen core from Lake Valencia in Venezuela extending back 13,000 y shows no rain forest pollen and presumably a very dry climate before 11,500 y ago (Salgado-Labouriau, 1982; Bradbury et al., 1981).

Evidence from lowland tropical regimes of South America is rather meagre and mostly undated. The only pollen data from the rain forests of the Amazon Basin apparently referring to the last ice age is that reported by Absy and Van der Hammen (1976) for Rondônia, Brazil. These data show that tropical forest was temporarily replaced by grass. There is, however, considerable geomorphological evidence for more seasonal rainfall and more arid conditions in the Amazon Basin presumed to have occurred earlier than 13,000 y ago, within the past ice age (Bigarella and de Andrade-Lima, 1982; Ab'Saber, 1982). "Stone-line" deposits have been found on the eastern and southern edge of the Amazon rain forest, as well as in the west central part of Amazonia, although they currently are formed only in the arid regions of the Brazilian northeast. Other evidence for more arid conditions in the past includes patches of white sand, fossil stream channels, river terraces and former riverbeds, rock outcrops, dissected slopes, fluvial gravel in an elevated location and gravel terraces (Ab'Saber, 1982), as well as offshore sediments (Damuth and Fairbridge, 1970).

The third line of evidence for arid conditions during the past ice age is the occurrence of centers of diversity of endemic biological species, that is, zones of very many different species interpreted in terms of refuges (Prance, 1982; Haffer, 1982). Such centers have been identified for trees, butterflies, birds, and variations of a species of lizard and other reptiles and amphibians. They indicate that during one or more previous geological periods, rain forest biota were isolated in several forest refuges corresponding approximately in location to the centers. The rain forest was apparently elsewhere replaced by seasonal forest or savanna as a result of sparser and more seasonal rainfall. This earlier climate of the refuges is usually associated with the last ice age or ice ages.

How much of apparent differences in the vegetation during the last ice age could have been a result of lower concentrations of carbon dioxide rather than climate change has not yet been considered. The lack within the Amazon Basin of well-dated evidence of forested localities where the refuges were present or of regions where savanna conditions prevailed (Bradley, 1985) indicates that caution must be exercised in interpreting or deducing climatic changes based on refuge theory. For example, some of the refuges are supposed to have been in sloped terrain where orographic rainfall could maintain the rain forest as is the case at present for the Atlantic coastal rain forest of central Brazil. However, colder temperatures in mountainous areas could have supported vegetation other than tropical rain forest. Liu and Colinvaux (1985) have examined pollen and plant megafossils in old forest beds 27,000–33,000 y old in the Ecuadorian Amazon forest at 1100 m elevation where a previous refuge has been suggested. They found evidence for a mountain Podocarpus forest at least 700 m lower than it grows today, implying conditions colder by about 3°C than today and the absence of the lowland moist forest species, but presumably still moist conditions.

## THE LAST TEN THOUSAND YEARS

The last ice age ended 10,000–12,000 y ago, and from that time to about 5000 y ago much of the tropics became considerably wetter than during the ice age or today (e.g., as inferred from lake-level fluctuations; Street-Perrott and Harrison, 1984). However, this period of general wetness was interrupted by severe dry episodes, at least on particular continents—for example, in Africa during the intervals 11,000–10,000 y ago, 8500–6500 y ago, and 6200–5800 y ago (Gillespie et al., 1983).

Because Earth's orbit about the sun is an ellipse rather than a circle, the total solar radiation received by Earth varies with time of year. Now we are closest to the sun in January, but 9000 y ago we were closest in July, and over a broad band of latitudes about 7% more solar radiation was received in July and that much less in January than now. Monsoon rainfalls appear to have been plentiful much of the time, as inferred from observed high lake levels and other evidence for increased rainfall in Africa, the Middle East, and Australia and confirmed by modeling studies for the Northern Hemisphere (Kutzbach, 1983; Kutzbach and Guetter, 1984).

Whereas summer monsoons were stronger in the Northern Hemisphere from around 12,000–5000 y ago, the same orbital changes may have led to exactly the opposite effect in the Southern Hemisphere. In the Southern Hemisphere, the seasonal cycle of solar radiation was reduced in amplitude; 10,000 y ago when perihelion was in July (instead of January as it is now), midsummer (January) radiation was 7% less than at present. In recent model studies, rainfall over land from 0° to 30° S in the southern tropics was slightly less 18,000 y ago than at present and reached lowest levels from 12,000–6000 y ago with cooler summers, before recovering to present values (Kutzbach and Guetter, 1986).

Thus, modeling arguments suggest enhanced summer rainfall 6000–12,000 y ago only north of the equator, but far enough south of the equator, a relatively dry period. Could this period have been one of extensive savanna in the southern Amazon forest? Or could the lowered concentrations of carbon dioxide during the last ice age have been more important for reducing these Amazon forests than more recent drought? Or has something important been left out of the models?

Northern South America apparently changed to more humid conditions starting at the end of the last ice age as indicated by the core from Lake Valencia, Venezuela (Bradbury et al., 1981). However, there is also abundant evidence further south for one or more dry periods over the last 10,000 y, in particular, shell middens, palynological profiles, and the stratigraphy of deposits covering the stone lines (Ab'Saber, 1982).

Campbell and Frailey (1984) have reported a thick blanket of alluvium in southwestern lowland Amazonia resulting from massive seasonal flooding from about 11,000 to about 5000 y ago. They suggest that, in the December–February season of maximum precipitation, lower solar radiation could have led to larger annual accumulation of snowpack, whereas in June to August, increased solar radiation would have accelerated melting of the snowpack. The ensuing floodwaters in combination with greater runoff from possible increases in seasonal precipitation may have formed a series of broad rivers crossing the Amazonia plains and developing swamplands over a large area. They also note two episodes of erosion and deposition within the last 5000 y.

Several other lines of evidence indicate climate fluctuations, especially lower effective precipitation, in tropical South America over the last 5000 y. Lower lake levels occurred in the Andean region between 4200 and 3500 y ago, between 2700 and 2000 y ago, and from A.D. 1200 to 1450 (Van der Hammen, 1982). Absy (1982) discusses pollen data from seasonal lakes of flooded river plains representing the past 5000 y. These data show no extension of savanna but suggest the same dry periods noted by Van der Hammen.

Colinvaux et al. (1985) describe the first permanent deep lakes found in the Amazon lowlands, located in western Amazonia in the rain forests of Ecuador. These lakes were apparently flooded by parent rivers between A.D. 800 and 1300. The pollen records of one of these lakes, Lake Kumpak show largely intact rain forest for the last 5200 y. The strata between 3800 and 4300 indicate increased erosion, probably from an increased frequency and intensity of storms.

The sampling of charcoal content in dry land forest areas of the Amazon gives further information on possible climate variations. Sanford et al. (1985) have sampled eight rain forest sites to 1-m depth with a large number of pits and cores near San Carlos in the Venezuelan Amazon forest. For comparison, they also sampled at three scrub (*caatinga*) forest sites. They found charcoal in seven of the eight rain forest sites and one of three scrub forest sites. Many other samples were taken in areas more distant from San Carlos, in most of which charcoal was also found. The charcoal was dated with ages of a few hundred years to 6000 y. It provides evidence for repeated burning of the rain forest sites, either through slash-and-burn agriculture or through wildfires. In view of the recent occurrence of wildfires during pronounced dry seasons, wildfires may have destroyed large areas of forest under drier climatic regimes.

Thompson et al. (1985) reports on an analysis of two ice cores recovered from the summit (5670 m) of the tropical Quelccaya Ice Cap containing 1500 y of consecutive paleoclimate information. Inferred records from these ice cores include such environmental parameters as drought episodes, volcanic activity, moisture stress, major El Niño–Southern Oscillation events, and glacier mass balance for Quelccaya. These records indicate that extended dry periods occurred during A.D. 1720–1860, 1250–1310, 570–610, and wet conditions prevailed during A.D. 1500–1720. Thompson's analysis indicates that recognized periods of global climate change, such as the little ice age (1520–1720), were accompanied by significant climatic changes in the equatorial Andes. Concomitant anomalous climatic conditions and significant changes in the rain forest regime probably occurred over the Amazon Basin as well.

In summary, the longest time scale climate variations since the last ice age are likely a result of the changes in the date of Earth's closest approach to the sun. The physical mechanisms responsible for more abrupt climate changes on century to millennia time scales are more poorly known.

## IMPLICATIONS

Although the extent of tropical rain forest degradation by human activities is a serious concern, at least it is susceptible to judicious management by the countries involved. On the other hand, the apparent near disappearance of tropical rain forests in the Amazon and elsewhere during the last ice age suggests that environmental conditions suitable for maintaining the rain forests must not be taken for granted. If natural climatic fluctuations associated with ice ages can nearly obliterate tropical forests, what is the likelihood that climate change caused by human activities may do likewise? Will conversion of forests to grasslands and agriculture, if carried too far, initiate an irreversible trend to conditions of greater aridity and more seasonal rainfall, leading to a collapse of the remaining forest system? Extensive wildfires promoted by the aridity could play a role in such a collapse.

Apparently, climate at some time since the last ice age was highly favorable to the expansion of rain forest. Whether such an expansion could happen today is unknown but could be less likely because of drier conditions. Furthermore, the climate of today is not the climate of tomorrow (the next 50–100 y). Increased warming from increases in atmospheric carbon dioxide and other trace gases should significantly change the climate in the tropics and elsewhere. Since the warming is global and not seasonal, as were the conditions of 9000 y ago, we cannot infer from the past climate record whether regions of tropical forests will be wetter or drier. Nevertheless, with the greater warmth, tropical convective rainfall will tend to be more intense and concentrated, possibly leading to greater flooding and erosion but leaving less moisture in the soil and giving more stressful dry seasons.

Further evidence for the degree of forest stability to climate change might be gained by better documentation of climate fluctuations and forest change, if any, over the last 5000–10,000 y. Considerably more study is also needed of the extent of the Amazon forest during the last ice age before we can assert with much confidence that it really shrank to the proposed refuges. Thus, paleoclimate studies of the Amazon and surrounding regions should continue to be a fertile source of information regarding climate, human, and vegetation interactions.

## ACKNOWLEDGMENTS

This manuscript has benefited from input and helpful critical comments by Ray Bradley, Paul Colinvaux, Tom Crowley, John Kutzbach, Pedro Silva-Dias, and Lonnie Thompson. We are most grateful to all of them.

## REFERENCES

Ab'Saber, A. N., 1982. The paleoclimate and paleoecology of Brazilian Amazonia, in G. T. Prance, Ed., *Biological Diversification in the Tropics*, Columbia University Press, New York.

Absy, M. L., 1982. Quaternary palynological studies in the Amazon basin, in G. T. Prance, Ed., *Biological Diversification in the Tropics*, Columbia University Press, New York.

Absy, M. L. and Van der Hammen, T., 1976. Some paleoecological data from Rondônia, southern part of the Amazon basin, *Acta Amazôn.* **6**, 293–299.

Barron, E. J. and Washington, W. M., 1984. The role of geographic variables in explaining paleoclimates: Results from Cretaceous climate model sensitivity studies, *J. Geophys. Res.* **89**, 1267–1279.

Berner, R. A. and Barron, E. J., 1984. Comments on the BLAG model: Factors affecting atmospheric $CO_2$ and temperature over the past 100 million years. *Amer. J. Sci.* **284**, 1183–1192.

Berner, R. A., Lasaga, A. C., and Garrels, R. M., 1983. The carbonate-silicate geochemical cycle and its effect on atmospheric carbon dioxide over the last 100 million years, *Amer. J. Sci.* **283**, 641–683.

Bigarella, J. S. and de Andrade-Lima, D., 1982. Paleoenvironmental changes in Brazil, in G. T. Prance, Ed., *Biological Diversification in the Tropics*, Columbia University Press, New York.

Box, E., 1978. Geographical dimensions of terrestrial net and gross primary productivity, *Rad. Environ. Biophys.* **15**, 305–322.

Bradbury, J. P., Leyden, B., Salgado-Labouriau, M., Lewis, W. M., Jr., Schubert,

C., Binford, M. W., Frey, D. G., Whitehead, D. R., and Weibezahn, F. H., 1981. Late Quaternary environmental history of Lake Valencia, Venezuela, *Science* **214**, 1299–1305.

Bradley, R. S., 1985. *Quaternary Paleoclimatology Methods of Paleoclimatic Reconstruction*, Allen & Unwin, Boston, MA.

Campbell, K. E. and Frailey, D., 1984. Holocene flooding and species diversity in southwestern Amazonia, *Quat. Res.* **21**, 369–375.

CLIMAP Project Members, 1976. The surface of the ice-age earth, *Science* **191**, 1131–1137.

Cloud, P. E., 1968. Atmospheric and hydrospheric evolution on the primitive Earth, *Science* **160**, 729–736.

Colinvaux, P. A., Miller, M. C., Liu, K.-b., Steinitz-Kannan, M., and Frost, I., 1985. Discovery of permanent Amazon lakes and hydraulic disturbance in the upper Amazon basin, *Nature* **313**, 42–45.

Crowley, T. J., 1983. The geologic record of climatic change, *Rev. Geophys. Space Phys.* **21**, 828–877.

Damuth, J. E. and Fairbridge, R. W., 1970. Equatorial Atlantic deep-sea arkosic sands and ice-age aridity in tropical South America, *Bull. Geol. Soc. Amer.* **81**, 189–206.

Flenley, J. R., 1979. *The Equatorial Rain Forest: A Geological History*, Butterworths, London.

Gillespie, R., Street-Perrott, F. A., and Switsur, R., 1983. Post-glacial arid episodes in Ethiopia have implications for climate prediction, *Nature* **306**, 678–682.

Haffer, J., 1982. General aspects of the refuge theory, in G. T. Prance, Ed., *Biological Diversification in the Tropics*, Columbia University Press, New York.

Imbrie, J., Hays, J. D., Martinson, D. G., McIntyre, A., Mix, A. C., Morley, J. J., Pisias, N. G., Prell, W. L., and Shackleton, N. J., 1984. The orbital theory of Pleistocene climate: Support from a revised chronology of the marine $\delta$ $^{18}$O record, in A. L. Berger, J. Imbrie, J. Hays, G. Kukla, and B. Saltzman, Eds., *Milankovitch and Climate*, Part I, D. Reidel, The Netherlands.

Keigwin, L. D. and Boyle, E. A., 1985. Carbon isotope in deep-sea benthic foraminifera: Precession and changes in low-latitude biomass, in E. T. Sundquist and W. S. Broecker, Eds., *The Carbon Cycle and Atmospheric $CO_2$: Natural Variations Archean to Present, Geophysical Monograph 32,* American Geophysical Union, Washington DC.

Kutzbach, J. E., 1983. Monsoon rains of the late Pleistocene and early Holocene: Patterns, intensity and possible causes of changes, in A. Street-Perrott, M. Beran, and R. Ratcliffe, Eds., *Variations in the Global Water Budget*, D. Reidel, Dordrecht, The Netherlands.

Kutzbach, J. E. and Guetter, P. J., 1984. The sensitivity of monsoon climates to orbital parameter changes for 9,000 years BP: Experiments with the NCAR general circulation model, in A. L. Berger, J. Imbrie, J. Hays, G. Kukla, and B. Saltzman, Eds., *Milankovitch and Climate*, Part 2, D. Reidel, The Netherlands.

Kutzbach, J. E. and Guetter, P. S., 1986. The influence of changing orbital parameters and surface boundary conditions on climate simulations for the past 18,000 years, *J. Atmos. Sci.* **41** (Sept. 1).

Kutzbach, J. E. and Street-Perrott, F. A., 1985. Milankovitch forcing in the level of tropical lakes from 18 to 0 K BP, *Nature* **17**, 130–134.

Liu, K.-b. and Colinvaux, P. A., 1985. Forest changes in the Amazon basin in the last glacial maximum, *Nature* **318**, 556–557.

Livingstone, D. A., 1982. Quaternary geography of Africa and the refuge theory, in G. T. Prance, Ed., *Biological Diversification in the Tropics*, Columbia University Press, New York.

Newkirk, G., Jr., 1983. Variations in solar luminosity, *Ann. Rev. Astron. Astrophys.* **21**, 429–467.

Oeschger, H., Beer, J., Siegenthaler, U., Stauffer, B., Dansgaard, W., and Langway, C. C., 1984. Late glacial climate history from ice cores, in J. E. Hansen and T. Takahashi, Eds., *Climate Processes and Climate Sensitivity*, Geophysical Monograph 29, American Geophysical Union, Washington, DC.

Peterson, G. M., Webb, T. III, Kutzbach, J. E., van der Hammen, T., Wijmstra, T. A., and Street, F. A., 1979. The continental record of environmental conditions at 18,000 yr B.P.: An initial evaluation, *Quat. Res.* **12**, 47–82.

Prance, G. T., Ed., 1982. *Biological Diversification in the Tropics*, Columbia University Press, New York.

Rind, D., and Peteet, D., 1985. Terrestrial conditions at the last glacial maximum and CLIMAP sea-surface temperature estimates: Are they consistent? *Quat. Res.* **24**, 1–22.

Salgado-Labouriau, M. L., 1982. Climatic change at the Pleistocene-Holocene boundary, in G. T. Prance, Ed., *Biological Diversification in the Tropics*, Columbia University Press, New York.

Sanford, R. L., Jr., Saldarriage, J., Clark, K., Uul, C., and Herrera, R., 1985. Amazon rainforest fires, *Science* **227**, 53–55.

Sarnthein, M., 1978. Sand deserts during glacial maximum and climatic optimum, *Nature* **272**, 43–46.

Smith, R. T., 1982. Quaternary environmental change in equatorial regions with particular reference to vegetation history: A bibliography, *Paleogeogr. Paleoclimatol. Palaeoecol.* **39**, 331–345.

Street, F. A., and Grove, G. T., 1979. Global maps of lake level fluctuations since 30,000 BP, *Quat. Res.* **12**, 83–118.

Street-Perrott, F. A. and Harrison, S. P., 1984. Temporal variations in lake levels since 30,000 BP: An index of the global hydrological cycle, in J. E. Hansen and T. Takahashi, Eds., *Climate Processes and Climate Sensitivity*, Geophysical Monograph 29, American Geophysical Union, Washington, DC.

Thompson, L. G., Mosley-Thompson, E., Bolzan, J. F., and Koci, B. R., 1985. A 1500-year record of tropical precipitation recorded in ice cores from the Quelccaya Ice Cap, Peru, *Science* **229**, 971–973.

Van der Hammen, T., 1982. Paleoecology of tropical South America, in G. T. Prance, Ed., *Biological Diversification in the Tropics*, Columbia University Press, New York.

Van der Hammen, T., Barelds, J., De Jong, H., and De Veer, A. A., 1981. Glacial sequence and environmental history in the Sierra Nevada Del Cocuy (Colombia), *Paleogeogr. Palaeoclimatol. Palaeoecol.* **32**, 247–340.

Verstappen, H. Th., 1980. Quaternary climatic changes and natural environment in SE Asia, *Geo. J.* **4.1,** 45–54.

Walker, J. C. J., Hays, P. B., and Kasting, J. F., 1981. A negative feedback mechanism for the long-term stabilization of the earth's surface temperature, *J. Geophys. Res.* **86,** 9776–9782.

Ward, M. W., 1973. Influence of climate on the early diagenesis of carbonate eolianties, *Geology* **1,** 171–174.

Webster, P. J., and Streten, N. A., 1978. Late Quaternary ice age climates of tropical Australia: Interpretations and reconstructions, *Quat. Res.* **10,** 279–309.

Williamson, P. G., 1985. Evidence for an early Plio-Pleistocene rainforest expansion in East Africa, *Nature* **315,** 487–489.

WMO/UNEP/ICSU, 1986. Report of the International Conference on the Assessment of the Role of Carbon Dioxide and Other Greenhouse Gases in Climate Variations and Associated Impacts. World Meteorological Organization No. 661, Geneva, Switzerland.

# PART II

# BIOGEOCHEMICAL CYCLES IN THE TROPICS

This part attempts to summarize our current understanding of biogeochemical cycles in the tropics, that is, the chemical processes of the atmosphere, soils, and rivers and their strong coupling to vegetation and microbiological processes.

Tropical soils and forests use and produce many chemicals. The vast numbers of secondary compounds produced by tropical forests continue to provide mankind with many medicines and other such valuable chemical products. Possible loss of these products is one of the arguments against widespread forest destruction. Various more common chemicals are recycled within forests in large quantities. Although the forests are nearly closed systems for much of their nutrient recycling, their release of various chemicals is still copious enough to exert major controls on the content of rivers and on important trace gases within the atmosphere.

Trace atmospheric constituents are important both for global climate and for vegetation. Global cycles of important tropospheric trace gases are fueled by emissions from tropical forests (Crutzen, Chapter 8). Forests, biomass burning, and tropical agriculture provide much of the carbon monoxide, methane, and other hydrocarbons entering the atmosphere. These compounds interact with the hydroxyl radical, the atmosphere's most important oxidizing compound, in cycles that depend crucially on the atmospheric concentrations of oxides of nitrogen. Methane concentrations in the atmosphere are increasing significantly, probably because of human activities. Crutzen argues that these increases of methane, together with increases of oxides of nitrogen from industrial activities, depress hydroxyl concentrations and shift the oxidation cycles of methane and other compounds into regions of the atmosphere that have greater concentrations of oxides of nitrogen. With less hydroxyl, many atmospheric hydrocarbon pollutants are removed less rapidly. Oxidation of methane in the presence of oxides of nitrogen generates large amounts of ozone, one of the most serious pollutants when abundant in surface air.

The exchange of various trace gases between different ecosystems and the atmosphere depends on complex and poorly understood interactions between production and destruction processes within the biosphere, and they are influenced by environmental factors such as light, temperature, moisture, and the oxidation state of the soil (Seiler and Conrad, Chapter 9). Tropical ecosystems act as both sources and sinks for trace gases and contribute a large fraction of the global budgets of many individual compounds, especially methane, carbon monoxide, nitrous oxide, and molecular hydrogen. Seiler and Conrad estimate contributions of the tropics to these compounds but emphasize their uncertainty and the urgent need for many more measurements of the strengths and environmental dependences of these sources and sinks. Harriss (Chapter 10) describes recent measurements of atmospheric profiles of ozone, carbon monoxide, and natural aerosol layers over the Amazon forest near the Atlantic coast. Further such measurements are needed to adequately document the chemistry of the air over the Amazon Basin.

Soils and their biology are of concern both because they can provide or destroy atmospheric constituents and because their mineral recycling is responsible for the maintenance or loss of the macro- and micronutrients responsible for plant growth and productivity. Tropical soils are part of natural and managed ecosystems (Lavelle, Chapter 11). Not only microorganisms but also other larger fauna such as earthworms and termites are important for the recycling of dead organic matter and hence the storage and release of nutrients for plant growth. Various pressures by human populations can degrade the soil systems and destroy the value of the land. Lavelle reviews land use systems currently employed and argues the need for better management of soils in the humid tropics using an ecological understanding of the processes involved.

A UNU-supported field project in Nigeria is attempting to quantify the local environmental changes and economic viability of various strategies for converting tropical forest to other uses (Ghuman and Lal, Chapter 12). Measurements are reported for rainfall, incident solar radiation, soil and air temperatures, relative humidity, pan evaporation, soil fauna, soil density, and water infiltration rates. Air and soil temperatures are several degrees cooler under the forest than in the open and have a much smaller diurnal variation. Relative humidity in the open drops to low values during the day but stays high under the forest except for late in the dry season.

Rivers and their chemical and sediment loads are of importance as the integrated leakage of water, soil, and nutrients from the land surfaces. They are also the habitat of important riverine fisheries, they supply the nutrients required for oceanic coastal fisheries, and they are agriculturally important for seasonally flooded lands. Rivers damage human and natural areas by excessive flooding and supply the waters for dams used for irrigation and generation of hydroelectricity. Silt or high acidity in rivers can have drastic economic impacts by greatly shortening the lifetimes of dams whose cost is sometimes many billions of dollars. Richey (Chapter 13) describes results of field measurements of various land-derived compounds in the Amazon River and its tributaries and relates these measurements to biogeochemical cycling processes in these regions.

# Chapter 8

# Role of the Tropics in Atmospheric Chemistry

**Paul J. Crutzen**

The role the tropics play in global atmospheric photochemistry is largely unexplored, but important because in this region of the atmosphere production of hydroxyl (OH) is most efficient. This highly reactive radical, although present at a mixing ratio of only $2 \times 10^{-14}$, is primarily responsible for the removal of many trace gases from the atmosphere, in particular, methane ($CH_4$) and carbon monoxide (CO). Radicals are fragments of more stable gases with an odd number of electrons. Many other radicals, which are produced in reaction chains initiated by reactions involving hydroxyl, are important for atmospheric chemistry.

The tropics, which contain the most productive ecosystems on earth, are also a dominant source region for these and other important trace gases. Human activities are major contributors, especially those related to agriculture. For example, carbon monoxide is produced in the tropics largely by biomass burning and by the oxidation of hydrocarbons emitted by tropical forests. Biospheric methane release is now mainly from human activities, with major contributions, maybe 80%, coming from tropical agricultural activities such as biomass burning, domestic cattle husbandry, and perhaps even more important, from rice production in the paddy fields of East Asia. Methane is now increasing in the atmosphere at a rate of 1–1.5% annually. With a projected annual population increase of almost 3% in many such areas, a continuing increase in atmospheric methane is probable.

Both methane and carbon monoxide are oxidized through different catalytic cycles, depending on the concentrations of oxides of nitrogen: with low levels of oxides of nitrogen, as are found in areas remote from human activity, OH and ozone are destroyed; with higher levels, tropospheric ozone is generated. It is probable that as increasing methane reduces tropical OH concentrations, more methane will be destroyed in regions of high nitric oxide outside the tropics and hence will take part in the catalytic cycles that involve oxides of nitrogen and thereby produce more tropospheric ozone. On the other hand, global average OH concentrations are probably decreasing.

Further study is needed of the tropical sources and sinks of methane, carbon monoxide, and other important trace gases and of the consequences, for the photochemistry of the atmosphere, of increasing emission of methane and carbon monoxide. In almost all respects, Brazil, and Amazonia in particular, is well suited for these studies of natural and anthropogenic releases to and chemical conversions in the atmosphere.

## THE HYDROXYL RADICAL

The destruction and production of many atmospheric gases are determined by photochemical reactions in which a major role is played by hydroxyl (OH). This radical is produced by photolysis of ozone ($O_3$) through absorption of solar ultraviolet radiation,

$$O_3 + h\nu \rightarrow O(^1D) + O_2 \qquad (\lambda \leq 310 \text{ nm}) \qquad (R1)$$

followed by the reaction of the electronically excited oxygen atom $O(^1D)$ with water vapor,

$$O(^1D) + H_2O \rightarrow 2OH \qquad (R2)$$

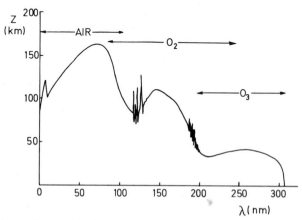

**FIGURE 1.** Approximate altitude at which incoming solar radiation is reduced by the factor $e$ ($\approx 2.8$) due to its absorption by various atmospheric gases. [Adapted from Friedman (1960) with permission of Academic Press, copyright, 1960.]

The efficiency of excited oxygen atom production by reaction (R1) is by far at its highest at low latitudes because the minimum in the overlying ozone column in the stratosphere allows considerable penetration to the earth's surface of photochemically active ultraviolet radiation at wavelengths shorter than about 310 nm (see Figs. 1 and 2).

The presence of hydroxyl in the troposphere is the only conceivable explanation for the observed brief lifetimes of many trace gases in the atmosphere. Most such compounds emitted at the earth's surface, for example, carbon monoxide, hydrogen sulfide, and the majority of organic gases, do not react at all with abundant molecular oxygen. They are not very soluble in water and so are not removed by rainfall. Thus, their residence times are only short because reaction with OH initiates their conversion into reaction products, many of which either do react with molecular oxygen or are easily dissolved in water and then efficiently removed from the atmosphere by precipitation.

The fundamental importance of the hydroxyl radical in tropospheric chemistry was postulated only about 15 y ago (Levy, 1971). Many unexplored questions remain about the photochemistry of the atmosphere, and only a handful of reliable observations of the hydroxyl radical are available. Its global average concentration is currently estimated to be about $5 \times 10^5$ molecules $cm^{-3}$, which corresponds to a molar mixing ratio of only $2 \times 10^{-14}$ in the lower atmosphere. This ultraminor constituent OH is formed

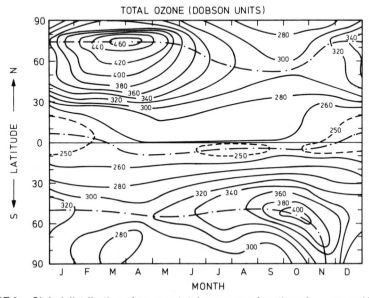

**FIGURE 2.** Global distribution of average total ozone as a function of season and latitude (London, 1980). Note the minimum at the equator (250 Dobson units correspond to 2.5 mm of ozone at standard temperature and pressure).

from ozone with a molar mixing ratio of only 10–40 ppbv (1 ppbv = 1 part per billion by volume = $10^{-9}$).

Without the action of the hydroxyl radical, the composition of the atmosphere would be entirely different. Many gases now present in low concentrations would be much more abundant, most likely at concentrations that would exert decisive influences on atmospheric quality and climate. In view of the critical role of such minute concentrations of OH, it is important to find out whether changes in its atmospheric concentration may be caused by changes in the distribution and emissions of much more abundant constituents that react with (are being oxidized by) hydroxyl, especially carbon monoxide (CO) and methane ($CH_4$).

## ATMOSPHERIC PHOTOCHEMISTRY

Although the hydroxyl radical is produced by reactions (R1) and (R2), its atmospheric concentration is determined by many additional reactions. In oceanic environments and in the free troposphere above the planetary boundary layer, the most important processes involve the oxidation of CO and $CH_4$, the detailed pathways of which are largely determined by the ambient concentrations of nitric oxide (NO) and nitrogen dioxide ($NO_2$).

### Ozone Production or Destruction by Carbon Monoxide Oxidation

In the case of oxidation of carbon monoxide, possible sets of gas phase reactions are

$$
\begin{array}{lll}
CO + OH & \rightarrow H + CO_2 & \text{(R3)} \\
H + O_2 + M & \rightarrow HO_2 + M & \text{(R4)} \\
HO_2 + NO & \rightarrow OH + NO_2 & \text{(R5)} \\
NO_2 + h\nu & \rightarrow NO + O \quad (\lambda \leq 400 \text{ nm}) & \text{(R6)} \\
O + O_2 + M & \rightarrow O_3 + M & \text{(R7)} \\
\hline
\text{C1:} \quad CO + 2O_2 & \rightarrow CO_2 + O_3 &
\end{array}
$$

or

$$
\begin{array}{lll}
CO + OH & \rightarrow H + CO_2 & \text{(R3)} \\
H + O_2 + M & \rightarrow HO_2 + M & \text{(R4)} \\
HO_2 + O_3 & \rightarrow OH + 2O_2 & \text{(R8)} \\
\hline
\text{C2:} \quad CO + O_3 & \rightarrow CO_2 + O_2 &
\end{array}
$$

The intermediates H and $HO_2$ are also free radicals. Together with OH, they are termed odd-hydrogen radicals. The M stands for any third molecule (e.g., $N_2$ or $O_2$) required to make a recombination reaction take place.

Where there are ample NO and $NO_2$, the first set of reactions (C1) takes place with a net production of ozone. Where there are very little NO and $NO_2$, the second set (C2) takes place with a net destruction of ozone (Crutzen, 1973). The first set (with ozone production) is more likely to occur than the second (with ozone destruction) if the ratio of the concentrations of NO to $O_3$ exceeds $2 \times 10^{-4}$, which at the earth's surface corresponds to NO volume mixing ratios larger than about $5 \times 10^{-12}$–$10 \times 10^{-12}$. Such relatively large NO concentrations probably occur in the vicinity of pronounced $NO_x$ sources, such as over the continents, especially in regions of fossil and biofuel combustion, and in the equatorial middle and upper troposphere, where lightning is an important source of NO. Production of NO by lightning is also concentrated over the continental areas because of the higher frequency of lightning there. From these considerations, it has been estimated that the production of NO in the atmosphere above the oceans is at most 10% of the entire global NO source (Borucki and Chameides, 1984; Crutzen et al., 1985; Crutzen, 1983), even though as much as 70% of the earth's surface and about 75% of the tropics are covered by oceans.

Because of reaction (R5), NO increases the amounts of OH and decreases $HO_2$, whereas CO does the opposite as a result of reactions (R3) and (R4).

## Methane Oxidation

Methane is by far the most abundant hydrocarbon gas in the atmosphere, with volume mixing ratios ranging between 1.5 and 2 ppmv (1 ppmv = one part per million by volume = $10^{-6}$). The reactions that take place during its oxidation are particularly important in the photochemistry of the background troposphere and will therefore be discussed in detail.

### With High NO Levels

The oxidation of methane also starts by reaction with OH. Subsequent oxidation steps and products depend decisively on the availability of nitric oxide (Levy, 1971, 1974; McConnell et al., 1971; Crutzen, 1973). If sufficient NO is present, the oxidation pathway to formaldehyde ($CH_2O$) goes mainly as follows:

$$
\begin{array}{lll}
CH_4 + OH & \rightarrow CH_3 + H_2O & (R9) \\
CH_3 + O_2 + M & \rightarrow CH_3O_2 + M & (R10) \\
CH_3O_2 + NO & \rightarrow CH_3O + NO_2 & (R11) \\
CH_3O + O_2 & \rightarrow CH_2O + HO_2 & (R12) \\
HO_2 + NO & \rightarrow OH + NO_2 & (R5) \\
2\times(NO_2 + h\nu & \rightarrow NO + O) & (R6) \\
2\times(O + O_2 + M & \rightarrow O_3 + M) & (R7) \\
\hline
\end{array}
$$

$$ C3: \quad CH_4 + 4O_2 \quad\quad\quad \rightarrow CH_2O + H_2O + 2O_3 $$

The net result is the production of two ozone molecules with no net loss of hydroxyl, nitric oxide, and nitrogen dioxide, which, therefore, are catalysts in the reaction cycle.

Formaldehyde will be oxidized further to carbon monoxide by any of three reaction pathways:

$$CH_2O + h\nu \rightarrow CO + H_2 \quad (\lambda < 360 \text{ nm}) \tag{R13a}$$

or

$$
\begin{array}{lll}
CH_2O + h\nu & \rightarrow CHO + H & (\lambda < 360 \text{ nm}) & (R13b) \\
H + O_2 + M & \rightarrow HO_2 + M & & (R4) \\
CHO + O_2 & \rightarrow CO + HO_2 & & (R14) \\
2 \times (HO_2 + NO & \rightarrow OH + NO_2) & & (R5) \\
2 \times (NO_2 + h\nu & \rightarrow NO + O) & & (R6) \\
2 \times (O + O_2 + M & \rightarrow O_3 + M) & & (R7) \\
\hline
\end{array}
$$

C4: $CH_2O + 4O_2 \quad \rightarrow CO + 2O_3 + 2OH$

or

$$
\begin{array}{lll}
CH_2O + OH & \rightarrow CHO + H_2O & (R15) \\
CHO + O_2 & \rightarrow CO + HO_2 & (R16) \\
HO_2 + NO & \rightarrow OH + NO_2 & (R5) \\
NO_2 + h\nu & \rightarrow NO + O & (R6) \\
O + O_2 + M & \rightarrow O_3 + M & (R7) \\
\hline
\end{array}
$$

C5: $CH_2O + 2O_2 \rightarrow CO + H_2O + O_3$

The average probabilities of these pathways are respectively 50–60%, 20–25%, and 20–30%. Altogether, in environments in which sufficient amounts of NO are present, the oxidation of methane to carbon monoxide yields an average net gain of about 2.7 ozone molecules and 0.5 hydroxyl radicals per methane molecule oxidized (Crutzen, 1973). Through reaction cycle C1, the oxidation of CO to $CO_2$ produces another ozone molecule without affecting the total odd-hydrogen concentration.

### With Low NO Levels

The situation is very different in environments with low NO volume mixing ratios, that is, much below about $10^{-11}$, or 10 pptv (parts per trillion by volume). There the most important reaction pathways to $CH_2O$ are

$$
\begin{array}{lll}
CH_4 + OH & \rightarrow CH_3 + H_2O & (R9) \\
CH_3 + O_2 + M & \rightarrow CH_3O_2 + M & (R10) \\
CH_3O_2 + HO_2 & \rightarrow CH_3O_2H + O_2 & (R17) \\
CH_3O_2H + OH & \rightarrow CH_2O + H_2O + OH & (R18a) \\
\hline
\end{array}
$$

C6: $CH_4 + OH + HO_2 \rightarrow CH_2O + 2H_2O$

or

$$
\begin{array}{lll}
CH_4 + OH & \rightarrow CH_3 + H_2O & \text{(R9)} \\
CH_3 + O_2 + M & \rightarrow CH_3O_2 + M & \text{(R10)} \\
CH_3O_2 + HO_2 & \rightarrow CH_3O_2H + O_2 & \text{(R17)} \\
CH_3O_2H + h\nu & \rightarrow CH_3O + OH \quad (\lambda < 340 \text{ nm}) & \text{(R19)} \\
CH_3O + O_2 & \rightarrow CH_2O + HO_2 & \text{(R12)} \\
\hline
\end{array}
$$

C7: $\quad CH_4 + O_2 \quad\quad \rightarrow CH_2O + H_2O$  (probability $\approx 20\%$)

Another possibility is the precipitation scavenging subcycle

$$
\begin{array}{lll}
CH_4 + OH & \rightarrow CH_3 + H_2O & \text{(R9)} \\
CH_3 + O_2 + M & \rightarrow CH_3O_2 + M & \text{(R10)} \\
CH_3O_2 + HO_2 & \rightarrow CH_3O_2H + O_2 & \text{(R17)} \\
CH_3O_2H + rain & \rightarrow CH_3O_2H \text{ (in rain)} & \text{(R20)} \\
\hline
\end{array}
$$

C8: $\quad CH_4 + OH + HO_2 \rightarrow CH_3O_2H$  (in rain)

Of great potential importance is the catalytic subcycle

$$
\begin{array}{lll}
CH_3O_2 + HO_2 & \rightarrow CH_3O_2H + O_2 & \text{(R17)} \\
CH_3O_2H + OH & \rightarrow CH_3O_2 + H_2O & \text{(R18b)} \\
\hline
\end{array}
$$

C9: $\quad OH + HO_2 \quad\quad \rightarrow H_2O + O_2$

Except for the oxidation set C7, all sets lead to a net loss of two odd-hydrogen (OH and $HO_2$) radicals. The catalytic reaction set C9 can be of particular importance because reaction (R18b) is 1.5 times faster than reaction (R18a). The reaction sequence C8, about which there is a major uncertainty, as for all heterogeneous reactions, also leads to the loss of two odd-hydrogen radicals. $CH_2O$ photolysis only partially compensates for this loss through the reaction sequence

$$
\begin{array}{lll}
CH_2O + h\nu & \rightarrow H + CHO & \text{(R13b)} \\
H + O_2 + M & \rightarrow HO_2 + M & \text{(R4)} \\
CHO + O_2 & \rightarrow CO + HO_2 & \text{(R14)} \\
2 \times (HO_2 + O_3 & \rightarrow OH + 2O_2) & \text{(R8)} \\
\hline
\end{array}
$$

C10: $\quad CH_2O + 2O_3 \quad\quad \rightarrow CO + 2O_2 + 2OH$

Besides the above reaction set C10 and reaction (R13a), which occurs both in NO-rich and NO-poor environments, further oxidation reactions of $CH_2O$ in NO-poor environments are

$$CH_2O + OH \rightarrow CHO + H_2O \qquad (R15)$$
$$CHO + O_2 \quad \rightarrow CO + HO_2 \qquad (R14)$$
$$HO_2 + O_3 \quad \rightarrow OH + 2O_2 \qquad (R8)$$

C11: $CH_2O + O_3 \rightarrow CO + H_2O + O_2$

Therefore, the oxidation of $CH_4$ to CO in low-NO environments leads, on the average, to a net loss of about 3.5 odd-hydrogen and 0.7 ozone molecules for each reacted $CH_4$ molecule. The further oxidation of CO to $CO_2$ via reaction cycle C2 leads to the loss of one additional ozone molecule without affecting odd hydrogen.

### Influence of NO on the Budgets of Tropospheric Ozone and Hydrogen Radicals

The above analysis shows how important the availability of NO is in the tropospheric ozone and odd-hydrogen radical budgets. The oxidation of one $CH_4$ molecule via CO to $CO_2$ yields approximately the following rather astonishing net results:

**a.** in NO-poor environments, to a net loss of 3.5 odd-hydrogen and 1.7 ozone molecules, and

**b.** in NO-rich environments, to a net gain of 0.5 odd-hydrogen and 3.7 ozone molecules.

The effects of cloud and precipitation scavenging processes will modify these results through the removal of intermediate products. For instance, if $CH_3O_2H$ is removed, the loss of one methane molecule removes only two odd-hydrogen radicals. The real atmospheric significance of scavenging processes is, however, difficult to quantify.

Our measurements during the dry season in Brazil (Crutzen et al., 1985) further demonstrate the importance of NO for tropospheric ozone formation. As shown in Fig. 3, boundary layer ozone concentrations in the savanna (*cerrado*) regions are much larger than those above the tropical forests (*selvas*). Biomass burning, which provides a widespread source for NO, is greater in the *cerrado* than in the *selvas*.

The lifetime of NO in the atmosphere is determined by reaction with OH, producing nitric acid through the reactions

$$NO + O_3 \qquad\qquad \rightarrow NO_2 + O_2 \qquad (R21)$$

$$NO_2 + OH (+M) \rightarrow HNO_3 (+M) \qquad (R22)$$

$$HNO_3 + rain \qquad \rightarrow HNO_3 \quad (in\ rain) \qquad (R23)$$

The lifetime of $NO_x$ (NO and $NO_2$) as determined by these reactions varies

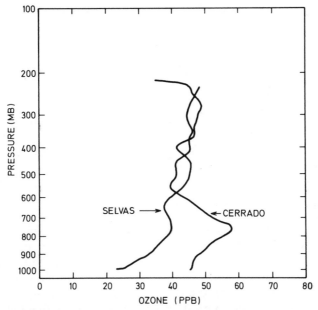

**FIGURE 3.** Average profiles of ozone volume mixing ratios over the tropical, humid forest, and savanna regions of Brazil. [Reprinted from Crutzen et al. (1985) with permission of D. Reidel Publishing Company, Dordrecht, Holland, copyright, 1985.]

from less than one day in the tropics to several days at middle and high latitudes. We may therefore expect a great variability in $NO_x$ concentrations and low concentrations in environments remote from $NO_x$ sources, especially the marine tropics and the Southern Hemisphere. The few available NO measurements support this conclusion (McFarland et al., 1979; Liu et al., 1983; Noxon, 1981, 1983; Stedman and McEwan, 1983; Bollinger et al., 1984; Drummond et al., 1985).

## Methane Is Increasing

We have devoted so much discussion to the several possible pathways for methane oxidation because worldwide observations show that global atmospheric methane concentrations are now increasing at the rate of 1–1.5% per year (Rasmussen and Khalil, 1984; Blake et al., 1982; Fraser et al., 1981; Seiler, 1984; Blake, 1984). Studies of air trapped in ice indicate constant $CH_4$ mixing ratios of 0.7 ppmv before A.D. 1560, an increase to 1.25 ppmv by 1950, and values approaching 2 ppmv at present (Robbins et al., 1973; Craig and Chou, 1982; Rasmussen and Khalil, 1984). Because of the demonstrated importance of methane for the photochemistry of the background atmosphere, especially its oxidative power, we must understand the atmospheric significance of the recorded methane increase and why it is occurring.

## THE TROPOSPHERIC OH DISTRIBUTION AND SOURCES AND SINKS OF CO AND CH$_4$

The distributions of CO and CH$_4$ are observed globally, but an estimate of their sources and sinks from this distribution requires also the distribution of OH, which is now best obtained from calculation because of lack of observations.

### Tropospheric Distribution of OH

Current ideas about atmospheric photochemistry are to a substantial degree still untested by atmospheric observations as only a few successful measurements have been made of OH, HO$_2$, NO, and NO$_2$. Nevertheless, it is possible to simulate the photochemistry of the background atmosphere outside the continental boundary layer by taking into account photochemical reaction schemes, atmospheric transport processes, estimated sources of NO$_x$, and observed concentrations of methane, carbon monoxide, and ozone (Crutzen and Gidel, 1983; Crutzen, 1983; Khalil and Rasmussen, 1983; Blake, 1984; Heidt et al., 1980; Seiler, 1974; Seiler and Fishman, 1981; Routhier et al., 1980). Ideally this simulation should be done in a three-dimensional model, but a suitable model is not yet available. Using a two-dimensional model that simulates the longitudinally averaged, meridional chemical distribution of the atmosphere, we obtained the daytime average meridional distributions of hydroxyl that are shown in Fig. 4 (Crutzen and Gidel, 1983). Calculated hydroxyl concentrations are largest for the tropics. The globally and diurnally averaged OH concentration corresponding to the calculated hydroxyl distributions equals $5.5 \times 10^5$ molecules cm$^{-3}$.

The few reliable hydroxyl measurements that have been made so far (e.g., Perner et al., 1976; Hübler et al., 1984) are insufficient to test the photochemical models of the background troposphere. However, the appropriateness of the calculated hydroxyl concentrations can be checked by a comparison between the calculated and observed global distributions and estimated atmospheric lifetimes of methylchloroform (CH$_3$CCl$_3$), a purely industrial gas with rather well-known sources, which is mainly removed by reaction with hydroxyl. The hydroxyl concentrations shown in Fig. 4 lead to a calculated global CH$_3$CCl$_3$ distribution in remarkably good agreement with that observed (Prinn et al., 1983), after improvements were made in the preparation of absolute calibration standards (Prinn, personal communication). There remain, however, some uncertainties in the release rates of CH$_3$CCl$_3$.

The atmospheric lifetime of CH$_3$CCl$_3$ can, however, also be determined

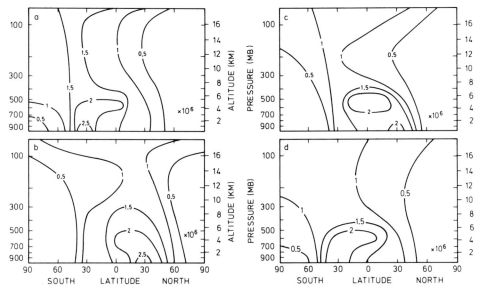

**FIGURE 4.** Calculated daytime average meridional distributions of OH (molecules cm$^{-3}$) for (*a*) January, (*b*) July, (*c*) April, and (*d*) October. [Reprinted from Crutzen and Gidel (1983), copyright by the American Geophysical Union.]

from its historical emission rates and the relative growth in its atmospheric abundance. Using this method, which does not depend on knowledge of the absolute concentrations of $CH_3CCl_3$, Prinn et al. (1983) estimated, from the worldwide ALE observations network, a most likely atmospheric removal time of 10.2 y with an uncertainty range of 7.6–15.4 y and a corresponding globally and diurnally averaged OH concentration of $(5 \pm 2) \times 10^5$ cm$^{-3}$. Our model calculations give a global average OH concentration within 10% of $5 \times 10^5$ cm$^{-3}$, similar to that derived by Volz et al. (1981) on the basis of global $^{14}$CO measurements. For the following numerical estimations we will therefore adopt the calculated OH distributions of Fig. 4, realizing that these could be uncertain by about 30%. The corresponding global average atmospheric lifetimes of methane and carbon monoxide for attack by OH are 16 y and 4 months, respectively. The global destruction rates of methane and carbon monoxide are $3.2 \times 10^{14}$ g y$^{-1}$ ($8 \times 10^{10}$ molecules cm$^{-2}$ s$^{-1}$) and $2.1 \times 10^{15}$ g y$^{-1}$ ($3 \times 10^{11}$ molecules cm$^{-2}$ s$^{-1}$), respectively.

### Tropical Sources for CO

The calculated global budget of sources and sinks of carbon monoxide, presented in Fig. 5, contains some well-known contributions, such as the production from methane oxidation, which can be estimated from the calculated OH and observed $CH_4$ distribution, the transport of CO from the Northern

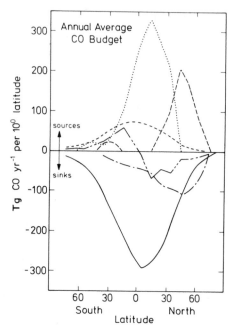

| Legend | Global | Process |
|---|---|---|
| ----- | 643 | Industrial Source |
| —·— | -636 | Deposition |
| ——— | -2054 | CO + OH oxidation sink |
| ....... | 566 | CH₄ + OH oxidation source |
| —··— | ±194 | Transport |
| ··········· | 1483 | Sources |

**FIGURE 5.** Annual CO budget calculated with the OH distributions of Fig. 4 and the observed CO distributions. [Reprinted from Crutzen and Gidel (1983), copyright by the American Geophysical Union.]

Hemisphere to the Southern Hemisphere, the uptake of CO by soils, and the oxidation of CO to $CO_2$ by reaction with OH, which is likewise estimated from the calculated global distribution of OH and the observed distribution of carbon monoxide. Consideration of these production and destruction terms indicates the need for an additional large source of CO in the tropics that equals about two thirds of the total source strength.

Our research over the past years points to two important tropical CO sources, that is, biomass burning and the oxidation of reactive (nonmethane) hydrocarbons that are emitted by tropical forests. The former source is predominately anthropogenic, takes place mostly in the dry season, and is due to (a) the cutting and burning of forests, which are turned into agricultural lands; (b) the annual burning of weeds, dry grass and other vegetation, mostly in the savanna regions; and (c) the combustion of firewood. The total mass of biomass burned for these purposes in the tropics is estimated to range from 2000 to 3300 Tg of carbon per year (1 Tg = $10^{12}$ g), but this estimate is quite uncertain and based on statistics prior to 1975 (Seiler and Crutzen, 1980). From our observations, the relative yield of CO to $CO_2$ molecules from biomass burning is 12–15% (Crutzen et al., 1985). Consequently, the annual production of carbon monoxide from biomass burning amounts to 500–1000 Tg CO, which corresponds to about one third to two thirds of the total CO source in the tropics. Similar estimates of CO production by biomass burning were presented by Crutzen et al. (1979) and Logan et al. (1981).

Our observations from Brazil have shown that an additional source of CO of 500–1000 Tg $y^{-1}$ might indeed be supplied by the oxidation of reactive hydrocarbons emitted from tropical forests (Crutzen et al., 1985). Measurements of carbon monoxide in the boundary layer to 3 km altitude over the Amazon forests (near Manaus) in August 1980 show average carbon monoxide volume mixing ratios of about 300 ppbv, indicating the existence of a large source of CO, since Atlantic and free tropospheric volume mixing ratios at the same latitudes are about 100 ppb. A trajectory analysis indicated a travel time of about two days for boundary layer air between the Atlantic and Manaus. Most prominent among the hydrocarbons emitted from forest vegetation is isoprene ($C_5H_8$), but other organics also contribute significantly. The exact oxidation reactions of the natural hydrocarbons are only approximately known and depend again on the availability of NO, about which there is very little observational knowledge. Although NO can be released from tropical soils by nitrification, as is $N_2O$ (Keller et al., 1983), little $NO_x$ is likely to penetrate through the dense tropical forest canopy to reach the free troposphere.

## Sources of Methane

The calculated global distribution of sources and sinks of methane, as shown in Fig. 6, also indicates dominant sources in the tropics. The global methane destruction by reaction with OH is estimated to be 320 Tg $y^{-1}$. The total mass of $CH_4$ in the atmosphere is about 5000 Tg. For methane to increase at the observed average rate of 1.2% per year, there must be a total input of about 380 Tg $CH_4$ per year. Several $CH_4$ sources can be confidently estimated. Enteric fermentation in domestic ruminants, especially cattle, produces about 80 Tg $CH_4$ per year with comparable contributions from the less developed and industrialized world. Coal mining produces worldwide 34 Tg $CH_4$ per year, given an emission of 18–19 $m^3$ methane per ton of coal (Dr. K. Noack, Westfälische Berggewerkschafts Kasse, GmbH, private communication). With a $CH_4$-to-$CO_2$ emission ratio between 0.8 and 1.6% and the previous estimates of carbon burned per year, biomass burning in the tropics produces 20–70 Tg $CH_4$ annually (Crutzen et al., 1985). An average of 45 Tg is adopted here. Leakage of natural gas from distribution systems could annually release 33 Tg if the 4% estimated for Switzerland (Dr. B. Gehr, Erdöl-Vereinigung, private communication) is assumed globally. Therefore, the total annual $CH_4$ production from these relatively well-known sources is about 170 Tg. Consequently, there remains an annual, mostly tropical source of about 210 Tg of methane to be accounted for, which

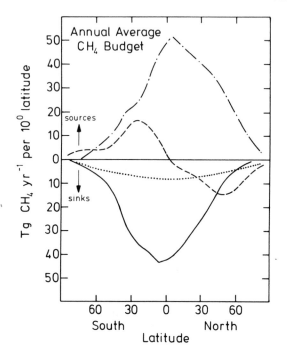

FIGURE 6. Annual CH₄ budget calculated with the OH distributions of Fig. 4 and the observed global CH₄ distributions. [Reprinted from Crutzen and Gidel (1983), copyright by the American Geophysical Union.]

| Legend | Global | Process |
|--------|--------|---------|
| – – – – | ± 71 | Transport |
| ·········· | 87 | CH₄ global increase |
| ——— | -322 | CH₄ + OH oxidation sink |
| –·—·– | 409 | Sources |

is presumably provided from rice fields, natural wetlands, termites and other processes. Recent studies, especially by Seiler, Conrad, and Scharffe (1984b), have indicated that the methane source from the digestion of plant material by termites is much less than the upper limit initially proposed by Zimmerman et al. (1982).

Seiler, Holzapfel-Pschorn, Conrad, and Scharffe (1984a) observed CH₄ release rates from rice fields in Andalusia, Spain, and determined an average emission of 12 g m$^{-2}$ during the rice-growing season. Cicerone et al. (1983) measured a CH₄ production of 25 g m$^{-2}$ in California rice fields. More recently, Holzapfel-Pschorn and Seiler (in press) made extensive measurements of CH₄ production from Italian rice fields and determined a release of 54 g m$^{-2}$ for the entire vegetation period of 140 days. They explained the lower production from Spain to be due to a lower organic matter content in the soils and a likely influx of some brackish water during drought conditions.

Extrapolation from this limited information to global conditions is clearly very uncertain, especially since rice production occurs overwhelmingly in South and East Asia, and no measurements are available from these areas. Holzapfel-Pschorn and Seiler (in press) estimate a possible annual release rate from rice fields of 70–170 Tg $CH_4$, with a central value of 120 Tg $CH_4$. This central value would account for more than half of the entire wetlands methane source required here.

The total area of marshes and swamps in the world equals about $2 \times 10^6$ $km^2$, of which 75% is located in the tropics. The tropical natural wetland area is about equal to the cultivated rice paddy area. Organic matter production in natural tropical wetlands is 4 kg $m^{-2}$ $y^{-1}$ (Bolin et al., 1979), a rate that extrapolates to an annual tropical wetland organic matter production of 6000 Tg, more than 80% of the total from all marshes and swamps in the world. A methane yield of about 1.5% from the decay of this material would, therefore, yield the required methane flux of 90 Tg $y^{-1}$. Such a low efficiency of $CH_4$ production indicates that many variable factors must influence the $CH_4$ release from different ecosystems and that results from global extrapolation of measurements at a handful of sites will probably forever remain extremely uncertain.

A compilation of past measurements from a few natural wetland systems in midlatitudes and extrapolated globally by Blake (1984) gives a higher range of annual emissions of 120–180 Tg $CH_4$. The agreement within a factor of 2 between this and our estimate is certainly fortuitous.

The various estimated or assumed methane production rates just discussed are given as estimate I in Table 1. Estimate I gives a current anthropogenic annual production of methane of 290 Tg and a natural production of about 90 Tg. A natural $CH_4$ contribution that is relatively small compared to the current total $CH_4$ release to the atmosphere would be in agreement with the $CH_4$ measurements in polar ice, which show a constant $CH_4$ mixing ratio of 0.7 ppmv between 400 and 2500 y ago (Craig and Chou, 1982; Rasmussen and Khalil, 1984). The annual $CH_4$ production of 380 Tg would be balanced by the sum of a global loss rate of 320 Tg by reaction with OH and an annual increase in the global amount of atmospheric $CH_4$ of 60 Tg.

## Reasons for Global Methane Increase

The simplest explanation for the observed global atmospheric $CH_4$ increase of 1–1.5% $y^{-1}$ would be an annual growth in global $CH_4$ production at about the same rate. This possibility is supported by some preliminary observations of changes in the $^{13}C$ content of atmospheric $CH_4$ over the past 30 y (Craig and Chou, 1982). An estimated annual $CH_4$ production of 380 Tg and an increase of about 1.2% per year suggests an annual growth in $CH_4$ emissions by 4.6 Tg, about 1.6% of the total anthropogenic $CH_4$ source. With the proposed $CH_4$ sources discussed so far and a constant lifetime for methane, this growth is difficult to explain. The annual growth rate in worldwide cattle

**TABLE 1.  Estimates of Global Sources of
Atmospheric Methane (Tg y$^{-1}$)$^a$**

|                    | Estimate I | Estimate II |
|--------------------|:----------:|:-----------:|
| Domestic ruminants | 80         | 80          |
| Biomass burning    | 45         | 60          |
| Natural gas leaks  | 33         | 33          |
| Coal mining        | 34         | 34          |
| Rice paddies       | 120        | 120         |
| Natural wetlands   | 70         | 50          |
| Total              | ~380       | ~380        |

$^a$ The main uncertainties are $CH_4$ releases from rice paddies and wetlands. Emissions from domestic ruminants (especially cattle) and biomass burning are better known, while those from natural gas are based on a 4% leakage. With the estimates presented in column 1 and a 0.7% annual increase for the rice paddy production, it is difficult to explain the currently observed average global $CH_4$ increase of about 1.2% per year without invoking increasing methane lifetimes. Column 2 assigns a greater weight to biomass burning. Growth in anthropogenic $CH_4$ production from estimate II sources at rates of 1, 2, 2.2, 2.2, and 1% per year, respectively, and a constant methane lifetime of 16 y would lead to the observed $CH_4$ increases in the atmosphere. Most likely, however, average global OH concentrations have decreased, so that too many unknowns exist to propose a satisfactory methane budget.

population between 1970 and 1980 was about 1% (FAO, 1979, 1983); in coal and in natural gas production, 2.2% (UN, 1981); and in rice paddy area about 0.7% (FAO, 1979, 1983). Given the methane production estimates for these categories in column 1 of Table 1, the total emission from these sources would currently increase by 2.9 Tg annually. An increase in the emission from biomass burning can account only for the remaining 1.7 Tg y$^{-1}$ if, worldwide, this source has been growing at a rate of 4% per year, at least over the past 5–10 y, which seems unlikely, although an acceleration of forest clearing activities in the Amazon is apparently taking place (Fearnside, Chapter 4).

Thus, either methane lifetimes are increasing or the anthropogenic contribution to the total $CH_4$ source is higher than that shown as Estimate I of Table 1 or both. The next section argues that increases of methane are reducing global hydroxyl concentrations and thus increasing methane lifetimes. Methane releases from biomass burning and rice paddies in the tropics are also likely to be larger than given in estimate I (Table 1). Although the worldwide harvested rice paddy area increased by only 0.7% annually in the 1970s, rice yields increased, thereby increasing the rice production by 3%, corresponding to the population growth (FAO, 1979, 1983; Watts, 1982).

The more efficient rice-growing practices that are being introduced world-wide may influence $CH_4$ release to the atmosphere. In one set of observations Cicerone and Shetter (1981) found enhanced $CH_4$ release rates from fertilized plots, but in other field experiments by Cicerone et al. (1983) and Seiler et al. (1984), such an enhanced rate was not observed.

Because the analysis of global biomass burning rates by Seiler and Crutzen (1980) was based on demographic and agricultural statistics before 1975, biomass burning is likely to be more than 3300 Tg C per year. Correspondingly, methane release from biomass burning may be higher than 45 Tg $CH_4$ per year.

To improve agreement with the observed rate of increase of methane without the need to invoke increasing methane lifetimes, the budget of $CH_4$ presented as estimate II in Table 1 would be a solution. Most probably, however, global average hydroxyl concentrations are decreasing as will be argued below. A definite $CH_4$ budget, therefore, cannot be proposed.


## PARTITIONING BETWEEN NO-POOR AND NO-RICH ENVIRONMENTS AND CHANGES IN ATMOSPHERIC PHOTOCHEMISTRY

If the entire atmosphere were to contain supercritical NO concentrations, the oxidation of CO (derived from $CH_4$ and other sources) would produce ozone globally at a rate of $3 \times 10^{11}$ molecules $cm^{-2} s^{-1}$, and the oxidation of $CH_4$ to CO another $2 \times 10^{11}$ molecules $cm^{-2} s^{-1}$. These potential production rates are much larger than the global mean ozone destruction rate by reaction (R2), which equals about $5 \times 10^{10}$ molecules $cm^{-2} s^{-1}$. They are also much larger than the estimated average downward flux of ozone from the stratosphere to the troposphere and the destruction rate at the earth's surface, which are also about $5 \times 10^{10}$ molecules $cm^{-2} s^{-1}$ (e.g., Galbally and Roy, 1980; Gidel and Shapiro, 1980).

In order to obtain a satisfactory tropospheric ozone balance, it is therefore necessary to postulate that roughly one half of the atmosphere contains subcritical and the other half supercritical NO concentrations.


### Changes in Global Odd Hydrogen

For each methane molecule oxidized in NO-poor environments, there is an average loss of about 3.5 odd-hydrogen radicals by gas phase reactions, while in NO-rich environments, there is a net gain of only 0.5 odd-hydrogen radicals. Consequently, with both such environments of about equal extent, the increase of methane will lead directly to a substantial decrease of global OH concentrations, probably further enhanced through reaction (R3) because CO concentrations may also be expected to increase with increasing methane in NO-poor environments. This lowering of OH concentrations depends on changing the globally averaged odd-hydrogen budget which balances roughly as follows.

The column production rate of odd hydrogen by reactions (R1) and (R2) in the troposphere is estimated rather accurately as about equal to $10^{11}$ molecules $cm^{-2}$ $s^{-1}$ as a global average. The loss rate of methane by reaction with hydroxyl, although far less certain, is estimated from the model calculations to be about $8 \times 10^{10}$ molecules $cm^{-2}$ $s^{-1}$. Half of this methane loss occurs in NO-rich environments in which there is a net gain of 0.5 odd-hydrogen radical for each $CH_4$ molecule oxidized. Consequently, in these regions, there is a mean global net gain of $0.5 \times 4 \times 10^{10} = 2 \times 10^{10}$ odd hydrogen $cm^{-2}$ $s^{-1}$. The global average production rate of odd hydrogen is, therefore, $1.2 \times 10^{11}$ molecules $cm^{-2}$ $s^{-1}$. This rate agrees rather well with the odd-hydrogen loss rate in NO-poor environments. In these, the oxidation of one $CH_4$ molecule leads to a net loss of 3.5 odd-hydrogen radicals, resulting in a net average loss rate of $3.5 \times 4 \times 10^{10} = 1.4 \times 10^{11}$ $cm^{-2}$ $s^{-1}$.

Because carbon monoxide and methane are the main reaction partners of hydroxyl in most of the background atmosphere, their oxidation is important for the atmospheric odd-hydrogen budget. The carbon monoxide oxidation cycles C1 and C2 merely recycle odd hydrogen. Additional reactions involving CO that are shown in the Appendix, however, do play some role in odd-hydrogen removal.

## Increasing Ozone at Northern Midlatitudes

A gradual shift of methane oxidation to regions of the atmosphere in which there are substantial sources of $NO_x$, such as the middle latitudes of the industrialized Northern Hemisphere, and the upper troposphere and the lower stratosphere, in which there are natural sources of $NO_x$, will enhance ozone production through the $CH_4$ oxidation cycles C3, C4, and C5 (and the CO oxidation cycle C1).

Such a shift in methane oxidation and a concomitant growth in industrial NO emissions may explain, at least partly, the observed increase in surface ozone concentrations, about 60% between 1967 and 1982 in the Federal Republic of Germany (Attmannspacher et al., 1984) and 12 and 16% between 1973 and 1983 at Barrow, Alaska, and Mauna Loa, Hawaii, respectively (Harris and Nickerson, 1984). The German data are reproduced in Fig. 7.

More tropospheric ozone implies more production of OH by reactions (R1) and (R2). The increase in anthropogenic NO emissions also tends to increase OH concentrations in midlatitude NO-rich environments because of the conversion of $HO_2$ to OH by reaction (R5). These tendencies may only partly have been lessened by a possible increase in CO concentrations. Altogether, a marked shift of photochemical activity to the northern midlatitudes must have occurred, especially during the last few decades with

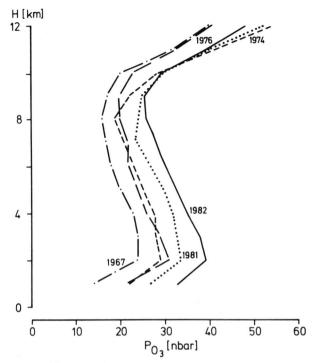

**FIGURE 7.** Observed increase in annual average ozone concentrations in the troposphere and lower stratosphere at Hohenpeissenberg, Bavaria, Federal Republic of Germany between 1967 and 1982. [Reprinted from Attmannspacher et al. (1984), reprinted with permission of Gebrüder Borntraeger, copyright 1984.]

increases of OH in northern midlatitudes and decreases elsewhere in regions of low $NO_x$.

## FURTHER IMPORTANT CONSEQUENCES OF METHANE INCREASE AND HYDROXYL DECREASE FOR ATMOSPHERIC PHOTOCHEMISTRY

Increases in atmospheric methane and resulting reduction in the OH concentrations in background air in which there is little $NO_x$ decrease overall the oxidative power of the atmosphere. Hence, not only will methane increase more rapidly than with constant OH concentrations but there will also be increases in the concentrations of many other compounds that require oxidation by OH for their removal. Given the probable continued growth in $CH_4$ production by human activities and a lowering of average global OH concentrations, the current imbalance between production and atmospheric destruction of $CH_4$ will probably continue.

## Impacts on Stratospheric Chemistry

Methane is important for the photochemistry of the stratosphere. An increase in stratospheric methane causes a decrease in active chlorine radicals, Cl and ClO, which destroy ozone through catalytic reactions. On the other hand, because of industrial emissions of various organic chlorine compounds, such as $CFCl_3$, $CF_2Cl_2$, and $CH_3CCl_3$, more active chlorine will accumulate in the stratosphere. The increase in stratospheric methane will, therefore, only partly offset the expected ozone decrease in the stratosphere. The oxidation of methane is an important source for stratospheric $H_2O$, which also has a large influence on stratospheric photochemistry.

## Climate Impact

Both methane and ozone are greenhouse gases whose increased tropospheric abundance will lead to an increase in temperatures at the earth's surface.

## SUMMARY OF THE ROLE OF THE TROPICS IN THE CHANGING INTERACTIONS BETWEEN OH, $CH_4$, NO, AND $O_3$

The tropics are very important for the photochemistry of the atmosphere and for the cycling and removal of many important atmospheric trace gases. This importance is due to the efficient production of hydroxyl radicals, the "cleaners" of the atmosphere. Hydroxyl radicals are increasingly being removed in the tropical atmosphere by reactions with methane and methane oxidation products. In these environments, the loss rate of methane from the atmosphere is no longer linearly dependent on its atmospheric concentrations. A continuing growth in atmospheric $CH_4$ is expected to lead to a decrease in global average hydroxyl radical concentrations and to an increase in the concentration of the many gases removed predominately by reaction with OH. On the other hand, in parts of the atmosphere containing supercritical NO concentrations, such as the upper troposphere and lower stratosphere and the continental boundary layer of the industrial midlatitudes as well as parts of the tropics, there will be more ozone production. These changes in methane, hydroxyl radical, and tropospheric ozone concentrations could clearly have important consequences for the future composition and photochemical functioning of the earth's atmosphere and global climate to the extent that it depends on the future composition.

The production and atmospheric release of $CH_4$ are apparently now dominated by land clearing and agricultural activities in the tropics, especially increasing biomass burning and rice production in the paddy fields of East Asia. With an expected annual population growth rate of 2.2% in the developing world, and in particular 2.5–3% in Latin America and almost 3% in East Asia, a continued growth, currently at 1–1.5% per year, in the atmospheric $CH_4$ content is likely. The consequences of this increase for the photochemistry of the earth's atmosphere should receive considerable attention. Studies of the sources and sinks of methane and many other important trace gases should have high priority so that the preliminary ideas presented in this chapter can be tested.

## APPENDIX

### Additional Mechanisms for Odd-Hydrogen Removal

Besides the reactions of oxidation of methane and its products in NO-poor regions, some loss of odd hydrogen also takes place through the reaction sequences

$$HO_2 + HO_2 \rightarrow H_2O_2 + O_2 \quad \text{(R24)}$$
$$H_2O_2 + OH \rightarrow H_2O + HO_2 \quad \text{(R25)}$$

C12:     Net:  $OH + HO_2 \rightarrow H_2O + O_2$

and

$$2 \times (CO + OH \rightarrow H + CO_2) \quad \text{(R3)}$$
$$2 \times (H + O_2 + M \rightarrow HO_2 + M) \quad \text{(R4)}$$
$$HO_2 + HO_2 \rightarrow H_2O_2 + O_2 \quad \text{(R24)}$$
$$H_2O_2 + \text{rain} \rightarrow H_2O_2 \text{ (in rain)} \quad \text{(R26)}$$

C13:  $2CO + O_2 + 2OH \rightarrow 2CO_2 + H_2O_2$  (in rain)

The efficiency of the "heterogeneous" removal process (C13) is difficult to estimate because little is known in general about chemical precipitation scavenging in the atmosphere. Loss of odd hydrogen in the methane oxidation sequence is, however, most important whenever gas phase reactions dominate, and the analysis presented in the main body of this essay applies for such conditions.

## REFERENCES

Attmannspacher, W., Hartmannsgruber, R., and Lang, P., 1984. Langzeittendenzen des Ozons der Atmosphäre aufgrund der 1967 begonnenen Ozonmeßreihen am Meteorologischen Observatorium Hohenpeißenberg, *Meteorol. Rdsch.* **37**, 193–199.

Blake, D. R., 1984. *Increasing Concentrations of Atmospheric Methane, 1979–1983*, Ph.D. dissertation, University of California, Irvine.

Blake, D. R., Mayer, E. W., Tyler, S. C., Montague, D. C., Makide, Y., and Rowland, F. S., 1982. Global increase in atmospheric methane concentration between 1978 and 1980, *Geophys. Res. Lett.* **9**, 477–480.

Bolin, B., Degens, E. T., Duvigneaud, P., and Kempe, S., 1979. The global biogeochemical carbon cycle, in B. Bolin, E. T., Degens, S. Kempe, and P. Ketner, Eds., *The Global Carbon Cycle, SCOPE*, Vol. 13, Wiley, Chichester, England.

Bollinger, M. J., Hahn, C. J., Parrish, D. D., Murphy, P. C., Albritton, D. L., and Fehsenfeld, F. C., 1984. NO$_x$ measurements in clean continental air and analysis of the contributing meteorology, *J. Geophys. Res.* **89**, 9623–9631.

Borucki, W. J. and Chameides, W. L., 1984. Lightning: Estimates of the rates of energy dissipation of nitrogen fixation, *Rev. Geophys. Space Phys.* **22**, 363–372.

Cicerone, R. G., and Shetter, J. D., 1981. Sources of atmospheric methane: Measurements in rice paddies and a discussion, *J. Geophys. Res.* **86**, 7203–7209.

Cicerone, R. J., Shetter, J. D., and Delwiche, C. C. 1983. Seasonal variation of methane flux from a Californian rice paddy, *J. Geophys. Res.* **88**, 11022–11024.

Craig, H. and Chou, C. C., 1982. Methane: The record in polar ice cores, *Geophys. Res. Lett.* **9**, 1221–1224.

Crutzen, P. J., 1973. A discussion of the chemistry of some minor constituents in the stratosphere and troposphere, *Pure Appl. Geophys.* **106–108**, 1385–1399.

Crutzen, P. J., 1983. Atmospheric interactions: Homogeneous gas reactions of C, N, and S containing compounds, in B. Bolin and R. B. Cook, Eds., *The Major Biogeochemical Cycles and Their Interactions, SCOPE,* Vol. 21, Wiley, Chichester, England.

Crutzen, P. J. and Gidel, L. T., 1983. A two-dimensional photochemical model of the atmosphere. 2: The tropospheric budgets of the anthropogenic chlorocarbons CO, CH$_4$, CH$_3$Cl and the effect of various NO$_x$ sources on tropospheric ozone, *J. Geophys. Res* **88**, 6641–6661.

Crutzen, P. J., Heidt, L. E., Krasnec, J. P., Pollock, W. H., and Seiler, W., 1979. Biomass burning as a source of atmospheric gases CO, H$_2$, N$_2$O, NO, CH$_3$Cl, and COS, *Nature* **282**, 253–256.

Crutzen, P. J., Delany, A. C., Greenberg, J., Haagenson, P., Heidt, L., Lueb, R., Pollock, W., Seiler, W., Wartburg, A., and Zimmerman, P., 1985. Tropospheric chemical composition measurements in Brazil during the dry season, *J. Atmos. Chem.* **2**, 233–256.

Drummond, J. W., Volz, A., and Ehhalt, D. H., 1985. An optimized chemiluminescence detector for tropospheric NO measurements, *J. Atmos. Chem.* **2**, 287–306.

Food and Agriculture Organization (FAO) of the United Nations, 1979. *Production Yearbook,* Vol. 33, FAO, Rome, pp. 46–47.

Food and Agriculture Organization (FAO) of the United Nations, 1983. *Production Yearbook,* Vol. 37, FAO, Rome, pp. 110–111, 216–218.

Fraser, P. G., Khalil, M. A. K., Rasmussen, R. A., and Crawford, A. Y., 1981. Trends of atmospheric CH$_4$ in the southern hemisphere, *Geophys. Res. Lett.* **9**, 1063–1066.

Friedman, H., 1960. The Sun's ionizing radiations, in J. A. Ratcliffe, Ed., *Physics of the Upper Atmosphere,* Academic, New York, p. 134.

Galbally, I. E. and Roy, C. R., 1980. Destruction of ozone at the earth's surface, *Quart. J. Roy. Meteor. Soc.* **106**, 599–620.

Gidel, L. T. and Shapiro, M., 1980. General circulation model estimates of the net vertical flux of ozone in the lower stratosphere and the implications for the tropospheric ozone budget, *J. Geophys. Res.* **85**, 4049–4058.

Harris, J. M. and Nickerson, E. C., 1984. *Geophysical Monitoring for Climatic Change,* No. 12, Summary Report 1983, NOAA, Boulder, CO.

Heidt, L. E., Krasnec, J. P., Lueb, R. A., Pollock, W. H., Henry, B. E., and Crutzen, P. J., 1980. Latitudinal distributions of CO and $CH_4$ over the Pacific, *J. Geophys. Res.* **85**, 7329–7336.

Holzapfel-Pschorn, A. and Seiler, W., in press. Methane emission during a vegetation period from an Italian rice paddy, *J. Geophys. Res.*

Hübler, G., Perner, D., Platt, U., Toennissen, A., and Ehhalt, D. H., 1984. Ground-level OH radical concentration: New measurements by optical absorption, *J. Geophys. Res.* **89**, 1309–1319.

Keller, M., Goreau, T. J., Wofsy, S. C., Kaplan, W. A., and McElroy, M. B., 1983. Production of nitrous oxide and consumption of methane by forest soils, *Geophys. Res. Lett.* **10**, 1156–1159.

Khalil, M. A. K. and Rasmussen, R., 1983. Sources, sinks, and seasonal cycles of atmospheric methane, *J. Geophys. Res.* **88**, 5131–5144.

Levy II, H., 1971. Normal atmosphere: Large radical and formaldehyde concentrations predicted, *Science* **173**, 141–143.

Levy II, H., 1974. Photochemistry of the troposphere, *Adv. Photochem.* **9**, 5325–5332.

Liu, S. C., McFarland, M., Kley, D., Zafiriou, O., and Huebert, B., 1983. Tropospheric $NO_x$ and $O_3$ budgets in the equatorial Pacific, *J. Geophys. Res.* **88**, 1360–1368.

Logan, J. A., Prather, M. J., Wofsy, S. C., and McElroy, M. B., 1981. Tropospheric chemistry: A global perspective, *J. Geophys. Res.* **86**, 7210–7254.

London, J., 1980. Radiative energy sources and sinks in the stratosphere and mesosphere, in *Proceedings of the NATO Advanced Study Institute on Atmospheric Ozone: Its Variation and Human Influences,* M. Nicolet and A. C. Aikin, Eds., U.S. Department of Transportation, Washington, DC.

McConnell, J. C., McElroy, M. B., and Wofsy, S. C., 1971. Natural sources of atmospheric CO, *Nature* **233**, 187–188.

McFarland, M., Kley, D., Drummond, J. W., Schmeltekopf, A. L., and Winkler, R. H., 1979. Nitric oxide measurements in the equatorial Pacific region, *Geophys. Res. Lett.* **6**, 605–608.

Noxon, J. F., 1981. $NO_x$ in the mid-Pacific troposphere, *Geophys. Res. Lett,* **8,** 1223–1226.

Noxon, J. F., 1983. $NO_3$ and $NO_2$ in the mid-Pacific troposphere, *J. Geophys. Res.* **88**, 11017–11021.

Perner, D., Ehhalt, D. H., Pätz, H. W., Platt, U., Röth, E. P., and Volz, A., 1976. OH radicals in the lower troposphere, *Geophys. Res. Lett.* **86**, 466–468.

Prinn, R. G., Rasmussen, R. A., Simmonds, P. G., Alyea, F. N., Cunnold, D. M.,

Lane, B. C., Cardelino, C. A., and Crawford, A. J., 1983. The atmospheric lifetime experiment. 5: Results for $CH_3CCl_3$ based on three years of data, *J. Geophys. Res.* **88**, 8415–8426.

Rasmussen, R. A., and Khalil, M. A. K., 1984. Atmospheric methane in the recent and ancient atmospheres: Concentrations, trends, and interhemispheric gradient, *J. Geophys. Res* **89**, 11599–11605.

Robbins, R. C., Cavanagh, L. A., Salas, L. J., and Robinson, E., 1973. Analysis of ancient atmospheres, *J. Geophys. Res.* **78**, 5341–5344.

Routhier, F., Dennett, R., Davis, D. D., Danielsen, E., Wartburg, A., Haagenson, P., and Delany, A. C., 1980. Free tropospheric and boundary layer airborne measurements of ozone over the latitude range of 58° S to 70° N, *J. Geophys. Res.* **85**, 7307–7321.

Seiler, W., 1974. The cycle of atmospheric CO, *Tellus* **26**, 117–135.

Seiler, W., 1984. Contribution of biological processes to the global budget of $CH_4$ in the atmosphere, in M. J. Klug and C. A. Reddy, Eds., *Current Perspectives in Microbial Ecology,* American Society for Microbiology, Washington, DC.

Seiler, W. and Crutzen, P. J. 1980. Estimates of gross and net fluxes of carbon between the biosphere and the atmosphere from biomass burning, *Climatic Change* **2**, 207–247.

Seiler, W. and Fishman, J., 1981. The distribution of carbon monoxide and ozone in the free troposphere, *J. Geophys. Res.* **86**, 7255–7265.

Seiler, W., Holzapfel-Pschorn, A., Conrad, R., and Scharffe, D., 1984a. Methane emissions from rice paddies, *J. Atmos. Chem.* **1**, 241–268.

Seiler, W., Conrad, R., and Scharffe, D., 1984b. Field studies of methane emission from termite nests into the atmosphere and measurements of methane uptake by tropical soils, *J. Atmos. Chem.* **1**, 171–186.

Stedman, D. H. and McEwan, M. J., 1983. Oxides of nitrogen at two sites in New Zealand, *Geophys. Res. Lett.* **10**, 168–171.

UN, 1981. Statistical Yearbook 1979/1980, United Nations, New York.

Volz, A., Ehhalt, D. H., and Derwent, R. G., 1981. Seasonal and latitudinal variation of [14]CO and the tropospheric concentration of OH radicals, *J. Geophys. Res.* **86**, 5163–5171.

Watts, J. A., 1982. The carbon dioxide question: Data sampler, in W. C. Clark, Ed., *Carbon Dioxide Review 1982,* Oxford University Press, Oxford.

Zimmerman, P. R., Greenberg, J., Wandiga, S. O., and Crutzen, P. J., 1982. Termites: A potentially large source of atmospheric methane, carbon dioxide and molecular hydrogen, *Science* **218**, 563–565.

# ☐ COMMENTS ON "ROLE OF THE TROPICS IN ATMOSPHERIC CHEMISTRY"

**Steven C. Wofsy**

Crutzen presents an interesting overview that emphasizes the global importance of gaseous emissions and atmospheric chemistry in the tropics.

The scope of the essay is very broad, and it is useful to summarize its major points here.

Tropical regions are important sources of carbon monoxide (CO) and methane ($CH_4$) emitted to the global atmosphere. Inputs of CO are associated with agricultural burning activities, with fossil fuel combustion, and with photooxidation of natural atmospheric hydrocarbons. Large inputs of $CH_4$ arise from agricultural activities, mainly cultivation of rice and raising of livestock, and from natural swamps such as the *varzea* of Amazonia. Atmospheric concentrations of CO and $CH_4$ are presently increasing because of increased rates of industrial and agricultural production. The OH radical is removed from the atmosphere primarily by reaction with CO and $CH_4$, and consequently global increases of these gases are important for the chemistry of the atmosphere.

Crutzen constructs a budget for CO in the tropics using his atmospheric photochemical model and data from atmospheric experiments conducted in Brazil during the dry seasons of 1979 and 1980. These experiments showed that CO and $O_3$ concentrations are greatly elevated in areas with extensive agricultural burning, and the data were used to estimate the global CO source due to biomass burning. The source reconstruction is evidently very uncertain; taken at face value, it leaves room for a very large source of CO due to oxidation of biogenic hydrocarbons.

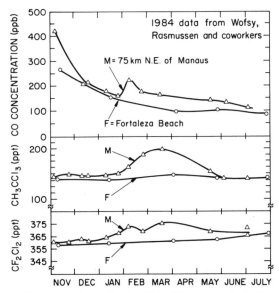

**FIGURE 1.** Observations over 9 months in 1984 of three atmospheric trace gases, taken in the Central Amazon (near Manaus) and on the northeast coast of Brazil (Fortaleza); the top frame shows carbon monoxide, the middle frame methylchloroform, and the bottom frame the chlorofluorocarbon F-12.

It seems to me that Crutzen's estimate of the CO source resulting from photodecomposition of hydrocarbons should be regarded with considerable caution. It is based on the observation that CO levels are significantly higher in the central Amazon Basin (Manaus) than at the Atlantic coast. Data obtained recently by Dr. Rei Rasmussen and me show that this excess is found only during the season of extensive agricultural burning in northern Brazil (August–November); see Fig. 1. At other times of the year, CO concentrations probably come from surrounding agricultural regions and not from decomposition of natural hydrocarbons.

Convergence of low-level winds over the Amazon Basin brings in air from surrounding areas and a variety of pollutants. Some of these pollutants, such as the halocarbons $CH_3CCl_3$ and $CF_2CCl_2$, appear to be imported from the Northern Hemisphere during the late Austral summer (see Fig. 1). Thus, it is often difficult to interpret observed concentrations of trace gases in the Amazon Basin since they are carried there by convergent winds from different regions.

# Chapter 9

# Contribution of Tropical Ecosystems to the Global Budgets of Trace Gases, Especially CH$_4$, H$_2$, CO, and N$_2$O

Wolfgang Seiler and Ralf Conrad

The biosphere is the most important source and/or sink for a variety of tropospheric trace substances and thus determines their mixing ratios and distributions. Observed fluxes at the biosphere–atmosphere interface are often the difference between simultaneous biospheric production and destruction. These net fluxes result from the activities of the living biomass in oxic and anoxic ecosystems and especially depend on microbial metabolism in soil, sediment, and water but also on chemical reactions involving biological materials and on biological and chemical processes in plants and animals. The interactions between the various organisms and the regulation of these processes are presently poorly understood or almost unknown.

The magnitude and direction of the net flux of trace constituents strongly depend not only on the environmental conditions within the particular ecosystem but also on the atmospheric mixing ratios. The large spatial and temporal variations of the fluxes make quantitative estimates of the global production or destruction rates very difficult.

Because the tropical regions of Earth contain more than 60% of the total global biomass (Schlesinger, 1977), and it is there that primary productivity reaches its maximum values (5000 Tg y$^{-1}$ dry matter, 1 Tg = 10$^{12}$ g; Lieth, 1975), these regions are probably the strongest sources of biospheric gases. The tropical biomass is mostly carbohydratelike materials but also contains large amounts of nitrogen, sulfur, and other trace substances, which are liberated in various gaseous forms into the troposphere. Tropical ecosystems contribute significantly to the global tropospheric budgets of carbon monoxide (CO), hydrogen (H$_2$), methane (CH$_4$), and nitrous oxide (N$_2$O). The fluxes of these trace gases are influenced by such environmental parameters as light, temperature, and soil moisture and may have strong seasonal and diurnal variations.

Biogenic gases are generally released in reduced form and are oxidized in the atmosphere by chemical and photochemical reactions, mainly by reactions with hydroxyl radical. The oxidized species are then removed from the atmosphere by dry and wet deposition. Oxidation of biogenic gases such as hydrocarbons, $CH_4$, CO, and dimethyl sulfide [$(CH_3)_2S$] help to form tropospheric ozone ($O_3$) when the atmospheric nitric oxide (NO) mixing ratio is higher than 11 pptv. At lower nitric oxide mixing ratios, oxidation of reduced trace constituents helps to destroy ozone and hydroxyl radical and thus diminishes the atmospheric abundance of these important species (Crutzen, Chapter 8). Some biogenic gases, for example, $N_2O$ and $CH_4$, have absorption bands in the infrared spectrum and therefore contribute to the radiation and heat budget of the atmosphere (Lacis et al., 1981). Consequently, changes in the biogenic production and decomposition rates by human activities such as deforestation, increased use of mineral fertilizers, and artificial irrigation will have some impact on the chemical composition of the troposphere and possibly on Earth's climate.

## CONTRIBUTIONS BY VEGETATION

Land vegetation consists mainly of trees, bushes, grass, and crops. The leaves are exposed to a wide range of irradiation, temperature, and humidity. These factors not only influence the metabolism of the cells in leaves but also the size of the stomata and thus the gas exchange rate between the leaves and the atmosphere. The regulation of the stomata depends on the photoassimilation of $CO_2$ and on the evapotranspiration of water. When the relative humidity of the surrounding air is high and the $CO_2$ concentration within the leaves is low, the stomata are completely open.

Higher plants appear not to exchange atmospheric $H_2$, $N_2O$, and $CH_4$ but do act as net sources for atmospheric CO (Seiler et al., 1978). Plants can also consume CO (Bidwell and Fraser, 1972; Bidwell and Bebee, 1974; Bzdega et al., 1981; Peiser et al., 1982), probably by oxidation to $CO_2$ or direct incorporation into cellular material, but CO production generally exceeds consumption.

Various reaction mechanisms have been proposed for CO production. It may be produced as a metabolite during the degradation of porphyrins (e.g., chlorophyll) (Troxler, 1972; Troxler and Dokos, 1973) or it may be formed during the degradation of glycolate, a product of photorespiration (Fischer and Lüttge, 1978; Lüttge and Fischer, 1980). The third and most likely mechanism of CO production is the photooxidation of plant cellular material (Bauer et al., 1979, 1980) following the photodynamic production of singlet oxygen in the chloroplasts (Krinsky, 1978; Elstner and Osswald, 1984).

Light intensity is the most important factor influencing CO emission into the atmosphere, according to field studies on trees in the Federal Republic of Germany (Bauer et al., 1979). Emission rates of CO increased linearly with irradiation intensity and did not show any light saturation even at intensities of 800 W m$^{-2}$, at which intensity net photosynthesis was already inhibited. After correction for this light dependence, CO emission was virtually independent of season and temperature and occurred with unaltered magnitude even during fall when discoloring of leaves began.

From measurements with higher plants (*Vicia faba, Platanus acerifolia, Pinus silvestris, Fagus silvatica*, and others) Seiler et al. (1978) determined net CO production rates of $3 \times 10^{-13}$ g s$^{-1}$ cm$^{-2}$ of leaf area for a radiation intensity of 50 W m$^{-2}$. The CO production by plants in tropical conditions is not known, but since the net CO production appears to be independent of many environmental processes, the figure of $3 \times 10^{-13}$ g s$^{-1}$ cm$^{-2}$ may apply globally. If so, the total CO emission by higher plants would be on the order of $75 \pm 25$ Tg y$^{-1}$. Model calculations by Logan et al. (1981) and Crutzen (1983) gave somewhat higher figures, an annual CO emission from plants of 50–200 and 20–200 Tg, respectively. Even so, plants contribute only 2–5% to the global CO budget and thus are of minor importance for the global CO cycle.

However, production of CO by plants may be more important locally, for example, in the tropics, where CO production is relatively high because of the abundance of plants, high solar radiation intensity, and the long growing season. Since land areas in the humid tropics are always covered with green plants, plant-dependent CO production occurs year-round. From data on the total surface area of tropical rain forests, seasonal forests, and savanna and data on the seasonal variation of solar radiation intensity, we estimate that more than 75% of the global net CO production by higher plants is emitted in the tropical belt, that is, $60 \pm 20$ Tg y$^{-1}$. Although this figure is uncertain because of lack of measurements in the tropics, it indicates that the CO production by higher plants in tropical areas is not negligible and most probably contributes to the elevated CO mixing ratios in the boundary layer in and over tropical forests (Crutzen et al., 1985).

## CONTRIBUTIONS BY SOILS

Soils are especially important in the exchange of compounds with the atmosphere. They may be classified into the aerated and the flooded or submerged soils. Most soils are well aerated, that is, they contain extensive air-filled pores through which gases are exchanged between the atmosphere and soil by molecular and turbulent diffusion, although some anoxic microenvironments may exist. Flooded soils, on the other hand, develop anaerobic conditions soon after flooding. Transport of gases from soil into the atmosphere is then either by diffusion through the overlying water or by emission of gas bubbles. Plants adapted for life in flooded anoxic soil have special structures to transport atmospheric oxygen to their roots. The transport of gases from the anoxic soil into the atmosphere occurs as a by-product. The importance of plant transport for the emission of gases from anoxic soils into the atmosphere has been established for mercury compounds via reed (*Phragmites communis*) (Kozuchowski and Johnson, 1978) and for methane via water lilies (*Nuphar lutheum*) (Dacey and Klug, 1979) or via rice plants (*Oryza sativa*) (Cicerone and Shetter, 1981; Seiler et al., 1984b). The transport of methane by a great variety of aquatic plants from water-logged soils into the atmosphere has most recently been studied by Sebacher et al. (1985).

## Exchange of Gases through Anoxic Soils

Flooding of soils establishes successive microbial populations that mineralize organic carbon by utilizing oxidants of decreasing redox potentials, for example, $O_2$, $Fe^{3+}$, $Mn^{4+}$, nitrate, sulfate, and $CO_2$ (Stumm, 1967; Tiedje et al., 1984). Thus soil conditions favor successively respiration, metal reduction, denitrification, sulfate dissimilation, and methanogenesis. The transition from an aerated soil into an anoxic soil is gradual and results in activities whose duration depends on the concentrations of organic carbon and particular oxidants in the soil as well as on temperature and pH. Hence, flooding is followed by periods of increased production of reduced nitrogen compounds (e.g., $NH_3$, $N_2O$, $N_2$), of reduced sulfur compounds (e.g., $H_2S$), and of methane. These periods usually follow each other successively but may occur simultaneously. Transformations of nitrogen and sulfur compounds in flooded soils have recently been reviewed by Reddy and Patrick (1984) and Freney et al. (1982), respectively. The onset of methanogenesis in flooded soils has been studied by Koyama (1964) and Yamane and Sato (1963, 1964, 1967).

### Flux of $H_2$ from Anoxic Soils

Flooded soils are potential sources for $H_2$, CO, $N_2O$, and $CH_4$. Hydrogen is produced during anaerobic fermentation of organic matter, especially of carbohydrates (Yamane and Sato, 1964). Emission of $H_2$ into the atmosphere is small, however, since it is rapidly consumed in the soil by denitrifiers, sulfate reducers, and methanogens as soon as populations of these microbes develop. After onset of methanogenesis and stabilization of the redox potential in the anoxic soil, $H_2$ is found only in traces (Zehnder, 1978). Our own experiments show that gas bubbles from paddy soils contain at most 50 ppmv of $H_2$, in contrast to up to 50% of methane. Hence, flooded soils are a marginal source for atmospheric $H_2$, although its turnover within the soil may be high.

### Flux of CO from Anoxic Soils

Carbon monoxide also escapes the soil only in small quantities. Its concentration in gas bubbles from paddy soil is lower than 40 ppmv. It is most probably formed by sulfate reducers (Lupton et al., 1984), acetogenic bacteria (Diekert et al., 1984), and methanogenic bacteria (Conrad and Thauer, 1983), which all are able to reutilize the CO as an energy source (Lupton et al., 1984; Lynd et al., 1982; Daniels et al., 1977). The result is a rapid turnover of CO at a low concentration.

### Flux of CH₄ from Anoxic Soils

In contrast to $H_2$ and CO, methane is emitted into the atmosphere in large quantities from flooded soils. This emission shows a significant seasonality, apparently different in California (Cicerone et al., 1983), Spain (Seiler et al., 1984b), and Italy (Holzapfel-Pschorn and Seiler, in press), and often shows a significant daily rhythm (Holzapfel-Pschorn and Seiler, in press). The $CH_4$ emission from rice paddies is influenced by soil temperature, organic carbon content of the paddy soil, sulfate concentration of floodwater, type and amount of applied nitrogen fertilizers (DeBont et al., 1978; Cicerone and Shetter, 1981; Seiler et al., 1984b; Holzapfel-Pschorn et al., 1985), and the oxidation of methane by methanotrophic bacteria in the upper layer of oxic soil and/or in the rhizosphere (Holzapfel-Pschorn et al., 1985).

From *in situ* measurements in California, Cicerone and Shetter (1981) estimated that the global $CH_4$ emission from rice paddies is about 59 Tg $y^{-1}$, a value considerably lower than the value of 280 Tg $y^{-1}$ previously published by Ehhalt and Schmidt (1978). Most recently, Seiler (1984) and Holzapfel-Pschorn and Seiler (in press) found seasonally averaged $CH_4$ emission rates of 0.4–0.5 g m$^{-2}$ day$^{-1}$ in Italian rice paddies. Extrapolation of these values globally results in a $CH_4$ flux of 120 ± 50 Tg for 1980 (Holzapfel-Pschorn and Seiler, in press), larger than any other individual source for $CH_4$. About 96% of the rice paddies are in tropical regions, particularly in East Asia. However, global estimates of the $CH_4$ emission from rice paddies is based on data obtained from higher latitudes and in countries with intensified agricultural practices. The actual $CH_4$ emission from rice paddies in tropical countries may be different since it depends on parameters that may differ considerably between soils. Because of the importance of $CH_4$ emissions from rice paddies, *in situ* measurements in tropical countries, especially countries in East Asia, are urgently needed.

The annual $CH_4$ emission rate from rice paddies has probably increased with time because of the increase of harvested rice paddy areas from $90 \times 10^{10}$ m$^2$ in 1950 to $150 \times 10^{10}$ m$^2$ in 1980 (FAO, 1983). Therefore, the $CH_4$ emission from rice paddies may have increased from 75 Tg $y^{-1}$ in 1950 to 117 Tg $y^{-1}$ in 1980 or about 1–2% per year during this period. This increase is comparable to the observed increase in tropospheric methane mixing ratios (Rasmussen and Khalil, 1981; Blake et al., 1982).

Methane emission is also significant in natural environments where the ground is flooded, for example, in swamps and other freshwater wetlands (Harriss and Sebacher, 1981; Harriss et al., 1982; Svensson, 1980; Svensson and Rosswall, 1984; Baker-Blocker et al., 1977). Methane emission rates reported for freshwater marshes and swamps are much more variable than those found for rice paddies, ranging from 0.001 to 0.35 g m$^{-2}$ day$^{-1}$. These $CH_4$ emission rates depend strongly on temperature and thus on season. Since most of the reported emission rates were measured in summer, the mean emission rates from swamps averaged over the whole year may be as low as 0.05–18 g $CH_4$ per square meter. Seiler (1984) estimated from these data that the global $CH_4$ emission from wetlands is about 34 ± 23 Tg y$^{-1}$.

The $CH_4$ emission rate from freshwater wetlands may also be inferred from the global average $CH_4$ flux measured in rice paddies. This approach seems reasonable since most rice paddies, swamps, and marshes are located in similar climatic regions and show comparable net primary productivities. On the basis of a $CH_4$ emission of 120 ± 50 Tg y$^{-1}$ from a rice paddy area of 150 × 10$^{12}$ m$^2$, we infer a global annual average $CH_4$ flux of 78 ± 32 Tg. Noting that large parts of the marshland in the Zaire and Amazon basins are flooded for only 6 months of the year, and assuming similar flooding periods for other large tropical swamps, we estimate the $CH_4$ flux from freshwater wetlands to be about 47 ± 22 Tg y$^{-1}$. This figure is tentative because of the uncertainties involved, such as result from basing it on data obtained exclusively in higher latitudes. Nevertheless, the actual $CH_4$ emission from swamps may be considerably lower than the previous estimates of 150 Tg y$^{-1}$ (Baker-Blocker et al., 1977) and 190–300 Tg y$^{-1}$ (Ehhalt and Schmidt, 1978). Since most swamps and marshes are located within the tropics and, furthermore, since the $CH_4$ emission rates depend on the soil temperature, it is likely that more than 80% of the $CH_4$ emitted from swamps is from tropical regions.

In summary, anoxic soils in the tropics emit 153 ± 64 Tg of $CH_4$ per year, accounting for nearly half of the total tropospheric $CH_4$ budget of about 430 ± 130 Tg y$^{-1}$.

### Flux of N₂O from Anoxic Soils

Flooded soils apparently emit little $N_2O$ to the atmosphere. The measured rate of $N_2O$ emission from an unfertilized flooded paddy field reached a maximum value of 10 μg N (i.e., nitrogen) m$^{-2}$ h$^{-1}$ (2.4 g ha$^{-1}$ day$^{-1}$) for a period of several days after flooding, but then decreased to less than 1 μg N m$^{-2}$ h$^{-1}$ (Smith et al., 1982). Low $N_2O$ emission rates were also observed after flooding of an organic-rich histosol in Florida, and in some cases flooding even caused a net uptake of atmospheric $N_2O$ (Terry et al., 1981). Treatment with nitrogen fertilizers such as urea (Smith et al., 1982) or ammonium sulfate (Freney et al., 1981) resulted in total losses as $N_2O$ of only 0.01–0.1% of the applied nitrogen. Measurements on a flooded field that had been under pasture for some years and thus had a high nitrate content indicated that only 1.4% of the total nitrate loss was due to $N_2O$ emission (Denmead et al., 1979a). Thus, the $N_2O$ emission from fertilized and unfertilized rice paddies as well as from swamps results in an $N_2O$ flux of less than 0.1 Tg y$^{-1}$, which is relatively small compared to other natural $N_2O$ sources. The most likely reason for the low $N_2O$ emission from flooded soils is that the strictly anoxic conditions favor the denitrification of nitrate to $N_2$ instead of to $N_2O$ (Firestone, 1982; Delwiche, 1978). Not only may available $N_2O$ be reduced by denitrifying bacteria (Garcia, 1975; Knowles, 1978) but also production of ammonia may replace denitrification (Delwiche, 1978; Buresh and Patrick, 1978).

## Exchange of Gases through Oxic Soils

Various biogeochemical processes in the soil produce or consume $H_2$, CO, $CH_4$, and $N_2O$, often simultaneously, and so affect their fluxes into the atmosphere. Equilibrium mixing ratios of these gases, established in soil air, are dependent on physicochemical soil parameters, soil moisture, and temperature. The direction and magnitude of the net flux into the atmosphere also depend on wind, atmospheric stability, and surface roughness and on the mixing ratios of the individual trace substances in the air close to the soil surface. Destruction processes are generally first-order reactions with respect to the mixing ratio of the atmospheric trace gases; that is, destruction rates increase in proportion to mixing ratio. Production processes, on the other hand, are independent of the atmospheric mixing ratio. Thus, the net flux ($F$) of a trace gas between soil and atmosphere is

$$F = P - d \cdot m_a$$

where $P$ is the gross production rate per unit area, $d$ is the deposition velocity, and $m_a$ is the concentration (i.e., air density times mixing ratio) in ambient air. At steady-state conditions, that is, $P = d \cdot m_a$, production and destruction balance, and the net flux is essentially zero. When the ambient mixing ratio is higher than its equilibrium value, the soils act as sinks; otherwise, they act as sources. This dependence on concentration controls, to a large extent, the chemical composition of the troposphere and regulates changes in the tropospheric concentrations of several trace constituents emitted by anthropogenic activities, such as burning, industry, and automobiles.

### Flux of $H_2$ through Oxic Soils

The ambient mixing ratios of atmospheric $H_2$ are generally higher than their equilibrium values so that the soil, on the average, removes atmospheric hydrogen (Seiler, 1978; Conrad and Seiler, 1980a, 1985a), by biological reactions (Liebl and Seiler, 1976; Conrad and Seiler, 1981) through soil enzymes rather than by soil microorganisms (Conrad and Seiler, 1981; Conrad et al., 1983a). Microorganisms would need metabolic systems with an extremely high affinity for $H_2$ in order to utilize atmospheric $H_2$ (Conrad, 1984). Such microorganisms have not yet been isolated. The so-called hydrogen bacteria (Bowien and Schlegel, 1981), which are able to grow by oxidizing

$H_2$ as an energy source, need $H_2$ mixing ratios much higher than ambient to exhibit activity (Conrad and Seiler, 1979b; Conrad et al., 1983d).

The oxidation of atmospheric $H_2$ in soil increases with temperature and exhibits a maximum at 30–40°C (Liebl and Seiler, 1976). This $H_2$-oxidizing activity depends on soil moisture, with maximum rates at about 10% water content. It decreases after prolonged dryness (Conrad and Seiler, 1981). Under field conditions, soil moisture has a major influence on $H_2$ loss (Conrad and Seiler, 1985a), especially in subtropical soils, which usually are extremely arid but may have a high water content for brief periods after heavy rain. High water content may limit the flux by reducing the diffusional transport through the uppermost soil layers. In contrast to soil moisture, surface soil temperature was found to have virtually no influence on $H_2$ deposition in subtropical soils (Conrad and Seiler, 1985a). Presumably, the $H_2$ oxidation occurs in deeper soil layers where daily temperature changes are very small and soil moisture is higher than in the surface soil. In the relatively humid soils of temperate regions, however, atmospheric $H_2$ usually is destroyed within the uppermost soil layers (Liebl and Seiler, 1976; Seiler et al., 1977).

As summarized by Conrad and Seiler (1985a), the $H_2$ deposition velocities measured in subtropical regions vary between $1 \times 10^{-2}$ and $14 \times 10^{-2}$ cm $s^{-1}$ with a most likely average value of $7 \times 10^{-2}$ cm $s^{-1}$. This value agrees reasonably well with average $H_2$ deposition velocities observed in temperate regions (Seiler, 1978; Conrad and Seiler, 1980a) so that the value of $7 \times 10^{-2}$ cm $s^{-1}$ may be applied globally. Thus the global $H_2$ uptake by soils is estimated to be in the range of $90 \pm 20$ Tg $y^{-1}$, and is the dominant sink for atmospheric $H_2$. The corresponding figure for the $H_2$ uptake in tropical areas is about $30 \pm 10$ Tg $y^{-1}$, more than a factor of 3 greater than the global oxidation of $H_2$ by OH radicals. In summary, the tropospheric $H_2$ cycle is strongly influenced by biological activities in soils, both in the tropics and elsewhere. For example, the $H_2$ mixing ratios in the planetary boundary layer over the Amazon Basin are significantly lower (~400 ppb) than the global average of 550 ppbv (our unpublished measurements).

Apparently, plants are not important for the removal of atmospheric $H_2$ by soils. However, soils vegetated with legumes can be a source of $H_2$ (Conrad and Seiler, 1979a, 1980a). Members of the legume plant family develop root nodules containing symbiotic *Rhizobium* bacteria, which are able to fix atmospheric $N_2$. This fixation is done by the enzyme nitrogenase, which catalyzes the reduction of $N_2$ to $NH_3$ (Burns and Hardy, 1975; Dalton, 1979). About 30% of the electron flow is diverted to reduce protons to $H_2$ (Schubert and Evans, 1976). Since this diversion of electrons is unavoidable in the nitrogenase reaction (Simpson and Buriss, 1984), most of the $N_2$-fixing microorganisms except those associated with legumes have developed an uptake hydrogenase that recycles the $H_2$ so formed (Robson and Postgate, 1980; Bothe and Eisbrenner, 1981). For example, *Azospirillum* associated with the roots of tropical grass and *Actinomyces* that form root nodules in trees (e.g.,

*Alnus*) have such microbes with active uptake hydrogenases and do not produce $H_2$ (Pedrosa et al., 1982; Lespinat and Berlier, 1981; Benson et al., 1980). Such hydrogenases are also found in free-living $N_2$-fixing microorganisms such as *Azotobacter* (Walker and Yates, 1978), *Derxia* (Pedrosa et al., 1980), and *Xantobacter* (Malik and Schlegel, 1980).

Most of the *Rhizobium* species, on the other hand, have no uptake hydrogenase (Uratsu et al., 1982; Li et al., 1980) and thus cannot recycle $H_2$ but release it into the environment where it is either oxidized or lost by diffusion into the atmosphere. Some such species inhabit tropical trees belonging to the legume family, such as *Acacia* (Van Kessel et al., 1983).

Emission of $H_2$ into the atmosphere from soils planted with legumes was observed only during approximately 2 months of the year when growth and nitrogen fixation by legumes were most active. During the rest of the year, the $H_2$ production was balanced by the $H_2$-oxidizing activity in soil, and the net exchange was from atmosphere to soil (Conrad and Seiler, 1980a). The total amount of atmospheric $H_2$ provided by biological $N_2$ fixation in soils is estimated to be in the range 2–5 Tg $y^{-1}$, of which about 70%, or 2 ± 1 Tg $y^{-1}$ may be emitted in the tropics.

### Flux of CO through Oxic Soils

Atmospheric CO is usually lost at soil surfaces. The destruction processes are biological, and are most probably due to microorganisms (Liebl and Seiler, 1976; Bartholomew and Alexander, 1979; Conrad and Seiler, 1980b). Any soil microbes that utilize atmospheric CO must have a remarkably high affinity for it (Conrad et al., 1981; Conrad, 1984). It is not known whether the responsible microbes are able to grow on atmospheric CO (Conrad and Seiler, 1982a; Conrad, 1984) or just oxidize it in a nonutilitarian way (Bartholomew and Alexander, 1982). Recent observations by Jones and Morita (1983a) and Jones et al. (1984) indicate that atmospheric CO may be partially oxidized by ammonium-oxidizing *Nitrosomonas* species and partially by still unknown microorganisms that possibly use CO for oligotrophic life (Conrad and Seiler, 1982a).

The consumption of CO by soil shows a temperature dependence similar to that of $H_2$ (Ingersoll et al., 1974; Liebl and Seiler, 1976); it is also dependent on soil moisture (Heichel, 1974; Conrad and Seiler, 1980b; Spratt and Hubbard, 1981). It is difficult to assess in the field the effect of temperature and moisture on CO destruction because of the simultaneous CO production, which affects the net flux.

Production of CO in soil is an abiotic process and is apparently due to chemical oxidation of humus material. It is strongly dependent on temperature, moisture, and pH of the environment (Conrad and Seiler, 1980b, 1982b, 1985c). Recently, Conrad and Seiler (1985a) developed a field technique to determine the roles of simultaneously occurring CO production and destruction for various soil temperatures and soil moisture. Initial measurements in arid subtropical soils showed that CO production was strongly dependent on soil surface temperature. By contrast, the CO destruction was independent of soil surface temperature. Apparently CO production processes are active predominantly in top soil, whereas CO destruction is more active in somewhat deeper soil layers (Conrad and Seiler, 1985a).

A minimum soil moisture is required for CO destruction but not for CO production, so desert soils are always a net source for atmospheric CO (Conrad and Seiler, 1982b) and savanna soils are a net source at least during the hot hours of the day (Conrad and Seiler, 1985a). In the relatively humid soils of temperate climates, however, CO production is insignificant compared to CO destruction (Seiler, 1978; Conrad and Seiler, 1980b). The CO destruction processes in the top soil layers of this region are sometimes so active that CO is not detectable at soil depths below 1 cm (Liebl and Seiler, 1976; Seiler et al., 1977).

Observations from humid tropical regions are not available. However, because these ecosystems have higher soil moisture and lower soil temperatures than deserts and savannas, we expect that their soils are a net sink rather than a net source for atmospheric CO. The global emission of CO from soils has been estimated to be in the range $17 \pm 15$ Tg y$^{-1}$ (Conrad and Seiler, 1985a) of which about $10 \pm 9$ Tg y$^{-1}$ are produced in the hot and dry tropical regions. This amount is but a small contribution to the atmospheric CO budget and may be only of local importance.

Deposition velocities for CO in temperate and dry subtropical climates as well as in savanna regions have been observed to be between 1 and $7 \times 10^{-2}$ cm s$^{-1}$ with average values from $2 \times 10^{-2}$ to $4 \times 10^{-2}$ cm s$^{-1}$, with no observed differences between different ecosystems. Apparently the CO deposition velocities are independent of climate as long as the soil moisture exceeds 0.5%.

The total CO consumption $S$ by soils in tropical humid regions can be calculated from

$$S = d \cdot m \cdot A$$

where $d$ is the average deposition velocity, $m$ is the CO concentration in the planetary boundary layer, and $A$ is the total soil surface area active in CO consumption. There is little information on the CO mixing ratios in tropical areas. Data obtained in tropical marine atmospheres show values on the order of 50–100 ppbv for regions south of the intertropical convergence zone (ITCZ) and 80–150 ppbv north of the ITCZ (Seiler et al., 1984c). Conditions within the planetary boundary layer of the tropical continental regions differ from those over marine areas. In these regions, the CO mixing ratios vary between 150 and 400 ppbv in totally unpolluted areas over the Amazon Basin (Crutzen et al., 1985) and exceed values of 500 ppbv in areas with burning from shifting agriculture or savanna fires. With an average CO mixing ratio of 200 ppbv, the total CO consumption within the humid tropical areas, including tropical deciduous and evergreen forests and tropical grasslands, is estimated to be $105 \pm 35$ Tg y$^{-1}$, compared with a total global CO uptake rate by soils of $390 \pm 140$ Tg y$^{-1}$.

### Flux of CH₄ through Oxic Soils

For a long time, aerated soils were believed insignificant for atmospheric $CH_4$ (Ehhalt and Schmidt, 1978), although it was known that large populations of methanotrophic bacteria exist in soil (Adamse et al., 1972; Wittenbury et al., 1976). Methanotrophic bacteria possess the metabolic capacity to grow with $CH_4$ as sole energy source (Higgins et al., 1981). Moreover, $CH_4$ is consumed by ammonium-oxidizing *Nitrosomonas* species (Hyman and Wood, 1983; Jones and Morita, 1983b), which are global in distribution (Belser, 1979). Field measurements made in different ecosystems now show that atmospheric $CH_4$ is actually deposited in aerated soils (Harriss et al., 1982; Keller et al., 1983; Seiler et al., 1984a) and that deposition may be a significant sink for atmospheric $CH_4$ (Seiler, 1984).

The processes responsible for the observed deposition of atmospheric $CH_4$ are still unknown. They are aerobic, requiring a well-aerated soil. For example, Harriss et al. (1982) observed a change from $CH_4$ emission to $CH_4$ deposition when a flooded soil in the Great Dismal Swamp slowly dried up. Hence, aerobic microorganisms such as the methanotrophic bacteria are possibly responsible for the loss of atmospheric $CH_4$ in soil. Atmospheric mixing ratios are too low for the growth of known methanotrophic bacteria, according to calculations comparing their kinetic parameters with those that would be required for growth (Conrad, 1984). A recently isolated methanotroph, however, exhibits a remarkably high affinity for $CH_4$, close to that required for growth on atmospheric $CH_4$ (Joergensen and Degn, 1983). Further studies are needed to clarify which microorganisms utilize atmospheric $CH_4$.

Only a few measurements have yet been made of uptake rates of atmospheric methane by soils, that is, those by Keller et al. (1983) in a temperate and a rain forest climate and by Seiler et al. (1984a) in a tropical savanna region. In addition, measurements have been made by our laboratory on different sites in the Federal Republic of Germany. All such measurements clearly indicate that soils remove atmospheric methane. Average loss rates reported by Keller et al. range between $1.2 \times 10^{10}$ and $1.6 \times 10^{10}$ molecules cm$^{-2}$ s$^{-1}$ for higher latitudes, with an overall daily average of $2.5 \times 10^{-4}$ g $CH_4$ per square meter. Higher $CH_4$ losses were observed in the savanna region ranging between $3 \times 10^{-4}$ and $24 \times 10^{-4}$ g m$^{-2}$ day$^{-1}$ (Seiler et al., 1984a). For an average of $12 \times 10^{-4}$ g m$^{-2}$ day$^{-1}$, the total $CH_4$ uptake in the tropical savanna regions and in the wood/shrub and desert areas is 21 Tg y$^{-1}$. Additional $CH_4$ uptake occurs in tropical forests, which have an overall area of about $24 \times 10^6$ km$^2$. If we assume that the $CH_4$ loss of $2.5 \times 10^{-4}$ g m$^{-2}$ day$^{-1}$ observed by Keller et al. in the Amazon Basin applies to the humid tropics in general, the $CH_4$ uptake rate within the whole tropics is about $25 \pm 12$ Tg y$^{-1}$. An additional $7 \pm 3$ Tg y$^{-1}$ is oxidized in higher latitudes, so the global $CH_4$ consumption by soils may account for $32 \pm 16$ Tg y$^{-1}$, about 10% of the $CH_4$ oxidation rate by reaction with OH.

### $N_2O$ Flux through Oxic Soils

It is evident that $N_2O$ is simultaneously produced and consumed in soils and that the observed $N_2O$ mixing ratios in soil are in equilibrium with these rates (Seiler and Conrad, 1981). Production and destruction of $N_2O$ occur within the metabolic pathways of denitrification, nitrification, nitrate dissimilation, and nitrate assimilation (Firestone, 1982; Knowles, 1982; Ritchie and Nicholas, 1972; Smith and Zimmerman, 1981; Yoshida and Alexander, 1970; Bleakley and Tiedje, 1982). Nitrous oxide is not only produced and consumed by single microbial species but also by microbial teams. It is usually reduced by microorganisms that use it as an electron acceptor when oxygen or nitrate is not rapidly available, that is, under anaerobic conditions. On the other hand, $N_2O$ may be oxidized by reactions involving soil catalase activity (Vedenina and Zavarzin, 1977; Vedenina et al., 1980). Thus, $N_2O$ production and destruction processes occur through many pathways and are affected by various environmental parameters such as temperature, moisture, redox potential, organic carbon content, pH, nitrate content, the presence of plants, carbonate content, and others (Smith and Patrick, 1983; Firestone et al., 1979; Letey et al., 1980, 1981; Blackmer and Bremner, 1978, 1979; Smith et al., 1983; Goodroad and Keeney, 1984b; McKenney et al., 1980; Minami and Fukushi, 1983). The $N_2O$ flux at the soil–atmosphere interface also depends on the location of the $N_2O$-producing and $N_2O$-consuming microorganisms and their relative activity within the soil column (Conrad and Seiler, 1985b).

Therefore, fluxes of $N_2O$ between soil and atmosphere can reliably be measured only under conditions that are as close as possible to natural conditions. In the past five years such studies have increased considerably our knowledge, especially of fluxes from agricultural land and of the impact of mineral fertilizers on the flux of $N_2O$ (e.g., Conrad et al., 1983e; Mosier et al., 1983). Very little is known, however, about the flux rates between uncultivated soils and the atmosphere (Denmead et al., 1979b; Mosier et al., 1981; Goodroad and Keeney, 1984a; Kaplan, 1984; Ryden, 1981; Seiler and Conrad, 1981).

Measurements on unfertilized soils indicate strong diurnal variation in the $N_2O$ emission rates, with maximum values during the afternoon and minimum values during the early morning (Conrad et al., 1983c; Slemr et al., 1984). In addition, considerable spatial (Matthias et al., 1980) and seasonal (Bremner et al., 1980) variability in rate was observed irrespective of soil type, soil moisture, and soil temperature. Seiler and Conrad (1981) found $N_2O$ emission rates of 0.5–2.5 $\mu$g N m$^{-2}$ h$^{-1}$ on loess loam, 1–3 $\mu$g N m$^{-2}$ h$^{-1}$ on loess, and 2–13 $\mu$g N m$^{-2}$ h$^{-1}$ on eolian sand at different stations in the Federal Republic of Germany. Mosier et al. (1981) obtained an $N_2O$

flux of 10 $\mu$g N m$^{-2}$ h$^{-1}$ from a native prairie in Colorado during summertime, and Goodroad and Keeney (1984a) found N$_2$O fluxes between 2 and 36 $\mu$g N m$^{-2}$ h$^{-1}$ from temperate grass and forest ecosystems. Conrad et al. (1983c) reported an average N$_2$O emission rate of about 4 $\mu$g N m$^{-2}$ h$^{-1}$ for uncultivated land near Mainz, Federal Republic of Germany, in reasonable agreement with an average N$_2$O emission rate of about 2 $\mu$g N m$^{-2}$ h$^{-1}$ found by Keller et al. (1983) at Hubbard Brook (United States). Significantly higher N$_2$O emission rates were found in the subtropical region of southern Spain (Andalusia), that is, 15 $\mu$g N m$^{-2}$ h$^{-1}$ (Slemr et al., 1984). Even higher values (43 $\mu$g N m$^{-2}$ h$^{-1}$) are reported for a tropical rain forest (Keller et al., 1983) so that there seems to be a tendency for increasing N$_2$O emission rate with decreasing latitude.

Slemr et al. (1984) calculated the N$_2$O emission from natural temperate and subtropical soils to be 4.5 Tg N per year. To this, about 1 to 2 Tg N per year may be added by the production in tropical soils, so that the total N$_2$O emission from natural soils may be about 6 $\pm$ 3 Tg N per year. This figure is tentative because of the very limited data base presently available and the large temporal and spatial variation of the N$_2$O emission rates from soils in different climates. Further studies, particularly on the tropics, are urgently needed to obtain a more reliable figure on the contribution of natural soils to the global N$_2$O budget.

## FRESHWATER SYSTEMS

As in the terrestrial ecosystems, H$_2$, CO, CH$_4$, and N$_2$O are also recycled in freshwater systems. Hydrogen is produced in the oxic epilimnion and metalimnion of lakes, most probably by N$_2$-fixing cyanobacteria (Conrad et al., 1983c; Dahm et al., 1983; Paerl, 1983; Schink and Zeikus, 1984) and is oxidized throughout the water column by small microorganisms (0.2–3.0 $\mu$m in size) with a high affinity for H$_2$ or by free enzymes (Conrad et al., 1983c).

The production of CO in water is generally due to photooxidative processes. These processes may be associated with phototrophic microorganisms serving as a target for photodynamic reactions or excreting substances that are then photooxidized (Conrad et al., 1983b; Bauer et al., 1980). Carbon monoxide is consumed by aquatic microorganisms acting like the soil microorganisms that oxidize atmospheric CO, that is, oligotrophic microorganisms and CO-oxidizing nitrifiers (Conrad and Seiler, 1982a; Jones et al., 1984).

Methane is produced in the anoxic sediments of lakes and rivers and diffuses upward until oxic water layers are reached. There, CH$_4$ is almost completely oxidized by methanotrophic bacteria, which usually concentrate at the oxycline (Hanson, 1980; Rudd and Taylor, 1980).

Very little is known about N$_2$O turnover in freshwater systems (Lemon and Lemon, 1981; Knowles et al., 1981; Yoh et al., 1983). As in soil, N$_2$O production and destruction depend on the availability of oxygen, organic carbon, and the different forms of inorganic nitrogen.

Surface water may sometimes be supersaturated with respect to atmospheric $H_2$, CO, $CH_4$, and $N_2O$, with saturation factors as high as 1000. However, even at these high supersaturations, it is very unlikely that freshwater systems are a significant source for these atmospheric compounds, since (a) the surface area of freshwater systems is small compared to the land surface and (b) the surface film layer that controls the diffusion of the gases from the water into the atmosphere (Liss and Slater, 1974) is up to 100 times thicker than in ocean water (Seiler et al., 1984b).

## TRACE GASES FROM ANIMALS

Trace gases are produced in large amounts during digestion of biomass by a variety of higher and lower animals having different diets and may be emitted into the atmosphere. What individual trace constituents are produced by animals is still poorly known, and more work is necessary to quantify the contribution of animals to the global budget of trace constituents in the troposphere.

Of particular interest is the formation of $CH_4$ during enteric fermentation, such as by ruminants. The microbial flora of the rumen degrade cellulose and other carbohydrate polymers under anaerobic conditions to compounds that can be digested by the animal. Hydrogen, produced during fermentation in stoichiometric amounts, is converted to methane by methanogenic bacteria using $CO_2$ as the electron acceptor. Methanogenesis occurs only in the absence of oxygen (Hungate, 1966).

Large amounts of $CH_4$ are produced in rumens, for example, those of cattle, sheep, and antelopes. How much methane escapes depends on the chemical composition of diet, feeding level, and type of animal. The $CH_4$ production rate per unit energy of food is low for cattle on a high-protein diet and/or with food intake above the maintenance level but is high for cattle on a roughage diet. The energy loss by formation of $CH_4$ ranges between 3 and 9% of the energy intake (Blaxter, 1962; Blaxter and Clapperton, 1965; Krishna et al., 1978). Using average $CH_4$ emission rates, Seiler (1984) estimated that the total $CH_4$ production by ruminants in 1975 is about $86 \pm 13$ Tg $y^{-1}$, the second largest individual source of tropospheric $CH_4$. The total $CH_4$ produced by animals has most likely increased by about 1% per year during the last 25 y because of the growth in the populations of cattle, sheep, and other domestic ruminants. Data on the total amount and distribution of domestic ruminants (FAO, 1983) suggest that about 30–50% of the global $CH_4$ emission by ruminants, or $35 \pm 10$ Tg $y^{-1}$, is emitted in the tropics.

Another important $CH_4$ source in the tropics is the degradation of biomass in the digestive tracts of termites and some wood-eating insects (Breznak,

1982, 1984). The first quantitative figures on the $CH_4$ formation by termites were given by Zimmerman et al. (1982), who calculated from laboratory experiments that their annual $CH_4$ emission is about 150 Tg $y^{-1}$. These authors also suggested that termites produce about 200 Tg $y^{-1}$ of $H_2$. These figures suggest that termites could make from 30 to 50% of the global tropospheric $CH_4$ and be the largest individual source within the tropospheric $H_2$ budget. According to more recent work (e.g., Rasmussen and Khalil, 1983; Collins and Wood, 1984), the contribution of termites to the $CH_4$ budget seems to be considerably lower than that proposed by Zimmerman et al.

Measurements on termite nests in a South African savanna suggest $CH_4$ emission rates by termites to be as low as 2–5 Tg $y^{-1}$. (Seiler et al., 1984a), considering the different digestion efficiencies and different $CH_4/CO_2$ ratios in gas emitted by different termite species. The fungi-growing *Macrothermes* are the most important consumers of dead biomass in savanna regions and show $CH_4/CO_2$ ratios one to two orders of magnitude lower than non-fungi-growing termites. There is still lively debate as to the contribution of termites to the global $CH_4$ budget (see, e.g., Zimmerman and Greenberg, 1983; Zimmerman et al., 1984), indicating many problems involved in the individual estimates that need to be resolved by more experiments in different climatic zones, different seasons, and different vegetation cover. As with $CH_4$, it appears that the CO and $H_2$ production by termites proposed by Zimmerman et al. (1982) is also considerably overestimated. We think, from our own unpublished results, that the contribution of termites to the tropical $H_2$ and CO budgets is negligible.

Possibly, CO, $H_2$, and $CH_4$ may also be produced by other animals, such as ants. Furthermore, other trace gases, particularly sulfur and nitrogen compounds, could be emitted by animals. However, these possibilities are not supported by any available data.


## CONTRIBUTION OF TROPICAL AREAS AS SOURCES AND SINKS OF TRACE GASES

Our current estimates of the global sources and sinks of carbon monoxide, methane, hydrogen, and nitrous oxide are given in Tables 1 to 4. Estimates are also given for the contribution of the tropical plus semitropical regions.

All the biological production of methane in Table 1 involves the mineralization of organic matter under strictly anaerobic conditions, such as in the digestive tracts of ruminants and termites as well as in the sediments of rice paddies and wetlands. Rice paddies are the dominant tropical source and contribute about one third of the global methane.

Additional methane is formed in the tropics during biomass burning, such as by savanna fires, clearing for shifting agriculture, and use of firewood (Seiler, 1984). All tropical sources together provide about 60% of the total tropospheric methane production (Table 1). Crutzen and Gidel (1983) in-

**TABLE 1. Global and Tropical Budget of Tropospheric Methane[a]**

|  | Global | Tropics (30° S–30° N) |
|---|---|---|
| Sources |  |  |
| Ruminants | 86 ± 13 | 35 ± 10 |
| Paddy fields | 120 ± 50 | 115 ± 47 |
| Swamps/freshwater wetlands | 47 ± 22 | 38 ± 17 |
| Lakes, ocean, termites, etc. | 25 ± 7 | 10 ± 5 |
| Biomass burning | 79 ± 23 | 60 ± 18 |
| Leakage of natural gas | 34 ± 5 | — |
| Coal mining | 35 ± 10 | — |
| Industry, volcanoes | 2 ± 1 | — |
| Total production | 428 ± 131 | 258 ± 97 |
| Sinks |  |  |
| Reaction with tropospheric OH | 300 ± 100 | 210 ± 70 |
| Flux into stratosphere | 60 ± 20 | 50 ± 20 |
| Soils | 32 ± 16 | 25 ± 12 |
| Total decomposition | 392 ± 136 | 285 ± 102 |

[a] Figures are for 1980 (in Tg $y^{-1}$)

ferred from model calculations that the methane loss by reaction with OH is about 300 Tg $y^{-1}$, 70% of which occurs in the tropics. Additional losses for methane include transport from the tropical troposphere into the stratosphere and unknown processes in aerated soils.

Since aerated tropical soils are apparently a net sink for atmospheric $CH_4$, at least part of the $CH_4$ produced by anaerobic mineralization of organic matter is removed from the atmosphere by processes other than photochemical reactions. This removal is the net result of simultaneously occurring production and destruction of $CH_4$ in soil, and its magnitude is very uncertain because of inadequate measurements.

Equilibrium mixing ratios of $CH_4$ range between 1.2 and 1.6 ppmv depending on the environmental soil conditions. Therefore, those soils that presently act as a net sink of atmospheric $CH_4$ at current mixing ratios of about 1.7 ppmv may have been a net source for $CH_4$ mixing ratios in prehistoric times when the tropospheric mixing ratios were about 0.7 ppmv (Craig and Chou, 1982). The existence of the $CH_4$ equilibrium in soils also indicates that the uptake rates by soils will increase more rapidly than will atmospheric methane. If the equilibrium value is 1.4 ppmv, an increase of the tropospheric $CH_4$ mixing ratio of 10% from 1.6 ppmv to 1.8 ppmv would almost double the $CH_4$ uptake by soils.

Because of the increasing cattle population, the rise in the annually harvested rice paddy area and the increasing amount of burned biomass, the

**TABLE 2. Global and Tropical Budget of Tropospheric Nitrous Oxide**[a]

|  | Global | Tropics (30° S–30° N) |
|---|---|---|
| Sources |  |  |
| Fossil fuel burning | 2 ± 1 | — |
| Biomass burning | 1.5 ± 0.5 | 1.2 ± 0.4 |
| Oceans, estuaries | 2 ± 1 | 1 ± 0.5 |
| Fertilized soils | 1.5 ± 1 | <0.2 |
| Natural soils | 6 ± 3 | 5 ± 3 |
| Plants | <0.1 | <0.1 |
| Gain of cultivated land | 0.4 ± 0.2 | 0.4 ± 0.2 |
| Total production | 14 ± 7 | 8 ± 4 |
| Sinks |  |  |
| Stratospheric loss | 9 ± 2 |  |

[a] Figures are for 1980 (in Tg y$^{-1}$)

$CH_4$ production in the tropics would have increased with time during the last 25 years and thus may have contributed substantially to the observed growth of atmospheric methane. Population growth, particularly in the developing countries, will require food and consequently higher cattle populations and the extension of the harvested rice paddy areas. Therefore, we expect a further increase in the $CH_4$ production rate and in the tropospheric $CH_4$ mixing ratios. These increases most likely will have a significant impact on tropospheric and stratospheric chemistry (Crutzen, Chapter 8).

In contrast to methane, there is generally a net production of atmospheric nitrous oxide by aerated tropical soils (Table 2). The total $N_2O$ emission from these soils is difficult to estimate because of the very limited data and the variability in the $N_2O$ emission rates. Because of the dependency of $N_2O$ emission rates on soil temperature, most of the global $N_2O$ is released from subtropical and tropical soils, perhaps about 3 Tg N per year and 2 Tg N per year, respectively. Additional $N_2O$ is also formed in the tropical regions by biomass burning, by oceans and estuaries, and by $N_2O$ emission during conversion of forests into cultivated land. The total $N_2O$ emission rate estimated for tropical areas in Table 2 is about 60% of the global $N_2O$ release. These estimates of $N_2O$ sources are highly uncertain and in some cases may only be guesses. They indicate, however, that tropical and subtropical areas contribute significantly to the global tropospheric $N_2O$ budget. More measurements are urgently needed to allow better estimates.

Tropical ecosystems are also important for the tropospheric $H_2$ and CO cycles. Hydrogen is rapidly destroyed by biochemical activities within the upper soil layers. The estimated loss in tropical areas (Table 3) is about 40% of the global tropospheric $H_2$ budget. More hydrogen is lost in soils in the

**TABLE 3. Global and Tropical Budget of Tropospheric Hydrogen (Tg y$^{-1}$)**

|  | Global | Tropics (30° S–30° N) |
|---|---|---|
| Sources |  |  |
| Technological sources | 20 ± 10 | — |
| Burning of biomass | 20 ± 10 | 16 ± 8 |
| Oceans | 4 ± 2 | 2 ± 1 |
| Plants | <0.1 | <0.1 |
| CH$_4$ oxidation by OH | 15 ± 5 | 10 ± 4 |
| Oxidation of nonmethane hydrocarbons | 25 ± 10 | 18 ± 7 |
| Microbial production in soil | <0.1 | <0.1 |
| Biological N$_2$ fixation | 3 ± 2 | 2 ± 1 |
| Total production | 87 ± 39 | 48 ± 21 |
| Sinks |  |  |
| Oxidation by OH | 8 ± 3 | 6 ± 2 |
| Uptake by soils | 90 ± 20 | 30 ± 10 |
| Total decomposition | 98 ± 23 | 36 ± 12 |

**TABLE 4. Global and Tropical Budget of Tropospheric Carbon Monoxide (Tg y$^{-1}$)**

|  | Global | Tropics (30° S–30° N) |
|---|---|---|
| Sources |  |  |
| Technological sources | 640 ± 200 | — |
| Biomass burning | 1000 ± 600 | 800 ± 500 |
| Vegetation | 75 ± 25 | 60 ± 20 |
| Ocean | 100 ± 90 | 50 ± 45 |
| CH$_4$ oxidation | 600 ± 300 | 400 ± 200 |
| Oxidation of nonmethane hydrocarbons | 900 ± 500 | 600 ± 300 |
| Production by soils | 17 ± 15 | 10 ± 9 |
| Total production | 3300 ± 1700 | 1900 ± 1100 |
| Sinks |  |  |
| Oxidation by OH | 2000 ± 600 | 1200 ± 400 |
| Uptake by soils | 390 ± 140 | 105 ± 35 |
| Flux into stratosphere | 110 ± 30 | 80 ± 20 |
| Total decomposition | 2500 ± 750 | 1400 ± 430 |

tropics than is gained from the photochemical destruction of $CH_4$ and of nonmethane hydrocarbons. In fact, the $H_2$ mixing ratio within the planetary boundary layer over the Amazon Basin has been found to be 10–20% less than the average $H_2$ mixing ratio above the planetary boundary layer. Biomass burning also gives $H_2$, particularly in the savanna regions.

Tropical ecosystems act both as sources and sinks for atmospheric carbon monoxide. It is destroyed at soil surfaces by microbial activities and is emitted into the atmosphere by plants as well as by photooxidative processes in freshwater systems and oceans (Table 4). Much more carbon monoxide is formed by photochemical oxidation of methane and nonmethane hydrocarbons emitted by plants. About two thirds of the global production by these sources occurs in the tropics (Crutzen, 1983). Biomass burning is another large tropical source. Table 4 clearly demonstrates that the tropics are also significant for the global budget and distribution of atmospheric CO.

## ACKNOWLEDGMENTS

We thank P. Crutzen and P. Haug for discussions and for reviewing the manuscript. We also thank the Bundesministerium für Forschung und Technologie (Grant No. KBF 68 and KF 1008) for financial support.

## REFERENCES

Adamse, A. D., Hoeks, J., de Bont, J. A. M., and van Kessel, J. F., 1972. Microbial activities in soil near natural gas leaks, *Arch. Microbiol.* **83**, 32–51.

Baker-Blocker, A., Donahue, T. M., and Mancy, K. H., 1977. Methane flux from wetland areas, *Tellus* **29**, 245–250.

Bartholomew, G. W. and Alexander, M., 1979. Microbial metabolism of carbon monoxide in culture and in soil, *Appl. Environ. Microbiol.* **37**, 932–937.

Bartholomew, G. W. and Alexander, M., 1982. Microorganisms responsible for the oxidation of carbon monoxide in soil, *Environ. Sci. Technol.* **16**, 300–301.

Bauer, K., Conrad, R., and Seiler, W., 1980. Photooxidative production of carbon monoxide by phototrophic microorganisms, *Biochim. Biophys. Acta* **589**, 46–55.

Bauer, Seiler, W., and Giehl, H., 1979. CO-Produktion höherer Pflanzen an natürlichen Standorten, *Z. Pflanzenphysiol.* **94**, 210–230.

Belser, L. W., 1979. Population ecology of nitrifying bacteria, *Ann. Rev. Microbiol.* **33**, 309–333.

Benson, D. R., Arp, D. J., and Burris, R. H., 1980. Hydrogenase in actinorhizal root nodules and root nodule homogenates, *J. Bacteriol.* **142**, 138–144.

Bidwell, R. G. S. and Bebee, G. P., 1974. Carbon monoxide fixation by plants, *Can. J. Bot.* **52**, 1841–1847.

Bidwell, R. G. S. and Fraser, D. E., 1972. Carbon monoxide uptake and metabolism by leaves, *Can. J. Bot.* **50**, 1435–1439.

Blackmer, A. M. and Bremner, J. M., 1978. Inhibitory effect of nitrate on reduction of $N_2O$ to $N_2$ by soil microorganisms, *Soil. Biol. Biochem.* **10**, 187–191.

Blackmer, A. M. and Bremner, J. M., 1979. Stimulatory effect of nitrate on reduction of nitrous oxide to nitrogen by soil microorganisms, *Soil Biol. Biochem.* **11**, 313–315.

Blake, D. R., Mayer, E. W., Tyler, St. C., Makide, Y., Montagne, D. C., and Rowland, F. S., 1982. Global increase in atmospheric methane concentration between 1978 and 1980, *Geophys. Res. Lett.* **9**, 477–480.

Blaxter, K. L., 1962. *The Energy Metabolism of Ruminants,* Hutchinson, London.

Blaxter, K. L. and Clapperton, J. L., 1965. Prediction of the amount of methane produced by ruminants, *Br. J. Nutr.* **19**, 511–522.

Bleakley, B. H. and Tiedje, J. M., 1982. Nitrous oxide production by organisms other than nitrifiers or denitrifiers, *Appl. Environ. Microb.* **44**, 1342–1348.

Bothe, H. and Eisbrenner, G., 1981. The hydrogenase–nitrogenase relationship in nitrogen-fixing organisms, in H. Bothe and A. Trebst, Eds., *Biology of Inorganic Nitrogen and Sulfur,* Springer, Berlin.

Bowien, B. and Schlegel, H. G., 1981. Physiology and biochemistry of aerobic hydrogen-oxidizing bacteria, *Ann. Rev. Microbiol.* **35**, 405–452.

Bremner, J. M. Robbins, S. G., and Blackmer, A. M., 1980. Seasonal variability in emission of nitrous oxide from soil, *Geophys. Res. Lett.* **7**, 641–644.

Breznak, J. A., 1982. Intestinal microbiota of termites and other xylophagous insects, *Ann. Rev. Microbiol.* **36**, 323–343.

Breznak, J. A., 1984. Biochemical aspects of symbiosis between termites and their intestinal microbiota, in J. M. Anderson, A. D. H. Rayner, and D. W. H. Walton, Eds., *Invertebrate-Microbial Interactions* Cambridge University Press, Cambridge, England.

Buresh, R. J. and Patrick, W. H., Jr., 1978. Nitrate reduction to ammonium in anaerobic soil, *Soil Sci. Soc. Am. J.* **42**, 913–918.

Burns, R. C. and Hardy, R. W. F., 1975. *Nitrogen Fixation in Bacteria and Higher Plants,* Springer-Verlag, New York.

Bzdega, T., Karwowska, R., Zuchmantowicz, H., Pawlak, M., Kleczkowski, L., and Nalborczyk, E., 1981. Absorption of carbon monoxide by higher plants, *Polish Ecol. Stud.* **7**, 387–399.

Cicerone, R. J. and Shetter, J. D., 1981. Sources of atmospheric methane: Measurements in rice paddies and a discussion, *J. Geophys. Res.* **86**, 7203–7209.

Cicerone, R. J., Shetter, J. D., and Delwiche, C. C., 1983. Seasonal variation of methane flux from a California rice paddy, *J. Geophys. Res.* **88**, 11022–11024.

Collins, N. M. and Wood, T. G., 1984. Termites and atmospheric gas production, *Science* **224**, 84–86.

Conrad, R., 1984. Capacity of aerobic microorganisms to utilize and grow on atmospheric trace gases ($H_2$, CO, $CH_4$), in M. J. Klug and C. A. Reddy, Eds., *Current Perspectives in Microbial Ecology,* American Society for Microbiology, Washington, DC.

Conrad, R. and Seiler, W., 1979a. Field measurements of hydrogen evolution by nitrogen-fixing legumes. *Soil Biol. Biochem.* **11**, 689–690.

Conrad, R. and Seiler, W., 1979b. The role of hydrogen bacteria during the decomposition of hydrogen by soil, *FEMS Microbiol. Lett.* **6**, 143–145.

Conrad, R. and Seiler, W., 1980a. Contribution of hydrogen production by biological nitrogen fixation to the global hydrogen budget, *J. Geophys. Res.* **85**, 5493–5498.

Conrad, R. and Seiler, W., 1980b. Role of microorganisms in the consumption and production of atmospheric carbon monoxide by soil, *Appl. Environ. Microbiol.* **40**, 437–445.

Conrad, R. and Seiler, W., 1981. Decomposition of atmospheric hydrogen by soil microorganisms and soil enzymes, *Soil Biol. Biochem.* **14**, 43–49.

Conrad, R. and Seiler, W., 1982a. Utilization of traces of carbon monoxide by aerobic oligotrophic microorganisms in ocean, lake and soil, *Arch. Microbiol.* **132**, 41–46.

Conrad, R. and Seiler, W., 1982b. Arid soils as a source of atmospheric carbon monoxide, *Geophys. Res. Lett.* **9**, 1353–1356.

Conrad, R. and Seiler, W., 1985a. Influence of temperature, moisture and organic carbon on the flux of $H_2$ and CO between soil and atmosphere. Field studies in subtropical regions, *J. Geophys. Res.* **90**, 5699–5709.

Conrad, R. and Seiler, W., 1985b. Localization of microbial activities relevant to the emission of nitrous oxide from soil into the atmosphere, *Soil Biol. Biochem.* **17**, 893–895.

Conrad, R. and Seiler, W., 1985c. Characteristics of abiological CO formation from soil organic matter, humic acids and phenolic compounds, *Environ. Sci. Technol,* **19**, 1165–1169.

Conrad, R. and Thauer, R. K., 1983. Carbon monoxide production by *Methanobacterium thermoautotrophicum, FEMS Microbiol. Lett.* **20**, 229–232.

Conrad, R., Meyer, O., and Seiler, W., 1981. Role of carboxydobacteria in consumption of atmospheric carbon monoxide by soil, *Appl. Environ. Microbiol.* **42**, 211–215.

Conrad, R., Weber, M., and Seiler, W., 1983a. Kinetics and electron transport of soil hydrogenases catalyzing the oxidation of atmospheric hydrogen, *Soil Biol. Biochem.* **15**, 167–173.

Conrad, R., Aragno, M., and Seiler, W., 1983b. Production and consumption of carbon monoxide in a eutrophic lake, *Limnol. Oceanogr.* **28**, 42–49.

Conrad, R., Aragno, M., and Seiler, W., 1983c. Production and consumption of hydrogen in a eutrophic lake, *Appl. Environ. Microbiol.* **45**, 502–510.

Conrad, R., Aragno, M., and Seiler, W., 1983d. The inability of hydrogen bacteria to utilize atmospheric hydrogen is due to threshold and affinity for hydrogen, *FEMS Microbiol. Lett.* **18**, 207–210.

Conrad, R., Seiler, W., and Bunse, G., 1983e. Factors influencing the loss of fertilizer-nitrogen into the atmosphere as $N_2O$, *J. Geophys. Res.* **88**, 6709–6718.

Craig, H. and Chou, C. C., 1982. Methane: The record in polar ice cores, *Geophys. Res. Lett.* **9**, 1221–1224.

Crutzen, P., 1983. Atmospheric interactions: Homogenous gas reactions of C, N, and S containing compounds, in B. Bolin and R. D. Cook, Eds., *The Major Biogeochemical Cycles and Their Interactions,* SCOPE, Vol. 21,Wiley, Chichester, England.

Crutzen, P. J. and Gidel, L. T., 1983. A two-dimensional photochemical model of the atmosphere. II. The tropospheric budgets of the anthropogenic chlorocarbons, CO, $CH_4$, $CH_3Cl$ and the effect of various $NO_x$ sources on tropospheric ozone, *J. Geophys. Res.* **88,** 6641–6661.

Crutzen, P. J., Delany, A. C., Greenberg, J., Haagenson, P., Heidt, L., Lueb, R., Pollock, W., Seiler, W., Wartburg, A., and Zimmerman, P., 1985. Tropospheric chemical composition measurements in Brazil during the dry season, *J. Atm. Chem.* **2,** 233–256.

Dacey, J. W. H. and Klug, M. J., 1979. Methane efflux from lake sediments through water lilies, *Science* **203,** 1253–1255.

Dahm, C. N., Baross, J. A., Ward, A. K., Lilley, M. D., and Sedell, J. R., 1983. Initial effects of the Mount St. Helens eruption on nitrogen cycle and related chemical processes in Ryan Lake, *Appl. Environ. Microbiol.* **45,** 1633–1645.

Dalton, H., 1979. Utilization of inorganic nitrogen by microbial cells, *Int. Rev. Biochem.* **21,** 227–266.

Daniels, L., Fuchs, G., Thauer, R. K., and Zeikus, J. G., 1977. Carbon monoxide oxidation by methanogenic bacteria, *J. Bacteriol* **132,** 118–126.

De Bont, J. A. M., Lee, K. K., and Bouldin, D. F., 1978. Bacterial oxidation of methane in a rice paddy, *Ecol. Bull.* **26,** 91–96.

Delwiche, C. C., 1978. Biological production and utilization of $N_2O$, *Pageoph* **116,** 414–422.

Denmead, O. T., Freney, J. R., and Simpson, J. R., 1979a. Nitrous oxide emission during denitrification in a flooded field, *Soil Sci. Soc. Amer. J.* **43,** 716–718.

Denmead, O. T., Freney, J. R., and Simpson, J. R., 1979b. Studies of nitrous oxide emission from a grass sward. *Soil Sci. Soc Amer. J.* **43,** 726–728.

Diekert, G., Hansch, M., and Conrad, R., 1984. Acetate synthesis from $2CO_2$ in acetogenic bacteria: Is carbon monoxide an intermediate, *Arch. Microbiol.* **138,** 224–228.

Ehhalt, D. H. and Schmidt, U., 1978. Sources and sinks of atmospheric methane, *Pageoph* **116,** 452–464.

Elstner, E. F. and Osswald, W., 1984. Fichtensterben in "Reinluftgebieten": Strukturresistenzverlust, *Naturwiss. Rundsch.* **37,** 52–61.

Firestone, M. K., 1982. Biological denitrification, *Agronomy* **22,** 289–326.

Firestone, M. K., Smith, M. S., Firestone, R. B., and Tiedje, J. M., 1979. The influence of nitrate, nitrite, and oxygen on the composition of the gaseous products of denitrification in soil, *Soil Sci. Soc. Amer. J.* **43,** 1140–1144.

Fischer, K. and Lüttge, U., 1978. Light-dependent net production of carbon monoxide by plants, *Nature* **275,** 740–741.

Food and Agriculture Organization (FAO) of the United Nations, 1983. *Production Yearbook,* Vol. 35, FAO, Rome.

Freney, J. R., Denmead, O. T., Watanabe, I., and Craswell, E. T., 1981. Ammonia and nitrous oxide losses following applications of ammonium sulfate to flooded rice, *Aust. J. Agric. Res.* **32,** 37–45.

Freney, J. R., Jacq, V. A., and Baldensperger, J. F., 1982. The significance of the biological sulfur cycle in rice production. *Dev. Plant Soil Sci.* **5**, 271–317.

Garcia, J. L., 1975. La dénitrification dans les sols, *Bull. Inst. Pasteur* **73**, 167–198.

Goodroad, L. L. and Keeney, D. R., 1984a. Nitrous oxide emission from forest, marsh, and prairie ecosystems, *J. Environ. Qual.* **13**, 448–452.

Goodroad, L. L. and Keeney, D. R., 1984b. Nitrous oxide production in aerobic soils under varying pH, temperature, and water content, *Soil Biol. Biochem.* **16**, 39–44.

Hanson, R. S., 1980. Ecology and diversity of methylotrophic organisms, *Adv. Appl. Microbiol.* **26**, 3–39.

Harriss, R. C. and Sebacher, D. I., 1981. Methane flux in forested freshwater swamps of the Southeastern United States, *Geophys. Res. Lett.* **8**, 1002–1004.

Harriss, R. C., Sebacher, D. I., and Day, F. P., Jr., 1982. Methane flux in the Great Dismal Swamp, *Nature* **297**, 673–674.

Heichel, G. H., 1974. Removal of carbon monoxide by field and forest soils, *J. Environ. Qual.* **2**, 419–423.

Higgins, I. J., Best, D. J., Hammond, R. C., and Scott, D., 1981. Methane-oxidizing microorganisms, *Microbiol. Rev.* **45**, 556–590.

Holzapfel-Pschorn, A. and Seiler, W., in press. Methane emission during a vegetation period from an Italian rice paddy, *J. Geophys. Res.*

Holzapfel-Pschorn, A., Conrad, R., and Seiler, W., 1985. Production, oxidation and emission of methane in rice paddies, *FEMS Microbiol. Ecol.* **31**, 343–351.

Hungate, R. E., 1966. *The Rumen and Its Microbes,* Academic, New York and London.

Hyman, M. R. and Wood, P. M., 1983. Methane oxidation by *Nitrosomonas europaea, Biochem. J.* **212**, 31–37.

Ingersoll, R. B., Inman, R. E., and Fisher, W. R., 1974. Soil's potential as a sink for atmospheric carbon monoxide, *Tellus* **26**, 151–159.

Joergensen, L. and Degn, H., 1983. Mass spectrometric measurements of methane and oxygen utilization by methanotrophic bacteria, *FEMS Microbiol. Lett.* **20**, 331–336.

Jones, R. D. and Morita, R. Y., 1983a. Carbon monoxide oxidation by chemolithotrophic ammonium oxidizers, *Can. J. Microbiol.* **29**, 1545–1551.

Jones, R. D. and Morita, R. Y., 1983b. Methane oxidation by *Nitrosococcus oceanus* and *Nitrosomonas europaea, Appl. Env. Microbiol.* **45**, 401–410.

Jones, R. D., Morita, R. Y., and Griffiths, R. P., 1984. Method for estimating in-situ chemolithotrophic ammonium oxidation using carbon monoxide oxidation, *Marine Ecol. Progr. Ser.* **17**, 259–269.

Kaplan, W., 1984. Sources and sinks of nitrous oxide, in M. J. Klug and C. A. Reddy, Eds., *Current Perspectives in Microbial Ecology,* American Society for Microbiology, Washington, DC.

Keller, M., Goreau, T. J., Wofsy, S. C., Kaplan, W. A., and McElroy, M. B., 1983. Production of nitrous oxide and consumption of methane by forest soils, *Geophys. Res. Lett.* **10**, 1156–1159.

Knowles, R., 1978. Common intermediates of nitrification and denitrification, and the metabolism of nitrous oxide, in D. Schlesinger, Ed., *Microbiology—1978,* American Society for Microbiology, Washington, DC.

Knowles, R., 1982. Denitrification, *Microbiol. Rev.* **46,** 43–70.

Knowles, R., Lean, D. R. S., and Chan, J. K., 1981. Nitrous oxide concentrations in lakes: Variations with depth and time, *Limnol. Oceanogr.* **26,** 855–866.

Koyama, T., 1964. Biogeochemical studies on lake sediments and paddy soils and the production of atmospheric methane and hydrogen, in: Y. Miyake and T. Koyama, Eds., *Recent Researches in the Fields of Hydrosphere, Atmosphere and Nuclear Geochemistry,* Maruzen, Tokyo.

Kozuchowski, J. and Johnson, D. L., 1978. Gaseous emissions of mercury from an aquatic vascular plant, *Nature* **274,** 468–469.

Krinsky, N. J., 1978. Non-photosynthetic functions of carotenoids, *Philos. Trans. Roy. Soc. London* **284B,** 581–590.

Krishna, G., Razdan, M. N., and Ray, S. N., 1978. Effect of nutritional and seasonal variations on heat and methane production, *Bos Indicus. Indian J. Anim. Sci.* **48,** 366–370.

Lacis, A., Hansen, G., Lee, P., Mitchell, T., and Lebedeff, S., 1981. Greenhouse effect of trace gases, 1970–1980, *Geophys. Res. Lett.* **8,** 1035–1038.

Lemon, E. and Lemon, D., 1981. Nitrous oxide in freshwaters of the Great Lakes Basin, *Limnol. Oceanogr.* **26,** 867–879.

Lespinat, P. A. and Berlier, Y. M., 1981. The dependence of hydrogen recycling upon nitrogenase activity in *Azospirillum brasilense* sp. 7, *FEMS Microbiol. Lett.* **10,** 127–132.

Letey, J., Valoras, N., Hadas, A., and Focht, D. D., 1980. Effect of air-filled porosity, nitrate concentration, and time on the ratio of nitrogen oxide ($N_2O$)/ nitrogen evolution during denitrification, *J. Environ. Qual.* **9,** 227–231.

Letey, J., Valoras, N. V., Focht, D. D., and Ryden, J. C., 1981. Nitrous oxide production and reduction during denitrification as affected by redox potential, *Soil Sci. Soc. Amer. J.* **45,** 727–730.

Li, Y. H., Chin, Y. H., Zhao, H. Y., Zhang, X. J., and Zhou, P. Z., 1980. Survey of hydrogen evolution by leguminoid rhizobial strains, *Wei Sheng Wu Hsuek Pao* **20**(2), 180–184.

Liebl, K. H. and Seiler, W., 1976. CO and $H_2$ destruction at the soil surface, in H. G. Schlegel, G. Gottschalk, and N. Pfennig, Eds., *Microbial Production and Utilization of Gases ($H_2$, $CH_4$, CO),* E. Goltze K G, Göttingen, FRG.

Lieth, H., 1975. Primary production of the major vegetation units of the world, in H. Lieth and R. H. Whittaker, Eds., Primary productivity of the Biosphere, Springer-Verlag, New York.

Liss, P. S. and Slater, P. G., 1974. Flux of gases across the air–sea interface, *Nature* **247,** 181–184.

Logan, J., Prather, M. J., Wofsy, S. C., and McElroy, M. B., 1981. Tropospheric chemistry: A global perspective, *J. Geophys. Res.* **86,** 7210–7254.

Lupton, F. S., Conrad, R., and Zeikus, J. G., 1984. CO metabolism of *Desulfovibrio vulgaris* strain Madison: Physiological function in the absence or presence of exogenous substrate, *FEMS Microbiol. Lett.* **23,** 263–268.

Lüttge, U. and Fischer, K., 1980. Light-dependent net carbon monoxide evolution by $C_3$ and $C_4$ plants, *Planta* **149**, 59–63.

Lynd, L., Kerby, R., and Zeikus, J. G., 1982. Carbon monoxide metabolism of the methylotrophic acidogen *Butyribacterium methylotrophicum, J. Bacteriol.* **149**, 255–263.

McKenney, D. J., Shuttleworth, K. F., and Findlay, W. I., 1980. Temperature dependence of nitrous oxide production from Brookston Clay, *Can. J. Soil Sci.* **60**, 665–674.

Malik, K. A. and Schlegel, H. G., 1980. Enrichment and isolation of new nitrogen-fixing hydrogen bacteria, *FEMS Microbiol. Lett.* **8**, 101–104.

Matthias, A. D., Blackmer, A. M., and Bremner, J. M., A simple chamber technique for field measurements of emissions of nitrous oxide from soils, *J. Environ. Qual.* **9**, 251–256.

Minami, K. and Fukushi, S., 1983. Effects of phosphate and calcium carbonate application on emission of $N_2O$ from soils under aerobic conditions, *Soil Sci. Plant Nutr.* **29**, 517–524.

Mosier, A. R., Parton, W. J., and Hutchinson, G. L., 1983. Modelling nitrous oxide evolution from cropped and native soils, *Ecol. Bull.* **35**, 229–241.

Mosier, A. R., Stillwell, M., Parton, W. J., and Woodmansee, R. G., 1981. Nitrous oxide emissions from a native shortgrass prairie, *Soil Sci. Soc. Am. J.* **45**, 617–619.

Paerl, H. W., 1983. Environmental regulation of hydrogen utilization (tritiated-hydrogen exchange) among natural and laboratory populations of nitrogen and non-nitrogen fixing phytoplankton, *Microbiol. Ecol.* **9**, 79–97.

Pedrosa, F. O., Döbereiner, J., and Yates, M. G., 1980. Hydrogen-dependent growth and autotrophic carbon dioxide fixation in *Derxia, J. Gen. Microbiol.* **119**, 547–551.

Pedrosa, F. O., Stephan, M., Döbereiner, J., and Yates, M. G., 1982. Hydrogen-uptake hydrogenase activity in nitrogen-fixing *Azospirillum brasilense, J. Gen. Microbiol.* **128**, 161–166.

Peiser, G. D., Lizada, C. C. and Yang, S. F., 1982. Dark metabolism of carbon monoxide in lettuce leaf disks, *Plant Physiol.* **70**, 397–400.

Rasmussen, R. A. and Khalil, M. A. K., 1981. Atmospheric methane ($CH_4$): Trends and seasonal cycles, *J. Geophys. Res.* **86**, 9826–9832.

Rasmussen, R. A. and Khalil, M. A. K., 1983. Global production of methane by termites, *Nature* **301**, 700–702.

Reddy, K. R. and Patrick, W. H., 1984. Nitrogen transformations and loss in flooded soils and sediments, *CRC Crit. Rev. Environ. Control* **13**, 273–310.

Ritchie, G. A. F. and Nicholas, D. J. D., 1972. Identification of the sources of nitrous oxide produced by oxidative and reductive processes in *Nitrosomonas europaea, Biochem. J.* **126**, 1181–1191.

Robson, R. L. and Postgate, J. R., 1980. Oxygen and hydrogen in biological nitrogen fixation, *Ann. Rev. Microbiol.* **34**, 183–207.

Rudd, J. W. M. and Taylor, C. D., 1980. Methane cycling in aquatic environments, *Adv. Aquat. Microbiol.* **2**, 77–150.

Ryden, J. C., 1981. $N_2O$ exchange between a grassland soil and the atmosphere, *Nature* **292**, 235–237.

Schink, B. and Zeikus, J. G., 1984. Ecology of aerobic hydrogen-oxidizing bacteria in two freshwater lake ecosystems, *Can. J. Microbiol.* **30**, 260–265.

Schlesinger, W. H., 1977. Carbon balance in terrestrial detritus, *Ann. Rev. Ecol. Syst.,* **8**, 51–81.

Schubert, K. R. and Evans, H. J., 1976. Hydrogen evolution: A major factor affecting the efficiency of nitrogen fixation in nodulated symbionts, *Proc. Nat. Acad. Sci. USA* **73**, 1207–1211.

Sebacher, D. I., Harriss, R. C., and Bartlett, K. B., 1985. Methane emission to the atmosphere through aquatic plants, *J. Environ. Qual.* **14**, 40–46.

Seiler, W., 1978. The influence of the biosphere on the atmospheric CO and $H_2$ cycles, in W. E. Krumbein, Ed., *Environmental Biogeochemistry and Geomicrobiology,* Vol. 3, *Methods, Metals and Assessment,* Ann Arbor Science, Ann Arbor, MI.

Seiler, W., 1984. Contribution of biological processes to the global budget of $CH_4$ in the atmosphere, in M. J. Klug and C. A. Reddy, Eds., *Current Perspectives in Microbial Ecology,* American Society for Microbiology, Washington DC.

Seiler, W. and Conrad, R., 1981. Field measurements of natural and fertilizer induced $N_2O$ release rates from soils, *J. Air Poll. Contr. Assoc.* **31**, 767–772.

Seiler, W., Liebl, K. H., Stöhr, W. T., and Zakosek, H., 1977. CO- und $H_2$-Abbau in Böden, *Z. Pflanzenernähr. Bodenkde.* **140**, 257–272.

Seiler, W., Giehl, H., and Bunse, G., 1978. The influence of plants on atmospheric carbon monoxide and dinitrogen oxide, *Pageoph* **116**, 439–451.

Seiler, W., Conrad, R., and Scharffe, D., 1984a. Field studies of methane emission from termite nests into the atmosphere and measurements of methane uptake by tropical soils, *J. Atmos. Chem.* **1**, 171–186.

Seiler, W., Holzapfel-Pschorn, A., Conrad, R., and Scharffe, D., 1984b. Methane emission from rice paddies, *J. Atmos. Chem.* **1**, 241–268.

Seiler, W., Giehl, H., Brunke, E. G., and Halliday, E., 1984c. The seasonality of CO abundance in the Southern Hemisphere, *Tellus* **36**, 219–231.

Simpson, F. B. and Burris, R. H., 1984. A nitrogen pressure of 50 atmospheres does not prevent evolution of hydrogen by nitrogenase, *Science* **224**, 1095–1097.

Slemr, F., Conrad, R., and Seiler, W., 1984. Nitrous oxide emissions from fertilized and unfertilized soils in a subtropical region (Andalusia, Spain), *J. Atmos. Chem.* **1**, 159–169.

Smith, C. J. and Patrick, W. H., Jr., 1983. Nitrous oxide emission as affected by alternate anaerobic and aerobic conditions from soil suspensions enriched with ammonium sulfate, *Soil Biol. Biochem.* **15**, 693–698.

Smith, M. S. and Zimmerman, K., 1981. Nitrous oxide production by nondenitrifying soil nitrate reducers, *Soil Sci. Amer. J.* **45**, 865–871.

Smith, C. J., Brandon, M. and Patrick, W. H., Jr., 1982. Nitrous oxide emission following urea-nitrogen fertilization of wetland rice, *Soil Sci. Plant Nutr. (Tokyo)* **28**, 161–171.

Smith, C. J., Wright, M. F., and Patrick, W. H., Jr., 1983. The effect of soil redox potential and pH on the reduction and production of nitrous oxide, *J. Environ. Qual.* **12**, 186–188.

Spratt, H. G., Jr. and Hubbard, J. S., 1981. Carbon monoxide metabolism in roadside soils, *Appl. Environ. Microbiol.* **41**, 1192–1201.

Stumm, W., 1967. Redox potential as an environmental parameter. Conceptual significance and operational limitation, in O. Jaag, Ed., *Advances in Water Pollution Research,* Vol. 1, Pergamon, New York.

Svensson, B. H., 1980. Carbon dioxide and methane fluxes from the ombrotrophic parts of a subarctic mire, *Ecol. Bull. (Stockholm)* **30**, 235–250.

Svensson, B. H. and Rosswall, T., 1984. In situ methane production from acid peat in plant communities with different moisture regimes in a subarctic mire, *Oikos* **43**, 341–350.

Terry, R. E., Tate, R. L., III, and Duxbury, J. M., 1981. The effect of flooding on nitrous oxide emissions from an organic soil, *Soil Sci.* **132**, 228–232.

Tiedje, J. M., Sextone, A. J., Parkin, T. B., Revsbech, N. P., and Shelton, D. R., Anaerobic processes in soil, *Plant Soil* **76**, 197–212.

Troxler, R. F., 1972. Synthesis of bile pigments in plants. Formation of carbon monoxide and phycocyanobilin in wildtype and mutants strains of the alga, *Cyanidium caldarium, Biochemistry* **11**, 4235–4242.

Troxler, R. F. and Dokos, J. M., 1973. Formation of carbon monoxide and bile pigment in red and blue-green algae, *Plant Physiol.* **51**, 72–75.

Uratsu, S. L., Keyser, H. H., Weber, D. F., and Lim, S.-T., 1982. Hydrogen uptake (HUP) activity of *Rhizobium japonicum* from major U.S. soybean production areas, *Crop Sci.* **22**, 600–602.

Van Kessel, C., Roskoski, J. P., Wood, T., and Montano, J., 1983. Nitrogen-15 fixation and hydrogen evolution by six species of tropical leguminous trees, *Plant Physiol.* **72**, 909–910.

Vedenina, I. Ya. and Zavarzin, G. A., 1977. Biological elimination of nitrous oxide under oxidative conditions, *Mikrobiologya* **46**, 898–903.

Vedenina, I. Ya., Miller, Yu. M., Kapustin, O. A., and Zavarzin, G. A., 1980. Oxidation of nitrous oxide during the decomposition of hydrogen peroxide by catalase, *Mikrobiologya* **49**, 5–8.

Walker, C. C. and Yates, M. G., 1978. The hydrogen cycle in nitrogen-fixing *Azotobacter chroococcum, Biochimie* **60**, 225–231.

Wittenbury, R., Colby, J., Dalton, H., and Reed, H. L., 1976. Biology and ecology of methane oxidizers, in H. G. Schlegel, G. Gottschalk, and N. Pfennig, Eds., *Microbial Production and Utilization of Gases,* E. Goltze KG, Göttingen, FRG.

Yamane, I. and Sato, K., 1963. Decomposition of organic acids and gas formation in flooded soil, *Soil Sci. Plant Nutr. (Tokyo)* **9**, 32–36.

Yamane, I. and Sato, K., 1964. Decomposition of glucose and gas formation in flooded soil, *Soil Sci. Plant Nutr. (Tokyo)* **10**, 127–133.

Yamane, I. and Sato, K., 1967. Effect of temperature on the decomposition of organic substances in flooded soil, *Soil Sci. Plant Nutr. (Tokyo)* **13**, 94–100.

Yoh, M., Terai, H., and Saijo, Y., 1983. Accumulation of nitrous oxide in the oxygen deficient layer of freshwater lakes, *Nature* **301**, 327–329.

Yoshida, T. and Alexander, M., 1970. Nitrous oxide formation by *Nitrosomonas europaea* and heterotrophic microorganisms, *Soil Sci. Soc. Proc.* **34**, 880–882.

Zehnder, A. J. B., 1978. Ecology of methane formation, in R. Mitchell, Ed., *Water Pollution Microbiology,* Vol. 2, Wiley-Interscience, New York.

Zimmermann, P. R., Greenberg, J. P., Wandiga, S. O., and Crutzen, P. J., 1982. Termites: A potentially large source of atmospheric methane, carbon dioxide, and molecular hydrogen, *Science* **218**, 563–565.

Zimmerman, P. R. and Greenberg, J. P., 1983. Termites and methane, *Nature* **302**, 354–355.

Zimmerman, P. R., Greenberg, J. P., and Darlington, J. P. E. C., 1984. Termites and atmospheric gas production, *Science* **224**, 86.

# ☐ COMMENTS ON CONTRIBUTION OF TROPICAL ECOSYSTEMS TO THE GLOBAL BUDGETS OF TRACE GASES, ESPECIALLY CH$_4$, H$_2$, CO, AND N$_2$O

**Ralph J. Cicerone**

This essay provides an up-to-date view of the state of knowledge of the role of the tropics for surface sources and sinks of atmospheric trace gases. It must be kept in mind, however, that the tropics have not been investigated yet with any thoroughness. For example, the authors have presented estimates of methane emission from world rice agriculture. These estimates are based on field experiments carried out exclusively in middle latitudes even though the authors note that their extrapolations imply that 95% of the world's emissions of methane from rice occurs in tropical zones. In almost every specific case and gas of interest, the apparent importance of the tropics is inferred from preliminary studies made only at higher latitudes.

Emissions of gases from animals is a topic that has been given too little attention in this contribution. The reader could conclude that there are few questions that require further research, yet in reality this is not the case. Most of the research results on methane releases from cows are from developed, midlatitude countries. For example, the methane released from cows and sheep probably varies a great deal with diet type and the nutritional adequacy of the diet. There are also interesting gaps in our knowledge of the actual emissions from termite colonies to the atmosphere. As it stands, the essay indicates that the early suggestions of global termite emissions by Zimmerman et al. were a large overestimate. The issue of the magnitude of global emissions by termites, however, is still unresolved. For a more complete view of the large remaining questions, the reader should consult not only the work of Rasmussen and Khalil, referenced in the essay, but also the reply of Zimmerman and Greenberg (1983). The Collins and Wood reference is a letter that discusses previous population measurements, and each of Collins and Wood's criticisms was answered in a response by Zimmerman, Greenberg, and Darlington (1984). The $CH_4/CO_2$ ratios that have been measured (by Zimmerman et al., Rasmussen and Khalil, and Seiler et al.) are not very different. Available estimates of methane emissions (into the atmosphere) from termites thus differ mostly because of the wide differences in estimates of how much carbon is processed annually by termites. None of the authors who have written on the subject to date is expert on such a question, except possibly Darlington. Interested readers should be aware that there are also unresolved issues of digestion efficiencies; the references cited above cite other papers that delve into interesting facets of methane production by living organisms. For example, it appears that termites emit as $CH_4$ only 1% of the carbon they process, while cows produce 8 or 10 times as much $CH_4$ per unit food intake.

Seiler and Conrad indicate that other xylophagous (wood-eating) insects also produce methane. A few xylophagous insects (e.g., *Cryptocercus*, a wood-eating cockroach phylogenetically related to termites) do produce $CH_4$; however, both their numbers and their production efficiencies are low. Many xylophagous insects break down sugars and starches and even some cellulose enzymatically. Because methane production in animals is a by-product of anaerobic fermentation, only animals that rely on fermentation products and maintain strict anaerobic conditions will be likely to produce much methane.

Seiler and Conrad discuss the temperature dependency of microbial gas production. A knowledge of how soil and water temperatures affect, say, methanogenesis is required for global extrapolations and for assessing the relative importance of the tropics. I believe that extrapolations such as those by Baker-Blocker et al. and Koyama are unlikely to represent the final correct answers. There is evidence, for example, that some microbes have adapted to colder environments and can produce methane at lower temperatures such as in tundra and high-latitude peat bogs (Svensson, 1983). A very interesting related question raised by Seiler and Conrad is the possibility of a compensation or equilibration point in soil gas pressures such that the soils might now be a net sink for atmospheric methane (at 1.7 ppmv) but could have been a net source when atmospheric methane was at 0.6 ppmv. Proving existence of either a constant or an average compensation point pressure could be very important but will be very difficult.

Figures quoted by Seiler and Conrad on annual methane sources (global total of 430 Tg $y^{-1}$) and the relative sizes of the soil methane sink and the atmospheric OH methane sink are, in reality, very uncertain. As to the total annual methane source, its value has generally been estimated as 500 Tg $y^{-1}$ or more (see, e.g., Mayer et al., 1982) when relevant $C_2H_3Cl_3$ data on production and latitudinal distributions are employed. Similarly, both the soil sink and atmospheric OH sink for methane are very uncertain so their ratio is risky to estimate, at best.

Finally, are not the *activities* of microbes in flooded soils much more important than the *populations*? Also, is not sulfate assimilation often an important process, not just dissimilation? The roles of plant roots in mediating gas exchange are as yet unclear but are not addressed in this essay, presumably because little relevant research has been performed to date.

## REFERENCES

Mayer, E. W., Blake, D. R., Tyler, S. C., Makide, Y., Montague, D. C., and Rowland, F. S., 1982. Methane: Interhemispheric concentration gradient and atmospheric residence time, *Proc. Natl. Acad. Sci., U.S.A.* **79,** 1366–1370.

Svensson, B. H., 1983. Microbial adaptability to lower temperatures, Ph.D. Dissertation, Swedish University of Agricultural Sciences, Uppsala.

Zimmerman, P. R. and Greenberg, J. P., 1983. Termites and methane, *Nature* **302,** 354–355.

Zimmerman, P. R., Greenberg, J. P. and Darlington, J. P. E. C., 1984. Reply to a comment by Collins and Wood, *Science* **224,** 84–86.

# Chapter 10

# Influence of a Tropical Forest on Air Chemistry

Robert C. Harriss

In recent years, we have seen increasing evidence of the important, possibly dominant, effects that biosphere–atmosphere interactions have on moisture and heat fluxes in the tropical atmosphere (e.g., Lettau et al., 1979; Dickinson, 1980; Rind, 1984) and on the chemistry of the atmosphere (e.g., Lovelock and Margulis 1974; McElroy, 1983; Cicerone et al., 1984). Changes in the atmospheric energy budget and circulation can result in changes in the character of the biosphere, such as vegetation distribution patterns, soil respiration and decomposition rates, and patterns of biomass burning (e.g., Holdridge, 1947; Meentemeyer, 1978; Meentemeyer et al., 1982; Box, 1981). The challenge now facing environmental scientists is to quantify these complex energy and chemical exchange processes between the biosphere and atmosphere and to use such knowledge in managing the earth's resources.

The biosphere–atmosphere interactions of the great tropical forest ecosystems are important because these ecosystems have large total area, net primary productivity, total standing biomass, and leaf area. However, because of their remoteness and relatively harsh environmental conditions, very little data are available on the chemistry of the atmospheric boundary layer over them.

The atmosphere ventilates the tropical biosphere, transporting respiratory (i.e., waste) products to regions of the atmosphere where they are oxidized and ultimately recycled back to the lithosphere and biosphere. Many important questions must be addressed in order to better understand these biosphere–atmosphere interactions, such as how important are turbulent transport processes for removing biogenic respiratory gases to critical sink regions in the atmosphere? Is the composition of the atmospheric boundary layer significantly different over different tropical ecosystems (such as forest versus agriculture)? What limits the capacity of the tropical atmosphere to remove reduced gases from the biosphere?

Tropical forests may also be important for regional and global budgets of primary and secondary aerosols and atmospheric chemical species such as sulfur, phosphorus, and potassium, which occur primarily in particulate form (Lawson and Winchester, 1979; Andreae, 1983). Most of the particulate organic carbon in the atmospheric boundary layer over remote oceanic regions is probably of continental origin (Hoffman and Duce, 1977; Chesselet et al., 1981) with epicuticular vascular plant waxes contributing a significant portion of this material (Gagosian et al., 1981).

The release of biogenic aerosols from forest vegetation to the tropical atmospheric boundary layer and the formation of secondary organic aerosols from nonmethane hydrocarbon photodecomposition in the boundary layer are particularly interesting since rapid vertical transport to upper tropospheric and stratospheric altitudes might occur in regions such as the intertropical convergence zone (ITCZ). Biogenic aerosols are potential ice nuclei (Schnell and Vali, 1972) and could play a role in global climatic processes.

The study of biosphere–atmosphere interactions in the tropics is only beginning.

Crutzen (Chapter 8) provides a theoretical framework for the role of the tropics in atmospheric chemistry, emphasizing the tropics as a source of hydroxyl (OH) and other key trace gases such as methane ($CH_4$), carbon monoxide (CO), and nonmethane hydrocarbons (NMHCs). Seiler and Conrad (Chapter 9) summarize the limited data base currently available on surface measurements of the exchange of gaseous compounds between tropical ecosystems and the atmosphere. The data are primarily for savanna and rice paddies. They conclude that tropical regions are important for the global budgets of CO, $CH_4$, and other gases.

This chapter summarizes the results of the first spatially extensive study of aerosols and selected trace gases over remote, undisturbed wet tropical forest. The study was conducted in Guyana in June 1984 as part of the NASA Global Tropospheric Experiment (GTE) Program.

## THE UTILITY OF AIRCRAFT FOR SAMPLING ATMOSPHERIC BOUNDARY LAYER OVER REMOTE AREAS

Two types of sampling are necessary for studies of biosphere–atmosphere interactions over any specific ecosystem: First, high-frequency (~1-h or better) sampling at fixed locations is needed for the investigation of processes such as diurnal variations in gaseous emissions from soils and vegetation and episodic, high-intensity meteorological events (e.g., frontal passage, thunderstorm). An example of this type of sampling in the Amazon forest is discussed by Molion (Chapter 14). Second, synoptic sampling of large areas (>$10^2$ km$^2$) is required for obtaining data on the variability of the boundary layer air in relation to the distribution of sources and sinks of specific chemicals at the surface. Samples integrated over large areas are also useful for characterizing the average chemical state of the atmosphere under a defined meteorological condition. Aircraft and satellite platforms are required for such rapid, large-area sampling.

## AIRCRAFT SAMPLING OVER TROPICAL FOREST OF GUYANA, JUNE 1984

On June 27, 1984, NASA conducted an aircraft research study of the distribution of aerosols, ozone ($O_3$), CO, aerosol chemical composition, and meteorological parameters over the wet tropical forest of Guyana. The portion of the flight path discussed in this paper ranged from the Guyana–Brazil border (2°12′ N, 56°50′ W) to a point (4°21′ N, 58°11′ W) approximately 200 km south of the Guyana coast where meteorological conditions changed abruptly; winds at the aircraft altitude changed from flow over forested surface (68°–80°) to flow from the Atlantic Ocean (330°–360°). The measurements reported here characterize approximately 260 km of boundary layer air over tropical forest at sampling altitudes of 244–457 m above the land surface and midtropospheric air over the same transect at a sampling altitude of 3.5 km above the land surface. The variation in boundary layer sampling altitude was due to variations in the cloud base; the aircraft was always kept below the cloud base.

The instrumentation used for measurements onboard the NASA Electra aircraft was as follows:

(a) Aerosols number and size were determined with a forward-scattering spectrometer probe (FSSP). The FSSP counts number density (aerosols per cubic centimeter) and sizes of aerosols (fifteen 0.5-$\mu$m wide bins from 0.5 to 7.5 $\mu$m) as they pass through the focused portion of a He–Ne laser beam. The measurements have a horizontal spatial resolution of approximately 5 km and a vertical resolution (during ascent or descent) of 150 m. A high-volume pump (0.85 $m^3$ $min^{-1}$) coupled to an isokinetic inlet, and 8-cm Zefluor Teflon filters were used to collect aerosols for chemical analysis. These filters have a collection efficiency of >99% for aerosols larger than 0.01 $\mu$m diameter. Aerosols were analyzed by ion chromatography for water soluble $Na^+$, $NH_4^+$, $K^+$, $Cl^-$, $PO_4^{3-}$, $SO_4^{2-}$, $C_2O_4^{2-}$, $HCOO^-$, $CH_3COO^-$, $CH_3SO_3^-$, and $F^-$. These techniques for our aerosol studies are described in detail by Talbot et al. (1986).

(b) CO was measured with a Trace Analytical chromatograph/reduction gas detection system that has a precision of $\pm 2\%$.

(c) The $O_3$ measurement system consisted of a Teflon-lined inlet and two simultaneously operating detectors, $C_2H_4$ chemiluminescence, and ultraviolet absorption. The $O_3$ data have a resolution of one measurement each 2s with an instrument precision of 2% (Gregory et al., 1983; Gregory et al., 1984).

(d) An airborne differential absorption lidar (DIAL) system was used on the aircraft to obtain continuous, remotely sensed aerosol distributions along each flight track. Aerosol profiles along the lidar line of sight are obtained in real time on the aircraft from an analysis of backscattered laser light at a wavelength of 600 nm. The spatial resolution for aerosol measurements is 15 m in the vertical and 20 m in the horizontal. A complete description of the DIAL system is given in Browell et al. (1983).

## METEOROLOGY AND AEROSOL DISTRIBUTION

During the period of our experiment (June 1984), the ITCZ was typically centered at approximately 5°N over the Atlantic Ocean. Precipitating clouds were present over Guyana almost every day. Daily analysis of satellite imagery and other weather data indicated a minimum in convective cloud activity for June 27, the day selected for our research flight. Large-scale weather features for the flight, which was conducted between 13:20 GMT and 19:20 GMT, are shown in Fig. 1.

During the transit from the project base at Barbados to Guyana, a line of cumulus clouds with tops to approximately 10 km was encountered between 8°15′ N, 57°50′ W and 5°30′N, 57°43′ W. On the south side of this line of tall cumulus, the weather over the Guyana forest was characterized by scattered clouds (25–50% cloud cover) with occasional precipitating clouds. The nonprecipitating clouds were generally confined to 0.5–1.0 km above the surface. At 3°25′N, the NASA aircraft began a straight and level data leg over tropical forest terrain at an altitude of 3.5 km. At 2°15′ N, 56°56′ W the aircraft executed a vertical descent to 450 m above the forest where a straight and level data leg was initiated for boundary layer measurements, retracing the high-altitude flight path. Winds along the 3.5-km leg were 8–12 knots, from 211° to 228° (SW); winds along the boundary layer leg were 16–21 knots, from 68° to 80° (E-NE). From the limited meteorological data available, we concluded that the boundary layer over the Guyana wet tropical forest was approximately 3–6 h old, on the average, with occasional exchange between the boundary layer and free troposphere in the vicinity of precipitating clouds. These conditions provided an opportunity to compare the chemical composition of relatively fresh boundary layer air over a wet tropical forest with free tropospheric conditions at 3.5 km immediately above the forest.

A lidar backscatter image obtained along the 3.5-km flight leg is shown in Fig. 2. The darker shades indicate relatively high aerosol concentrations; white areas under dark patches result from clouds that have such high aerosol concentrations that the laser beam does not penetrate through the cloud to the boundary layer air. The data in Fig. 2 are important for two purposes.

1601 27JN84 17A-4    00101 19111 WC1

**FIGURE 1.** Geostationary satellite image of atmospheric conditions during the NASA/ GTE research flight over tropical forest in Guyana, June 27, 1984.

First, the distribution of clouds (including a precipitating cloud at 2°28′ N) and aerosol concentrations is strong visual documentation of the qualitative meteorological description given above. The major features of clean, low-aerosol air above 1.8 km and aerosol-rich boundary layer air below 1.5 km are obvious. Between 0.75 and 1.5 km, the lidar data show a very hetero-geneous distribution of aerosols resulting from atmospheric mixing processes (e.g., cloud formation–evaporation, vertical transport associated with pre-cipitating clouds). The combined effects of mixing processes and cloud evap-oration apparently produced an irregular aerosol maximum between 0.75 and 1.5 km. Second, the lidar data document the free troposphere and bound-ary layer conditions at flight altitudes selected for *in situ* sampling. A vertical profile of aerosol, static air temperature, and dew point temperature (Fig. 3) provides a more detailed description of atmospheric structure, albeit for a single location. In these data, we again see evidence of a subcloud boundary

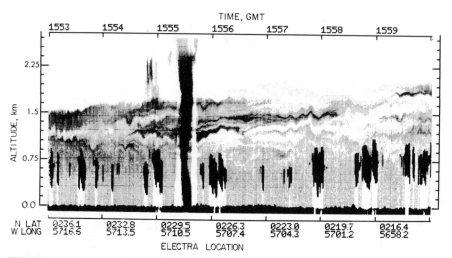

**FIGURE 2.** Lidar aerosol measurements over Guyana, June, 27, 1984. Darker shades indicate higher aerosol concentrations. Black areas are clouds (note that the lidar does not penetrate through clouds; white areas below clouds indicate no data). The white areas above 0.75 km are a result of very low aerosol concentrations.

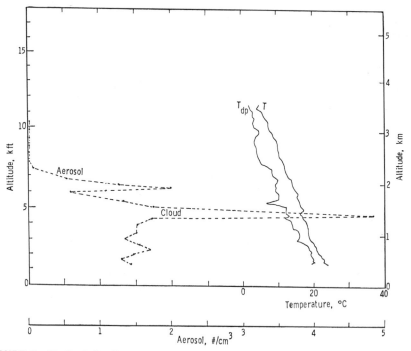

**FIGURE 3.** Vertical distribution of aerosol (0.5–7.5 μm), air temperature ($T$), and dew point temperature ($T_{dp}$) at 2°12′ N, 56°50′ W over wet tropical forest.

**168**

layer (0–0.5 km), a nonprecipitating cloud layer (0.5–1.0 km), a layer of active mixing (0.5–1.5 km), and the free troposphere (>2.0 km).

## ATMOSPHERIC CHEMISTRY OVER WET TROPICAL FOREST

Synoptic sampling of CO, $O_3$, and aerosols over an extensive area of tropical forest in Guyana has demonstrated that the wet tropical forest can have a pronounced influence on the chemistry of the atmospheric boundary layer. The forest vegetation emits NMHCs, which are a source for CO and a sink for $O_3$ as a result of photochemical processes outlined by Crutzen (Chapter 8). Forest vegetation also appears to be a major source for nutrient-rich boundary layer aerosols.

### Carbon Monoxide and Ozone

The variability and vertical structure in the distribution of CO and $O_3$ are illustrated in Fig. 4. The most striking feature in these data is the decrease in $O_3$ and increase in CO in the tropical forest boundary layer relative to the overlying free troposphere. When placed in the qualitative meteorological framework, discussed previously, which indicates a relatively

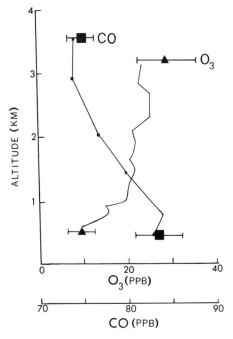

**FIGURE 4.** Vertical distribution of CO and $O_3$ over wet tropical forest. The vertical profiles were obtained at 2°12′ N, 56°50′ W. The average value and standard deviation for CO (■) and $O_3$ (▲) measurements along straight and level flight legs at 3.5- and 0.4-km altitudes are also illustrated.

"young" boundary layer, these data suggest the possibility of a strong source of CO and sink for $O_3$ in the wet tropical forest boundary layer.

Isoprene and several other NMHC species emitted by vegetation are a likely source for the enhancement of CO over the forest. The concentration of isoprene over the Guyana forest was high (Rasmussen and Khalil, 1985); it is the likely source of the enhanced CO in the boundary layer (Kleindlenst et al., 1982; Zimmerman et al., 1978). The approximately linear decrease in CO in the layer of active mixing (0.5–2.5 km) suggests conservative mixing with no appreciable sources or sinks active at these altitudes.

The $O_3$ concentration over the Guyana tropical forest decreases from 30 ± 7 ppb in the free troposphere to 19 ppb at the cloud base and then rapidly to an average of 10 ± 2 ppb at 0.4 km. This rapid decrease below the cloud base suggests active boundary layer removal processes but does not distinguish between *in situ* consumption (e.g., NMHC oxidation) and surface deposition of $O_3$.

Crutzen et al. (1985) observed an enhancement of CO and a depletion in $O_3$ in the Amazon boundary layer relative to concentrations in the overlying free troposphere and suggested that the boundary layer CO came from oxidation of isoprene and other hydrocarbons emitted by the forest vegetation. They speculated that 2–3% of the total carbon fixed in net primary productivity is returned to the atmosphere as CO. Theoretical investigations by Volz, Ehhalt, and Derwent. (1981) and Crutzen and Gidel (1983) imply a large production of CO from hydrocarbon oxidation in the tropics. In contrast to wet tropical forests, dry tropical savanna areas appear to be a source of tropospheric $O_3$ as a result of photochemical processes associated with emissions from biomass burning (Delany et al., 1985).

### Aerosol Chemistry

Particulate material in the boundary layer over tropical forests can originate from direct emission from vegetation surfaces, wind erosion of exposed soils, and atmospheric transport from distant sources. The composition of the water-soluble fraction of boundary layer and free tropospheric aerosols over Guyana is presented in Table 1. The most striking features of the forest boundary layer aerosol are the pronounced enrichments of $Na^+$, $NH_4^+$, $NO_3^{2-}$, $SO_4^{2-}$, $CH_3SO_3^-$, $PO_4^{3-}$, $F^-$, $C_2O_4^{2-}$, and $CH_3COO^-$. Scanning electron microscopy of the aerosols from the forest boundary layer showed evidence of organic particulates up to approximately 20 μm in diameter.

The chemical species have various origins. We hypothesize that the $Na^+$, $NH_4^+$, $NO_3^{2-}$, $PO_4^{3-}$, $F^-$, and $CH_3COO^-$ are primarily associated with the organic particulates derived from the forest vegetation. The sulfur species, $SO_4^{2-}$ and $CH_3SO_3^-$, are most probably secondary products derived from the photooxidation of gaseous $H_2S$ and dimethyl sulfide emitted from anaerobic sites in the forest soils. Previous studies in humid forest of the Ivory Coast demonstrated that wet-season tropical forest soils can be a sig-

**TABLE 1. Chemical Composition of Water-Soluble Fraction of Atmospheric Aerosols Collected at 3.5 and 0.4 km over Wet Tropical Forest in Guyana, June 27, 1984[a]**

| Species | Free Troposphere | Forest Boundary Layer |
|---|---|---|
| Na | 51 | 162 |
| K | 13 | 20 |
| $NH_4$ | 8 | 105 |
| Cl | 69 | 74 |
| $NO_3$ | 3 | 13 |
| $SO_4$ | 22 | 256 |
| $CH_3SO_3$ | 0.91 | 2.7 |
| $PO_4$ | 20 | 157 |
| F | 0.74 | 5.1 |
| $C_2O_4$ | 4 | 25 |
| HCOO | 1 | <0.5 |
| $CH_3COO$ | 2 | 11 |

[a] All concentrations are in nanograms per standard cubic meters.

nificant source of $H_2S$ (Delmas et al., 1980; Delmas and Servant, 1983). Lawson and Winchester (1979) analyzed total aerosol composition of ground-based samples from tropical forest and hypothesized that sulfur, potassium, and phosphorus were probably associated with biogenic particulates. Aerosols derived from the tropical forest and transported to other areas by the atmosphere may serve as important nutrient sources (e.g., to oligotrophic oceanic areas; Talbot et al., 1986).

## REFERENCES

Andreae, M. O., 1983. Soot carbon and excess fine potassium: Long-range transport of combustion-derived aerosols, *Science* **220,** 1148–1152.

Box, E. O., 1981. *Macroclimate and Plant Forms: An Introduction to Predictive Modeling in Phytogeography. Tasks for Vegetation Science*, Vol. 1, W. Junk, The Hague, Netherlands, p. 258.

Browell, E. V., Carter, A. F., Shipley, S., Allen, R., Butler, C., Mayo, M., Siviter, J., and Hall, W., 1983. NASA multipurpose airborne DIAL system and measurements of ozone and aerosols profiles, *Appl. Opt.* **22,** 522–534.

Chesselet, R., Foutugne, M., Buat-Menard, P., Ezat, U., and Lambert, C. E., 1981.

The origin of particulate organic carbon in the marine atmosphere as indicated by its stable carbon isotopic composition, *Geophys. Res. Lett.* **8**, 345–348.

Cicerone, R., Delwiche, R., Harriss, R. C., and Dickinson, R., 1984. Biological and surface sources, in *Global Tropospheric Chemistry*, National Academy of Sciences, National Academy Press, Washington, DC.

Crutzen, P. J. and Gidel, L. T., 1983. A two-dimensional photochemical model of the atmosphere, 2. The tropospheric budgets of the anthropogenic chlorocarbons, CO, $CH_4$, $CH_3Cl$ and the effect of various $NO_x$ sources on tropospheric ozone, *J. Geophys. Res.* **88**, 6641–6661.

Crutzen, P. J., Delany, A. C., Greenberg, J., Haagenson, P., Heidt, L., Lueb, R., Pollock, W., Seiler, W., Wartburg, A., and Zimmerman, P., 1985. Tropospheric chemical composition measurements in Brazil during the dry season, *J. Atmos. Chem.* **2**, 30–102.

Delany, A. C., Haagensen, P., Walters, S. and Wartburg, A. F., 1985. Photochemically produced ozone in the emission from large-scale tropical vegetation fires, *J. Geophys. Res.* **90**, 2425–2429.

Delmas, R. and Servant, J., 1983. Atmospheric balance of sulfur above an equatorial forest, *Tellus* **35B**, 110–120.

Delmas, R., Boudet, J., Servant, J., and Baziard, Y., 1980. Emissions and concentrations of hydrogen sulfide in the air of the tropical forest of the Ivory Coast and of temperate regions in France, *J. Geophys. Res.* **85**, 4468–4474.

Dickinson, R. E., 1980. Effects of tropical deforestation on climate, *Blowing in the Wind: Deforestation and Long-Range Implications*, Studies in Third World Societies, Publication No. 14, College of William and Mary, Williamsburg, VA, pp. 411–441.

Gagosian, R. B., Peltzer, E. T., and Zafiriou, O. C. 1981. Atmospheric transport of continentally derived lipids to the tropical North Pacific, *Nature* **291**, 312–314.

Gregory, G. L., Beck, S. M., and Williams, J. A., 1984. Measurements of free tropospheric ozone: An aircraft survey from 44° north to 46° south latitude, *J. Geophys. Res.* **89**, 9642–9648.

Gregory, G. L., Hudgins, C. H., and Edahl, R. A., 1983. Laboratory evaluation of an airborne ozone instrument which compensates for altitude/sensitivity effects, *Environ. Sci. Technol.* **17**, 100–103.

Hoffman, R. J. and Duce, R. A., 1977. Organic carbon in marine atmosphere particulate matter: Concentration and particle size distribution, *Geophys. Res. Lett.* **4**, 449–452.

Holdridge, L. R., 1947. Determination of world plant formations from simple climatic data, *Science* **105**, 267–269.

Kleindlenst, T. E., Harris, G. W., and Pitts, J. N., 1982. Rates and temperature dependences of the reaction of OH with isoprene, its oxidation products, and selected terpenes, *Environ. Sci. Technol.* **16**, 844–846.

Lawson, D. R. and Winchester, J. W., 1979. Sulfur, potassium, and phosphorus associations in aerosols from South American tropical rain forests, *J. Geophys. Res.* **54**, 3723–3727.

Lettau, H., Lettau, K., and Molion, L. C. B., 1979. Amazonia's hydrologic cycle and the role of atmospheric recycling in assessing deforestation effects. *Mon. Weather Rev.* **107**, 227–238.

Lovelock, J. E. and Margulis, L., 1974. Atmospheric homeostasis by and for the biosphere: The gaia hypothesis, *Tellus* **26**, 2–10.

McElroy, M. B., 1983. Atmospheric composition: Influence of biology, *Planet. Space Sci.* **31**, 1065–1074.

Meentemeyer, V., 1978. Macroclimate and lignin control of litter decomposition rates, *Ecology* **59**, 465–472.

Meentemeyer, V., Box, E. O., Thompson, R., 1982. Terrestrial plant litter production: Climatic correlates, world patterns, and estimated annual amounts, *Bio. Sci.* **32**, 125–129.

Rasmussen, R. A. and Khalil, M. A. K., 1985. Atmospheric isoprene, *EOS* **66**, 39.

Rind, D., 1984. The influence of vegetation on the hydrologic cycle in a global climate model, in J. E. Hansen and T. Takahashi, Eds., *Climate Processes and Climate Sensitivity*, Geophysical Monograph 29, American Geophysical Union, Washington, DC.

Schnell, R. C. and Vali, G., 1972. Atmospheric ice nuclei from decomposing vegetation, *Nature* **236**, 163–165.

Talbot, R. W., Harriss, R. C., Browell, E. V., Gregory, G. L., Sebacher, D. I., and Beck, S. M., 1986. Distribution and geochemistry of aerosols in the tropical North Atlantic troposphere: Relationship to Saharan dust, *J. Geophys. Res.* **91**, 5173–5182.

Volz, A., Ehhalt, D. H., and Derwent, R. G., 1981. Seasonal and latitudinal variation of $^{14}CO$ and the tropospheric concentration of OH radicals, *J. Geophys. Res.* **86**, 5163–5171.

Zimmerman, P. R., Chatfield, R. B., Fishman, J., Crutzen, P. J., and Hanst, P. L., 1978. Estimates of the production of CO and $H_2$ from the oxidation of hydrocarbon emissions from vegetation, *Geophys. Res. Lett.* **5**, 679–682.

# Chapter 11

# Biological Processes and Productivity of Soils in the Humid Tropics

**Patrick Lavelle**

In terrestrial ecosystems, soil recycles dead organic matter and provides physical support and nutrients for plant production. Optimization of these functions depends on a balance between the release of nutrients by mineralization and the accumulation of nutrient and energy reserves through humification (humus formation). Good soil structure facilitates these processes by improving the circulation of water, solutes, and gases.

In the humid tropics, heavy rains and constantly high temperatures, although conducive to plant production, tend to rapidly degrade soils where they are exposed. Natural ecosystems are sheltered by vegetation, and their soil processes are regulated by biological systems that optimize the release of nutrients or their accumulation in stable forms and also conserve the soil structure. The efficiency of natural ecosystems results from a temporal and spatial match (synchrony) between nutrient release and plant needs. The activity of the soil biota is also strongly attuned to the microscale soil state. In such systems, plant production is sustained at very high levels and erosion is extremely low.

Inadequate soil management under humid tropical conditions impairs biological regulation systems. The resulting perturbation of chemical and physical processes in the soil leads to soil degradation.

Nowadays, soil as an agricultural resource faces increasing pressure. Population growth will increase demand for new cultivated land, much of which will be on marginal soils. Meanwhile, degradation from misuse reduces the available arable land.

It is expected that demand for food in the tropics will double in 20 y. It is doubtful that this demand can be met with the present technology and economics of tropical agriculture (FAO, 1981). The present rate of increase

**175**

of food production is too small. In sub-Saharan Africa, the per-capita food production has even decreased during the last 15 y (Swaminathan, 1983). Thus progress in soil management is needed to obtain significant increases of productivity.

Tropical soils are both ecological systems and limited and degradable resources. This chapter considers

**a.** the functioning of tropical soils as ecological systems,

**b.** the present and coming pressures on the soil resources because of human activities and

**c.** the present management options and their possible effects on the soil resource.

## FUNCTIONING OF THE SOIL SYSTEM IN NATURAL ECOSYSTEMS

Ecological systems have physical components (climate, soil) and biological components (microorganisms, plants, animals) structured through such elements as food chains or nutrient cycles. Ecosystems may be seen as open thermodynamic systems that dissipate energy (solar radiation) and their functioning described in terms of fluxes of matter and energy and of structural maintenance.

### Soil Environment

Most of the soils in the tropics pose serious problems for annual crop agriculture. Many pose problems even for use as pasture. In the older shield areas of the humid tropics, tens of millions of years of heavy, warm rainfall have deeply altered, weathered, and leached substrates, leaving low-nutrient-status clay soils. Weathering is less complete on younger soils and in arid or wet-dry climates, and soils may suffer instead from shallowness, salinity, or structural problems such as the tendency to form pans. The violent nature of tropical rains makes most tropical soils sensitive to erosion when exposed. Rapid decomposition results in relatively low levels of humus, which is made of highly complex and thus largely inaccessible organic molecules.

Despite such problems, humid tropical soils generally sustain natural ecosystems with high plant productivity. In these soils, biological conservation systems ensure rapid nutrient recycling, conserve soil structure, and strictly regulate soil humic reserves by activation or inhibition of humus mineralization.

#### Soil Types

With the high temperature and moisture in the tropics, underlying rocks are deeply and strongly weathered. Intense leaching removes silica and nutrient cations, leaving soils dominated by aluminum and iron in the form of oxy-hydroxides. Clays poor in silica (kaolinites and gibbsites) appear. The intense alteration of the original minerals tends to make all soils similar regardless of the nature of the original bedrock (Volobuyev, 1962; Lelong and Souchier, 1979; Duchaufour, 1979).

Such processes, when complete, lead to the formation of desaturated ferralitic soils (oxisols). Under less humid conditions or when leaching is limited by topographic or lithologic conditions, alteration is less complete and ferruginous soils (alfisols) or vertisols appear. Permanent or temporary waterlogging, alluvium or colluvium deposition, volcanic activities, and pod-zolization diversify the soil types. Nevertheless, ferralitic (oxisols and ul-tisols) and ferruginous (alfisols) soils cover 58% of the humid tropics. Apart from these, two groups of relatively fertile soils, alluvial (entisols) and brown tropical soils (inceptisols) cover another 30% of the area, the rest being occupied by more special, rather fertile soils (vertisols, mollisols) or highly infertile soils (podzols) (Sanchez and Salinas, 1983).

### Nutrient Reserves

Soils formed under tropical conditions may have high clay content, but they are poor clays with a low ability to retain nutrients. Furthermore, intense leaching often drives cation retention below the cation exchange capacity (CEC, an important parameter of soil fertility) as, for instance, for the highly desaturated ferralitic soils (oxisols). As a result, these soils are poor in nu-trients and low in pH. This soil acidity promotes high levels of aluminum toxicity. Ferruginous tropical soils (alfisols) and alluvial soils (alluvisols) may have better nutrient status but are still not very fertile. Examples of the nutrient content of different Amazon soils are shown in Fig. 1.

In spite of their low nutrient levels, natural ecosystems on tropical soils often have high primary productivity, and standing biomass is large in rain forests. Much of the nutrient stock of these ecosystems is contained in the plant biomass: in an extreme case, in the Amazonian rain forest at San Carlo de Rio Negro (Venezuela), on a poor tropical podzol, Herrera (1979) found that as much as 92% of the magnesium, 90% of the potassium, 74% of the calcium, 66% of the phosphorus, and 62% of the nitrogen was stored in the plant biomass. Even in richer soils, large proportions of nutrients, especially potassium, calcium, and magnesium, are accumulated in the plants (Table 1). Such nutrient sequestering helps prevent nutrient loss by leaching.

### Humic Reserves

In contrast to the mineralization process that releases nutrients for plant nutrition, humification accumulates in the soil more complex organic com-pounds acting as energy and nutrient reserves. Humic reserves are definitely beneficial for the soil (Swift and Sanchez, 1984). As organic molecules, they provide nutrients for plant growth, improve the ability of soils to retain cations (i.e., increase CEC) by as much as 20–70%, and buffer pH changes.

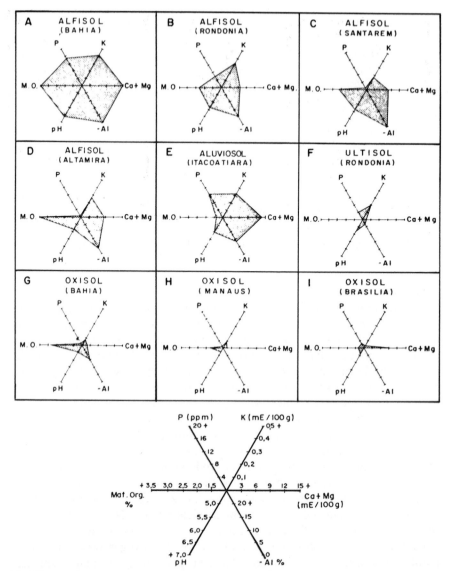

**FIGURE 1.** Graphic representation of fertility of different kinds of tropical soils from Brazil. [Reprinted from Alvim (1978), *Interciencia*, vol. 3, copyright Interciencia, 1978.]

As colloid complexes, they have many of the good features of clays: increasing the moisture-retaining properties of soil, improving structural stability, and forming complexes with soil pollutants (heavy metals, pesticides) and helping to alleviate the problems of poor drainage and high erodability commonly associated with heavy clays. Humic reserves may be especially

**TABLE 1.** **Total Soil Nutrient Reserves as Percentage of Total Stock Contained in Soil and Above-Ground Vegetation in Different Tropical Forests**[a]

| Locality | N | P | K | Ca | Mg | Author |
|---|---|---|---|---|---|---|
| Banco (Ivory Coast) | 82.2 | 50.0 | 13.3 | 8.3 | 15.1 | Bernhard-Reversat et al., 1979 |
| Kade (Ghana) | 69.2 | | | | | Nye, 1961 |
| | | (8.6) | (41.6) | (49.1) | (49.6) | |
| Mountain forest (Porto Rico) | | | 15.6 | 28.3 | 55.0 | Jordan et al., 1972 |
| San Carlos de Rio Negro (Venezuela) | 62.6 | 59.3 | 18.1 | 38.9 | 20.2 | Herrera, 1979 |
| | (37.6) | (33.8) | (10.0) | (26.2) | (7.8) | |
| Panama | | 11.6 | 10.1 | 84.3 | 84.3 | Golley et al., 1975 |
| El Verde (Porto Rico) | | 83.6 | 8.9 | 47.1 | 69.3 | Odum and Pigeon, 1970 |
| Yangambi (Zaïre) | 91.5 | 98.6 | 74.6 | 37.8 | 64.4 | Bartholomew et al., 1953 |
| | (89.5) | (98.0) | (66.3) | (33.8) | (42.0) | |

[a] Data in parentheses are the nutrient reserves as percentage of total stock including roots; from Lavelle (1984).

important in soils that are very poor in clay, such as many sandy ferruginous tropical soils (alfisols), sandy soils (arenosols), and podzols (spodosols).

Decomposition is very rapid in the tropics: Leaf litter disappears totally in as little as 2.5–17 months (UNESCO, 1979) or in about 8 months on the average. Mineralization occurs much more readily than humification, leading to low organic content (Fig. 2). In ferruginous soils of the African savanna, as well as in grassland soils of Brazil, for example, the upper horizons usually contain well below 2% organic matter (see for example Goodland, 1971; Jones and Wild, 1975; Kowal and Kassam, 1978; Darici, 1978; Lasebikan, 1982; Abbadie, 1983). In forest soils, organic contents are generally greater than in savannas and may vary from 1 to 6%, exceeding 3% in many cases (see Sanchez, 1976; Alvim, 1978; Puig, 1979). Leaf litter is often mineralized at the soil surface and little, if any, is converted to soil humus. Thus, dead roots are the main contributors to this organic stock. However, since tropical plant production is often much greater than in temperate countries, soil organic matter resulting from its decomposition may sometimes compare favorably with temperate standards despite the low humification (Sanchez et al., 1982b; Schlesinger, 1977).

### *Moisture and Thermal Regimes*

Temperatures are always warm in the humid tropics, and the diurnal amplitude is much greater than the seasonal amplitude (Lecordier, 1974). Annual means may be as high as 25–28°C. At Lamto (Ivory Coast), for example,

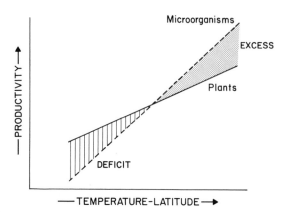

**FIGURE 2.** Microorganism activity increases more rapidly than plant productivity with increasing temperatures. [From Beck (1971), redrafted with permission of Dr. Ludwig Beck.]

in a region of moist guinean savannas, the warmest month is February (28.3°C) and the coldest is August (25.2°C).

Cover strongly affects soil temperatures. At Lamto, just after bush fires, under conditions of blackened surface and impaired shading and evapotranspiration, the temperature may rise above 50°C in the upper 2 cm of soil, and the diurnal amplitude may reach 28°C. Such variations decrease with depth: The annual mean of daily amplitude in burnt savannas decreases from 14°C in the top 2 cm to 4°C at 10 cm. In unburned savanna, mean annual diurnal amplitudes are only 2.6°C in the 0–2-cm stratum (Athias, 1974). In forest soils, temperatures are nearly constant. Thus, the first effect of clearing is a dramatic change in soil temperatures, with a much larger diurnal range and becoming hotter on the average.

Soil moisture depends on four main variables: rainfall, the water-retaining capacity of soil (field capacity), infiltration rates, and vegetative cover. Field capacity and the usable water range may be low in many tropical soils because of a low clay content and/or the low field capacity of many tropical clays. However, vertisols and some oxisols with high clay content may have better field capacities (Table 2).

Infiltration rates in undisturbed systems are often rather high: values up to 25 cm h$^{-1}$ are reported for savannas and forests (Kowal and Kassam, 1978); among other factors, earthworm (Wilkinson, 1975; Hurault, 1971; Aina, 1984) and termite (Lepage, 1981; Lee and Wood, 1971; Wielemaker, 1984) activities modify the soil porosity and hydraulic conductivity. In cultivated areas, the initial infiltration rate rapidly declines as a result of modifications of the surface structure, decrease of the overall volume of pores, and formation of surface crusts (Kowal, 1970; Aina, 1984).

Vegetative structure also affects soil moisture. For example, trees may

**TABLE 2.   Field Capacity (pf 2.5 or $\frac{1}{3}$ bar), Wilting Point (pf 4.2 or 15 bars), and Usable Water Range in Some Grassland Soils (0–10 cm)**[a]

|  | Lamto (Ivory Coast) | | | Laguna Verde, Mexico (Vertisol) |
|---|---|---|---|---|
|  | Ferruginous Hydromorphic Soil | Well-Drained Ferruginous Soils | Vertisol |  |
| pf 2.5 (%) | 9 | 11.5 | 18.2 | 34.6 |
| pf 4.2 (%) | 4.5 | 4 | 4.9 | 17.2 |
| Usable water range (%) | 4.5 | 7.5 | 13.3 | 17.4 |

[a] From Lavelle (1978) and Barois (1982); water contents in percentage of dry soil.

have much higher evapotranspiration rates than grasses. As a result, forest soils will frequently be drier than savannas despite higher rainfalls (Fig. 3). At Lamto, in 1969, a dry year, soil was physiologically dry during 80 days in a lowslope grassland and 140 days in an adjacent gallery forest (Lavelle, 1978).

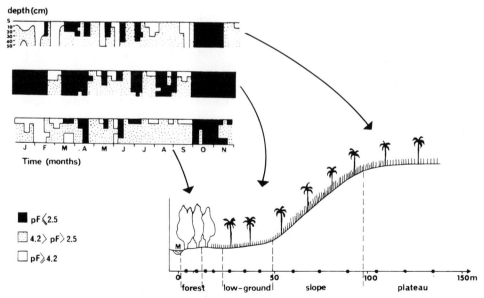

**FIGURE 3.**   Moisture regime of soils at different topographic levels in the same savanna landscape (Lamto, Ivory Coast, 1969; after Lavelle, 1978). Soil water potential is measured logarithmically by pF (pF of 2.5 is field capacity at $\frac{1}{3}$ bar, pF of 4.3 is the wilting point of 15 bars).

## Biological Components

### Plants

Various aspects of plant ecology are especially important for the soil. First, dead leaves and roots provide the energy and nutrients to the soil system. Living roots produce exudates, a complex mixture of energetic compounds, which have a considerable impact on the soil organisms within the rhizosphere (i.e., the soil influenced by root activity). Finally, plants have a dramatic effect on climate and microclimate as well as on soil water and temperature.

In the humid tropics, litter fall ranges between 6.3 and 12.4 t ha$^{-1}$ y$^{-1}$ according to the forest type and is more or less seasonal. Decomposition is rapid so that mean annual litter accumulation generally does not exceed 2.3–5.7 t ha$^{-1}$ (Jenny et al., 1949; Laudelout and Meyer, 1954; Nye and Greenland, 1960; Devineau, 1976). Forest litter is a relatively abundant resource steadily renewed and rather uniformly distributed. Frequent and heavy rains may leach out the hydrosoluble organic matter and nutrients.

In savannas, much dead plant material is destroyed by fire. Litter is present on the soil surface only part of the year. Its maximum weight varies from 0.9 to 5.7 t ha$^{-1}$ in moist savannas of the Ivory Coast (Cesar, 1971; Fournier, 1982).

Root biomass is difficult to evaluate. Available measurements indicate it varies greatly in tropical forests. Values of 48–255 t ha$^{-1}$ have been reported that constitute, respectively, 9–60% of the total plant biomass (Muller and Nielsen, 1965; Fittkau and Klinge, 1973; Bernhard-Reversat et al., 1979; Herrera, 1979). Tap roots and lateral roots may be distinguished (Golley, 1983). Lateral roots develop close to the soil surface and even in the litter itself and take up nutrients released by litter decomposition. In forests with infertile soils, lateral roots may form a mat 20–30 cm thick, which prevents nutrient leaching. They are generally associated with abundant mycorrhizae that link the roots and the dead leaves and thus ensure a direct cycling from the leaf to the root. In such cases, root biomass is large and as much as 80–90% of it may be concentrated in the upper 20 cm. Factors other than poor nutrient content, such as poor drainage or soil texture, may also contribute to this surface root accumulation (Went and Stark, 1968; Medina et al., 1977; Stark and Jordan, 1978; Herrera et al., 1978).

A deep root system extracts the nutrients released by the mineralization of the organic reserves and leached down from the surface. In their rhizosphere, the deep roots produce exudates, poorly characterized mixtures of assimilable organic compounds, complex mucopolysaccharides, and growth factors that might play a very important, though still unknown, role in soil functioning.

The root biomass in savannas is generally less than that of forests but is highly variable: In the same year, a minimum value of 5 t ha$^{-1}$ and a maximum of 19 t ha$^{-1}$ were recorded by Fournier (1982) in a guinean savanna of the Ivory Coast. For such humid savannas, root production and decay, estimated at between 10 and 19 t ha$^{-1}$ annually, is the main input to soil organic matter.

### Microbial and Invertebrate Communities

Invertebrates and microorganisms use the energy and cycle the nutrients held in soil humus systems. Soil animals transform materials mechanically, whereas microorganisms are responsible for most of the chemical transformations of mineralization and humification. Fauna and microflora work in tandem. Animals disseminate materials, bring in new organic resources, and activate microorganisms; microorganisms digest complex organic compounds (e.g., cellulose or humic acids) and make assimilable compounds available to the animals.

Associations among microorganisms and invertebrates take very diverse (and largely uninvestigated) forms. They may be obligatory or not, specific or general, and develop inside or outside the gut of the invertebrate. In many cases, the relationships seem to be mutually advantageous, but this does not exclude selective inhibition, predation, or competition (Barois and Lavelle, 1986).

*Microbial Populations.* Microbial populations have seldom been evaluated in humic tropical soils, and methodological difficulties are such that the available data are not very reliable (see, e.g., Kaiser, 1983). The overall microbial activity may, however, be evaluated by oxygen consumption or carbon dioxide production. Tropical soils generally have potentially high mineralization rates. However, in natural conditions mineralization is often reduced by climatic conditions (drought or waterlogging) and especially by the lack of assimilable carbon sources (Darici, 1978; Lavelle, 1984; Abbadie, 1983). Such conditions may result in low nitrogen mineralization, as in the case of savannas. Thus, one of the main problems of many tropical soils seems to be the paradoxical need to activate mineralization of the humic reserves.

*Invertebrate Communities.* Soil invertebrate communities are highly diverse and variable. Soil animals may be classified into ecological categories according to their food sources and their habitats (Bouche, 1971; Lavelle, 1981, 1984) (Fig. 4).

(a) Epigeics live in and feed in the litter, whether they be detritivorous or predatory. They include microarthropods (Acarina, Collembola, and a great variety of other small insects), myriapods, Diptera larvae, and ants.

(b) Anecics feed on litter but live in the soil (e.g., earthworms that dig galleries or termites that nest in the soil) or in nests established outside the litter (e.g., termites that nest on the trees). Their main contribution is to export litter to different decomposing systems.

(c) Endogeics live in the soil and feed on soil organic matter. They have

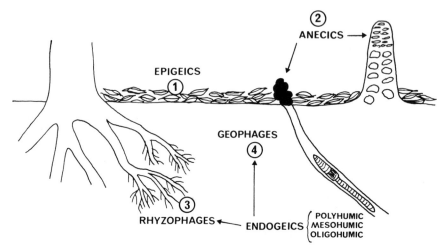

**FIGURE 4.** Functional categories of soil animals. [From Lavelle (1984), reprinted with permission of Biology International, The IUBS News Magazine.]

been classified into three subcategories depending on the relative organic richness of the soil they ingest. Mesohumics ingest the soil of the upper 10–20 cm as it is. Oligohumics ingest the poor soil of the deep horizons (20–60 cm depth), and polyhumics ingest a soil enriched in organic matter, for example, surface organic pellicles, live or dead roots, or the richer soil of the rhizosphere. Earthworms are the most important endogeic group, especially in the oligohumic and mesohumic subcategories. Humivorous termites, a large number of rhizophagous insect larvae, and endogeic microarthropods are polyhumics.

The density and biomass of these communities differ greatly between forests and savannas (Tables 3 and 4). Total macrofauna communities sampled in forests of Mexico and Nigeria have mean densities of about 1000–3000 individuals and a biomass of 16–34 g fresh mass per square meter. They are rather diverse, with no particular group showing dominance. Epigeic animals may constitute up to 62.5% by mass, whereas anecics are of little importance. Endogeics are mostly soil-eating animals; root-eating ones do not exceed 5.4% of the total biomass of soil invertebrates.

In moist grasslands of the Ivory Coast and Mexico, densities of soil macrofauna communities are comparable to forest ones (1800–3000 per square meter), but biomass is generally greater (30–96 g fresh mass per square meter) because of large earthworm populations. These communities are clearly dominated by earthworms, which may constitute up to 91% of the living macrofauna biomass. Termites are very often important (9% of the macrofauna biomass in some savannas of the Ivory Coast), and Coleoptera larvae may be locally abundant (47% of the macrofauna biomass in a Mexican pasture). As a result, the trophic (feeding) structure of these communities

**TABLE 3.  Soil Macrofauna Communities in Three Tropical Grasslands from Africa and America[a]**

| | Lamto, Ivory Coast | | | Foro-Foro, Ivory Coast | | | Laguna Verde, Mexico | | |
|---|---|---|---|---|---|---|---|---|---|
| | d | bm | % bm | d | bm | % bm | d | bm | % bm |
| Earthworms | 230 | 49.00 | 91.10 | 460.0 | 22.30 | 71.10 | 700 | 47.00 | 49.00 |
| Myriapoda | 50 | 0.36 | 0.70 | 103.0 | 0.73 | 2.50 | 33 | 0.70 | 0.73 |
| Arachnida | 4 | 0.03 | 0.06 | 3.2 | 0.10 | 0.30 | 74 | 0.90 | 0.94 |
| Coleoptera | 230 | 0.29 | 0.50 | 28.0 | 1.30 | 4.30 | 320 | 45.00 | 46.90 |
| Diptera | 16 | 0.03 | 0.06 | 0.5 | 0.05 | 0.17 | 60 | 0.10 | 0.10 |
| Termites | 910 | 1.95 | 3.60 | 1200.0 | 2.80 | 9.40 | 2 | $\epsilon$ | $\epsilon$ |
| Ants | 500 | 2.00 | 3.70 | 1400.0 | 2.10 | 7.10 | 570 | 1.09 | 1.14 |
| Others | 75 | 0.09 | | 12.0 | 0.30 | | 71 | 1.20 | |
| Total | 2015 | 53.80 | — | 3207 | 29.70 | — | 1830 | 96.0 | — |

[a] From Athias, Josens, and Lavelle, (1975); Lavelle, Maury, and Serrano (1981); and Lavelle, (1983). Density (d) in units per $m^2$ and biomass (bm) in g fresh mass per $m^2$ (in Lavelle, 1984).

**TABLE 4.  Soil Macrofauna Communities in Humid Tropical Forests[a]**

| | Nigeria | | Laguna Verde, Mexico (average) | | | Bonampak (Mexico) | | | Gunung Mulu, Sarawak (Malaysia) | | |
|---|---|---|---|---|---|---|---|---|---|---|---|
| | d | bm | d | bm | %bm | d | bm | %bm | d | bm | %bm |
| Earthworms | 34 | 10.2 | 132 | 9.8 | 29.2 | 7.9 | 10.7 | 56.8 | 31 | 0.68 | 15.2 |
| Myriapoda | 1255 | 0.83 | 417 | 13.3 | 39.6 | 118 | 2.0 | 10.5 | 63 | 0.30 | 6.7 |
| Arachnida | ? | ? | 129 | 1.4 | 4.2 | 45 | 0.5 | 2.8 | 29 | 0.10 | 2.2 |
| Coleoptera | 260 | 3.17 | 122 | 2.4 | 7.1 | 58 | 2.0 | 10.3 | 21 | 0.76 | 17.0 |
| Diptera | 1540 | 2.72 | 79 | 0.6 | 1.8 | 19 | $\epsilon$ | — | 8 | 0.03 | 0.7 |
| Termites | 30 | 0.15 | 500 | 1.1 | 3.2 | 10 | $\epsilon$ | — | 928 | 1.96 | 43.8 |
| Ants | ? | ? | 1400 | 1.6 | 4.8 | 467 | 0.7 | 3.5 | 497 | 0.29 | 6.5 |
| Others | 120 | 0.07 | 232 | 3.4 | 10.1 | — | — | — | 96 | 0.36 | 8.0 |
| Total | 3119 | 16.4 | 3011 | 33.6 | — | 888 | 18.9 | — | 1673 | 4.48 | — |

[a] Abbreviations as in Table 3 (Madge, 1969; Lavelle and Kohlmann, 1984; Collins, 1980).

**185**

is greatly dominated by endogeics, especially mesohumics. Epigeics are rather limited, and their mass depends greatly on litter availability and shrub cover. Anecics may be locally important, where large termite and anecic earthworm populations are present. Root eaters are of negligible mass unless local population explosions occur, possibly related to soil management techniques.

Compared to temperate communities, humid tropical soil macrofauna communities have generally lower densities and biomass and a much more diversified vertical distribution in the soil profile. Biological activity that occurs mainly in the litter in temperate regions clearly tends, in the tropics, toward the utilization of soil organic reserves; in some Mexican rain forests, only 20% of the total macroinvertebrate community was found in the litter. Also interesting are suspended soils in palm trees and epiphytes (e.g., Bromeliaceae), increasing the vertical range of the soil macrofauna. Furthermore, a greater horizontal diversity is observed as a result of specialization for particular microhabitats (Lavelle and Kohlmann, 1984).

## Biological Regulation Systems

There are three main systems for biological regulation representing a functional adaptation to the adverse nutrient status and climatic conditions of tropical soils: a litter and surface-roots subsystem in which leaf litter may be directly cycled, thus preventing nutrient losses and two subsystems that regulate the mineralization and humification of humic reserves and help conserve the soil structure, the "zoosphere" and the rhizosphere subsystems, that is, the root and soil invertebrates and the soil under their control (Lavelle, 1984).

### The Litter and Surface-Roots Subsystem

The litter and surface-roots subsystem includes litter as a food supply, surface lateral roots, epigeic invertebrates, and microorganisms. It cycles the energy and nutrients from the litter to the surface roots. Leaf litter is colonized by microorganisms and transformed by epigeic or anecic invertebrates. These divide, ingest litter, and sometimes mix it into the soil. As a result, the surface available for microbial attacks is dramatically increased, and microbial colonization is favored. Water-soluble organic compounds and nutrients are released, nutrients are absorbed by the roots, and water-soluble organic matter is made insoluble and added to the soil reserves or leached out.

This type of litter utilization may be found in soils rather rich in nutrients. Where soil nutrients are less, root mats are thicker and, in the most extreme cases, surface roots cease to avoid light, and fungi bridges develop between the root and the dead leaves. (Fig. 5). Thus nutrients may pass directly from the leaf to the root (Herrera et al., 1978). Stark and Jordan (1978) have found

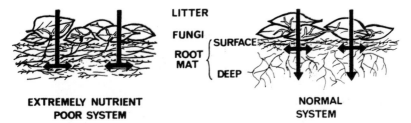

**FIGURE 5.** The litter and surface-roots subsystem (arrows represent flux of soluble organic matter and nutrients).

that in such a system virtually 100% of a solution of labeled phosphorus sprayed over the root mat was incorporated into the plant.

The role of epigeic and anecic soil invertebrates in such systems may be relatively minor since microbial activity is high and litter rarely accumulates.

### Rhizosphere Subsystem

In humid and tropical savannas, lack of assimilable carbon is the primary limitation to mineralization (see, e.g., Darici, 1978; Lavelle, Zaidi, and Schaefer, 1983; Lavelle, 1984). In particular, it limits organic nitrogen mineralization and perhaps also nitrogen fixation and humification.

Nevertheless, since primary production is very high, nitrates are being released in sufficient amounts to allow plant growth (Abbadie, 1983). Possibly mineralization is locally activated and thus nutrients are provided at the right place and time where and when they are needed. Such an activation could be initiated by organisms able to produce assimilable carbon, for example, root exudates or earthworm intestinal and cutaneous mucus. Microorganisms develop on these energetic substrates and then a "priming effect" enables them to degrade the highly complex molecules of the humic reserves.

Precise data on the production of exudates are available for only a few cultivated plants: Exudates may represent up to 10% of the gross primary production, and their total production may be on the order of several tons per hectare per year (see, e.g., Rovira, 1969; Oades, 1978; Chaboud and Rougier, 1981). Nothing is known about root exudates from tropical plants.

Root exudates increase both the density and activity of the microflora in the rhizosphere (see, e.g., Barois, 1982; Kaiser, 1983). The rhizosphere is also the place where roots are decomposed. Invertebrates seem to be of little importance in this process. Dead roots are immediately colonized by the abundant microflora of the rhizosphere and decomposed under the favorable temperature and moisture conditions of the subsoil.

Finally, roots and vegetation as a whole are the main factors that prevent erosion in areas of intense rainfall.

### Invertebrate Activities: Zoosphere Subsystem

Soil invertebrates have three major effects on the soil: (a) provide assimilable carbon, for example, earthworms produce mucus; (b) participate in nutrient

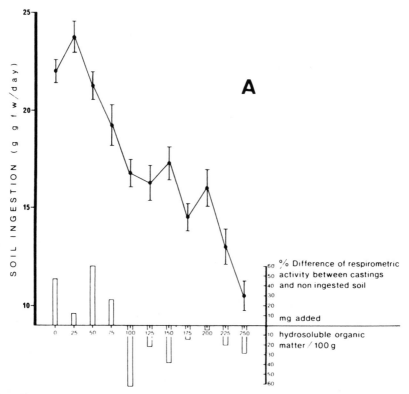

**FIGURE 6.** (*a*) Variations of soil ingestion by earthworms (points) and differences of respirometric activity between castings and noningested soil (blocks) as a function of initial hydrosoluble contents. Earthworms ingest greater amounts of soil and activate soil microflora when the soil is low in assimilable carbon compounds.

conservation systems; and (c) prevent erosion by increasing soil porosity and improving the soil structural stability.

*Regulation of Microbial Activity of Soil by Geophagous Earthworms.*    Endogeic earthworms digest soil organic matter through a mutually beneficial relationship with the soil microflora. In the anterior part of the gut of *Pontoscolex corethrurus*, a very common endogeic earthworm, water (+ 120% of the soil weight) and water-soluble organic matter (16% of the soil weight) are added to the ingested soil. As a result, pH is increased, and overall microbial respiratory activity increases up to 8 times that of undigested soil. This microbial activity first develops within the highly energetic substrates produced by the worm. Then, by a well-known priming effect, microbes begin to digest the complex organic matter of the soil to the benefit of the earthworm. On the whole, about 20% of the total initial organic matter is mineralized (Barois, 1982; Barois and Lavelle, 1986) in the 2–4 h of a gut transit.

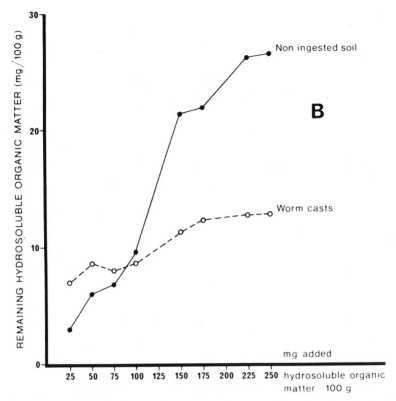

**FIGURE 6.** (*b*) Hydrosoluble organic contents of worm casts and noningested soil as a function of initial hydrosoluble contents. The hydrosoluble organic matter is increased by earthworm activity when it is initially sufficiently low. [From Lavelle, Zaidi, and Schaefer (1983), reprinted with permission of Ph. Lebrun.]

In fresh casts, microbial activity is still 40–50% greater than in noningested soil and may remain greater for 30–40 days. Water-soluble organic compounds are more abundant as a result of this increased mineralization (Lavelle, Sow, and Schaefer, 1980).

The activity of earthworms thus activates the soil microflora in the ingested soil by producing assimilable carbon compounds in the form of intestinal mucus. However, the process is homeostatic. When the water-soluble organic content of the soil exceeds a certain threshold, the action of earthworms on microflora may shift to inhibition, and/or there may be a decrease in the role of soil ingestion by the worm. This limits mineralization when it is too intense (Lavelle, Zaidi, and Schaefer, 1983) (Fig. 6). Such effects are observed in the rhizosphere (Barois, 1982). Earthworms' regulation of humus mineralization is localized in time and space according to the soil microclimatic conditions and population dynamics patterns (Lavelle and Meyer, 1983).

Such regulating effects may be very significant for the overall functioning of the soil system. In the humid savannas of Lamto (Ivory Coast), with poor sandy ferruginous soils, a mean number of 190,000 endogeic earthworms weighing 380 kg fresh mass per hectare ingest in one year 1200 t dry soil, the equivalent of a 10-cm-thick soil layer containing 70% of the organic matter of the upper 10 cm, or 33%, of the total stock. In the process, they produce an annual total of between 50 and 100 t of intestinal mucus per hectare compared to the humic stock of about 45 t ha$^{-1}$ (Lavelle, Kanyonyo, and Rangel, 1983). Thus, over a short time interval, the whole soil organic matter of the upper soil layer is acted upon by this process of microbial regulation.

*Nutrient Conservation by Termites.*   Most termites, whether fungi growing or foraging, are anecics; they take litter into their nests, and after consuming it, add the remaining organic matter and nutrients to their nests, which become enriched in carbon, nitrogen, and exchangeable bases. Nutrients are thus stocked and slowly released into the soil after the death of the termite colony.

Termites may take away as much as 30% and even up to 70% of the total litter (Josens, 1983; Ohiagu and Wood, 1979; Lepage, 1981). Some investigators consider this litter removal deleterious to the soil system (Ohiagu, 1982); others argue that termites only modify the spatial and temporal distribution of the nutrient release from litter that in most cases would have been burnt and but little incorporated into the soil humus (Menaut et al., 1985).

*Elaboration and Conservation of Soil Structure by Termites and Earthworms.*
Termites are a major factor in soil formation in the humid tropics (see Roose et al., 1981; Nye, 1955; Watson, 1974). They contribute to mixing of soil horizons and development of physical properties. Particularly, they help form horizons that are free of gravel and underlain by stones (Wielemaker, 1984). Such soil horizons are also promoted by earthworms that ingest only fine-grained soil and cast part of it onto the soil surface. In the Lamto savannas, up to 1200 t ha$^{-1}$ y$^{-1}$ dry soil are ingested and excreted by endogeic earthworms. This process ensures a constant mixing of soil horizons. About 25–30 t ha$^{-1}$ are excreted as casts on the soil surface, creating a volume of about 30 m$^3$ of voids in the soil (Lavelle, 1978). More empty spaces are created by termites and ants that dig galleries and nests. For example, Lepage (1981) calculated that foraging holes made by termites during 1 y in a dry savanna in Kenya occupy an area of 2–4 m$^2$ ha$^{-1}$. Most of the regulation of soil porosity is due to invertebrate activities. Such activities help balance the progressive natural compression of the soil. The consequent increased infiltration of water into the soil diminishes the runoff and helps prevent erosion.

### Variations in Relative Importance of Functional Subsystems

The relative importance of the above-described subsystems varies greatly between ecosystems. The litter and surface-roots subsystem is rarely well developed in savannas, whereas in forests it varies: In soils with high nutrient status, plants invest less energy in root development than in nutrient-poor systems. Furthermore, the structure and abundance of the epigeic fauna seem to be quite variable. Finally, anecics are extremely variable. For example, anecic earthworms are apparently uncommon except in some parts of the Amazonian forest. Termites also have quite variable communities, mostly undescribed.

The functioning of the rhizosphere is very poorly known. A few studies have been made of spatial and seasonal changes in root biomass in savannas and forests. However, little is yet known about the details of rhizospheres in the tropics.

The zoosphere subsystem is also highly variable: The *drilosphere* (endogeic earthworms) is especially important in humid savannas such as at Lamto (Ivory Coast) or Laguna Verde (Mexico). In moist forest, it is generally much less important: Earthworms have an average biomass that ranges from 300 to 600 kg fresh mass per hectare in humid savannas and generally drops down to about 100 kg fresh mass or less in most tropical forests (Lavelle, 1983a). However, there are some exceptions, such as in the Lacandon forest (Mexico), where the mean annual biomass is 389 kg fresh mass per hectare (Fragoso and Lavelle, in press).

Anecic termites have important and as yet largely unexplained variations. Their relative importance seems to increase in drier areas (Menaut et al., 1985), but the factors that determine their distribution, abundance, and trophic structure on local and regional scales are still poorly understood.

## Heterogeneity and Diversity in Tropical Soil Systems

Natural ecosystems are heterogeneous: Varying environmental conditions create a mosaic of elements whose structure and functioning may vary greatly. Within these structural units, single functions such as, for example, eating and fractionating litter by epigeic invertebrates may be done by a variable number of species: The more numerous they are, the more diverse will be their communities and their resulting activities.

### Catena Effect

Broad soil types (i.e., soil classifications for a large area) often conceal complex distributions at a local scale. Local topography affects drainage, decomposition, mineral leaching, and accumulation. Acting over many thousands of years, these processes can result in major variations from the mean regional soil type, creating successions along toposequences, a phenomenon known as the catena effect (Milne, 1935; Menaut et al., 1985; Van Wambeke, 1978) (Fig. 7). As a consequence, diversity of soils on a landscape scale may

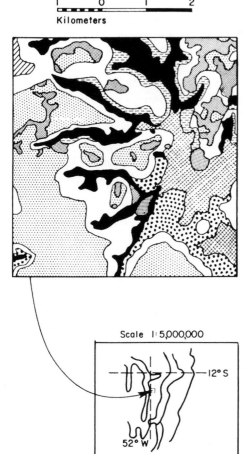

Scale 1:50,000

Kilometers

Scale 1:5,000,000

12° S

52° W

**FIGURE 7.** Apparent uniformity and actual diversity of soils as represented on small- and large-scale soil maps (Van Wambeke, 1978): in an apparently uniform square of 5 × 5 km (below), seven different soil types may be distinguished (above) that correspond to local geological and topographic heterogeneity.

be much greater than the variation observed on a broad geographic scale where only dominant soil types are represented.

### Species Diversity: A Useful Characteristic to Favor Synchrony and Prevent Leakage

Species richness is generally much higher in the tropics than in other parts of the world. More species should result in more ecological functions and a greater functional diversity.

Thus differences in the physical and chemical qualities among leaves from different plant species result in variations in the time of decomposition and subsequent timing of the nutrient release. Diversity in the decomposer organisms increases these timing variations. On the whole, the greater the diversity of plants and decomposers, the more diverse and biologically regulated the timing of nutrient release. Thus, there is less risk in such diverse systems of an imbalance between nutrient production and their utilization by plants and subsequent losses by leaching (Swift and Sanchez, 1984; Swift, 1984).

## PRESSURES ON SOIL RESOURCE

In the year 2000, human population is projected to exceed 6 billion and demand for food to increase by 100% in tropical areas. The need for timber and fuel wood will also increase. More land will be required for cultivation, and more productive cultivation techniques will have to be developed. However, most of the more fertile and easily cultivated soils in the tropics are already in cultivation. Thus, pressures on the forest resource and its soils will increase: New and increasingly marginal land will be deforested and brought into cultivation, and soil may be degraded or lost unless suitable management options are chosen.

### Deforestation: Present Situation of Tropical Forests and Woodlands and Expected Evolution

In 1980, tropical forested areas and woodlands covered an estimated 2970 million hectares, approximately 20% of the total land surface of the earth and approximately 40% of the tropical area. They comprise 1201 million hectares of broad-leaved forest (40%), 734 million hectares of "open" forest (25%), 624 million hectares of bush (20%), 240 million hectares (8%) of fallow within broad-leaved forests, 170 million hectares (6%) of open forests, and a comparatively small area of 11 million hectares occupied by forest plantations (Hadley and Lanley, 1983, and Fig. 8).

The Global Environmental Monitoring System of FAO and UNEP estimated the present annual rate of deforestation at 6.9 million hectares (0.6%) (FAO, 1982). However, this value only includes totally deforested areas and thus does not take into account badly degraded forest created by logging, failures at cultivation, and pasture that reverts to scrub forest. Myers (1983a) gives a quite different figure of about 24.5 million hectares deforested annually (i.e., an area the size of Wales or Massachusetts each month and 46 ha min$^{-1}$!). At this rate, the entire tropical forest biome could disappear in as little as 38 y (Sommer, 1976). Melillo et al. (1985) conclude that the differences between the FAO/UNEP estimates and those of Myers are explained by differences in assumptions and definitions. In particular, Myers only included $7.5 \times 10^6$ ha y$^{-1}$ of closed forest; the rest of his estimate applied to disturbance of fallow forest, which was not included by FAO/UNEP. In some countries, deforestation rates are much higher and some-

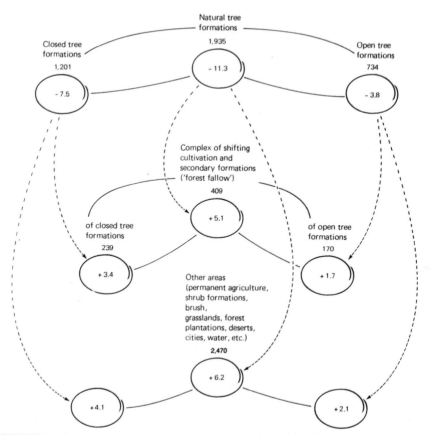

**FIGURE 8.** Arrows show paths of deforestation in the humid tropics. The center ovals represent total forest, whereas closed and open forest are represented by the left and right sides, respectively. Numbers inside the ovals give percentage of deforestation change by 1980 relative to total forest. Numbers above the ovals give the 1980 coverage, in hectares [From Hadley and Lanley, 1983, and earlier in FAO Forestry Paper No. 30, FAO, 1982, with permission of the Food and Agricultural Organization of the United Nations.]

times increasing; Myers (1983b) gives a list of 19 areas in which tropical forests are likely to disappear by 1990 or earlier.

There are large local and regional variations in the importance of the different causes of deforestation as well as considerable differences of emphasis between researchers. Many authors emphasize clearing new land for shifting cultivation: Hadley and Lanley (1983) estimate 70% of deforestation is due to shifting cultivation in Africa, 50% in Asia, and 35% in the Americas. Other causes include commercial exploitation of timber, which would affect $530 \times 10^6$–$870 \times 10^6$ ha $y^{-1}$, fuelwood gathering (of $1100 \times 10^6$ m$^3$ y$^{-1}$ or 8 times the production of industrial timber), and cattle ranching, whose effect is especially important in Latin America (Myers, 1983a; Hecht, 1981; Fearnside, Chapter 4).

Whatever the exact rate of deforestation may be, it "will represent a biological debacle to surpass . . . any other that has ever occurred" and "it will happen in the twinkling of a geologic eye" (Myers, 1983b).

## Soil Losses by Erosion

While forests are cleared for crops and pasture, increasing areas of soils are lost by erosion, generally the result of inadequate management techniques. Little erosion occurs in undisturbed ecosystems. For example, in many savannas and forests of West Africa from 0.05 to 1.2 t ha$^{-1}$ y$^{-1}$ is lost (Roose and Lelong, 1976). In Puerto Rico, values of 0.45–3.0 t ha$^{-1}$ y$^{-1}$ have been reported by Smith and Stamey (1965).

Taking into account the physical properties of a wide range of tropical soils, Lombardi Neto and Bertoni (1975) estimated from 4.2 to 15 t ha$^{-1}$ y$^{-1}$ as the acceptable limits of erosion. However, El-Swaify et al. (1982) argue that limits should be lower, as nutrients and humic reserves tend to be concentrated in the topmost horizons, and slight erosion may seriously deplete nutrients and humic reserves and impair further evolution of soil and vegetation.

Several studies show a dramatic increase of erosion in cultivated soils at regional levels (see Roose and Lelong, 1976). Precise data on present soil losses are scattered; however, some maps already exist that show the current state of erosion and maximum risk of future erosion under conditions of low plant covering and inadequate land shaping (El-Swaify et al., 1982; Jansson, 1982). Pimentel et al. (1976) estimate that mean soil losses in the tropics are 54 t ha$^{-1}$—twice as severe as in the United States. However, this rough estimate of soil loss and more accurate ones at a regional level calculated from the sediment loads of the rivers (Fournier, 1960; Jansson, 1982) include erosion from a wide variety of situations. As stated by the universal soil loss equation (Wischmeier and Smith, 1960),

$$A = R \times K \times L \times S \times C \times P$$

where soil loss $A$ is a function of rainfall erosivity $R$, soil erodibility $K$, the length of the slope $L$, the slope $S$, the vegetative cover $C$, and conservation practices $P$.

Rainfall erosivity $R$ is a particularly important factor in the tropics. An index of rainfall erosivity has been designed by Wischmeier and Smith (1960), and maps showing the distribution of this index have been drawn for some parts of the world (Roose and Lelong, 1976; Dunne and Leopold, 1978; Jansson, 1982). Erosivity index contours for western Africa closely correspond to the rainfall isohyets.

The erodibility $K$ of most tropical soils is not particularly high by temperate or mediterranean standards. Estimates or measurements of the $K$ parameter vary from 0.10 to 0.30 for most soils, as compared with 0.05 to

0.60 for soils of the Great Plains in the United States (Birot et al., 1968; Wischmeier et al., 1971; El-Swaify, et al., 1982; Roose and Lelong, 1976). A larger review including 13 different tropical soils gives values ranging from 0.004 to 0.48 (Jansson, 1982).

Surface runoff and consequent erosion depend on both slope steepness $S$ and length $L$. Where slopes are steep, these terms may become the overriding factors in the equation. In Senegal, Roose (1967) showed that runoff increases from 16.3 to 30% when slope steepens from 1.25 to 2%. The length of the slope determines the volume and velocity of runoff. Kowal (1970) estimated 55 m to be the maximum safe length for a 1.4% slope. However, such an effect of slope length has been questioned (Rattan Lal, commentor on this chapter, personal communication).

After rainfall erosivity, the major erosion factor is vegetative cover $C$. Many studies have shown that changes in vegetation cover resulting from land cultivation drastically affect erosion rates. Roose (1967), for example, found that erosion at Sefa (Senegal), which is as low as 0.1–0.2 t ha$^{-1}$ for natural cover, increases up to 4.9 t ha$^{-1}$ in fallows, to 7.8 t ha$^{-1}$ in cotton fields, and to 10.3 t ha$^{-1}$ in maize and millet fields. Charreau (1974), reviewing different savanna stations from western Africa, estimated soil erosion at 0.03–0.2 t ha$^{-1}$ under natural vegetation, 0.1–99.0 t ha$^{-1}$ in cropped land, and 4–170 t ha$^{-1}$ in bare fallows. Roose (1975) estimated relative erosion rates of different crop systems in percentage of values measured for bare soil: Dense forest or culture with a thick mulch would have a relative rate of 0.1; ungrazed savanna, 1; rice, 10–20; palms, coffee, and cocoa with cover crops, 10–30; cassava (first year), 20–80; groundnuts, 40–80; and maize, sorghum, and millet, 30–90.

In a broad review of 14 papers on tropical erosion, Jansson (1982) found erosion rates of up to 334 t ha$^{-1}$ y$^{-1}$. Erosion in crops may increase from natural systems by factors of from 1.5 to 2500, depending on the slope, the annual rainfall, and the nature of the crop and cultivation techniques and with a mean increase factor of about 7. Hudson (1971) states that erosion hazard is highest in the semiarid tropics because vegetation cover is often inadequate to prevent erosion. In the arid tropics, scarcity of rain makes rainfall erosion unlikely to occur, and in the humid tropics, natural plant production is very high and thus the plant cover gives good protection from erosion (Fig. 9).

Finally, conservation practices $P$ may help prevent soil losses by improving cover $C$, slope $S,L$, and erosivity $K$ (Moldenhauer and Onstad, 1975; Dumsday and Flinn, 1975). The most efficient practices are either control of the land cover or physical manipulation of slope and drainage through means such as terraces, grass strips, contour farming, surface protection by mulches, or conditioners that improve the structure of the surface soil (Greenland and Lal, 1975).

## Conclusions Regarding Soils

Population pressure and the subsequent demands for crop production, timber, and fuelwood lead to rapid deforestation. More fertile and easily cul-

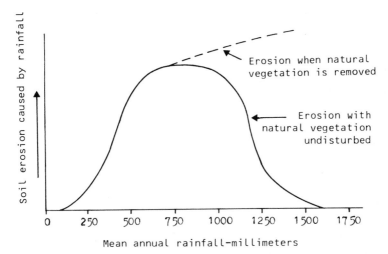

**FIGURE 9.** Changes in soil erosion trends with rainfall amount. (Reprinted from Norman Hudson: *Soil Conservation*, 2nd ed. Copyright © 1971, 1981 by Norman Hudson. Used by permission of Cornell University Press.)

tivated soils are already being utilized in much of the tropics; thus, the soils removed from protection of natural cover and maintenance by natural biological systems are increasingly marginal and fragile. Increasing amount of soils are lost because of poor vegetation and nonconservative cultivation techniques. These soil losses create even more demand for new land and new deforestation. Such a vicious circle has to be broken to prevent the total disappearance of tropical forest, which would have unwelcome effects on climate and hydrological systems, not to speak of the extinction of extraordinarily rich genetic resources (20–40% of the earth's species). Part of this forest (10–20% as suggested by Myers, 1983b) should be rigorously protected as a reserve of special and genetic pools and for scientific research. At present, only 2% is officially preserved. More management options must be found that promote both development for human populations and forest conservation. Improved management in timber exploitation and pasture management are also required to prevent soil losses by erosion and to allow sustained utilization.

## PRINCIPAL MANAGEMENT OPTIONS AND THEIR EFFECTS ON SOIL SYSTEM

Deforestation is largely the result of three human activities: timber exploitation, cultivation with low- or high-input techniques, and pasture conversion. Each of these activities has different implications for deforestation and for possible regrowth of the original forest because they affect differently the physical and chemical properties of the soil and the biological regulation systems.

## Lumbering

The demand of developed countries for tropical wood has increased tremendously in the last decade and is a primary reason for the rapid deforestation, particularly in southeast Asia (Myers, 1983a). Exports have increased from $4 \times 10^6$ m$^3$ in 1950 to $53 \times 10^6$ m$^3$ in 1973 to $66 \times 10^6$ m$^3$ in 1980, and by the year 2000, FAO (1982) estimates they will reach $95 \times 10^6$ m$^3$. Timber exploitation is most often selective; for example, only 50 of Amazonia's 2500 tree species are regularly exploited for timber, though a much larger number are used for charcoal making. Thus, only a few trees are lumbered, but many more are damaged: In Kalimantan (Indonesia), where about 5% of the trees are taken, 41% of the total individuals are damaged (Hadley and Lanley, 1983). This proportion of damaged trees varies between one third and two thirds (Myers, 1983a). In addition, lumbering roads greatly facilitate human colonization and promote erosion. Where forests do not contain easily exploitable timber, clear cutting for paper, charcoal, or fuelwood production is of greater importance.

## Clearing: A Critical Stage

Felling may be done manually or with heavy machinery such as bulldozers. Felled trees may be removed, burned, or left. Many studies (e.g., Sanchez, 1976; Hecht, 1981) have shown that burning is desirable in that it releases nutrients as ash and raises pH, which helps make insoluble the toxic soluble aluminum (Fig. 10).

Burning is normally harmless to soil structure. However, approximately 20% of the nitrogen is volatilized in burning (de las Salas, 1978), and part of the nutrients contained in the ashes may be washed away or leached. Under drought conditions, fire may escape control, and areas much larger than needed may be thus burned. Such uncontrolled fires have recently had dramatic effects in Kalimantan, where about 3.5 million hectares were burned in 4 months. Furthermore, fire adversely affects the seeds of some species and may thus disturb further regeneration (De Foresta et al., 1984; Mori and Prance, Chapter 6).

Mechanical clearing appears, in almost all cases, to be more destructive than manual cutting and burning. Mechanical clearing first results in organic matter exportation and removal of part of the nutrient-rich and biologically active topsoil. Lal et al. (1975; Sanchez, 1979) showed that crop yield decreases by 50% when the top 2.5 cm of soil are removed by erosion. Clearcutting without burning leads to a dysynchrony between nutrient release and their use by plants. The decomposition of low-quality organic matter (wood, roots) may immobilize nitrogen and phosphorous and thus decrease the

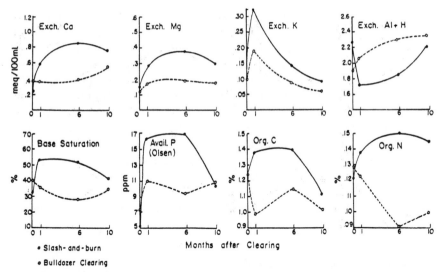

**FIGURE 10.** Changes in top soil nutrients and organic matter after clearing by two methods (Seubert et al., 1977, in Sanchez, 1979). All the nutrients and organic carbon are seen to stay at higher levels with slash-and-burn than with bulldozer clearing, whereas the harmful aluminum plus hydrogen ion content is less.

leaching hazard (Swift, 1984). Heavy machinery also tends to cause compaction, which may diminish infiltration rates by 8–38 times (Sanchez, 1979).

## Shifting Cultivation

Shifting cultivation, preceded or not by timber exploitation, is blamed for from 30 to 70% of the global deforestation. Data problems and questions of interpretation leave such statements open to question. In 1960, the area of tropical soils under shifting cultivation was estimated at $36 \times 10^6$ km$^2$, that is, 30% of the world's soils (Nye and Greenland, 1960). Soil fertility rapidly declines after the nutrient pulse from burning has passed through the system. Cropping may be abandoned because of weed proliferation as much as the decrease of fertility. In any case, the productive phase for annual crops rarely exceeds 2–4 y (Sanchez, 1979). However, in more complex systems, useful perennials may be planted or encouraged in the swidden plot, thus extending its productive phase by at least a decade (cf. Denevan et al., 1984).

After cultivation, the fallow period may last 10–16 (or many more) years until original soil is restored. A new succession of plant species takes hold that includes first pioneer and then progressively more closed forest species. The increase of plant diversity stops losses by restoring the synchrony between nutrient release and nutrient utilization. Nutrient exportation and leaching stop, and organic carbon and nitrogen gradually accumulate in the soil until they reach their former equilibrium.

Shifting cultivation is an ancient and very diverse system of forest exploitation. In present forms, it includes everything from traditional systems of exploitation based on very old cultural, sociological, and economic bases, to systems recently evolved to utilize the growing expanse of *Imperata* grasslands, to landless peasants who may or may not be equipped to take on the forest. It is facilitated by the absence of property titles. Traditional shifting cultivators have been observed to have a good knowledge of soils and forest ecology that has made shifting cultivation a relatively efficient and sustainable system (Gouron, 1952; Nye and Greenland, 1960; Greenland, 1975; Lal, 1974). Pests, diseases, and weed problems are well controlled by these practices (Ofori, 1974). However, many consider shifting cultivation unsuitable because of its relatively low productivity. Also, when demographic pressures shorten the fallow period or cultural practices are not ecologically sound, it may degrade the soil.

## Continuous Sustained Production

The forms of continuous production are crop rotation systems with restorative fallow crops, agroforestry, alley cropping, no-till farming, intensive crop production using fertilizers, and pastures.

Experimental studies have demonstrated that soil stability can be maintained under reduced fallow if fallow crops are planted instead of permitting the plot to revert to natural vegetation. These crops may be composite shrubs such as *Chromolaena odorata*, whose introduction can shorten the fallow period from 7–15 y to only 3 y in the Philippines (Sajise and Cuevas, 1984). Similarly, the use of *Pueraria phaseolides* (kudzu), a nitrogen-fixing creeper in managed fallows, may have in 1–2 y the same restorative effect as 25 y of natural fallow (Sanchez et al., 1982). More generally, many nitrogen-fixing nodulated legumes have similar properties, such as *Sesbania cannabina*, which may fix up to 524 kg $N_2$ per hectare per crop (Gibson et al., 1982).

Agroforestry is a general term for cultivation systems in which trees, crops, and living stock are associated. Such systems may provide crop products, fuelwood, and livestock. At the same time, interactions among the different components have a conservative effect on soil physical and chemical fertility. The deleterious effect of crops on soil fertility may be balanced by microclimatic modification and nutrient and organic matter inputs from the trees. In such systems, soil carbon content may reach an equilibrium in which losses under crops are balanced by gains under forest while the soil carbon stock is held at a stable, though lower, level (Fig. 11) (Young, 1984). There is a great variety of such systems, including traditional "home gardens" and coffee or cocoa plantations.

Continuous crop production may be achieved by the careful use of fertilizers. Successful experiments were realized at Yurimaguas (Peru) on ultisols (Sanchez et al., 1982a) (Fig. 12). Under the conditions of complete fertilization that were established after 3 y, crop production was high and the total system beneficial. However, such cropping systems require regular monitoring of soil chemistry and response to deficiencies as they appear. Fertilizers may be replaced in part by kudzu as mulch or green manure, thereby reducing costs. Such experiments suggest that even in poor oxisols continuous cropping is feasible provided that fertilization is correctly conducted. However, economic and sociological factors tend to make correct fertilization the exception rather than the rule in most of the poor soils of the tropics.

Low-input continuous production may be feasible on favorable soils by intercropping practices using legumes as a mulch or green manure or by alley cropping. Combined cropping of cassava, corn, soybeans, and peanuts has been shown to produce 30% more yield per year than equivalent monocultures. On the other hand, the adequate use of kudzu mulch may lead to yields that are 80–90% of the yields obtained by heavy fertilization (Wade, 1978).

### Cattle Raising

Transformation of forest to pastures in order to produce cheap beef is apparently the main factor of deforestation in Latin America. Myers (1983a) estimates that 20,000 km$^2$ y$^{-1}$ of forests are thus cleared, and in the Brazilian Amazon region alone, well over 100,000 km$^2$ of forest were cleared for pas-

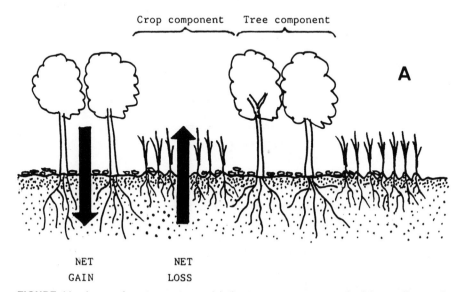

**FIGURE 11.** In agroforestry systems, (a) the tree component replenishes soil organic matter destroyed by the crop component. In such a system, (b) soil carbon is initially lost but eventually equilibrates at lower values. [From Young (1984), redrafted with permission of A. Young.]

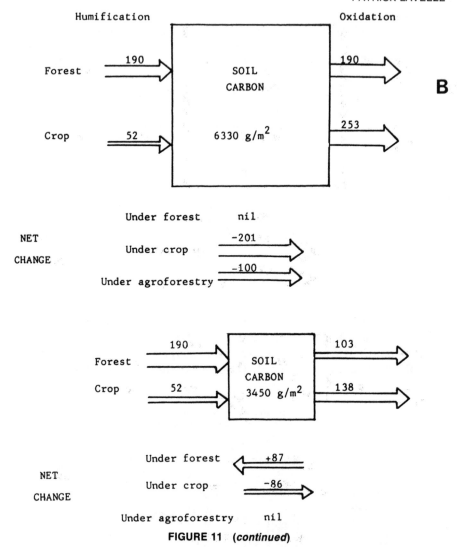

FIGURE 11  (*continued*)

ture between 1966 and 1983. This practice, which is supported by very important economic and political lobbies, has led to the deforestation of nearly one third of Costa Rica, where tropical forests might disappear totally by 1990.

Pasture establishment entails total removal of forest cover. Sustainability and productivity (i.e., livestock carrying capacity) are complex and controversial topics. LANDSAT-based estimates for areas indicate that in 1975–1976 44% of pastures were degraded at Barra de Carcas and Luciara, Mato Grosso, and in 1977–1978, 54% were degraded in Paragominas, Pará (Fearnside, 1986, Table 1–4). As much of the pasture observed at these sites was

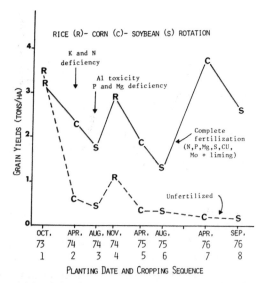

**FIGURE 12.** Crop yields of the rice–corn–soybean system after clearing in Yurimaguas (Peru) (Sanchez et al., 1982a). The unfertilized plots (dashed line) gave low and declining yields after 1 y. The plots fertilized in response to observed deficiencies (solid line) gave high and sustainable yields.

newly created, these estimates probably understate fractions of pasture that will become degraded.

Changes in soil properties over a decade or more under conversion from forest to pasture have been studied in Amazonia by Serrao et al. (1979), Falesi (1976), and Hecht (1981). Data are generally noisy and are open to varying interpretations. However, most sources agree that phosphorus decline is critical and may be exacerbated by overstocking, soil compaction, erosion, and declines in other nutrients. Soil nutrient levels under pasture seem to be similarly low to those in forest, but the store of nutrients held in the forest vegetation is much greater than that in pasture vegetation.

Limited efforts are being undertaken to reclaim such degraded pastures (Schubart, 1977; Sanchez, 1979). Sanchez (1979) asserts that the degradation of these pastures is easy to prevent by clearing the regrowth and fertilizing with phosphorus. Complementary management options such as introduction of legume species (*Stylosanthes capitata, P. phaseoloides*, etc.) may increase the forage value and retard soil degradation. Sanchez (1979) reports that the continuous use of fertilizers on mixed grass–legume pastures led to production of 149 kg ha$^{-1}$ y$^{-1}$ with a carrying capacity of 2.1 animals per hectare. On the other hand, Fearnside (1979) calculates a short-term (3–7 y) feeding capacity for pasture on the Transamazon Highway in the range of 0.19–0.32 head per hectare, given the prevailing management practices, and notes that lower stocking rates would have to be used to prevent degradation over the longer term.

A further problem with conversion of forest to pasture is drastic regression of land tenure and social dynamics, as emphasized in "La Deforestacion" (Anonymous, 1985).

## CONCLUSIONS AND PERSPECTIVES

The soil system in the humid tropics is characterized by great diversity of the biological components and a very strict biological regulation. Species diversity, generally considered as a key factor of ecosystem stability and resilience, favors the multiplication of ecological functions and their spreading over time and space.

Microflora–invertebrate and microflora–root interaction systems ensure at every moment the necessary match between the chemical conditions of each soil microsite and the plant needs for nutrients, while conserving the soil structure. The activity of these systems is regulated by physical factors of the environment, such as soil moisture and temperature, and by chemical factors such as nutrients and assimilable carbon concentration (see Lavelle and Meyer, 1983). According to prevailing conditions, the activity of these interactive systems varies in intensity, and their resulting effects can be qualitatively and quantitatively different. Thus, the needed function may always be performed at the right place, at the right time, and with the right intensity thanks to the flexibility of the biological activities.

Plant production in the tropics is the highest of the biosphere; tropical rain forests produce, on the average, half again as much as do temperate forests, despite frequent low fertility of their soils. Jordan (1983) notes that foliage production is remarkably high, whereas wood production is comparable to that of temperate forests. Vegetation cover and root systems are well developed, and thus erosion hazard is lowest despite the outstanding erosivity of rains and erodibility of some of the soils.

Water retention capacity and infiltration rates maintained by biological activities are such that much of the rainfall infiltrates the soil and is taken by roots and evapotranspired, maintaining a permanently wet climate. As much as 50% of rainfall in tropical rain forests originates from local water cycling (Salati et al., 1978).

The only nearly nondegrading exploitation system is gathering of forest products, but such systems do not provide a reasonably high or stable standard of living. In Mexico, some forest products such as *chicle*, the natural chewing gum, or *barbasco*, which was for many years utilized to make contraceptive products, have given rise to local economic development, though limited (Diechtl, 1980). Large areas of undisturbed forest should be preserved so that still unknown resources represented by hundreds of thousands of plant and animal species will be available to future generations.

Some forms of shifting cultivation are sustainable provided that demographic pressure does not reduce the fallow period to below regeneration time. Inadequate duration of fallow commonly reduces soil fertility, and degradation of soils may be even more rapid when new colonizers who have no idea of the local ecological conditions start cultivating new forest land. Moran (1977) observed that indigenous cultivators along the Transamazon Highway chose the better soils than did new settlers and grew more adapted crops.

Extensive timber exploitation is somewhat comparable to shifting cultivation since its impact depends on its intensity and the time allowed for restoration before new trees are felled. However, clearings are typically larger, and hence microclimatic alteration is more severe, and there is a very strong tendency in many parts of the world for logging to be followed by spontaneous settlement, which prevents forest regrowth.

On the other extreme, sustained high-input cultivation and cattle raising are technically feasible even in the poorest soils. However, they require both technological and financial means. The existing economics and transport infrastructure do not always allow high inputs, and more often than not, what is achieved fails disasterously short of the technically possible. This shows up, for example, in the large and rapidly growing amount of degraded pasture in Amazonia (Hecht, 1981; Fearnside, 1980). Moreover, the economic failure of Ludwig's Jari project demonstrates that even high technology and adequate financing do not guarantee success in forest utilization schemes (Fearnside and Rankin, 1982). Some cases of severe degradation by uncontrolled use of heavy machines have also been reported.

New alternatives must be found to these two major options with a limited future; for example, improving the traditional land use to allow low-input continuous cropping systems. This practice may be facilitated with limited use of fertilizers. More promising, however, are methods that maintain or increase the fertility of tropical soils by conserving, improving, and even manipulating the biological processes.

The effect of management practices on soil has been evaluated in the past only in terms of crop production, nutrient content, and soil losses. Nothing is yet known about changes occurring in the biological regulation systems, which are clearly of dominant importance in natural ecosystems. A knowledge of how such systems change under modified conditions will help determine alternative management options that can preserve the necessary synchrony between nutrient release and uptake and can improve the biological mechanisms of the soil structure conservation.

For example, the drilosphere (earthworm) subsystem is much more limited in forests than in savannas. After deforestation, soil microclimatic conditions are of savanna type, and most of the already limited earthworm populations will disappear. Introducing adaptable species of earthworms into these new savannalike areas would have a very positive effect on soil and nutrient conservation.

Among other manipulations that would be of interest are the activation of nitrogen fixation by introducing nitrogen-fixing plants and inoculating

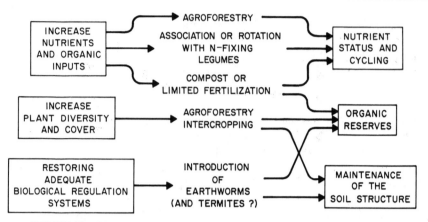

**FIGURE 13.** Biological bases for low-input continuous cropping systems.

them with selected strains of nitrogen-fixing bacteria. A collaborative program of research is now being developed by the International Union of Biological Sciences and the Man and Biosphere (IUBS/MAB) UNESCO Program to promote international research on these topics (tropical soil fertility and biological processes) (Swift, 1984; 1985).

The significance of species diversity and its connection with ecosystem functioning and conservation problems is the central theme of another international ecological program for the same "Decade of the Tropics" IUBS/MAB general program (Solbrig and Golley, 1983; Maury-Lechon et al., 1984).

Thus, ecological foundations for a better management of humid tropical soils are expected to be available in the near future. A more complete knowledge of the structure and functioning of the main subsystems under natural and managed field conditions will help the design of efficient continuous-cropping systems that combine old wisdom with some of the more advanced ecological results (Fig. 13).

It will then be necessary to transfer such new techniques to the small farmers. The success of this transfer will require sensitivity to sociological, political, and economic aspects of land use and a general improvement in the currently low, though rapidly increasing, educational level of many countries. Agricultural technicians will be needed in the villages to transfer the knowledge and accelerate the introduction of progressively improved management options. Financial support will also be essential. These approaches may be the only way to win the race against deforestation and soil losses by erosion.

## REFERENCES

Abbadie, L., 1983. Contribution à l'étude de la production primaire et du cycle de l'azote dans les savanes de Lamto (Côte d'Ivoire), *Trav. Cherch. Lamto (RCI)* **1**, 1–136.

Aina, P. O. 1984. Contribution of earthworms to porosity and water infiltration in a tropical soil under forest and long-term cultivation, *Pedobiologia* **26**, 131–136.

Alvim, P. de T., 1978. Perspectives de produçao agricola na regiao amazonica. *Interciência* **3**(4), 243–251.

Anonymous, 1985. La deforestacion: Los costos sociales. *Cult. Survi.* **6**, 4–9.

Athias, F., 1974. Les conditions microclimatiques dans le sol, *Bull. Liaison Cher. Lamto*, **5**, 5–27.

Athias, F., Josens, G., and Lavelle, P., 1975. Traits généraux du peuplement endogé de la savane de Lamto (Côte d'Ivoire), in *Progress in Soil Zoology*, Academia, Prague.

Barois, I., 1982. Interrelations entre *Pontoscolex corethrurus* (Oligochète), la microflore et la matière organique d'un vertisol du Mexique. Laguna Verde, Vera Cruz. DEA, Univ. P. et M. Curie.

Barois, I. and Lavelle, P., 1986. Mutualistic digestion systems between geophagous earthworms (*Pontoscolex corethrurus*), Glossoscolecidae), and microorganisms in soils of the humid tropics, *Soil. Biol. Biochem.*, in press.

Bartholomew, M. V., Meyer, J., and Laudelout, H., 1953. Mineral nutrient immobilization under forest and grass fallow, INEAC publications, series 1–27.

Beck, L., 1971. Bodenzoologische gliederung und Charakterisierung des amazonischen Regenwaldes, *Amazoniana* **3**(1), 69–132.

Bernhard-Reversat, F., Huttel, C., and Lemee, G., 1979. Structure et fonctionnement des écosystèmes de la forêt pluvieuse sempervirente de la Côte d'Ivoire, *Rech. Res. Nat.* **14**, 605–625, UNESCO: Paris.

Birot, Y., Galabert, J., Roose, E., and Arrivets, J., 1968. Deuxième campagne sur la station de mesure de l'érosion de Gampela, CTFT report, Paris.

Bouché, M. B., 1971. Relations entre les structures spatiales et fonctionelles des écosystèmes, illustrées par le rôle pédobiologique des vers de terre, in P. Pesson, Ed., *La Vie dans les Sols, Aspects Nouveaux, Etudes Expérimentales*, Gauthier-Villars, Paris.

Cesar, J., 1971. Etude quantitative de la strate herbacée de la savane de Lamto (Moyenne Côte d'Ivoire), Thèse 3e cycle, University of Paris, Paris, France.

Chaboud, A. and Rougier, M., 1981. Sécrétions racinaires mucilagineuses et rôle dans la rhizosphère, *Ann. Biol.* **20**, 313–323.

Charreau, C., 1974. *Soils of Tropical Dry and Dry-Wet Climatic Areas and Their Use and Management*, Cornell University, Department of Agronomy, Mimeo 74-26.

Collins, N. M., 1980. The distribution of soil macrofauna on the west ridge of Gunung Mulu. Sarawak, *Oecologia*, **44**, 263–275.

Darici, C., 1978. Effet du type d'argile sur quelques activités microbiennes dans divers sols tropicaux. Comparaison d'un sol à allophanes, d'un vertisol à montmorillonite et d'un sol ferrugineux tropical à illite et kaolinite, Thèse 3d cycle, University of Paris, Paris, France.

DeForesta, H., Charles-Dominique, P., Erard, C., and Prevost, M. F., 1984. Zoochorie et premiers stades de la régénération naturelle aprés coupe en forêt guyanaise, *La Terre et la Vie* **39**(4), 369–400.

Denevan, W. M., Treacy, J. M., Alcorn, J. R., Padoch, J. D., and Paitán, S. F.,

1984. Indigenous agroforestry in the Peruvian Amazon: Boro Indian management of swidden fallows, *Interciência* **9**, 346–357.

Devineau, J. L., 1976. Données préliminaires sur la litière et la chute des feuilles dans quelques formations forestières semi-décidues de moyenne Côte d'Ivoire, *Oecol. Plant.* **11**(4), 375–395.

Diechtl, S., 1980. *El Barbasco Mexicano: Condiciones y Perspectivas para su Aprovechamiento*, INIF, Publication No. 24, Mescico.

Duchaufour, Ph., 1979. *Pédologie*, Vol. 1, *Pédogénèse et Classification*, Masson, Paris.

Dumsday, R. G. and Flinn, J. C., 1975. Evaluating systems of soil conservation through bioeconomic modelling. In D. J. Greenland and R. Lal, Eds., *Soil Conservation and Management in the Humid Tropics*, Wiley, New York.

Dunne, T. and Leopold, L. B., 1978. *Water in Environmental Planning*, Freeman, San Francisco, CA.

El-Swaify, S. A., Dangler, E. W., and Armstrong, C. L., 1982. *Soil Erosion by Water in the Tropics*, University of Hawaii Research Extension Series 024 Honolulu.

Falesi, I., 1976. *Ecossistema de Pastagem Cultivada na Amazonia Brasiliera*, Technical Bulletin No. 1 EMBRAPA CPATU, Belém, Brazil.

FAO, 1981. *Agriculture: Horizon 2000*, Vol. 23, *Développement Economique et Social*, FAO, Rome.

FAO, 1982. *Tropical Forest Resources*, Forestry Paper No. 30, FAO, Rome.

Fearnside, P. M., 1979. Cattle yield prediction for the Transamazon Highway of Brazil, *Interciência* **4**, 220–225.

Fearnside, P. M., 1980. The effect of cattle pasture on soil fertility in the Brazilian Amazon: Consequences for beef production sustainability, *Trop. Ecol.* **21**, 125–137.

Fearnside, P. M., 1986. *Human Carrying Capacity of the Brazilian Rainforest*, Columbia University Press, New York.

Fearnside, P. M. and Rankin, J. M., 1982. The new Jari: Risks and prospects of a major Amazonian development, *Interciência* **7**, 329–339.

Fittkau, J. and Klinge, M., 1975. On biomass and trophic structure of the central Amazonian rain forest ecosystem, *Biotropica* **5**(1), 2–14.

Fournier, A., 1982. Cycle saisonnier de la biomasse herbacée dans les savanes de Ouango-Fitini (Côte d'Ivoire), *Ann. Univ. Abidjan*, **15**, 64–94.

Fournier, M. F., 1960. *Climat et Erosion*, Presses Universitaires de France, Paris.

Fragoso, C. and Lavelle, P., in press. *The Earthworm Community of a Tropical Rainforest from Mexico (Chajul, Chiapas), International Symposium on Earthworms, Bologna, Italy, March 1985. Boll. Zool.*

Gibson, A. H., Dreyfus, B. L., and Dommergues, Y. R., 1982. Nitrogen fixation by legumes in the tropics, in Y. R. Dommergues and H. G. Diem, Eds., *Microbiology of Tropical Soils and Plant Productivity*, Junk, The Hague, Netherlands.

Golley, F. B., 1983. Nutrient cycling and nutrient conservation, in F. B. Golley, Ed., *Ecosystems of the World*, Vol. 14, *Tropical Rain Forest Ecosystems*, Elsevier, Amsterdam.

Golley, F. B., McGinnis, J. T., Clements, R. G., Child, G. I., and Duever, M. J.,

1975. *Mineral Cycling in a Tropical Moist Forest Ecosystem*, University of Georgia Press, Athens, GA.

Goodland, R., 1971. The cerrado oxisols of the Triangulo Mineiro, central Brazil, *Ann. Acad. Bras. Cienc.* **43**, 407–414.

Gouron, P., 1952. Referenced in Nye, P. H. and Greenland, D. J., 1960. *The Soil under Shifting Cultivation*.

Greenland, D. J., 1975. Bringing the green revolution to the shifting cultivator, *Science* **190**, 841–844.

Greenland, D. J. and Lal, R., Eds., 1975. *Soil Conservation and Management in the Humid Tropics*, Wiley, New York.

Hadley, M. and Lanly, J. P., 1983. Ecosystèmes des forêts tropicales: Différences et similitudes, *Nat. Res.* **19**, 1–19.

Hecht, S. B., 1981. Deforestation in the Amazon Basin: Magnitude, dynamics and soil resource effects, in V. H. Sutlive, N. Altshuler, and M. Zamora, Eds., *Where Have All the Flowers Gone? Deforestation in the Third World*, Studies in Third World Societies Publication 13, College of William and Mary, Department of Anthropology, Williamsburg, VA.

Herrera, R. A., 1979. Nutrient distribution and cycling in an Amazon Caatinga forest on spodosols in southern Venezuela, Thesis, University of Reading, England.

Herrera, R. A., Jordan, C. F., Klinge, H., and Medina, E., 1978. Amazon ecosystems: Their structure and functioning with particular emphasis on nutrients. *Interciência* **3**, 233–230.

Hudson, N. W., 1971. *Soil Conservation*, Cornell University Press, Ithaca, NY.

Hurault, J., 1971. The erodibility of overgrazed soils in the Adamama high plateaux, *Bull. Ass. Fr. Etude Sol* **1**, 23–56.

Jansson, M. B., 1982. *Land Erosion by Water in Different Climates*, UNGI Report No. 57, Department of Physical Geography, Uppsala University, Uppsala, Sweden.

Jenny, H., Gessel, S. P., and Bingham, F. T., 1949. Comparative study of decomposition rates of organic matter in temperate and tropical regions, *Soil Sci.* **68**, 419–432.

Jones, M. J. and Wild, A., 1975. *Soils of the West African Savannas, C.A.B. Techn. Commun.* **55**, 1–146.

Jordan, C. F., 1983. Productivity of tropical rain forest ecosystems and the implications for their use as future wood and energy sources, in F. B. Golley, Ed., *Ecosystems of the World,* Vol. 14A, *Tropical Rainforest Ecosystems: Structure and Function*, Elsevier, Amsterdam.

Jordan, C. F., Kline, J. R., and Sasscer, D. S., 1972. Relative stability of mineral cycles in forest ecosystems. *Amer. Nat.* **106**(948), 237–253.

Josens, G., 1983. The soil fauna of tropical savannas. III. The termites, in F. Bourliere, Ed., *Ecosystems of the World*, Vol. 13, *Tropical Savannas,* Elsevier, Amsterdam.

Kaiser, P., 1983. The role of microorganisms in savanna ecosystems, in F. Bourliere, Ed., *Ecosystems of the World*, Vol. 13, *Tropical Savannas,* Elsevier, Amsterdam.

Kowal, J. M., 1970. The hydrology of a small catchment basin at Samaru, Nigeria. I–IV. *Niger. Agric. J.* **7**, 27–147.

Kowal, J. M. and Kassam, A. H., 1978. *Agricultural Ecology of Savanna: A Study of West Africa*, Clarendon, Oxford, England.

Lal, R., 1974, Soil erosion and shifting cultivation, Shifting cultivation and soil conservation in Africa, *FAO Soils Bull.* **24**, 48–72.

Lal, R., Kang, B. T., Moorman, F. R., Juo, A. S. R., and Moomaw, J. C., 1975. Problemas de manejo de suelos y posibles soluciones en Nigeria Occidental, in E. Bornemisza and A. Alvarado, Eds., *Manejo de Suelos en America Tropical*, North Carolina State University, Raleigh, NC.

Lasebikan, A., 1982. Soil microarthropods in savanna ecosystems, in W. Sanford et al., eds., *Nigerian Savannas*, MAB-UNESCO, Paris.

Laudelout, H. and Meyer, J., 1954. Les cycles d'éléments minéraux et de matière organique en forêt équatoriale congolaise, *Trans. Fifth Int. Congr. Soil Sci.* **2**, 267–272.

Lavelle, P., 1978. Les vers de terre de la savane de Lamto (Côte d'Ivoire): Peuplements, populations et fonctions dans l'écosystème, *Publ. Lab. Zool. ENS* **12**, 1–301.

Lavelle, P., 1981. Stratégies reproductives chez les vers de terre, *Acta Oecol. Oecol. Gener.* **2**, 117–133.

Lavelle, P., 1983. The soil fauna of tropical savannas. II. The earthworms, in F. Bourliere, Ed., *Tropical Savannas*, Elsevier, Amsterdam.

Lavelle, P., 1984. The soil system in the humid tropics, *Biol. Int.* **9**, 2–17.

Lavelle, P. and Kohlmann, B., 1984. Etude quantitative de la macrofaune du sol dans une forêt tropicale mexicaine (Bonampak, Chiapas), *Pedobiologia* **27**, 377–393.

Lavelle, P. and Meyer, J. A., 1983. Allez-les-Vers, a simulation model of dynamics and effect on soil of populations of *Millsonia anomala* (Oligochaeta, Megascolecidae), in P. Lebrun et al., Eds., *New Trends in Soil Biology*, Dieu Brichart, Louvain-la-Neuve, France.

Lavelle, P., Kanyonyo, J., and Rangel, P., 1983. Intestinal mucus production by two species of tropical earthworms: *Millsonia Lamtoiana* (Megascolecidae) and *Pontoscolex corethrurus* (Glossoscolecidae), in P. Lebrun et al., eds., *New Trends in Soil Biology*, Dieu-Brichart, Louvain-la-Neuve, France.

Lavelle, P., Maury, M. E., and Serrano, V., 1981. Estudio cuantitativo de la fauna del suelo en la region de Lagune Verde, Vera Cruz, Epoca de Iluvias, *Inst. Ecol. Publ.* **6**, 75–105.

Lavelle, P., Sow, B., and Schaefer, R., 1980. The geophagous earthworms community in the Lamto savanna (Ivory Coast): Niche partitioning and utilization of soil nutritive resources, in D. Dindal, Ed., *Soil Biology as Related to Land Use Practices*, EPA, Washington, DC.

Lavelle, P., Zaidi, Z., and Schaefer, R., 1983. Interactions between earthworms, soil organic matter and microflora in an African savanna soil, in P. Lebrun et al., Eds., *New Trends in Soil Biology*, Dieu-Brichart, Louvain-la-Neuve, France.

Lecordier, C., 1974. Le climat de la région de Lamto. *Publ. Labo. Zool. E.N.S., No. Spécial Lamto* **II**, 45–104.

Lee, K. E. and Wood, T. G., 1971, Physical and chemical effects on soils of some Australian termites and their pedological significance, *Pedobiologia* **11**, 376–409.

Lelong, F., and Souchier, B., 1979. Méthodes d'identification et de quantification des constituants, in M. Bonneau and B. Souchier, Eds., *Pédologie,* Vol. 2, *Constituants et Propriétés du Sol,* Masson, Paris.

Lepage, M., 1981. L'impact des populations récoltantes de *Macrotermes michaelseni* (Sjostedt) (Isoptera, Macrotermitinae) dans un écosystème semi-aride (Kajiado-Kenya). I. L'activité de récolte et son déterminisme, *Ins. Soc.* **28**, 297–308.

Lombardi Neto, F. and Bertoni, J., 1975. Tolerancia de perdas de terra para solas do Estado de Sao Paulo, *Bol. Tec. Inst. Agron.* **28**, 1–12.

Madge, D. S., 1969. Field and laboratory studies on the activities of two species of tropical earthworms, *Pedobiologia,* **9**, 188–214.

Maury-Lechon, G., Hadley, M., and Younes, T., Eds., 1984. The significance of species diversity in tropical forest ecosystems, *Biol. Int.* **6**(special issue), 1–74.

Medina, E., Herrera, R., Jordan, C., and Klinge, H., 1977. Man and the Amazon rain forest, *Nat. Resourc.* **13**(3), 4–6.

Melillo, J. M., Palm, C. A., Houghton, R. A., Woodwell, G. M., and Myers, N., 1985. A comparison of two recent estimates of disturbances in tropical forests, *Environ. Cons.* **12**, 37–40.

Menaut, J. C., Barbault, R., Lavelle, P., and Lepage, M., 1985. African savannas: Biological systems of humidification and mineralization, in J. C. Tothill and J. J. Mott, Eds., *Management of the World Savannas*, Australian Academy of Sciences, Canberra.

Milne, G., 1935. Some suggested units of classification and mapping, particularly for east African soils, *Soil Res.* **4**, 183–189.

Moldenhauer, W. C. and Onstad, C. A., 1975. Engineering practices to control erosion, in D. J. Greenland and R. Lal, Eds., *Soil Conservation and Management in the Humid Tropics*, Wiley, New York.

Moran, F. F., 1977. Estrategias de sobrevivência: O uso de recursos ao longo da rodovia Transamazônica, *Acta Amazôn.* **7**, 363–379.

Muller, D. and Nielsen, J., 1965. Production brute, pertes par respiration et production nette dans la forêt ombrophile tropicale, *Det Forst. Forss. Danmark* **29**, 69–160.

Myers, N., 1983a. Conversion rates in tropical moist forests, in F. B. Golley, Ed., *Ecosystems of the World,* Vol. 14A, *Tropical Rain Forest Ecosystems: Structure and Function*, Elsevier, Amsterdam, pp. 289–299.

Myers, N., 1983b. Conservation of rain forests for scientific research, for wildlife conservation, and for recreation and tourism, in F. B. Golley, Ed., *Ecosystems of the World,* Vol. 14A, *Tropical Rain Forest Ecosystems: Structure and Function*, Elsevier, Amsterdam.

Nye, P. H., 1955. Soil forming processes in the humid tropics. IV. The action of the soil fauna, *J. Soil Sci.* **6**, 51–83.

Nye, P. H., 1961. Organic matter and nutrient cycle under moist tropical forest, *Plant and Soil* **13**, 333–346.

Nye, P. H. and Greenland, D. J., 1960. The soil under shifting cultivation, *Commonwealth Agricultural Bureau Tech. Comm.* **51**, 1–156.

Oades, J. M., 1978. Mucilages at the root surface, *J. Soil Sci.* **29**, 1–16.

Odum, H. T. and Pigeon, R. F., 1970. *A Tropical Study of Irradiation and Ecology at El Verde*, U.S. Atomic Energy Commission, Washington, DC.

Ofori, C. S., 1974. Shifting cultivation: Reasons underlying its practice, *FAO Soils Bull.* **24**, 14–20.

Ohiagu, C. E., 1982. Grass- and deadwood-feeding termites in Nigerian savanna: A review, in W. S. Sanford, H. M. Yesufu, and J. S. O. Ayeni, Eds., *Nigerian Savanna*, MAB-UNESCO, Paris.

Ohiagu, C. E. and Wood, T. G., 1979. Grass production and decomposition in Southern Guinea savanna, Nigeria, *Oecologia* **40**, 155–165.

Pimentel, D., Terhune, E. C., Dyson-Hudson, R., Rochereau, S., Samis, R., Smith, E. A., Denman, D., Reifschneider, D., and Shepard, M., 1976. Land degradation effects on food and energy resources, *Science* **194**, 149–155.

Puig, H., 1979. Production de litière en forêt guyanaise, *Bull. Soc. Hist. Nat. Toulouse* **115**, 338–346.

Roose, E. J., 1967. Dix années de mesure de l'érosion et du ruissellement au Sénégal, *Agron. Trop.* **22**, 123–152.

Roose, 1975. Application of the universal soil loss equation of Wischmeier and Smith in West Africa, in D. J. Greenland and R. Lal, Eds., *Soil Conservation and Management in the Humid Tropics*, Wiley, New York.

Roose, E. J. and Lelong, F., 1976. Les facteurs de l'érosion hydrique en Afrique tropicale. Etudes sur petites parcelles expérimentales de sol, *Rev. Geogr. Phys. Geol. Dyn.* **4**, 365–374.

Roose, E. J., Fauck, R., Lelong, R., and Pedro, G., 1981. Modifications fondamentales de la dynamique actuelle de sols ferrallitiques et ferrugineux d'Afrique occidentale sous l'influence de la mise en culture, *C.R. Acad. Sci. Paris II* **292**, 1457–1460.

Rovira, A. D., 1969. Plant root exudates, *Bot. Rev.* **35**, 35–57.

Sajise, P. E. and Cuevas, V. C., 1984. Some soil biological processes in traditional agriculture, MAG/IUBS Workshop on Soil Biological Processes in Tropical Ecosystems, Lancaster, England.

Salas, G. de las, 1978. El sistema forestal Carare-Opon, *Conif. Ser. Tec.* **8**, 1–25.

Salati, E., Marques, J., and Molion, L. C. B., 1978. Origem e distribuicao das chuvas na Amazonica, *Interciência* **3**, 200–205.

Sanchez, P. A., 1976. *Properties and Management of Soils in the Tropics*, Wiley, New York.

Sanchez, P. A., 1979. Soil fertility and conservation considerations for agroforestry systems in the humid tropics of Latin America, in H. O. Mongi and P. A. Huxley, Eds. *Soils Research in Agroforestry*, ICRAF, Nairobi, Kenya.

Sanchez, P. A. and Salinas, J. G., 1983. Low input technology for managing oxisols and ultisols in tropical America, *Adv. Agron.* **34**, 279–405.

Sanchez, P. A., Bandy, D. E., Villachica, J. H., and Nicholaides, J. J., 1982a. Amazon basin soils: Management for continuous crop production, *Science* **16**, 821–827.

Sanchez, P. A., Gichuru, M. P., and Katz, L. B., 1982b. Organic matter in major soils of the tropical and temperate regions, *Proc. 12th Int. Congr. Soil Sci., New Delhi.*

Schlesinger, W. H., 1977. Carbon balance in terrestrial detritus, *Ann. Rev. Ecol. Syst.* **8**, 51–58.

Schubart, H., 1977. Criterios ecologicos para o desenvolvemento agricola das terras firmes da Amazônia, *Acta Amazôn.* **7**, 559–567.

Serrao, E. A. S., Falesi, L. C., Vaiga, J. B., and Texeira, J. F., 1979. Productivity of cultivated pastures in low fertility soils of the Amazon of Brazil, in P. A. Sanchez and L. E. Tergas, Eds., *Pasture Production in Acid Soils of the Tropics,* Centro Internacional de Agricultura Tropical, Cali, Colombia.

Seubert, C. E., Sanchez, P. A., and Valverde, C., 1977. Effects of land clearing methods on soil properties and crop performances in an ultisol of the Amazon jungle of Peru, *Trop. Agric. (Trin.)* **54**, 307–321.

Smith, R. M. and Stamey, W. L., 1965. Determining the range of tolerable erosion, *Soil Sci.* **100**, 414–424.

Solbrig, O. T. and Golley, F. B., 1983. A decade of the tropics, *Biol. Int.* **2**(special issue), 1–15.

Sommer, A., 1976. Attempt at an assessment of the world's tropical moist forests, *Unasylva* **28**(112/113), 5–24.

Stark, N. and Jordan, C. F., 1978. Nutrient retention by the root mat of an Amazonian rain forest, *Ecology* **59**, 434–437.

Swaminathan, M. S., 1983. Our greatest challenge: Feeding the hungry world, in G. Bixler and L. W. Shemilt, Eds., *Chemistry and the World Food Supplies: The New Frontiers, CHEMRAWN II, Perspectives and Recommendations,* International Rice Research Institute, Los Banos, Philippines.

Swift, M. J., Ed., 1984. Soil biological processes and tropical soil fertility: A proposal for a collaborative programme of research, *Biol. Int.* **5**(special issue), 1–38.

Swift, M. J., Ed. 1985. Tropical Soil Biology and Fertility (TSBF). Planning for research, *Biology International* **9**, 24 p.

Swift, M. J. and Sanchez, P. A., 1984. Biological management of tropical soil fertility for sustained productivity, *Nat. Resourc.,* **20**, 4, Oct.–Dec., 2–10.

UNESCO, 1979. *Ecosystèmes forestiers tropicaux, Rech. Res. Nat.* **14**, 1–740.

Volobuev, V. R., 1962. *Pochvovedeniye* **5**, 73–82.

Van Wambeke, A., 1978. Propiedades et potencial dos solos na bacia Amazonica, *Interciência* **3**, 233–242.

Wade, M. K., 1978. Soil management practices for increasing crop production for small farms in the Amazon jungle of Peru, Ph.D. Thesis, North Carolina State University, Raleigh, NC.

Watson, J. P., 1974. Termites in relation to soil formation, groundwater and geochemical prospecting, *Soils and Fert.* **5**, 111–114.

Went, F. W. and Stark, N., 1968. Mycorrhiza, *Bioscience* **18**, 1035–1039.

Wielemaker, W. G., 1984. Soil formation by termites: A study in the Kisii area, Kenya. Doctoral Thesis, Wageningen, Netherlands.

Wilkinson, G. E., 1975. Rainfall characteristics and soil erosion in the rainforest area of Western Nigeria, *Exp. Agric.* **11**, 247–255.

Wischmeier, W. H. and Smith, D. D., 1960. A universal loss equation to guide conservation farm planning, *Trans. 7th Int. Congr. Soil. Sci.* **1**, 418–415.

Wischmeier, W. H., Johnson, C. B., and Cross, B. V., 1971. A soil erodibility nomograph for farmland and construction sites, *J. Soil Water Conserv.* **26**, 189–192.

Young, A., 1984. The role of soil biological processes in agroforestry, MAB/IUBS Workshop on Soil Biological Processes in Tropical Ecosystems, Lancaster, England.

# ☐ COMMENTS ON "BIOLOGICAL PROCESSES AND PRODUCTIVITY OF SOILS IN THE HUMID TROPICS"

**Rattan Lal**

Lavelle emphasizes the role of biological processes in maintenance of soil fertility in the tropics. However, nutrient availability and toxicity are not the only severe constraints imposed by the soils of the humid tropics on agricultural development and production. Microclimate and the physical properties of soils are also important to the productivity and need further discussion. Neglect of these factors has been responsible for rapid degradation of soil quality and decline in agronomic productivity. If soil physical properties are not maintained at optimum levels, other inputs (new cultivars, fertilizers and amendments, etc.) are easily wasted.

## SOIL-RELATED CONSTRAINTS TO CROP PRODUCTION

The predominant soil chemical and nutritional shortcomings in acidic oxisols and ultisols are low pH, lack of major plant nutrients, and excess aluminum and manganese. Adverse effects of nutritional imbalance are aggravated by rapid declines in soil organic matter content under cultivation and the resultant decline in soil physical properties. Nitrogen deficiency is common in all tropical soils, and phosphorus availability is a major problem in soils of the Amazon Basin. The predominant physical defects of soils of the lowland humid tropics are low water-holding capacity, rapid decline with cultivation of the stability of structural aggregates, formation of crust and surface seals, and susceptibility to compaction and accelerated soil erosion (see Table 1). Recognition of the major soil physical constraints allows the development of management strategies for their alleviation.

**TABLE 1. Soil-Related Constraints on New Agricultural Land in Humid Tropics**

| Region | Constraints |
|--------|-------------|
| 1. Tropical America | Phosphorus fixation and availability, aluminum toxicity, acidity, erosion and compaction, and drought stress |
| 2. West and Central Africa | Erosion, compaction, crusting, drought stress, nitrogen deficiency and high soil temperatures |
| 3. Sumatra | Erosion, compaction, soil acidity, and nutrient imbalance |

## Structural Properties and Clay Minerals

Oxisols, ultisols, and alfisols are soils with predominantly low activity clays, that is, clays composed mainly of kaolinite, halloysite with hydrous oxides of iron and aluminum. Part of the clay in alfisols and ultisols is readily dispersible but that in oxisols is more resistant to dispersion. Oxisols, therefore, are more structurally stable than are alfisols and ultisols. The alfisols of West Africa, south Asia, and northern Australia have the least favorable soil physical conditions. Once cultivated, these can develop crust and surface seal, are easily compacted, and are easily eroded. The pale and rhodic great groups of alfisols are, however, more stable.

Because of their susceptibility to compaction, the infiltration rate of most uplands declines rapidly with cultivation, especially with the adoption of motorized farm operations. Lal (in press) observed a decline of infiltration rate from 71 cm h$^{-1}$ in 1976, to 33 cm h$^{-1}$ in 1978, to 18.5 cm h$^{-1}$ in 1979, and to 8.5 cm h$^{-1}$ in 1980 (Fig. 1). This drastic decline in infiltration rate is attributed to structural collapse and elimination of transmission pores and formation of surface crust. Soil compaction and decline in infiltration rate are also severe in oxisols, but the relative susceptibility to structural degradation is somewhat less. In general, soils of the lowland humid tropics have structural properties that are easily degraded by intensive land use.

## Particle Size Distribution

Coarse texture is typical of the surface soil horizons of most tropical uplands, containing as much as 60–80% sand. The clay fraction has either been washed downward or removed in water runoff. The clay fraction is greatly influenced by the soil turnover by soil fauna. Some oxisols and nitosols have relatively higher clay content, but they do not behave like a clayey soil because the clay is strongly aggregated into silt- or sand-sized particles.

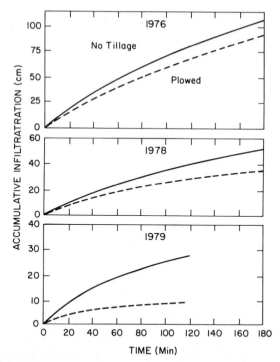

**FIGURE 1.** Changes in infiltration over 3 y for intensively cultivated soil. The drastic decline in infiltration rate is a result of structural collapse, elimination of transmission pores, and development of surface seal.

## Soil Erodibility

Soils with low-activity clays are less susceptible to erosion than those containing high-activity clays. Among soils with low-activity clays, those with stable structure (e.g., rhodic paleustult) have a lower erodibility than those with less stable structure (e.g., oxic paleustalf). For example, oxisols with relatively stable structure have a lower erodibility than alfisols or ultisols (Table 2). The low erodibility index of some soils, however, does not necessarily imply that these soils erode less. The magnitude of soil erosion in the field depends not only on the erosivity but also on the slope steepness and length and the soil surface management.

In soils of the humid tropics, where nutrients are located primarily in the surface horizon, productivity decline from soil erosion is often more drastic than in soils with a more equitable nutrient distribution (Fig. 2). Irreversible soil degradation, for example, can occur in soils where plinthite, that is, hardened iron pan, is located at a shallow depth in the soil profile. Effects of erosion on crop productivity are less drastic in soils with favorable subsoil conditions.

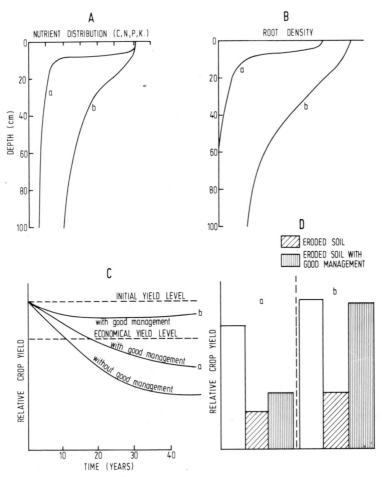

**FIGURE 2.** The nutrient profile (A) edaphological properties (B) determine the soil loss tolerance. If nutrients and organic matter are confined to the top few centimeters (as in soil "a"), erosion causes severe yield reductions. Consequently the soil loss tolerance of soil "a" is lower than soil "b", because soil "b" has more favorable nutrient profile and soil edaphological properties. Crop yield in soil "a" declines rapidly with cultivation even with good management (C), and yields are lower than in soil "b" regardless of amendments and inputs made (D).

## Water Reserves Available to Plants

Despite the humid climate and high rainfall, the available water reserves of most alfisols, ultisols, and oxisols are low. The upper limit of available water content, or "the field capacity," is attained at low suctions of 30–50 cm water. Most of the available soil moisture is released at low suctions of less than 1 bar (Fig. 3). Consequently, drought stress is commonly responsible for low yields of seasonal crops even in regions of high annual rainfall.

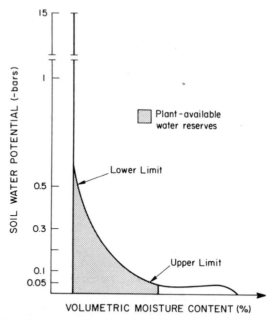

**FIGURE 3.** Soil moisture content versus soil potential in a typical tropical soil with low-activity clay. The *field capacity* is often attained at 50–60 cm of water suction and most of the plant available water is released below 0.5 bar suction.

Frequent and severe drought stress is caused by the shallow effective rooting depth and by the high temperatures of the surface soil layers. The soil temperature in the surface layer can be as high as 40–45°C, especially before the onset of the rainy season, as seen in Fig. 4. The hardness of these soils with low soil moisture is partly a result of the ultradesiccation and high soil

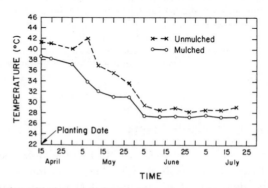

**FIGURE 4.** Variation with time of surface soil temperature for a mulched and unmulched plot. The soil temperature on the surface layer of the unmulched plot is often above the optimum range for crop production. The practice of ridging also raises the surface soil temperature, and early plant crops suffer from high temperatures.

TABLE 2. Erodibility of Some Low-Activity Clay Soils Determined on Field Plots

| Country | Climate | Erodibility | Reference |
|---------|---------|-------------|-----------|
| A. Alfisols: | | | |
| Benin | Subhumid | 0.10 | Roose, 1977 |
| Ivory Coast | Subhumid | 0.10 | Roose, 1977 |
| Kenya | Subhumid | 0.03–0.49 | Barber et al., 1979 |
| Nigeria | Subhumid | 0.06–0.36 | Lal, 1976 |
| Nigeria | Subhumid | 0.058 | Wilkinson, 1975 |
| Tanzania | Semiarid | 0.121–0.60 | Ngatunga et al., 1984 |
| B. Ultisols: | | | |
| Hawaii | Humid | 0.09 | Dangler and El-Swaify, 1976 |
| Nigeria | Humid | 0.04 | Vanelslande et al., 1984 |
| Thailand | Subhumid | 0.09–0.19 | Taugtham, 1983 |
| Trinidad | Humid | 0.03–0.06 | Lindsary and Gumbs, 1982 |
| C. Oxisols: | | | |
| Costa Rica | Humid | 0.103–0.155 | Amezquita and Forsythe, 1975 |
| Hawaii | Humid | 0.14–0.22 | Dangler and El-Swaify, 1976 |
| Ivory Coast | Humid | 0.10 | Roose, 1977 |
| Puerto Rico | Humid | 0.01 | Barnett et al., 1971 |

temperatures. The range of moisture content over which soil is friable is narrow. Both the plant-available soil water reserves and the range of moisture content over which soil is friable depend on the organic matter content of the soil. In spite of deep weathering, plant roots can exploit only a shallow soil volume. Root penetration into the subsoil horizons is restricted by physical and/or chemical factors.

## ROLE OF SOIL FAUNA

The soil fauna (e.g., earthworms, termites, and other soil dwellers) are important for soil physical properties, soil turnover, mineralization of biomass, nutrient recycling, and so for soil productivity. Those management systems that undermine the role of soil fauna are often unsuccessful and have been responsible for a rapid degradation in soil quality. Soil macrofauna keep soils porous and able to absorb high-intensity rains and so prevent erosion. A soil devoid of intense activity is easily compacted.

High biotic activity of soil fauna depends on a regular supply of organic matter to the soil surface and on optimum soil temperature and soil moisture.

A high frequency of natural or man-induced fires and an unthinking use of some agrochemicals (e.g., the use of soil-acidifying ammonium sulfate and soil applications of pesticides) have severe adverse effects on soil fauna. Mechanical soil manipulation, such as plowing and other mechanized farm operations, also decrease soil biotic activity. Many tropical soils have been rendered compact and inert following mechanized farm operation and heavy and frequent doses of agrochemicals.

## MICROCLIMATE AND ITS EFFECTS ON AGRICULTURE IN THE TROPICS

Not only soil physical properties but also microclimatic factors affect crop growth. Rainfall, temperature, and relative humidity also are important for the physical and chemical properties of soil. Tropical rains are generally intense with a relatively high energy load. The latter is related to the drop size distribution. Some data obtained on drop size distribution of tropical rains have indicated that a median drop size ($D_{50}$) of above 2.5 mm is common. Lal (1981) reported that most erosive rains received at Ibadan, Nigeria, had a $D_{50}$ ranging between 1.70 and 2.55 mm. As a consequence of a relatively big drop size and high intensity, tropical rains often have higher energy loads than temperate rains. For example, Kowal and Kassam (1976) reported much higher values ($34.6 \, \text{J m}^{-2} \, \text{mm}^{-1}$) of energy load than those reported from subtropical (Elwell and Stocking, 1975) and temperate regions. The high-energy load of tropical rains is a major factor responsible for severe erosion hazard and soil compaction.

The frequent occurrence of dry spells lasting for 5–20 days is common during the rainy season. Because upland soils are coarse textured and have a low available water-holding capacity, crops suffer from drought stress even during the rainy season. The effects of drought stress are aggravated by supraoptimal soil temperatures. Shallow-rooted seasonal crops (e.g., upland rice, maize, soybeans, and cowpea) are susceptible to the lack of adequate water.

Prevalence of year-round high ambient temperatures affects crop growth both directly and indirectly. Since the nocturnal temperatures are high, the net photosynthesis is often low. Because of rapid growth, the rate of water supply to plant roots often lags behind the demand—another reason for the incipient wilting observed in actively growing crops. The high rate of mineralization of soil organic matter in the tropics is also due to high temperatures.

The low radiation level is another important factor that affects crop production in the humid tropics. Low yields obtained in the equatorial humid tropical region in comparison with the midlatitudes are partly due to low levels of radiation. There is thus scope to develop varieties with suitable plant architecture that effectively intercepts the available sunlight.

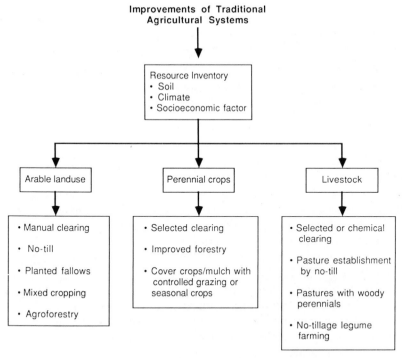

**FIGURE 5.** The traditional farming practices should be gradually changed into improved agriculture by no-till/mulch farming, agroforestry, integrating livestock with crops, and an ecological approach to tropical agriculture.

## LOW-INPUT MANAGEMENT STRATEGY

Most small-plot landholders are subsistence farmers. High-input technology is often unsuitable for them because it is not financially affordable, technically suitable, or ecologically compatible. Management of their soils requires (i) a regular supply of organic matter to the soil surface, (ii) maintenance of soil structure through enhanced biotic activity, (iii) effective recycling of nutrients, and (iv) supplemental application of lime, phosphorus, and other essential plant nutrients. Improvements in farm tools and implements enable subsistence farmers to increase the land area under cultivation. Equally important is the introduction of improved varieties and plant species and cropping systems that are adapted to the acid soils and low nutrients. Nitrogen buildup in soil can be achieved through incorporation, in rotation, of leguminous covers and woody perennials with ability to fix atmospheric soil nitrogen. Thus, the components of improved low-input technology for subsistence farmers, as shown in Fig. 5, are

    **i.** ecologically compatible land-clearing methods, such as manual clearing followed by *in situ* burning;

ii. improved cultivars and species adapted to acid soil conditions and low inherent fertility;

iii. improved crop rotations including the use of woody perennials, agroforestry, and frequent use of cover crops;

iv. mulch farming with a no-till system;

v. the use of better tools for improving the productivity of labor; and

vi. integration of livestock and crops.

The objective is to maximize output per unit input and minimize the dependence on chemicals and other high-energy inputs that are not available. Innovations based on these principles have proven successful in maintaining high and sustained productivity on fragile soils in harsh environments.

Careful land use planning and soil management are needed in order to achieve high and sustained production with minimum of soil degradation. The sequence of steps shown in Fig. 5 indicates planning and soil management and land use strategies. Whether the lands now under forest should be cleared or not depends on the resource inventory. The choice of appropriate land use also depends on the soil capability and environmental factors. The guidelines for management of land and water resources should be based on the ecological approach that considers sustainable and stable returns while preserving the resource base.

## REFERENCES

Amezquita, E. C., and Forsythe, W. F., 1975. Application de la ecuacion universal de perdade de suelo en Turrialba, Costa Rica, paper presented at *V. Latin Amer. Congr. Soil Sci.* Medellin, Columbia.

Barber, R. G., Moore, T. R., and Thomas, D. B., 1979. The erodibility of two soils from Kenya, *J. Soil Sci.* **30**, 579–591.

Barnett, A. P., Carreker, J. R., Abruwa, F., and Dooley, A. E., 1971. Erodibility of selected tropical soils, *Trans. Amer. Soc. Agric. Engr.* **14**, 496–499.

Dangler, E. W. and El-Swaify, S. A., 1976. Erosion of selected Hawaii soils by simulated rainfall, *Soil Sci. Soc. Amer. J.* **40**, 769–779.

Elwell, H. A. and Stocking, M. A., 1975. Parameters for estimating annual runoff and soil loss from agricultural lands in Rhodesia, *Water Resourc. Res.* **11**, 601–605.

Kowal, J. M. and Kassam, A. H., 1976. Energy and instantaneous intensity of rainstorms at Samaru, northern Nigeria, *Trop. Agric.* **53**, 185–198.

Lal, R., 1976. Soil erosion problems on Alfisols in Western Nigeria and their control, in *IITA Monogr.* **1**.

Lal, R., 1981. Analysis of different processes governing soil erosion by water in the tropics, *IAHS Publ.* **133**, 351–364.

Lal, R., in press. Mechanized tillage systems effects on properties of a tropical Alfisol in watersheds cropped to maize, *Soil Till. Res.*

Lindsary, J. I. and Gumbs, F. A., 1982. Erodibility indices compared to measured values of selected Trinidad soils, *Soil Sci. Soc. Amer. J., 46,* 393–396.

Ngatunga, E. L. N., Lal, R., and Uriyo, A. P., 1984. Effects of surface management on runoff and soil erosion from some plots at Mlingano, Tanzania, *Geoderma* **33,** 1–12.

Roose, E. J., 1977. Use of the Universal Soil Loss. Equation to predict erosion in West Africa, *SCCA Spec. Publ.* **21,** 60–74.

Taugtham, N., 1983. Estimating K- and C-factor in the USLE for Hill evergreen forest in northern Thailand, paper presented at *Malama Aina Conf.* Honolulu, Hawaii.

Vanelslande, A., Roussea, P., Lal, R., Gabriels, D., and Ghuman, B. S., 1984. Testing the applicability of soil erodibility nomogram for some tropical soils, *IAHS Publ.* **144,** 463–473.

Wilkinson, G. E., 1975. Rainfall characteristics and soil erosion in the rainforest area of western Nigeria, *Expl. Agric.* **11,** 247–255.

# Chapter 12

# Effects of Deforestation on Soil Properties and Microclimate of a High Rain Forest in Southern Nigeria

## B. S. Ghuman and Rattan Lal

Conversion of forested land to other uses produces a broad range of ecological effects including alterations in energy and water balance and disruption of the pathways of major nutrient elements. Most of the literature relevant to the humid tropics is, however, speculative, laced with emotions, and supported by few experimentally determined facts on the ecological effects. Despite the paucity of basic scientific knowledge of the effects, the tropical rain forests are increasingly being perturbed. About 11 million hectares of tropical forests are being cleared annually for various uses.

The effects of forest conversion depend on the land use and management practices. For example, the effects on soils, hydrology, and microclimate are different when the forest is cleared by shifting cultivators, for selective logging, by mechanized versus manual or chemical clearing for arable land use, or plantation crops or pastures. Furthermore, the effects can be local, regional, or global, depending on the extent of forest removed.

We report the preliminary results from a project to quantify the magnitude and trends in alterations of soil, hydrology, microclimate, and biotic environments resulting from conversion of a tropical rain forest to different land use systems and agricultural practices. The general project objectives are to strengthen the basic scientific body of knowledge that enables the rational use of land and water resources; to develop guidelines for the management of land resources for economically viable and sustained productivity; to evaluate agronomic potential and constraints of the lowland humid tropics; and to provide training opportunities.

More specifically, the project is aimed at evaluating the effects of forest conversion on the physical, chemical, and biological processes of the forest ecology; alterations in soil physical, chemical, and biological properties; the effects on water and energy balance and micro- and mesoclimate, runoff rate and erosion; and the effects on biotic environments including soil fauna and flora and agronomic productivity.

## SITE

The 75-ha site is located on the premises of the Okomu Oil Palm Co. Ltd., about 75 km southwest of Benin City, Nigeria, approximately at 5°12′ E and 6°24′ N. The rainy season lasts from March to October. The mean annual rainfall of the region is about 2.0 m with a range of 1.8–2.9 m. The vegetation is a mature high forest with three distinct strata: the upper stratum exceeding 40 m, the middle stratum between 16 and 40 m, and the understory at less than 16 m. The predominant tree species of the upper stratum are *Afzelia africana, Klainedoxa gabonensis, Antiaris africana, Ceiba pentandra, Amphimas pterocarpoides, Combretodendron macrocarpum*, and *Poga oleosa*. The predominant tree species in the middle stratum are *Albizia, Enantia, Elaeis, Guarea, Monodora, Polyathia, Strombosia, Scottellia*, and *Trichilia*. The understory is a shrub layer consisting of climbers, *Calamus*, and thickets of young trees. Predominant species in the understory are *Stromosia, Scottellia, Diospyros, Enantia, Guarea*, and *Anthonotha*. The mean basal area of the trees ranges between 386 and 462 $m^2$ $ha^{-1}$.

The geological strata are composed mainly of Eocene sediments. The rocks are very poorly exposed, and only ferruginized rock fragments can be seen through deep cuttings. The terrain is fairly flat to gently undulating, with an average slope ranging from 2 to 4%. The soils of the experimental site are classified as Ultisols with low pH and low base saturation (Table 1).

## MICROCLIMATE OF OKOMU TROPICAL RAIN FOREST

### Rainfall

The rainy season at Okomu is short, with the least amount of rain received in December and January (Fig. 1). Studies are being conducted to determine how the rainfall received over the forest canopy is partitioned into its components: throughfall, stem flow, and canopy interception. The preliminary data of rainfall partitioning from July through December 1984 are shown in Table 2. On an average, throughfall under the forest canopy was about 12.2% less than in the open. From June to December 1984, canopy interception plus stemflow accounted for about 13 cm of the rainfall received.

### Solar Radiation

Solar radiation received under the forest canopy and in the open is compared in Fig. 2 and Table 3 for the rainy season during May and for the dry season

**TABLE 1. Soil Chemical Analysis of Site To Be Cleared**

| Location | Depth (cm) | pH | Organic Carbon (%) | Total Nitrogen (%) | Available Phosphorus (ppm) | Exchangeable Cations (meq per 100 g) | | | | | Total Acidity | Cation Exchange Capacity |
|---|---|---|---|---|---|---|---|---|---|---|---|---|
| | | | | | | Ca | Mg | K | Na | Mn | | |
| Valley | 0–5 | 4.3 | 1.61 | 0.194 | 3.9 | 1.57 | 0.46 | 0.11 | 0.04 | 0.04 | 1.03 | 3.25 |
| | 5–10 | 4.2 | 0.91 | 0.125 | 3.2 | 1.12 | 0.31 | 0.09 | 0.05 | 0.02 | 1.10 | 2.69 |
| Midslope | 0–5 | 4.6 | 2.70 | 0.348 | 6.5 | 2.62 | 1.38 | 0.19 | 0.05 | 0.00 | 1.87 | 6.11 |
| | 5–10 | 4.6 | 1.11 | 0.113 | 4.5 | 0.97 | 0.57 | 0.09 | 0.05 | 0.03 | 0.73 | 2.44 |
| Up slope | 0–5 | 5.7 | 3.48 | 0.286 | 2.4 | 12.63 | 2.34 | 0.19 | 0.06 | 0.03 | 1.27 | 16.52 |
| | 5–10 | 5.7 | 1.45 | 0.141 | 1.5 | 4.49 | 1.10 | 0.09 | 0.06 | 0.02 | 0.47 | 6.25 |

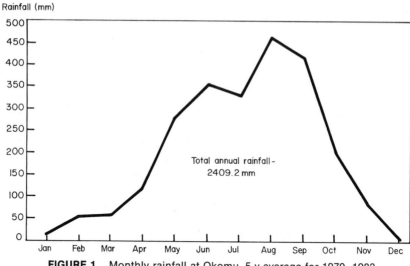

**FIGURE 1.**  Monthly rainfall at Okomu, 5-y average for 1979–1983.

during December, respectively. The data in Fig. 2 for a sunny and a cloudy day show that the forest canopy effectively intercepts the radiation received. During the dry season in December, only 10 cal cm$^{-2}$ day$^{-1}$ (0.04 kJ cm$^{-2}$ day$^{-1}$) of radiation reached the ground surface under forest as compared to 250 cal cm$^{-2}$ day$^{-1}$ (1.0 kJ cm$^{-2}$ day$^{-1}$) received in the cleared area. Consequently, there is little undergrowth beneath the forest canopy.

## Soil and Air Temperatures

The temperature profiles within the forest canopy were measured during rainy and dry seasons. The rainy season temperature profiles within the

**TABLE 2.**  Monthly Rainfall (cm) from June to December 1984 at Okomu

| Month | Cleared Area | Under Forest | |
|---|---|---|---|
| | | Throughfall | Stem Flow + Canopy Intercepted |
| June 21–28 | 4.86 | 3.90 | 0.96 |
| July | 25.51 | 19.87 | 5.64 |
| August | 23.23 | 21.15 | 2.08 |
| September | 32.07 | 28.63 | 3.44 |
| October | 20.36 | 19.51 | 0.85 |
| November | 0.00 | 0.00 | 0.00 |
| December | 0.00 | 0.00 | 0.00 |
| Total | 106.03 | 93.06 | 12.97 |

**TABLE 3. Solar Radiation Received Under Forest and in Cleared Area at Okomu During Some Days of Dry Season of 1984–1985**

| | Solar Radiation (cal cm$^{-2}$ day$^{-1}$) | | |
| Day | Forest | Cleared Area | Forest Cleared |
|---|---|---|---|
| December 4 | 10 | 270 | 0.037 |
| December 6 | 9 | 229 | 0.039 |
| December 8 | 8 | 229 | 0.035 |
| December 10 | 10 | 243 | 0.041 |
| December 12 | 10 | 229 | 0.043 |
| December 14 | 11 | 270 | 0.041 |
| December 16 | 10 | 283 | 0.035 |
| Average | 9.7 ± 0.9 | 250.4 ± 21.6 | 0.039 ± 0.003 |

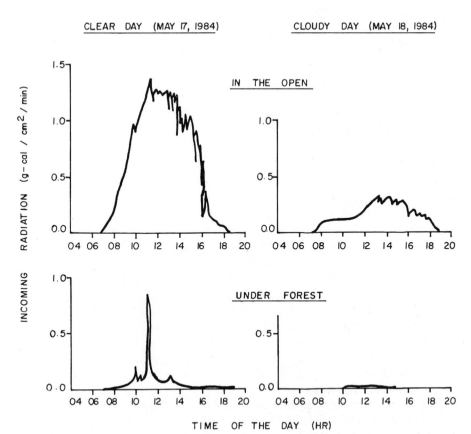

**FIGURE 2.** Incoming solar radiation under forest canopy and on cleared land measured on May 17 and 18, 1984, which were clear and cloudy days, respectively.

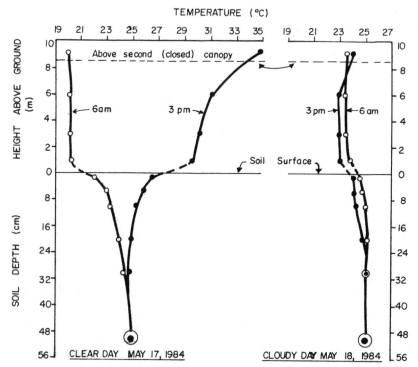

**FIGURE 3.** Temperature profile within the forest canopy from 50 cm below to 9 m above the ground surface during the rainy season for the same two days of Fig. 2.

forest canopy from 50 cm below to 9 m above the ground surface, for a sunny and a cloudy day, are shown in Fig. 3. On the clear day, the soil temperature exceeded the air temperature at 6 a.m. but was lower than the air temperature at 3 p.m. On the cloudy day, however, the soil temperature was slightly more than the air temperature regardless of the time of day. The diurnal fluctuations in soil temperature within the forest canopy for the rainy season are compared in Fig. 4 with that of the cleared site for a cloudy and a sunny day. The soil temperature at the 50-cm depth is approximately 28°C for the cleared site and 25°C under the forest cover at all times. The soil temperature at the 1-cm depth on a sunny day fluctuated diurnally from a minimum of 22°C to a maximum of 37°C for the cleared site compared with a minimum of 20°C and a maximum of 26.5°C under the forest cover. The amplitude of air temperature fluctuation was about 15°C for the cleared site and 10°C for the forest cover.

Soil and air temperatures for cleared and forested areas on six consecutive days during the dry season in December 1984 are shown in Fig. 5. At a 5-cm depth, the average soil temperature under the forest was 3°C lower than in the open. However, the maximum daytime temperature under forest was

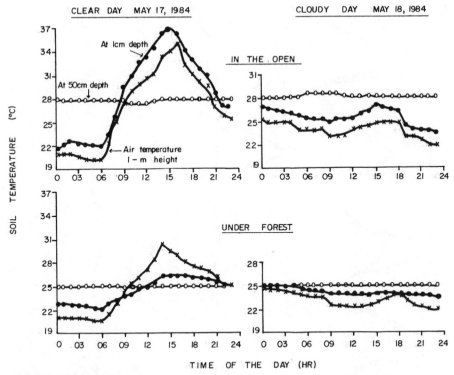

**FIGURE 4.** Diurnal fluctuations in soil and air temperature under forest and on cleared land for the same two days of Fig. 2.

generally lower by 6°C than at the cleared area. There was also a phase lag of about 1–2 h in the occurrence of the maxima at the 5-cm depth under forest compared to cleared sites. Soil temperatures under forest at 5- and 20-cm depths were identical. The difference between average temperatures in the open and forest was reduced to 2.5°C at the 20-cm depth. In the cleared area, the maximum temperature diminished to 32°C at the 20-cm depth. Maxima occurred nearly 2–3 h later at the 20-cm depth than at the 5-cm depth.

During daytime, air temperature measured at 1-m height above the soil surface was always lower by 3–6°C under forest than in the open. However, the forest at 1 m was relatively warm at night, though the temperature difference was never more than 0.5°C. With the advance of the dry season, the difference between the maximum air temperatures in the open and forest decreased; for instance, the difference was 5.5°C on December 4, and it decreased to 3°C on December 11.

Temperature profiles from 20 cm below the soil surface to 10 m above are illustrated in Fig. 6 At 6 a.m. (time of the minimum temperature occurrence), air temperature in the canopy was nearly constant at 26.2°C, about

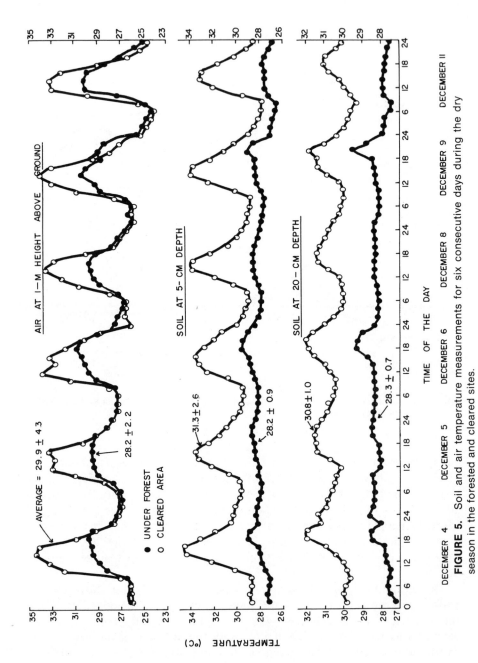

**FIGURE 5.** Soil and air temperature measurements for six consecutive days during the dry season in the forested and cleared sites.

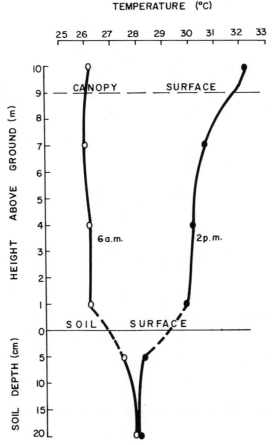

**FIGURE 6.** Temperature profile within the forest canopy from 20 cm below to 10 m above the ground surface at 6 a.m. and 1 p.m.

2°C lower than the soil temperature. However, soil temperature increased with depth at 6 a.m., indicating that the soil was losing heat to the atmosphere at night. At 2 p.m., the air temperature in the canopy was relatively variable and increased with height. At the 10-m height (i.e., 1 m above tree canopy), air temperature was 1.6°C more than at 7 m (i.e., 2 m below the canopy surface). In contrast to 6 a.m., the soil temperature at 2 p.m. was lower than the air temperature in the canopy. Thus, soil was receiving energy from the air above it during the daytime. At 6 a.m. and 2 p.m., the soil temperature profiles below the 20-cm depth were essentially the same (Fig. 6).

## Relative Humidity

Air temperature and humidity in the forest are compared with those of cleared land for May 23 during the rainy season. Figure 7 shows the contrast

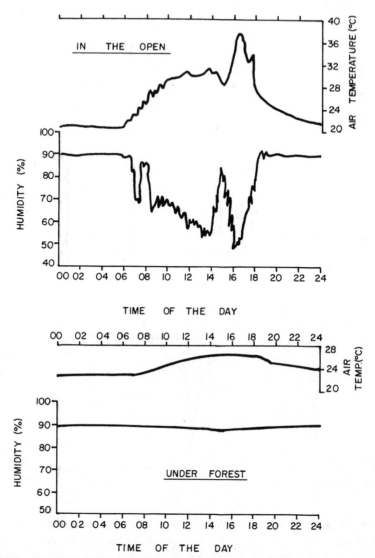

**FIGURE 7.** Relative humidity and air temperature measured under forest and in cleared land on May 23, 1984.

in microclimates of the forested and the open sites merely 50 m apart. The minimum relative humidities of 87 and 49% corresponded to the maximum air temperatures of 26 and 37°C on forested and cleared sites, respectively.

The relative humidity in the cleared area also dropped to 30–40% during daytime in the dry season until December 8 (Fig. 8). However, later in the dry season, the daytime minimum values were lower. In spite of the extremely dry conditions, relative humidity still increased to about 95% toward

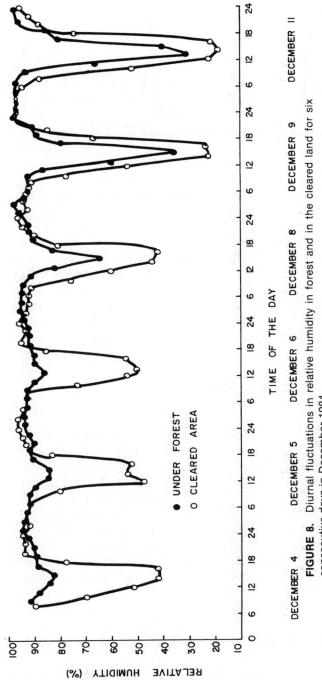

**FIGURE 8.** Diurnal fluctuations in relative humidity in forest and in the cleared land for six consecutive days in December 1984.

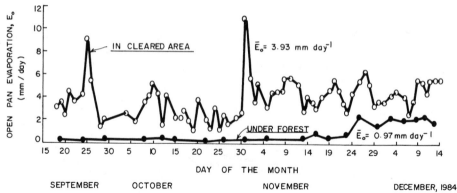

**FIGURE 9.** Effect of forest cover on the open-pan evaporation from September to December 1984.

evening. Relative humidity under the forest canopy varied more in the dry season than it did during the rainy season. On December 4 (1 month after the beginning of the dry season), the minimum forest relative humidity was 82%, much higher than that in the open. But as the severity of the dry season was increased by dust-laden winds coming from the Sahara desert, the day-time forest relative humidity dropped sharply. The difference between relative humidity values for the cleared and forested sites narrowed to 12% on December 11.

## Evaporation

The effect of forest canopy on open-pan evaporation is also considerable, as is shown by data in Fig. 9. During the rainy season, the evaporation rate ($E_0$) was lower in the forest than in the cleared area. However, $E_0$ in the forest increased with the advancing dry season, although there was not much increase in $E_0$ in the cleared area. In spite of the dry climate (Fig. 8), the solar heating decreased during the dry season because of prevailing hazy conditions in the atmosphere. This decrease might help maintain $E_0$ in the cleared area at a level existing before the beginning of the dry season. On the other hand, air inside the forest was desiccated by increased evaporative demand. For the period considered, $E_0$ inside the forest averaged 25% of that in the cleared area.

## TREE DENSITY AND LITTER FALL UNDER RAIN FOREST

The number of trees with trunk girth equal to or more than 15 cm at a 1-m height ranged from 100 to 2100 per hectare. The distribution of tree density was described by a normal frequency function. The mean rate of leaf fall

TABLE 4. Rate of Leaf Fall in Forest During 1984 at Okomu

| Interval | Rate of Leaf Fall ($kg\ ha^{-1}\ day^{-1}$) |
|---|---|
| June 8–20 | 20.0 |
| June 20–27 | 17.9 |
| June 27–July 9 | 21.5 |
| July 9–17 | 11.6 |
| July 17–August 1 | 14.7 |
| August 1–17 | 16.3 |
| August 1–16 | 13.8 |
| August 16–23 | 25.6 |
| August 23–27 | 16.6 |
| August 27–September 10 | 27.2 |
| September 10–19 | 23.6 |
| September 19–October 3 | 13.9 |
| October 3–15 | 20.1 |
| October 15–29 | 22.1 |
| October 29–November 9 | 13.8 |
| November 9–19 | 23.0 |
| Average | 18.8 ± 4.5 |

under the forest canopy from June to November, 1984 was 18.8 kg ha$^{-1}$ day$^{-1}$ with a range from 11.6 to 25.6 kg ha$^{-1}$ day$^{-1}$ (Table 4). The rate of leaf fall is more during the dry season, that is, December and January. These measurements show that about 7 t ha$^{-1}$ year$^{-1}$ of dry leaves fall from the trees in this system.

## SOIL PROPERTIES UNDER A TROPICAL RAIN FOREST

### Soil Fauna

#### Termites
Preliminary data are being collected for density of termite hills and the earthworm population under the forest cover. The termitarium density ranges from 60 to 1020 per hectare with a mean of 280 hills per hectare (Fig. 10). The predominant mound-building species is tentatively classified as *Cubitermes fungifaber*. We are estimating the rate of soil turnover by termites for different land use systems and investigating the effects of deforestation and of intensive land use on species diversity and activity.

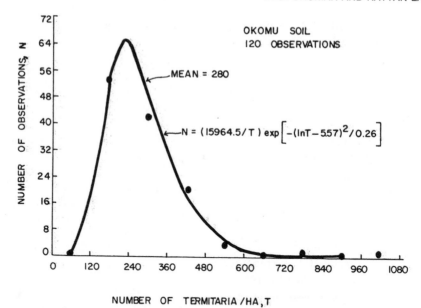

**FIGURE 10.**  Distribution of termite mounds under the forest cover.

The temperature and humidity conditions within a termitarium often differ from the outside environment. The differences are presumably less within the forest cover than in the cleared site. For example, the data in Fig. 11 show the dampening effect of a termitarium on the maximum daytime temperature, especially on a sunny day. Not only was the maximum temperature on a sunny day lower within the termite mound than outside but there was also a phase difference of about 2 h. The differences in temperature were rather small on a cloudy day. In order to calculate soil turnover by termites, empirical relations have been developed relating weight and volume of the termitarium with its outside dimensions, that is, with the product X of its height (cm) and diameter (cm). These relationships for *Cubitermes fungi-faber* are

$$\text{Weight (g)} = -195 + 3.84X + 6.89 \times 10^{-3}X^2 \qquad (r = 0.99) \quad (1)$$

$$\text{Volume (cm}^3) = -200 + 4.35X + 8.12 \times 10^{-3}X^2 \qquad (r = 0.99) \quad (2)$$

These empirical relations for the *Nausitermes triodiae* are

$$\text{Weight (kg)} = -0.98 + 7.9 \times 10^{-3}X + 4.7 \times 10^{-6}X^2$$
$$(r = 0.99) \qquad\qquad\qquad\qquad (3)$$

$$\text{Volume (cm}^3 \times 10^{-3}) = -1179 + 9.63X + 0.0057X^2$$
$$(r = 0.99) \qquad\qquad\qquad\qquad (4)$$

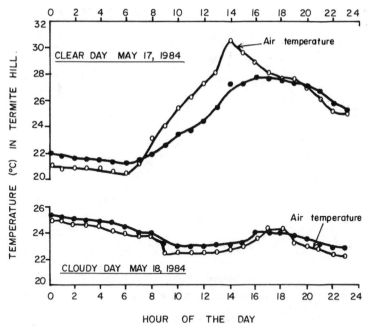

**FIGURE 11.** Outside air temperature (open circles) versus that inside a termite mound (solid circles).

### Earthworms

The earthworm population in the forested soil was determined during the rainy season of 1984 using a formaldehyde solution. The earthworm population varied from 30 to 210 individuals per square meter with a mean of 90 (Fig. 12). On a hectare basis, there were $9 \times 10^5$ earthworms. The rate of cast production varied with the rainfall and soil plot (Table 5). There was no casting activity during the dry season. The mean soil turnover from earthworm activity was calculated to be 21.5 t ha$^{-1}$ y$^{-1}$.

## Soil Physical Properties

The soil texture is mostly sand to sandy clay loam with the particle size distribution ranging from 72 to 96% sand, 0 to 7% silt, and 7 to 25% clay. The textural composition makes this soil highly susceptible to compaction and rapid decline in total porosity. The pH of the surface soil (240 samples) varies from 4.2 to 6.2, organic carbon from 0.92 to 3.54%, and cation exchange capacity from 1.75 to 13.28 me/100 g.

### Bulk Density

The frequency analysis of bulk density measured at 268 sites in the project area still under forest is shown in Fig 13. Spatial distribution of bulk density

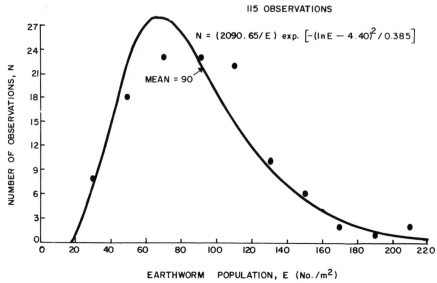

**FIGURE 12.** Distribution of earthworm population in a soil supporting high forest.

was adequately described by a normal frequency function, $f(x)$, given by

$$f(x) = \frac{1}{\sigma\sqrt{2\pi}} \exp\left[-\frac{(x-\mu)^2}{2\sigma^2}\right] \tag{5}$$

where $\mu$ is the mean bulk density (1.28 g cm$^{-3}$), $\sigma$ is the standard deviation (0.13 g cm$^{-3}$) and $x$ is the bulk density.

Bulk density varied from 0.9 to 1.7 g cm$^{-3}$ with a mean of 1.28 g cm$^{-3}$. The surface layer usually had a lower bulk density, perhaps maintained by high organic matter content, roots of shrubs and trees, and the high biotic activity of soil fauna. The highest bulk density values were measured in the 20–40-cm layer. Below 40 cm, bulk density remained around 1.40 g cm$^{-3}$.

### Infiltration Rate

The infiltration rate was measured at 154 points in the 120 plots. Distribution of steady infiltration rate is presented in Fig. 14. The majority of the plots had infiltration rates of 114.5 cm h$^{-1}$ or less. Only two sites had infiltration rates of more than 300 cm h$^{-1}$. Variation in the infiltration rate was random and did not depend on the bulk density of the surface layers. Since the entire soil profile is involved in the infiltration process, the least permeable horizon in the profile controls the infiltration rate.

Mathematically, steady infiltration rate variation was described by a log-

**TABLE 5. Rate of Cast Production (kg ha⁻¹ day⁻¹) by Earthworms under Forest at Okomu**

| Period (1984) | 16 | 17 | 18 | 19 | 20 | 21 | 22 | 23 | 24 | 25 | Average |
|---|---|---|---|---|---|---|---|---|---|---|---|
| August 16–23 | 137.8 | 142.7 | 109.7 | 94.3 | 108.0 | 95.6 | 122.0 | 50.7 | 68.4 | 23.0 | 95.2 |
| August 23–27 | 280.0 | 264.7 | 174.2 | 117.2 | 163.2 | 91.2 | 240.0 | 41.5 | — | 47.0 | 157.0 |
| August 27–September 10 | 63.1 | 83.8 | 24.9 | 28.6 | 76.6 | 38.1 | 55.8 | 24.4 | 53.3 | 19.1 | 46.8 |
| September 10–19 | 39.4 | 59.3 | 32.3 | 32.4 | 87.4 | 38.9 | 43.4 | 28.3 | 64.1 | 2.4 | 42.8 |
| September 19–October 3 | 11.1 | 21.2 | 3.8 | 6.4 | 24.4 | 24.1 | 57.1 | 20.8 | 56.8 | 10.2 | 23.6 |
| October 3–15 | 31.3 | 36.4 | 12.1 | 24.6 | 37.7 | 22.9 | 92.6 | 61.2 | 73.3 | 9.1 | 40.1 |
| October 15–29 | 5.8 | 13.1 | 7.6 | 5.2 | 14.6 | 2.8 | 4.9 | 6.6 | 11.8 | — | 8.0 |
| Average | 81.2 | 88.7 | 52.1 | 44.1 | 57.7 | 44.8 | 88.0 | 33.3 | 43.2 | 19.4 | 59.1 |

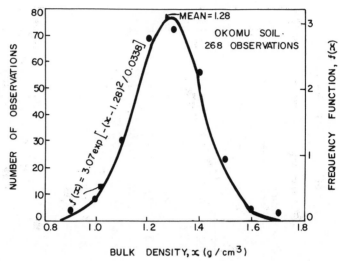

**FIGURE 13.** Distribution of 268 soil bulk density measurements made under the forest cover.

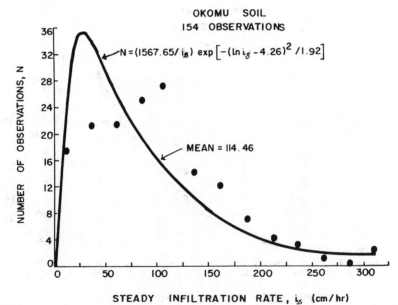

**FIGURE 14.** Distribution of the equilibrium infiltration rate measured on 154 sampling sites within a 30-ha forested watershed.

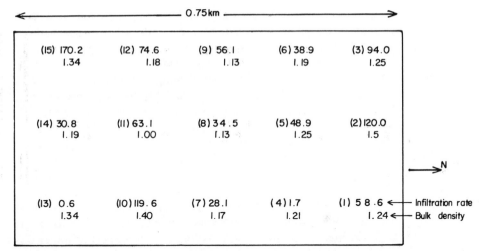

**FIGURE 15.** Spatial variation in infiltration rate in relation to bulk density of the surface horizon. The upper figure refers to the equilibrium infiltration rate and the lower to soil bulk density.

normal distribution function, presented in Fig. 14. The log-normal function is given by

$$N = \frac{n \, \Delta i_s}{i_s \sigma \ln \sqrt{2\pi}} \exp\left[ -\frac{(\ln i_s - \mu \ln)^2}{2\sigma \ln^2} \right] \tag{6}$$

where $N$ is the number of observations expected to fall within a class $\Delta i_s$, $i_s$ is the steady infiltration rate, $\mu \ln$ and $\sigma \ln$ are the mean and standard deviation of the $\log_e$ values of $i_s$, and $n$ is the total number of observations (154 in the present case). The mean value of $i_s$ from the log-normal curve is given by $\exp(\mu \ln + \frac{1}{2} \sigma \ln^2)$, which equals 114.46 cm h$^{-1}$ and is different from the arithmetic mean of the observed $i_s$ values, which was 90 cm h$^{-1}$.

The data in Fig. 15 show the spatial variation in infiltration rate and soil bulk density for 15 locations within a 750 × 400-m forest area. The infiltration rate ranged from 0.6 to 170 cm h$^{-1}$. The variability observed is random and is not related to soil bulk density because the soil bulk density values at the locations of the minimum (0.6 cm h$^{-1}$) and the maximum (170 cm h$^{-1}$) infiltration rates were the same, that is, 1.34 g cm$^{-3}$.

## FUTURE PLANS

The land was cleared January 9–21 1985, using a front-mounted shear blade on a track-type tractor. Detailed observations were made in order to assess the economics of land clearing. The soil properties immediately after clearing are also being observed. Each of the eight land use treatments is located on a watershed measuring 200 × 50 m and equipped with a 3-ft rate measuring H-flume, water stage recorder, water runoff sampler, and monolith lysimeter to measure evapotranspiration and percolation losses. The land use treatments are (i) forest control, (ii) traditional farming, (iii) improved forestry, (iv) oil palm plantation, (v) plantain, (vi) grazed pastures, (vii) agroforestry, and (viii) food crops. Each of these land use treatments is replicated thrice. A total of 24 plots is located within a delineated watershed of about 30 ha.

The observations planned are (a) hydrology: runoff discharge and its physical (sediment load) and chemical (dissolved load) properties, rainfall analyses over different ground covers, water percolation and its chemical composition, and plant water use; (b) microclimate: soil and ambient temperatures, relative humidity, heat flux, radiation penetration at different levels in the canopy, evaporation, and wind velocity; (c) soils: evolutions of physical, hydrological, chemical, and biological soil properties under different land uses; and (d) biotic environments: agronomic and economic evaluation of different land use systems.

## ACKNOWLEDGMENTS

The authors are grateful for the generous financial support received from the UNU. The logistic support by the staff of the Okomu Oil Palm Co. (i.e., Mr. D. O. Igbinovia, Dr. C. S. O. Agbakoba, Mr. R. Delogu, and Mr. Nwolu) is gratefully acknowledged.

# Chapter 13

# Element Cycling in the Amazon Basin: A Riverine Perspective

Jeffrey E. Richey and Maria de Nazaré Góes Ribeiro

The Amazon River basin has a vast central plain bordered by highlands and a drainage network including different-sized tributaries that provide inputs to the main channel and its extensive floodplain.

The water of the Amazon and its tributaries carries dissolved and suspended chemical materials, both organic and inorganic in composition. These materials are washed by runoff into the river from the land, are formed by chemical transformations within the river, or originate in exchanges with the atmosphere. The material from land may be biological debris or mineral nutrients lost from the land vegetation.

Heavy rainfall, of which about 50% is recycled via evapotranspiration (Salati et al., 1978), mobilizes sediments and leaches nutrients from the lithologically and topographically distinct subdrainages of the Amazon (Gibbs, 1972; Stallard and Edmond, 1983). These elements, the majority of which is Andean derived, provide the critical nutrients needed for primary production of phytoplankton and the extensive vegetation in the floodplain along the river (Schmidt, 1973; Sioli, 1975; Fisher and Parsley, 1979).

Thus, sufficiently detailed sampling and chemical analyses of the composition of the water from the Amazon and its tributaries, if properly interpreted, should provide considerable information on overall ecological properties of the land–river system and, if continued over time, show how these properties change with land use change.

## ELEMENT CYCLING: THE MICRO- AND LARGE-SCALE APPROACHES

The most common approach to the study of element cycling is to consider nutrient cycling for an individual process or site. On a slightly larger scale, such studies have been integrated to provide a view of cycling in "small watersheds" (Bormann and Likens, 1967). Examples of this approach include the Hubbard-Brook forest of the northeastern United States, the Coweeta watershed of the southeastern United States, and the Reserva Ducke watershed near Manaus, Brazil. The other extreme is represented by the study of the global patterns of such elements as carbon and nitrogen.

Microscale studies have shown the Amazon region to be a dense rain forest growing on highly leached, impoverished soils, with most of the nutrients contained in the vegetation. Plant growth is maintained through rapid and efficient recycling of dead plant materials (Klinge, 1976; Herrera et al., 1978; Jordan, 1982).

## ELEMENT CYCLING: A MESOSCALE RIVERINE PERSPECTIVE

The sheer size of the Amazon (over $6 \times 10^6$ km$^2$) and its diversity make it difficult to extrapolate from any site-specific study. Global-scale analyses do not provide information at fine enough resolution to describe unique regional details. To obtain such details, we must apply a regional-scale approach that incorporates the spatial and temporal variability of the basin with sufficient resolution to be "useful," while coupling to changes in driving functions (climate) and ultimately to changes in global cycles. This approach should be done efficiently because of the considerable logistic problems inherent in any large-scale study of the Amazon.

These requirements are fulfilled by study of the water and material fluxes from their input as precipitation in the respective subdrainages to the output of the river system to the ocean. Rivers act as integrators of basinwide properties: Their loads are a composite of organic and inorganic materials representing a spectrum of sizes and chemical characteristics. Richey (1983) outlined a conceptual model of the biogeochemistry of river basins, which considers the river as a series of linked reaches, with each homogeneous reach receiving inputs from its catchment and exchanging materials with its floodplain. From discrete river samples integration information is obtained on the source of that material, which could be differentiated back to a description of the source properties.

The potential of this approach can be demonstrated with results from the CAMREX (Carbon in the AMazon River EXperiment) project—a cooperative research program between the University of Washington (Seattle, USA), the Instituto Nacional de Pesquisas da Amazônia (Manaus, Brazil), and the Centro de Energia Nuclear na Agricultura (Piracicaba, Brazil). Eight sampling cruises were conducted at different stages of the hydrograph from Santo Antônio do Içá to Obidos (Fig. 1). The spatial resolution was approximately 100 km over a 1750-km stretch of river, with time scales on the order of weeks. This work has been reported in a series of papers (Meade et al., 1985; Richey et al., 1986; Devol et al., in press; Hedges et al., in

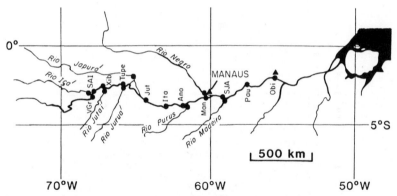

FIGURE 1. CAMREX station locations. VGR = Vargem Grande, SAI = Santo Antônio do Içá, Xib = Xibeco, Tup = Tupe, Jut = Jutica, Ita = Itapeua, Ano = Anori, Man = Manacapuru, SJA = São José do Amatari, Pau = Paura, and Obi = Obidos. Points on tributaries indicate tributary sampling stations.

press). Briefly, a series of parameters varies systematically over space and time; these distributions have been analyzed to deduce some of the key processes operating within the river itself. The tributaries are assumed to provide discrete inputs to the main channel.

Outflow from a tributary represents the sum of the biogeochemistry of its drainage, as transformed during its residence in the river. The concentration of major ions in the tributaries and subsequently in the mainstem is strongly influenced by the weathering regimes in the respective catchments. Superimposed on these patterns are the effects of nutrient cycling by the vegetation. If the Amazon had a homogeneous distribution of primary production and nutrient cycling, the tributaries draining the different subbasins would exhibit similar patterns of carbon and nutrient fluxes. We would expect to see low levels of the limiting nutrient, for example, nitrogen, in the draining waters, with little annual variance in flux.

To compare drainage basins of different sizes, we have computed the area-normalized flux of water and nitrate for the different tributaries (Fig. 2). Water discharge at Vargem Grande (representing primarily the Andean drainage) ranged between 0.0002 and 0.0006 $m^3$ $ha^{-1}$ $s^{-1}$, which was comparable to that of the Rios Japurá, Içá and Jutaí (although the timing varied). Unit discharge was slightly lower in the Rio Purus and even lower in the Rios Juruá and Madeira. The Rio Negro had the greatest temporal variation in discharge, from 0.0001 to 0.0009 $m^3$ $ha^{-1}$ $s^{-1}$.

The patterns of nitrate flux in the tributaries were more variable than was the discharge. At Vargem Grande, nitrate followed the discharge hydrograph, even showing increasing concentrations on the ascending limb, with a maximum flux of 0.009 mmol $ha^{-1}$ $s^{-1}$. Less accentuated patterns were seen for the Rios Japurá and Madeira; the Rio Juruá apparently was diluted

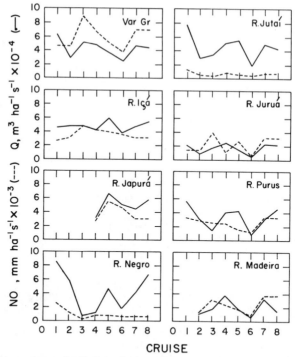

**FIGURE 2.** Comparison of tributary fluxes of water (Q) and $NO_3$ per unit of drainage basin. Vargem Grande (Var Gr) can be considered as the "Andean" tributary.

at high water. Fluxes in these rivers were generally less than 0.005 mmol $ha^{-1}$ $s^{-1}$. More damped patterns were characteristic of the Rios Içá, Jutaí, Purus, and Negro, with particularly low fluxes of less than 0.002 mmol $ha^{-1}$ $s^{-1}$ in the Jutaí and Negro.

The chemical composition of their organic matter provides another perspective on the tributaries. The CAMREX project analyzed water samples for a series of tracers that are uniquely characteristic of the different possible origins of the organic material carried by the river (Hedges et al., 1986). The ratio of the stable carbon isotopes $^{13}C$ to $^{12}C$ (that is, $\delta$ $^{13}C$, which is 1000 times the ratio of $^{13}C$ to $^{12}C$ divided by the standard PDB ratio minus one) versus lambda (the total carbon-normalized phenols produced by lignin oxidation; Ertel et al., 1984) indicates the composition of the material in transport (Fig. 3). The outstanding characteristics of particulate carbon in the Amazon itself are its nearly uniform composition and relative concentrations, with material larger than 0.063 mm mostly composed of undegraded leaf (80%) and wood (20%) remains and with material smaller than 0.063 mm mostly refractory, soil-derived substances. However, the tributaries exhibit a much wider variability. Therefore, the organic matter at Vargem Grande is mixed with tributary material of varying compositions that is generally

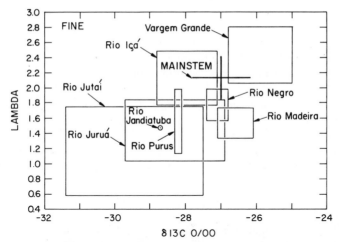

**FIGURE 3.** Plot of lambda (total mg lignin-derived phenols per 100 mg organic carbon) versus δ $^{13}$C for Amazon mainstem ( + ) and tributary fine suspended sediments. Rectangles represent mean ± 1 standard deviation.

isotopically lighter, with lower lambda, modifying the Amazon composition downstream.

Examination of area- and discharge-normalized nitrate flux and the indices of organic composition indicate several properties of importance: (1) Tributary chemistry is considerably more variable and dynamic than would be expected if the "uniform production and tight nutrient-cycling" hypotheses were entirely true. (2) The variability clearly occurs on a systematic and analytically tractable basis. Our mesoscale biogeochemical approach holds considerable promise for elucidating some of the overall properties of water, sediment, and chemical fluxes through the system, as necessary to assess the potential consequences of land use change in Amazonia.

## ACKNOWLEDGMENTS

This research was supported by NSF Grants DEB-8017522 and BSR-8416478 and the Conselho Nacional de Desenvolvimente Cientifico e Tecnologico, Contribution No. 11 of the CAMREX program.

## REFERENCES

Bormann, F. H. and Likens, G. E., 1967. Nutrient cycling, *Science* **155,** 424–429.

Devol, A., Richey, J., Quay, P., and Martinelli, L., in press. Dissolved gases and air–water exchange in the Amazon River, *Limnol. Oceanogr.*

Ertel, J. R., Hedges, J. I., and Perdue, E. M., 1984. Lignin signature of aquatic humic substances, *Science* **223**, 485–487.

Fisher, T. R. and Parsley, P. E., 1979. Amazon lakes: Water storage and nutrient stripping by algae, *Limnol. Oceanogr.* **243**, 547–553.

Gibbs, R. J., 1972. Water chemistry of the Amazon River, *Geochim. Cosmochim. Acta* **36**, 1061–1066.

Hedges, J. I., Clark, W., Quay, P., Richey, J. E., Devol, A., and Ribeiro, N., in press. Composition and fluxes of particulate organic matter in the Amazon River, *Limnol. Oceanogr.*

Herrera, R., Jordan, C. F., Klinge, H., and Medina, E., 1978. Amazon ecosystems: Their structure and functioning with particular emphasis on nutrients, *Interciência* **3**, 223–232.

Jordan, C. F., 1982. The nutrient balance of an Amazonian rainforest, *Ecology* **63**, 647–654.

Klinge, H., 1976. Bilanzierung von Hauptnahrstoffen in Okosystem tropischer Regenwald (Manaus)-vorlaufige, *Daten. Biogeogr.* **7**, 59–77.

Meade, R. H., Dunne, T., Richey, J. E., dos Santos, U., and Salati, E., 1985. Storage and remobilization of suspended sediment in the lower Amazon River of Brazil, *Science* **228**, 488–490.

Richey, J. E., 1983. Interactions of C, N, P, and S in river systems: A biogeochemical model, in B. Bolin and R. B. Cook, Eds., *The Major Biogeochemical Cycles and their Interactions,* Wiley, Chichester, England.

Richey, J. E., Meade, R. H., Devol, A., Nordin, C., Salati, E., and dos Santos, U. 1986. Water discharge and suspended sediment concentrations in the Amazon River: 1982–1984, *Water Resourc. Res.* **22**, 756–764.

Salati, E., Marques, J., and Molion, L., 1978. Origem distribuição das chuvas na Amazônia, *Interciência* **3**, 200–205.

Schmidt, G. W., 1973. Primary production of phytoplankton in the three types of Amazonian waters. III. Primary production of phytoplankton in a tropical floodplain lake of central Amazonia, Lago Castanho, Amazonas, Brazil, *Amazoniana* **4**, 379–404.

Sioli, J., 1975. Amazon tributaries and drainage basins, in A. D. Hasler, Ed., *Couplings of Land and Water Systems,* Springer-Verlag, New York.

Stallard, R. F. and Edmond, J. M., 1983. Geochemistry of the Amazon: 2. The influence of geology and weathering environment on the dissolved load, *J. Geophys. Res.* **88**, 9671–9688.

# PART III

# CLIMATE, MICROMETEOROLOGY, AND THE HYDROLOGICAL CYCLE IN THE MOIST TROPICS

This part considers the connections between vegetation and climate through the micrometeorological processes in the forest canopy and through the hydrological cycle. In order to develop capabilities to predict consequences of future changes, scientists must improve their descriptions of these processes in the tropical forests.

Tropical forests are linked to atmospheric meteorology and climate through exchanges of energy, in particular, solar and infrared radiation fluxes and the transfer of sensible and latent heat. Latent heat, that is, the energy carried by water in its vapor form, is released when the vapor condenses into rainfall in tropical showers and storms. Sensible heat, the internal energy of air, is convected away from a heated surface. These energy exchange processes must not only be understood in detail but also modeled mathematically before quantitative estimates can be made of the impacts of forest change on regional and global climates. Intuitively most obvious are the effects of forest removal on the micrometeorology of local sites (e.g., Chapter 12), for example, drying out and heating the ground because of lack of shading or reducing the infiltration of rainfall into the soil and hence increasing runoff.

Molion (Chapter 14) reports the results of the first field campaign of an Anglo-Brazilian collaborative study of the micrometeorology of undisturbed Amazonian rain forest from a site 25 km northeast of Manaus, Brazil, during September 1983. The rain forest reflected about 12% of incident solar energy, 75% of the available energy was used for evapotranspiration on dry days, and the ratio of sensible to latent heat flux from the canopy was about 0.3. About 17% of rainfall was intercepted by the canopy during the study period, and 48% of the rainfall returned to the atmosphere through evapotranspiration. Wind profile parameters were in close agreement with results reported for temperate forests. Molion also discusses the daily cycles of temperature, humidity, and humidity deficit. Such field studies, along with similar ones of sites deforested into other land uses, help provide an observational basis for modeling the effects of the forest and its removal on climate.

Salati (Chapter 15) reviews the evidence for the role of the forests in the hydrological cycle over the Amazon region. Besides micrometeorological studies such as reported by Molion, and small-basin hydrological studies, the water budget of the Amazon Basin as a whole has been estimated with various approaches, including use of large-scale meteorological data, isotopic tracer measurements, and measurements of river flow. A consistent picture is obtained. On the average, over the basin as a whole, about half the rain that falls is returned to the atmosphere by evapotranspiration and about half is lost by runoff. Equivalently, about half the water in the rainfall originates from the Amazon region itself and about half from the Atlantic Ocean. (The Amazon region is isolated from the Pacific by the Andes and from other regions of South America by lower mountain barriers.) Over local forest sites, as much as three fourths of the incident rainfall is returned locally to the atmosphere by evaporation or transpiration. Since much of the water in rainfall originates from the land, large-scale modifications of the land surface in Amazonia, especially through deforestation, would likely change the intensities, distributions, and amounts of rainfall over the Amazon and possibly elsewhere in South America.

Such changes would depend not only on the micrometeorological properties of the forest but also on those of the deforested regions. For example, conversion to savanna might have a much larger climatic effect than conversion to secondary or managed forest, though ecological damage could be equally drastic. Most lines of argument suggest that extensive forest removal would promote increased aridity and seasonality of soil moisture and rainfall in the Amazon, leading to increased flooding and drought. How noticeable these changes would be or what would be the effects on the climate of the rest of South America or North America cannot yet be said.

Sellers (Chapter 16) discusses the importance of some of the interactions between land surface and atmosphere and then briefly reviews the history of land surface–atmosphere modeling. He has developed a simple biosphere model with realistic mathematical representations of land surface–atmosphere interactions for implementation in global general circulation models (GCMs). Surface properties (roughness length, stomatal resistance, albedo, soil properties, etc.) are determined from an assigned vegetation category at each model point and affect the exchange of energy and momentum at the land–atmosphere interface. The parameterization explicitly resolves the interaction of vegetation with diffuse and direct radiation in the visible, near-infrared, and thermal wavelength intervals, the conduction of soil water through the root–stem–leaf system of vegetation, the interaction of photosynthetically active radiation with the integrated stomatal functioning of the canopy, rainfall interception and evaporation, and aerodynamic transport of heat, moisture, and momentum between the terrestrial surface and the planetary boundary layer.

His model, when coupled to a GCM, is designed to produce prognostic ground and vegetation canopy temperatures, soil moisture content, and fluxes of sensible and latent heat at each model time step. The performance of the model uncoupled from a GCM has been tested using local site data.

# Chapter 14

# Micrometeorology of an Amazonian Rain Forest

Luiz C. B. Molion

Much of the energy that drives physical processes in the troposphere, particularly the general circulation of the atmosphere, which produces weather and climate, is provided by the earth's surface through its interaction with incident solar radiation. This energy enters the atmosphere through the boundary layer, mainly in the form of vertical fluxes of latent and sensible heat. The equatorial portions of the continents, which are mostly covered with natural forests, are major sources of this heat. Although the role of tropical forests as heat sources for the general circulation is widely recognized, there have been only a few experimental studies to quantify this exchange of energy between the forest and the atmosphere, such as those of Jackson (1971) in Tanzania, Read (1977) in the Panama Canal zone, and Heuveldop (1979) in Venezuela.

To quantify this exchange and to see the details of the mechanisms involved, it is necessary to make micrometeorological measurements at sites with climates representative of the region. The micrometeorological measurements reported here for one such site include radiation fluxes, temperature, humidity, wind within and above the canopy, fluxes of sensible and latent heat, and incident and intercepted rainfall. The radiation measurements include incident and absorbed solar radiation and downward longwave radiation. Net absorption of radiation drives fluxes of energy to the atmosphere, divided between sensible and latent heat. Sensible heat is the energy carried by the warmth of the air, and latent heat is that energy derived from the evaporation of water. The total latent heat of evaporation comes from both transpiration and from interception, that is, the reevaporation of water from leaves wetted by rainfall.

The measurements reported here are from the first field campaign of a major Anglo-Brazilian collaborative study of the micrometeorology and plant physiology of the Amazonian rain forest. Most of the results were published by Shuttleworth et al. (1984a,b, 1985). The objective was to give a picture of the diurnal cycle and daily mean balances between the various radiative, sensible and latent fluxes, and possible changes in canopy energy storage. They were also intended to describe the microclimate within the canopy in terms of radiative fluxes, temperature, humidity and wind structure, and the transfer of momentum from atmospheric winds to the canopy.

## THE SITE

Instruments were mounted on a 45-m scaffolding tower located at a site selected as representative of the natural vegetation and regional topography in the Ducke Reserve (INPA/CNPq), 25 km northeast of Manaus, at latitude 2°57′ S, longitude 59°57′ W. Plant density is high, up to 3000 stems per hectare, but less than 10% of the trees have girths of 0.2 m or more. The forest canopy around the tower extends to a height of about 35 m, with occasional emergent trees reaching over 40 m. There are no obvious substories. The middle and lower parts of the canopy are made up of more numerous but individually smaller plants. Ground-level vegetation is scarce, and rooting in the yellow laterite soil is shallow, with a dense root mat down to 0.15 m, and a few tap roots deep in the soil. The rainfall reaching the ground was measured with 16 raingauges relocated randomly along a linear transect after each storm.

## RADIATION BALANCE

The net radiation $R_n$ for the *active canopy* surface is

$$R_n = S{\downarrow} - S{\uparrow} - L{\uparrow} + L{\downarrow} - RL{\downarrow} \tag{1}$$

where $R_n$ is the radiation imbalance or net radiation, $S{\downarrow}$ is the incoming solar radiation, $S{\uparrow}$ is the reflected solar radiation, $L{\uparrow}$ is the long-wave radiation emitted by the surface, $L{\downarrow}$ is the downward long-wave radiation, and $RL{\downarrow}$ is the reflected downward long-wave radiation. All quantities are in flux units.

Using the definitions of surface albedo $a$, surface emissivity $\epsilon$, and the Stefan–Boltzmann law with constant $\sigma$, equation (1) is rewritten as

$$R_n = S{\downarrow}(1 - a) - \epsilon\sigma T_S^4 + L{\downarrow} - (1 - \epsilon)L{\downarrow} \tag{2}$$

where $T_S$ is the surface temperature. The emissivity of natural vegetation usually lies between 0.95 and 0.98, and for practical purposes it can be considered that of a black body ($\epsilon = 1$) so that the last term in equation (2) may be neglected.

A unidirectional radiometer was used to measure all-wavelength downward radiation ($U = S\downarrow + L\downarrow$). For this instrument, the lower plastic dome on a standard Funk-type net radiometer has been replaced by an optically black hemisphere, the temperature of which is measured with a calibrated thermistor. The values of $L\uparrow$ and $L\downarrow$ were derived from combinations of the measured fluxes. The upward component of long-wave radiation agrees with that calculated assuming that the mean surface temperature and the mean measured air temperature at canopy level are equal and that the surface emissivity equals 1. The long-wave components are particularly sensitive to error since they are calculated as a combination of several measured fluxes. A net radiation measurement at a single location may have an error of about ±5% (Federer, 1968; McNeil and Shuttleworth, 1975).

The average diurnal variation of short and long-wave components of the radiation flux, and the net radiation for six days of continuous data, measured at the site near Manaus are shown in Fig. 1 (from Shuttleworth et al., 1984a). On the average, solar radiation peaks before midday and then falls slightly in the afternoon, presumably in response to increasing cloudiness. Hourly average solar radiation exceeded 900 W m$^{-2}$ on rare occasions, but peak daily values of 500–700 W m$^{-2}$ were more common. During the day, the net radiation followed the behavior of solar radiation very closely, with an average maximum around 500 W m$^{-2}$, and through the nighttime was rather constant with values around $-40$ W m$^{-2}$. The upward and downward long-wave radiation fluxes have a small diurnal variation, with the net long-wave radiation loss slightly increased around midday because of higher canopy temperature. The mean upward flux was approximately 452 W m$^{-2}$ and the mean downward flux equal to 412 W m$^{-2}$. The angstrom ratio, that is, the fractional net loss, was about 9%.

Figure 2 (Shuttleworth et al., 1984a) shows the above- and below-canopy fluxes of solar and net radiation in the form of hourly means and standard errors for the same period. The below-canopy solar radiation reaches a peak before midday, probably because of sunlight penetration at low solar angles. A second peak in the afternoon does not occur, probably because of cloudiness.

On the average, the solar radiation reaching the ground was 1.2% of that above the canopy, that is, an average flux of about 4 W m$^{-2}$. The below-canopy net radiation lags behind the above-canopy net radiation by about an hour and provides averages of about 0.06 MJ m$^{-2}$ over 24 h, approximately equal to the input of below-canopy solar radiation. The observed morning peak is related to the structure of the main canopy, which allows penetration of sunlight at low solar angles; the afternoon peak results not only from light penetration but also from main canopy heating since maximum temperature is observed near this time of the day.

The relative variation in the below-canopy fluxes is significantly greater

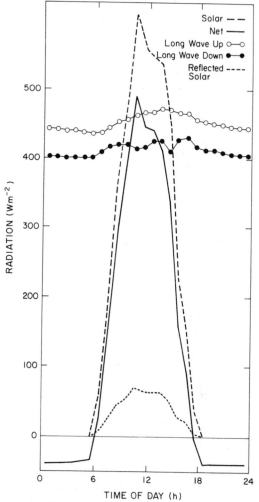

**FIGURE 1.** Mean value of radiation components above an Amazonian rain forest for six days of continuous data. [From Shuttleworth et al. (1984a), redrafted with permission of the Royal Meteorological Society.]

than that in the above-canopy fluxes, as the error bars in Fig. 2 indicate. These fluxes are subject to sampling errors. In addition, the data may represent a less than perfect spatial average.

The major factors that regulate the albedo of tall vegetation are the solar zenith angle, cloudiness, wetness, and spectral properties of the vegetation. The density, height, and geometric configuration are also important. For an ideal rough surface, the albedo would be independent of the direction of the radiation beam. Pinker et al. (1980) analyzed a large amount of solar radiation data to determine the mean albedo of a tropical evergreen forest in Thailand.

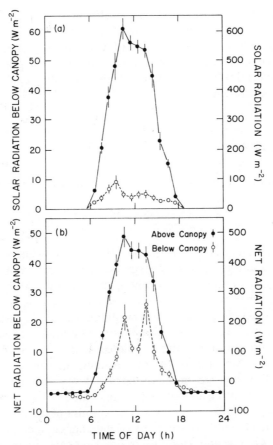

**FIGURE 2.** Mean values of (*a*) solar and (*b*) net radiation above and beneath the canopy of an Amazonian rain forest for six days of continuous data. Above- and below-canopy fluxes are plotted on different scales. The bars indicate the standard error for each flux. [From Shuttleworth et al. (1984a), redrafted with permission of the Royal Meteorological Society.]

They found a mean albedo of 13% with a strong diurnal variation during clear days, that is, with an albedo ranging from about 11% around midday to as high as 18–19% in early morning or late afternoon. The variation is largely suppressed on overcast days, and the midday albedo is higher than on the clear days. On overcast days, the solar radiation is all diffuse, that is, incident at all angles, with the angular distribution of radiation nearly independent of time of day.

Shuttleworth et al. (1984a) reported a mean albedo value of about 12% for the Amazon rain forest and less diurnal variation than did Pinker et al. (1980). For a tropical forest in Nigeria, Oguntoyinbo (1970) reported a value of 13%.

As pointed out in Shuttleworth et al. (1984a), changes in measured reflection ratio for the sun near the horizon are very sensitive to experimental errors. Fortunately, common practice for daily energy budget calculations is to use the mean albedo, which is calculated from integrated daily fluxes of incoming and reflected solar radiation, thus avoiding consideration of the solar altitude dependence.

## ENERGY FLUXES

The energy flux ($A$) from the forest to the atmosphere is written as

$$A = \lambda E + H = R_n - G - S \tag{3}$$

where $\lambda E$ is the latent heat into the air, $H$ is the sensible heat into the air, $R_n$ is the net radiation, $G$ is the energy going into the ground, and $S$ is the energy going into storage (i.e., warming the canopy). All quantities are in flux units. The energy used in photochemical reactions is neglected, and horizontal homogeneity, that is, no energy advection, is assumed.

As stated before, the net radiation flux can be measured with an error of ±5% or less with net radiometers mounted at the end of long booms. The heat flux into the Amazon forest soil is small; Shuttleworth et al. (1984a) reported an hourly average on the order of 4 W m$^{-2}$ entering the soil during the day and leaving it during the night. This value is typically 1% of the net radiation for dense forest vegetation. The amount of energy going into storage is determined from measurements of the change in canopy temperature and humidity with time and from the canopy heat capacity (see, e.g., Stewart and Thom, 1973; McNeil and Shuttleworth, 1975). Spittlehouse and Black (1980) discussed the difficulty in estimating $G$ and $S$ for forests. Nevertheless, they claim that, except for periods around sunrise and sunset, $G + S$ is less than 5% of the net radiation flux, so that even a 50% error in this sum would result in a minor error in the measurement of available energy.

For a tropical forest, however, the presence of storage terms in the energy budget may add considerable complexity to the computation of the available energy and its partitioning. Simple modeling of this component proved incapable of describing sustained nighttime radiation (Thompson, 1979). Recent sophisticated computer models (e.g., Goudriaan, 1979) suggest that storage can be a significant contribution to the energy budget, both in terms of magnitude and of duration. The size, complexity, and density of tropical forest are such that energy storage is likely to be a particularly important component but difficult to calculate.

One possible way of avoiding the calculation of $S$ is to assume that the cumulative sum of daily $S$ values over a period of several days is approximately zero. Equation (3) then is rewritten as

$$\sum A = \sum (\lambda E + H) = \sum R_n \qquad (4)$$

This equality is not completely definitive in that it cannot rule out the possibility of a fortuitous numerical cancellation between daytime and nighttime errors. With this equality, the problem is reduced to one of partitioning the available energy between latent and sensible heating, as reviewed by Spittlehouse and Black (1980). Two methods were applied to the Amazon tropical forest, the eddy correlation and the Bowen ratio methods. The eddy correlation technique used a measuring system named Hydra, consisting of a vertical sonic anemometer (Shuttleworth et al., 1982), a single-beam infrared hygrometer (Moore, 1983), a 50-$\mu$m thermocouple thermometer and, two Gill propeller anemometers mounted orthogonally to measure the horizontal wind. This system measures the latent heat flux ($\lambda E$) and the sensible heat flux ($H$) directly. The comparison of cumulative net radiation and the cumulative sum of $\lambda E + H$ was satisfactory for the eight complete days; that is, the integration over all eight days indicated a difference of 6.3 MJ m$^{-2}$ between the net radiation and fluxes from the eddy correlation measurements. This difference is about 7% of the total radiant input of 96.5 MJ m$^{-2}$. The *evaporative fraction* is defined either as

$$\alpha = \frac{\sum \lambda E}{\sum (\lambda E + H)} \qquad (5a)$$

or

$$\alpha' = \frac{\sum \lambda E}{\sum R_n} \qquad (5b)$$

For the eight fine days, the average daily value, for the average of $\alpha$ and $\alpha'$ was $0.72 \pm 0.06$ with values of $\alpha$ generally higher than those of $\alpha'$ because of the difference between the net radiation and integrated eddy flux loss mentioned above. Figure 3 (from Shuttleworth et al., 1984b) illustrates the energy partitioning for the eight days considered in their analyses.

The Bowen ratio $B$ is defined as the ratio of sensible heat flux to the latent heat flux ($B = H/\lambda E$). If it is assumed that the fluxes obey a diffusion law and that the eddy diffusivities for heat and water vapor are equal, then near neutral conditions, the Bowen ratio reduces to

$$B = \frac{c_p}{\lambda} \frac{\Delta \theta}{\Delta q} \qquad (6)$$

where $\theta$ is the potential temperature, $q$ is the specific humidity, $c_p$ is the specific heat of air at constant pressure, and $\lambda$ is the latent heat of vaporization of water.

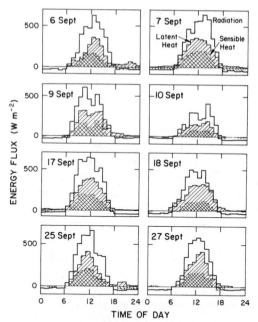

**FIGURE 3.** Daily variation in measured net radiation and latent and sensible heat fluxes for eight fine days in an Amazonian forest during September 1983. Thick line indicates net radiation; latent and sensible heat fluxes are shown as lightly shaded and darkly shaded portions, respectively. [From Shuttleworth et al. (1984b), redrafted with permission of the Royal Meteorological Society.]

The evaporative fraction is readily calculated from this ratio through the expression $\alpha = (1 + B)^{-1}$. Differential measurements of temperature and humidity were made using a reversing psychrometers system (TIS) described by McNeil and Shuttleworth (1975). Vertical gradients over a rough forest surface tend to be small and therefore difficult to measure accurately. By reversing the psychrometers, systematic errors cancel and a more accurate gradient is obtained. The daily $\alpha$ values resulting from TIS measurements are in general agreement with the ones calculated through the eddy correlation method, with the TIS results tending to show slightly lower values of evaporative fraction. The average evaporative fraction of about 0.75 on dry days corresponds to a Bowen ratio of about 0.3. The data collected imply that, on the average, about 75% of the energy available to the Amazonian forest goes into evaporating water, and the remaining 25% is used to heat the air. For a daily average of 4.96 mm water equivalent of radiation, 3.70 mm of water was evaporated into the air.

The evaporation from tropical forests consists of both transpiration by plants and interception of rainfall by the canopy. Direct soil evaporation does not appear to contribute significantly to moisture fluxes. Tropical forest interception ranges from as low as 13% of incident rainfall (Jordan and Heu-

veldop, 1981) for the Amazon forest at San Carlos de Rio Negro to as high
as 50% (Read, 1977) for the Panama Canal forest.

Shuttleworth et al. (1984b) reported a preliminary value of 17% for interception loss measured during 25 days in September 1983 at a site near
the tower. Franken et al. (1982), at a different site 40 km from Manaus but
with a similar environment, found an average value of 22% for a 1-y period.
Shuttleworth et al. (1984b) also estimated that, during the period of measurement, 48% of the precipitation falling on the site returned to the atmosphere by evapotranspiration.

This value of 48% is in close agreement with the results for total evapotranspiration published by Jordan and Heuveldop (1981). If the interception loss is 17% and direct soil evaporation can be disregarded, then transpiration is responsible for 31% of the rainfall loss.

## VERTICAL STRUCTURE OF WIND, TEMPERATURE, AND HUMIDITY

### Wind

The profile of the mean horizontal wind in the atmospheric surface layer
over natural surfaces is generally logarithmic in neutral stability conditions,
that is, above tall vegetation,

$$u(z) = \frac{u_*}{k} \ln \left\{ \frac{z - d}{z_0} \right\} \tag{7}$$

where $u(z)$ is the mean horizontal wind at a height $z$ above the ground, $u_*$
is the friction velocity, $k$ is von Karman's constant, $z_0$ is the roughness
length, and $d$ is the zero-plane displacement. The values of $d$ were computed
together with $u_*$ and $z_0$ using the mass conservation method in conjunction
with least squares (Molion and Moore, 1983).

The Amazonian forest measurement site presents no problem of fetch,
having height–fetch ratios smaller than 1:700. For the data set collected in
September 1983, only 24 profiles were found to be in near neutral conditions
($0.008 \leq -dT/dz < 0.012°C \text{ m}^{-1}$). Speeds were above 2.0 m s$^{-1}$ at the
highest measurement level, which was about 10 m above the mean canopy.
The estimated values of $d = 25.3 \pm 0.6$ m and $z_0 = 5.0 \pm 0.4$ m correspond
to $(0.72 \pm 0.02)h$ and $(0.14 \pm 0.01)h$, respectively, where $h$ is the mean
canopy height, which is equal to about 35 m.

The values of $u_* = 0.79 \pm 0.13$ m s$^{-1}$ calculated from equation (7) seem
to be high considering that in the set of profiles the uppermost-level wind
did not exceed 4.0 m s$^{-1}$. The $u_*$ values measured with the Hydra had an
average that is about half of the $u_*$ calculated from equation (7).

The zero-plane displacement and aerodynamic roughness, however, seem
to be in good agreement with values reported for temperate forests. It is still

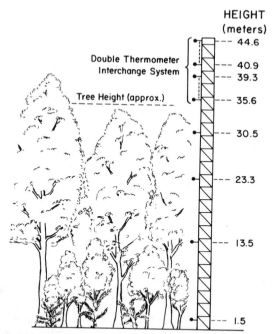

**FIGURE 4.** Schematic diagram illustrating heights of aspirated wet- and dry-bulb psy-chrometer systems (indicated by black circles) mounted on the tower and their relationship to the forest canopy. [From Shuttleworth et al. (1985), redrafted with permission of the Royal Meteorological Society.]

difficult to draw conclusions about these parameters, and it is expected that coming field experiments will elucidate the question.

Below the canopy, the mean horizontal wind speeds were usually between 0.0 and 1.0 m s$^{-1}$. In this range, the cup anemometers are not accurate, so the wind profile below the canopy was not estimated.

### Temperature and Humidity

The temperature and humidity data were collected with psychrometers de-scribed by Gash and Stewart (1975). Figure 4 illustrates their arrangement on the tower with the double reversing psychrometers system (TIS), which was located above the canopy surface. Although wet and dry bulb ther-mometers were well calibrated, it would be unrealistic to assume that the measurements represent the spatial average at each level to accuracies better than, say, 0.1°C in temperature and 0.2 g kg$^{-1}$ in humidity.

Figure 5 (from Shuttleworth et al., 1985) presents data of temperature and humidity for two consecutive days that are of particular interest because they provide a comparison between a dry day and a day when two short rainstorms occurred. These data suggest that, in dry conditions, mixing in

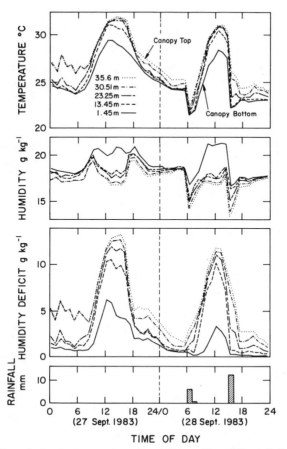

**FIGURE 5.** Daily variation in temperature, humidity, and humidity deficit from saturated values measured at five heights within and just above the forest canopy and the above-canopy rainfall for September 27 and 28, 1983. [From Shuttleworth et al. (1985), redrafted with permission of the Royal Meteorological Society.]

the top two thirds of the canopy is quite efficient during daylight hours, with temperature, humidity, and humidity deficit (i.e., the difference between saturated and actual humidity) following those of the air above to within about 1°C and 2 g kg$^{-1}$, respectively. On the other hand, the bottom third seems to undergo a less pronounced daily cycle, the amplitude of temperature being about 60% of that at the canopy top, specific humidity higher by about 2 g kg$^{-1}$ and humidity deficit only 30–50% of upper canopy values.

At night, the behavior is reversed, with temperature of the air in the upper part of the canopy significantly decoupled from that in the lower two thirds. Possibly, the air at the canopy top cools by radiative losses and sinks down, replacing the warmer air, which is forced to rise. The nighttime radiation losses may be sustained by this energy from the warmer air stored below the canopy during the day. In dry nighttime conditions, there is a small variation in temperature and specific humidity deficit through the bottom two thirds of the canopy. Above this level, the variation has significantly higher values. The specific humidity changes little throughout the canopy.

When rain started at 6:00 and 15:00 local time, both temperature and specific humidity fell sharply at all levels, perhaps because of cool downdrafts and cooling by evaporation. The humidity deficit at the top level was significantly reduced, by about 3 g kg$^{-1}$, compared to its value during the previous day. However, a few hours later, the humidity deficit in the upper two thirds exhibited remarkably little difference from that of the previous day, as if the canopy were already dry. The bottom level showed a noticeable reduction in the humidity deficit throughout the wet day.

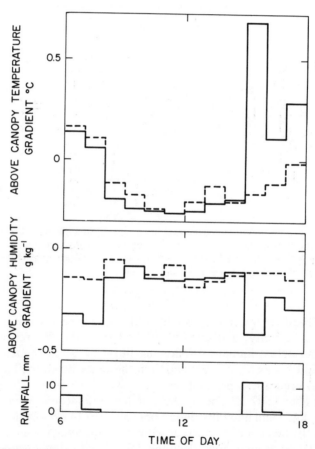

**FIGURE 6.** Differential gradients of temperature and humidity measured above the forest canopy for daylight hours of September 27 (broken line) and 28 (solid line), 1983, and the above canopy rainfall measurement. [From Shuttleworth et al. (1985), redrafted with permission of the Royal Meteorological Society.]

Figure 6 shows the gradients in temperature and specific humidity above the canopy as measured with TIS. The broken line indicates the behavior on the dry day (September 27) and the full line that on the following day, when the two storms occurred. A positive temperature gradient as seen in the early morning hours indicates a downward sensible heat flux from the warmer atmosphere above, suggesting that the radiant input at this time is insufficient to support the losses through long-wave radiation and possibly evaporation. The humidity gradients are always negative and indicate an upward flux of latent heat, that is, evaporation. When the storm occurred at 15:00 on September 28, the temperature gradient reversed and the humidity differences were significantly increased. Presumably, the wet canopy was evaporating water at a rate that could not be supported by radiation alone so that it drew energy from the atmosphere, causing local advection, and from the forest storage.

Hourly computations of energy balance assuming no horizontal temperature gradients, that is, no advection term, can be therefore quite erroneous in the presence of these small rain showers. Convective cells of equivalent diameter smaller than, say, 5 km are common in the Amazonian forest and may introduce a serious problem of surface heat source heterogeneity that is impossible to solve with a single-tower setup.

## ROLE OF FOREST

The first field measurements of the micrometeorological experiment in an Amazonian rain forest near Manaus yielded the following information. On dry days, about 75% of the absorbed radiative energy is consumed in evapotranspiration and the remaining 25% in heating the air. The assumption that over a daily cycle both storage and net horizontal energy advection terms are zero may not be true, particularly on occasions when short-duration rain showers occur. These convective cells have an equivalent diameter smaller than 5 km. If the rain shower is at the tower site, the forest surface acts as a sink of both sensible heat and storage energy, which are used for evaporation. Horizontal convergence of sensible heat at the tower site presumably supplies this energy deficit. On the other hand, if the rain-shower is elsewhere but near the tower, the opposite occurs and there will be a net horizontal divergence of sensible heat from the air layer over the tower site. On a daily basis, the evaluation of variation of energy storage in the forest and the net horizontal energy advection terms is a difficult task using only one tower. The assumption of horizontal homogeneity of the surface with respect to sources and sinks is questionable.

From an analysis of wind profiles near neutral conditions, values are obtained of the surface aerodynamic roughness and zero-plane displacement that are in agreement with published results for temperate forests. The values of friction velocity computed with a mass conservation method were higher than expected and exceeded the values measured with the eddy correlation system by a factor of 2. The mean wind flow in the air layer above the site was generally weak and from the east northeast–east southeast quadrant. Sometimes, a single convective cell to the west of the tower was sufficient to reverse the flow direction. At times, deep penetration of frontal systems into the tropics enhances the wind field for several hours, for example, on September 26, when a frontal system was observed to the south of the Amazon region.

The influence of forests on climate is poorly known. For the Amazon region as a whole, Molion (1976) and Salati et al. (1979) have shown that, on the average, 50% of the precipitation is recycled back into the atmosphere through evapotranspiration. The present analysis indicated that during the 25 observed days of September, 48% of the rainfall returned to the atmosphere as evapotranspiration. Of this, 17% was due to evaporation of intercepted rainfall by the canopy.

Nowadays, man can transform the geography of large land masses, particularly through the removal of natural forests. Scientific studies have indicated that deforestation usually reduces evaporation locally. Since in the Amazon the local source of water vapor for precipitation is, on the average, of the same magnitude as the net advected vapor, a reduction of evaporation would reduce the regional precipitation. Furthermore, a decrease in evaporation over land is nearly balanced by an increase in sensible heat flux (Nobre, 1983). Sensible heat, however, warms the air only in a relatively shallow layer whereas the latent heat warms the entire troposphere through the condensation of vapor in tall cumulus clouds. Thus, large-scale deforestation in the Amazon Basin could affect the global weather and climate patterns by changing tropical latent heating and hence the planetary-scale tropical circulations and the subtropical jet stream that links tropical and extratropical circulations.

There is an urgent need to quantify the interaction between the Amazon forest and the atmosphere, especially as it affects the latent heating of the atmosphere, and to model possible climate changes resulting from a large-scale deforestation. The micrometeorological experiment near Manaus is a contribution to this effort.

## ACKNOWLEDGMENTS

The author would like to thank his British colleagues W. J. Shuttleworth, J. H. C. Gash, C. R. Lloyd, C. J. Moore, J. M. Roberts, D. D. McNeil, and H. R. Oliver and his Brazilian colleagues L. F. Aguiar, O. M. R. Cabral, G. Fisch, A. O. Marques Filho, J. C. Moraes, C. A. Nobre, S. Patel, M. N. G. Ribeiro, L. D. A. Sá, V. P. Silva Filho, and A. O. Manzi, who worked diligently and contributed to make this micrometeorological experiment a reality. He also wishes to thank and acknowledge the financial support provided by the following British Institutions: the Institute of Hydrology, the Natural Environment Research Council and the British Council; and the following Brazilian Institutions: the National Research Council (CNPq) and its affiliated institutes INPA and INPE, the Brazilian Company for Agricultural Research (EMBRAPA), through its National Research Center CNPSD, and the University of Amazonas. Special thanks to his colleague C. A. Nobre, who kindly reviewed this manuscript, and Sueli A. F. V. Camargo Pinto for the expert typing.

## REFERENCES

Federer, C. A., 1968. Spatial variation of net radiation, albedo and surface temperature of forests, *J. Appl. Meteor.* **7**, 789–795.

Franken, W., Leopoldo, P. R., Matsui, E., and Ribeiro, M. N. G., 1982. Interceptação das Precipitações em Floresta Amazônica de Terra Firme, *Acta Amazon.* **12**(3), 15–22.

Gash, J. H. C. and Stewart, J. B., 1975. The average surface resistance of a pine forest derived from Bowen ratio measurements, *Bound. Lay. Met.* **8**, 453–464.

Goudriaan, J., 1979. Micro Weather Simulation Model Applied to a Forest, in: S. Halldin, Ed., *Comparison of Forest Water and Energy Exchange Models*, International Society of Ecological Modelling, Copenhagen.

Heuveldop, R., 1979. The International Amazon MAB Rainforest Ecosystem Pilot Project at San Carlos de Rio Negro: Micrometeorological studies, in S. Adisoemarto and E. F. Brunig, Eds., *Transactions of the Second International MAB-IUFRO Workshop on Tropical Rainforest Ecosystem Research,* Reinbeck, Hamburg.

Jackson, I. J., 1971. Problems of throughfall and interception under tropical forest, *J. Hydrol.* **12**(3), 234–254.

Jordan, C. F. and Heuveldop, J., 1981. The water budget of an Amazonian rainforest, *Acta Amazôn.* **11**(1), 87–92.

McNeil, D. D. and Shuttleworth, W. J., 1975. Comparative measurements of the energy fluxes over a pine forest, *Bound. Lay. Meteor.* **9**, 297–313.

Molion, L. C. B., 1976. *A Climatonomic Study of the Energy and Moisture Fluxes of the Amazonas Basin with Considerations of Deforestation Effects*, INPE-923-TPT/035, São José dos Campos.

Molion, L. C. B. and Moore, C. J., 1983. Estimating the zero-plane displacement for tall vegetation using a mass conservation method, *Bound. Lay. Meteor.* **26**, 115–125.

Moore, C. J., 1983. On the calibration and temperature behaviour of single-beam infrared hygrometers, *Bound. Lay. Meteor.* **25**, 245–269.

Nobre, C. A., 1983. The Amazon and climate. In *Proceedings of the Climate Conference for Latin America and the Caribbean*, World Meteorological Organization, Geneva, Switzerland.

Oguntoyinbo, J. S., 1970. Reflection coefficients of natural vegetation crops and urban surfaces in Nigeria, *Quart. J. Roy. Meteor. Soc.* **96**, 430–441.

Pinker, R. T., Thompson, O. E., and Eck, T. F., 1980. The albedo of a tropical evergreen forest, *Quart. J. Roy. Meteor. Soc.* **106**, 551–558.

Read, R. G., 1977. Microclimate as background environment for ecological studies of insects in a tropical forest, *J. Appl. Met.* **16**, 1282–1291.

Salati, E., Dall'Olio, A., Matsue, E., and Gat, J. R., 1979. Recycling of the water in the Brazilian Amazon Basin, *Wat. Resourc. Res.,* **15**, 1250–1258.

Shuttleworth, W. J., McNeil, D. D., and Moore, C. J., 1982. A switched continuous-wave sonic anemometer for measuring surface heat fluxes, *Bound. Lay. Meteor.* **23**, 425–448.

Shuttleworth, W. J., Gash, J. H. C., Lloyd, C. R., Moore, C. J., Roberts, J., Marques Filho, A. O., Fish, G., Silva Filho, V. P., Ribeiro, M. N. G., Molion, L. C. B., Nobre, C. A., Sá, L. D. A., Cabral, O. M. R., Patel, S. R., and Moraes, J. C., 1984a. Observation of radiation exchange above and below Amazonian forest, *Quart. J. Roy. Meteor. Soc.* **110**, 1163–1169.

Shuttleworth, W. J., Gash, J. H. C., Lloyd, C. R., Moore, C. J., Roberts, J., Marques Filho, A. O., Fish, G., Silva Filho, V. P., Ribeiro, M. N. G., Molion, L. C. B., Nobre, C. A., Sá, L. D. A., Cabral, O. M. R., Patel, S. R., and Moraes, J. C., 1984b. Eddy correlation measurements of energy partition for Amazonian forest, *Quart. J. Roy. Meteor. Soc.* **110**, 1143–1162.

Shuttleworth, W. J., Gash, J. H. C., Lloyd, C. R., Moore, C. J., Roberts, J., Marques Filho, A. O., Fish, G., Silva Filho, V. P., Ribeiro, M. N. G., Molion, L. C. B., Nobre, C. A., Sá, L. D. A., Cabral, O. M. R., Patel, S. R., and Moraes, J. C., 1985. *Daily Variations of Temperature and Humidity Within and Above Amazonian Forest, Weather,* **40**, 102–108.

Spittlehouse D. L. and Black, T. A., 1980. Evaluation of the Bowen ratio/energy balance method for determining forest evapotranspiration, *Atmos. Oc.* **18**(2), 98–116.

Stewart, J. B. and Thom, A. S., 1973. Energy budgets in pine forest, *Quart. J. Roy. Meteor. Soc.* **99**, 154–170.

Thompson, N., 1979. Turbulence measurements above a pine forest, *Bound. Lay. Meteor.* **16**, 293–310.

# ☐ COMMENTS ON "MICROMETEOROLOGY OF AN AMAZONIAN RAIN FOREST"

## William E. Reifsnyder

There are few ecosystems in the world that have had more pronouncements made about them based on as little hard information as has the Amazon forest. The news media are hungry for information on the health of our world ecosystem and are all too ready to print any snippet, especially if it is at least mildly sensational. And too many self-styled experts are willing to make pseudo-scientific statements, especially in fields they know little about. It is refreshing, therefore, to see a high level of good scientific research on the

Amazon ecosystem, some of which is being reported and discussed in this book. It is especially gratifying to see the preliminary results of a major micrometeorology experiment (reported in Molion's essay).

One of the major controversies surrounding the development and exploitation of the Amazon region concerns the role of the moist tropical forest in the hydrological cycle. Many attempts have been made to predict the environmental consequences of *deforestation* at various predicted rates. One of the problems in predicting the hydrological effects of deforestation is the uncertainty over long-range ecological and hydrological consequences of such land cover manipulation. For example, some scientists have made the ecologically questionable straight-line extrapolation from the area of forest cut per year to the time of *complete forest destruction*; (see, e.g., Lovejoy and Salati, 1983, p. 211). Such an extrapolation ignores the role of regrowth of the forest, something I suspect is difficult to prevent in much of Amazonia. Most of these attempts have made tacit assumptions about the hydrometeorological consequences of such land use modification; namely that removing the forest drastically reduces the evapotranspiration from the area, and that the land surface modification is irreversible, at least for many years, if not forever. The latter question is one for ecologists and political scientists to answer; the first is in the province of the micrometeorologist.

Perhaps the most significant finding of the work of the joint Brazilian–British research team of which Molion was a member (Shuttleworth, et al., 1984) is that the tropical rain forest studied behaves pretty much as one might have expected based on experience in other forests, both temperate and tropical. That is, the dense canopy allows only about 1–2% of incident sunlight to reach the forest floor (cf. Aoki et al., 1975); that the variability of below-canopy solar radiation is greater than the above-canopy flux (Reifsnyder et al., 1971); that the mean albedo of the canopy is about 12% (Pinker et al., (1980), with highest albedos at low solar angles (although the lowest albedo was measured at solar altitudes of about 55°); that the roughness length is about 5 m (Rauner, 1976); that the ratio of evaporative flux to net radiation is about 0.7; and that precipitation is distributed about one quarter to direct evaporation of leaf-intercepted water, about one half returned to the atmosphere by transpiration, and the remaining quarter to runoff and groundwater. These figures compare closely with those for mature hardwood forests in temperate zones and with the few measurements in other moist tropical forests.

What is not known is what happens to these figures when the tropical forest is converted to grazed pasture, slash-and-burn agriculture, partially cut forest, or clear-cut and abandoned forest. And what happens over time as land use changes? It is no criticism of the current effort to point out that applying the Molion–Shuttleworth data to the entire Amazon Basin would be like applying the micrometeorological data obtained for a Douglas fir forest in the Pacific Northwest to the entire United States. My point here is twofold: There is a need for replications and extensions to other parts of the Amazon ecosystem of the kind of high-quality work reported on by Molion; and, no less important, current predictions of the hydrometeorological functioning of the Amazon Basin based on meagre data and fanciful scenarios must be treated with some skepticism.

This brings me to my last point and to the only major criticism I have of the work of the research group. In order ultimately to apply their data to other places and other times, we must have detailed quantitative descriptions of the forest at the measurement site. In the work published so far, about all we get is one short paragraph with statements of the sort, "The forest canopy is of very varied species and typical of undisturbed natural forest"! I urge that they produce a detailed ecological and mensurational description of the forest under observation.

To close the circle, we need to expand efforts to monitor land use changes over the basin. Only after developing a clear picture of such changes and putting this together with knowledge of the hydrological cycle will we be able to make useful predictions of the trends in basin hydrometeorology. The research of Molion and Shuttleworth is critical for this effort and should be continued and expanded.

## REFERENCES

Aoki, M., Yabuki, K., and Koyami, H., 1975. Micrometeorology and assessment of primary production of a tropical rain forest in West Malaysia, *J. Agr. Met. (Japan)* **31**, 115–124.

Campbell, G. S., 1977. *An Introduction to Environmental Biophysics*, Springer-Verlag, New York.

Lovejoy, T. E. and Salati, E., 1983. Precipitating change in Amazonia, in E. J. Moran, Ed., *The Dilemma of Amazonian Development*, Westview, Boulder, CO.

Pinker, R. T., Thompson, O. E., and Eck, T. F., 1980. The albedo of a tropical evergreen forest, *Quart. J. Roy. Meteor. Soc.* **106**, 551–558.

Rauner, Ju. L., 1976. Deciduous forests, in J. L. Monteith, Ed., *Vegetation and the Atmosphere*, Vol. 2, *Case Studies*, Academic, New York.

Reifsnyder, W. E., Furnival, G. M., and Horowitz, J. L., 1971. Spatial and temporal distribution of solar radiation beneath forest canopies, *Agric. Meteorol.* **9**, 21–37.

Shuttleworth, W. J., Gash, J. H. C., Lloyd, C. R., Moore, C. J., Roberts, J., Marques Filho, A. O., Fish, G., Silva Filho, V. P., Ribeiro, M. N. G., Molion, L. C. B., Nobre, C. A., Sá, L. D. A., Cabral, O. M. R., Patel, S. R., and Moraes, J. C., 1984. Eddy correlation measurements of energy partition for Amazonian forest, *Quart. J. Roy. Meteor. Soc.* **110**, 1143–1162.

# Chapter 15

# The Forest and the Hydrological Cycle

**Eneas Salati**

Over the past 20 y, efforts have been made to turn agriculture in the humid tropics into an economically productive activity. Intensive colonization, particularly of the Amazon region, started toward the end of the 1960s. Exploitation of the Brazilian Amazon has occurred along navigable rivers for many centuries. However, with the construction of roads crossing the forest from north to south and from east to west in the last two decades, it has become possible to use *terra firme* (never flooded) forest areas, and so agriculture has expanded considerably in the region. The main highways used are Belém-Brasília (BR-010), Transamazônica (BR-230), Porto Velho/Manaus/Boa Vista (BR-319), and Cuiabá/Porto Velho (BR-364).

About 2–3 million ha of forest are now being converted annually into agricultural production (pasture, coffee, annual crops, cacao, rubber, etc.). With increased clearing, the question of possible ecological changes that might be introduced into the region was raised (Goodland and Irwin, 1975).

Research has greatly increased during the past 15 y in an effort to find adequate answers to the questions raised by the ecologists and to help in government planning for colonization and agricultural development. The objective is to determine what changes might occur and to what degree these changes would influence the water cycle and other biogeochemical cycles both in the region itself and in adjacent areas.

Research to answer such questions can be subdivided into several categories:

a. energy balance on a microclimatic scale,
b. regional energy balance,
c. water balance on a microclimatic scale,

**d.** water balance in representative hydrographic basins,

**e.** water balance on a regional level (Amazon Basin),

**f.** biogeochemical cycles on basin and regional scales, and

**g.** interactions among water, *terra firme* forest, and flooded-land forest.

Research institutions operating in the Amazon region are now studying these topics through programs and special projects. Researchers in Brazil and in the other countries comprising the Amazon Basin have written over 100 papers (these were reviewed, e.g., by Salati and Vose, 1984).

What are the changes that might occur in this area of approximately $6 \times 10^6$ km$^2$, which constitutes the last and greatest tropical rain forest reserve of the world?

Among the projects attempting to provide answers to this question are the following (meaning of abbreviations is given at the end of this chapter):

(i) Northwest Pole Project: to study the ecological impact of the Cuiabá/Porto Velho (BR-364) highway; coordinated by CNPq; started in March 1982.

(ii) Amazon Erosion Project: to quantify average erosion in the Amazon by measuring the sediments transported by the Amazon River and its main tributaries; coordinated by CENA and INPA in collaboration with the University of Washington (UW); started in 1983.

(iii) Isotope-Aided Studies of the Effects of Changing Land Use on the Ecology and Climate of the Brazilian Amazon: to establish baseline data for the water and nutrient cycles, to find out more about how the Amazon Basin's natural systems function, and to develop guidelines for conservation and sustainable agriculture; coordinated by the Brazilian Nuclear Energy Agency (CNEN), to be implemented by CNPq/INPA, EMBRAPA/CPATU, and USP/CENA; started in 1985; executing Agency: International Atomic Energy Agency (IAEA), Vienna, Austria.

(iv) Biogeochemistry of the Carbon Cycle: to quantify the carbon exported from the oceanic Amazon Basin and the changes suffered by organic compounds during transportation; Coordinated by UW, INPA, and CENA; started in 1982.

(v) Micrometeorology Experiment in the Amazon Region: (a) to quantify micrometeorological and plant physiological measures of energy and vapor exchange between the tropical forest and the atmosphere as a basis for studies and modeling of the surface atmospheric layer; (b) collaboration between Brazilian and British scientists for the transfer to Brazilian scientists of techniques for experimental sampling and analysis of the surface atmospheric layer, which will make it possible to proceed with environmental research work. Coordinated by British Council Institute of Hydrology, Wallingford, England, CNPq/INPA, and INPE; started in April 1983.

This chapter gives a general view of the current questions and research on the hydrological cycle in the Brazilian Amazon.

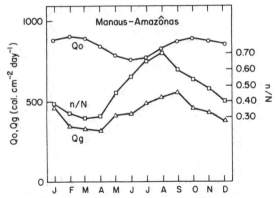

**FIGURE 1.** Manaus (AM): latitude 3°8' S, longitude 60°2' W. Mean monthly values of insolation ratio (n/N), solar energy at top of atmosphere ($Q_0$), and global radiation at canopy top ($Q_g$). [From Salati (1985) with permission of Pergammon Press.]

## SOLAR RADIATION

The energy available at the top of the plant canopy in the Amazon region is far from being known with sufficient accuracy. Only a few measurements have been made using an Eppley pyranometer. Data for Manaus are published in Ribeiro et al. (1982) and shown in Table 1. The annual mean incident energy is about 373 cal cm$^{-2}$ day$^{-1}$, the peak being in August, with 444 cal cm$^{-2}$ day$^{-1}$, and the minimum in December, with 365 cal cm$^{-2}$ day$^{-1}$.

Figures 1, 2, and 3 show, for three different locations, estimates of the seasonal variation of the solar radiation at the top of the earth's atmosphere ($Q_0$), the global radiation at canopy top, and their ratios (Villa Nova et al.,

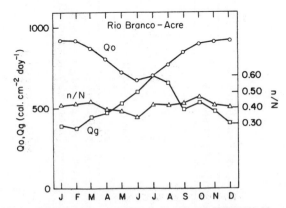

**FIGURE 2.** Rio Branco (AC): latitude 9°58' S, longitude 67°48' W. Mean monthly values of insolation ratio (n/N), solar energy at top of atmosphere ($Q_0$), and global radiation at canopy top ($Q_g$). [From Salati (1985) with permission of Pergammon Press.]

**TABLE 1. Global Radiation at Surface ($Q_s$) in Manaus[a]**

| Year | January | February | March | April | May | June | July | August | September | October | November | December |
|---|---|---|---|---|---|---|---|---|---|---|---|---|
| 1977 | — | — | — | — | — | — | — | 425 (51) | 348 (40) | 325 (36) | 360 (41) | 267 (30) |
| 1978 | 295 (33) | 277 (31) | 305 (34) | 323 (38) | 335 (42) | 432 (57) | 404 (52) | 462 (56) | 486 (56) | 499 (56) | 407 (46) | 363 (41) |
| 1979 | 337 (38) | 395 (36) | 412 (44) | — | — | — | — | — | — | — | — | — |

Source: Ribeiro et al. (1982).

[a] Measurements made with an Eppley pyranometer (in cal·cm$^{-2}$·day$^{-1}$). The numbers in parentheses show the percentage in relation to solar radiation reaching the top of local atmosphere ($Q_0$).

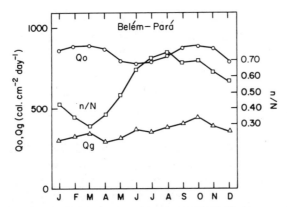

**FIGURE 3.** Belém (PA): latitude 1°28′ S, longitude 67°48′ W. Mean monthly values of insolation ratio (n/N), solar energy at top of atmosphere ($Q_0$), and global radiation at canopy top ($Q_g$). [From Salati (1985) with permission of Pergammon Press.]

1976). The solar energy at the top of the canopy is a function of cloudiness. Average cloudiness in the region is about 50%. The influence of solar declination is small, since the length of daylight in the Amazon Basin varies little (Salati and Marques, 1984). Some measurements of the spectral distribution of solar radiation, made in Manaus on clear days, are shown in

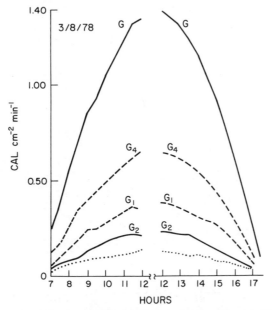

**FIGURE 4.** Spectral distribution of global radiation at ground level, in Manaus: $G$ = grand total, $G_1$ = violet-blue, $G_2$ = green-yellow, $G_3$ = red, $G_4$ = infrared. [From Almeida et al. (1979) with permission of Acta Amazônica, Manaus, Brazil.]

Fig. 4 (Almeida et al., 1979). Further precise measurements of incident solar and net radiation are needed, not only for the Brazilian Amazon but also for the other countries of the Amazon Basin for which published data are almost nil.

## PRECIPITATION

The sun moves between parallels 23°27' N and 23°27' S and crosses the equator every 6 months, strongly influencing the distribution of weather patterns in the Amazon region. During summer in the Southern Hemisphere, the area of maximum precipitation extends from 0° to 10°S, south of the Amazon River, and from that period onward, the area of maximum precipitation moves progressively toward the Northern Hemisphere. Maximum values of annual precipitation are observed in the coastal region of the Amapa Territory (Brazil). Somewhat lower values are observed in the central Amazon and larger values again on the westward edge of the Amazon in the mountains of Peru and Colombia (Salati et al., 1978). In some regions, it reaches 8 m, almost four times the mean annual precipitation of the basin. Figures 5 and 6 show isohyets for January and July, respectively. Figure 7 shows annual isohyets, and Figure 8 shows the rain distribution within the Amazon Basin. Jordan and Heuveldop (1981) made measurements in the tropical rain forest of Venezuela (1°56' N, 67°03' W) in the period September 1975 to August 1977 and found a mean annual value of 3.7 m.

Kouski (1980) suggests that the occurrence of rain induced by the sea breeze may affect the annual mean distribution of precipitation in the basin.

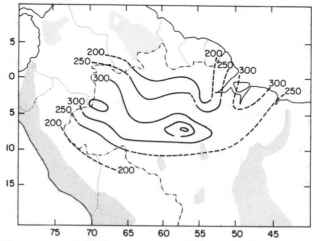

**FIGURE 5.** Normal precipitation in the Amazon Basin in January; isohyets in millimeters. Shaded area: altitudes above 500 m. [From Salati et al. (1978), *Interciencia*, vol. 3, no. 4, pp. 200–206, with permission of Interciencia, Caracus, Venezuela.]

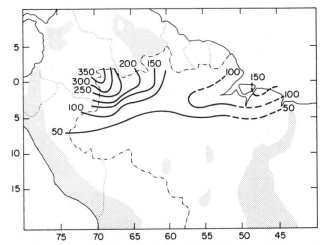

**FIGURE 6.** Normal precipitation in the Amazon Basin in July; isohyets in millimeters. Shaded area: altitudes above 500 m. [From Salati et al. (1978), *Interciencia*, vol. 3, no. 4, pp. 200–206, with permission of Interciencia, Caracus, Venezuela.]

The nighttime maximum along the East Coast is probably due to the convergence between trade winds and the land breeze. The annual totals at approximately 500 km from the coast are considerably smaller because of reduced daily convection. At night, there is some precipitation in this region, although it is less intense than that during the day because of reduction in

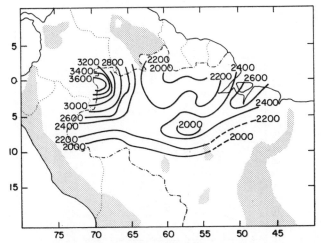

**FIGURE 7.** Normal precipitation in the Amazon Basin; annual isohyets in millimeters. Shaded area: altitudes above 500 m. [From Salati et al. (1978), *Interciencia*, vol. 3, no. 4, pp. 200–206, with permission of Interciencia, Caracus, Venezuela.]

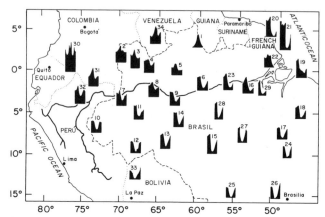

**FIGURE 8.** Rain distribution within the Amazon Basin at the following stations: 1-Boa Vista; 2-Iauaretê; 3-Taracuá; 4-Uaupa; 5-Barcelos; 6-Manaus; 7-Benjamin Constant; 8-Fonte Boa; 9-Coarí; 10-Cruzeiro do Sol; 11-Caruarí; 12-Rio Branco; 13-Porto Velho; 14-Humaitá; 15-Alto Tapajós; 16-Taperinha; 17-Conceição do Araguaia; 18-Imperatriz; 19-Belém; 20-Clevelândia; 21-Amapá; 22-Macapá; 23-Parintins; 24-Porto Nacional; 25-Cuiabá; 26-Pirenópolis; 27-Serra do Cachimbo; 28-Jacareacanga; 29-Altemira; 30-Tema; 31-Mean of region; 32-Iquitos; 33-Apolo; 34-Mean of region. [From Salati et al. (1978), *Interciencia*, vol. 3, no. 4, pp. 200–206, with permission of Interciencia, Caracus, Venezuela.]

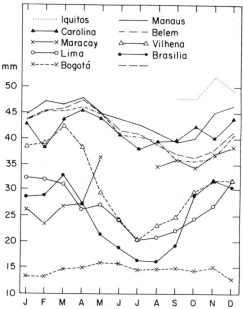

**FIGURE 9.** Mean monthly values of precipitable water, in millimeters. [From Marques (1978), with permission of Interciencia, Caracus, Venezuela.]

thermal contrast. Convective activity again intensifies further west along the Amazon.

## WATER VAPOR

Radiosonde data have been used to determine the distribution of atmospheric water vapor in the Amazon Basin and thus the precipitable water, which is graphed in Figs. 9 and 10 and summarized by station in Table 2.

The distributions of the total water vapor flux in the Amazon Basin for the months of March, June, September, and December are shown in Fig. 11. The flow is predominantly from the east, but its direction varies from northeast to southeast.

The convergence of the flux of water vapor integrated over the Amazonian hydrographic basin should correspond to the Amazon River discharge. Data obtained for the period 1972–1975 (Marques et al., 1980a) are summarized

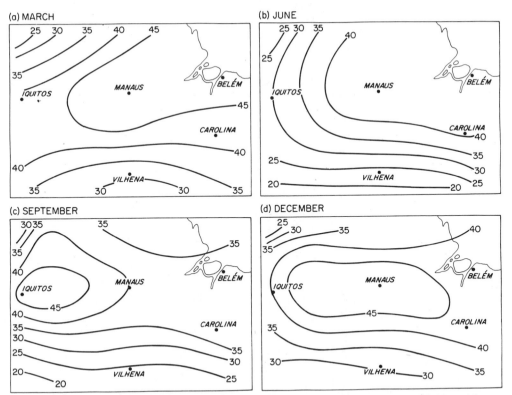

**FIGURE 10.** Spatial distribution of precipitable water (mm) for (*a*) March, (*b*) June, (*c*) September, and (*d*) December. [From Marques et al. (1979a), with permission of Acta Amazônica, Manaus, Brazil.]

**TABLE 2. Mean Monthly Values of Precipitable Water ($W_p$, in mm), 1972–1975[a]**

| Stations | January | February | March | April | May | June | July | August | September | October | November | December | Mean | Annual Amplitude | When Observed[b] |
|---|---|---|---|---|---|---|---|---|---|---|---|---|---|---|---|
| Belém | 43.4 | 45.6 | 46.1 | 47.5 | 45.0 | 41.7 | 41.0 | 38.9 | 37.2 | 36.5 | 37.9 | 41.5 | 41.9 | 11.0 | — |
| Bogotá | 13.3 | 13.3 | 14.7 | 14.9 | 15.9 | 15.7 | 14.3 | 14.6 | 14.9 | 14.5 | 15.2 | 12.8 | 14.5 | 3.1 | — |
| Brasília | 28.8 | 29.1 | 33.0 | 27.4 | 21.4 | 18.8 | 16.3 | 16.1 | 19.3 | 29.0 | 32.0 | 30.8 | 25.2 | 16.9 | — |
| Carolina | 42.8 | 38.5 | 43.7 | 45.6 | 44.1 | 40.9 | 35.3 | 39.4 | 39.8 | 42.5 | 40.2 | 43.9 | 41.4 | 10.3 | — |
| Iquitos | — | — | — | — | — | — | — | — | 47.8 | 47.9 | 52.2 | 49.3 | — | — | 3 |
| Lima | 33.5 | 39.2 | 42.6 | 38.3 | 29.5 | 24.3 | 20.4 | 21.0 | 22.3 | 24.4 | 27.0 | 31.9 | 30.0 | 8.2 | — |
| Manaus | 44.7 | 47.2 | 46.7 | 47.9 | 44.9 | 43.8 | 42.8 | 41.1 | 39.4 | 40.2 | 45.2 | 46.5 | 44.2 | 8.5 | — |
| Maracay | 26.3 | 23.5 | 27.0 | 27.4 | 35.4 | 35.8 | 35.0 | 34.5 | 36.0 | 34.4 | 35.2 | 28.4 | 31.3 | 12.9 | 5 |
| S. Antonio | — | — | — | — | — | — | — | — | 34.9 | 40.1 | 38.3 | 31.1 | — | — | 1 |
| S. Elena | — | — | — | — | — | — | — | — | 30.2 | — | — | — | — | — | 2 |
| Vilhena | 32.5 | 33.2 | 31.3 | 26.3 | 27.2 | 24.3 | 20.4 | 23.3 | 24.8 | 29.7 | 32.1 | 31.8 | 28.1 | 12.8 | 4 |

[a] Source: Marques (1978).
[b] 1, Only 1973 and 1974; 2, only 1974; 3, only 1975; 4, only 1972; 5, only 1972, 1973, and 1974.

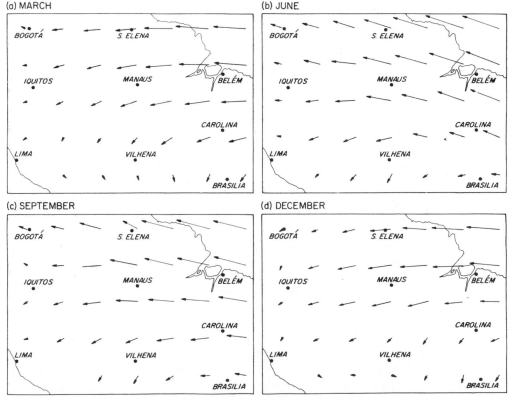

**FIGURE 11.** Vector field values $\mathbf{Q} = \mathbf{Q}_\lambda + \mathbf{Q}_\phi$. Mean monthly values for the 1972–1975 period obtained for the 5° latitude × 5° longitude little squares. 1 cm = 2000$g_v$ cm$^{-1}$ s$^{-1}$. Months of (a) March, (b) June, (c) September, and (d) December. [From Marques et al. (1979b), with permission of Acta Amazônica, Manaus, Brazil.]

graphically in Fig. 12. The average precipitation and the discharge of the Amazon River according to the data of Oltman (1967) are also shown on the graph.

The measured river outflow agrees reasonably well with the convergence of the vapor flux, which is estimated to be three and one-half months earlier in phase relative to the outflow. These data suggest the possibility of determining flooding in the low Amazon once the water vapor flux in the basin is known, especially the values at the Atlantic Coast. Research to better understand the connections between water vapor flux and Amazon flooding is needed.

## WATER BALANCE

The water balance of the Amazon Basin has been a challenge to scientists and engineers concerned with soil problems in the region. The accurate determination of water balance is made difficult by

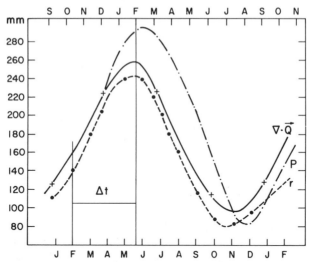

**FIGURE 12.** Monthly values of the water vapor convergence (Δ · **Q**) estimated using the aerological method; of precipitation P, mean of 1972–1975 period; of discharge r, according to Oltman (1967) data (values in millimeters). [From Marques et al. (1980b).]

  **a.** lack of continuous temporal and spatial precipitation data,

  **b.** lack of simultaneous measurements of river discharge along the Amazon Basin,

  **c.** lack of meteorological data for calculations with more adequate spatial distribution, and

  **d.** little available information on incident and reflected solar radiation and surface energy balances.

In spite of these difficulties, several authors have attempted to determine the water balance using different methods.

The water balance in the Amazon Basin as a whole has been determined using meteorological methods by Molion (1975), Villa Nova et al. (1976), and Lettau et al. (1979). Marques et al., (1980a) estimated water balance using water vapor flux divergence. More recently, direct plant transpiration measurements were made by Jordan and Heuveldop (1981), and water balance in a model basin was measured by Leopoldo et al. (1982a,b).

More detailed consideration of water balance is given below since understanding the effects of its alteration is important for determining the effects of forest removal on climate.

## Model Basin

The water balance in an experimental basin in the Amazon region was determined for the first time in a forest reserve of INPA located 60 km north

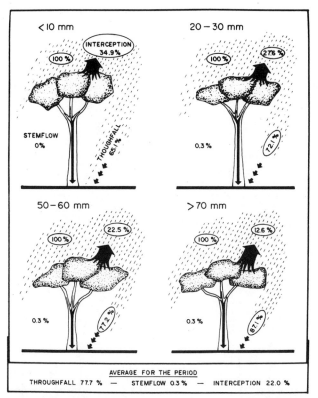

**FIGURE 13.** Interception of rain by tree canopy in the model basin, as a function of intensity of precipitation. [Based on Franken et al. (1982).]

of Manaus. The program was established through collaboration between INPA and CENA/USP and was supported by the WMO and the OEA.

The flora, fauna, and soil species of this model basin (area of about 25 km$^2$) have been described in a special issue of *Acta Amazônica*. This region consists of dense forest with trees up to 40 m high. The Project Coordinator was Dr. Maria de Nazaré Góes Ribeiro, Head, Ecology Department, INPA. The water balance was measured using pluviometers placed above tree tops and others distributed randomly at ground level. Stemflow measurements were also made. Detailed descriptions of the methodology used and measurements taken can be found in Franken et al. (1982) and Leopoldo et al. (1982a).

Figure 13 shows the water intercepted by the plants, stemflow, and throughfall. Interception depends on rain intensity, varying from 35 to 13%, the average being 22%. Heavy rains have little influence on stemflow, which averages about 0.3%. Throughfall varies with rain intensity, from 65 to 87% and averaging 78%.

The water balance obtained from the above figures and runoff are shown

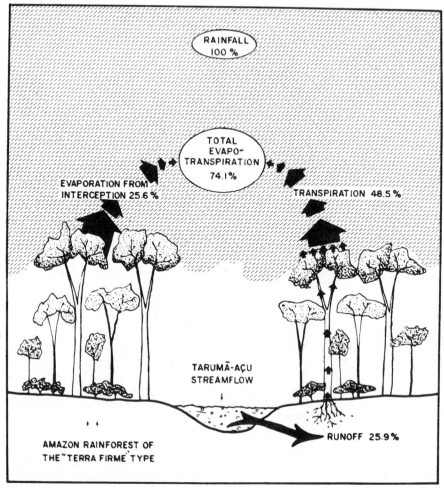

**FIGURE 14.** Water balance of the model basin. [Based on Salati and Marques (1984).]

in Fig. 14. For a 2-y period, streams (*igarapé*) drained off 26% of the total precipitation. Transpiration removed about 48.5%, and evaporation of water intercepted by the leaves removed about 26%. The values obtained for the water balance measured at the Ducke Reserve of INPA, 20 km from Manaus (Franken et al., 1982), are quite similar to the above. On the average, interception is about 25%, plant transpiration 50%, and runoff 25% of the incident rainfall. Thus, in a dense forest, 75% of the precipitation is returned to the atmosphere by evapotranspiration.

### Amazon Basin

The water balance in the Amazon Basin as a whole is very difficult to measure, as mentioned earlier. It can only be determined by successive approximation using different methods.

**FIGURE 15.** Water balance and storage of water vapor in the Amazon Basin. [Based on Salati and Marques (1984).]

To determine the water balance using classical methods, it is necessary to make measurements of precipitation and river discharge throughout the Amazon. Evapotranspiration can be estimated by the difference between these two quantities and compared with that obtained by independent methods.

Precipitation in the Amazon region has been studied using data from the meteorological stations of the different institutes operating in the region (Brazil and other countries). Average total precipitation was estimated as $11.9 \times 10^{12}$ m$^3$ y$^{-1}$ (Villa Nova et al., 1976).

The Amazon River discharge has been measured with good accuracy by Oltman (1967). Measurements were taken at Obidos, and the estimated average was based on data recorded from water level readings. The discharge from Obidos to the estuary was indirectly estimated. The best mean value obtained for the Amazon River discharge is $5.5 \times 10^{12}$ m$^3$ y$^{-1}$.

Evapotranspiration, estimated by the Penman method, was $6.4 \times 10^{12}$ m$^3$ y$^{-1}$, which is in good agreement with the difference between precipitation and discharge. The Amazon River discharge was also determined independently by calculation of water flux convergence (Marques et al., 1980a), in complete agreement with the measurements by Oltman at Obidos.

The water balance of the Amazon Basin is summarized in Fig. 15. Table 3 gives a summary of the evapotranspiration values obtained by different authors.

TABLE 3. Summary of Results Obtained by Different Researchers on Hydrological Cycle of Amazon Region[a]

| Research | Rainfall (mm) | | Transpiration | | | Evapotranspiration | | | Runoff | |
|---|---|---|---|---|---|---|---|---|---|---|
| | | | mm | % | mm day⁻¹ | mm | % | mm day⁻¹ | mm | % |
| Marques et al., 1980 | (1) | 2328 | — | — | — | 1260 (r) | 54.2 | 3.5 | 1068 | 45.8 |
| | (2) | 2328 | — | — | — | 1000 (r) | 43.0 | 2.7 | 1328 | 57.0 |
| | (3) | 2328 | — | — | — | 1330 (p) | 57.1 | 3.6 | 998 | 42.9 |
| Villa Nova et al., 1976 | (4) | 2000 | — | — | — | 1460 (p) | 73.0 | 4.0 | 540 | 27.0 |
| | (5) | 2101 | — | — | — | 1168 (r) | 58.4 | 3.2 | 832 | 41.6 |
| Molion, 1975 | (6) | 2379 | — | — | — | 1569 (p) | 73.4 | 4.3 | 532 | 26.6 |
| Ribeiro et al., 1979 | (7) | 2478 | — | — | — | 1146 (r) | 48.2 | 3.1 | 1233 | 51.8 |
| | | | — | — | — | 1536 (p) | 62.0 | 4.2 | 942 | 38.0 |
| IPEAN, 1972 | (8) | 2179 | — | — | — | 1508 (r) | 60.8 | 4.1 | 970 | 39.2 |
| | | | — | — | — | 1475 (r) | 67.5 | 4.0 | 704 | 32.5 |
| | | | — | — | — | 1320 (r) | 60.6 | 3.6 | 859 | 39.4 |
| DMET, 1978 | (9) | 2207 | — | — | — | 1452 (p) | 65.8 | 4.0 | 755 | 34.2 |
| | | | — | — | — | 1306 (r) | 59.2 | 3.6 | 901 | 40.8 |
| Jordan and Heuveldop, 1981 | (10) | 3664 | 1722 | 47.0 | 4.7 | 1905 (r) | 52.0 | 5.2 | 1759 | 48.0 |
| Leopoldo et al., 1981 | (11) | 2089 | 1014 | 48.5 | 2.7 | 1542 (r) | 74.1 | 4.1 | 541 | 25.9 |
| Leopoldo et al., 1982a | (12) | 2075 | 1287 | 62.0 | 3.5 | 1675 (r) | 80.7 | 4.6 | 400 | 19.3 |

[a] Observations: (r), real evapotranspiration; (p), potential evapotranspiration; (1), aerological method, applied for all Amazon Basin, period 1972–1975; (2), same as (1), for the region between Belém and Manaus; (3), by Thornthwaite method for the region between Belém and Manaus; (4), Penman method, mean for the period 1931–1960; (5), same as (4), for Manaus Region; (6), climatonomic method, for all Amazon region, mean for the period 1931–1960; (7), water balance by Thornthwaite and Mather method for the Ducke Forest Reserve, mean for the period 1965–1973; (8), Thornthwaite method for all Amazon region and estimated for a period over 10 y; (9) same as (8), for various periods; (10), water balance, with transpiration estimated by class A pan-evaporation for San Carlos Region; (11), Model Basin water balance; (12), Barro-Branco water balance (Ducke Forest Reserve).

## EVIDENCE OF WATER RECYCLING

We tried to find out the origin of the water vapor generating precipitation in the Amazon region. Figure 12 clearly shows that the water vapor entering the Amazon region comes from the Atlantic Ocean and generally moves westward with easterly winds.

The total water vapor flux during the year corresponds, however, to only about 50% of the total precipitation in the region (Marques et al., 1981a,b). Therefore, there should be another source of water vapor. Table 3 shows that the evapotranspiration estimated by different authors is over 50% of precipitation and especially in dense forests can reach an average of 75%. Evapotranspiration is thus a source of water vapor of the same magnitude as the water vapor from the ocean. The water vapor generated in the forest mixes with the water vapor from the ocean to form clouds that later precipitate in the region.

The Amazon region is bounded on the west by the Andean mountains, which form a barrier 4 km in height, to the north by the Guyana plateau with altitudes of around 1 km, and to the south by the central plateau of Brazil with altitudes of about 700–800 m. The winds penetrating the Amazon Basin from the Atlantic must move over these barriers with resulting large amounts of precipitation, especially on the western edge, where annual precipitation as high as 5 m has been reported. The Amazon region may also provide vapor to the neighboring regions, such as the central plateau of Brazil.

Further evidence of water vapor recycling in the region has been obtained using isotope techniques (Salati et al., 1979). The isotopic method is simply explained. Water consists of hydrogen and oxygen isotopes. The stable hydrogen isotopes are $^1H$ and $^2H$ or D. The stable oxygen isotopes are $^{16}O$, $^{17}O$, and $^{18}O$. Different species of water molecules are formed by the combination of these various isotopes, for example, $H_2^{16}O$, $H_2^{18}O$, and $H_2^{17}O$. Of these molecules, the most important for the study of recycling are $H_2^{16}O$ and $H_2^{18}O$. When water is evaporated from the ocean, molecules of the type $H_2^{16}O$ with a molecular mass of 18 are evaporated before molecules of the type $H_2^{18}O$ with a molecular mass of 20.

An isotopic fractionation thus occurs during evaporation, and the vapor from the sea water has an $^{18}O$ concentration about 8% less than that of the ocean. As this water vapor enters the continent, it will condense and precipitate and then become soil and river water. Since the heavier molecules condense first, they are depleted from the remaining water vapor by cloud formation and precipitation. Consequently, the water vapor of the more westward regions in the Amazon should have a lower concentration of $^{18}O$.

A special study during the 1970s systematically measured the $^{18}O$ and D isotope composition in river and rain water and the atmospheric water vapor. The isotopic gradient from east to west was smaller than would be expected if the Atlantic Ocean were the only source of water vapor.

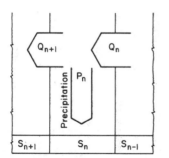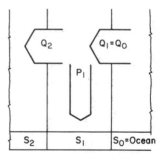

**FIGURE 16.** Precipitation model of Amazon, considering only one source of water vapor. The water vapor would come from the ocean ($Q_0$) and be removed by rain ($P$) when it penetrates the continent. [From Dall'Olio et al. (1979), with permission of Acta Amazônica, Manaus, Brazil.]

Two models (as sketched in Figs. 16 and 17) have been developed to explain the spatial and temporal distribution of isotopes in the Amazon region. The model indicated in Fig. 16 assumes the Atlantic Ocean as the primary and only source of water vapor, the rain being formed by continuous removal of the residual water vapor. The model shown in Fig. 17 suggests that rain in a certain region is formed by a mixture of the original water vapor from the Atlantic Ocean and the water vapor generated in the forest by evapotranspiration.

Calculations made by Dall'Olio et al. (1979) were critically interpreted by Salati et al. (1979), who concluded that there is evidence of water vapor recycling in the region; 1972 and 1973 data were used, and the isotope composition of the water vapor from the ocean was calculated from precipitation levels at several cities along the Brazilian coast bordering the Amazon region.

Matsui et al. (1983) presented direct measurements of the isotope com-

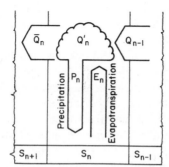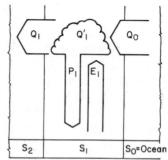

**FIGURE 17.** Model to explain the distribution of rain ($P$) in the Amazon, considering two sources of water vapor: first, from the ocean ($Q_0$); second, water vapor from evapotranspiration ($E$). [From Dall'Olio et al. (1979), with permission of Acta Amazônica, Manaus, Brazil.]

position of the water vapor collected daily at Belém during the years 1978, 1979, and 1980. The results obtained are in good agreement with those calculated and used in the models by Dall'Olio et al. (1979).

Based on data obtained both with the water balance and the isotopic model, it has been concluded that there should be water recycling in the Amazon region and that this recycling is not negligible in relation to total precipitation but might represent up to 50% of the water vapor generating rain in the region.

## DEFORESTATION AND CLIMATIC CHANGES

It is not difficult to explain to biologists and ecologists that a change in land use through deforestation of tropical rain forests will result in changes in flora, fauna, and soil nutrient cycles. Meteorologists, however, are more skeptical of the suggestion that replacement of the forest by pasture or permanent agriculture might cause climatic changes on regional or even global scales.

The present equilibrium of the water and energy cycles in the Amazon forest is obviously related to the present vegetation cover.

The Amazon can be developed in several different ways, some of which would lead to a regeneration of the forest, but the time of total regeneration will always be uncertain. However, the new equilibrium that is reached might involve drastic differences in the water and energy cycles.

Until the 1970s, the Amazon was typically occupied by shifting agriculture, which cleared an area of the forest to plant subsistence crops. Under shifting cultivation the soil fertility rapidly decreases, and in 3–4 y the area is abandoned. A secondary forest called *capoeira* is formed that tends to regenerate the original forest. The time necessary for this recovery is about 100 y, but about 200–300 y would be necessary to reach a dynamic equilibrium similar to the original one. This type of land use, long employed by Indians and other indigenous peoples of low population density, has not noticeably changed the total equilibrium of the region.

During the 1970s, more intensive colonization began, with large areas cleared for annual crops and pastures. Around 2–3 million hectares per year of forest are now cleared in the Brazilian Amazon alone. Such land use not only greatly modifies the soil nutrient cycles but also destroys many plant species and the germplasm necessary for their natural regeneration. Where pastures are not adequately managed and abandoned to natural regeneration, then regeneration will take a long time, from 300 to 1000 y, depending on the deforested area and the type of soil.

Where permanent agriculture is established, ecosystem changes are even more drastic as very few species replace the thousands of species previously present. Soil nutrient cycles are altered and productivity can only be maintained with continuous application of fertilizer. Modifications in water and

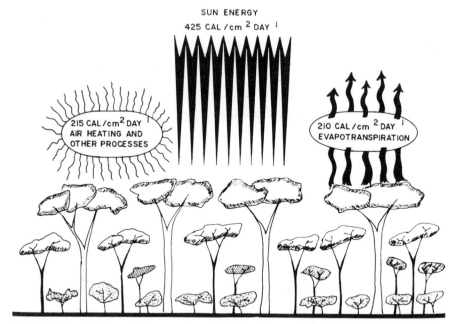

**FIGURE 18.** Balance of daily average energy in the Amazon Basin. [Based on Salati and Marques (1984).]

energy cycles are a natural consequence of the change in plant cover. There will be a greater loss of water through rivers during rainy seasons, especially when rainfall is heavier, and therefore less water will be available for evaporation and transpiration.

The water and energy cycles will be modified on the microclimatic scale. Some experiments (Ribeiro et al., 1982) have shown that in areas where vegetation cover is reduced, the relative humidity is reduced and the temperature is higher.

As stated earlier, about 50% of the precipitation in the Amazon region returns to the atmosphere as water vapor through evapotranspiration which depends on the forest cover. The current balance estimated for the Amazon between net radiative heating of the surface and sensible and evaporative energy fluxes is shown in Fig. 18. Changing land use to permanent agricultural systems will alter the water and energy balances so that there will be months with a greater water deficit and higher temperatures, and in general the equilibrium reached will be different from the present one.

Variations in the amount of vapor condensing in the higher part of the troposphere may also influence climate on a global scale; during evaporation, solar energy is transformed into latent heat. This heat is subsequently released in the atmosphere where the water vapor condenses to form clouds. This energy is partially responsible for the circulation of the upper troposphere. On the other hand, part of this vapor is transferred to higher latitudes where, upon condensation, it releases energy. This is one of the important mechanisms for transferring energy from the equatorial to the polar regions. We do not know the extent to which the deforestation of the Amazon would influence the atmospheric general circulation. However, it is clear that some changes would be introduced.

The large amounts of water vapor in the atmosphere, coming in part from the forests, control not only the energy balance but also cloud formation and therefore rainfall over the Amazon Basin. Thus, a decrease in the forested area might lead to a decrease in the water vapor in the atmosphere and, consequently, also in the precipitation. The extent of these changes would depend on the level of the disturbance taking place. Attempts to quantify the changes through modeling have been made but with somewhat contradictory conclusions (Potter et al., 1975, 1981; Lettau et al., 1979; Henderson-Sellers and Gornitz, 1984, as reviewed by Henderson-Sellers, Chapter 20).

The effects of deforestation on the existing dynamic equilibrium of the water, energy, and biogeochemical cycles can be minimized by the following scientifically based procedures:

1. Use the most fertile soils for agriculture in which the modifications of the biogeochemical cycles are smallest.
2. Use resources according to a rational development plan for the existing hydrographic basins, always leaving intact forest surrounding the rivers and level strips of intact forest between cultivated areas. These forest strips will diminish the effects of deforestation on the water transit time and on the energy balance.
3. Always use soil conservation techniques, avoiding as much as possible erosion and runoff to ensure replenishment of groundwaters and diminish the effects on the biogeochemical cycles.
4. In areas of very poor soils and especially in the central Amazon, give preference to forestry, which maintains the existing water, energy, and nutrient equilibria, and considerable storage of carbon in the ecosystem.
5. In the case of exploitation of forests where there are exotic species, always leave level strips of the primary forest of adequate size. These strips will help preserve the germplasm of the original forest, protect flora and fauna, and diminish the effects of deforestation on the water, energy, and nutrient cycles.

## LIST OF ABBREVIATIONS

CENA            Center of Nuclear Energy in Agriculture, Brazil (University of São Paulo)

CNPq        National Council for Technological and Scientific Development, Brazil

CNEN        Brazilian Nuclear Energy Agency

CPATU       Center for Agricultural Research of the Humid Tropics, Belém, Brazil (EMBRAPA)

EMBRAPA     Ministry of Agriculture, Network of Research Institutions, Brazil

IAEA        International Atomic Energy Agency, Vienna, Austria

INPA        National Institute of Amazon Research, Manaus, Brazil (CNPq)

INPE        National Institute of Space Research, São José dos Campos, Brazil (CNPq)

OEA         Organization of American States

USP         University of São Paulo, São Paulo, Brazil

UW          University of Washington, Seattle, United States

WMO         World Meteorological Organization

## REFERENCES

Almeida, R., Salati, E., and Villa Nova, N. A., 1979. Distribuição espectral e coeficiente de transmissão da radiação solar para condições de céu limpo em Manaus, *Acta Amazôn.* **9**, 279–285.

Dall'Olio, A., Salati, E., Azevedo, C. E., and Matsui, E., 1979. Modelo de fracionamento isotópico da água na Bacia Amazônica, *Acta Amazôn.* **9**, 675–687.

Departmento Nacional de Meteorology (DMET), 1978. *Balanço Hidrico do Brazil*, DMET,

Franken, W., Leopoldo, P. R., 1984. Hydrology of catchment area of Central-Amazonian forest streams, in H. Sioli, Ed., *The Amazon: Limnology and Landscape Ecology of a Mighty Tropical River and its Basin.* W. Junk, Dordrecht, The Netherlands.

Franken, W., Leopoldo, P. R., Matsui, E., and Ribeiro, M. N. G., 1982. Interceptação das precipitacões em floresta Amazônica de terra firme, *Acta Amazôn.* **12**, 15–22.

Goodland, R. J. A. and Irwin, H. S., 1975. *Amazon Jungle: Green Hell to Red Desert?* Elsevier, Amsterdam.

Henderson-Sellers, A. and Gornitz, V., 1984. Possible climatic impacts on land cover transformations, with particular emphasis on tropical deforestation, *Climatic Change* **6**, 231–258.

IPEAN, 1978. Instituto de Pesquisas Agropecuárias do Norte 1972, Zoneamento Agricola da Amazônia, *Bol. Téc.,* Belem, Brazil.

Jordan, C. F. and Heuveldop, J., 1981. The water balance of an Amazonian rain forest, *Acta Amazôn.* **11**, 87–92.

Kagano, M. T., 1979. Um estudo climatológico e sinótico utilizando dados de radiossondagens, 1968–1976, de Manaus e Belém, INPE Report No. 1559-TDL/013, São José dos Campos, Brazil.

Kousky, V. E., 1980. Diurnal rainfall variation in Northeast Brazil, Mon. Wea. Rev. 108, 488–498.

Leopoldo, P. R., Franken, W., Matsui, E., and Salati, E., 1982a. Estimativa da evapotranspiração de floresta Amazonica de terra firme, Acta Amazôn. 12, 23–28.

Leopoldo, P. R., Matsui, E., Salati, E., Franken, W., and Ribeiro, M. N. G., 1982b. Composição isotopica das precipitações e d' água do solo em floresta Amazônica do tipo terra firme na região de Manaus, Acta Amazôn. 12, 7–13.

Lettau, H., Lettau, K., and Molion, L. C. B., 1979. Amazonia's hydrologic cycle and the role of atmosphere recycling deforestation effects, Mon. Wea. Rev. 107, 227–238.

Marques, J., 1978. A transferência horizontal de vapor d' água na troposfera e a hidrologia da Bacia Amazônica, Doctoral Thesis, ESALQ, University of São Paulo, Piracicaba.

Marques, J., Santos, J. M., and Salati, E., 1979a. O armazenamento atmosférico de vapor d' água sobre a região Amazônica, Acta Amazôn. 9, 715–721.

Marques, J., Santos, J. M., and Salati, E., 1979b. O campo do fluxo de vapor d' água atmosférico sobre a região Amazônica, Acta Amazôn. 9, 701–713.

Marques, J., Salati, E., and Santos, J. M., 1980a. Cálculo de evapotranspiração real na bacia Amazônica através do método aerológico, Acta Amazôn. 10, 357–361.

Marques, J., Salati, E., and Santos, J. M., 1980b. A divergência do campo do fluxo de vapor dágua e as chuvas na Região Amazônica, Acta Amazôn. 10, 133–140.

Matsui, E., Salati, E., Ribeiro, M. N. G., Reis, C. M. dos, Tancredi, A. C. S. N. F., and Gat, J. R., 1983. Precipitation in the Central Amazon Basin: The isotopic composition of rain and atmospheric moisture at Belém and Manaus, Acta Amazôn. 13, 307–369.

Molion, L. C. B., 1975. A climatonomic study of the energy and moisture fluxes of the Amazonas basin with consideration of deforestation effects, Doctoral Thesis, University of Wisconsin.

Oltman, R. E., 1967. Reconnaissance investigations of the discharge and water quality of the Amazon, in Atas do Simp. sobre Biota Amazônica, Rio de Janeiro, CNPq, Vol. 3, pp. 163–185.

Potter, G. L., Ellsaesser, H. W., MacCracken, M. C., and Luther, F. M., 1975. Possible climatic impact of tropical deforestation, Nature 258, 697–698.

Potter, G. L., Ellsaesser, H. W., MacCracken, M. C., and Ellis, J. S., 1981. Albedo change by man: Test of climatic effects, Nature 291, 47–50.

Ribeiro, M. N. G., Salati, E., Villa Nova, N. A., and Demetrio, C. G., 1982. Radiçao solar disponivel em Manaus (AM) e sua relação com a duração do brilho solar, Acta Amazôn. 12, 339–346.

Salati, E., 1985. The climatology and hydrology of Amazonia, in G. T. Prance, Ed., Amazonia, Pergammon, Oxford, England.

Salati, E. and Marques, J., 1984. Climatology of the Amazon region, in H. Sioli,

Ed., *The Amazon: Limnology and Landscape Ecology of a Mighty Tropical River and its Basin*, W. Junk, Dordrecht, The Netherlands.

Salati, E. and Vose, P. B., 1984. Amazon basin: A system in equilibrium, *Science* **225**, 129–138.

Salati, E., Marques, J., and Molion, L. C. B., 1978. Origem e distribuição das chuvas na Amazônia, *Interciência* **3**, 200–206.

Salati, E., Dall'Olio, A., Matsui, E., and Gat, J. R., 1979. Recycling of water in the Amazon basin: An isotopic study, *Water Resourc. Res.* **15**, 1250–1258.

Villa Nova, N. A., Salati, E., and Matsui, E., 1976. Estimativa da evapotranspiração na Bacia Amazônica, *Acta Amazôn.* **6**, 215–228.

## ☐ COMMENTS ON "THE FOREST AND THE HYDROLOGICAL CYCLE"

**John C. Rodda**

The author should be applauded for the quality of his essay, for the topics he has covered, and for the aptness of his illustrations. His discussion of the subject follows a logical path, and he has drawn his conclusions together in a sound and concise fashion.

However, the basic hydrological data for the Amazon Basin are so inadequate that any conclusions must be suspect. There are simply not the records available of the necessary precision and length to justify some of this author's conclusions. This inadequacy is not the fault of the author: It is a problem for the hydrological and meteorological services of the countries concerned. Lack of funds, difficulties of access, problems of making the basic measurements in a hostile environment, questions of representativeness and extrapolation, lack of staff, and other difficulties are only too well known to the agencies involved. Use of remote-sensing techniques provides some means of overcoming the basic lack of data and the difficulties of interpreting the data that exist. However, remote sensing will not provide the complete answer. What is needed is for the hydrological network to be upgraded.

In this context, the author refrains from making any comment on the number of raingauges situated in the Amazon and their density, nor on the density of the other networks such as the radiosonde stations. The problem of measuring the flow of the Amazon is not considered. He does, however, consider the difficulties of measuring solar radiation. (Are there any reliable continuous measurements?) Yet the errors inherent in these measurements of the components of the hydrological cycle will have a significant impact on the water balance values quoted and could alter some of the conclusions reached now and in the future.

# Chapter 16

# Modeling Effects of Vegetation on Climate

Piers J. Sellers

Until recently, little attention was paid to the effects of differing surface types on local and regional climate; the vegetation (or lack of it) in a given region was assumed to be solely the result of climatic forcing with minimal feedback onto the climate itself (Tivy, 1977; Walter, 1973). This view was reflected in the methodologies adopted by meteorologists and agronomists–biophysicists in modeling their respective lower and upper boundary conditions: Meteorologists have continued to develop more complex general circulation models (GCMs) with crude representations of the significant processes on the earth's land surface (see Carson, 1981) while agronomists and biophysicists have used prescribed micrometeorological conditions or, at best, one-dimensional climate models to simulate the effects of changing the vegetation on the local energy and water balance, thus neglecting the feedback effects on the local climate (e.g., Sellers and Lockwood, 1981). *Two-way* interactions were not investigated in much detail, partly because such interactions were thought to be of minimal importance when compared to the large-scale atmospheric processes.

Recent work has demonstrated, however, that the interactions between land surface and atmosphere are significant and complex. The land surface influences the atmosphere via three principal modes of exchange: radiation, transfer of momentum, and transfer of sensible and latent heat. Early GCM experiments were done to determine the extent of the sensitivity of the global and regional climate to changes in these fluxes. Often, these sensitivity experiments assumed drastic and unrealistic changes in the land surface properties by the simple alteration of a specific surface parameter, for example, albedo, roughness length, and soil moisture fraction. However, the results of these early efforts showed that the different kinds and scales of surface–

atmosphere interactions could have significant effects on atmospheric circulation. Three of these experiments, concerned with radiative, heat, and momentum transfer, respectively, serve as useful illustrations.

Charney (1975) hypothesized that the removal of vegetation in arid regions would increase the surface albedo, reduce the amount of radiation absorbed, lower the equivalent surface temperature, and further promote subsiding motion in the overlying air mass. This chain of events (which assumes that any other processes influenced by the presence or absence of vegetation are negligible) would act to maintain the area in a desertlike state. Simulations using GCMs with different prescribed surface albedos have qualitatively supported this thesis (Charney et al., 1977; Mintz, 1984).

Shukla and Mintz (1982) conducted a simple experiment with a GCM in which the land surface was assumed to be evaporating freely (first case) and completely dry (second case). The resultant fields of precipitation, air temperature, and wind vector were found to be considerably different.

Sud and Smith (1985) conducted a numerical experiment wherein the roughness length assigned to the Sahara desert (usually taken to be 44 cm in their model, i.e., representative of a tall vegetation cover) was changed to a lower value of 0.2 mm, a more realistic value for bare sand. This change reduced the frictional drag on the boundary layer and moved the simulated rainfall band further south to a latitude more consistent with observations.

Mintz (1984) provides a general review of the history of such studies by summarizing the results of 11 experiments conducted with GCMs wherein the nature of the land surface parameterization (albedo, soil moisture, roughness length, etc.) was changed from a "control" condition to a physically different state. The results obtained by different research groups using different GCMs were qualitatively similar in their predictions of the changes induced in the regional fields of air temperature, humidity, winds, pressure, and precipitation for similar alterations in the drag, radiation absorption, and energy partition properties of the land surface.

These studies all used relatively simple descriptions of the various processes occurring at the land surface–atmosphere interface. More sophisticated and realistic models of the energy and mass balance of the vegetated land surface have been developed by a separate scientific community concerned with biophysics, agrometeorology, and hydrometeorology. Generally, their purpose was the local one-dimensional description of biophysical processes applicable to small areas.

A number of these studies used prescribed atmospheric conditions to drive soil–plant–atmosphere models (SPAMs) capable of simulating the effects of changing the vegetation type of an area. Sellers (1981) and Sellers and Lockwood (1981) demonstrated that the energy and water balance of a region could be highly dependent on plant physiology and morphology: The former factor controls the transpiration rate while the latter has a marked effect on the annual interception loss rate (that proportion of rainfall that is held on plant leaves as liquid water and then reevaporates to the atmosphere without reaching the bulk soil moisture store). Otterman (1981), Goudriaan (1977), and Ross (1975), who gives earlier references, have shown how plant structure affects the absorption of radiation in a region by the trapping of light in multiple reflections between plant elements.

These one-dimensional studies have simulated exchange processes in a biophysically realistic way, but most of them are far too elaborate and site specific to be considered for implementation in a GCM. What is required is a generally applicable, realistic, but simple representation of the biophysical elements that control such exchanges. In this chapter, I review the simpler models used up to now in GCMs, discuss their successes and shortcomings, and then briefly describe the Simple Biosphere model of Sellers et al. (1986) as an example of the trend toward biophysically realistic formulations.

The Simple Biosphere model is intended to be as physically and biologically realistic as is feasible to incorporate into a GCM given the constraints of computer resources. Initially, this model will be physiologically reactive to atmospheric conditions, but the type, density, and health of the vegetation will be prescribed as functions of season and location. It should provide more realistic fields of sensible and latent heat fluxes, and drag over the continents than do existing formulations provided it is coupled to a GCM with an adequate simulation of the planetary boundary layer, distribution of rainfall, and other climatic features.

Subsequent studies will explore the possibility of simulating growth and changes of vegetation interactively with the GCM, which will permit the simulation of the effects of atypical climatic conditions on the surface. If the goal of a truly interactive biosphere–atmosphere model were achieved, simulation studies of complex global problems would become feasible.

## MODELING STRATEGIES

Three broad strategies are open to the would-be modeler of land-surface processes in GCMs. These are (i) the prescription of land surface parameters, (ii) the use of conceptual models and (iii) the use of biophysically based models. Until the work of Dickinson (1984), all GCM surface parameterizations had been confined to the first two approaches. (The sensitivity studies described in the preceding section all used such formulations.) The methodologies used in these approaches are summarized below.

### Prescription of Land Surface Parameters

The global fields of terrestrial albedo, roughness length, and the Bowen ratio are specified and held constant for a given model run.

The equations describing the exchanges of radiation, momentum, and heat are:

*Radiation*:

$$R_n = \int_0^\infty F_l(1 - \alpha_l) \cdot dl + \epsilon_s F_t - \epsilon_s \sigma_s T_s^4 \tag{1}$$

where $R_n$ = net radiation flux absorbed by the land surface, W m$^{-2}$

$\quad\quad F_l$ = solar radiative flux density at wavelength $l$ incident on the surface, W m$^{-2}$

$\quad\quad \alpha_l$ = spectral albedo

$\quad\quad \epsilon_s$ = emissivity of the surface

$\quad\quad F_t$ = long-wave flux downward from the atmosphere, W m$^{-2}$

$\quad\quad \sigma_s$ = Stefan–Boltzmann constant, W m$^{-2}$ K$^{-4}$

$\quad\quad T_s$ = surface radiative temperature, K

*Momentum*:

$$\boldsymbol{\tau} = \rho C_D u_r \mathbf{u}_r \tag{2a}$$

where $\boldsymbol{\tau}$ = shear stress, kg m$^{-1}$ s$^{-2}$

$\quad\quad \rho$ = density of air, kg m$^{-3}$

$\quad\quad C_D$ = surface drag coefficient

$\quad\quad \mathbf{u}_r$ = wind velocity at reference height $z_r$, m s$^{-1}$

$\quad\quad u_r$ = absolute value of $\mathbf{u}_r$.

Here $C_D$ may either be prescribed or obtained from

$$C_D = \left\{ \frac{k}{\ln(z_r/z_0) - \phi_1} \right\}^2 \tag{2b}$$

where $k$ = von Karman's constant, 0.41

$\quad\quad z_r$ = reference height, m

$\quad\quad z_0$ = roughness length, m

$\quad\quad \phi_1$ = nonneutral Paulson (1970) coefficient.

All existing models prescribe fields of either $C_D$ or $z_0$ and hold them constant over the annual cycle. Indeed, one constant value of $z_0$ is often specified over the entire land surface. In the case of the GLAS (Goddard Laboratory for Atmospheric Sciences) GCM, this is 44 cm, representative of a tall forest cover (Sud and Smith, 1985).

*Heat fluxes*:

$$R_n - G = \lambda E + H \tag{3a}$$

where $G$ = soil heat flux, W m$^{-2}$

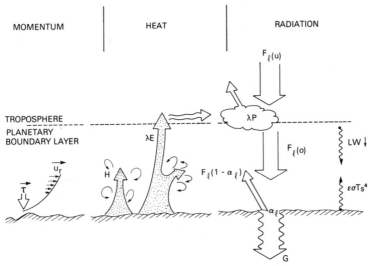

**FIGURE 1.** Schematic diagram of interactions between the land surface and the atmosphere. The net radiation absorbed by the surface ($R_n$) is partitioned into storage ($G$), sensible ($H$) and latent ($\lambda E$) heat terms. The latent heat flux is released into the atmosphere upon condensation ($\lambda P$). The resulting cloud cover may intercept and reflect significant amounts of downcoming radiation.

$E$ = evaporation rate, kg m$^{-2}$ s$^{-1}$
$\lambda$ = latent heat of vaporization, J kg$^{-1}$
$H$ = sensible heat flux, W m$^{-2}$

$$B = \frac{H}{\lambda E} \tag{3b}$$

where $B$ = Bowen ratio

$$G = C_g \frac{dT_g}{dt} \tag{3c}$$

where $C_g$ = ground heat capacity, J m$^{-2}$ K$^{-1}$
$T_g$ = ground temperature, K.

The processes described by equations (1)–(3) are shown in Fig. 1. This equation set was used in the early GCMs with prescribed (sometimes seasonally varying) fields of the parameters $\alpha_l$ and $C_D$ or $z_0$, $B$, and $C_g$. (Often, the ground heat flux term $G$ was omitted by setting $C_g = 0$.) These surface parameterizations could be tuned to give acceptable results and were frequently used for sensitivity studies. However, the utility of the approach as a research tool is extremely limited because of the following:

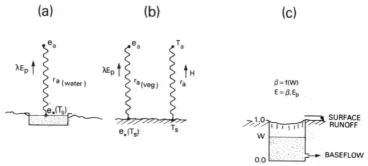

**FIGURE 2.** Surface hydrology as used in most contemporary GCMs. The resistance $r_a$ between surface and air is indicated as in electric circuit theory. An estimate of evapotranspiration appropriate to either (a) an open water lysimeter or (b) a saturated surface with temperature $T_s$ is used to calculate the *potential evapotranspiration* rate. This quantity is then multiplied by a function of the soil moisture fraction, $W$, to account, along with runoff, for the depletion of soil moisture as sketched in (c).

**a.** No feedback effects (from climate to surface) can be simulated with prescribed surface properties; for example, the specification of a fixed Bowen ratio will yield an evaporative flux even if the historical time integral of precipitation minus evaporation is large and negative in a region.

**b.** Obtaining *realistic* climatological fields of the surface parameters necessitates an enormous data collection effort; in many regions, some of these quantities vary drastically from year to year.

## Conceptual Models

Conceptual models were designed and implemented in an attempt to incorporate some of the feedback effects operating between the land surface and atmosphere and hence overcome the shortcomings of the *prescribed field* approach described above. A review of these models is presented by Carson (1981), and so only a general outline of their common features is presented here.

Generally, the broad form of equations (1)–(3) was retained in these models, but the parameters in these equations were made to depend on the land surface condition as predicted by the model, in particular, on the soil moisture storage. The soil moisture storage is usually represented as a "bucket" filled by precipitation and emptied by evaporation and runoff. Most models define runoff as the surplus water produced when the bucket overflows (see Fig. 2). Some surface hydrology models incorporate leakage terms to describe the runoff rate when the bucket is less than full. The governing equation for the soil moisture wetness fraction $W$ is

$$\frac{dW}{dt} = \frac{1}{\theta_s D}\left(P - \frac{E}{\rho_w} - R_0\right) \tag{4}$$

where $W$ = soil moisture wetness fraction ($= \theta/\theta_s$)
    $\theta$ = volumetric soil water content, $m^3 \, m^{-3}$
    $\theta_s$ = value of $\theta$ at saturation, $m^3 \, m^{-3}$
    $D$ = thickness of the hydrologically active soil layer, m
    $P$ = precipitation rate, $m \, s^{-1}$
    $\rho_w$ = density of water, $kg \, m^{-3}$
    $R_0$ = runoff rate, $m \, s^{-1}$.

The maximum moisture storage of the soil is given by the product $\theta_s D$.

The addition of equation (4) to the set allows the modeler to specify some of the feedback effects explicitly in the surface formulation.

A few examples of such feedback effects are given below.

### Radiation
Surface albedo can be made a function of soil moisture, for example,

$$\alpha_l = 0.30 - 0.15W \tag{5}$$

Carson and Sangster (1981) used equation (5) in a British Meteorological Office (MO) GCM simulation run and found it enhanced contrasts between wet and dry regions when compared to runs using prescribed albedos. Qualitatively, equation (5) is reasonable in that dead vegetation or bare ground is more reflective in the visible spectral region (0.4–0.7 μm) than is live vegetation, where chlorophyll absorbs this higher energy radiation. Furthermore, the vegetation albedo may have a highly nonlinear dependence on soil moisture content, related to the survival strategy of the dominant species in a region; for example, deciduous versus coniferous forests and opportunistic species (desert grasses) versus perennials (cacti).

### Momentum
To the author's knowledge, no feedback effects of surface changes on momentum transfer have ever been incorporated into a GCM simulation.

### Latent Heat Fluxes
The conceptual surface models yield their greatest improvement over the prescribed field approach in the calculation of surface fluxes. The most common methodology is as follows: a potential evaporation rate is calculated using either

$$\lambda E_{\mathrm{p}} = \frac{(e_*(T_s) - e_r)}{r_a} \frac{\rho c_p}{\gamma} \tag{6a}$$

or

$$\lambda E_{\mathrm{p}} = \frac{\Delta(R_n - G) + [e_*(T_r) - e_r]\rho c_p/r_a}{\Delta + \gamma} \tag{6b}$$

where $E_p$ = potential evaporation rate, kg m$^{-2}$ s$^{-1}$
    $e_*(T)$ = saturated vapor pressure at temperature $T$, mbars
    $e_r$ = vapor pressure at reference height, mbars
    $T_r$ = air temperature at reference height, K
    $c_p$ = specific heat of air, J kg$^{-1}$ K$^{-1}$
    $\Delta$ = slope of saturation vapor pressure versus temperature curve, mbar K$^{-1}$
    $\gamma$ = psychrometric constant, mbar K$^{-1}$
    $r_a$ = aerodynamic resistance to the turbulent transfer of heat and vapor, s m$^{-1}$

and

$$r_a \approx \frac{1}{k^2 u_r} \left( \ln \frac{z_r}{z_0} - \phi_1 \right) \left( \ln \frac{z_r}{z_0} - \phi_2 \right) \tag{6c}$$

where $\phi_2$ = Paulson (1970) nonneutral correction factor for vapor transfer

or

$$r_a \simeq \frac{1}{C_D C_V u_r} \tag{6d}$$

where $C_V$ = vapor or heat transfer coefficient.

Equations (6a)–(6d) are modifications of the Penman (1948) expression for evaporation from an open-water surface. With appropriate values of $r_a$ and $R_n - G$, (6) will yield identical results when applied to a surface completely covered with free water.

The potential evaporation rate given by (6) is usually adjusted for the limiting effects of soil moisture by

$$E = \beta E_p \tag{7}$$

where $\beta$ is a prescribed function of $W$ and decreases with decreasing $W$.

The combination of equations (6) and (7) would appear to place realistic bounds on the evaporation rate and also to describe its decline with soil moisture depletion in a reasonable way. In fact, neither conclusion is correct.

First, if a value of the aerodynamic resistance $r_a$ for an open-water surface is used (see Fig. 2$a$), both (6a) and (6b) will underestimate the evaporation rate from a saturated natural surface, which is almost always rougher. Use of the $r_a$ value for open water gives an evaporation rate near that of a freely ventilated surface covered with well-watered short grass. (The evaporation rate for both surfaces is limited primarily by the amount of available energy,

$R_n - G$.) Alternatively, if an $r_a$ value appropriate to vegetation is used (i.e., with a $z_0$ on the order of a few centimeters to meters), excessively large evaporation rates will be predicted (see Fig. 2b), often exceeding the net radiation. While such a large rate would be typical of the evaporation rate from a wetted vegetation canopy, it will differ considerably from the transpiration rate of most natural surfaces, even when $W = 1$. Thus, the value of $E_p$ given by (6) may be either that of an open-water surface or of a saturated canopy but not of a freely transpiring vegetation canopy.

The combination of equations (6) with (7) will yield different estimates of the evapotranspiration rate depending on whether one uses equation (6a) or (6b). In most GCMs, the surface temperature $T_s$ is a prognostic variable. If (6a) is used with this value of $T_s$, the derived value of $E_p$ will be too high in arid regions so that even when $W$ is small, excessive evaporation is predicted. On the other hand, (6b) refers to a surface temperature representative of an open-water lysimeter, which is different from the $T_s$ carried by the model. The shortcomings of the (6a) and (7) combination have prompted many workers to use (6b) and (7) even though the predicted surface temperatures are then not consistent with evaporation rates. As stated by Y. Mintz, University of Maryland (personal communication), "in nature, there are no telephonic connections between lysimeters and the rest of the land surface."

More recently, the Penman–Monteith equation (Monteith, 1973) has been used within a GCM. This modification of the original Penman (1948) formula defines the evapotranspiration rate from a vegetated surface in terms of a surface resistance $r_c$ that is roughly equivalent to the resistance imposed by all the leaf stomata acting in parallel. Figure 3 illustrates the action of a stomatal pore:

$$\lambda E = \frac{\Delta(R_n - G) + \rho c_p[e_*(T_r) - e_r]/r_a}{\Delta + \gamma \dfrac{r_a + r_c}{r_a}} \tag{8}$$

where $r_c$ = surface or canopy resistance, s m$^{-1}$.

The use of (8) within a model is consistent with the prediction of a single prognostic ground temperature $T_s$. Sud and Smith (1984) used this surface resistance formulation in a GCM along with a soil moisture term that reduced the predicted evapotranspiration rate, thereby introducing an inconsistency similar to that produced by the combination of (6) and (7).

Equation (8) is a physically more acceptable description of the partition of energy at the surface than the combination of (6) and (7). One may obtain an understanding of the "real" components of the $\beta$ function of (7) by com-

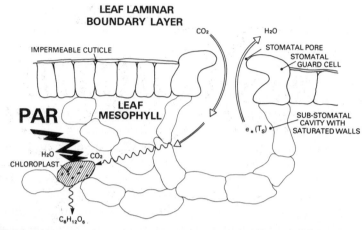

**FIGURE 3.** Processes of gas exchange and photosynthetically active radiation (PAR) interception at the leaf level. Carbon dioxide diffuses in through the stomatal pore, the aperture of which is under active control. There is an inevitable loss of water vapor over the same route since the internal tissues are saturated. Carbon dioxide and cellular water are combined into organic molecules in the mesophyll chloroplasts. These have chlorophyllous structures that are highly absorbent in the 0.4–0.7-μm spectral region.

bining (8) with (6b) (the commonly used expression for $E_p$) and expressing β as

$$\beta = \frac{\Delta(R_n - G) + [e_*(T_r) - e_r]\rho c_p/r_{a_1}}{\Delta(R_n - G) + [e_*(T_r) - e_r]\rho c_p/r_{a_2}} \frac{\Delta + \gamma(r_{a_2} + r_c)/r_{a_2}}{\Delta + \gamma} \tag{9}$$

where $r_{a_1}$ = assumed aerodynamic resistance for $E_p$ calculation in (7), s m$^{-1}$

$r_{a_2}$ = aerodynamic resistance for the vegetated surface, s m$^{-1}$.

Equation (9) shows that if a value of $r_a$ appropriate to the actual surface is used in (7), that is, $r_{a_1} = r_{a_2}$, as opposed to the much higher value for an open-water surface usually used, the value of β is a function of $r_a$ and $r_c$ only. If instead the value of $r_{a_1}$ is set to the original Penman open-water form, then β depends on the values of all of the micrometeorological input variables $(R_n - G)$, $T_r$, and $e_r$ and on $r_{a_1}$, $r_{a_2}$ and $r_c$. The dependence of β on all of these variables as shown in (9) explains why attempts to fit β functions to evapotranspiration data sets have produced less than satisfactory formulations.

In spite of the above failings, conceptual models can provide some accounting for the past accumulation of precipitation minus evaporation and runoff. Nevertheless, they are unreliable for the prediction of soil moisture, and the questionable physical significance of their various parameters discourages elaboration and experimentation beyond the crudest formulations. It is doubtful whether land-surface-change experiments conducted with such models give more than merely qualitative indications of the importance of various surface-related processes.

## Biophysically Based Models

Both of the preceding methodologies specify the transfer of radiation, momentum, and heat as independent processes, that is, the albedo, momentum, and heat transfer coefficients and the soil hydrology formulations (if any) are presented as separate attributes of the land surface rather than as complementary facets of the vegetation–soil system. Since such models are limited as predictive tools, a more fundamental approach to the problem is required. Ideally, the perfect model should be based entirely on biological and physical principles, but the limitations of current biophysical knowledge and the diversity of plant form and function to be found within a given region discourage such a stringent approach, and such exactness would be too expensive in terms of computer resources. A more realistic approach would be to base the model design on biophysical principles and to attempt to capture the important aspects of the biophysical controls over the surface–atmosphere exchanges. Although harder to design and implement than the two previous classes, a biophysical model may have the following benefits.

It may be used to study more realistically the various feedback processes acting between the atmosphere and the vegetated surface.

It offers a better prospect for the use of coupled surface–atmosphere models for prediction.

The model may provide physical-state variables (rather than their conceptual analogs) for comparison with actual measurements and therefore allow model verification and initialization. In this respect, remotely sensed data with global coverage and high temporal resolution may be immensely useful.

However, the complexity of any such proposed model is severely limited by the constraints of computer storage and operation. For the model to be *simple without being trivial* and hence to satisfy computer storage, execution time, and vectorization constraints, it must also be capable of representing any land surface condition by an adjustment of its input parameters. With these constraints in mind, we should try to model radiation interception, momentum exchange, and heat flux transfer as processes linked via the physical and biophysical properties of the vegetation cover. In pursuing this methodology, it is necessary to discard the view of plants as passive, damp surfaces evaporating at rates governed solely by the atmospheric demand and soil moisture condition. Rather, they are living organisms that regulate the passage of water and gas through their systems in an efficient manner in order to maximize their prospects of growth and survival. If we are to understand the links between surface and atmosphere, we must introduce some of the influences of the physiology and morphology of the vegetation to be found in a given region.

A discussion of the principal ways in which terrestrial plants may interact with the atmosphere follows.

### Radiation

The chlorophyll molecule in green plants absorbs the visible, or photosynthetically active (0.4–0.7 μm), radiative flux energy in order to combine water and $CO_2$ into organic compounds needed for growth and maintenance. Green, healthy leaves are highly absorbent in this wavelength region (scattering coefficient ≤ 0.2) but weakly absorbent in the adjacent near-infrared (0.7–3.0-μm) region (scattering coefficient of about 0.8) where the lower energy radiation cannot drive photosynthesis. Bare ground, on the other hand, usually exhibits a flatter scattering response with increasing wavelength and reflectances of about 0.1–0.3 over the spectral region 0.4–3.0 μm. The differing orientations of leaves within the canopy and the effect of multiple reflection and reinterception of radiation between the leaves make the canopy an effective radiation trap.

### Biophysical Control of Evapotranspiration

For $CO_2$ to reach the chlorophyll reaction sites, leaves must maintain an open pathway between the atmosphere and their saturated tissues and so inevitably lose water via evaporation over the same route (see Fig. 3). Higher plants control the amount of gas exchange (and hence water loss) by means of valvelike structures on the leaf surface (stomata). Since only a small fraction of the radiant energy absorbed by leaves goes into photosynthesis or other storage terms, any decrease in the evaporation rate will be approximately balanced by a concomitant increase in the sensible heat loss.

### Momentum Transfer

Some plants grow tall in order to compete for light and, in some environments, to avoid being eaten by grazing animals. The vertically extended canopy of tall vegetation presents a rough porous medium to the planetary boundary layer airflow when compared to short herbaceous vegetation or bare soil. The resultant turbulence enhances the transport of sensible and latent heat away from the surface while exerting a drag force on the air mass.

### Insulation

The soil surface under a dense vegetation canopy intercepts less radiation and may also be aerodynamically sheltered. As a result, the net radiation available to the covered soil will be smaller, and the component terms of the soil energy budget (evaporation, sensible heat, and ground heat flux) will be correspondingly reduced.

### Summary

The interactions described above are merely different manifestations of the same thing: optimal design of an integrated system (the plant) that can access and utilize various resources (radiation, soil moisture, $CO_2$, nutrients, etc.) in order to maximize the organism's chances of survival and growth. In modeling such a system, we should take account of its linked integrated nature and represent the separate interactions in terms of a common self-consistent set of parameters. For example, the leaf area index has an influence on the radiative transfer, momentum flux, and energy partition properties of the vegetation in the Simple Biosphere model.

## STRUCTURE OF SIMPLE BIOSPHERE MODEL (SiB)

A schematic diagram of the Simple Biosphere (SiB) model is shown in Fig. 4. The land surface is represented by a vegetation canopy (upper story) that may be separated from the soil surface by a "trunk" space. The underlying soil surface may be bare or covered by ground vegetation and litter. Either or both of these vegetative layers may be continuous, broken, or absent (e.g., as in tropical rain forest, savanna and desert, respectively). This structure may be adapted to describe crudely the morphological characteristics of the major vegetation formations (as defined by de Laubenfels, 1975, and Kuchler, 1949) by an adjustment of the heights, densities, and cover fractions of the two vegetative layers. The parameters necessary for the operation of the model are obtained by classifying terrestrial biomes according to their vegetation and assigning physical and physiological properties to each. This structure is the simplest method for providing the interactions summarized in the previous section.

The complete model uses boundary conditions set at the height of the lowest layer of the GCM, $z_r$, to calculate dynamically the partition of energy at the surface. Of the seven prognostic variables in the SiB model, two are considered to undergo significant time rates of change over a model time step that may feed back onto the partition of energy. These are the canopy and ground temperatures, $T_c$ and $T_g$, which are directly associated with the "fast" processes of radiation interception and partitioning into latent, sensible, and storage heat terms. The remaining five prognostic variables are moisture stores: $M_c$ and $M_g$ are the amount of intercepted precipitation held as liquid water on leaves of the canopy or of the ground vegetation, respectively; $W_1$ is the soil wetness fraction of the surface store, $W_2$ that of the root zone, and $W_3$ that of the recharge zone, that is, the water-holding soil and rocks below the root zone. These "slow" variables are updated between time steps since the feedback effects induced by their time rates

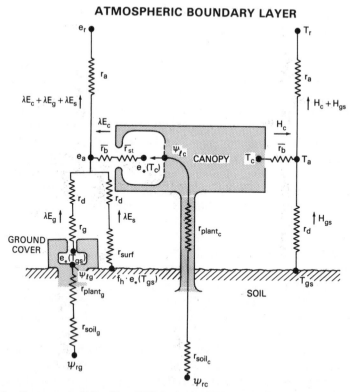

**FIGURE 4.** Framework of the Simple Biosphere (SiB) model. The transfer pathways for latent and sensible heat flux are shown on the left and right sides of the diagram, respectively. Fluxes are proportional to differences in temperature $T$ or water vapor pressure $e$ divided by the appropriate resistance. The subscript $r$ refers to reference height, $a$ to canopy air space, $b$ to canopy element boundary layer, $g$ to ground, $d$ to air space between canopy and ground, and st to stomatal. Resistances are shown in terms of an analogous electrical circuit. These are defined in detail in the text. The treatment of interception loss is excluded from this diagram for clarity.

of change on the fast processes are taken to be negligible. Moisture stores change their levels by the redistribution of water between themselves, by input from precipitation, and by losses to runoff and evapotranspiration.

The relegation of the five moisture stores to the status of accounting variables considerably simplifies the treatment of the surface energy balance. We now must use the initial state of the seven prognostic variables (see Table 1) in combination with the atmospheric forcing to calculate the time rates of change of the fast variables $T_c$ and $T_g$, following which the values of the slow variables may be updated.

In the model, the upper story and ground intercept, reflect, and absorb the incoming radiation in accordance with the physical structure of the canopies and the optical properties of the plant elements and soil. The absorbed

**TABLE 1. Prognostic and Forcing Variables and Variables Associated with Flux Calculations in the SiB Model**

A. Prognostic variables

$T_c$ = canopy temperature, K
$T_g$ = ground temperature, K
$M_c$ = liquid water stored on canopy foliage, m
$M_g$ = liquid water stored on ground foliage, m
$W_1$ = soil moisture wetness fraction of surface store
$W_2$ = soil moisture wetness fraction of root zone
$W_3$ = soil moisture wetness fraction of recharge zone

B. Forcing variables

$F_0$ = incident radiative flux (spectral and angular components), W m$^{-2}$
$P$ = precipitation, m s$^{-1}$
$u_r$ = wind speed at reference height, m s$^{-1}$
$T_r$ = air temperature at reference height, K
$e_r$ = vapor pressure at reference height, mbar

C. Fluxes

| Flux | Potential Difference | Resistances |
|---|---|---|
| $H_c$ | $(T_c - T_a)\rho c_p$ | $\bar{r}_b$ |
| $H_g$ | $(T_g - T_a)\rho c_p$ | $r_d$ |
| $H_c + H_g$ | $(T_a - T_r)\rho c_p$ | $r_a$ |
| $\lambda E_c$ | $[e_*(T_c) - e_a]\rho c_p/\gamma$ | $f(\bar{r}_{st}, \bar{r}_b, M_c)$ |
| $\lambda E_g$ | $[e_*(T_g) - e_a]\rho c_p/\gamma$ | $f(r_{surf}, r_g, r_d, M_g)$ |
| $\lambda E_c + \lambda E_g$ | $(e_a - e_r)\rho c_p/\gamma$ | $r_a$ |

where $T_a, e_a$ = air temperature, vapor pressure in canopy air space, K, mbar
$\rho, c_p$ = density, specific heat of air; kg m$^{-3}$, J kg$^{-1}$ K$^{-1}$
$\gamma$ = psychrometric constant, mbar K$^{-1}$
$\bar{r}_b$ = bulk boundary layer resistance, s m$^{-1}$
$r_d$ = aerodynamic resistance between ground and canopy air space, s m$^{-1}$
$r_a$ = aerodynamic resistance between canopy air space and reference height, s m$^{-1}$
$\bar{r}_{st}$ = bulk stomatal resistance of upper-story vegetation, s m$^{-1}$
$r_g$ = bulk stomatal resistance of ground vegetation, s m$^{-1}$
$r_{surf}$ = bare soil surface resistance, s m$^{-1}$
$e_*(T)$ = vapor pressure at temperature T, mbar

energies, $Rn_c$ and $Rn_g$, are partitioned into latent, sensible, and storage heat terms as shown below.

$$Rn_c = \lambda E_c + H_c + C_c \frac{dT_c}{dt} \tag{10}$$

$$Rn_g = \lambda E_g + H_g + C_g \frac{dT_g}{dt} \tag{11}$$

where $C_c$, $C_g$ = effective heat capacity, J $K^{-1}m^{-2}$
$T_c$, $T_g$ = temperatures, K
$Rn_c$, $Rn_g$ = net radiation absorbed, W $m^{-2}$
$\lambda E_c$, $\lambda E_g$ = latent heat fluxes, W $m^{-2}$
$H_c$, $H_g$ = sensible heat fluxes, W $m^{-2}$.

The subscripts $c$ and $g$ refer to the upper story canopy and ground (ground cover and soil), respectively. The terms in (10) and (11) are functions of (a) the prognostic variables, that is, canopy temperature, ground temperature, and the five moisture stores; (b) the boundary forcings of incoming radiation, precipitation, air temperature, humidity, and wind speed at a reference height $z_r$; and (c) six resistances, three aerodynamic resistances ($r_a$, $\bar{r}_b$, and $r_d$) and three surface resistances ($\bar{r}_{st}$, $r_g$, and $r_{surf}$). Figure 4 illustrates the various resistances used in the SiB model.

The heat fluxes $H_c$, $H_g$, $\lambda E_c$, and $\lambda E_g$ are obtained from the above resistances and the differences between the surface (i.e., canopy or ground) and canopy air temperatures in the case of sensible heat and the corresponding differences in vapor pressure for the transfer of latent heat.

The resistances are equivalent to the integrals of inverse conductances per unit length over a specified length. In the cases of the aerodynamic resistances, $r_a$, $\bar{r}_b$, and $r_d$, the conductances correspond to the turbulent transfer coefficients for heat and vapor. The surface resistances $\bar{r}_{st}$ and $r_g$ are the additional resistances to the transfer of vapor from the saturated tissues in the plants, and $r_{surf}$ is the equivalent resistance limiting the transfer of water from within the soil surface store to the air just above the soil. The aerodynamic resistances $r_a$, $\bar{r}_b$, and $r_d$ are calculated from the morphology of the vegetated surface; the wind speed at reference height, $u_r$; and the temperature differences $T_a - T_r$, $T_c - T_a$, and $T_g - T_a$, respectively. The surface resistances $\bar{r}_{st}$, $r_g$, and $r_{surf}$ are calculated from a combination of plant physiological and morphological parameters, incident radiation, temperature, vapor pressure, and soil moisture. A full listing of the prognostic, diagnostic, and forcing variables is given in Table 1.

From the calculations just outlined and described further in subsequent sections, equations (10) and (11) are reduced to a pair of coupled differential equations in $T_c$ and $T_g$ that are solved by a numerical method.

## Classification of the World's Biomes

The vegetation communities covering the earth's surface have been classified and identified on a $1° \times 1°$ grid scale (Willmott et al., 1984) using data originating from Matthews (1983). Currently, the classification identifies 32 surface-cover types, but for the initial implementation of SiB, these categories are combined into eight biomes. Each of these biomes has values for the surface properties listed in Table 2. In the noninteractive version of SiB,

**TABLE 2. Biome Surface Properties from which SiB Parameters Are Derived**

*Vegetation* (upper story)

$z_2$ = height of canopy top, m
$z_1$ = height of canopy base, m
$L_d$ = leaf area density as a function of time, $m^2 \ m^{-3}$
$\alpha, \delta$ = leaf optical properties (reflection and transmission)
$O(\xi,\theta)$ = leaf angle distribution function
$C_d, p_s$ = drag coefficient of leaves, shelter factor
$C_s$ = leaf transfer coefficient
$a, b, c$ = stomatal resistance coefficients (light dependence)
$T_l, T_h, T_0$ = minimum, maximum, and optimum temperatures for stomatal functioning, K
$h_5$ = parameter governing stomatal response to vapor pressure, $mbar^{-1}$
$h_6, \psi_c$ = parameters governing stomatal response to leaf water potential $m^{-1}$, m
$S_c$ = precipitation interception capacity, m
$V_c$ = extent of surface covered by upper story
$C_c$ = heat capacity of vegetation, taken to be equivalent to 0.2 mm water per unit leaf area index, $J \ m^{-2} \ K^{-1}$
$z_d, D_d$ = rooting depth and density as functions of time, m, $m \ m^{-3}$
$r_{plant}$ = resistance imposed by plant vascular system, $s \ m^{-1}$
$R$ = root resistance per unit root length, $s \ m^{-1}$

Where there is significant ground cover underneath the upper-story vegetation, parameters corresponding to the above list are also required for the lower story except for $z_2$, $z_1$, $L_d$, $C_c$, $C_d$, $p_s$, and $C_s$ and with the addition of:

$L_t$ = total leaf area index, $m^2 \ m^{-2}$
$z_s$ = roughness length of ground, m
$C_{D_g}$ = drag coefficient of the ground

*Soil*

$C_g$ = effective heat capacity of the ground, $J \ m^{-2} \ K^{-1}$
$D_1$ = depth of interception layer, m
$D_2$ = depth of upper story root zone, m
$D_3$ = depth of recharge zone, m
$K_s$ = saturated conductivity, $m \ s^{-1}$
$\theta_s$ = pore space
$\psi_s$ = soil moisture potential at saturation, m
$B$ = soil moisture potential parameter
$\alpha_s$ = soil optical properties

phenological variations in the surface properties are specified at 1-month time resolutions.

These basic data for each biome class give secondary parameters used by the SiB model (see following sections). This preliminary task, which need be done once only for each biome, is performed by the SiB preprocessor.

## Radiation Balance

The interception and scattering of solar radiation by vegetation may be modeled in a variety of ways (see the review of Dickinson, 1983), but a simple, economical method is appropriate to SiB.

The two-stream approximation description as described in Meador and Weaver (1980), Coakley and Chylek (1975), and Dickinson (1983) allows for the multiple scattering of light by leaves. Equations (12) and (13) were proposed by Dickinson (1983) as appropriate for vegetation:

$$-\bar{\mu}\frac{dI\uparrow}{dL} + [1 - (1 - \beta)\omega]\,I\uparrow\, - \omega\beta I\downarrow\, = \omega\bar{\mu}K\beta_0 e^{-KL} \tag{12}$$

$$\bar{\mu}\frac{dI\downarrow}{dL} + [1 - (1 - \beta)\omega]\,I\downarrow\, - \omega\beta I\uparrow\, = \omega\bar{\mu}K(1 - \beta_0)e^{-KL} \tag{13}$$

where $I\uparrow$, $I\downarrow$ = upward and downward diffuse radiative fluxes, normalized by incident flux

$K$ = optical depth of the direct beam per unit leaf area $[= G(\mu)/\mu]$

$G(\mu)$ = projected area of leaf elements in direction $\mu$

$\mu$ = cosine of the zenith angle of the incident beam

$\bar{\mu}$ = average inverse diffuse optical depth per unit leaf area $(= \int_0^1 [\mu'/G(\mu')]\,d\mu')$

$\mu'$ = direction of scattered flux

$\omega$ = scattering coefficient

$L$ = cumulative leaf area index

and $\beta$ and $\beta_0$ are the upscatter parameters for the diffuse and direct beams, respectively. The value of $\omega\beta$ is inferred from the analysis of Norman and Jarvis (1975):

$$\omega\beta = \tfrac{1}{2}[\alpha + \delta + (\alpha - \delta)\cos^2\bar{\theta}] \tag{14}$$

where $\omega = \alpha + \delta$

$\alpha$ = leaf reflection coefficient

$\delta$ = leaf transmission coefficient

$\bar{\theta}$ = mean leaf angle inclination above horizontal plane

The value of $\beta_0$, the direct beam upscatter parameter, was suggested by Dickinson (1983) to be

$$\beta_0 = \frac{1 + \bar{\mu}K}{\omega\bar{\mu}K} a_s(\mu) \tag{15}$$

where the single scattering albedo, $a_s(\mu)$, is given by

$$a_s(\mu) = \omega \int_0^1 \frac{\mu'\Gamma(\mu, \mu')}{\mu G(\mu') + \mu' G(\mu)} d\mu' \tag{16}$$

where $\Gamma(\mu, \mu') = G(\mu)G(\mu')P(\mu, \mu')$
$P(\mu, \mu')$ = scattering phase function

A full discussion of the various terms in equations (12)–(16) is presented in the comprehensive review of Dickinson (1983).

A number of simplifying assumptions are made for calculating some of the above parameters for use within SiB. For example, all the individual scattering interactions are taken to be isotropic, which makes the scattering phase function independent of the angle of the incoming beam. The physical implications of these assumptions and the method of obtaining solutions to (12) and (13) are discussed in Sellers (1985). After some manipulation, (12) and (13) may be modified and solved with suitable boundary conditions for the albedo and transmission coefficient of the canopy (see Sellers, 1985) for both direct beam and diffuse incident radiation. To take account of the effects of nonuniform plant cover, we let $V_c$ and $V_g$ represent the fractional cover of the upper story and ground vegetation, respectively. The area averaged leaf area index, $\bar{L}_t$, is related to the local leaf area index, $L_t$, used in the radiation calculation by $L_t = \bar{L}_t/V$, where $V = V_c, V_g$ and $L_t = L_{tc}, L_{tg}$. The albedo of the ground (ground cover plus bare soil) is then given by

$$A_{\Lambda,\mu} = I{\uparrow}_g V_g + (1 - V_g)\alpha_s(\Lambda) \tag{17}$$

where $A_{\Lambda,\mu}$ = ground albedo as a function of wavelength interval $\Lambda$ and angle of incident radiation, $\mu$
$\alpha_s$ = soil reflectance
$I{\uparrow}_g$ = upward diffuse radiation flux above ground cover, normalized by incident flux

and $A_{\Lambda,\mu}$ for diffuse and direct fluxes is $A_{\Lambda,d}$ and $A_{\Lambda,b}$, respectively.

The radiation absorbed by the canopy and ground is then

$$F_{\Lambda,\mu}(c) = V_c[1 - I{\uparrow}_c - I{\downarrow}_g^c(1 - A_{\Lambda,d}) - \exp(-KL_{tc})(1 - A_{\Lambda,b})]{\cdot}F_{\lambda,\mu}(0) \tag{18}$$

and

$$F_{\Lambda,\mu}(g) = \{(1 - V_c)(1 - A_{\lambda,\mu})$$
$$+ V_c[I\downarrow_g^c(1 - A_{\Lambda,d}) + \exp(-KL_{tc})(1 - A_{\Lambda,b})]\} \cdot F_{\Lambda,\mu}(0) \quad (19)$$

where $F_{\Lambda,\mu}(0)$ = incident radiant energy of wavelength interval $\Lambda$ and direction $\mu$, W m$^{-2}$

$F_{\Lambda,\mu}(c)$, $F_{\Lambda,\mu}(g)$ = amount of $F_{\Lambda,\mu}(0)$ absorbed by the canopy and by the ground cover and soil, W m$^{-2}$

$I\uparrow_c$ = diffuse flux leaving top of canopy

$I\downarrow_g^c$ = diffuse flux leaving base of canopy

$\exp(-KL_{tc})$ = direct flux penetrating canopy (0 for incident diffuse light)

$L_{tc}$ = local leaf area index of canopy, m$^2$ m$^{-2}$

$d, b$ = subscripts for diffuse and direct beam components, respectively.

[*Note*: The diffuse terms in (18) and (19) are normalized by the incident flux $F_{\Lambda,\mu}(0)$. Also, $A_{\Lambda,b}$ will vary with the solar angle while $A_{\Lambda,d}$ is constant for a given surface condition.]

The above calculations are done for five components of the incoming radiation: visible (diffuse and direct), near infrared (diffuse and direct), and thermal infrared (diffuse only). Mean values of the reflection and transmission coefficients for the leaves and soil are used within each wavelength interval.

Finally, the net radiation terms are calculated by subtracting the emitted thermal radiative loss from the absorbed radiative terms.

$$Rn_c = \langle F_c \rangle - 2\sigma_s T_c^4 \cdot V_c + \sigma_s T_g^4 \cdot V_c \quad (20)$$

$$Rn_g = \langle F_g \rangle - \sigma_s T_g^4 + \sigma_s T_c^4 \cdot V_c \quad (21)$$

where $\langle F_c \rangle$, $\langle F_g \rangle$ = sum of five absorbed radiation components, W m$^{-2}$

$\sigma_s$ = Stefan–Boltzmann constant, W m$^{-2}$ K$^{-4}$

$T_c$, $T_g$ = canopy and ground temperatures, K.

In equations (20) and (21), the emissivities of ground and canopy are assumed to be unity.

Figure 5 indicates the performance of the surface albedo calculation. The hemispherical albedo observed over a spring wheat crop in the Federal Republic of Germany is shown for two summer days in 1979 (van der Ploeg et al., 1980). Also shown is the predicted albedo for a wheat cover at a similar growth stage at a nearby site as given by (12) and (13). The diurnal trend and magnitudes of the predicted global albedo agree with the observations.

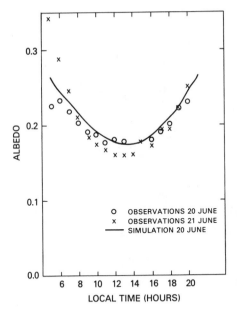

**FIGURE 5.** Measured and simulated albedo values for shortwave radiation above a wheat crop. The observed points were calculated from observations of incoming and outgoing shortwave radiation taken at Volkenrude, Federal Republic of Germany, June 20–21, 1979, by van der Ploeg et al. (1980). The simulation for the wheat crop at Ruthe (50 km away) for June 20, 1979, is also shown. [From Sellers, 1985, with permission of the *International Journal of Remote Sensing*, Taylor and Francis.]

## Aerodynamic Resistances

Figure 4 shows how the SiB model transfers heat and vapor from canopy and ground via three aerodynamic resistances and two surface resistances. The turbulent transport of momentum and other quantities between the atmosphere and the surface is a complex process and not simply modeled (see Raupach and Thom, 1981). In SiB, flux-gradient equations describe all such transfers, although such methods are not completely realistic.

Some of the parameters listed in Table 2 are used to solve diffusion equations that describe the absorption of momentum by the surface. Figure 6 shows how the upper-story canopy is represented as a block of constant-density porous material from $z_1$ to $z_2$ and sandwiched between two constant-stress layers. Extrapolation of the log profile yields underestimates of the turbulent transfer coefficient close to the top of the canopy. Thus, the log profile is only valid above a certain transition height, $z_m$, which is taken to be a function of surface morphology. Below this level, an empirical adjustment to the profile must be made. Data from Garratt (1978) and Raupach and Thom (1981) are used to estimate the value of $z_m$ as equal to $z_2 + 2(z_2 - d)$ and the ratio of the actual turbulent transfer coefficient at $z_2$ to that predicted by the log profile as 1.75. Under neutral conditions, equations for the transfer of momentum above and within the canopy are:

*Above the canopy*: $z > z_m$.

$$\tau = \rho u_*^2 = \rho \left\{ \frac{ku}{\ln\left(\dfrac{z - d}{z_0}\right)} \right\}^2 \tag{22}$$

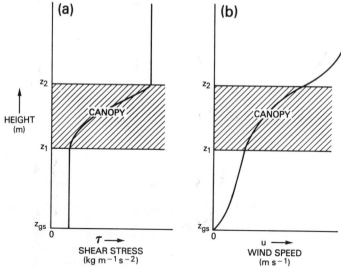

**FIGURE 6.** Profiles of (a) shear stress and (b) wind speed above, within and below the canopy as represented in SiB.

where $\tau$ = shear stress, kg m$^{-1}$s$^{-2}$
$\rho$ = air density, kg m$^{-3}$
$u_*$ = friction velocity, m s$^{-1}$
$k$ = von Karman's constant ($=0.41$)
$u$ = wind speed, m s$^{-1}$
$d$ = zero-plane displacement height, m
$z_0$ = roughness length, m
$z_m$ = transition height, m.

*Within the canopy*: $z_1 < z < z_2$.

$$\frac{\partial \tau}{\partial z} = \rho \frac{C_d \overline{L}_d}{p_s} \cdot u^2 \tag{23}$$

where $C_d$ = leaf drag coefficient
$\overline{L}_d$ = area-averaged leaf area density, m$^2$ m$^{-3}$
$p_s$ = leaf shelter factor.

*Also*:

$$\tau = \rho K_m \frac{\partial u}{\partial z} \tag{24}$$

where $K_m$ = momentum transfer coefficient, m$^2$ s$^{-1}$

and

$$d = \frac{\displaystyle\int_{z_1}^{z_2} u^2 z \, dz}{\displaystyle\int_{z_1}^{z_2} u^2 \, dz + \tau/\rho \left.\right|_{z_1} \frac{p_s}{\overline{L}_d \, C_d}} \tag{25}$$

Equations (22) and (23) are commonly used to describe the absorption of momentum by a rough surface and are derived in Monteith (1973). Equation (25) was first suggested by Thom (1971), where $d$, the zero-plane displacement height, is defined as the moment height for momentum absorption. The second term in the denominator of (25) has been added to the original form to account for the momentum absorbed by the ground. In contrast to the approach used in describing radiative transfer, the effects of vegetation morphology on turbulent transfer are described in terms of the area-averaged (denoted by an overbar) properties of the plant cover.

In order to calculate the momentum transfer characteristics of the surface, $z_0$ and $d$, and to estimate the values of the resistances $\overline{r}_b$, $r_d$, and $r_a$, equations (22)–(25) are closed by adding another equation describing the variation of $K_m$ within the canopy air space. (Currently, the assumption that $K_m$ is proportional to the local wind speed is used within the canopy.) There are then five equations and five unknowns, $u$, $K_m$, $z_0$, $d$, and $\tau/\rho$ evaluated at $z_1$. Although the use of $K$-theory within the canopy is physically unrealistic, it yields reasonable results, so this simple analysis is to be used until suitable second-order closure models are applied to the problem.

Finally, boundary conditions must be imposed on the five equations. The upper boundary condition is that $u = u_r$ and the lower one is that shear stress at the ground surface equals the downward transport to the ground by eddy mixing, that is,

$$\tau \left.\right|_{z_1} = \rho C_{D_g} u \left.\right|_{z_1} = \rho K_m \frac{\partial u}{\partial z} \bigg|_{z_1} \tag{26}$$

where $C_{D_g}$ is the drag coefficient of the ground estimated from the size of the ground roughness elements.

Equations (22)–(26) are solved for any set of input values of $z_2$, $z_1$, $\overline{L}_d$, $C_d$, $p_s$, and $C_{D_g}$ to yield wind profile parameters and estimates of $z_0$ and $d$; see Fig. 7. The input parameters that are hardest to quantify are the shelter factor $p_s$, reported to be between 2 and 4 depending on vegetation density, and the ratio of $K_m$ at $z_2$ to the extrapolated log-linear value, here taken as equal to 1.75 throughout. The solution of the equation set (see Sellers et al., 1986) yields a predicted relationship between $z_0$, $d$, and variations in the leaf area density that agrees qualitatively with the results obtained by Shaw and Pereira (1982) using a second-order closure model.

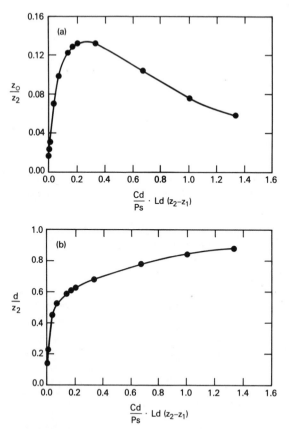

**FIGURE 7.** (a) Roughness length $z_0$ and (b) zero-plane displacement height $d$, both normalized by canopy height $z_2$ and versus a nondimensional parameter given by the product of the drag coefficient, leaf area index, and shelter factor, which is equivalent to the total drag coefficient of the canopy as used by Shaw and Pereira (1982, Figs. 4 and 5).

The calculated profiles of $u$ and $K_m$ give the aerodynamic resistances $r_a$, $\bar{r}_b$, and $r_d$. The explicit forms of $r_a$, $\bar{r}_b$, and $r_d$ are not reproduced here but may be found in the appendix of Sellers et al. (1986).

The laminar boundary layer resistance for a single leaf, $r_b$, has been determined experimentally for many species (Goudriaan, 1977) and commonly yields an expression of the form

$$r_{bi} = \frac{C_s}{L_i \sqrt{u_i}} \tag{27}$$

where $C_s$ = transfer coefficient (dependent on leaf shape and size)
$L_i$ = leaf area of $i$th leaf, m$^2$

$u_i$ = local wind speed, m s$^{-1}$
$r_{b_i}$ = boundary layer resistance of $i$th leaf, s m$^{-1}$.

A bulk boundary layer resistance may be assigned to a group of leaves if the individual resistances $r_{b_i}$ are assumed to act in parallel. As the variation of $u$ with height within the canopy is known from the solution of equations (22)–(26), we may write

$$\frac{1}{\bar{r}_b} = \int_{z_1}^{z_2} \frac{\overline{L_d}\sqrt{u(z)}}{p_s C_s}\, dz \tag{28}$$

where $\bar{r}_b$ = area-averaged bulk boundary layer resistance, s m$^{-1}$.

For neutral stability, equation (28) gives

$$\bar{r}_b = \frac{C_1}{\sqrt{u_2}} \tag{29}$$

where $u_2$ = wind speed at $z_2$
$C_1$ = surface-dependent constant obtained by integrating (28).

The vapor and sensible heat source height, $h_a$, is the center of action of $\bar{r}_b$ in the canopy such that

$$\int_{z_1}^{h_a} r_b^{-1}\,dz = \int_{h_a}^{z_2} r_b^{-1}\,dz$$

The neutral value of the aerodynamic resistance $r_d$ for the transfer of heat and water vapor between the soil surface and $h_a$ is simply

$$r_d = \int_0^{h_a} \frac{0.74}{K_m}\, dz = \frac{C_2}{u_2} \tag{30}$$

where 0.74 = factor accounting for different diffusivities of heat or vapor and momentum
$C_2$ = surface/canopy-dependent constant.

The aerodynamic resistance between $h_a$ and $z_r$ is $r_a$, defined as

$$r_a = \int_{h_a}^{z_r} \frac{1}{K_s}\, dz = \int_{h_a}^{z_2} \frac{1}{K_s(z)}\, dz + \int_{z_2}^{z_r} \frac{1}{K_s(z)}\, dz \tag{31}$$

where $K_s$ = heat and vapor transfer coefficient, m$^2$ s$^{-1}$

Under neutral conditions,

$$r_a = \frac{C_3}{u_r} \qquad (32)$$

where $C_3$ = surface-dependent constant
$u_r$ = wind speed at reference height, m s$^{-1}$.

The above expressions for $\bar{r}_b$, $r_d$, and $r_a$ are modified to account for the effects of nonneutrality, and in the case of $\bar{r}_b$ and $r_d$, $u_2$ is replaced by $u_r$. The relationships between $u_2$ and $u_r$ and the full forms of the nonneutral resistances are given in the appendix of Sellers et al. (1986).

The coefficients $C_1$, $C_2$, $z_0$, and $d$ are calculated only once for a given surface configuration by a preprocessor program. The nonneutral calculation of $r_a$ depends on $z_0$, $d$, and the Monin–Obukhov length; equation (32) is valid only under neutral conditions.

## Surface Resistances and Vapor Fluxes

### Transpiration and Evaporation from Soil Surface

The resistances to the transport of moisture from a theoretically saturated air space at the temperature of the canopy or from the ground to the free air are defined as the canopy resistance $\bar{r}_{st}$, ground vegetation resistance $r_g$, and soil surface resistance $r_{surf}$, respectively. When the canopy is dry, $\bar{r}_{st}$ is assumed to be equivalent to the resistances of all the leaf stomata acting in parallel. Similarly, the resistance to vapor transfer at the ground level is a combination of the bulk stomatal resistance of the ground vegetation, $r_g$, and the diffusion resistance of the soil surface, $r_{surf}$.

Jarvis (1976) summarized his own and other researchers' work on the stomatal function of coniferous trees. The stomatal resistance of an individual leaf, $r_s$, was taken to be a function of the normal incident visible flux, vapor pressure deficit $(T_a, e_a)$, leaf temperature $T$, and leaf water potential, $\psi_l$. Rearrangement of Jarvis's original expression yields

$$r_s = \left[ \frac{a}{b + F_s \sin \phi} + c \right] \cdot f(\psi_l)^{-1} \cdot f(T)^{-1} \cdot f(T_a, e_a)^{-1} \qquad (33)$$

where $a, b, c$ = constants determined from observations
$F_s$ = total short-wave flux, W m$^{-2}$ (0.4–0.7 μm wavelength interval)
$\phi$ = angle between leaf and incident flux
$f(\psi_l), f(T), f(T_a, e_a)$ = factors limiting stomatal resistance depending on leaf water potential $\psi_l$, leaf temperature $T$, and air vapor pressure deficit, $e_*(T_a) - e_a$; all factors limited to $0 \leq f(\ ) \leq 1$.

Following a methodology similar to that used for the derivation of $r_b$ in (26), we define the *bulk* stomatal resistance for the canopy by

$$\frac{1}{\overline{r}_{st}} = \int_0^{\overline{L}_t} \int_0^{\pi/2} \int_0^{2\pi} \frac{O(\xi, \theta)}{r_s} \sin \theta \, d\xi d\theta dL \tag{34}$$

where $O(\xi, \theta)$ = leaf angle distribution function
$\xi, \theta$ = leaf azimuth and inclination angles.

The extinction of short-wave or photosynthetically active radiation (PAR) down through the canopy has been described by equations (12) and (13). In view of the small amount of scattering by leaves in this wavelength interval ($\omega \leq 0.2$), the extinction of PAR is approximated by Goudriaan's (1977) semiempirical expression to yield a more manipulable function:

$$F_s(L) \simeq F_s(0)\exp(-\kappa L) \tag{35}$$

where $\kappa$ = extinction coefficient ($=[G(\mu)/\mu] (1 - \omega_s)^{1/2}$)
$F_s(0)$ = short-wave flux above canopy, W m$^{-2}$
$F_s(L)$ = short-wave flux within canopy below a leaf area index of $L$, W m$^{-2}$
$\omega_s$ = leaf scattering coefficient for PAR.

With an appropriate value of $G(\mu)$ used in equation (35) and with the assumption that leaf water potential, air temperature, and humidity vary only slightly within the canopy when compared to the extinction of radiation, equation (34) is simplified to

$$\frac{1}{\overline{r}_{st}} \simeq V_c f(\psi_l) f(T) f(T_a, e_a) \cdot \int_0^{L_{tc}} \int_0^{\pi/2} \int_0^{2\pi} \frac{O(\xi, \theta)\sin \theta}{r_s(F_s(0), \kappa, \xi, \theta)} d\xi d\theta dL \tag{36}$$

Some analytical solutions to the integral part of the above equation for a number of leaf angle distribution functions are discussed by Sellers (1985). The dependences on leaf water potential, vapor pressure deficit, and leaf temperature are currently the same as in Jarvis (1976), whereby optimum conditions result in setting the respective factor to 1 and less than optimal conditions reduce it, thus increasing the total resistance.

The factor $f(\psi_l)$ accounts for the effects of soil moisture stress and excessive evaporative demand.

$$f(\psi_l) = 1 - \exp(-h_6\delta_\psi) \tag{37}$$

where $\delta_\psi = \psi_l - \psi_0$
$\psi_0$ = leaf water potential at which stomata close completely, m

$h_6$ = species-dependent constant, $m^{-1}$.
$\psi_l$ = leaf water potential, m

The quantity $\psi_l$ is calculated with a catenary model of the water transfer pathway from root zone to leaf given by van den Honert (1948):

$$\psi_l = \psi_r - z_T - \frac{E_d}{\rho_w}(\bar{r}_{plant} + \bar{r}_{soil}) \tag{38}$$

where $z_T$ = height of transpiration source ($= h_a$ for upper story and 0 for ground vegetation), m
$\psi_r$ = soil moisture potential in root zone, m
$\bar{r}_{plant}$ = area-averaged resistance imposed by plant vascular system, $s\ m^{-1}$
$\bar{r}_{soil}$ = area-averaged resistance of soil and root system, $s\ m^{-1}$
$\rho_w$ = density of water, $kg\ m^{-3}$
$E_d$ = transpiration rate, $kg\ m^{-2}\ s^{-1}$.

The soil moisture potential in the root zone, $\psi_r$, is an average term obtained by summing the weighted soil moisture potentials of the soil layers from the surface to the rooting depth $z_d$:

$$\psi_r = \sum_0^{z_d} \frac{\psi_i D_i}{z_d} \tag{39}$$

where $\psi_i$ = soil moisture potential of $i$th layer, m
$D_i$ = depth of $i$th layer, m
$z_d$ = rooting depth, m.

The soil moisture potential of a layer, $\psi_i$, is given by the empirical expression of Clapp and Hornberger (1978):

$$\psi_i = \psi_s W_i^{-B} \tag{40}$$

where $W_i$ = soil moisture wetness fraction
$\psi_s$ = soil moisture potential at saturation, m
$B$ = empirical constant.

The area-averaged resistance imposed on the flow of water from the soil to the root cortex, $\bar{r}_{soil}$, is described by a depth-averaged form of the expression proposed by Federer (1979):

$$\bar{r}_{soil} = \frac{R/D_d + \alpha_f/K_r}{z_d} \tag{41}$$

$$\alpha_f = \frac{1}{8\pi D_d}\left(V_r - 3 - 2\ln\frac{V_r}{1 - V_r}\right)$$

where $R$ = resistance per unit root length, s m$^{-1}$
$D_d$ = root density, m m$^{-3}$
$V_r$ = volume of root per unit volume of soil, m$^3$ m$^{-3}$
$K_r$ = mean soil hydraulic conductivity in the root zone, m s$^{-1}$.

The soil hydraulic conductivity in the root zone, $K_r$, is obtained by a manipulation of the expressions of Clapp and Hornberger (1978) and Milly and Eagleson (1982), which yields $K_r$ as a function of $\psi_r$:

$$K_r = K_s \left(\frac{\psi_s}{\psi_r}\right)^{(2B+3)/B} \tag{42}$$

where $K_s$ = soil saturated hydraulic conductivity, m s$^{-1}$.

Values of $B$, $\psi_s$, and $K_s$ for a number of different soils are listed in Clapp and Hornberger (1978). The transpiration rates from the dry portions of the vegetation are given by

$$\lambda E_{dc} = \frac{e_*(T_c) - e_a}{\bar{r}_{st} + \bar{r}_b} \frac{\rho c_p}{\gamma} (1 - W_c) \tag{43}$$

$$\lambda E_{dg} = \frac{e_*(T_g) - e_a}{r_g + r_d} \frac{\rho c_p}{\gamma} (1 - W_g)V_g \tag{44}$$

where $E_{dc}$, $E_{dg}$ = transpiration rates of upper story and ground vegetation, kg m$^{-2}$ s$^{-1}$
$e_*(T_c)$, $e_*(T_g)$ = saturated vapor pressure at temperatures $T_c$ and $T_g$, mbar
$\rho$, $c_p$ = density and specific heat of air, kg m$^{-3}$, J kg$^{-1}$ K$^{-1}$
$\gamma$ = psychrometric constant, mbar K$^{-1}$
$\lambda$ = latent heat of vaporization, J kg$^{-1}$
$W_c$, $W_g$ = wetness fraction of upper story and ground vegetation.

Following the calculation of the transpiration rates, the abstraction of water from the different soil layers is given by

$$E_{di} = \frac{D_i}{z_d} \frac{\psi_i - \psi_l}{\bar{r}_{plant} + \bar{r}_{soil}} \rho_w \tag{45}$$

where $E_{di}$ = extraction rate of transpired water from $i$th soil layer, kg m$^{-2}$ s$^{-1}$

Equation (45) must be applied with values of $E_d$, $\psi_l$, and $\bar{r}_{soil}$ appropriate to the upper story and ground vegetation in turn. In the case of the ground

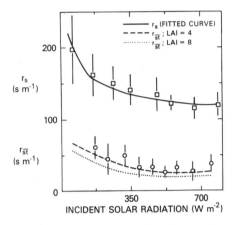

**FIGURE 8.** Data showing variation of leaf stomatal resistance $r_s$ (top leaves) and canopy resistance $\bar{r}_{st}$ for a barley crop (from Monteith et al., 1965). Lines show fit to $r_s$, using equation (31), and estimate of $\bar{r}_{st}$ as given by equation (34) for leaf area indices (LAI) of 4.0 and 8.0. [From Sellers, 1985, with permission of the *International Journal of Remote Sensing*, Taylor and Francis.]

vegetation, the rooting depth may not extend down to the bottom of $D_2$; $\psi_r$ and $E_{d_i}$ are then calculated using equations (39) and (45) except that the $D_i$ terms are multiplied by the fractional depth of the soil layer occupied by the roots. All of the above calculations that relate stomatal resistance to the abstraction of soil water are performed for both the upper story and the ground vegetation.

There are few available data with which to test the efficacy of the above description of the plant water transfer system, in particular, the expression for bulk stomatal resistance. Monteith et al. (1965) measured the stomatal resistance of barley leaves with a viscous flow porometer and estimated the surface resistance of the crop as a residual of an energy balance calculation. Figure 8 shows their estimate of the surface resistance and the calculated value of $\bar{r}_{st}$ as provided by equation (36) assuming a spherical leaf distribution. The values of $a$, $b$, and $c$ were fitted onto the porometer data (see the upper points and solid line in Fig. 8). The model appears to reproduce the trend in surface resistance reasonably well and also illustrates the diminishing effect of adding further increments of leaf area index; the predicted difference in $\bar{r}_{st}$ for leaf area indices of 4 and 8 is relatively small as the additional leaves are shaded and hence have correspondingly high values of $r_s$.

Evaporation from the soil surface depends on the difference between the vapor pressure in the surface soil store $W_1$ and that of the canopy air space, $e_a$. Since the gradient of vapor pressure in the soil changes sharply near the surface, an empirical surface resistance term, $r_{surf}$, is used to account for the difference between the actual surface vapor pressure and the value associated with $W_1$, which is a mean value for the top few centimeters of soil (see Shu Fen Sun, 1982). Camillo and Gurney (1986) demonstrated that the specification of such an apparent soil surface resistance improved the performance of their multilayer soil model.

The evaporation rate from the soil is then expressed by

$$\lambda E_s = \frac{f_h \cdot e_*(T_g) - e_a}{r_d + r_{\text{surf}}} \frac{\rho c_p}{\gamma} \cdot (1 - V_g) \qquad (46)$$

where $E_s$ = soil evaporation rate, kg m$^{-2}$ s$^{-1}$

$\quad f_h$ = relative humidity of water vapor in surface soil moisture store
$\quad\quad [= \exp(\psi_1 g / RT_g)]$

$\quad \psi_1$ = soil moisture potential of surface soil moisture store from (40), m with $i = 1$.

$\quad g$ = acceleration due to gravity, m s$^{-2}$

$\quad R$ = gas constant for water vapor, J kg$^{-1}$ K$^{-1}$.

## Interception and Interception Loss

The interception and evaporation of precipitation held on the leaf surfaces are modeled simply in SiB. The interception of rainfall is calculated using the same cross section as for the interception of vertically incident radiation by black leaves. The inflow (interception) and outflow (drainage) of water stored on the canopy are then given by

$$P_c = P[1 - \exp(-K_c L_{tc})]V_c$$

$$D_c = 0, \qquad M_c < S_c \qquad (47)$$

$$D_c = P_c, \qquad M_c = S_c$$

where $P$ = rainfall rate, m s$^{-1}$

$\quad P_c$ = rainfall interception rate of canopy, m s$^{-1}$

$\quad D_c$ = canopy drainage rate, m s$^{-1}$

$\quad M_c$ = water held on the canopy, m

$\quad S_c$ = maximum value of $M_c$ [$\approx (0.0002-0.0005)L_{tc}$], m

$\quad K_c$ = extinction coefficient for canopy for black leaves and a vertical flux [$= G(\mu)/\mu$ where $\mu = 1$].

For the ground vegetation,

$$P_g = (P - P_c + D_c)[1 - \exp(-K_g L_{tg})]V_g$$

$$D_g = 0, \qquad M_g < S_g \qquad (48)$$

$$D_g = P_g, \qquad M_g = S_g$$

where $P_g$ = rainfall interception rate of ground vegetation, m s$^{-1}$

$\quad D_g$ = drainage rate of ground vegetation, m s$^{-1}$

$\quad M_g$ = water held on ground vegetation, m

$S_g$ = maximum value of $M_g$, m
$K_g$ = as for $K_c$ but for ground vegetation.

The input of precipitation into the soil surface moisture store is then given by

$$P_w = P - P_c - P_g + D_c + D_g \qquad (49)$$

where $P_w$ = rainfall interception of soil surface moisture store, m s$^{-1}$.

The transfers described by equations (47)–(49) are performed at the beginning of the time step so that the vegetation water storage values, $M_c$ and $M_g$, are determined prior to the energy balance calculations for the time step. The quantities $M_c$ and $M_g$ determine the fractional wetted areas of the canopy, $W_c$, and ground cover, $W_g$. Wetted areas have a surface resistance of zero. The evaporation rates from the wetted parts of the vegetation are given by

$$\lambda E_{wc} = \frac{e_*(T_c) - e_a}{\bar{r}_b} \frac{\rho c_p}{\gamma} W_c$$

$$W_c = \frac{M_c}{S_c} \qquad 0 \leqslant W_c \leqslant 1 \qquad (50)$$

$$\lambda E_{wg} = \frac{(e_*(T_g) - e_a)}{r_d} \frac{\rho c_p}{\gamma} W_g V_g$$

$$W_g = \frac{M_g}{S_g} \qquad 0 \leqslant W_g \leqslant 1 \qquad (51)$$

where $E_{wc}, E_{wg}$ = evaporation rates from wet parts of the upper story and ground vegetation, kg m$^{-2}$ s$^{-1}$.

The wet and dry parts of the canopy in (50) and (51) are assumed to be at the same temperature. A number of arguments and some evidence (see Hancock et al., 1983) indicate that this assumption is more reasonable than assuming separate temperatures. The interception loss terms are implicit in the energy balance equations in Section 4 where they are combined with transpiration and soil evaporation terms to yield the total latent heat fluxes from canopy and ground.

The simplified approach outlined above is thought to provide acceptable estimates of interception loss rates and is considerably less complex than combined approaches (see Sellers and Lockwood, 1981) where interception, drainage and evaporation are described simultaneously. Provided the time step of simulation is short (1 h or less), the two methods should not produce widely differing predictions. The interception, evaporation, and melting of snow have not yet been included in the model.

## Soil Model

A three-layer isothermal model is used to describe the vertical transfer of water in the soil. Transfer of water from one layer to another is calculated by the method of Milly and Eagleson (1982), and the soil heat capacity is represented by a diurnal skin depth, as outlined in Arakawa (1972). (The heat capacity of the soil slab, $C_g$, is thermally equivalent to about 25–40 mm of water, depending on soil wetness.) The drainage rate out of the bottom layer is controlled by the soil hydraulic conductivity and gravity.

These interlayer exchanges are calculated at the end of the time step since these processes are slow compared to the interception and partition of radiation. The extraction of transpired water from the root zones is also performed at this time.

## DYNAMIC EQUATION SET FOR SiB

The framework of SiB as outlined in Figure 4 has been used to write the dynamic equations describing $T_c$ and $T_g$ as functions of time [see equations (10) and (11)]. Assuming no storage of heat or moisture at any of the junctions of the resistance network, we write the area-averaged fluxes from soil and vegetation as follows:

## From Canopy Air Space to Reference Height

### Sensible Heat

$$H_c + H_g = \frac{T_a - T_r}{r_a} \cdot \rho c_p \tag{52}$$

where $T_a, T_r$ = air temperature at canopy source height and reference height, respectively, K

$H_c, H_g$ = sensible heat flux from canopy and soil, respectively, W m$^{-2}$

$\rho, c_p$ = density and specific heat of air, respectively, kg m$^{-3}$, J kg$^{-1}$ K$^{-1}$.

### Latent Heat

$$\lambda E_c + \lambda E_g = \frac{e_a - e_r}{r_a} \cdot \frac{\rho c_p}{\gamma} \tag{53}$$

where $e_a, e_r$ = vapor pressure at canopy source height and reference height, respectively, mbars

$\lambda E_c, \lambda E_g$ = latent heat flux from canopy and soil, respectively, W m$^{-2}$

$\gamma$ = psychrometric constant, mbar K$^{-1}$.

### Canopy-to-Canopy Air Space

$$H_c = \frac{2(T_c - T_a)}{\bar{r}_b} \cdot \rho c_p \tag{54}$$

$$\lambda E_c = [e_*(T_c) - e_a] \cdot \frac{\rho c_p}{\gamma} \left(\frac{W_c}{\bar{r}_b} + \frac{1 - W_c}{\bar{r}_b + \bar{r}_{st}}\right) \tag{55}$$

where $e_*(T_c)$ = saturated vapor pressure at $T_c$, mbar

$r_a$ = aerodynamic resistance between canopy source height and reference height, s m$^{-1}$

$\bar{r}_b$ = bulk leaf boundary resistance, s m$^{-1}$

$\bar{r}_{st}$ = bulk stomatal resistance, s m$^{-1}$

$W_c$ = wetted fraction of canopy.

### Soil-to-Canopy Air Space

$$H_g = \frac{T_g - T_a}{r_d} \cdot \rho c_p \tag{56}$$

$$\lambda E_g = [e_*(T_g) - e_a] \frac{\rho c_p}{\gamma} \left(V_g \left[\frac{W_g}{r_d} + \frac{1 - W_g}{r_d + r_g}\right] + \frac{(1 - V_g)h_s}{r_{\text{surf}} + r_d}\right) \tag{57}$$

where $W_g$ = ground vegetation wetness fraction

$r_g$ = surface resistance of ground vegetation (calculated in a similar way as $\bar{r}_{st}$), s m$^{-1}$

$e_*(T_g)$ = saturated vapor pressure at $T_g$, mbar

$h_s$ = factor to correct for soil dryness ($=[e_*(T_g)f_h - e_a]/[e_*(T_g) - e_a]$)

$f_h$ = $\exp(\psi_1 g/RT_g)$

$R$ = gas constant for water vapor, J kg$^{-1}$ K$^{-1}$.

$\psi_1$ = soil moisture potential in top layer, m.

In (55), stomata are assumed to be present on one side of the leaf only. Sensible heat is transferred from both sides of the leaf, hence the factor 2 in combination with the inverse of $\bar{r}_b$ in (54).

The preceding sections showed how the five resistances $r_a$, $\bar{r}_b$, $r_d$, $\bar{r}_{st}$, and $r_g$ could be estimated. Given these values and the estimates of $Rn_c$ and $Rn_g$ from (20) and (21), (10) and (11) may be combined with the above expressions to eliminate $T_a$ and $e_a$ and yield two equations in $T_c$ and $T_g$ which may then be solved by an implicit backward method (see Sellers et al., 1986).

Solution for the temperatures and application of (53), (55), and (57) over a time step will yield values of the latent heat fluxes $\lambda E_{wc}$, $\lambda E_{wg}$ (interception losses), $\lambda E_{dc}$, $\lambda E_{dg}$ (transpiration losses), and $\lambda E_s$ (soil surface loss). These fluxes are included in the calculation of the change of the five moisture stores.

A backward implicit method was chosen for the solution of (52)–(57) because of its stability; however, it has been found that under changing radiative conditions and using time steps of more than half an hour, the solutions of $T_c$ and $T_g$ show slight oscillation if no iterative corrections are made for the effects of nonneutrality on $r_a$.

## MODEL VERIFICATION

A thorough evaluation of the performance of the various subcomponents of the model and their functioning as a separate ensemble is essential before implementing SiB in a GCM where unanticipated feedbacks between the boundary layer and surface models might obscure serious errors in the formulation.

Since few experimental studies have been conducted in natural vegetated sites where all of the variables necessary to drive and validate the SiB model

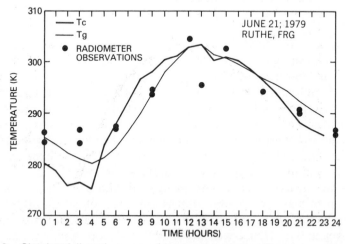

**FIGURE 9.** Simulated diurnal courses of canopy temperature $T_c$ and ground temperature $T_g$ for a barley field near Ruthe, Federal Republic of Germany, June 20, 1979. [Micro-meteorological data and surface temperature measurements (hand-held radiometers) from van der Ploeg et al. (1980).] Long-wave radiation (downward) radiometer malfunctioned, leading to erroneous simulation of nighttime temperatures. [Surface properties of barley crop from van der Ploeg et al. (1980) and Monteith et al. (1965).]

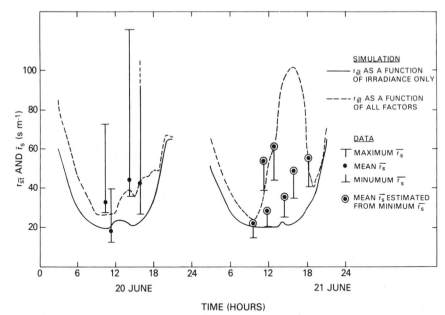

**FIGURE 10.**  Predicted ($\bar{r}_{st}$) and estimated ($\bar{r}_s$) values of the bulk stomatal resistance for the barley crop near Ruthe, Federal Republic of Germany, June 20–21, 1979. Values of $\bar{r}_s$ were derived by summing the area-weighted conductances measured for upper, middle, and lower leaves and then inverting the total. (A diffusion porometer was used to obtain the conductance values.) Minimum $\bar{r}_s$ corresponds to $\bar{r}_s$ for the topmost leaves weighted by total leaf area index; maximum $\bar{r}_s$ is calculated in the same way except that $r_s$ values for leaves at the canopy base were used.

were measured, the first tests used micrometeorological and biophysical data gathered over an agricultural site. The data described in van der Ploeg et al. (1980) and Gurney and Camillo (1984) were recorded over a barley field in the Federal Republic of Germany as part of a remote sensing experiment. Accordingly, the model parameters were fixed to represent a barley crop for which the necessary data sets were available. The morphological and physiological properties of the vegetation and the physical properties of the vegetation and soil were measured or estimated for the experimental site and were used to derive the model's surface parameters.

Since the measurements were associated with a uniform, monoculture vegetation, it was not possible to perform a test of SiB in its full form as specified in this text; that is, with an upper-story canopy and underlying ground vegetation. Hence we "promoted" the crop canopy to the status of upper-story vegetation and took the ground surface as bare so that $V_g = 0$. Initial soil moisture conditions were taken from van der Ploeg et al. (1980), and the micrometeorological data were then applied as the boundary forcing to the model in order to generate time series of the radiation exchanges, heat fluxes, and surface temperatures.

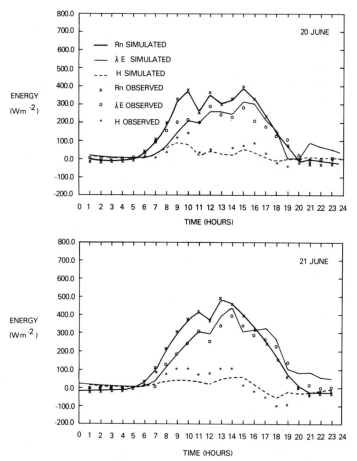

**FIGURE 11.** Observed and predicted values of net radiation $R_n$, latent heat flux $\lambda E$, and sensible heat flux $H$ for the barley test site, Ruthe, Federal Republic of Germany for June 20–21, 1979. (The net radiation has been forced onto the observed values.)

Figure 9 shows the simulated diurnal course of the canopy temperature $T_c$ and the ground temperature $T_g$ for the barley field. The model provides a realistic time series of $T_c$ and $T_g$ when compared to bulk surface temperature measurements obtained from hand-held radiometers. The large departure of the simulated temperatures from the observed ones at night is due to the erroneous measurement of the downward long-wave radiative flux, which gives rise to large negative net radiation values in the absence of short-wave radiation.

Figure 10 compares the simulated course of $\bar{r}_{st}$ for the barley crop and some estimated bulk stomatal resistance values derived from individual leaf stomatal resistance observations. The predicted rise in $\bar{r}_{st}$ away from its light-limited value in the afternoon, because of the falling leaf water potential and decrease in $f(\psi_l)$, is in accordance with the trend of the observations.

Finally, Figure 11 shows the observed and predicted partitioning of the surface energy balance for the barley field. (The simulated net radiation was forced onto the observations to circumvent the erroneous long-wave radiation flux measurements.) Again, the diurnal course and magnitudes of the predicted fluxes agree with the measurements.

## USE FOR MODELING AND COMPARISONS TO SATELLITE DATA

The use of simple land surface parameterizations in GCMs of the atmosphere has shown that vegetation is an important factor influencing the exchanges of radiation, momentum, and heat at the local scale and, by extension, the regional climate. To date, the parameterizations implemented within GCMs have consisted of either prescribed fields of albedo, momentum, and moisture transfer coefficients or of simple conceptual models of the land surface. While these biophysically unrealistic models have indicated that the atmosphere is sensitive to the condition of the land surface, they should not be relied on for any quantitative predictive experiments.

Dickinson (1984) and Sellers et al. (1986) have attempted to incorporate biophysical principles into simple surface formulations appropriate for use within GCMs. The SiB model, described in this chapter, is an attempt to design a scheme simple and robust enough to operate within the computing constraints of a GCM, yet not so simple as to be totally unrealistic in its representation of the biophysics of land surface–atmosphere interaction. So far, the model has been tested only against local micrometeorological observations, but it appears that its separate elements (radiation interception, turbulent transport, stomatal functioning, etc.) operate realistically and with an acceptable accuracy. The model will be linked to a GCM for fully interactive studies in the near future. The model of Dickinson (1984), not discussed here for reasons of brevity, has the same essential approach to the problem and is comparable in the design of many of its components. It is currently implemented within the Community Climate Model of the National Center for Atmospheric Research and is undergoing sensitivity tests.

The advantages of using a biophysically realistic model lies in the specification of measurable parameters and the output of physical state variables as part of the model prognostic calculations. There are two obvious areas where the specified or calculated fields of these quantities (as given by SiB or any comparable model) may be compared with remotely sensed data obtained from satellite platforms for the purposes of model initialization and validation. First, we may compare the model initialization data set with narrow-band visible (0.55–0.68-$\mu$m) and near-infrared (0.73–1.1-$\mu$m) surface reflectance data as gathered by polar orbiting meteorological and earth observation satellites [see Tucker et al. (1985) and Tucker (1978)]. It will be

**FIGURE 12.** AVHRR Normalized Vegetation Index (NDVI) image as compiled from 27 days of aggregated data over South America, August 1982. Western Amazonia shows high values of NDVI while northeastern Brazil shows lower values, consistent with the state of the vegetation in the dry season. (Image provided by C.J. Tucker, NASA Goddard Space Flight Center. Reproduced with permission.)

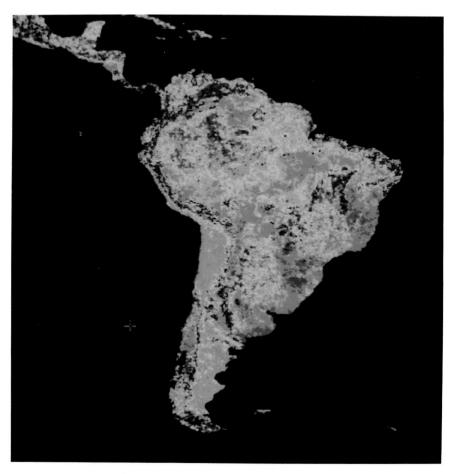

**FIGURE 13.** AVHRR Normalized Vegetation Index (NDVI) image as compiled from 29 days of aggregated data over South America, February—March 1983. NDVI has increased in northeastern Brazil as the green vegetation density peaks during the wet season. (Image provided by C.J. Tucker, NASA Goddard Space Flight Center. Reproduced with permission.)

remembered that green leaves are highly absorbent in the visible wavelength interval and scatter strongly in the near infrared. The normalized vegetation index of Tucker et al. (1985) is a dimensionless quantity that increases with chlorophyll density:

$$NDVI = \frac{I\eta_{(NIR)} - I\eta_{(VIS)}}{I\eta_{(NIR)} + I\eta_{(VIS)}} \qquad (58)$$

where $NDVI$ = normalized difference vegetation index
$I\eta_{(NIR)}, I\eta_{(VIS)}$ = nadir or near-nadir surface reflectance in near infrared and visible wavelength intervals.

The value of the NDVI generally increases from ~0.3 for bare ground to 0.9 for a full green cover of vegetation. Figures 12 and 13 show fields of NDVI for August 1982 and February/March 1983 for the South American continent as obtained by J. Tucker of NASA Goddard (personal communication) from the Advanced Very High Resolution Radiometer (AVHRR) mounted on the NOAA-7 meteorological satellite. The two images show a striking contrast in NDVI in those regions with a strong seasonality in precipitation as is the case in northeastern Brazil. Those areas with little or no seasonality in precipitation, for example, the western Amazon Basin, display minimal differences in NDVI over the year. The NDVI may be interpreted as an area-averaged photosynthetic capacity and hence related to a value of the minimum canopy resistance ($\bar{r}_{st}$ in the absence of stress factors) for continuous vegetative cover (see Sellers, 1985). The high temporal resolution of the meteorological satellite system makes feasible the use of such data for model initialization and validation.

Second, satellite data may be directly useful for the estimation of fields of surface temperature (equivalent to a combination of the SiB-predicted prognostic variables of $T_c$ and $T_g$). From (54) and (56), it is clear that the air–surface temperature difference is proportional to the sensible heat flux and, if the surface net radiation is known, can be used to estimate the evapotranspiration rate. Thus, soil moisture storage could be inferred from a combination of satellite data, mesometeorological data, and modeling. Susskind et al. (1984) and Carlson et al. (1984) review current capabilities in the estimation of surface temperatures and regional evapotranspiration from satellite data. In the near future, microwave remote sensing (passive and active) may yield estimates of the surface soil moisture content and the vertical structure of the vegetation canopy (Schmugge, 1983).

In summary, little can be expected from unrealistic surface formulations in GCMs in the way of quantitative understanding of the interactions operating between the surface and the atmosphere. This understanding can only be achieved by biophysically based models where the important features of the transfers of radiation, momentum, and heat are described in a realistic fashion. Such an approach predicts physical state variables that can be compared with satellite data for the purposes of model initialization and validation.

## ACKNOWLEDGMENTS

Piers Sellers was a National Academy of Sciences/National Research Council Resident Research Associate during the period when this work was done. The author would like to extend his gratitude to the following researchers for useful discussions: Y. Mintz, Y. C. Sud, R. E. Dickinson, A. Dalcher, T. J. Schmugge, J. Shukla, R. J. Gurney, P. J. Camillo, B. J. Choudhury, V. V. Salomonson, and C. J. Willmott. Special thanks go to J. Tippett and L. A. Wright for typing the manuscript. R. E. Dickinson is to be warmly thanked for his encouragement throughout this work and for providing considerable help with the radiative transfer component of SiB. Figures 12 and 13 were provided by C. J. Tucker using the NASA Goddard Space Flight Center (Laboratory for Terrestrial Physics) data processing facility.

## REFERENCES

Arakawa, A., 1972. Design of the UCLA general circulation model, *Technical Report 7*, Department of Meteorology, University of California, Los Angeles, CA.

Camillo, P. J. and Gurney, R. J., 1986. A resistance parameter for bare soil evaporation models, *Soil Sci.* **141**, 95–105.

Carlson, T., Rose, F. G., and Perry, E. M., 1984. Regional scale estimates of soil moisture availability from GOES satellites, *J. Agron.* **16**, 972–979.

Carson, D. J., 1981. Current parameterizations of land surface processes in atmospheric general circulation models, in P. S. Eagleson, Ed., *Land Surface Processes in Atmospheric General Circulation Models*, Cambridge University Press, Cambridge, England.

Carson, D. J. and Sangster, A. B., 1981. The influence of land-surface albedo and soil moisture on general circulation model simulations, *Numerical Experimentation Program Report No. 2*, 5.14–5.21, Meteorological Office (U.K.), Bracknell, Surrey, England.

Charney, J. G., 1975. Dynamics of deserts and droughts in the Sahel, *Quart. J. Roy. Meteor. Soc.* **101**, 193–202.

Charney, J. G., Quirk, W. J., Chow, S. H., and Kornefield, J., 1977. A comparative study of the effects of albedo change on drought in semi-arid regions, *J. Atmos. Sci.* **34**, 1366–1385.

Clapp, R. B. and Hornberger, G. M., 1978. Empirical equations for some soil hydraulic properties, *Water Resourc. Res.* **14**, 601–604.

Coakley, J. A., Jr., and Chylek, P., 1975. The two stream approximation in radiative transfer: Including the angle of incident radiation, *J. Atmos. Sci.* **32**, 409–418.

de Laubenfels, D. J., 1975. *World's Vegetation: Formations and Flora*, Syracuse University Press, Syracuse, NY.

Dickinson, R. E., 1983. Land surface processes and climate-surface albedos and energy balance, in B. Saltzman, Ed., *Advances in Geophysics*, Vol. 25, *Theory of Climate*, Academic Press, New York.

Dickinson, R. E., 1984. Modeling evapotranspiration for three-dimensional global climate models, in J. E. Hansen, Ed., *Climate Processes and Climate Sensitivity*, Geophysical Monograph 29, American Geophysical Union, Washington DC.

Federer, C. A., 1979. A soil-plant-atmosphere model for transpiration and availability of soil water, *Water Resourc. Res.* **15**, 555–562.

Garratt, J. R., 1978. Flux profile relations above tall vegetation, *Quart. J. Roy. Meteor. Soc.* **104**, 199–211.

Goudriaan, J., 1977. *Crop Micrometeorology: A Simulation Study*, Wageningen Center for Agricultural Publishing and Documentation, Wageningen, The Netherlands.

Gurney, R. J. and Camillo, P. J., 1984. Modeling daily evapotranspiration using remotely sensed data, *J. Hydrol.* **69**, 305–324.

Hancock, N. H., Sellers, P. J., and Crowther, J. M., 1983. Evaporation from a partially wet forest canopy, *Ann. Geophys.* **1**, 139–146.

Jarvis, P. G., 1976. The interpretation of the variations in leaf water potential and stomatal conductance found in canopies in the field, *Philos. Trans. Roy. Soc. London B.* **273**, 593–610.

Kuchler, A. W., 1949. A physiognomic classification of vegetation, *Ann. Assoc. Amer. Geogr.* **39**, 201–210.

Matthews, E., 1983. Global vegetation and land use: New high-resolution data bases for climate studies, *Clim. Appl. Meteor.* **22**, 474–487.

Meador, W. E. and Weaver, W. R., 1980. Two-stream approximations to radiative transfer in planetary atmospheres: A unified description of existing methods and a new improvement, *J. Atmos. Sci.* **37**, 630–643.

Milly, P. C. and Eagleson, P. S., 1982. Parameterization of moisture and heat fluxes across the land surface for use in atmospheric general circulation models, Report Number 279, Department of Engineering, Massachusetts Institute of Technology, Cambridge, MA.

Mintz, Y., 1984. The sensitivity of numerically simulated climates to land-surface conditions, in J. Houghton, Ed., *The Global Climate*, Cambridge University Press, Cambridge, England.

Monteith, J. L., 1973. *Principles of Environmental Physics*, Edward Arnold, London.

Monteith, J. L., Szeicz, G., and Waggoner, P. E., 1965. The measurement and control of stomatal resistance in the field, *J. Appl. Ecol.* **2**, 345–355.

Norman, J. M. and Jarvis, P. G., 1975. Photosynthesis in Sitka spruce (*Picea sitchensis* (Bong.) Carr.). V. Radiation penetration theory and a test case, *J. Appl. Ecol.* **11**, 839–878.

Otterman, J., 1981. Plane with protrusions as an atmospheric boundary, *J. Geophys. Res.* **86**, 6627–6630.

Paulson, C. A., 1970. Mathematical representation of wind speed and temperature profiles in the unstable atmospheric surface layer, *J. Appl. Meteor.* **9**, 857–861.

Penman, H. L., 1948. Natural evaporation from open water, bare soil and grass, *Proc. Roy. Soc. London So. A.* **193**, 120–145.

Raupach, M. R. and Thom, A. S., 1981. Turbulence in and above plant canopies, *Ann. Rev. Fluid Mech.* **13**, 97–129.

Ross, J., 1975. Radiative transfer in plant communities, in J. L. Monteith, Ed., *Vegetation and the Atmosphere*, Vol. 1, Academic, London.

Schmugge, T. J., 1983. Remote sensing of soil moisture: Recent advances, *IEEE Trans.* **GE-21, 3**, 336–344.

Sellers, P. J., 1981. Vegetation type and catchment water balance: A simulation study, Ph.D. Thesis, Department of Geography, Leeds University, Leeds, England.

Sellers, P. J., 1985. Canopy reflectance, photosynthesis and transpiration, *Int. J. Rem. Sens.* **6**, 1335–1372.

Sellers, P. J. and Lockwood, J. G., 1981. A computer simulation of the effects of differing crop types on the water balance of small catchments over long time periods, *Quart. J. Roy. Meteor. Soc.* **107**, 395–414.

Sellers, P. J., Mintz, Y., Sud, Y. C., and A. Dalcher, 1986. A Simple Biosphere model (SiB) for use within general circulation models, *J. Atmos. Sci*, **43**, 505–531.

Shaw, R. H. and Pereira, A. R., 1982. Aerodynamic roughness of a plant canopy: A numerical experiment, *Agric. Meteor.* **26**, 51–65.

Shu Fen Sun, 1982. Moisture and heat transport in a soil layer forced by atmospheric conditions, M.Sc. Thesis, University of Connecticut, Storrs, CT.

Shukla, J. and Mintz, Y., 1982. Influence of land-surface evapotranspiration on the earth's climate, *Science* **215**, 1498–1501.

Sud, Y. C. and Smith, W. E., 1984. Ensemble formulation of surface fluxes and improvement in evapotranspiration and cloud parameterizations in a GCM, *Bound. Layer Meteor.* **29**, 185–210.

Sud, Y. C. and Smith, W. E., 1985. The influence of surface roughness of· deserts on the July circulation: A numerical study, *Bound. Layer Meteor.*, **33**, 15–49.

Susskind, J., Rosenfield, J., Reuter, D., and Chahine, M. T., 1984. Remote sensing of weather and climate parameters from HIRS2/MSU on TIROS-N, *J. Geophys. Res.* **89**, 4677–4697.

Thom, A. S., 1971. Momentum absorption by vegetation, *Quart. J. Roy. Met. Soc.* **97**, 414–428.

Tivy, J., 1977. *Biogeography: A Study of Plants in the Ecosystem*, 3rd ed., Oliver & Boyd, Edinburgh, Scotland.

Tucker, C. J., 1978. A comparison of satellite sensor bands for vegetation monitoring, *Photogramm. Eng. Rem. Sens.* **44**, 1369–1380.

Tucker, C. J., Townshend, J. R. G., and Goff, T. E., 1985. African land-cover classification using satellite data, *Science* **227**, 369–375.

van den Honert, T. H., 1948. Water transport as a catenary process, *Discuss. Faraday Soc.* **3**, 146–153.

van der Ploeg, R. R., Tassone, G. and von Hoyningen-Heure, J., 1980. *The Joint Measuring Campaign 1979 in Ruthe (West Germany)—Description of Preliminary Data*, European Economic Commission of Joint Research Center, Ispra.

Walter, H., 1973. *Vegetation of the Earth*, Heidelberg Science Library, Springer-Verlag, New York.

Willmott, C. J., Klink, K., Legates, D., and Rowe, C., 1984, personal communication.

## ☐ COMMENTS ON "MODELING EFFECTS OF VEGETATION ON CLIMATE"

**Keith G. McNaughton**

As Sellers points out in his introduction, until recently, creators of GCM models have used very poor representations of the energy exchange processes at land surfaces. The model presented in Sellers's paper represents an early attempt to rectify this situation and to make use of the extensive body of knowledge developed by many agricultural and forest meteorologists over several decades. It is therefore a valuable contribution to GCM modeling. It is also a pioneering contribution, with all that that implies about the lack of any consensus on the best way to proceed.

Sellers's model represents a particular level of sophistication and complexity. A simpler or more complex model could have been constructed using results from the wide range of models that have been developed to describe heat and mass exchanges at vegetated surfaces. The simplest models treat the canopy as one layer, with water availability described by a single-canopy resistance (Monteith, 1965). More complicated models subdivide the canopy into many layers and consider the energy exchange from each layer (e.g., Waggoner and Reifsnyder, 1968; Lemon et al., 1971). Some have stressed the need to treat separately the energy exchanges of sunlit and shaded leaves at the same level of the canopy (Sinclair et al., 1976), while others have emphasized the importance of evaporation from the ground in the overall energy balance (Denmead, 1973). Similarly, soil water storage and movement may be represented at many levels of complexity, from single reservoir models (Thornthwaite, 1948) to multilayer diffusion models (Feddes et al., 1978).

Sellers has taken a middle course in designing his model and used a single-layer canopy with an understory and three soil layers. We might ask whether this general choice of level of complexity is the most appropriate one for use in a GCM model. In this commentary, I shall argue that it is not.

Plant communities are complex in ways that the atmosphere is not. If we had the wit and the computing power, then we might solve the equations of atmospheric motion and thermodynamics to a very close approximation, since the equations and properties of the system are quite well known. The biosphere, on the other hand, is replete with particular adaptations and special cases to such an extent that some biologists and ecologists deny that any general and quantitative predictions can be made. Such people seem unduly pessimistic, of course, but they do have a point. There are no general laws of plant response to environment. Plant form and function are both highly variable. Our basic knowledge consists of a collection of empirical examples, all different but with some common trends which can be interpreted using some unifying conservation principles. Models, if they are to claim generality, must necessarily be approximate.

An example will illustrate what I mean. It is widely accepted that the "big leaf" canopy model is a useful description of vegetation for hydrological purposes. The canopy conductance in such a model is taken to represent the total conductance of all of the leaves above unit area of ground. Analysis shows that this would be true only if the whole canopy were perfectly ventilated so that each leaf surface "sees" the same saturation deficit. Real canopies, particularly dense canopies with large leaves, are imperfectly ventilated. Experimental comparisons of canopy resistance, measured by micrometeorological methods, usually agree with measurements by porometry and leaf area measurement to $\pm 20\%$ or thereabouts. The discrepancy is due partly to model error and partly to measurement error, either instrumental or statistical, from the sampling program adopted. In either case, we must accept that the canopy resistance is never perfectly known. More detailed measurements could possibly support a more complex model including, perhaps, changes of stomatal response with depth in the canopy and age of the leaves as well as an account of turbulent transport within the canopy. But as detail increases, the model becomes more specific to the particular canopy. In the context of Sellers's model, we might ask the purpose of an understory compartment, whose presence in his model might contribute only a few percentage points to the modeled fluxes, when the bulk stomatal resistance of the upper story is unknowable to comparable accuracy.

Not only is the exact definition of model components uncertain, but quantitative information on individual elements is difficult to obtain. Sellers's model contains 49 settable constants, plus a leaf angle distribution function. Ideally, values for these would be obtained by experiment, but in practice they will be an eclectic selection of values from a variety of experiments on a variety of different plants and soils, since a complete set of measurements on any particular vegetation type required in Sellers's model will not be available. There is great scope for imagination here, and although it cannot be doubted that a careful selection of 49 values will give a good fit to almost any data available, the relationship between the model and the world can become tenuous.

Let us, however, suppose that the model is accurate for a given canopy and soil and that values for the constants have been selected. A GCM grid square of $10^5$ km$^2$ contains many such units, so we must address the problem of averaging the model over the whole range of vegetation and soil types. A possible averaging procedure would be to assume that the individual land units are small enough and randomly enough mixed that conditions at the lowest level of the GCM solution net remain the same for all. Then we could calculate the behavior of each of the different canopies separately and so form an average by weighting their individual contributions according to their fractional areas. But this is of course absurd. We would need an accurate set of 49 constants for each of the many vegetation and soil types, and computing costs would get out of hand. But if we do not do this, we must ask questions like "What is the root resistance for a vegetation type characterized on an eight-point scale for the world's vegetation?" and, more fundamentally, "What would such a resistance mean?" The finer parts of the model cease to have any clear relationship with measurable things.

If these arguments were accepted, then many parts of a reasonably complete model, such as Sellers's, would have conceptual value only, signifying real processes but not describing them in any interpretable fashion. But what, in the context of a GCM, is the conceptual significance of a root resistance or a stomatal response to saturation deficit? Surely something simpler is indicated.

It is not yet clear how complex a vegetation model should be for use in a GCM, but my feeling is that it should be no more complex than the models now sometimes used in hydrology. These use single-layer descriptions of both canopy and soil. The canopy is characterized by a canopy resistance, a roughness length, an albedo, and perhaps an interception storage capacity. The soil is a simple reservoir with a storage capacity that overflows when overfilled, generating runoff. Some simple arrangements are made to have transpiration limited when soil water content falls below some low level. This type of model is lamentably crude in many respects, but I find it difficult to argue that any further elaboration is justifiable, given the difficulties outlined in the preceding paragraphs.

In this commentary, my purpose has been to provoke discussion on the type of model that might be appropriate to investigations with a GCM. The level of sophistication of Sellers's model, even if carried further than I would have recommended, is a large step forward in representing surface interactions in GCMs. One must compare his model with other current representations, such as that by Sud and Smith (1984) where the whole land area of the world is taken to have the same surface resistance. Surely the direction taken by Sellers is correct. But GCM modelers find it difficult to provide experimental checks of their predictions, and we must find other means to decide where realism and fantasy meet.

## REFERENCES

Denmead, O. T., 1973. Relative significance of soil and plant evaporation in estimating transpiration, in *Plant Response to Climatic Factors, Proceedings of the Uppsala Symposium, 1970*, UNESCO, Paris.

Feddes, R. A., Stewart, P. J., and Zaradny, H., 1978. *Simulation of Field Water Use and Crop Yield*, PUDOC, Wageningen, The Netherlands.

Lemon, E., Stewart, D. W., and Shawcroft, R. W., 1971. The sun's work in a cornfield, *Science* **174**, 371–378.

Monteith, J. L., 1965. Evaporation and environment, in G. E. Fogg, Ed., *The State and Movement of Water in Living Organisms*, Cambridge University Press, Cambridge England.

Sinclair, T. R., Murphey, C. E., and Knoerr, K. R., 1976. Development and evaluation of simplified models for simulating canopy photosynthesis and transpiration, *J. Appl. Ecol.* **13**, 813–829.

Sud, Y. C. and Smith, W. E., 1984. Ensemble formulation of surface fluxes and improvements in evapotranspiration and cloud parameterizations in a GCM, *Bound. Lay. Meteor.* **29**, 185–210.

Thornthwaite, C. W., 1948. An approach toward a rational classification of climate, *Geogr. Rev.* **38**, 55–94.

Waggoner, P. E. and Reifsnyder, W. E., 1968. Simulation of the temperature, humidity and evaporation profiles in a leaf canopy, *J. Appl. Meteor.* **7**, 400–409.

# REPLY TO COMMENTS

## Piers J. Sellers

McNaughton's commentary and review have been immensely helpful in clearing up a number of badly expressed ideas in my essay. I am more grateful, however, for the lucid statement of his dissenting viewpoint, which has prompted me to reassess and defend the basic approach and methodology used in constructing the Simple Biosphere model.

As McNaughton says, the biosphere is complex in ways the atmosphere is not. I would argue that although the plethora of adaptations observed in the life forms making up the biosphere is intimidating to the would-be modeler, the underlying principles governing mass and energy flow should be tractable. For example, in any ecosystem there will be many species of plants, but the constraints of $C_3$ or $C_4$ chemistry and the range of environmental forcings to which the biota are subjected must limit the range of responses. More generally, any system that evolves and functions in the physical world must be predictable to a greater or lesser degree; our failure to achieve more fundamental understanding of the functioning of the biosphere to date does not preclude the eventual possibility of being able to do so. To assume otherwise comes close to a resignation to mysticism.

McNaughton has discussed the suitability of an approach based on the big leaf model. I concur: SiB is essentially two big leaf models, one in direct contact with the soil and the other distributed as a tall porous upper-story canopy. His assumption that the lower layer (grass and herbaceous species) contributes only a few percentage points to the total fluxes is clearly invalid in the partial or complete absence of upper-story vegetation! The other most crucial element in the model structure is the derivation of the canopy and ground bulk stomatal resistances. It would appear that the treatment presented in the essay is a reasonable and economic one since what we do know about stomatal function links it closely to photosynthetic activity and hence the local flux density of PAR. Any treatment of $r_s$ that fails to account for the effects of different leaf angle inclinations on the PAR flux and the attenuation of the latter down through the canopy will be severely in error. The criticism that the model is less than realistic in ignoring the differential effects of vapor, air temperature, and surface temperature gradients within the canopy is entirely valid. However, a scale analysis will quickly reveal that usually $r_s > r_b$ within most canopies and that such effects are second order. To model these details more realistically would entail the use of multilayer turbulent transfer models, probably closing at higher orders—clearly beyond the scope of any work conducted within the context of a GCM.

It is suggested by McNaughton that there are 49 settable constants in SiB that may be tuned to give any desired result. This and the associated remarks about realism and fantasy I find hard to accept with any grace. It seems to me that it is simpler to estimate the height and density of the upper-story vegetation in a region than the associated roughness length and turbulent transfer parameters directly. Additionally, it seems simpler to model radiative transfer using estimates of leaf transmission and reflectance (which allows one to take such factors as leaf browning, leaf fall, and snow interception directly into account) than to prescribe surface albedos. With the suspicion that tundra vegetation may have a different morphology and level of activity in its root system than, say, tropical rain forest, it seems that some approximate specification of the root length density and resistance and other components is appropriate for even the simplest global model.

McNaughton suggests that simpler models with a specified canopy resistance, a roughness length, an albedo, and perhaps an interception storage capacity and a single soil moisture store would be adequate. Maybe so. But, and this is an enormous *but*, how would one begin to specify the values of the above terms (with their responses to environmental conditions) on the global scale? To cover the range of temporal and spatial conditions properly, one would have to compile a huge table of values (with probably more individual values than in SiB) with few direct linkages to the actual physical quantities concerned. This proposal is not only indefensible from a modeling viewpoint (as we are thrown straight back to *independently* specifying albedos, turbulent transfer coefficients, and Bowen ratio formulations instead of modeling the vegetation itself) but would be more difficult to complete than collecting the equivalent set of biophysical data for SiB. It would also be far more open to the abuse of tuning. My feeling is that one would get out of such an approach precisely what one had put in: more uncertainty and less understanding. Another point arises when considering the volume of data required by SiB, that of model sensitivity to the input parameters. The submodels in SiB (radiative, momentum, and heat flux transfer) are crude and approximate but have the advantage of operating on physical input data. It is clear from preliminary work that the submodels are relatively insensitive to the exact specification of leaf angle distribution, leaf area index (at high values of LAI), shelter factor, and a number of other parameters. To my mind it is better to start with a complete system that is physically reasonable and then to pursue the questions of sensitivity and redundancy than to progress from a simple parameterization where the physical meaning of the various parameters is less clear. In the latter case, tuning would be essential and the future possibility of climate–surface feedback modeling excluded.

Ultimately, the approach one adopts in tackling such a problem is a matter of personal judgment and faith apart from anything else. As far as judgment is concerned, I am more comfortable pursuing a biophysically based approach than one founded on a set of tunable conceptual variables although *initially* there may be little to choose between the two methods in terms of practical dividends. As for faith, the last two decades have seen an enormous increase in our understanding of the biochemical functioning of organisms and the mechanism of natural selection. As a result, the direction of ecological research is tending toward a more even balance of theory, observations, and experiment. The pursuit of theoretical understanding, which is where faith in the existence of governing principles is required, is a process marked by model construction, testing, rejection, and improvement. Physically based models are far more likely to contribute in this respect than are conceptual parameterizations.

# PART IV

# TROPICAL CLIMATE AND GENERAL CIRCULATION: ITS SUSCEPTIBILITY TO HUMAN INTERVENTION

In this part we review present knowledge of the meteorology and climate of the Amazon and other humid tropical regions, survey our present capabilities for modeling these processes, and address the question of what, if anything, can now be said regarding the impacts of tropical deforestation on regional and global climate systems.

Micrometeorological processes and the hydrological cycle (Part III) interact with large-scale climatic processes and the general circulation of the tropical atmosphere to determine the climate elements that affect tropical forests and other vegetation, in particular, precipitation, solar radiation, and surface temperature and wind. Convective rainfall systems show this interaction between various scales of motion. Normal patterns of rainfall depend on surface features and especially the large-scale terrain, as well as on seasonal and diurnal cycles of solar heating.

Paegle (Chapter 17) considers the interactions between large-scale and convective motions within the tropics in general and Amazonia in particular. The large-scale meteorological processes that modulate tropical convection include cold fronts from extratropical latitudes, various waves and vortices, and large-scale circulation systems such as the Hadley circulation, the intertropical convergence zone, and the Walker circulation. The term *Walker circulation* refers to large east–west oriented systems along the equatorial belt with maximum updrafts and precipitation in the western Pacific (Paegle) or over the Amazon (Molion, Chapter 18). Large changes from normal conditions involving these systems and occurring for a year or two are referred to as the El Niño–southern oscillation (ENSO) phenomenon.

Various surface processes control tropical convection, including especially the effects of ocean surface temperatures. The Walker circulations and ENSO phenomena are related to ocean temperature variations. Land processes, in particular the diurnal cycle of surface heating, soil moisture, and large-scale terrain features, are also shown to be important controls. Paegle suggests the possible importance of boundary layer jets for Amazonian meteorology.

Tropical convection can affect larger scales of motions. Paegle suggests links not only to large-scale tropical circulations but also to weather patterns in midlatitudes. He considers possible connections between Amazon rainfall and weather systems in the United States.

Molion (Chapter 18) also discusses large-scale and mesoscale circulation patterns over the Amazon region, driven primarily by latent heat from convective rainfall systems. He suggests how spatial, seasonal, and interannual variations of rainfall might be related to these circulations.

Shukla (Chapter 19) reviews simulations of the time-dependent general circulation using three-dimensional numerical models. He compares with observations the results of one model for such global fields as sea level pressure, zonal winds and temperature, surface winds, and various time and space fluctuations of atmospheric circulations. The interannual variability of circulation statistics consists of two parts: first, that resulting from the atmosphere's internal dynamics for seasonally varying surface conditions, and second, that resulting from interannual variability of ocean and land surface processes. Various model integrations indicate that much of the year-to-year variation in atmospheric climate in the tropics can be modeled only by including the observed year-to-year variations in ocean surface temperatures. These ocean temperature variations modulate the fluxes of latent and sensible heat from the ocean to the atmosphere. Modeling results show that tropical ocean surface temperature anomalies have not only local but also global influences.

Effects similar to those from ocean temperature anomalies are expected as large land areas are modified to change the fluxes of latent and sensible heat. Modeling studies have shown that major changes in precipitation, and circulation patterns result from drastic changes in land surfaces. The effects of more realistic changes of land surfaces have not yet been modeled because of inadequate treatments of land processes within the models.

Henderson-Sellers (Chapter 20) reviews past modeling of the effects of deforestation on the climate of the humid tropics. She argues that in order to assess probable effects, we must be able to establish current and future land use changes and have available an effective predictive model, but that neither of these requirements is currently satisfied. Data pertaining to land use change are difficult to obtain and verify, whereas the global climate models that might be applied to the study of tropical deforestation differ in their land surface input data and their land surface parameterization schemes. She indicates that differences among past model simulations of the climatic effects of tropical deforestation are as great as their similarities. Because of these and other problems, past studies of the impact of tropical land use change upon climate have not been very definitive, but further efforts should lead to more meaningful answers.

# Chapter 17

# Interactions Between Convective and Large-Scale Motions Over Amazonia

Jan Paegle

The Amazon Basin is a region approximately 2000 × 2000 km containing one of the world's largest rain forests. It is one of two or three large-scale tropical areas that are convectively active at any given time around the world, and thus its contribution is important to the global atmospheric energy cycle. Because of this contribution and likelihood of interactions with other regions, the circulation over this area may affect global atmospheric processes and cannot be treated in isolation.

Complete analyses of the role of Amazonia for global weather are possible only in computerized general circulation simulations. While such simulations have been made (as discussed in this essay), their complexity limits their utility for explaining the atmosphere's behavior in conceptually simple terms. Furthermore, the model simulations do not allow unequivocal conclusions because computer technology cannot yet resolve all potentially important elements in the necessary detail. For example, there is still no published computer simulation of the coupled atmosphere–ocean interaction that successfully simulates both atmospheric and oceanic evolution during El Niño events, starting from prior initial conditions.

Although the soil–vegetation–atmosphere coupling is in some respects simpler because only the surface thermodynamics (rather than the dynamics) interacts with the atmosphere, it is not clear that even this coupling is adequately resolved. Nevertheless, several calculations now point to the same conclusion: that a desertification trend in the tropics and subtropics produces positive feedbacks on the local system, as first suggested for the question of African desertification by the study of Charney (1975), which emphasized the effect of albedo change. Further computer simulations have shown that lack of moisture input by evapotranspiration can significantly reduce rainfall over continental areas, suggesting that deforestation of a large tropical region, such as Amazonia, might promote aridity.

This review emphasizes those aspects of tropical weather that control Amazon Basin convection, surface effects that modify it, and the extra-tropical response to the presence or absence of convection over Amazonia.

## LARGE-SCALE CONTROLS OF TROPICAL CONVECTION

Tropical precipitation is usually from heavy showers or thunderstorms produced by convective cumulus clusters [reviewed by Houze and Hobbs (1982)]. Figure 1 displays a schematic cross section of a typical mesoscale convective cluster. This structure covers a horizontal scale on the order of $2 \times 10^5$ km$^2$. Most of the latent heat released by tropical convection is released on the cluster scale (Fig. 1, bottom). The clusters are highly complex phenomena, poorly resolved by the current meteorological observing systems over Amazonia. At times they assume the form of propagating squall lines; on other occasions, they display strong diurnal fluctuations. In certain respects, they are similar to midlatitude convective clusters that are known to be strongly modulated by synoptic scale disturbances.

Deep convection requires three conditions: (i) an unstable thermal stratification for moist processes, (ii) sufficient low-level moisture to produce condensation in air parcels that rise from a low level and cool by expansion, and (iii) low-level convergence that forces the moist low-level air upward toward eventual condensation.

Unstable stratification is an ambient atmospheric temperature structure that cools more rapidly with height than would an isolated rising air parcel. Such a parcel cools adiabatically by expansion, without external heat input except for latent heat release. Unstable stratification occurs in tropical regions and drives moist convection (e.g., Yanai, 1964).

Low-level moisture provides water for the precipitation that is produced over tropical rain forests. Convective clouds obtain moisture through updrafts originating in the subcloud boundary layer.

Low-level convergent motions producing uplift primarily reflect the dynamic response of the air motion to force fields, in contrast to the vertical temperature stratification and moisture availability, which represent essentially thermodynamic controls on convection. In the tropics, low-level convergence may be produced by several apparently distinct dynamical processes. These include fronts, the intertropical convergence zone (ITCZ) found at the confluence of equatorward-moving air of the two hemispheres, various tropical vortices and waves, and large-scale overturning flows of the tropics.

This review is about variable weather patterns. Kousky and Ferreira (1981) have decomposed daily mean surface pressure data with annual mean and annual cycle removed into patterns that characterize the most commonly

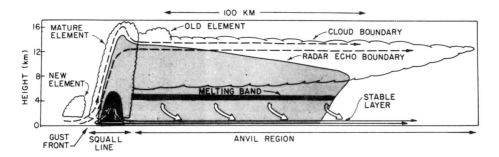

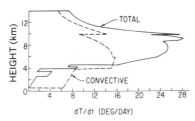

**FIGURE 1.**  Schematic of a typical cross section through a tropical squall system. Dashed streamlines show convective-scale updraft and downdraft motions associated with the mature squall-line element. Wide solid arrows show mesoscale downdraft circulation. Wide dashed arrows show mesoscale updraft circulation. Dark shading shows strong radar echo in the melting band and in the heavy precipitation zone of the mature squall-line element. Light shading shows weaker radar echoes. Scalloped line indicates visible cloud boundary. [Adapted from Houze (1977) with permission of *Monthly Weather Review*, the American Meteorological Society.] (*bottom*) Total heating of large-scale region ($2 \times 10^5$ km$^2$ in area) by a mature cloud cluster (solid curve). The total heating by the convective towers in the cluster (dashed curve) is shown for comparison. [From Houze (1982) with permission of the Meteorological Society of Japan.]

occurring variable structures over Brazil. Although the computed patterns may not precisely correspond to individual weather maps with great precision, there are some similarities to particular weather types that are commonly seen on surface weather charts. They conclude that the dominant, essentially zonal (i.e., independent of longitude) pattern corresponds to the large-scale planetary circulation, while other patterns reflect various types of frontal wave intrusions into the tropics.

## Frontal Activity in Amazonia

The theory of fronts was developed for midlatitudes by Bergeron (1928) and others who noted abrupt air mass changes across the boundary separating cold and warm air in different segments of midlatitude cyclones. Warmer

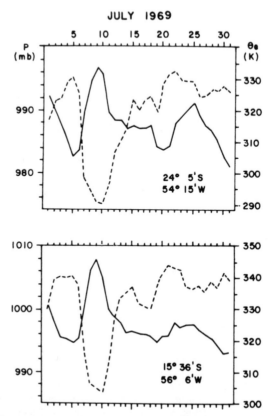

**FIGURE 2.** Station pressure (solid line) and equivalent potential temperature (dashed line) for July 1969. Stations used are indicated by their latitude and longitude coordinates. The frontal passage is marked by the strong pressure rise and equivalent potential temperature drop occurring around July 10. [From Kousky and Ferreira (1981) with permission of *Monthly Weather Review*, the American Meteorological Society.]

air is forced upward over the frontal surface, sometimes producing clouds and precipitation, especially in maritime air masses. It is relatively easy to explain the formation of fronts in regions of strong temperature gradient, such as the middle latitudes, where deformation of low-level air flow may bring air masses together and tighten low-level thermal gradients (e.g., Williams, 1967; Hoskins, 1976).

The fact that fronts exist in the tropics is more difficult to explain because tropical temperature gradients are weaker and deformations of low-level flows are ordinarily weaker. Air masses do often converge at low levels in the ITCZ, but the thermal gradient across this region is weak, and frontal lifting does not occur.

Kousky and Ferreira (1981) show satellite images of clouds with obvious frontal characteristics above the Amazon Basin. Figure 2 shows the time evolution of pressure and equivalent potential temperature ($\theta_e$) as the front crosses two tropical stations. The quantity $\theta_e$ is proportional to the temperature the air would have if all the moisture were condensed out of it, heating the air mass through the liberation of latent heat. The changes in pressure and $\theta_e$ display the obvious frontal signatures associated with air mass displacements.

Kousky (1979) also shows that much of the winter precipitation at some stations of the Amazon Basin is triggered by fronts and suggests that years with more fronts may be wetter than those with fewer frontal episodes. Kousky studied situations with cold fronts in which the equatorward-moving colder air of midlatitudes replaces the warm tropical air, producing heavy precipitation in the region of strong uplift of the humid tropical air at the boundary. Although the cooler air behind such fronts may have originated as polar air, it is considerably modified in its equatorward track.

Most polar air masses of the Southern Hemisphere are of maritime origin. Consequently, they are not as cold as the wintertime air masses of the Northern Hemisphere, where extensive continents at high latitudes result in much colder low-level temperatures.

Cold fronts of the Northern Hemisphere and associated troughs from the northern storm track also penetrate the deep tropics and enhance the rainfall there. Such fronts are mentioned by Riehl (1977) in relation to weather events around northern portions of South America and extensively studied by Chang and Lau (1980, 1982) in association with the "cold surges" that emanate from China, cross the China Sea, and produce heavy convection around Indonesia. Frontal penetration from the Northern Hemisphere into the tropics may be explained by the very cold temperatures over the extensive continents of Asia and North America. This very cold air has been associated with a highly stable cold dome, which promotes rapid equatorward propagation (e.g., Lim and Chang, 1981).

South American fronts, however, lack extensive cold air masses. Hence, other explanations of the equatorward displacement of midlatitude air masses must be sought. At present, there are two main suggestions.

First, topography may steer midlatitude disturbances anticyclonically around the periphery of mountains, thus equatorward east of high mountain ranges. This "edge wave" dynamics has been suggested by Bannon (1981) for midlatitude disturbances that track counterclockwise around the periphery of the South African high terrain and by Murakami (1982) for topographically bound cyclonic swirls moving around the Tibetan plateau. Such disturbances carry with them midlatitude air that may support fronts in the tropics. This suggestion of topographic influence may explain a higher frequency of tropical fronts on the east side of the Andes but does not distinguish the reasons for active frontal years, nor does it explain the tropical frontal activity that is occasionally noted in midocean.

Second, ambient low-level convergence or divergence may provide important modulations of frontal clouds and precipitation within the tropics.

In particular, the Walker circulation (to be discussed further) may modify the resulting frontal rains in important ways. Kousky and Ferreira (1981) indicate that Amazon Basin fronts are important in the deep tropics in the winter, but other mechanisms (to be discussed further) also modulate precipitation in the summer when most of the precipitation occurs.

### Vortices and Waves

Vortices and waves are among the most important causes of rain in the tropics. In many tropical regions they also lead to hurricanes. Although the tropical South Atlantic Ocean does have active waves and vortices that affect the weather of South America, hurricanes do not form there.

The tropical flows of low levels are commonly directed equatorward and westward in each hemisphere. This meridionally converging, westward-moving stream is sometimes perturbed by waves that represent weak swirls (or vortices) superposed upon the general current. The resulting pattern is an *easterly wave*. When the swirls are sufficiently strong to produce closed circulation centers, the pattern is a *vortex*, and when the vortex has sufficiently large amplitude, it becomes a *tropical storm* or, with even larger amplitude, a *hurricane*.

An excellent basic review of waves, vortices, and their transition to hurricanes is given by Yanai (1964), and hurricane development is studied as an instability of the tropical atmosphere by Charney and Eliassen (1964), Kuo (1965), and Ooyama (1969). Theories of the last three authors treat hurricane development as a cooperative interaction between the cyclone-scale flow and the convective cumulus clouds within the disturbance. Low-level moisture convergence organized by the cyclone-scale flow supplies moisture to the clouds that produce locally heavy precipitation. The associated latent heat release warms the atmosphere, providing the heating necessary to drive the circulation. The increased circulation sometimes is relatively localized; but at other times it occurs over a larger domain extending into the extratropics.

At some critical point of its evolution (attained by only a small fraction of the weaker vortices), the vortex core that was initially kept cool by adiabatic decompression in rising air and by raindrop evaporation warms by latent heating of condensation, and the system assumes a warm-core structure, which may continue to develop into a hurricane. It is not now possible to distinguish incipient vortices and ambient states that may produce hurricanes from those that do not in otherwise similar, highly convective circumstances. The previously cited instability studies were performed with respect to resting ambient states and do not explicitly consider sensitivity to ambient flow. Likewise, numerical simulations that have successfully treated hurricane evolution (e.g., Anthes, 1972; Kurihara and Tuleya, 1974) produce fully developed hurricanes in states that characterize both developing and nondeveloping tropical waves.

In contrast to the stability studies, the investigation of Schubert et al. (1980) emphasizes energy dispersion and suggests that some states may be less prone to develop hurricanes than others because they may more effectively allow outward *radiation* of the energy released by convection and therefore allow a weaker, remote response rather than an energetic, local development.

The South Atlantic is the only extensive tropical ocean region where hurricanes are not observed (e.g., Gray, 1983). Consequently, Amazonia is not subject to the violent tropical cyclones that produce frequent inundations around southeast Asia, India, northern Australia, East Africa, Madagascar, and occasionally strike Central and North America. The reasons for the absence of hurricanes are not entirely clear, but Gray's (1983) studies over other regions suggest that a necessary (but not always sufficient) condition for their development is the presence of upper-tropospheric easterly winds.

Such winds are observed over all other regions where tropical storms grow to hurricane strength. However, above the tropical South Atlantic, where hurricanes do not develop, the upper-level winds tend to be westerly. The upper-level westerlies of the South Atlantic are probably, at least in part, a consequence of the upper-level outflow from heavy convection over the Amazon Basin. Meteorologists do not yet understand how easterly flow can influence hurricane formation, but the tropical South Atlantic provides a good control setting that can be used to test theories of hurricane development. Another basic condition—ocean temperatures of at least 26–27°C— seems to be marginally satisfied in the South Atlantic.

Although tropical storms do not grow to hurricanes over the South Atlantic, they do organize heavy rain bands and contribute to precipitation over Amazonia (Kousky and Gan, 1981). Many of these systems originate as extratropical cyclones that drift into the tropics from southern midlatitudes. Latent heating is likely important to their dynamics as in the case of the easterly waves of the east Atlantic (Norquist et al., 1977). The rainfall rates produced by tropical storms and other mechanisms may be strongly modulated by changes of the Walker and Hadley ambient circulations and sea surface temperatures.

### Intertropical Convergence Zone and the Hadley Circulation

The intertropical convergence zone (ITCZ), the Hadley circulation, and large-scale flows with which they interact display both long-term changes and short-term variations, some of which may affect the cumulus convection of Amazonia. A longitudinal average of the tropical circulation shows low-level air moving equatorward in the subtropics of each hemisphere, converging and rising near the equator and then flowing poleward in the upper levels, a circulation referred to as the *Hadley cell*. At low levels, winds are light and tropical air rises with absolute angular momentum approximately equal to that at the earth's surface near the equator. In moving poleward, it shrinks in radius, and with this poleward movement, it is accelerated eastward to conserve angular momentum.

In many regions, especially over the oceans, the rising branch of the Hadley circulation corresponds to the ITCZ, an east–west band of heavy convection. Longitudinal asymmetries in its location are associated with easterly waves that occasionally develop into active tropical storms and drift into higher latitudes.

The position of the ITCZ is governed by the location of the *thermal equator* and lags seasonally the passage of the sun across the actual equator. The most active tropical convection tends to be colocated with the largest local buoyancy and hence with the warmest oceans or humid continental settings. However, desert climates often experience subsidence although they are hotter than their surroundings. This subsidence warming is balanced by strong radiative losses producing relative cooling [see, e.g., Blake et al. (1983) and Charney (1975) for discussion of heat balance in deserts].

The most active segments of the ITCZ have the greatest net heating rates (resulting from latent heat of condensation). Latent heating can be locally much greater than radiative effects. For example, 2 cm of rain commonly produced by a rainy day in the tropics are sufficient to warm the entire troposphere by about 6°C through latent heat release. On the other hand, insolation is sufficient to warm the entire air column by less than 2°C day$^{-1}$, and infrared radiative losses largely cancel this heating.

Humid warm regions are particularly likely to produce ascent in the tropics; thus, precipitation over Amazonia may be related to sea surface temperatures. For example, Hastenrath and Heller (1977) show that the ITCZ is locally displaced toward warm sea surface temperature anomalies. They suggest that the region of northeast Brazil, which is particularly prone to drought, is sensitively dependent on the placement of the ITCZ over the Atlantic Ocean. A slight northward displacement of a positive sea surface temperature (SST) anomaly apparently shifts the rain band sufficiently to the north to produce serious drought conditions over northeast Brazil (see also Moura and Shukla, 1981).

However, short-term SST anomalies may also follow, rather than lead, weather patterns. Furthermore, remote extratropical weather events may influence the rainfall around Brazil (Namias, 1972), and the structure of the Hadley circulation depends on the rate of extratropical heat and momentum removal at its poleward perimeter (Dickinson, 1971a). Rather than considering the complete global system, we here emphasize those components of the atmospheric circulation that are most relevant to the tropics and that depend on the presence or absence of tropical forcing.

## East–West Overturnings

As previously noted, the vertically averaged latent heating in tropically precipitating regions is much larger than the radiative heating or cooling that is usually the major nonadiabatic effect in other regions. Furthermore, it rains heavily in some tropical regions (such as the rain forests of Amazonia and Africa and the warm western oceans), and rains hardly at all in other regions (such as the cooler eastern oceans). Consequently, the tropical east–west heating gradients are almost as large as the north–south heating gradients. The nearly steady temperature field of the tropical atmosphere is sustained against such heating gradients by the adiabatic warming of sinking air over the eastern tropical oceans and by the adiabatic cooling of ascending air over the western oceans and rain forests. The east–west circulations that close these vertically overturning motions, referred to as the Walker circulation, are almost as strong as the meridional Hadley circulations, about 1–2 m s$^{-1}$ for the seasonal average (Krishnamurti et al., 1973). They are accompanied by global precipitation and surface pressure oscillations, first studied by Walker and Bliss (1932), now referred to as the southern oscillation and associated with changes in the tropical motion field during SST anomalies (Bjerknes, 1969, 1972).

Figure 3 displays the Walker circulation in an east–west plane for the average of the years 1979–1981. There are major rising centers over the western tropical Pacific Ocean and above Amazonia, with the latter being somewhat weaker.

Gill (1980) and Geisler (1981) present theoretical analyses of the Walker circulation that reproduce its basic aspects and explain its structure in terms of idealized tropically trapped wave modes. Some aspects of these results are supported by projections of the observed fields upon atmospheric normal modes (Silva-Dias and Paegle, 1984; Paegle et al., 1984).

El Niño is the occurrence of relatively warm SST anomalies in the eastern or central Pacific Ocean and the eastward displacement of the large Pacific heating center along with its surrounding subsiding branches. These episodes occur every few years. On such occasions, the subsidence that occurs east of the Pacific heating region blocks upward motion over Amazonia and so suppresses convection as was first suggested by Walker (1928) in association with the droughts over northeast Brazil and also indicated in the analyses by Kousky et al. (1984). The latter study also indicates apparent connection between the southern oscillation (Trenberth, 1976) and El Niño events, both of which have similar phase and sensitivity. The acronym ENSO refers to the combined El Niño–southern oscillation, recently reviewed by Rasmusson and Wallace (1983).

Although the correlation of the droughts of northeast Brazil and ENSO events appears to be statistically significant, the variance of the precipitation that is explained by the El Niño phenomena is only about 10% (Kousky et al., 1984). Consequently, while a knowledge of the phase of the ENSO cycle may help forecast some precipitation trends around the Amazon Basin, it cannot produce accurate estimates of the rainfall deviation from climatology.

The time scale for the Walker circulation to adjust to changed heating can be estimated by dividing the scale of the phenomenon ($10^7$ m) by the

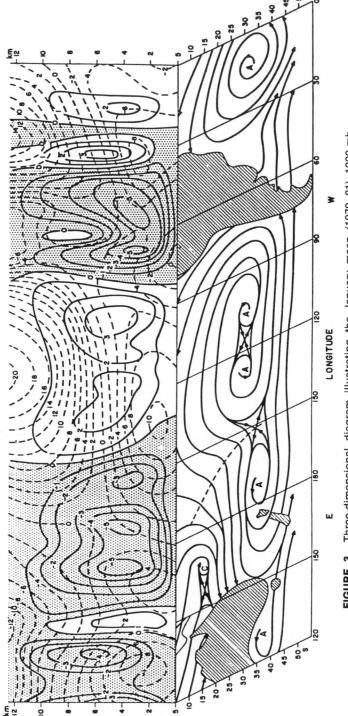

**FIGURE 3.** Three-dimensional diagram illustrating the January mean (1979–81) 1000-mb streamline pattern (horizontal portion of diagram), vertical motion *w* (solid lines, in units of $10^{-7}$ mb s$^{-1}$, with regions of upward motion shaded) and zonal wind (dashed lines in m s$^{-1}$), at 5°S. [From Kousky et al. (1984) with permission of *Tellus*.]

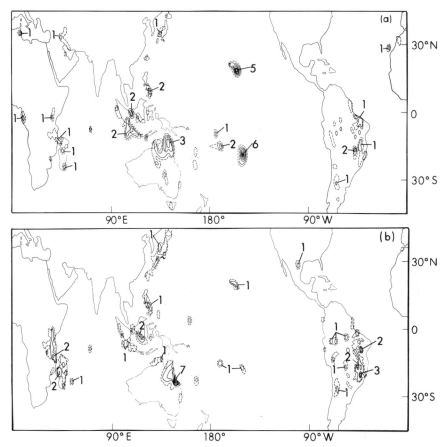

**FIGURE 4.** (a) Precipitation (cm day$^{-1}$) averaged over the period January 10 to January 23, 1979. (b) As in (a), averaged over the period January 26 to February 7, 1979. [From Paegle et al. (1983b) with permission of Birkhäuser Verlag.]

propagation rate of the wave modes that are most important for its structure. Silva-Dias (1983) shows that most of the amplitude of the vertically reversing modes over the Amazon Basin projects upon structures that have phase speeds on the order of 30 m s$^{-1}$ in the analyses of Gill (1980) and Geisler (1981). Therefore, adjustment time scales for these global-scale overturnings should be on the order of a few days.

Large adjustments of the Walker circulation occur on the interannual time scales of the ENSO phenomena, but whether they also occur on much shorter periods has not been so obvious. The data of the global weather experiment (GWE) suggest pronounced changes similar to the ENSO phenomena on time scales as short as two weeks (Paegle and Baker, 1982a).

Figure 4, from Paegle et al. (1983b), presents precipitation data averaged over successive two-week periods of the First Special Observing Period of the GWE and averaged over spherical grid squares that are 1.875° on a side. Each grid point value is obtained by averaging all precipitation observations within a grid square centered on the grid point. If there are no precipitation observations around the point (as is the case over most of the ocean regions), no values are calculated.

Extreme rainfall rates exceed 6 cm day$^{-1}$ in the tropical South Pacific Ocean during the first period of 14 days (Fig. 4, top), and peak rates exceed 7 cm day$^{-1}$ on the northeast coast of Australia during the second period (Fig. 4, bottom). The latent heating associated with this precipitation rate

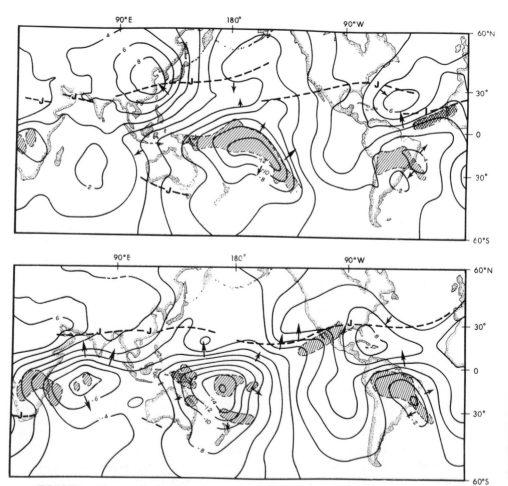

**FIGURE 5.** Velocity potential (solid curves) and divergent wind (arrows) for the same two periods in Fig. 4. Note westward shift of Pacific outflow center and development of Indian Ocean and Amazon Basin outflows from the first to the second period. Hatched regions denote extensive deep clouds. [From Paegle et al. (1983b) with permission of Birkhäuser Verlag.]

could warm the tropospheric column from 850 to 200 mb by about 20°C day$^{-1}$.

The pronounced changes of the rainfall distribution between frames in Fig. 4 are similar to those that occur between different phases of the ENSO phenomenon on longer time scales. Note the eastward displacement of the Pacific sector activity during the first period (which is somewhat analogous to the El Niño phase of the ENSO) and the westward return of this pattern in the second period. Suppression of the Amazon Basin rainfall and latent heating are not strongly evident here. However, the divergent overturning pattern changes significantly from the first period to the second (see Fig. 5) and presumably results in greater outflow from the South American sector during the second period.

The oscillation just described may be a component of a rather prominent (and as yet largely unexplained) 40–50-day tropical oscillation (Madden and Julian, 1972). Tropical convection can also change with changes at the earth's surface, as discussed in the next section. Highly transient convective activity does not allow a distant response, but Buchmann et al. (1984) and Silva-Dias et al. (1983) display calculations that suggest important short-term local connections across the Amazon Basin. The nonlinear model integration of Buchmann et al. (1984) suggests that precipitation in northeast Brazil may be inhibited by the subsidence next to enhanced precipitation over the Andes bordering Amazonia.

## SURFACE CONTROLS OF TROPICAL CONVECTION

The importance of high humidity and warm temperatures to tropical convection has already been described. Both requisites for deep convection are typically satisfied over the warm western tropical oceans and above humid rain forests of tropical land masses. Additionally, both these surface controls are likely to be important for long-time-scale changes.

However, land surfaces affect at least one very important high-frequency oscillation in convection: the diurnal cycle. Furthermore, evapotranspiration from vegetated surfaces can recycle the boundary layer water vapor on time scales as short as one week. This rapid recycling is of obvious relevance to rain forests such as Amazonia, which are affected by cumulus convection that is in turn fueled mainly by boundary layer water vapor.

### Sea Surface Temperature

Maritime tropical convection is strongly enhanced in regions of locally warm sea surface temperatures (SSTs). The near-surface maritime air temperature tends to adjust to the temperature of the sea surface because of the relatively high heat capacity of water. Thus, the air temperature above warmer water is relatively warm, and the air's positive buoyancy carries it upward. Even slight surface temperature perturbations on the order of 1°C are apparently sufficient to organize convective activity over the oceans.

In addition to simple buoyancy, elevated SSTs produce greater evaporation from the water surface because the saturation vapor pressure increases rapidly with temperature. For example, a 5°C increase of temperature from 25 to 30°C (a typical range in the tropics) increases the saturation vapor pressure by about 35% and the saturation mixing ratio by about 7 g water vapor per kilogram of air, contributing to potentially greater rainfalls and latent heat release; a temperature change from 10 to 15°C, typical of midlatitudes, produces only half as great a change of saturation mixing ratio as that from 25 to 30°C. Consequently, tropical SST variability has greater potential for modifying the atmosphere through latent heating than does midlatitude SST variability. Additionally, because atmospheric thermal advections are larger in middle latitudes than in low latitudes, the SST-driven latent heat of midlatitudes is more likely to be canceled by horizontal thermal advection. In the tropics, adiabatic expansion of strongly overturning, divergent flows largely compensates for latent heat release.

The influence of prescribed SST anomalies has been studied in atmospheric model integrations. Rowntree (1976) assumed SST anomalies in the Atlantic Ocean, Julian and Chervin (1978) assumed anomalies in the tropical Pacific Ocean, and Moura and Shukla (1981) focused on the region around northeast Brazil. The integrations of Moura and Shukla (1981) suggest that regional rainfall over Amazonia may be greatly modified by local SST anomalies.

Large-scale SST anomalies of the east central Pacific sector peaked at about 4°C during March 1983 (Quiroz, 1983), during one of the most active El Niño periods on record. At this time, many of the heavy rainfall records in normally dry regions of the western coast of South America were broken (Almeyda, 1983), and the quasi-stationary atmospheric wave pattern had maximum deviations as large as the amplitude of the climatological long-wave pattern (Quiroz, 1983). An association between tropical SST anomalies and changes of the long-wave pattern and rainfall cannot be proven because of the low statistical reliability of only a few events, both for data and for model simulations of the phenomena (e.g., Blackmon et al., 1983).

The role of oceanic dynamics in determining SST anomalies is uncertain. Slowly propagating global-scale wave modes that are trapped near the equator (Wyrtki, 1975) and propagate across the tropical Pacific Ocean may be involved, as well as local radiative, advective, and turbulent heat balances. Because of the potential impact of the SST anomalies on the weather and current deficiencies in our understanding of their influences, the Tropical Ocean Global Atmosphere field program is currently being mounted. The project will last 10 y in order to obtain at least one reasonably active El Niño event.

## Diurnal Oscillations

Our descriptions of tropical convection have thus far emphasized organizing mechanisms such as fronts, waves, vortices, the ITCZ, Walker circulations, and their modulation by SST. These phenomena are rather irregular, both in amplitude and location. By contrast, the annual and diurnal oscillations are highly regular cycles in convection. Summer is the wettest season over the Amazon Basin in both hemispheres. In the summer, the surface heating is greatest, as are the evaporation and evapotranspiration, producing unstable stratification and the low-level moisture needed to drive convection.

Likewise, these effects could be expected to be most pronounced during midday. Kousky (1980) finds that the diurnal cycle of convection is very pronounced over some stations of Brazil. An example for Soure and Belém is displayed in Fig. 6. However, the lack of hourly rainfall data for much of interior Amazonia makes comprehensive analyses of the diurnal precipitation cycle difficult. The strength of this cycle over other tropical regions such as Africa (Reed, 1983) and tropical islands (Gray and Jacobson, 1977) and areas bordering Amazonia suggest its importance for Amazonia.

Paegle et al. (1983a) have studied the diurnal convective cycles over Argentina, whose northern sections contain semitropical forests. Figure 7 shows the diurnal cycle of precipitation with a vector display; the direction indicates the hour of maximum convection; the magnitude is proportional to the amplitude of the first diurnal Fourier mode normalized by the daily average. A vector pointing from the north indicates a midnight maximum, while vectors from the east, south, and west indicate, respectively, maxima at 6:00, 12:00, and 18:00 local standard time. Each barb perpendicular to the vector denotes a contribution to the daily variation equaling 10% of the daily average. A station with four such barbs denotes a location where the occurrence of precipitation at the wettest time of day is 1.4 times the daily average, while it is only 0.6 times the daily average at the driest time or less than half as wet as during the wettest time. Since most stations have at least this magnitude, diurnal cycles in rainfall are evidently quite important in practically all of Argentina.

Stations on the east coast exhibit afternoon maxima, as do stations near the Andes mountains, while those in the broad valley east of the Andes have nocturnal maxima. The latter cannot depend on atmospheric destabilization by surface heating because the maximum convection occurs at night. Here, as well as on the east coast and over the Andes, the principal control is essentially dynamical, involving diurnal cycles of low-level convergence induced by the diurnal cycle of solar heating above sloping terrain and coastal regions.

The daytime sea breeze is formed by the greater heating of the land, vertical displacement of the air over land, and a resulting pressure field that drives the sea air toward land. Enhanced convergence and vertical lifting

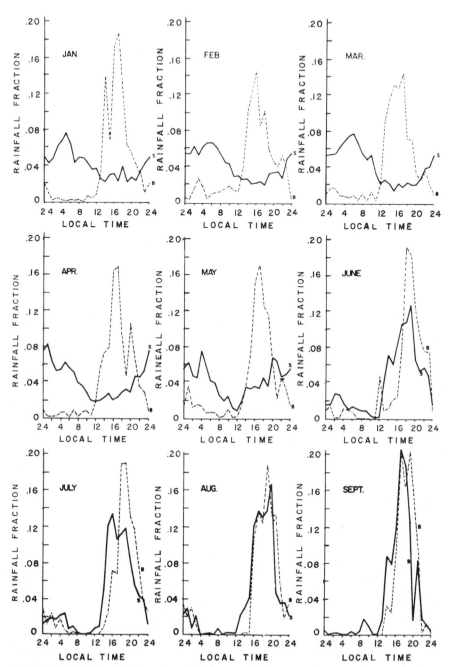

**FIGURE 6.** Hourly rainfall fractions for Soure (solid line) and Belém (dashed line) for the months of January–September. [From Kousky (1980) with permission of *Monthly Weather Review*, the American Meteorological Society.]

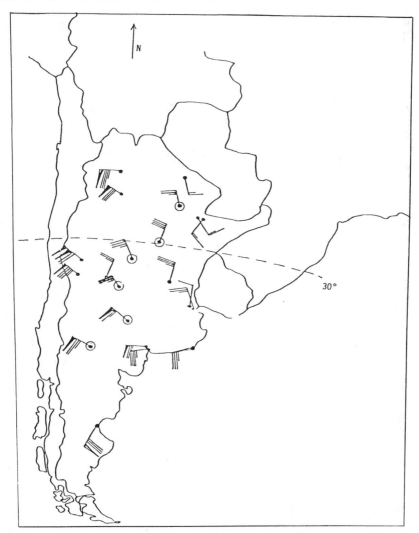

**FIGURE 7.**   Diurnal convective precipitation oscillations over Argentina. See text for description of symbols. [From Paegle et al. (1983a).]

near coastal stations where the sea breeze impinges on the calmer air over the land accentuate daytime showers. At night, the sea breeze is missing (or located over water as a "land breeze").

Sea breezes may explain the diurnal cycles in some of Kousky's (1980) results and those of the North American coastal regions in Wallace's (1975) study. The sea breeze over Brazil penetrates about 100 km inland during the afternoon, and diurnal precipitation cycles over interior Amazonia could be affected only indirectly. Minnis et al. (1983) show that cloud cover over Amazonia is greatest in the evening and night, but lack of hourly rainfall data precludes a comprehensive analysis of diurnal precipitation cycles over the interior of Amazonia. However, the data over Argentina (Fig. 7) and also Wallace's (1975) studies over North America indicate that the interior plains of these regions have pronounced enhancement of nocturnal convection.

Two mechanisms appear to be especially important for these enhancements. First, interior plains are broad valleys where drainage convergence from adjacent mountain slopes is accentuated at night, producing uplift and favoring nocturnal showers. Second, a low-level jet, typically situated about 500 m above the surface and especially pronounced at night, may produce strong convergence at its leading edge. This nocturnal low-level jet has been documented in great detail over the Great Plains of the United States (Bonner, 1968) and is also evident over Argentina (M. L. Altinger, University of Buenos Aires, personal communication) and Amazonia (Virji, 1981). Figure 3 of the latter study displays a clear example of this jet.

Recent model integrations (Paegle and McLawhorn, 1983; Astling et al., 1985) suggest that the low-level jet convergence is the most important factor for diurnal modulation of convection over the Great Plains of the United States. Anthes et al. (1982) also show that the low-level jet modulates severe weather in mesoscale model integrations. Afternoon rainfall maxima over mountains may reflect the upslope, buoyancy-driven convergence of low-level air toward the mountain peaks. Because the Amazon Basin is flanked on the east by the Atlantic Ocean, on the west by the Andes, and on the south and north by large plateaus, all of the mechanisms discussed above may act to produce diurnally oscillating precipitation.

Not all of the diurnal cycles are entirely regular. For example, Kousky (1980) finds evidence that regions of preexisting convection may inhibit subsequent convection because solar heating is used mainly to evaporate the wetter surface, which remains cooler than the surroundings and consequently produces a local air mass with negative buoyancy. Adjacent drier regions warm more strongly during the day, and a weak analog of the sea breeze may form over these regions, enhancing the precipitation there.

The diurnal convective cycles are important for two reasons. First, the diurnal cycle may be strongest when heaviest convection occurs (Wallace, 1975). Thus, the problem of diurnal convective cycles may be of considerable importance to severe weather events. Second, the diurnal cycle is often the most common single tropical convection cycle, dominating the occurrence of tropical rain. Consequently, inadequate resolution of the surface effects leading to the diurnal cycles may seriously degrade model simulations of tropical processes. Kuo and Qian (1981) find that the summer monsoon of Asia develops more rapidly in their model if the diurnal convective cycle is maintained rather than suppressed.

## Soil Moisture

As already discussed, the SST may have long-term impacts on the weather. The soil moisture over land may also have substantial influence on both long- and short-term changes. Soil moisture gradients produce surface temperature gradients during the day because most of the incident radiation on the wet surface is used to evaporate water and less is available for sensible heating. Thus, a local sea-breeze-like effect may modulate low-level convection in regions of soil moisture gradient.

Continental precipitation may involve, in large part, water vapor from recent evaporation and evapotranspiration occurring in the same region (Mintz, 1984). Some prior estimates of the local surface contributions of precipitation have suggested continental evapotranspiration as low as 14% of the local precipitation. These estimates are probably low for tropical convection because they include stable midlatitude winters when there is no evapotranspiration from plants (in part for lack of net radiative heating). Some of the estimates are based on pan evaporation rates that can be smaller than evapotranspiration rates from vegetated surfaces exposed to full sunlight.

A vegetated surface (such as grass) will remain relatively cool under strong insolation only if the latent heat used for evapotranspiration balances most of the radiative heating. This temperature-regulating mechanism of leaf and blade surfaces ensures that a large fraction of the incident solar heating is used to pull water through the root system in regions of heavy vegetative cover, such as the Amazon Basin.

The potential evapotranspiration is on the order of 0.5 cm day$^{-1}$ during the summer. The actual evapotranspiration is a small fraction of this amount over desert regions lacking vegetation and, on the average, up to 80% of this value over highly vegetated surfaces such as the eastern United States or the Amazon Basin.

To the extent that the average rainfall over either of these continental regions is not much larger than 0.5 cm day$^{-1}$, much of the moisture supply for rain must come from regional evapotranspiration. Such moisture input should restore the ambient moisture supply of the tropical boundary layer in about one week. Finally, because convective clouds receive their moisture mainly from the subcloud boundary layer, moisture that is evaporated locally is likely to be more important for convective clouds than for stably stratified clouds.

Nevertheless, there are questions motivated by the earlier lower estimates of evapotranspiration in the hydrological cycle and the possibility that advective processes may somehow provide significant moisture influx from oceanic regions in ways that are not adequately resolved by previous budget studies. In particular, direct estimation of evapotranspiration over large regions such as the eastern United States (where some of the studies have been performed) is difficult, and budget studies are used instead. In the budget study approach, the moisture flux across the coastlines is obtained from the observed wind and humidity fields, the net continental deposition is estimated from rainfall data (supplemented by runoff estimates), and the

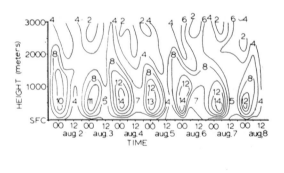

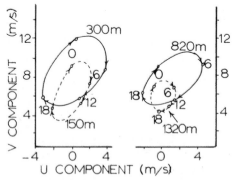

**FIGURE 8.** Time section of wind speeds (m s⁻¹) at Fort Worth, Texas, for August 2–8, 1960 (*top*). Mean wind oscillation (m s⁻¹) at various levels for August 2–8, 1960, at Fort Worth, Texas (*bottom*). Times are CST. [From Paegle and Rasch (1973) with permission of *Monthly Weather Review*, the American Meteorological Society.]

residual represents the continental input of moisture through evapotranspiration.

Mintz (1984) summarizes estimates of this residual over the eastern United States, which show that most of the summer precipitation of this region is water recycled by evapotranspiration from the land. Among the difficulties of such estimates is their sensitivity to the calculated inflow of water vapor from the Gulf of Mexico. Much of this influx is accomplished in the southerly low-level jet, which has a rather detailed vertical and temporal structure that may not be well resolved in gross budget calculations. Figure 8 displays the typical wind field over Fort Worth, Texas, during eight consecutive days of August. The strongest inflow occurs at night at a level well below the first mandatory reporting level of the radiosonde data set. If such a wind structure were not well resolved, budget calculations would give excessive sinks of moisture and evapotranspiration rates.

The available budget studies showing a large contribution to precipitation from evapotranspiration have provided partial motivation for various general circulation experiments in which soil moisture is suppressed, and the results are compared to experiments where this parameter is realistically retained.

These integrations, as reviewed by Mintz (1984), show great sensitivity of the continental precipitation to evapotranspiration, not only in their long-term climate evolution but also in their short-term trends. In particular, continental rainfall in most places, including the Amazon Basin, is strongly suppressed in simulations lacking soil moisture.

Riehl (1977) reports that the evaporation during field experiments performed over Venezuela during the summers of 1969 and 1972 is approximately half of the total precipitation during these experiments. This result is similar to the water balance calculations for the entire Amazon Basin (e.g., Molion, 1975; see also Salati, Chapter 15).

In summary, evapotranspiration is most likely an important agent for determining the tropical distribution of convection. Soil moisture may also help to determine the structure of the Walker circulation and thus have a substantial regional and possible global impact on the weather. Presumably, the characteristics of vegetated surfaces, which are important for the availability of the soil moisture, are also important.

## Boundary Layer Transports

Boundary layer water vapor is transported by turbulent mixing and by vertical and horizontal winds. These processes are usually poorly resolved in global general circulation models, which must compromise vertical resolution in order to accommodate a global forecast domain. In particular, low-level, diurnally oscillating jets (see Fig. 8) that transport and converge large amounts of moisture are not well resolved by large-scale forecast models (Astling et al., 1985).

A numerical model has been designed to resolve the boundary layer structure in great detail. The lowest 3 km of this model are represented by a total of 30 computational levels, the lowest of which is less than 1 m above the roughness height. The model also has 10 levels below the surface where the temperature is forecast. Heat balance is imposed at the atmosphere–surface interface. This high resolution helps to accurately depict the shallow, nocturnal, low-level jets and their attendant moisture transports (Paegle and McLawhorn, 1983; Yeh, 1983).

With such fine vertical resolution, the model can be run only over regional forecast domains, and unlike the previously mentioned global models, it does not resolve the feedback between moisture convergence, convective weather, and global-scale flow modifications. Consequently, it is applicable only for short time scales before such feedback effects become important.

An example of diurnally fluctuating boundary layer jets is given in Fig. 9, which displays the observed 850-mb winds in a region east of the Rocky mountains for May 9, 1979. The nocturnal (1200 GMT) speeds are faster than those of the previous afternoon (0000 GMT) by approximately a factor of 2. The nocturnally enhanced convergence downwind of the southerly jet accentuates the convection over Nebraska at night (see radar charts in Fig.

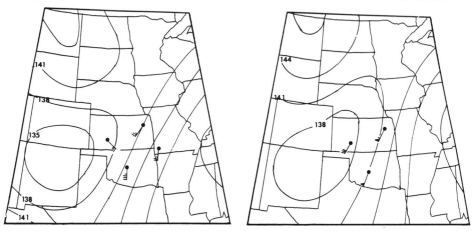

**FIGURE 9.** Height contours (in dm)) and selected wind observations at 0000 GMT (*left*) and 1200 GMT, May 9, 1979 (*right*) over U.S. Great Plains. [From Miller (1982).]

10). The winds within the southerly jet ($\sim 25$ m s$^{-1}$) can move air over the 1000-km distance between Nebraska and the Gulf of Mexico in only about 12 h.

This case has also been studied in greater detail by Astling et al. (1985), who used the boundary layer model developed by Paegle and McLawhorn (1983) to investigate the predictability of the nocturnal jet and the rising motion at its leading edge. The model prediction of the nocturnal jet is displayed in Fig. 11 as is the day-to-night change of the forecast winds. These

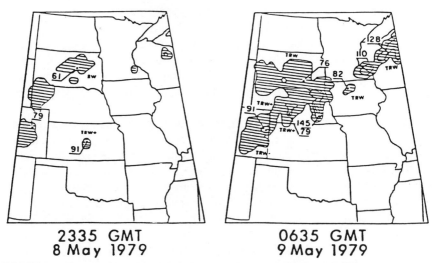

**2335 GMT**
**8 May 1979**

**0635 GMT**
**9 May 1979**

**FIGURE 10.** Radar composites for afternoon (left) and night (right). The numbers indicate echo tops in hundreds of feet over U.S. Great Plains. [From Miller (1982).]

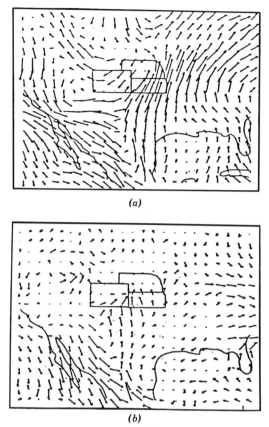

(a)

(b)

**FIGURE 11.** Model wind fields at 529 m above the surface over Central U.S. (a) Forecast for 0200 CST, where one grid interval represents 12 m s$^{-1}$. (b) Difference between forecasts for 0200 and 1400 CST. Afternoon values are subtracted from nighttime values and one grid interval represents 6 m s$^{-1}$. [From Paegle (1984).]

fields display a substantial southerly jet east of the Rocky Mountains that has a strong nighttime acceleration and produces rising motion of 4 cm s$^{-1}$ at its leading edge, around the region of nocturnal convection over Nebraska.

Similar nocturnally enhanced low-level jets have been successfully predicted by this model around the Alps (Paegle et al., 1984a) and around Somalia in East Africa (Paegle and Geisler, 1986). These studies find that the jets are produced by topography that can block and channel a stably stratified flow and by the elevated heat sources determined by the mountains but that the former effect is dominant around these rather small mountain barriers.

We next describe applications of the model to South America and consider the two limiting cases of very wet and very dry surfaces. In the limit of a swamp surface with an evapotranspiration that is sufficiently efficient to convert all surface radiative imbalances to latent heat of evaporation, the solar influence would not change the temperature at low levels. This surface is similar to the ocean, which also does not react to radiation changes over time scales of a few days. Consequently, in this limit, an initially uniform field of temperature would remain uniform, so that there would be no buoyancy differences to induce vertical motion, and radiative effects would produce no motion from an initial resting state.

At the other extreme is a surface devoid of vegetation and moisture and composed of a weakly conducting, low-heat-capacity substance such as dry sand, which reacts strongly to radiation changes. This lower boundary is assumed for the terrain of South America. As time proceeds, insolation heats the region, and the relatively buoyant atmosphere is displaced upward. This displacement would be most pronounced around the elevated heat source of the Andes and would produce lateral inflow at low levels to eventually fill the area near the heat source with a maritime air mass and ultimately produce clouds and rain. Because central Amazonia is a broad, relatively low basin, the surrounding elevated heat sources and associated clouds and rain on their slopes may induce subsidence further in the basin and promote aridity.

Although our boundary layer model cannot describe cloud and precipitation processes, it estimates the rate of inflow that would be produced. Model integrations by Paegle (1984) for a dry surface, but without ambient flow fields, predict divergence (i.e., subsidence) over central Amazonia that would accentuate the dry, warm conditions, in agreement with the above

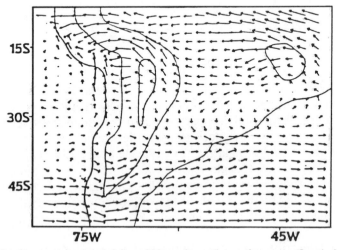

**FIGURE 12.** Forecast horizontal flow 500 m above the surface over South America. A vector length equaling the north–south separation between grid points represents a speed of 10 m s$^{-1}$. [From Paegle (1984).]

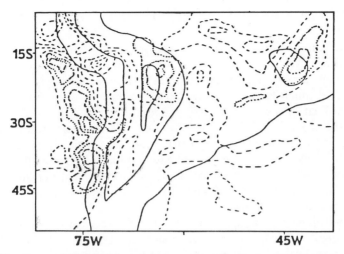

**FIGURE 13.** Forecast horizontal convergence over South America averaged over the layer from the surface to 3 km for the case with a zonal ambient flow. The analysis interval is 3 × 10⁻⁶ s⁻¹, convergence is displayed by dashed contours, divergence by dotted contours, and the zero contour is dashed. [From Paegle (1984).]

arguments and GCM studies. However, this divergence depends on the motion of the initial and ambient states.

A more realistic calculation includes a nonzero ambient flow field with tropical easterlies and extratropical westerlies at low levels. Paegle (1984) has also calculated model results with dry surface conditions imposed, including an easterly wind of 10 m s⁻¹ at the north boundary (located around 5°S) and a westerly flow of 10 m s⁻¹ at the south boundary (around 55°S) with a zero value at 30° S. The horizontal flow after three days is displayed in Fig. 12 for the level of strongest forecast winds (around 500 m above the surface), and the horizontal convergence is shown in Fig. 13.

A moderate easterly jet (about 15 m s⁻¹) develops over eastern Amazonia and an active convergent area spreads into much of the Amazon Basin. At transport rates of 15 m s⁻¹, the Amazon Basin would be replenished by maritime air in only a few days' time, and the convergent motion would ensure its ascent to higher levels, (i.e., a doubling of boundary layer moisture in about two days.) Thus, this case and the case study of Fig. 9 suggest more flux of water vapor from the oceans than do past GCM studies of the Amazon (reviewed by Henderson-Sellers, Chapter 20).

It is not yet clear whether this discrepancy is a consequence of the inadequate resolution of boundary layer transports by the GCM simulations or the excessively localized application of our planetary boundary layer model. It would be useful to run the boundary layer model using actual surface parameters and evapotranspiration processes to establish its applicability to the Amazon Basin.

## FEEDBACK OF TROPICAL CONVECTION ON LARGER SCALES

The major energy source in tropical regions such as the Amazon Basin is the latent heat release associated with precipitation. As shown in Fig. 4, local rainfall rates in excess of 4 cm day$^{-1}$ are not uncommon for weekly periods, and much larger rates are observed locally over shorter periods. The latent heat released by the daily condensation of 4 cm rain is sufficient to heat the troposphere by about 10°C day$^{-1}$. The temperature changes observed in the midtroposphere of the tropics are typically on the order of 1°C day$^{-1}$ or less, even in regions of heavy rainfall. Consequently, the latent heating of local tropical disturbances is not locally realized but is spread over a large area and it may influence circulations that are rather far removed from the precipitation area.

Regions of heavy precipitation are typically concentrated in relatively narrow squalls with horizontal dimension on the order of a few hundred kilometers or less. The temperature change occurring in the cloudy region is an almost negligibly small balance of the diabatic effect of strong latent heat release and the adiabatic cooling effect experienced by rising air undergoing strong decompression.

The air rising into the upper troposphere spreads laterally outward and subsides in the nonprecipitating regions surrounding the rain bands. These regions occupy an area much larger than the precipitating zone, and the total heating is diluted over the much larger subsiding area where the air warms adiabatically by compression.

Much of the subsiding flow occurs outside the tropics where the distance from the earth's polar axis of revolution is less than at the equator. Because of the atmosphere's tendency to conserve angular momentum, poleward movement of air accelerates the zonal velocity, producing westerly jet streams outside the tropics.

During the solstices, most of the tropical latent heating occurs in the summer hemisphere, while the strongest Hadley cell occurs across the equator in the winter hemisphere, where the strongest atmospheric jet streams of the upper troposphere are also found. Much of this asymmetry may be a consequence of the more effective radiative cooling of the winter hemisphere. However, even in the presence of similar external heating rates, the principal impact of the tropical heating of the summer hemisphere may be in the winter hemisphere.

The release of latent heat over the Amazon Basin should contribute to both the generation of the zonally symmetric Hadley cell and to more localized wave effects. It may also contribute to the shifting of the storm tracks and jet streams around North America. The conventional view, however, has been that the long atmospheric waves of the northern midlatitudes and their attendant jet streams and storm tracks are principally consequences of the distribution of the mountain ranges, continents, and seas within the midlatitudes.

Nevertheless, the modifications of the jet stream and storm tracks that are apparently attributable to pronounced El Niño events, such as that of 1983, the presence of strong stationary waves in the Southern Hemisphere (Paegle et al., 1983b; Kalnay and Halem, 1981), and the observed winter–spring transitions of the long waves of the Northern Hemisphere demand other explanations. Although all of these events are consistent with the redistribution of latent heat release within the tropics, we do not yet have satisfactory theoretical explanations for the regional extratropical effects of tropical heating.

## Amazon Basin Rainfall Cycles and Large-Scale Flow Changes

It is easier to identify potential connections between the tropics and elsewhere for long-term climatic changes than for short-term weather transitions. We now present evidence suggesting extratropical impacts from rainfall transitions over Amazonia on the time scales of the 40–50-day oscillation over Brazil for February and March 1981. Precipitation over Amazonia (Kousky, 1984b) was much heavier during March 1981. Kousky notes a pronounced rearrangement of the extratropical circulation pattern during this period (Fig. 14) with strong subtropical jet enhancements over both the North Atlantic and South Atlantic, with the former being greater. Much of the change appears to be related to a prominent 40–50-day oscillation that occurred at this time.

The apparent location of the 40–50-day oscillation in the tropics suggests that changes in the tropical latent heating redistribution produced an extratropical effect. However, Kousky (1984b) concludes that the events could also be interpreted by enhanced storm activity over the east coast of North America eventually enhancing the rainfall over northeast Brazil (Namias, 1972). The extratropical transitions and Brazilian rainfall redistributions occur almost simultaneously, complicating any explanation of cause.

On a longer time scale, the tropical rainfall changes are probably the result of local tropical surface heating changes and associated low-level convergence changes dominated by local tropical effects rather than of extratropical influences. Figures 15 and 16 display the seasonal transition of rainfall as estimated from satellite imagery using empirical relationships between observed precipitation and remote satellite sensing. This technique of rainfall estimation is rather new, and an extensive climatology of the rain data is not available. We display results for the winter, spring, summer, and fall of 1984 in the illustrations.

The driest season over most of Amazonia is the southern winter (June, July, and August) when the precipitation maximum shifts northward toward the tropical northeast Pacific Ocean in the vicinity of a relative maximum in SST. This shift is the result of the northward, cross-equatorial solar passage and the associated reduction of low-level buoyancy over Amazonia.

The shift generally begins in the northern spring, and by April and May

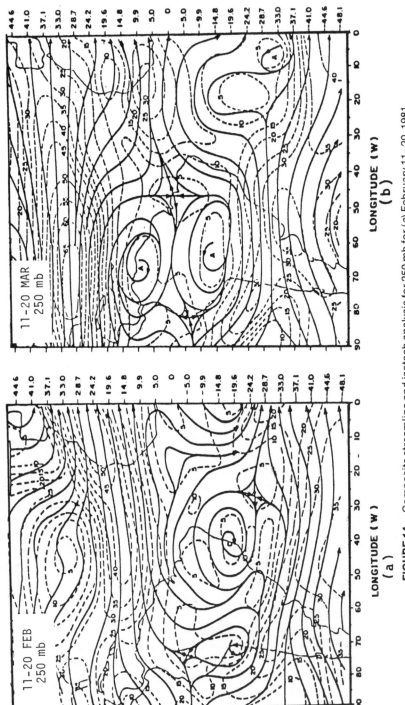

**FIGURE 14.** Composite streamline and isotach analysis for 250 mb for (a) February 11–20, 1981, and (b) March 11–20, 1981. Units for isotachs are m s⁻¹. [From Kousky (1984a).]

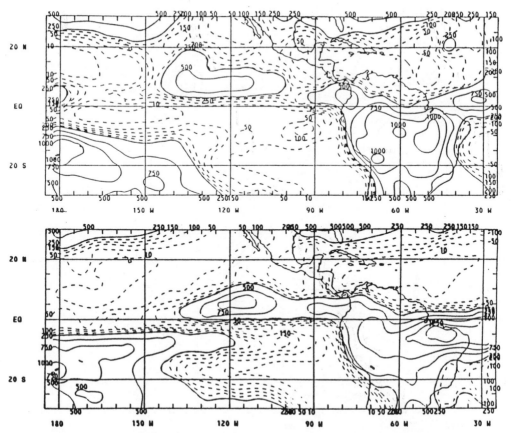

**FIGURE 15.(top)**   GOES precipitation index, for December–February 1983–1984. Estimated tropical precipitation (mm) for 2.5° areas derived from fractional coverage of cloud colder than 235 K by method of Arkin (*Tropical Ocean-Atmosphere Newsletter*, March, 1983). Solid contours at 100-mm intervals; dashed contours at 4, 20, 40, 60 and 80 mm. (*Bottom*) for March, April, and May, 1984. [From NOAA (1984a).]

the precipitation maximum west of Central America is often already greater than that over Amazonia. The March, April, and May data for 1984 suggest more clouds and precipitation over Amazonia and less over the tropical eastern Pacific than does climatology.

If there is an extratropical response to tropical heating changes, as Kousky's (1984b) study implies, we should expect a westward shift of the subtropical jet stream from the east coast of North America in winter to the west coast in spring and a concomitant westward shift of the North American long-wave trough. Such shifts are observed in the data of the global weather experiment conducted in 1979 and also in climatological data on North American trough and ridge positions (Table 1).

This shift in trough locations has a notable effect on the weather of North

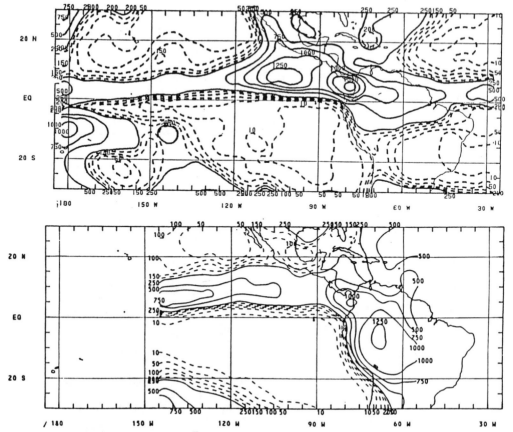

**FIGURE 16. (top)** GOES precipitation index (derived as in Fig. 15), September–November 1984. Solid contours at 100-mm intervals; dashed contours at 4, 20, 40, 60 and 80 mm (from NOAA, 1984d). (*Bottom*) June–August, 1984. Solid contours at 100-mm intervals; dashed contours at 10, 50, 100, 150, and 200 mm (from NOAA, 1984c).

America. For example, the wettest month in Salt Lake City is April, when the trough has been displaced westward toward this region. The time of most frequent severe weather on the Great Plains east of the Rocky Mountains is also in spring, when the southerly flow ahead of the mountain trough supplies large amounts of moisture from the Gulf of Mexico.

Amazon Basin convection may be important for the North American jet stream and storm tracks. It is, therefore, useful to summarize evidence for the suggested connection. Although the data are suggestive, it is difficult to draw further conclusions because of the brief period for which the seasonal precipitation transitions are known and the few cases for which analyses of the sort shown in Fig. 14 are available. Furthermore, although simple mathematical models display extratropical responses similar in pattern to those of

**TABLE 1.  Distribution of Monthly Averaged Trough Axes at 30°, 40°, and 50°N over North America, 1960–1980**[a]

|         | 130–110°W | 110–90°W | 90–70°W |
|---------|-----------|----------|---------|
| **January–February** | | | |
| 50°N    | 0         | 7        | 29      |
| 40°N    | 1         | 23       | 17      |
| 30°N    | 9         | 22       | 9       |
| **April–May** | | | |
| 50°N    | 7         | 9        | 8       |
| 40°N    | 19        | 18       | 1       |
| 30°N    | 34        | 5        | 1       |

[a] Counts are number of months with trough axes located in given longitude sectors at these latitudes. [Adapted from Paegle et al. (1983c) with permission from *Journal of the Atmospheric Sciences*, the American Meteorological Society.]

Fig. 14, none of them predicts important aspects of the total apparent structure.

For example, the theories by Webster (1982), Gill (1980), and Simmons (1982) show greater tropical flow than extratropical flow for tropical heating in calm or easterly upper-level flow, while the observations (Fig. 14) indicate the opposite. Instability theories (Simmons et al., 1983) may help to explain the midlatitude response on time scales of a month or more, but their relevance to the subtropical jet changes (which are rapid and apparently strong in the wind field) is not yet clear. Paegle et al. (1983b) note that heavily convective areas of the tropics are fundamentally different in character from other regions in that the upper-level motion is largely divergent, rather than rotational, as shown in Fig. 17, during a time of particularly active convection over Amazonia. Such divergent flow appears to be dynamically analogous to the Hadley cell.

## Hadley Cell and Related Symmetric Circulations

The Hadley cell refers to the longitudinally averaged meridional circulation of the tropics and subtropics and is determined in part by the large contribution made by Amazon Basin convection to net tropical heating. The tropical atmosphere typically displays rising motion in association with the heating at the ITCZ. This air is replaced at low levels by the equatorward flow converging from each hemisphere and evacuated at upper tropospheric lev-

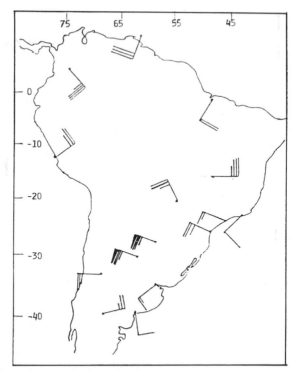

**FIGURE 17.** Example of radiosonde winds at 200 mb for February 9, 1976, 1200 GMT. A full barb represents 10 knots, a half barb is 5 knots.

els by poleward-moving circulations that ultimately descend around 30° latitude to close the cell. The rising warm air near the equator and subsiding cooler air in the subtropics lower the system's center of mass and convert potential to kinetic energy to drive the zonal flow against frictional dissipation and momentum extraction by midlatitude waves.

Around the solstices, the Hadley circulations are asymmetric with respect to the equator, with the strongest rising being in the summer hemisphere and the strongest sinking in the winter hemisphere, so that the Hadley cell circulations cross the equator. Around the equinoxes, the Hadley cells are considerably weaker and more nearly symmetrical with respect to the equator.

Because of the atmosphere's tendency to conserve angular momentum, the zonal winds increase at upper levels as the Hadley cell streams poleward. Strong subtropical jets are thus produced in the upper troposphere at the poleward perimeter of the Hadley circulation.

The momentum balance is also influenced by wave effects at higher latitudes. Waves transfer large amounts of zonal momentum meridionally and redistribute heat. A quantitatively accurate depiction of the zonal flow acceleration consequently requires detailed analysis (Dickinson, 1971a), but it appears that the strongest zonal tropospheric jets tend to occur on the poleward flank of the strongest cross-equatorial Hadley cells.

The tropical circulations are rather variable, as has already been indicated in Fig. 4. Detailed examination of the daily evolution of the tropical charts of the global weather experiment reveals alternating cycles of relatively active episodes and calmer periods. An especially active sequence of tropical events occurred in mid-January 1979, when there was locally enhanced convection in the central Pacific accompanied by strong cross-equatorial flow (Paegle and Baker, 1982a,b). These events motivated in part the forecast model tropical impact experiments conducted by Baker and Paegle (1983) and Paegle and Baker (1983).

The subtropical jet stream displayed marked intensification at this time (Paegle and Baker, 1983), suggesting short-term connections between the zonal flow and tropical activity and increasing the globally integrated kinetic energy by about 10% (Sampson, 1982). We now present model results that suggest that these changes may be consequences of tropical heating changes.

The Hadley cell is driven by meridional heating gradients produced and modified by (i) the meridional gradient of radiative heating, (ii) the meridional gradient of latent heating, (iii) the meridional gradient of heat flux by waves, and (iv) meridional momentum flux by waves. Theories of the Hadley circulation are summarized by Lorenz (1967). Subsequent calculations with models emphasize various forms of the forcing mechanisms and dissipation (Dickinson, 1971a,b; Schneider and Lindzen, 1977; Schneider, 1977; Held and Huo, 1980). Global observations of the Hadley cell were presented by Newell et al. (1972).

The meridional gradient of radiative heating is rather small and, in the absence of other effects, can drive only a very weak Hadley cell with meridional winds on the order of a few centimeters per second (Kuo, 1956) rather than several meters per second, as observed. On the other hand, the meridional gradient of latent heating is quite large within the tropics because of the strongly concentrated rain band around the ITCZ. The annual zonally averaged precipitation and evaporation estimates (Lorenz, 1967) suggest a sharp gradient of latent heating from the equator to 30° latitude. Heating of this magnitude and shape produces strong Hadley cells in the linear models studied by Dickinson (1971a,b) and Schneider and Lindzen (1977).

Subtropical jets produced by such forcings alone are excessively large but can be realistically damped by meridional wave fluxes of momentum into higher latitudes (Dickinson, 1971a) or by imposition of internal momentum mixing, intended to represent the vertical turbulent transfer of cumulus clouds (Schneider and Lindzen, 1977). Dickinson's results show that poleward momentum transfer from the subtropical jet into midlatitudes by the midlatitude waves produces important modifications of the symmetric circulation compared to that driven entirely by thermal forcing.

Hadley cell circulations across the equator are further addressed in two real data experiments conducted by Paegle and Baker (1983b) using the Goddard Laboratory for Atmospheres GCM. One experiment was run for five days from January 15, 1979, and included all model physical processes. In a parallel experiment, latent heating within the tropics was suppressed. The largest heating differences and heating gradient differences between the two experiments occur in the southern (summer) hemisphere. Nevertheless, the largest differences in the predicted Hadley cell evolution occur in the upper troposphere of the northern (winter) hemisphere through the five days of the forecast.

The fact that the Hadley cell responds in the winter hemisphere to changes in the summer hemisphere suggests that short-term transitions of the Hadley cell in this model are practically independent of midlatitude processes. Furthermore, using the general circulation model of the National Center for Atmospheric Research (NCAR) and integrations as long as 10 days using initial data from the same period, we have found that the subtropical jet streams change more in the Northern Hemisphere than in the Southern Hemisphere in response to Southern Hemisphere heating changes. Thus, the response to tropical heating changes of one hemisphere may be most pronounced in the opposite hemisphere, at least for intermediate forecast periods. Local subtropical jet stream cores ordinarily located around the east coasts of continents may be similarly sensitive to the amount and location of tropical heating, as now discussed.

## Local Hadley Cell and Jet Stream Structure

Although a zonally symmetric circulation may satisfy the equations for atmospheric processes, it is not a stable solution, and an incipient disturbance about this state inevitably grows at the expense of the zonally averaged state and contributes to the longitudinal variation of the flow. Baroclinic instability (Charney, 1947; Eady, 1949) and barotropic instability (Kuo, 1952) are especially important. These instabilities transfer energy between the longitudinally symmetric portion of the flow field and growing waves.

The fraction of atmospheric wave energy that can be assigned to such instabilities (as well as to other mechanisms that perturb the zonal flow, such as mountains), compared to direct thermal forcing of the wave pattern, is still poorly known. The energy transformation diagram discussed by Kung and Tanaka (1983) from one global weather experiment analysis suggests that the potential energy of the zonally averaged state is transformed into potential energy of waves about as strongly as the latter is transformed into kinetic energy and dissipated. Thus, no wave generation is required other than the unstable conversion of energy from the zonally averaged state (although this is not necessarily the only explanation of the diagram).

Another analysis of the data gives quite a different result, with potential energy of the zonally averaged state providing only about half of the potential energy required to maintain the wave potential energy against a substantially larger conversion to wave kinetic energy (Kung and Tanaka, 1983). The other half of the energy must be supplied by a direct thermal input, perhaps corresponding to the input of sensible heat in midlatitudes and latent heat release in the tropics.

The longitudinal asymmetry of tropical heat release and the possibility of tropical wave momentum flux led Dickinson (1971c) to conjecture that extratropical responses should not only occur in a zonally symmetric mode (as discussed in the last two sections) but also have a longitudinally asymmetric structure. The strongest northern winter jet streams occur in the western Pacific and around the east coast of North America, in the approximate longitudinal location of the tropical latent heating maxima. Are these jet streams produced by the enhanced rainfall of the corresponding tropical regions?

Figure 5 depicts the upper-level outflow pattern for a two-week period beginning January 10, 1979. This pattern displays a marked divergent outflow from the western and central Pacific Ocean and a secondary outflow from the Amazon Basin. These outflow patterns are presumably produced by air rising in these regions in association with enhanced convection. The rainfall data (Fig. 4) support this association. During the subsequent 10-day period, the divergent outflow from the Amazon Basin increases, the central Pacific center shifts westward, while a new outflow center develops over the Indian Ocean. These changes are consistent with the observed rainfall and heating changes.

A local Hadley cell teleconnection interpretation of these results (e.g., Bjerknes, 1966, 1969; Ramage, 1968) predicts that the winter jet stream patterns should adjust consistently with the tropical heating rearrangements. In particular, the subtropical jet stream over North America should increase from the first to the second period, while the North Pacific jet should be displaced westward with increased winds over India. Such changes actually occurred in this period (see Paegle et al., 1983b). Similar short-term tropical–extratropical connections have been cited in association with Brazilian rainfall and subtropical jets (Kousky, 1984a), the Asian monsoon and the Australian jet (Wilde, 1984), and the Southern Hemisphere monsoon and the Asian jet (Chang and Lau, 1982).

Whereas tropical heating distributions evidently affect the position of the subtropical jet, it is much less clear whether midlatitude long waves may be locked to the subtropical jet enhancements in simple ways (Simmons et al., 1983) and thus whether there is a direct association between the winter–spring long-wave transitions of North America (Table 1) and the rearrangement of the tropical heating of the western hemisphere.

## REFERENCES

Almeyda, G. F., 1983. Cloud systems and weather forecasting in Peru. Presented at the First Conference on Southern Hemisphere Meteorology, São José dos Campos, Brazil, August 1983.

Anthes, R. A., 1972. Development of asymmetries in a three-dimensional numerical model of the tropical cyclone, *Mon. Wea. Rev.* **100**, 461–476.

Anthes, R. A., Kuo, Y. H., Benjamin, S. G., and Li, Y. F., 1982. The evolution of the mesoscale environment of severe local storms: Preliminary modeling results, *Mon. Wea. Rev.* **110**, 1187–1213.

Astling, E. G., Paegle, J., Miller, E., and O'Brien, C. J., 1985. Boundary layer control of nocturnal convection on a synoptic scale system, *Mon. Wea. Rev.* **113**, 540–552.

Baker, W. E. and Paegle, J., 1983. The influence of the tropics on the prediction of ultra-long waves. Part I: Tropical wind field, *Mon. Wea. Rev.* **111**, 1341–1355.

Bannon, P. R., 1981. Synoptic-scale forcing of coastal lows: Forced double Kelvin waves in the atmosphere, *Quart. J. Roy. Meteor. Soc.* **107**, 313–327.

Bergeron, T., 1928. Über die dreidimensional verknupfende Wetteranalyse I. *Geofys. Publikasjoner* **5**, 1–111.

Bjerknes, J., 1966. A possible response of the atmosphere Hadley circulation to equatorial anomalies of ocean temperature, *Tellus* **18**, 820–829.

Bjerknes, J., 1969. Atmospheric teleconnections from the equatorial Pacific, *Mon. Wea. Rev.* **97**, 163–172.

Bjerknes, J., 1972. Large-scale atmospheric response to the 1964–65 Pacific equatorial warming, *J. Phys. Oceanogr.* **2**, 212–217.

Blackmon, M. L., Geisler, J. E., and Pitcher, E. J., 1983. A general circulation model study of January climate anomaly patterns associated with interannual variation of equatorial Pacific sea surface temperature, *J. Atmos. Sci.* **40**, 1410–1425.

Blake, D. W., Krishnamurti, T. N., Low-Nam, S. V., and Fein, J. S., 1983. Heat low over the Saudi Arabian desert during May 1979 (Summer MONEX), *Mon. Wea. Rev.* **111**, 1759–1775.

Bonner, W. D., 1968. Climatology of the low level jet, *Mon. Wea. Rev.* **96**, 833–850.

Buchmann, J., Silva-Dias, P. L., and Moura, A. D., 1984. Transient convection over the Amazon/Bolivia region and the dynamics of droughts over Northeast Brazil, presented at the WMO Symposium on Meteorological Aspects of Tropical Droughts, Fortaleza, C. E., September 24–28, 1984.

Chang, C.-P., and Lau, K. M., 1980. Northeasterly cold surges and near equatorial disturbances over the Winter MONEX area during December 1974. Part II: Planetary-scale aspects, *Mon. Wea. Rev.* **108**, 298–312.

Chang, C.-P., and Lau, K. M., 1982. Short-term planetary scale interactions over the tropics and midlatitudes during Northern Winter. Part I: Contrasts between active and inactive periods. *Mon. Wea. Rev.* **110**, 933–946.

Charney, J. G., 1947. The dynamics of long waves in a baroclinic westerly current, *J. Meteor.* **4**, 135–162.

Charney, J. G., 1975. Dynamics of deserts and droughts in the Sahel. *Quart. J. Roy. Meteor. Soc.* **101**, 193–202.

Charney, J. G., and Eliassen, A., 1949. A numerical method for predicting the perturbations of the middle-latitude westerlies, *Tellus* **1**, 38–54.

Charney, J. G. and Eliassen, A., 1964. On the growth of the hurricane depression, *J. Atmos. Sci.* **21**, 68–75.

Dickinson, R. E., 1971a. Analytic model for zonal winds in the tropics, I: Details of the model and simulation of gross features of the zonal mean troposphere, *Mon. Wea. Rev.* **99**, 501–510.

Dickinson, R. E., 1971b. Analytic model for zonal wind in the tropics, II: Variation of the tropospheric mean structure with season and differences between hemispheres, *Mon. Wea. Rev.* **99**, 511–523.

Dickinson, R. E., 1971c. Cross-equatorial momentum fluxes as evidence of tropical planetary wave sources. *Quart. J. Roy. Meteor. Soc.* **97**, 554–558.

Eady, E. J., 1949. Long waves and cyclone waves, *Tellus* **1**, 33–52.

Geisler, J. E., 1981. A linear model of the Walker Circulation, *J. Atmos. Sci.* **38**, 1390–1400.

Gill, A. E., 1980. Some simple solutions for heat induced tropical circulations, *Quart. J. Roy. Meteor. Soc.* **106**, 447–462.

Gray, W. M., 1983. Association of global tropical cyclone activity with the El Niño stratospheric QBO, and winter hemisphere surge influences, in *Proceedings of the First International Conference on Southern Hemisphere Meteorology*, American Meteorological Society, Boston, MA.

Gray, W. M. and Jacobson, R. W., Jr., 1977. Diurnal variation in deep, oceanic convection, *Mon. Wea. Rev.* **105**, 1171–1188.

Grose, W. L. and Hoskins, B. J., 1979. On the influence of orography on large-scale atmospheric flow, *J. Atmos. Sci.* **36**, 223–234.

Hastenrath, S. and Heller, L., 1977. Dynamics of climatic hazards in Northeast Brazil, *Quart. J. Roy. Meteor. Soc.* **103**, 77–92.

Held, I. M. and Hou, A. Y., 1980. Nonlinear axially symmetric circulation in a nearly inviscid atmosphere, *J. Atmos. Sci.* **37**, 515–533.

Hoskins, B. J., 1976. Baroclinic waves and frontogenesis. Part I: Introduction and Eady waves, *Quart. J. Roy. Meteor. Soc.* **102**, 103–122.

Houze, R. A., Jr., 1977. Structure and dynamics of a tropical squall-line system, *Mon. Wea. Rev.* **105**, 1540–1567.

Houze, R. A., Jr., 1982. Cloud clusters and large scale vertical motions in the tropics, *J. Meteor. Soc. Japan* **60**, 396–410.

Houze, R. A., Jr. and Hobbs, P. V., 1982. Organization and structure of precipitating cloud systems, *Adv. Geophys.* **24**, 225–315.

Julian, P. R., and Chervin, R. M., 1978. A study of the Southern Oscillation and Walker Circulation phenomonen, *Mon. Wea. Rev.* **106**, 1433–1451.

Kalnay, E. and Halem, M., 1981. Large amplitude stationary Rossby waves in the Southern Hemisphere, Proceedings of the International Conference on Early Results of FGGE and Large-Scale Aspects of its Monsoon Experiments, January 12–17, Tallahassee, FL.

Kousky, V. E., 1979. Frontal influences on Northeast Brazil, *Mon. Wea. Rev.* **107**, 1140–1153.

Kousky, V. E., 1980. Diurnal rainfall variation in Northeast Brazil, *Mon. Wea. Rev.* **108**, 488–498.

Kousky, V. E., 1984a. Atmospheric circulation changes associated with rainfall anomalies over tropical Brazil, presented at the First Meeting of Principal Investigators of the USA–Brazil Cooperative Program in Meteorology: Studies of Convection over the Amazon River Basin and Interaction with Large Scale Circulations in Higher Latitudes, March 5–6, 1984.

Kousky, V. E., 1984b. Atmospheric circulation changes associated with rainfall anomalies over tropical Brazil, presented at the WMO Symposium on Tropical Droughts, September 22–26, 1984, Fortaleza, Brazil.

Kousky, V. E. and Ferreira, N. J., 1981. Interdiurnal surface pressure variation in Brazil: Their spatial distributions, origins and effects, *Mon. Wea. Rev.* **109,** 1999–2008.

Kousky, V. E. and Gan, M. A., 1981. Upper tropospheric cyclonic vortices in the tropical South Atlantic, *Tellus* **33,** 538–551.

Kousky, V. E., Kagano, M. T., and Cavalcanti, I. F. A., 1984. A review of the southern oscillation: Oceanic-atmospheric circulation changes and related rainfall anomalies, *Tellus* **36A,** 490–504.

Krishnamurti, T. N., Kanamitsu, M., Koss, W. J., and Lee, J. D., 1973. Tropical east–west circulation during the northern winter, *J. Atmos. Sci.* **31,** 780–787.

Kung, E. C. and Tanaka, H., 1983. Energetics analysis of the global circulation during the special observing periods of FGGE, *J. Atmos. Sci.* **40,** 2575–2592.

Kuo, H. L., 1952. Three-dimensional disturbances in a baroclinic zonal current, *J. Meteor.* **9,** 260–278.

Kuo, H. L., 1956. Forced and free meridional circulations in the atmosphere, *J. Meteor.* **13,** 561–568.

Kuo, H. L., 1965. On the formation and intensification of tropical cyclones through latent heat release by cumulus convection, *J. Atmos. Sci.* **22,** 40–63.

Kuo, H. L. and Qian, Y. F., 1981. Influence of Tibetan Plateau on cumulative and diurnal changes of weather and climate in summer, *Mon. Wea. Rev.* **109,** 2337–2358.

Kurihara, Y. and Tuleya, R. E., 1974. Structure of a tropical cyclone developed in a three-dimensional numerical simulation model, *J. Atmos. Sci.* **31,** 893–919.

Lim, H. and Chang, C. P. 1981. A theory for mid-latitude forcing of tropical motions during winter monsoons, *J. Atmos. Sci.* **38,** 2377–2392.

Lorenz, E. N., 1967. *The Nature and the Theory of the General Circulation in the Atmosphere,* Word Meteorological Organization, Publication No. 218, T.P. 115, Geneva, Switzerland.

Madden, R. A. and Julian, P. R., 1972. Description of global-scale circulation cells in the tropics with a 40–50 day period, *J. Atmos. Sci.* **29,** 1109–1123.

Miller, E. R., 1982. Diurnal oscillation of boundary layer flow over synoptic scale sloping terrain, Master's thesis, Department of Meteorology, University of Utah, Salt Lake City, UT.

Minnis, P., Gibson, G. G., and Denn, F. M., 1983. Diurnal cloud variations over South America, presented at First International Conference on Southern Hemisphere Meteorology of the American Meteorological Society, São José dos Campos, Brazil, August 1983, pp. 329–332.

Mintz, Y., 1984. The sensitivity of numerically simulated climates to land-surface boundary conditions, in J. T. Houghton, Ed., *The Global Climate*, Cambridge University Press, Cambridge England.

Molion, L. C. B., 1975. A climatonomic study of the energy and moisture fluxes of the Amazonia Basin with consideration of deforestation effects, Doctoral Dissertation, University of Wisconsin.

Moura, A. and Shukla, J., 1981. On the dynamics of droughts in Northeast Brazil: Observations, theory and numerical experiments with a general circulation model, *J. Atmos. Sci.* **38**, 2653–2675.

Murakami, T., 1982. Large scale aspects of topography, Paper presented at *Winter Monex Workshop*, Monterey, CA, June 14–15, 1982.

Namias, J., 1972. Influence of Northern Hemisphere general circulation on drought in Northeast Brazil, *Tellus* **24**, 336–343.

Newell, R. E., Kidson, J. W., Vincent, D. G., and Boer, G. J., 1972. *The General Circulation of the Tropical Atmosphere and Interactions with Extratropical Latitudes*, vols. 1 and 2, MIT, Cambridge, MA.

NOAA, 1984a. *Climate Diagnostics Bulletin, February 1984*, NOAA/National Weather Analysis Center, Washington, DC.

NOAA, 1984b. *Climate Diagnostics Bulletin, May 1984*, NOAA/National Weather Analysis Center, Washington, DC.

NOAA, 1984c. *Climate Diagnostics Bulletin, August 1984*, NOAA/National Weather Analysis Center, Washington, DC.

NOAA, 1984d. *Climate Diagnostics Bulletin, November, 1984*, NOAA/National Weather Analysis Center, Washington, DC.

Norquist, D. C., Recker, E. E., and Reed, R. J., 1977. The energetics of African wave disturbances as observed during phase III of GATE, *Mon. Wea. Rev.* **105**, 334–342.

Ooyama, K., 1969. Numerical simulation of the life cycle of tropical cyclones, *J. Atmos. Sci.* **26**, 3–40.

Paegle, J., 1978. A linearized analysis of diurnal boundary layer convergence over the topography of the United States, *Mon. Wea. Rev.* **106**, 492–502.

Paegle, J., 1984. Topographically induced low-level jets, presented at the Third Conference on Mountain Meteorology of the American Meteorogical Society, Portland, Oregon, October 1984, pp. 85–88.

Paegle, J. and Baker, W. E., 1982a. Planetary-scale characteristics of the atmospheric circulation during January and February 1979, *J. Atmos. Sci.* **39**, 2521–2538.

Paegle, J. and Baker, W. E., 1982b. Global-scale weekly and monthly energetics during January and February 1979, *J. Atmos. Sci.* **39**, 2750–2759.

Paegle, J. and Baker, W. E., 1983. The influence of the tropics on the prediction of ultra-long waves. Part II: Latent heating, *Mon. Wea. Rev.* **111**, 1356–1371.

Paegle, J. and Geisler, J. E., 1986. The effect of East African topography on flow driven by zonally symmetric forcing, *J. Atmos. Sci.* **43**, in press.

Paegle, J. and McLawhorn, D. W., 1983. Numerical simulation of diurnal convergence oscillations above sloping terrain, *Mon. Wea. Rev.* **111**, 67–85.

Paegle, J. and Rasch, G., 1973. Three-dimensional characteristics of diurnally varying boundary-layer flows, *Mon. Wea. Rev.* **101**, 746–756.

Paegle, J., Paegle, J. N., Ereno, C., and Collini, E. A., 1983a. Diurnal oscillations of convective weather and boundary-layer flows in South America, presented at Anais 2° Congreso Brasileiro de Meteorologia.

Paegle, J., Paegle, J. N., and Lewis, F. P., 1983b. Large scale motions of the tropics in observations and theory, *Pageoph* 121(5/6), 947–982.

Paegle, J., Paegle, J. N., and Hong, Y. 1983c. The role of barotropic oscillations within atmospheres of highly variable refractive index, *J. Atmos. Sci.* **40**, 2251–2265.

Paegle, J. N., Paegle, J., and Zhao, Z. 1984. Intercomparison of 200 mb global wind fields from level III-b data sets, presented at the WMO, GWE Workshop on Tropical Meteorology, October 1984.

Paegle, J., Paegle, J. N., McCorcle, M., and Miller, E., 1984. Diagnoses and numerical simulation of a low-level jet during ALPEX, *Beitr. Phys. Atmos.* **57**, 419–430.

Quiroz, R. S., 1983. The climate of the "El Niño" winter of 1982–83. A season of extraordinary climate anomalies, *Mon. Wea. Rev.* **111**, 1685–1706.

Ramage, C. S., 1968. Role of tropical "maritime continent" in the atmospheric circulation, *Mon. Wea. Rev.* **96**, 365–370.

Rasmusson, E. M. and Wallace, J. M., 1983. Meteorological aspects of the El Niño Southern Oscillation, *Science* **222**, 1195–1202.

Reed, R. J., 1983. The diurnal variation of precipitation in the tropics, presented at the First International Conference on Southern Hemisphere Meteorology of the American Meteorological Society, São José dos Campos, Brazil, August 1983, pp. 312–319.

Riehl, H., 1977. Venezuelan rain systems and the general circulation of the summer tropics I: Rain system, *Mon. Wea. Rev.* **105**, 1402–1420.

Rowntree, P. R., 1976. Response of the atmosphere to a tropical Atlantic Ocean temperature anomaly, *Quart. J. Roy. Meteor. Soc.* **102**, 607–625.

Sampson, G. W., 1982. Selected analyses of the first global atmospheric research project global experiment special observing period one data, Master's Thesis, Department of Meteorology, University of Utah, Salt Lake City, UT.

Schneider, E. K., 1977. Axially symmetric steady-state models of the basic state for instability and climate studies. Part II: Nonlinear calculations, *J. Atmos. Sci.* **34**, 263–279.

Schneider, E. K. and Lindzen, R. S. 1977. Axially symmetric steady-state models of the basic state for instability and climate studies, *J. Atmos. Sci.* **34**, 263–279.

Schubert, W. H., Hack, J. J., Silva-Dias, P. L., and Fulton, S. R., 1980. Geostrophic adjustment in an axi-symmetric vortex, *J. Atmos. Sci.* **37**, 1464–1484.

Silva Dias, P., 1983. Diurnally forced tropical tropospheric circulation over South America. Presented at the First Conference on Southern Hemisphere Meteorology, São José dos Campos, Brazil.

Silva-Dias, P. and Paegle, J. N., 1984. The partition of energy associated with tropical heat sources, presented at the First National Workshop on the Scientific Results of the Global Weather Experiment, Woods Hole, MA, July 9–20, 1984.

Silva-Dias, P., Schubert, W. H., and DeMaria, M., 1983. Large scale response of a tropical atmosphere to transient convection, *J. Atmos. Sci.* **40**, 2689–2707.

Simmons, A. J., 1982. The forcing of stationary wave motion by tropical diabatic heating, *Quart. J. Roy. Meteor. Soc.* **108**, 503–534.

Simmons, A. J., Wallace, J. M., and Branstator, G. W., 1983. Barotropic wave propagation and instability, and atmospheric teleconnection patterns, *J. Atmos. Sci.* **40**, 1363–1392.

Smagorinsky, J., 1953. The dynamical influence of large-scale heat sources and sinks on the quasi-stationary mean motions of the atmosphere, *Quart. J. Roy. Meteor. Soc.* **79**, 342–366.

Trenberth, K. E., 1976. Spatial and temporal variations of the Southern Oscillation, *Quart. J. Roy. Meteor. Soc.* **102**, 639–653.

Virji, H., 1981. A preliminary study of summertime tropospheric circulation patterns over South America estimated from cloud winds, *Mon. Wea. Rev.* **109**, 599–610.

Wagner, 1977. Weather and circulation of January 1977: The coldest month on record in the Ohio Valley, *Mon. Wea. Rev.* **105**, 553–560.

Walker, G. T., 1928. Ceara (Brazil) famines and the general air movement, *Beitr. Phys. Frein. Atmos.* **14**, 88–93.

Walker, G. T. and Bliss, E. W., 1932. World weather V, *Mem. Roy. Meteor. Soc.* **4**, 53–84.

Wallace, J. M., 1975. Diurnal variations in precipitation, and thunderstorm frequency over the coterminous United States, *Mon. Wea. Rev.* **103**, 406–419.

Webster, P. J., 1982. Seasonality in the local and remote atmospheric response to sea surface temperature anomalies, *J. Atmos. Sci.* **39**, 41–52.

Wilde, T., 1984. Hemispheric interactions associated with the Asiatic summer monsoon, Master's thesis, University of Utah, Salt Lake City, UT.

Williams, R. T., 1967. Atmospheric frontogenesis: A numerical experiment, *J. Atmos. Sci.* **24**, 627–641.

Wyrtki, K., 1975. El Niño: The dynamic response of the Equatorial Pacific Ocean to atmospheric forcing, *J. Phys. Oceanogr.* **5**, 572–584.

Yanai, M., 1964. Formation of tropical cyclones, *Rev. Geophys.* **2**, 367–413.

Yeh, E. N., 1983. Prediction of atmospheric flow and dispersion over sloping terrain, Doctoral dissertation, University of Utah, Salt Lake City, UT.

# ☐ COMMENTS ON "INTERACTIONS BETWEEN CONVECTIVE AND LARGE-SCALE MOTIONS OVER AMAZONIA"

**John M. Wallace**

Jan Paegle's essay entitled "Interactions between Convective and Large-Scale Motions over Amazonia" provides a number of revealing glimpses into the causes and effects of the deep, precipitating cloud masses that often obscure the skies above the forest canopy.

   The contribution first discusses a wide range of tropical motion systems that play a role in organizing precipitation; the list includes fronts, waves, vortices, hurricanes, the intertropical convergence zone, the Hadley cell, the Walker circulation, and 30–50-day oscillations; then it deals with the influence of sea surface temperature and soil moisture on tropical precipitation; finally, it considers the remote response to changes in the distribution of tropical precipitation, such as might be caused by deforestation. Some of the material is rather technical in content, but the interdisciplinary reader who has the fortitude to work through it will be rewarded with some interesting and useful perspectives on current research in tropical meteorology. The author has made a concerted effort to keep the discussion focused on a few main themes so that the reader does not lose sight of the forest for the trees. The essay provides some good illustrations of the important role that numerical models are playing in this research, but the author is careful to point out the limitations of the models and the inherent ambiguities in many of the results derived from them. With only a few minor exceptions, the discussion is balanced and the scientific arguments are basically sound.

   As one who works with atmospheric observations, as opposed to models, I view the interactions between convective and large-scale motions over Amazonia from a somewhat different perspective than Professor Paegle. I am continually struck by how little we know about day-to-day weather in this part of the world. Our ignorance is well justified: The weather systems that produce precipitation over the Amazon Basin are complex and subtle phenomena that are not adequately resolved by the kind of surface meteorological data routinely available from this region.

   The complexity and subtlety of these systems are fully apparent when they are viewed from space. Convective cloudiness over the tropical oceans tends to be organized in the waves and vortices as Paegle mentions. The satellite imagery reveals discrete "cloud clusters," 5000–10,000 km across, with lifetimes much longer than the individual convective cells from which they are formed. These features can be tracked over periods of days or longer as they move across the oceans, and they can be identified with well-defined perturbations in the wind field. Episodes of heavy rainfall occurring at widely separated tropical islands several days apart can sometimes be identified with the same weather disturbance and its attendant cloud cluster. When the same satellite images are averaged together for a week or longer, cloud clusters tend to merge together to form remarkably continuous bands of cloudiness extending across the Atlantic and most of the Pacific, a few hundred kilometers in width. These bands, which usually lie between 4°N and 10°N, correspond to the intertropical convergence zone (ITCZ) as mentioned by Paegle.

   The satellite imagery shows evidence of widespread cloudiness over Amazonia, but it is much more difficult to identify and track discrete cloud clusters over the region than it is over the oceans. The predominant features evident in the imagery are the convective complexes themselves, which have spatial dimensions up to a few hundred kilometers and characteristic lifetimes on the order of 3–12 h. The features most evident in the imagery are the stratiform anvils, which consist of cirroform clouds in the upper troposphere. The anvils are formed when the updrafts in the cumulonimbus clouds encounter an increasingly stable environment as they approach the tropical tropopause, which causes them to lose their buoyancy and spread out horizontally. It is now believed that much of the rainfall over Amazonia and other parts of the tropics falls from such cloud layers. Their existence profoundly influences the nature of the interactions between convective and large-scale motions. The explosive growth of these anvils in the satellite imagery inspired the term *popcorn cumulonimbus*, which was widely used to describe the cloud patterns over Amazonia in the early satellite imagery. In time-lapse infrared-imagery the diurnal rhythm is evident as a pervasive but complex redistribution of convective activity through the course of the day. There are also regional and day-to-day variations in the intensity of convective activity, but they are much more subtle than their oceanic counterparts discussed in Paegle's essay.

The difficulty of the problem of understanding the large-scale organization of precipitation over Amazonia is compounded by the fact that remarkably little hourly and daily rainfall data from Amazonia have found its way into the open literature. Hence it has not been possible to carry out fundamental analyses such as the documentation of the diurnal cycle in rainfall or the comparison of spatial and temporal autocorrelation functions of rainfall over Amazonia with their oceanic counterparts. Paegle mentions some recent studies of the role of fronts and cyclones in organizing rainfall patterns over Amazonia, but I would have enjoyed more discussion of this topic.

The seasonal distribution of rainfall over Amazonia, which is not discussed by Paegle, is an important aspect of the climate that poses some challenging problems for theoreticians and modelers. In common with monsoon climates throughout the subtropics, the northern and southern reaches of Amazonia experience pronounced wet (summer) and dry (winter) seasons. However, the northern wet season appears to be centered in May and June, about two months earlier than its counterparts in Africa and Asia. In the equatorial zone of eastern Brazil, the heaviest rainfall occurs in the period from February through June for reasons that are not at all obvious. Understanding these seasonal variations is important because the climatic effects of deforestation may well prove to be seasonally dependent. Seasonal climate changes such as the prolongation of the dry season may have greater ecological impacts than decreases in mean annual rainfall.

Paegle argues that the climatic impacts of the deforestation of Amazonia may be felt beyond the confines of the region itself and that the climate of the United States, in particular, may be sensitive to the presence or absence of heavy rainfall over Amazonia. The results that he presents are suggestive and, I might add, constitute only part of the modeling evidence that could be put forward in support of this argument. However, I fully agree with Paegle's overall assessment that the modeling results are as yet inconclusive with regard to specific remote effects of Amazon basin deforestation.

# Chapter 18

# On the Dynamic Climatology of the Amazon Basin and Associated Rain-Producing Mechanisms

**Luiz C. B. Molion**

The climate of a region is determined by factors acting on both global and regional scales. The most important are the general circulation of the atmosphere acting on the region, the local topography, the nature of surface cover, the hydrological cycle, and the influence of ocean currents if the region is coastal.

The general circulation of the atmosphere, which is a consequence of the latitudinal distribution of solar energy and the asymmetric distribution of land and oceans, imposes the general characteristics of a region's climate. The hydrological cycle is not only a component of climate itself but also of the biogeophysical landscape. Its influence on climate is more than the interaction between the atmospheric moisture, rainfall, and runoff.

This chapter deals with the macro- and mesoscale tropospheric circulations acting on the Amazon region and the associated dynamical mechanisms that promote rainfall in the area.

## LARGE-SCALE MEAN CIRCULATION

Until recently, the mean tropospheric circulation over the Amazon Basin had been studied using conventional radiosonde data of just a few stations. For instance, Newell, Kidson, Vincent, and Boer (1972) analyzed the streamline fields for 850 and 200 mb between 45°N and 45°S, but their analyses included less than 2 y of data from Manaus and Belém. More recent works on the Amazon troposphere used longer data series but still only a few stations (e.g., Sobral, 1979; Kagano, 1979).

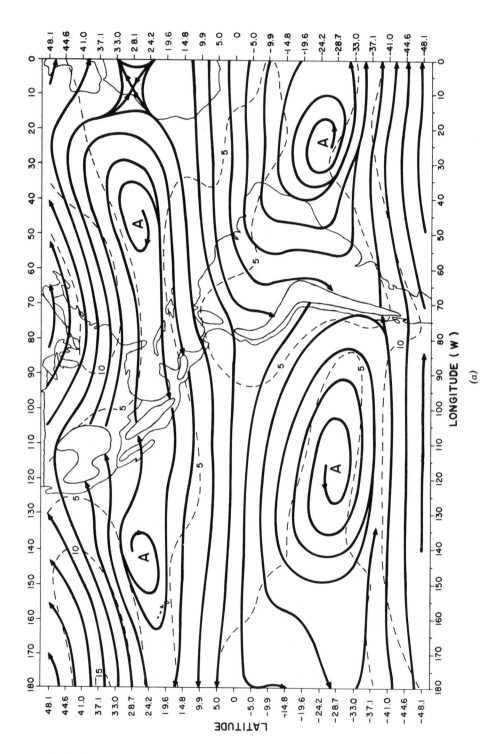

**FIGURE 1.** (a) Streamlines representing the mean tropospheric flow for January (summer) at 850 mb (Kousky, 1983); "A" refers to the center of a high pressure cell.

LONGITUDE ( W )

LATITUDE

*(a)*

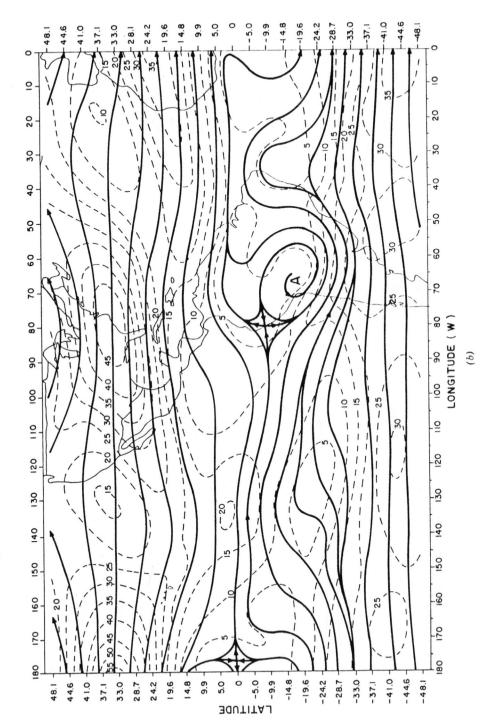

**FIGURE 1.** (b) Streamlines representing the mean tropospheric flow for January (summer) at 250 mb (Kousky, 1983).

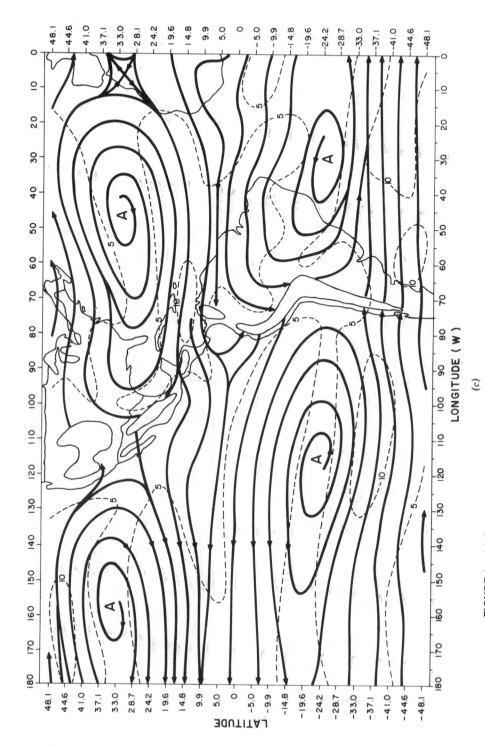

**FIGURE 1.** (c) Streamlines representing the mean tropospheric flow for July (winter) at 850 mb (Kousky, 1983).

394

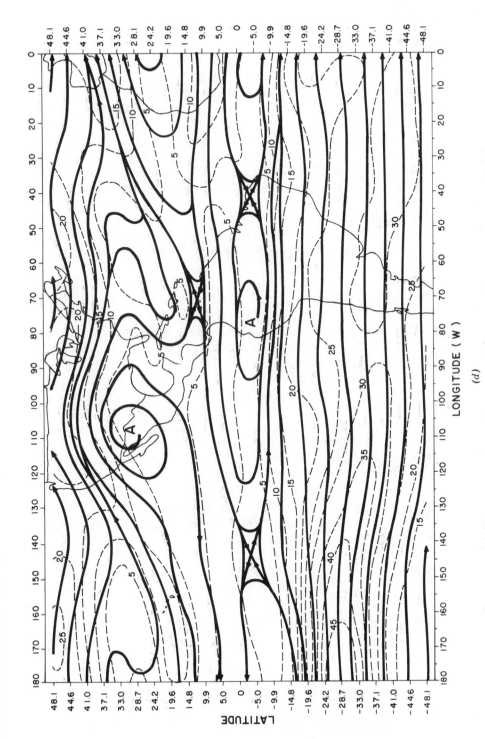

**FIGURE 1.** (*d*) Streamlines representing the mean tropospheric flow for July (winter) at 250 mb (Kousky, 1983).

On the other hand, the geostationary satellites (SMS/GOES series) with a high-frequency coverage can be used to compute the wind fields from cloud motion. Virji (1980) was the first to use this technique to study the patterns of the summer circulation over South America. Kousky (1983) used the U.S. National Meteorological Center data set for the 1970–1975 period, which combines conventional and satellite data, and produced revised mean streamline charts for two levels, 850 and 250 mb, and for two typical months—January (summer) and July (winter). These are reproduced as Fig. 1. Comparison of the Southern Hemisphere streamlines in Figs. 1a and 1c shows that at the 850-mb level the subtropical Atlantic and Pacific anticyclones (A) are present in both seasons. In the winter, the Pacific anticyclone center is displaced slightly equatorward from its summer position, whereas the Atlantic anticyclone center remains at approximately the same latitude but approaches the South American coast. There seems to be no significant difference in the mean low-level tropospheric flow between these seasons.

At the 250-mb level, however, there is a strong seasonal variation in the mean tropospheric flow, from basically meridional motion during January (Fig. 1b) to a highly zonal motion during July (Fig. 1d). The meridional nature of the summer flow is a direct result of the strong heating of the surface (releasing sensible heat) and of latent heat release by condensation of water vapor throughout the tropospheric column. This heating produces a thermally driven circulation cell with hot humid air rising over the continent and dry air descending over the adjacent oceanic areas. Figure 2 is a schematic representation of this direct circulation cell. According to Gill (1980), however, the eastern branch of the zonal component of such a circulation, known as a Walker circulation, may be more extended than the western one. Thus, air subsides over a large region eastward of the center of the ascending air. In the case of South America, the sinking motion extends from the eastern Amazon to western Africa, including the northeastern part of Brazil. The ascending branch of this Walker circulation causes an intense development of deep convective clouds and high rainfall, whereas the descending branch

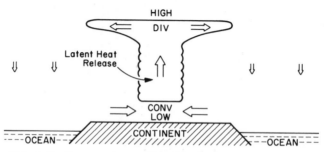

**FIGURE 2.**  Schematic diagram representing the circulation that results from the differential heating of the continent and oceans in the summer.

SMØØTHED   MINTZ/JAEGER MØNTHLY MEAN PRECIPITATIØN   SMØØTHED

## MEAN RAIN (MM/DAY) FOR ANNUAL

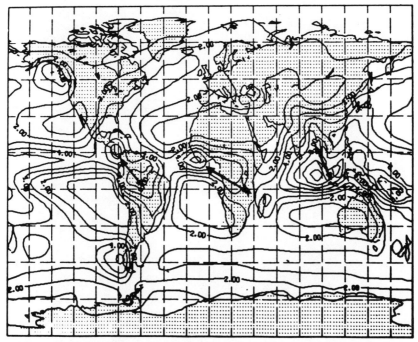

**FIGURE 3.**   Global annual precipitation (in mm day$^{-1}$) (map prepared at GLAS based on data from Jaeger, 1976). Arrows indicate the direction of displacement of maximum precipitation centers between summer and winter. (Courtesy of Dr. C. A. Nobre, INPE, Brazil.)

inhibits cloud formation and rainfall. This pattern is evident in the mean global rainfall distribution pattern (Fig. 3): more than 6 mm day$^{-1}$ in the Amazon Basin (ascending branch) and less than 1 mm day$^{-1}$ in the subtropical oceans (descending branch).

The thermally driven circulation over the heated region gives convergence of air and low atmospheric pressure at low levels and divergence of air and high pressure at high levels. The seasonal variability, both in intensity and position, of the high-pressure system in the upper troposphere is directly related to the spatial and temporal distribution of rainfall (Kousky and Kagano, 1981). As the high pressure weakens and moves north in the winter (see Figs. 1*b* and 1*d*), the southern and eastern portions of the Amazon experience their dry season, as seen in the mean brightness maps from satellite-visible imagery (Fig. 4). Northwest South America has no dry season. By October the high-pressure system starts moving back to the mean summer position, and the end of the dry season progresses from central to eastern Amazon.

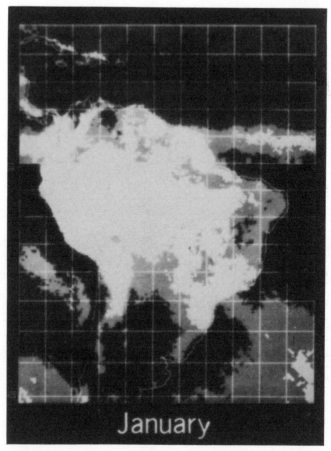

**FIGURE 4.** Mean cloudiness over South America. Mosaic prepared with polar orbiting satellite imagery (14:00 LT) for the period 1967–1970 (Miller and Feddes, 1971).

Another general circulation feature related to rainfall on the northeastern coast of Amazonia is the intertropical convergence zone (ITCZ) over the equatorial Atlantic. The ITCZ is formed by the confluence of Northern Hemisphere and Southern Hemisphere trade winds. Hastenrath and Lamb (1977) showed that, over the Atlantic, the ITCZ moves southward progressively from its northernmost position during the Southern Hemisphere winter and reaches its southernmost position by the end of summer (March). Thus, the ITCZ is responsible for most of the rainfall in Amazon coastal areas. Some authors (e.g., Trewartha, 1961; Ratisbona, 1976) mention the existence of a continental ITCZ during the summer. Figure 5 shows the region of high rainfall along the coast near the mouth of the Amazon River, but other maxima occur inland in the central–southern and northwestern portions of the basin, with a noticeable minimum in between. There is no evidence from

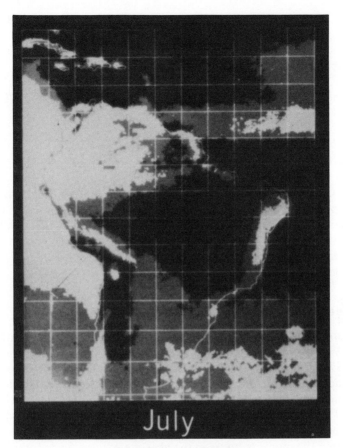

**FIGURE 4.** *(continued)*

ANNUAL RAINFALL (m) NORTHERN BRAZIL

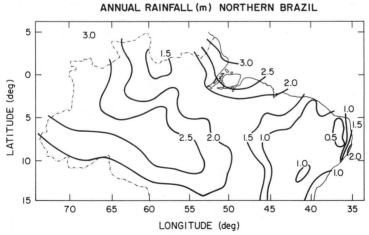

**FIGURE 5.** Isolines of mean annual rainfall over Brazil. [Redrafted from Ratisbona (1976) with permission of Elsevier Science Publishers, copyright 1976.]

satellite imagery (Fig. 4) for the existence of an east–west cloud band over the continent.

The low tropospheric flow from the two hemispheres may mix laterally and vertically in storms without maintaining a clear boundary zone (Taljaard, 1972).

## TRANSIENT DISTURBANCES

Transient disturbances might be classified according to their time scale, varying from local mesoscale convection, which has lifetimes of minutes to hours, to cumulonimbus clusters, which are organized by the extratropical large-scale features of the tropospheric flow and may last for several days. In this section, the regional mesoscale disturbances are treated first and then those associated with the synoptic-scale circulation.

### Mesoscale Tropical Systems

A fairly large number of studies on the behavior and structure of mesoscale tropical systems over Africa have been made (e.g., Aspliden et al., 1976; House, 1977; Fortune, 1980) as a result of GATE. Adequate conventional data are lacking for the Amazon Basin. The only resource available for the study of the formation and propagation of cloud systems is satellite imagery. Johnson (1970) noticed the presence of a large number of cloud clusters that develop and dissipate daily. The development of convective cells normally begins during the morning hours in the absence of large-scale forcing. These cells undergo a selection process by which the larger ones grow, forming clusters or lines, whereas the smaller ones are suppressed. The formation of a line or a cluster depends on the tropospheric flow pattern, as shown schematically in Fig. 6. With a moderate wind field, the new convective cells form downwind of the original cell. The cooler downdrafts of the original cell act as mini–frontal zones raising the ambient humid air. The new cells form in an arched line (Fig. 6a). When the wind is weak, the new cells surround the decaying original cell as a ring or a cluster that continues to grow at the expense of downdrafts (Fig. 6b).

Recently, Cavalcanti (1982) demonstrated that the sea breeze circulation

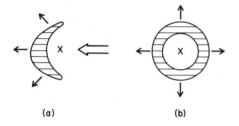

(a)                                (b)

**FIGURE 6.** Schematic diagram showing the formation of instability lines and cumulonimbus clusters: (a) with moderate wind field; (b) with weak wind field. The × indicates the position of the original convective cell.

organizes convection over coastal areas near the mouth of the Amazon River. The convective lines form outside the coast because of sea breeze convergence and propagate inland, reaching Belém in the afternoon and decaying after sunset, as a result of reduced thermal contrast. There are times, however, when these instability lines remain active for more than 48 h and propagate inland as far as the Andes Mountains. During the night they become less active, but the next day they intensify because of the strong surface heating. They may propagate with speeds of about 10° longitude per day. Figure 7 (Kousky, 1983), showing an example of these lines, was constructed using the technique described by Wallace (1970). The mosaic is composed of GOES satellite image sections extending from 5°N to 5°S latitude, starting at 03:18 GMT on January 21, 1980, and ending at 21:18 GMT on January 25 with a 3-h time interval. The propagation of the instability lines is indicated by bright diagonal bands of cloudiness. These lines may be over 1000 km long, whereas the ones formed by the process depicted in Fig. 6a seldom reach 500 km.

The sea breeze convergence may not be the only dynamical mechanism forming these mesoscale traveling disturbances. Some of the lines form along the coast during the evening and appear to be associated with deep penetration of Northern Hemisphere frontal systems in the subtropics near the equator. This deep penetration appears to cause disturbances in the trade winds field, which propagate westward and meet the land breeze, creating a convergence zone and deep convection along the coast. They eventually propagate inland, as shown in Fig. 7.

One interesting aspect of the mean rainfall distribution in the Amazon Basin is the minimum of rainfall, oriented northwest–southeast, between the coastal maximum and central southern maximum. The propagation of the mesoscale disturbances may contribute to this dryness. Their passage over the region of minimum rainfall occurs during nighttime, when they are less intense and, therefore, produce less precipitation.

### Synoptic-Scale Influence

Several authors have described the effects of Southern Hemisphere cold front penetration into the Amazon during the Southern Hemisphere winter (e.g., Trewartha, 1961; Brinkmann et al., 1971; Parmenter, 1976; Ratisbona, 1976). Most of these descriptions emphasized the sharp 15–20°C decrease in temperature, which lasts for 3–5 days, and its consequence to the environment.

These fronts influence rainfall and penetrate the Amazon throughout the year. Kousky (1979), for example, reports a case study of a January frontal system moving equatorward along the eastern coast of South America, shifting the rainfall maximum from its mean position in western Amazon toward the eastern Amazon and northeast Brazil. Precipitation in the western Amazon was reduced by compensating subsident motion, which inhibits con-

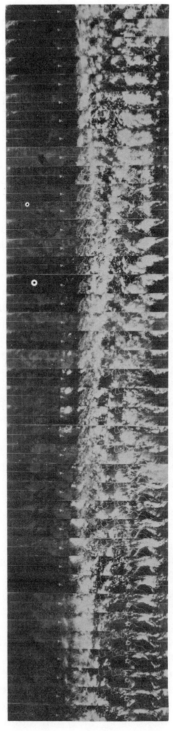

**FIGURE 7.** Composite of satellite images showing the propagation of instability lines in the Amazon. See text for details. (From Kousky, 1983.)

vection. An inspection of geostationary satellite imagery reveals that many frontal systems behave as this one did, especially during the Southern Hemisphere summer.

There are years when frontal systems remain quasi-stationary during the summer, oriented northwest–southeast near 20°S latitude. They organize the convective activity over southern Amazonia, and as a consequence of large rainfall, all the right-bank tributaries of the Amazon River have high flood peaks. These stationary frontal systems are caused by blocking in the Southern Hemisphere tropospheric flow over the Pacific at about 30–40°S latitude and 90–100° W longitude. This situation is associated with an enhanced subtropical jet stream over the eastern coast of Brazil at around 20°S latitude.

## INTERANNUAL VARIABILITY OF RAINFALL

In the tropics, the most important climatological parameter is rainfall. The physical causes of its interannual variability in the Amazon are not yet well known but are certainly tied up with large-scale fluctuations, mainly of the intensity of the high-pressure system (A in Figs. 1b and 1d) in the upper troposphere. In turn, these fluctuations are related to the variability of the latent heat sources over tropical continents.

Large reductions in the annual amount of precipitation appear to be related to the occurrence of strong El Niño–southern oscillation (ENSO) events. The possible relationship between ENSO and droughts or reduction of precipitation has been explained recently (e.g., Kousky et al., 1984): Stronger than normal convection is established over the abnormally warm waters of the eastern equatorial Pacific. The ascending branch of the Walker circulation, which normally is over the western portion of the Amazon, is shifted westward to the warmer ocean and is enhanced by the strong convection. The descending branch covers practically the entire Amazon and reaches the west coast of Africa, causing noticeable reductions in precipitation.

Moura and Kagano (1983) studied the rainfall distribution of 1958 when there was a strong ENSO event. Figure 8, from their work, shows the isolines of standard deviation normalized with respect to the long-term mean precipitation for the period from February to May. Over portions of the western Amazon, northeast Brazil, and central and southern Africa, there were negative deviations exceeding −1.8. Kousky et al. (1984) demonstrated that the 1983 ENSO also affected precipitation in the Amazon. The precipitation totals for the January–May period were about 30% lower than normal for some selected stations in the region.

Other dynamical mechanisms may cause rainfall variability, for example, the enhancement of the Hadley circulation when the ITCZ is located farther north than its normal position. Moura and Shukla (1981) showed that when

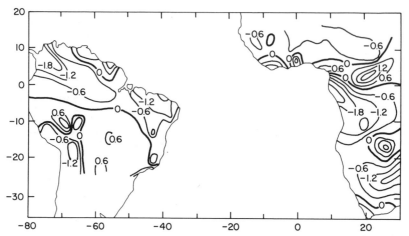

**FIGURE 8.** Patterns of deviations from the mean rainfall total for the 1958 wet season (February–May) normalized with respect to the standard deviation (Moura and Kagano, 1983).

the sea surface temperature (SST) in the subtropical North Atlantic is warmer than normal, and at the same time the SST is colder in the subtropical South Atlantic, the descending branch of the Hadley cell is enhanced, causing strong sinking motions over the central and eastern Amazon. As previously mentioned, deeply penetrating frontal systems of the Southern Hemisphere organize convection over the Amazon. This penetration is affected by tropospheric blocking occurring over southern South America and adjacent Pacific waters. In years with a high frequency of blocking, a small number of frontal systems reach the Amazon, and precipitation is reduced.

## CONNECTIONS TO THE EFFECTS OF DEFORESTATION ON CLIMATE

Weather in Amazonia is affected by a broad spectrum of meteorological phenomena that vary from small-scale cumulus convection to global-scale circulation patterns. Instability lines, associated with sea breezes and disturbances in the easterlies, may explain the alternating maxima and minima in the annual mean rainfall distribution. The interaction among the broad range of processes is important for determining rainfall and its annual variability. One of our main concerns for climate change is the role of man in transforming inadvertently the surface of large land masses by the removal of natural forest. Large-scale deforestation of the Amazon Basin may interfere with the regional climate and possibly also with global climate.

   It is likely that deforestation reduces evaporation locally as indicated by numerical experiments (e.g., Henderson-Sellers and Gornitz, 1984). Since the local source of water vapor for precipitation in the Amazon is of the same magnitude as the advected vapor, a reduction in evaporation would change the hydrological cycle, probably reducing precipitation. The forest, composed of several strata and a litter layer, intercepts about 20% of the annual rainfall. The intercepted rainfall cycles directly back to the atmosphere by evaporation without taking part in the soil moisture cycle. When forest cover is removed, the previously intercepted water will be available to increase the overland flow, changing drastically the monthly runoff pattern, with larger flood peaks in the rainy season and possibly lower river levels in the dry season. The Amazon Basin, with an area of about $7 \times 10^6$ km$^2$, is one of the most important regions on the global scale providing heat to the general circulation (Kasahara and Mizzi, 1983). However, we do not know very well the magnitude of this latent heat contribution and in what way a reduction of precipitation or, equivalently, latent heat release would affect the total amount of heat being transported poleward and consequently the global climate.

In conclusion, there is an urgent need to quantify the interaction between the forest and the atmosphere and to model the possible changes in the hydrological cycle and the global climate resulting from large-scale deforestation.

## ACKNOWLEDGMENTS

The author wishes to thank his colleague Dr. V. B. Rao, who kindly reviewed the manuscript, and Maria de Fátima Santana Massunaga for the expert typing. This work is based on an INPE Technical Report by V. E. Kousky and L. C. B. Molion written in Portuguese.

## REFERENCES

Aspliden, C. I., Tourre, Y., and Sabine, J. B., 1976. Some climatological aspects of West African disturbance lines during GATE, *Mon. Wea. Rev.* **104,** 1029–1035.

Brinkmann, W. L., Weinman, J. A., and Ribeiro, M. N. G., 1971. Air temperatures in central Amazonia. I. *Acta Amazôn.* **1,** 51–56.

Cavalcanti, I. F. A., 1982. Um estudo sobre interações entre sistemas de circulação de escala sinótica e circulações locais, MSc thesis, INPE-2494-TDL/097, São José dos Campos, São Paulo.

Fortune, M., 1980. Properties of African squall lines inferred from time-lapse satellite imagery, *Mon. Wea. Rev.* **108,** 153–168.

Gill, A. E., 1980. Some simple solutions for heat-induced tropical circulation, *Quart. J. Roy. Meteor. Soc.* **106,** 447–462.

Hastenrath, S. and Lamb, P., 1977. *Climatic Atlas of the Tropical Atlantic and Eastern Pacific Oceans*, University of Wisconsin Press, Madison, WI.

Henderson-Sellers, A. and Gornitz, V., 1984. Possible climatic impacts of land cover transformations, with particular emphasis on tropical deforestation, *Clim. Change* **6**, 231–258.

House, R. A., Jr., 1977. Structure and dynamics of a tropical squall-line system, *Mon. Wea. Rev.* **105**, 1540–1567.

Johnson, D. H., 1970. The role of the tropics in the global circulation, in G. A. Corby, Ed., *The General Circulation of the Atmosphere*, Royal Meteorological Society, London.

Kagano, M. T., 1979. Um estudo climatológico e sinótico utilizando dados de radiossondagem (1968–1976) de Manaus e Belém, INPE-1559-TDL/013, INPE, São José dos Campos, São Paulo.

Kasahara, A. and Mizzi, A. P., 1983. On the evaluation of the heating/cooling rate from ECMWF Level III-b analysis data, *The Global Weather Experiment Newsletter*, Vol. 2, USC-GARP, NAS, Washington, DC.

Kousky, V. E., 1979. Frontal influences on Northeast Brazil, *Mon. Wea. Rev.* **107**, 1140–1153.

Kousky, V. E., 1980. Diurnal rainfall variation in Northeast Brazil, *Mon. Wea. Rev.* **108**, 488–498.

Kousky, V. E., 1983. Personal communication.

Kousky, V. E. and Kagano, M. T., 1981. A climatological study of the tropospheric circulation over the Amazon Region, *Acta Amazôn.* **11**, 743–758.

Kousky, V. E., Kagano, M. T., and Cavalcanti, I. F. A., 1984. A review of the southern oscillation: Oceanic atmospheric circulation changes and related rainfall anomalies, *Tellus* **36A**, 490–504.

Miller, D. B. and Feddes, R. G., 1971. *Global Atlas of Relative Cloud Cover 1967–1970*, U.S. Air Force (AWS) Department of Commerce, NOAA, Washington, DC.

Moura, A. D. and Kagano, M. T., 1983. Teleconnections between South America and Western Africa as revealed by monthly precipitation analysis, *First International Conference on Southern Hemisphere Meteorology*, São José dos Campos, São Paulo, Brasil, pp. 120–122, American Meteorological Society, Boston, MA.

Moura, A. D. and Shukla, J., 1981. On the dynamics of droughts in Northeast Brazil: Observations, theory and numerical experiment with a general circulation model, *J. Atmos. Sci* **38**, 2653–2675.

Newell, R. E., Kidson, J. W., Vincent, D. G., and Boer, G. J., 1972. *The General Circulation of the Tropical Atmosphere*, Vol. 1, The Massachusetts Institute of Technology Press, Cambridge, MA.

Parmenter, F. C., 1976. A Southern Hemisphere cold front passage at the Equator, *Bull. Amer. Meteorol. Soc.* **57**, 1435–1440.

Ratisbona, L. R., 1976. The climate of Brazil, in W. Schwerdtfeger, Ed., *World Surveys of Climatology*, Vol. 12, *Climates of Central and South America*, Elsevier, Amsterdam.

Sobral, Z. R., 1979. Um estudo climatológico dos campos de vento e temperatura nos níveis superiores sobre a América do Sul, MSc thesis, INPE-1672-TDL/017, INPE, São José dos Campos, São Paulo.

Taljaard, J. J., 1972. Synoptic meteorology of the Southern Hemisphere, in C. W. Newton, Ed., *Meteorology of the Southern Hemisphere*, American Meteorological Society, Boston, MA.

Trewartha, G. T., 1961. *The Earth's Problem Climates*, University of Wisconsin Press, Madison, WI.

Virji, H., 1981. A preliminary study of summertime tropospheric circulation patterns over South America estimated from cloud winds, *Mon. Wea. Rev.* **109**, 599–610.

Wallace, J. M., 1970. Time-longitude sections of tropical cloudiness December 1966–November 1967, *ESSA Technical Report NESC 56*, National Environmental Satellite Center, Washington, DC.

# Chapter 19

# General Circulation Modeling and the Tropics

**Jagadish Shukla**

General circulation models (GCMs) are used to simulate atmospheric climate. These models are three-dimensional and represent the atmosphere by layers in the vertical dimension, typically about 10, and by grid points or Fourier (spectral) waves in the horizontal dimension, with typical resolution of about five degrees of latitude and longitude. Atmospheric winds are obtained by solution of the fluid equations of motion with numerical approximations defined on the model grid. Likewise, the distributions of temperature, humidity, pressure, and rainfall are calculated by numerical approximations to the continuum equations and parameterizations of the subgrid-scale processes. GCMs are used for sensitivity studies of atmospheric circulation. Models can be integrated with and without a prescribed change (e.g., deforestation) to calculate responses to the prescribed change.

The main emphasis in this essay is the simulation of tropical climate and its interannual variability. However, since tropical and extratropical variability are closely related, it is difficult to isolate the tropics in a global GCM. Therefore, we present the modeling of global circulation with particular emphasis on the tropics.

The ability and limitations of the GCMs to simulate climate and its variability are discussed in terms of

- **a.** mean climate;
- **b.** space–time fluctuations within a season;
- **c.** interannual variability of monthly, seasonal, and annual means; and
- **d.** interannual variability of intraseasonal space–time fluctuations.

**409**

For a description of the simulation of the mean climate, we have summarized the results of Shukla et al. (1981a) and for interannual variability the results of Manabe and Hahn (1981), Charney and Shukla (1981), Lau (1981), Lau and Oort (1984), Malone et al. (1984) and Lau (1985). For additional discussion of simulation of tropical mean and transient circulations, the reader is referred to pioneering works of Manabe and his colleagues (Manabe and Smagorinsky, 1967; Manabe et al., 1970; Manabe et al., 1974; Hayashi, 1974; Hayashi and Golder, 1980).

## MEAN CLIMATE

The time-averaged circulation or the *mean climate* of the atmosphere is determined by a balance between the radiative forcing (shortwave and long-wave radiation), the stationary forcing at the earth's surface (resulting from mountains and land, ocean, and ice distribution), and the horizontal and vertical fluxes of heat, momentum, and moisture. For a realistic simulation of the mean climate, it is therefore necessary to calculate each of these components accurately. Calculation of radiative fluxes requires vertical profiles of temperature, moisture, $O_3$, $CO_2$, other trace gases and aerosols, and a treatment of cloud–radiation interaction for variable clouds. To accurately calculate the stationary forcing at the earth's surface, it is necessary to model correctly the thermal and mechanical effects of mountains and the heat and moisture fluxes across land–air, sea–air, snow–air, and ice–air interfaces. And finally, an accurate calculation of the dynamical fluxes requires the simulation of the correct amplitudes and phases of stationary and transient eddies, their growth and decay, and their interactions among themselves and with the mean circulation.

One of the primary objectives of general circulation modeling studies has been to simulate the mean climate realistically by incorporating these complex processes in a single model. All the physical-dynamical processes discussed above have not been treated with a uniform degree of sophistication. Some processes have been treated in detail, whereas other processes are highly simplified. The large number of parameters and processes has made it difficult to conduct extensive integrations to determine the appropriate levels of complexity for treatment of physical processes. Therefore, it is very difficult to compare the models with each other; rather, each model is compared individually with observations.

The discussions in this chapter are confined to comparisons with observations, and no attempt is made to describe the model sensitivity to external forcings, parameterizations of physical processes, and chemical composition.

We present here a summary of simulation results from the GLAS (Goddard Laboratory for Atmospheric Sciences) climate model, which has been extensively described in Shukla et al. (1981a).

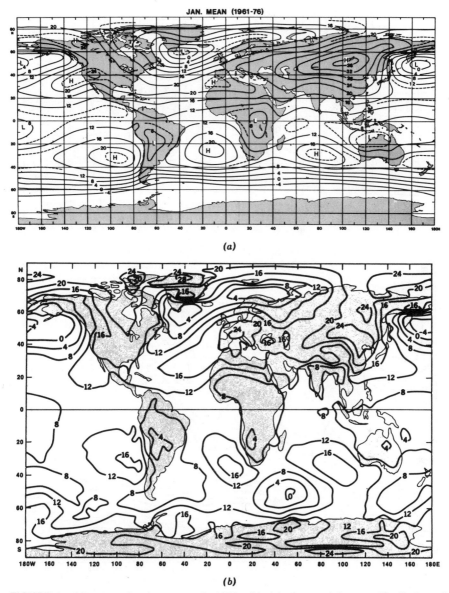

**FIGURE 1.** Mean sea level pressure (− 1000 mb): (*a*) observed January (Godbole and Shukla, 1981); (*b*) GCM February; (*c*) observed July (Godbole and Shukla, 1981); (*d*) GCM July.

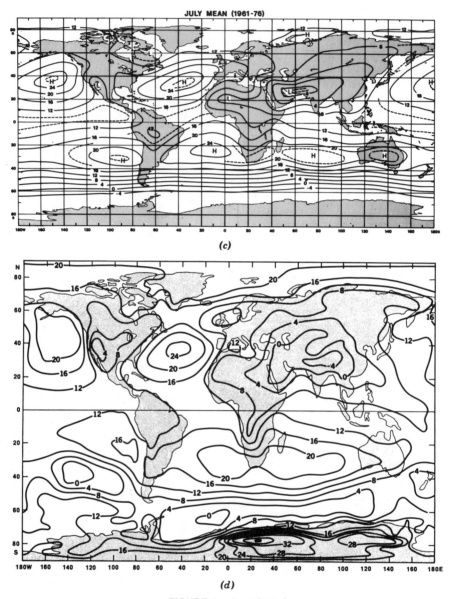

FIGURE 1. (*continued*)

## Sea Level Pressure

Figures 1*a* and 1*c* show the observed 16-y mean sea level pressure for Jan-uary and July reproduced from Godbole and Shukla (1981), and Figures 1*b* and 1*d* show the model's simulated mean sea level pressure for a single February and July, respectively. For February, the simulation of the prominent Northern Hemispheric circulation features, such as the Aleutian and Icelandic lows, is fairly realistic, but the discrepancy in the structure and intensity of the Siberian high is too large to be accounted for by interannual variability or by differences between January and February. The most serious deficiency of the simulated field is in the Southern Hemisphere, south of 60°S, where the simulated field shows a large eddy structure whereas the observed field is zonally uniform. For July, the high-pressure cell over the North Atlantic and the monsoon low are well simulated, but the orientation of the North Pacific high is not as observed. The subtropical high-pressure cells in the Southern Hemisphere are well simulated over the Indian Ocean, Atlantic Ocean, and eastern Pacific but not over Australia. For both summer and winter, the models show a common deficiency of distinct nonzonal isobar configurations in the Southern Hemispheric mid-to-high latitudes.

## Geopotential Height

Figure 2 shows the observed and simulated geopotential height field at 200 mb. For February, the simulated trough over northeast United States and eastern Canada, the ridge over the eastern Atlantic, the jet stream over Japan, and the anticyclonic circulation over the tropics are quite realistic. However, the ridge over the west coast of the United States is displaced to the east, and the Southern Hemisphere midlatitudes show more eddy structure than is observed. For July, there are several deficiencies in the simulated field. Large-amplitude short waves are seen over North America and adjacent Pacific Ocean, and the geopotential heights in the tropical belt are higher by about 200 geopotential meter (gpm) than is observed.

The surface circulation during July and the upper-level circulation during February are, in general, better simulated than the surface circulation during February and the upper-level circulation during July.

## Zonal Wind and Temperature

Figure 3 shows the observed and simulated zonal wind and zonally averaged temperature. For February, the locations of the strongest zonal wind maxima in both hemispheres are well simulated. The most conspicuous deficiency is the absence of the closed maximum near 200 mb that is seen in the observed zonal winds. This deficiency is related to the very low model temperatures in the upper troposphere of the polar regions. The model-simulated tropical atmosphere is considerably warmer than the observed atmosphere. Cooling near the poles and large zonal winds near the upper boundary have been one of the common deficiencies of GCMs, and their precise cause is yet to be determined.

## Stationary Wave Variance

Figure 4 shows the observed and simulated variances around a latitude circle of the winter and summer mean stationary geopotential height summed over

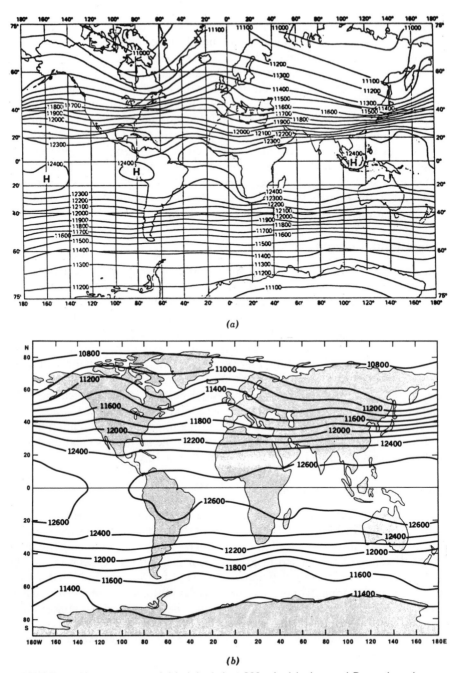

**FIGURE 2.** Mean geopotential height (m) at 200 mb: (a) observed December, January, and February; (b) GCM February; (c) observed June, July, and August; (d) GCM July.

414

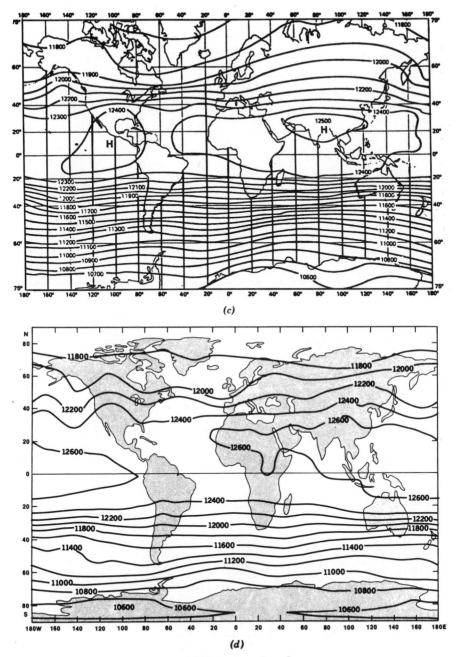

(c)

(d)

**FIGURE 2.** (*continued*)

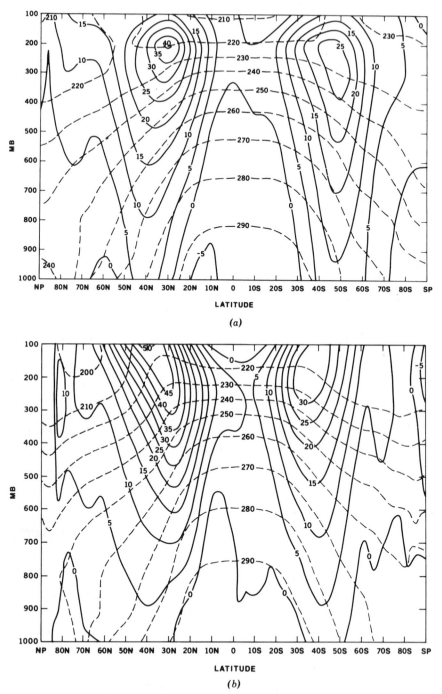

**FIGURE 3.** Zonally averaged zonal wind (m s$^{-1}$ solid lines) and temperature (K, dashed lines): (a) observed February, 1979; (b) GCM February; (c) observed July 1979; (d) GCM July.

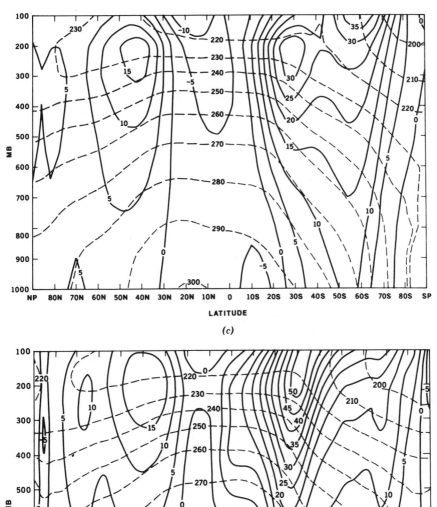

FIGURE 3. (*continued*)

417

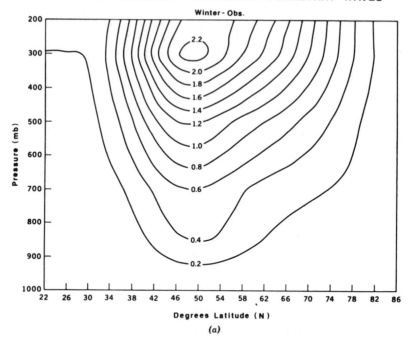

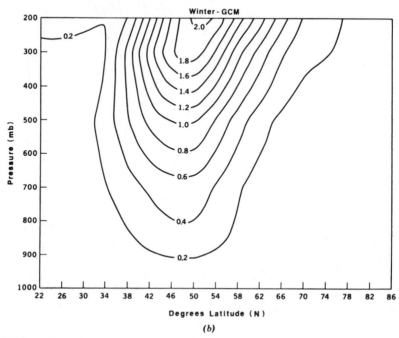

**FIGURE 4.** Stationary planetary wave variance of the geopotential height in the Northern Hemisphere: (*a*) observed winter (units of $10^4$ m$^2$); (*b*) GCM winter (units of $10^4$ m$^2$); (*c*) observed summer (units of $10^3$ m$^2$); (*d*) GCM summer (units of $10^3$ m$^2$).

## 15 YEAR AVERAGE : STATIONARY PLANETARY WAVES

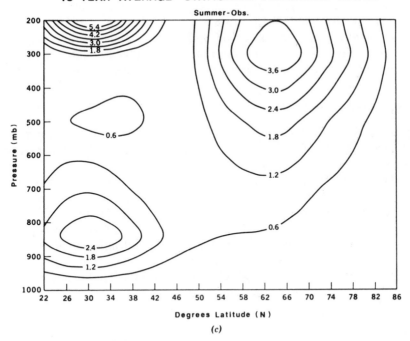

(c)

## GEOPOTENTIAL STATIONARY PLANETARY WAVES

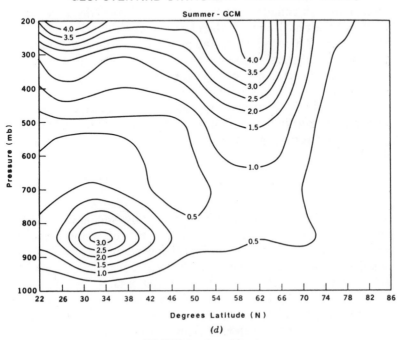

(d)

**FIGURE 4.** (*continued*)

the planetary waves (wave number 1–4). The latitudinal and height distributions of the simulated variance are in good agreement with the observations for both seasons. The observed decrease of variance above 300 mb is not satisfactorily simulated. This discrepancy is probably related to the low polar temperatures and strong zonal winds at the upper levels.

## Surface Winds and ITCZ

Figures 5 and 6 show the observed and simulated surface winds reported in the modeling study of Halem et al. (1979). The corresponding maps from Shukla et al. (1981a) are quite similar to these. The observed fields are from Mintz and Dean (1952). The agreement between the observed and the simulated intertropical convergence zone (ITCZ) is very good, especially with regard to its longitudinal variation. The structure and locations of anticyclonic centers are also well simulated. The seasonal reversal from northeasterly winds during winter to southwesterly winds during summer over the north Indian Ocean is correctly simulated by the model. The main discrepancy in the latitudinal location of ITCZ occurs during winter over the eastern part of the Pacific and over the Indian Ocean.

## Rainfall

Figures 7 and 8 show the observed (from Jaeger, 1976) and simulated monthly mean rainfall for winter and summer, respectively. Given the large variability of rainfall and the uncertainty in the observations, the agreement between the simulated and the observed rainfall patterns is very good. Areas of very large and very small rainfall are well reproduced. The most obvious discrepancies are the excessive February precipitation over the Tibetan plateau and the overprediction of July rainfall over eastern North America. Partition of the total precipitation between large-scale and convective (cumulus) precipitation (not shown) indicates that in both seasons cumulus precipitation dominates in the tropics but large-scale precipitation dominates in higher latitudes.

## Upper-Level Flow

The simulation of the 200-mb flow (not shown) by Shukla et al. (1981a) is in good agreement with the observations. For February, the locations and the intensities of the jet streams in both hemispheres are well simulated, although the simulated jet stream speeds were stronger than those observed for 1979, to which they are compared in Shukla et al.

Manabe et al. (1979) have presented simulation results from spectral models with 15, 21, and 30 wave numbers. They found that the increase in spectral resolution improved the simulation of tropical rain belts and subtropical dry zones. An example of one of the better simulations of the upper-

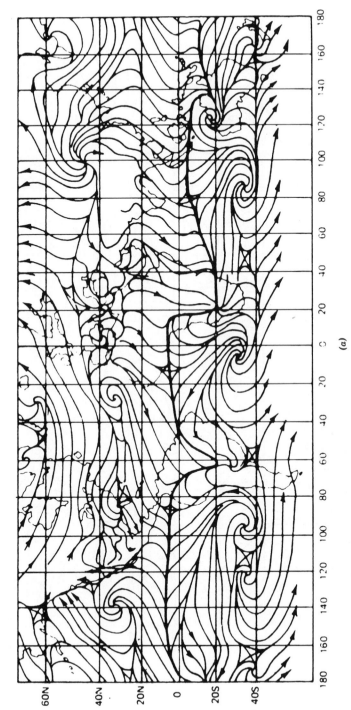

**FIGURE 5.** Streamlines at earth surface: (*a*) observed January (Mintz and Dean, 1952); (*b*) GCM February. [From Halem et al. (1979) with permission of the World Meteorological Organization.]

(*a*)

421

FIGURE 5. (continued)

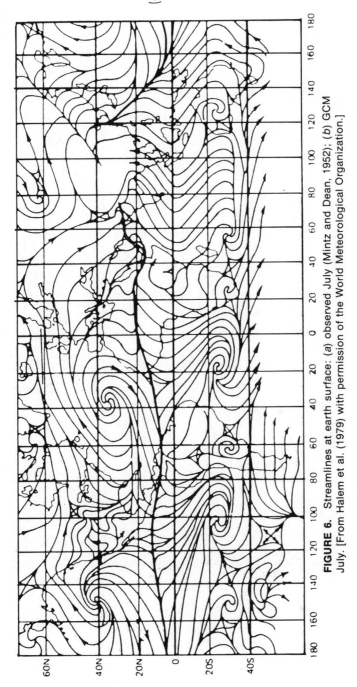

(a)

**FIGURE 6.** Streamlines at earth surface: (a) observed July (Mintz and Dean, 1952); (b) GCM July. [From Halem et al. (1979) with permission of the World Meteorological Organization.]

423

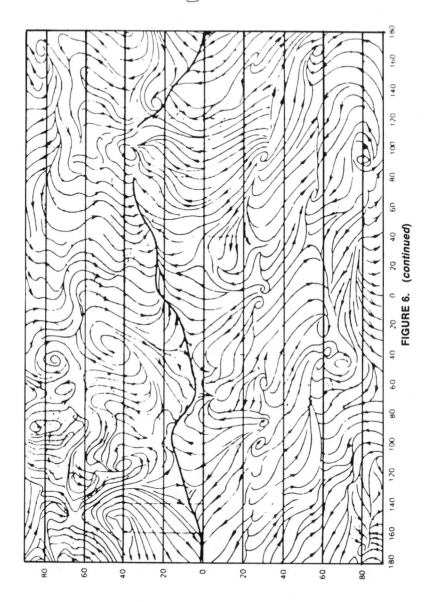

(b)

FIGURE 6. *(continued)*

424

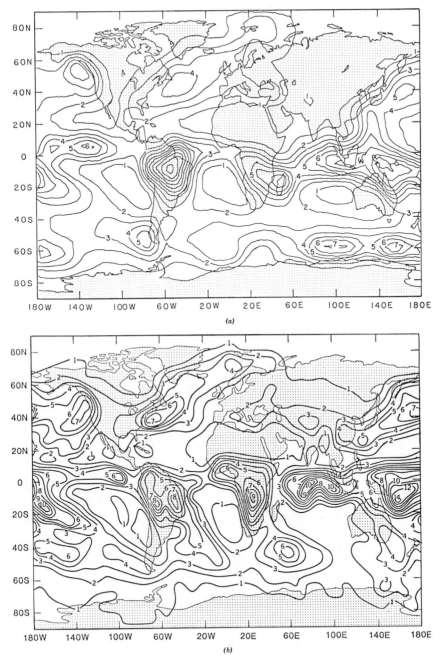

**FIGURE 7.** Precipitation (mm day$^{-1}$): (a) observed February (Jaeger, 1976); (b) GCM February.

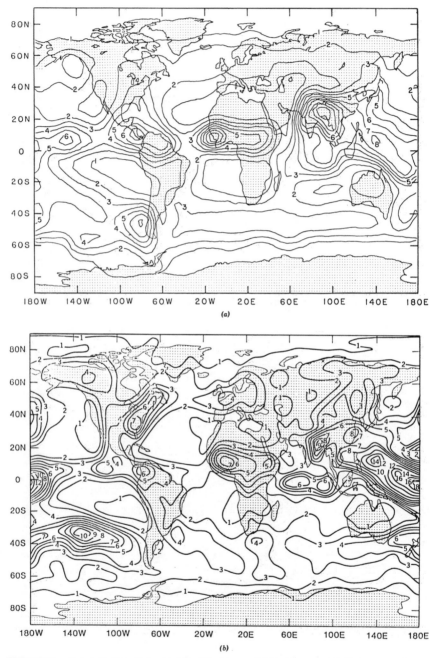

**FIGURE 8.** Precipitation (mm day$^{-1}$): (*a*) observed July (Jaeger, 1976); (*b*) GCM July.

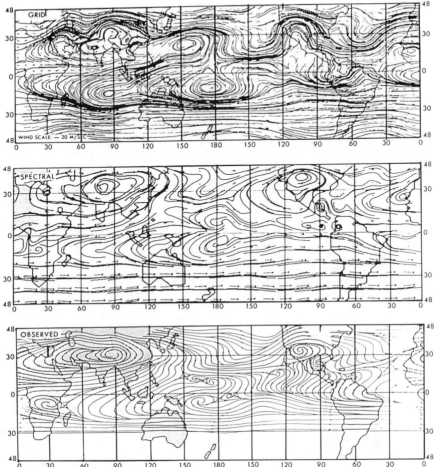

**FIGURE 9.** July mean streamlines: (*top*) computed at 190 mb (grid model, Manabe et al., 1974; (*middle*) computed at 205 mb [spectral model, from Manabe et al. (1979)]; (*bottom*) observed at 200 mb (Sadler, 1975).

level flow with a 30-wave-number spectral model is shown in Fig. 9, reproduced from Hayashi (1980). The large-scale features of the Tibetan and Mexican highs, the mid-Pacific and mid-Atlantic troughs, and the easterly jet off southern Asia are better simulated in the spectral model than in the grid model.

## SPACE–TIME FLUCTUATIONS WITHIN A SEASON

For GCMs to be useful for sensitivity and predictability studies, they must simulate accurately not only the time-averaged circulation but also the transient circulation. We present here the simulation of low-frequency planetary wave variance and the local bandpass variance from the GLAS climate model and the Geophysical Fluid Dynamics Laboratory of NOAA (GFDL) grid point model.

## Low-Frequency Planetary Wave (LFPW) Variance

The LFPWs consist of wave numbers 1–4 with periods of 7.5–90 days. Figure 10 shows the observed and simulated latitude–height structure of the LFPWs. There is general agreement in the overall structure for both winter and summer seasons. The discrepancy near the upper level is the same as discussed for Figure 4; in addition, the model variances are somewhat too small.

## Bandpass Variance

Figure 11 shows the observed and simulated local bandpass filtered variance of the 500-mb geopotential height in the Northern Hemisphere for the winter season. The bandpass variance is defined as the spatially local root-mean-square (rms) deviation in time for fluctuations of 2.5–6 days. The bandpass variance is related to the frequency, intensity, growth, and decay of cyclonic storms and indicates the location of "storm tracks" (Blackmon et al., 1977). The observed and simulated bandpass rms for winter are in excellent agreement in both the location and the strength of the major areas of cyclonic activity in the north central Pacific and western Atlantic. For summer (not shown) the Atlantic maximum has been realistically simulated, both with respect to position and to magnitude, but the simulated Pacific maximum is too weak and is located too far to the west.

Blackmon and Lau (1980) have analyzed the variance and covariance of bandpass filtered and low-pass filtered data from simulations of a GFDL model earlier described by Manabe et al. (1974). They found good agreement between the observations and the model-simulated location and intensity of storm tracks, vertical structure of the disturbances, and transport of heat and potential vorticity by transient eddies. The total rms and the low-pass filtered rms of the 500-mb height were weaker in the model simulations than in the observations.

Malone et al. (1984) have presented the results of simulation of stationary and transient eddies using the spectral general circulation model (Pitcher et al., 1983). In general, simulation of stationary waves is more realistic in the Northern Hemisphere than in the Southern Hemisphere. The transient eddies are better simulated in the winter hemisphere; however, for geopotential height the total variance at 400 mb is too high and bandpass variance at 1000 mb is too low over the Northern Hemisphere for January simulation. The structure of the transient wave variability in the summer hemisphere also shows some discrepancies from the observations.

## 15 YEAR AVERAGE : LOW FREQUENCY PLANETARY WAVES

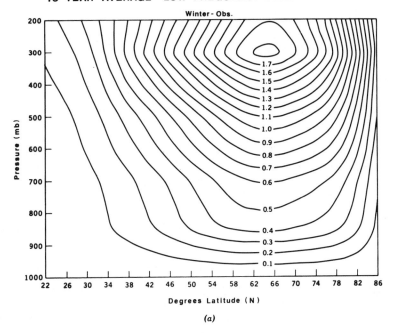

(a)

## GEOPOTENTIAL HT : LOW FREQUENCY PLANETARY WAVES

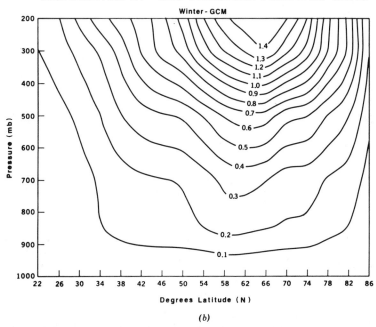

(b)

**FIGURE 10.** Geopotential height variance in low-frequency planetary waves in the Northern Hemisphere: (a) observed winter (in units of $10^4$ m$^2$, contour interval is $0.1 \times 10^4$ m$^2$); (b) GCM winter ($10^4$ m$^2$, contour interval $0.1 \times 10^4$ m$^2$); (c) observed summer ($10^3$ m$^2$, contour interval $0.9 \times 10^3$ m$^2$); (d) GCM summer ($10^3$ m$^2$, contour interval $1.0 \times 10^3$ m$^2$).

## 15 YEAR AVERAGE : LOW FREQUENCY PLANETARY WAVES

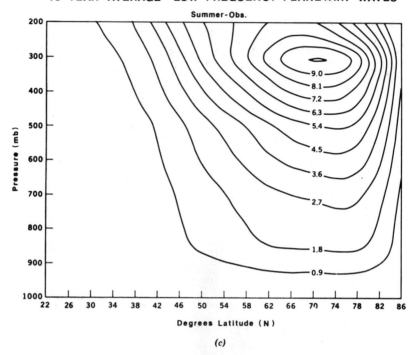

(c)

## GEOPOTENTIAL HT : LOW FREQUENCY PLANETARY WAVES

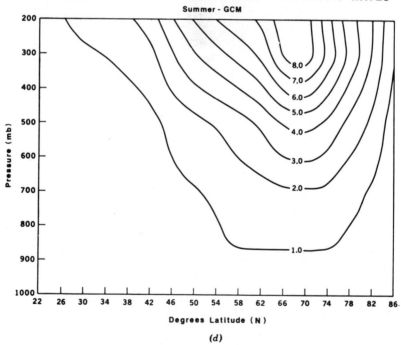

(d)

FIGURE 10. (*continued*)

*(a)*

**FIGURE 11.** RMS deviation of the winter 500-mb bandpass geopotential height field in the Northern Hemisphere (units of m, contour interval is 5 m): (*a*) observed winter; (*b*) GCM winter.

From such studies as just discussed, we conclude the following:

(a) GCMs show a remarkable degree of success in simulating the geographical location, intensity, and life cycle of synoptic scale disturbances, as inferred from the similarities in observed and model-simulated bandpass filtered height variances. The geographical locations of the storm tracks in relation to mean field structures are also well simulated.

(b) GCMs do not simulate as well the low-pass filtered variance. The amplitudes are less in every model and sometimes even the geographical locations are not well simulated. Since the maxima in low-pass variance are coincident with the maxima in the frequency of blocking in all seasons

(b)

FIGURE 11. (*continued*)

(Shukla and Mo, 1981; Dole, 1982) it is unlikely that the models will simulate the amplitude, location, and duration of observed blocking events correctly.

### Simulation of Blocking

The midlatitude atmospheric flow pattern is occasionally dominated by quasi-persistent features whose time scale is larger than the life cycle of individual storms but shorter than the length of a season. These features, generally referred to as blocking, are of great importance to medium-range and monthly prediction. Shukla and Mo (1981) and Dole (1982) have examined the geographical and seasonal occurrences of persistent anomalies in the geopotential height field over the Northern Hemisphere. They found that large positive anomalies (>100–200 m) persist at three distinctly different geographical locations: from the Pacific to the west of the Rockies, from the Atlantic to the west of the Alps, and from the Scandinavian mountain ranges to the west of the Ural Mountains of the USSR. The local structure of blocking in all three regions is very similar, and these preferred locations do not change with season.

A preliminary analysis of climatology of blocking in the GLAS climate model is presented by Shukla et al. (1981b). They examined 17 winter and 7 summer short-term simulations to determine the frequency and geographical locations of the model-simulated blocking events. A blocking event was identified at any grid point that a 500-mb geopotential height anomaly (departure from the mean seasonal cycle) of 100 gpm or more persisted for 7 days or more. The geographical locations of the maximum blocking events were not in good agreement with observed locations. The model underestimated the intensity of blocking ridges. Several blocking features appeared, but they did not persist with amplified magnitude. Chen and Shukla (1983) have analyzed a strong blocking situation, the strongest that was simulated by the GLAS climate model, which occurred in a winter simulation with large sea surface temperature (SST) anomalies in the northern Pacific such as observed during January 1977. Mansfield (1981) and Gilchrist (1982) have also examined the blocking situations in the British Meteorological Office GCM. Some of the factors that affect the location, intensity, and duration of blocking events in a GCM are described below.

### Resolution

If the maintenance of the blocks were due to interactions between the large-scale circulation and small-scale waves, and if the model resolutions were not adequate to resolve the latter and their interactions with the former, the inadequate resolution might be one of the causes for unrealistic simulation. Examination of blocking in high-resolution models could shed further light on this matter.

### Structure of Zonal Flow

Tung and Lindzen (1979) have suggested that the vertical structure of zonal winds, especially at higher levels, is very important for setting up stationary waves and blocking. Since most of the models do not simulate the zonal winds and temperatures at the higher levels, they may not produce realistic blocking events either.

### Diabatic Heat Sources

If some of the observed blocking events were due to either the influence of anomalous midlatitude stationary thermal forcings (because of anomalies of SST, snow, or sea ice, etc.) or to tropical heat sources (because of anomalies of SST or soil moisture), the models would not be able to simulate them because they use climatological boundary forcing. We do not understand the precise role of slowly varying boundary forcing in the generation and maintenance of blocking events. Possibly, although the large-scale quasi-stationary flow patterns are initiated by stationary forcing, the small-scale waves and their interactions may be important for the maintenance of the blocks.

Even in the absence of quasi-stationary thermal forcing, blocks may be generated by interactions between fluctuating zonal winds and mountains (Charney and Devore, 1979; Charney and Straus, 1980; Charney et al., 1981), and in this context, lack of GCM's ability to simulate blocking can be attributed to inadequate treatment of interactions between the zonal flow and orography. The apparent regional nature of the blocking and locally amplified ridges could be due to the longitudinal variations of zonal flow (an opinion of the late Professor Charney), which are in turn caused by the longitudinal variations of diabatic heating. If GCMs were not able to simulate the heat sources and the asymmetric zonal flows, they would also be deficient in simulating the blocking events. A more thorough analysis of blocking phenomena in GCM simulations could clarify the mechanisms of blocking in GCMs.

Lau (1981) has shown that the so-called Pacific/North American pattern of monthly mean height anomalies is present in a simulation without SST anomalies. This does not necessarily mean that the SST anomalies are not important for blocking, because the Pacific/North American pattern is not the same as blocking. D. Gutzler AER (personal communication) has shown that the Pacific/North American pattern can be found even if all the days identified as blocking were removed from the data set before the calculations for the pattern were made.

## INTERANNUAL VARIABILITY OF MONTHLY, SEASONAL, AND ANNUAL MEANS

The interannual variability of the time mean or transient circulation consists of two parts: that due to the internal dynamics with prescribed seasonally varying boundary forcing and that due to the interannual variability of boundary forcing itself. The boundary conditions of SST, soil moisture, snow, sea ice, and so on can be prescribed to have their mean seasonal variation, and GCMs can then be integrated for several years to calculate the interannual variability due to internal dynamics. Similarly, GCMs can be integrated with time-varying (interannually as well as seasonally) boundary forcing to determine the total interannual variability due to the combined effects of internal dynamics and boundary forcing. To our knowledge, neither of the above two integrations has been performed with any large complex GCM for a simulated time period of 10 y or more. The model simulation of Manabe and Hahn (1981) is a hybrid of both approaches. Manabe and Hahn prescribed the seasonally varying (but not interannually varying) SST but allowed the soil moisture and snow cover to vary interannually as determined by the model parameterizations. We shall describe their results in the next section.

## GFDL Spectral Model Results for a 15-Year Integration

Manabe and Hahn (1981) have presented the results of a simulation of atmospheric variability from the last 15 y of a 17.75-y integration of the GFDL spectral climate model. The description of the model and simulation of mean fields is given in Manabe et al. (1979). Sea surface temperature, cloud amounts, insolation, and ozone are prescribed for each calendar day of the year and have no interannual variability; therefore, the simulated interannual variability is mainly due to internal dynamics and changes in snow cover and soil moisture. This simulation has been examined further by Lau (1981) to study recurrent meteorological anomalies.

The studies find that the geographical structure of the simulated variability of daily and monthly means is in good agreement with the observations. The magnitude of the variability is systematically underestimated in the tropics and is either comparable to or less than is observed in the middle latitudes. In the regions of systematic underestimation of simulated sea level pressure, daily and monthly variability is overestimated. According to Lau (1981), the rms amplitude of 500-mb monthly mean heights is about 70–80% of that observed in the atmosphere. They have not presented results of interannual variability of seasonal means.

Figure 12a shows the zonal means of observed and simulated standard deviation of daily and monthly mean 1000-mb geopotential height (m) for the December–February season. The model systematically underestimates the observed variability in the tropics. As the averaging period increases from one day to one month, the model-simulated tropical variability decreases further. For example, at the equator, the model variability is ~70% of the daily and only about 45% of the monthly observed variability. It is likely that most of the monthly variability in the model is due to the sampling of daily values, which have rather large autocorrelation decay times of 4–8 days (see Figure 5.13 of Manabe and Hahn 1981). The interannual variability of simulated seasonal means was probably also too low in the tropics.

Figure 12b shows latitude–pressure distributions of the zonal mean standard deviation of the monthly mean geopotential height (m) for the December–February season. Although the extratropical variability is underestimated only slightly, the simulated tropical variability in the upper troposphere and stratosphere is smaller by factors of 2 and 3, respectively.

The ratio of the observed to simulated standard deviation of Northern Hemisphere mean surface air temperature is about 1.8 for daily, 2.0 for 3 month running means, and 3.0 for 12-month running means. It is not clear whether this difference is genuine or just a result of differences in sampling of observed and model-simulated data.

The first eigenvector of the normalized monthly mean 500-mb height field

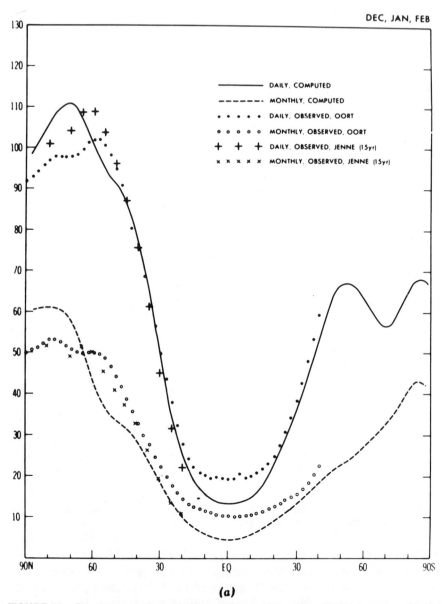

(a)

**FIGURE 12.** Zonal means of standard deviation for December–February season for: (a) daily and monthly mean 1000-mb geopotential height; (b) latitude–pressure distribution for monthly mean geopotential height (m). [From Manabe and Hahn (1981) with permission of *Monthly Weather Review*, the American Meteorological Society.]

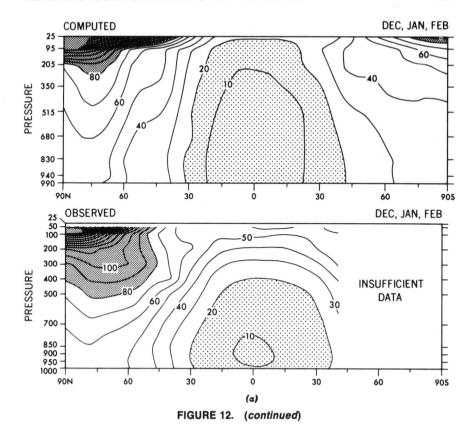

**FIGURE 12.** (*continued*)

for winter looks similar to the corresponding eigenvector from observations, although there are some differences in the locations and amplitudes of anomaly centers. The model-simulated first eigenvector explains 22.4% of the hemispherically integrated variance.

Thus, even in the absence of variable SST anomalies, large-scale, though poorly understood fluctuations do occur in the model atmosphere. The basic mechanisms for such fluctuations could involve the interactions of fluctuating zonal winds with orography, the instability of the three-dimensional flow, or the tropical and midlatitude transient diabatic heat sources associated with episodes of enhanced or reduced precipitation caused by the internal dynamics itself. A more detailed analysis of the model-simulated rainfall is needed in order to investigate the possible role of tropical heat sources in causing these large-scale fluctuations.

Figure 13 shows the structure of the first eigenvector of the normalized monthly mean geopotential height at (a) 300 and (b) 1000 mb for all 12 months of the year over the tropics. The most conspicuous features are the lack of zonal variation and a complete absence of any signature of the southern

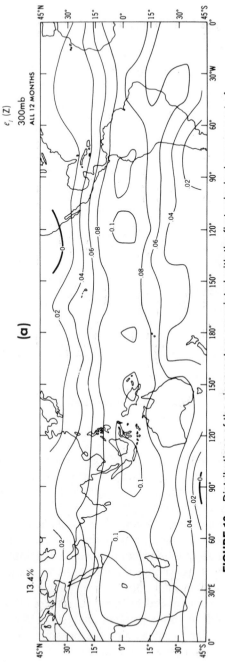

**FIGURE 13.** Distributions of the eigenvectors associated with the first principal component of normalized monthly mean geopotential height at (*a*) 300 mb and (*b*) 1000 mb for all 12 months of the year over the tropics. [From Lau (1981) with permission of *Monthly Weather Review,* the American Meteorological Society.]

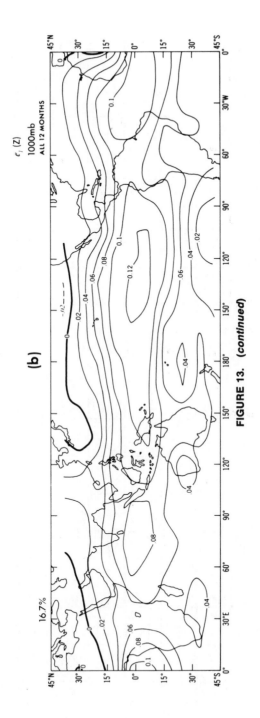

FIGURE 13. *(continued)*

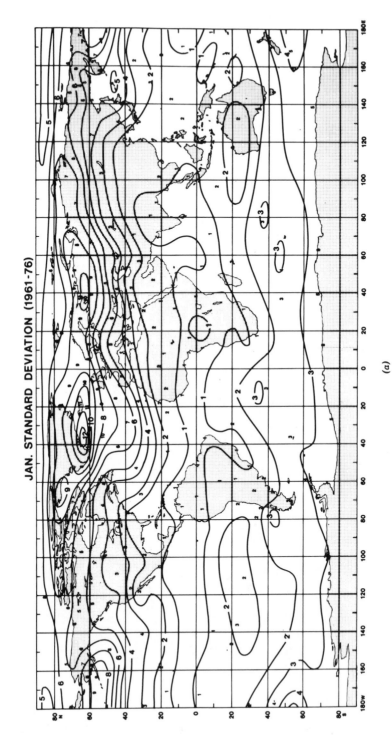

**FIGURE 14.** Standard deviation of monthly mean sea level pressure (mb): (a) observed January (Godbole and Shukla, 1981); (b) GCM February [from Shukla (1981a) with permission of *Journal of the Atmospheric Sciences*, the American Meteorological Society].

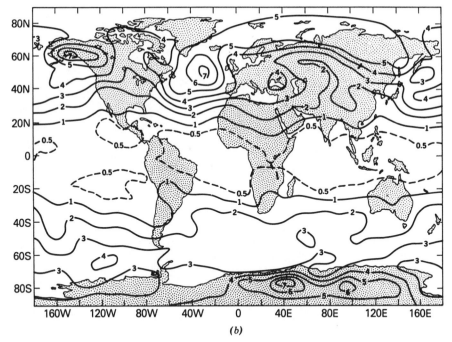

*(b)*

**FIGURE 14.** (*continued*)

oscillation (not shown), which would give opposite signs over the Indian Ocean and the eastern tropical Pacific. According to Lau (1981), the pattern based on simulated winter data alone is very similar to the one shown here, and the next few eigenvectors also do not show any signature of the southern oscillation.

## Simulations with Different Initial Conditions

Shukla (1981a) integrated the GLAS climate model for 60 days with nine different initial conditions but identical boundary conditions. Three of these initial conditions were the observed atmospheric conditions on January 1 of 1975, 1976, and 1977, and six other initial conditions were obtained by superimposing over the observed initial conditions a random perturbation for which the rms error for all the grid points was 3 m s$^{-1}$ in $u$ and $v$ components of wind. Figure 14$b$ shows the global map of standard deviation of the nine monthly means for the second month (February) of the model integration. Figure 14$a$ shows the standard deviation of the observed monthly mean sea level pressure for 16 y (1961–1976) from Godbole and Shukla (1981). The model-simulated variability is uniformly smaller than the observed variability. This difference is partly due to the absence of anomalous boundary forcing and partly due to the limited duration of the model integrations, which

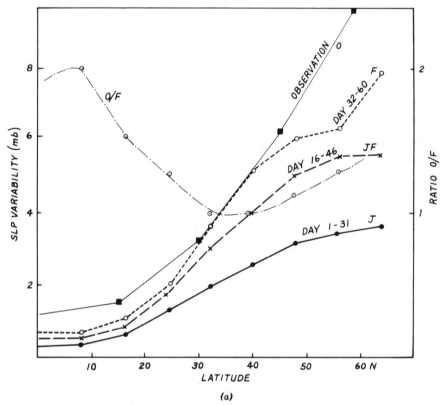

**FIGURE 15.** (*a*) Zonally averaged rms deviation of sea level pressure (mb) between control
and perturbation runs averaged for days 1–31, 16–46, and 32–60 (O/F = ratio of observations and model for days 32–60). (*b*) Zonally averaged standard deviation of daily grid
point values for sea level pressure (mb) for January (upper panel) and February (lower
panel) for model (solid line) and observations (dashed line). [From Shukla (1981a) with
permission of *Journal of the Atmospheric Sciences*, the American Meteorological Society.]

does not allow very low frequency internal dynamical processes to affect
the monthly means. Figure 15*a* shows the zonally averaged standard deviations for observed and model-simulated monthly mean sea level pressure
and the ratio of observed-to-simulated zonally averaged standard deviations.
The ratio is about 2 in the low latitudes and about 1 in the middle latitudes.
Figure 15*b* shows the zonally averaged daily standard deviations of sea level
pressure for observations and model simulations, which are in good
agreement.

   Figure 16*b* shows the standard deviation of model-simulated monthly
mean rainfall (mm day$^{-1}$) for February, and Fig. 16a shows the observed
standard deviation of mean rainfall (cm month$^{-1}$) for the winter season over
land for 16 y (1963–1976). Although the general pattern of the simulated
standard deviations (locations of large maxima and minima) shows some

STANDARD DEVIATION OF DAILY VALUES OF SEA LEVEL PRESSURE

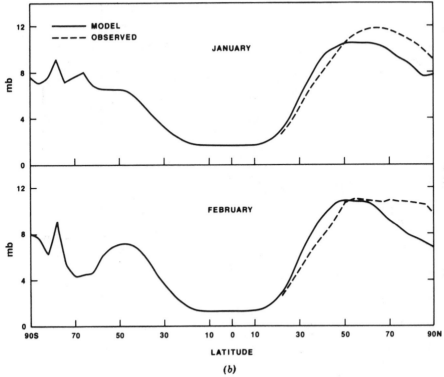

*(b)*

**FIGURE 15.** *(continued)*

similarity to the observations, the magnitudes, especially in the tropics, are clearly underestimated. Evidently, interannual variability of boundary forcing is quite important for the interannual variability of monthly and seasonal mean rainfall.

Charney and Shukla (1981) examined the variability of the monthly mean (July) circulation for four model runs for which the boundary conditions were kept identical but the initial conditions randomly perturbed. Although the observed and model variabilities were comparable at middle and high latitudes, the variability among the four model runs for the monsoon region was far less than the observed interannual variability of the atmosphere, possibly because of fixed boundary conditions. Manabe and Hahn (1981) gave a similar explanation for the model-simulated low variability in the tropics. However, for inferring such conclusions about the role of boundary forcing, it is more appropriate to make integrations with and without the influence of the boundary forcing, so that two properties of the same model can be directly compared and any intrinsic model deficiency will not bias

STANDARD DEVIATION OF WINTER (D J F) RAINFALL (cm/MONTH)

(1961–1976)

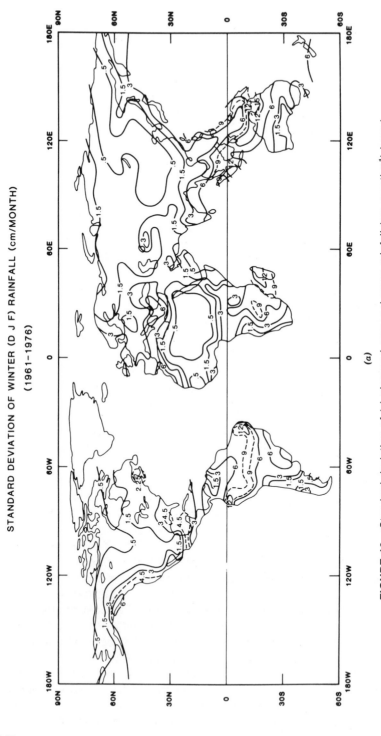

(a)

**FIGURE 16.** Standard deviation of (a) observed seasonal mean rainfall (cm month$^{-1}$) based on 16 years (1962–1977) and (b) GCM February mean rainfall (mm day$^{-1}$) for nine model runs (Shukla, 1981a).

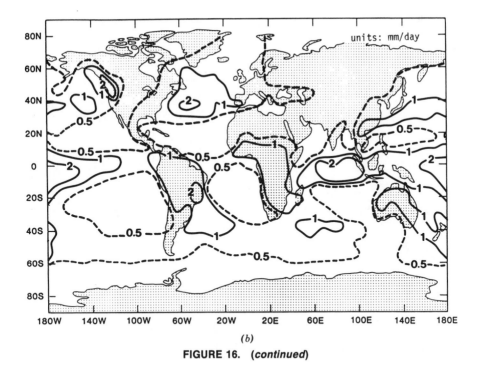

(b)

**FIGURE 16.** (*continued*)

the results. The results of a preliminary study along these lines by Shukla (1981b) are summarized below.

### Effect of Different Sea Surface Temperature Distributions

The GLAS climate model was integrated for 45 days starting from the observed initial conditions in the middle of June and with climatological mean boundary conditions [referred to as the control ($C$) run]. Three additional integrations for 45 days were done by randomly changing the initial conditions of $u$ and $v$ at each of the nine model levels but retaining the same boundary conditions. The random errors corresponded to a Gaussian distribution with zero mean and a standard deviation of 3 m s$^{-1}$ for $u$ and $v$ separately. These integrations are the predictability ($P_1$, $P_2$, $P_3$) runs. Three additional integrations for 45 days were made in which, in addition to randomly perturbed initial conditions, the boundary conditions of SST between the equator and 30°N were replaced by the observed SST during July of 1972, 1973, and 1974. These integrations are the boundary forcing ($B_1$, $B_2$, $B_3$) runs. The variance ($\sigma_P^2$) among monthly means of $C$, $P_1$, $P_2$, and $P_3$ gives a measure of the natural variability of the model, that is, the variability caused by internal dynamics alone. The variance ($\sigma_B^2$) among monthly means of $C$, $B_1$, $B_2$, and $B_3$ gives a measure of the variability including

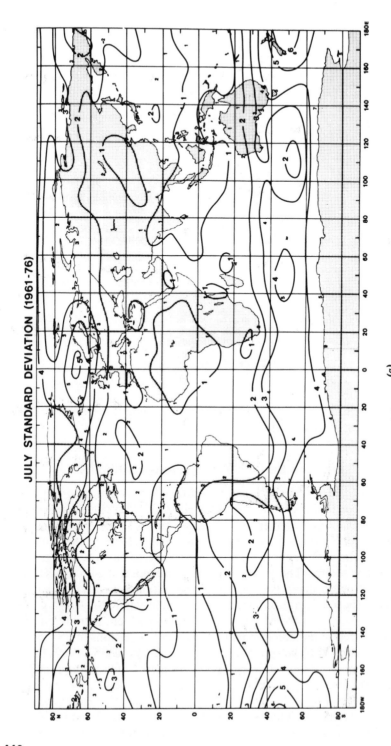

**FIGURE 17.** Standard deviation of monthly mean sea level pressure (mb): (*a*) observed July (Godbole and Shukla, 1981); (*b*) GCM July (Shukla, 1981b)

(*a*)

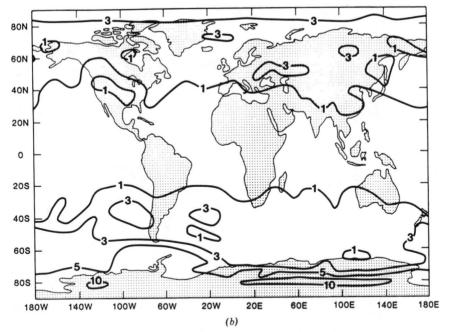

(b)

**FIGURE 17.** (*continued*)

boundary forcing of SST. We have compared $\sigma_p$ and $\sigma_B$ with the observed standard deviation ($\sigma_o$) for 10 y of monthly means. Figure 17 shows the global maps of $\sigma_o$ and $\sigma_p$. The July standard deviation fields for the model are considerably smaller than is observed, with the most pronounced discrepancy occurring in the tropics.

Figure 18a shows plots of zonally averaged values of $\sigma_p$, $\sigma_B$, and $\sigma_o$ and the ratios $\sigma_o/\sigma_p$ and $\sigma_p/\sigma_B$. In agreement with the results of Charney and Shukla (and Manabe and Hahn), the ratio $\sigma_o/\sigma_p$ is more than 2 in the tropics and close to 1 in the middle latitudes. The ratio $\sigma_B$ lies nearly halfway between $\sigma_o$ and $\sigma_p$, which suggests that nearly half of the remaining variability was accounted for by changes in SST between the equator and 30°N. The influence of other variable boundary forcing by soil moisture or snow cover would further bring $\sigma_B$ closer to $\sigma_o$. These results, although for short period integrations, are in remarkable agreement with those of Manabe and Hahn, which are based on 15 y of model integration. We have calculated the ratio $\sigma_o/\sigma_M$ (where $\sigma_M$ refers to model-simulated standard deviations) from the two curves of Manabe and Hahn (shown in Fig. 12a of this essay) and the results are shown in Fig. 18b. The ratio $\sigma_o/\sigma_M$ is again about 2 in the near equatorial regions and is reduced to about 1 in the middle and high latitudes. The corresponding ratio for the height field in the tropical troposphere and stratosphere is more than 3 (see Fig. 12b).

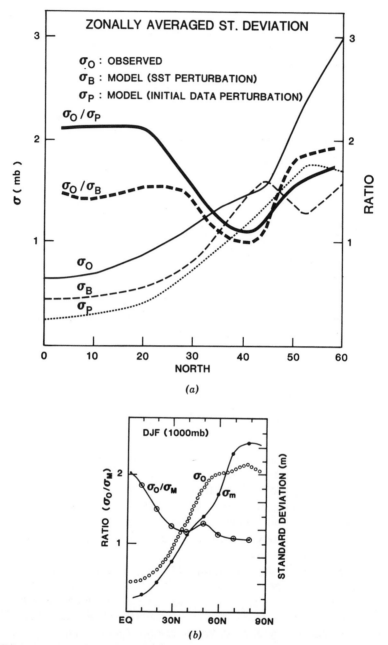

**FIGURE 18.** (*a*) Zonally averaged standard deviation among monthly mean (July) sea level pressure (mb) for 10 y of observations ($\sigma_o$, thin solid line); four model runs with variable boundary conditions ($\sigma_B$, thin dashed line); and four model runs with identical boundary conditions ($\sigma_p$, thin dotted line). Thick solid line and thick dashed line show the ratio $\sigma_o/\sigma_p$ and $\sigma_o/\sigma_B$, respectively. (*b*) Zonal means of standard deviation of monthly mean 100 mb geopotential height (m) from Manabe and Hahn (1981). On the left side is the ratio ($\sigma_o/\sigma_m$) of observed and model standard deviations.

The additional variability explained by ocean temperature variations, taken together with the analysis of Lau (1981), which showed that the southern oscillation was not simulated by the model simulations of Manabe and Hahn, suggests that the slowly varying boundary forcings are the most important mechanisms for determining the interannual variability of the monthly and seasonal means in the tropics. However, more systematic GCM simulation studies with and without boundary forcing are needed to understand better the relative importance of internal dynamics and boundary forcing and whether or not tropical boundary forcing can also influence the simulation of midlatitude variability.

A recent paper by Lau (1985) is a good example of work in this direction. Using the observed SST in the tropical Pacific for a 15-y integration of a GFDL spectral model, he has shown that the interannual variability of the southern oscillation is simulated rather well. Correlation coefficients between the prescribed SST anomalies in the tropical Pacific and midlatitude circulation over the Northern Hemisphere are also in good agreement with the observations.

## INTERANNUAL VARIABILITY OF INTRASEASONAL SPACE–TIME FLUCTUATIONS

The interannual variability of model-simulated intraseasonal space–time fluctuations has yet been little studied. Figure 17 in Lau (1981) is the only such result that we could find. Lau presents composite charts of rms of bandpass filtered 500-mb height for five simulated winter seasons that had large positive amplitudes of the first eigenvector of normalized monthly mean 500-mb height and compared it with a composite of another five winter seasons that had large negative amplitude of the same eigenvector. He found that the displacements of maxima of bandpass filtered rms (which represent storm tracks) are consistent with shifts in large-scale circulation features such as the location of jet streams and regions of enhanced baroclinicity.

## PREDICTABILITY OF TROPICAL ATMOSPHERE

The large-scale time-mean tropical atmosphere is potentially more predictable than the extratropical atmosphere, because its planetary-scale circulations are dominated by Hadley, Walker, and monsoon circulations, which are intrinsically more stable than is the midlatitude Rossby regime. Interaction of these large-scale overturnings with tropical disturbances (easterly waves, depressions, cyclones, etc.) is not strong enough to make the former unpredictable because of the unpredictability of the latter.

Tropical disturbances are initiated by barotropic–baroclinic instabilities, but their main energy source is the latent heat of condensation. Although their growth rate is fast and they are deterministically less predictable than midlatitude disturbances, their amplitude equilibration is also quite rapid and they attain only moderate intensity.

The intensity and geographical location of Hadley and Walker cells are primarily determined by the boundary conditions and not by synoptic-scale disturbances. Thus, frequency and tracks of depressions and easterly waves are likely controlled by the location and intensity of Hadley and Walker cells and by the distribution of SST and soil moisture fields. It is unlikely that details of tropical disturbances have much influence on the large-scale tropical circulation. By contrast, in midlatitudes, synoptic-scale instabilities interact with planetary-scale circulations to such an extent as to make them less predictable. The circulation in midlatitudes consists of baroclinic waves, long waves, and planetary waves of different wave number and frequency, whereas in the tropics the circulation is clearly separated between the large-scale Hadley and Walker cells and the synoptic-scale disturbances. In other words, tropical spectra in space, as well as in time, are redder than are midlatitude spectra.

The interannual variability of the seasonal mean tropical circulation and rainfall results largely from changes in the location and intensity of the thermally driven Hadley and Walker circulations (Moura and Shukla, 1981). Although the reasons for the positions and intensities of the climatological mean rainfall maxima (corresponding to the ascending branches of Hadley and Walker cells) are not well understood, it appears that the interannual fluctuations of these thermally driven circulations are closely related to the changes in the boundary conditions (viz. SST and soil moisture) at the earth's surface. Much of the local interannual variability over different parts of the tropics is in fact a regional manifestation of the planetary-scale El Niño–southern oscillation–monsoon phenomena resulting from interactions among the atmosphere, the oceans, and the land processes. Some of the largest anomalies in circulation and rainfall, comprising a major portion of the interannual variability, are strongly phase locked with the seasonal cycle. Thus, the major tropical droughts and floods are due either to an amplification of the annual cycle or to shifts in the locations of maximum amplitude.

## Atmosphere–Ocean Interactions

The winter of 1982–1983 witnessed the most outstanding example of large persistent SST anomalies over the equatorial Pacific and related circulation anomalies over many parts of the globe. Since the influence of tropical SST anomalies on atmospheric circulation, locally as well as globally, may be important for prediction of short-term climate, we should understand the mechanisms through which SST anomalies influence the atmospheric circulation. Several climate modeling groups have conducted sensitivity experiments for tropical Pacific SST anomalies using their respective GCMs (Blackmon et al., 1983; Shukla and Wallace, 1983). During the Sixteenth

Liège Colloquium on Hydrodynamics (May 1984), a session was devoted to intercomparison of the results from the various modeling groups.

Papers were presented by the following authors reporting on the GCMs of the listed institutions: M. Blackmon, National Center for Atmospheric Research; G. Boer, Canadian Climate Center; V. Cubash, European Centre for Medium Range Weather Forecasts; S. Esbensen, Oregon State University; M. Fennessy, L. Marx, and J. Shukla, Goddard Laboratory for Atmospheric Sciences; A. Oort and N. C. Lau, Geophysical Fluid Dynamics Laboratory; T. N. Palmer and D. Mansfield, British Meteorological Office; R. Sadourny and R. Michaud, Laboratoire de Météorologie Dynamique; and M. Suarez, University of California, Los Angeles.

All the models correctly simulated the general eastward shift of the rainfall maximum over the central equatorial Pacific but with some quantitative differences. The consistency of the results using such widely different GCMs confirmed the earlier hypothesis that tropical SST anomalies can produce significant and predictable changes in tropical rainfall and circulation. Similarities among the simulations of the midlatitude response were not so obvious.

We shall present here, as an example, a sensitivity study with the GLAS climate model using the observed SST anomalies over the tropical Pacific during the winter of 1982–1983 (Fennessy et al., 1985). Figure 19 (top panel) shows the observed SST anomaly during January 1983, which was added to the climatological SST with the model integrated for 60 days. This integration is referred to as the *anomaly run*, and a similar integration with climatological SST is referred to as the *control run*. Such pairs of integrations were made for three different initial conditions. Figure 19 also shows the difference in precipitation between the anomaly and control runs averaged for these three pairs for the period of days 11–60 (middle panel) and the rainfall anomaly calculated from the observed outgoing long-wave radiation for the 1982–1983 winter (bottom panel). The outgoing long-wave radiation anomalies are converted to rainfall anomalies using empirical relations. It is remarkable that the model calculations have been able to simulate the location as well as the intensity of the rainfall anomaly rather well.

To study the role of tropical SST anomalies, Lau and Oort (1984) and Lau (1985) examined a 15-y integration of the GFDL model with the observed SST anomalies over the equatorial Pacific. In the simulation without the SST anomalies (Lau, 1981), there was no evidence for the planetary-scale see-saw of surface pressure referred to as the southern oscillation, which is one of the most dominant modes of tropical variability, whereas in the simulation with the SST anomalies, the southern oscillation is simulated remarkably well. The observed correlations between the tropical SST anomalies and midlatitude circulation are also simulated remarkably well in the 15-y simulation with the SST anomalies.

Philander and Seigel (1985) and Latif (1985) have shown that realistic simulation of oceanic circulation and SST anomalies in tropical oceans can

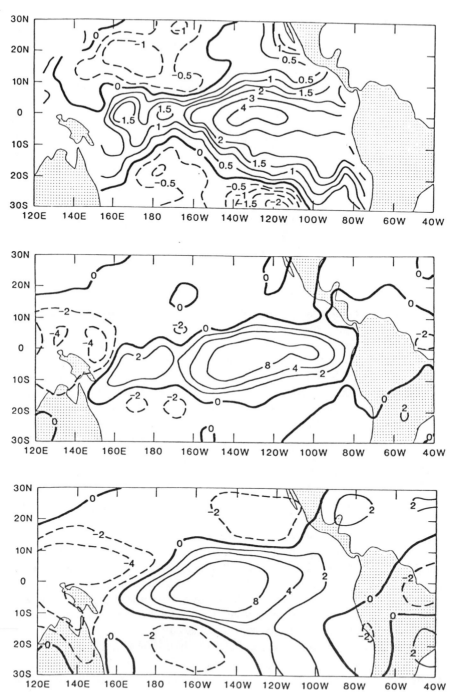

**FIGURE 19.** Observed SST anomaly (°C) for January 1983 (*top*), model-simulated rainfall (mm day$^{-1}$) (*middle*), and observed rainfall anomalies (*bottom*).

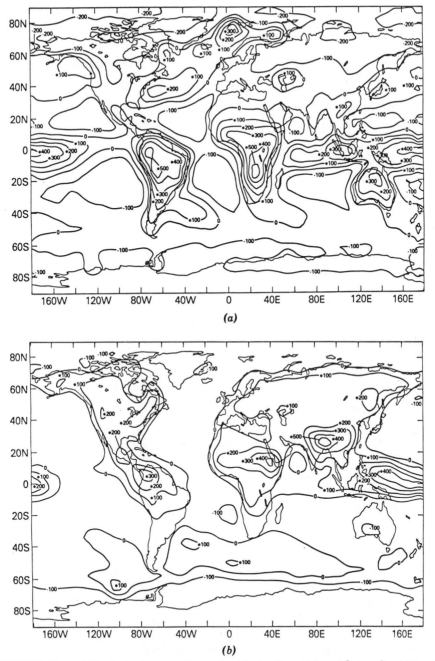

**FIGURE 20.** (*a*) Vertically integrated net diabatic heating (cal cm$^{-2}$ day$^{-1}$) of the atmosphere during winter, as simulated by the GLAS climate model. (*b*) Vertically integrated net diabatic heating (cal cm$^{-2}$ day$^{-1}$) of the atmosphere during summer, as simulated by the GLAS climate model.

be obtained by using the prescribed wind stress from the atmospheric observations. These results of one-way forced ocean models are quite encouraging and suggest that the predictability of the coupled ocean–atmosphere system could be longer than the predictability of the atmosphere alone.

### Atmosphere–Land Interactions

Several model sensitivity studies suggest that changes in the land surface boundary conditions influence the tropical circulation on regional as well as on planetary scales (Shukla and Mintz, 1982; Mintz, 1984). Changes in soil moisture, albedo, or vegetation change the partitioning of the incoming radiant energy into sensible and latent heat. Changes in the ground temperature, evaporation, and cloudiness can produce regional effects, but changes in rainfall can produce planetary-scale effects because they represent changes in the deep diabatic heat sources that drive the atmospheric circulation. Although the land surface area is smaller than the ocean surface area, the influence of the land surface forcing functions can be very large because the maxima of the vertically integrated heat sources occur over the land (see Fig. 20a for winter and 20b for summer), and therefore, for the same fractional change in the intensity of the heat source, the absolute value of the change in the forcing, and consequently the response, may be larger over the land.

### FURTHER PROGRESS NEEDED

Although GCMs can realistically simulate the observed large-scale circulation features of summer and winter, some systematic errors remain to be removed. Seasonal cycle simulations still need a detailed analysis of such structural features as seasonal transitions and seasons other than summer and winter. The simulations of low-pass filtered variance and location and intensity and duration of blocking events need further improvement. Interannual variability of model-simulated intraseasonal variability still needs to be examined.

Presumably, the most important mechanism for midlatitude variability is the internal dynamics, while boundary forcing is the most important mechanism for the tropical variability. However, the model integrations necessary to answer these questions still need to be done, as well as further analysis of existing model integrations. We cannot rule out the influence of midlatitude and/or tropical boundary forcing in producing large circulation anomalies in midlatitudes.

Evidently, a significant portion of the variability over different tropical regions is a regional manifestation of the planetary-scale low-frequency disturbances, and major tropical droughts and floods are related to changes in the amplitude and phase of the annual cycle. Detailed analyses of these connections are still to be developed.

Most of the existing general circulation models do not have an adequate treatment of the physical processes at the land surface, especially the role of vegetation in determining the energy and moisture balance at the earth's surface. These models must be improved before modeling experiments on the impact of regional land surface anomalies would be meaningful. For example, in order to study the impact of deforestation on local and global climate, the model must be integrated first with an adequate treatment of forest. A model climate resulting from deforestation cannot be meaningfully interpreted without a model climate with the forest. The spatial resolution of the models also must be adequate for a description of the physical effects associated with regional changes in land surface properties. In these respects, modeling of atmosphere–land interactions is about 10 y behind the state of modeling of atmosphere–ocean interactions. Several modeling groups are beginning to implement realistic models of the biosphere in general circulation models, and it is hoped that within the next several years there will be systematic numerical sensitivity studies on the effects of changes in land surface conditions and the role of land surface forcing in determining the variability and predictability of the tropical atmosphere.

## REFERENCES

Blackmon, M. L., Geisler, J. E., and Pitcher, E. J., 1983. A general circulation model study of January climate anomaly patterns associated with interannual variation of equatorial Pacific sea surface temperatures, *J. Atmos. Sci.* **40,** 1410–1425.

Blackmon, M. L. and Lau, N. C., 1980. Regional characteristics of the Northern Hemisphere wintertime circulation: A comparison of the simulation of a GFDL general circulation model with observations, *J. Atmos. Sci.* **37,** 497–514.

Blackmon, M. L., Wallace, J. M., Lau, N. C., and Mullen, S. L., 1977. An observational study of the Northern Hemisphere wintertime circulation, *J. Atmos. Sci.* **34,** 1040–1053.

Charney, J. G. and Devore, J. G., 1979. Multiple flow equilibria in the atmosphere and blocking, *J. Atmos. Sci.* **36,** 1205–1216.

Charney, J. G. and Straus, D. M., 1980. Form-drag instability, multiple equilibria and propagating planetary waves in baroclinic, orographically forced, planetary wave systems, *J. Atmos. Sci.* **37,** 1157–1176.

Charney, J. G. and Shukla, J., 1981. Predictability of monsoons, in Sir James Lighthill and R. P. Pearce, Eds., *Monsoon Dynamics*, Cambridge University Press, London, England.

Charney, J. G., Shukla, J., Mo, K. C., 1981. Comparison of a barotropic blocking theory with observation, *J. Atmos. Sci.,* **38,** 762–779.

Chen, T. C. and Shukla, J., 1983. Diagnostic analysis and spectral energetics of a blocking event in the GLAS climate model simulation, *Mon. Wea. Rev.* **111,** 3–22.

Dole, R. M., 1982. Persistent anomalies of the extratropical Northern Hemisphere wintertime circulation, Ph.D. Thesis, Massachusetts Institute of Technology, Cambridge, MA.

Fennessy, M. J., Marx, L., and Shukla, J., 1985. General circulation model sensitivity to 1982–83 equatorial Pacific sea surface temperature anomalies, *Mon. Wea. Rev.* **113,** 858–864.

Gilchrist, A., 1982. Aspects of the simulation of climate and climate variability in middle latitudes, in *Proceedings of the Study Conference on the Physical Basis for Climate Prediction on Seasonal, Annual and Decadal Time Scales*, Leningrad (USSR), 13–17 September 1982, *World Climate Program Series, WCP-47*, World Meteorological Organization, Geneva, Switzerland.

Godbole, R. V. and Shukla, J., 1981. *Global Analysis of January and July Sea Level Pressure*, NASA Technical Memo. 82097 (NTIS N8124674), Goddard Space Flight Center, Greenbelt, MD.

Halem, M., Shukla, J., Mintz, Y., Wu, M. L., Godbole, R., Herman G., and Sud, Y., 1979. Comparisons of observed seasonal climate features with a winter and summer numerical simulation produced by the GLAS general circulation model, in *GARP Publication Series No.* **22,** World Meteorological Organization, Geneva, Switzerland.

Hayashi, Y., 1974. Spectral analysis of tropical disturbances appearing in a GFDL general circulation model, *J. Atmos. Sci.* **31,** 180–218.

Hayashi, Y., 1980. Studies of the tropical general circulation with a global model of the atmosphere, in *Proceedings of the Seminar on Impact of GATE on Large-Scale Numerical Modeling of the Atmosphere and Ocean, Woods Hole, Massachusetts, August 20–29, 1979*, National Academy of Sciences, Washington, D.C.

Hayashi, Y., and Golder, D. G., 1980. The seasonal variation of tropical transient planetary waves appearing in a GFDL general circulation model, *J. Atmos. Sci.* **37,** 705–716.

Jaeger, L., 1976. Monatskarten des Niederschlags für die ganze Erde, in *Berichte des Deutschen Wetterdienstes*, Vol. 18, No. 139, Offenbach, FRG.

Latif, M., 1985. Western and eastern variability in a model of the equatorial Pacific, Ph.D. thesis, Max-Planck-Institut für Meteorologie, Hamburg, FRG.

Lau, N. C., 1981. A diagnostic study of recurrent meteorological anomalies appearing in a 15-year simulation with a GFDL general circulation model, *Mon. Wea. Rev.* **109,** 2287–2311.

Lau, N. C., 1985. Modeling the seasonal dependence of the atmospheric response to observed El-Niños in 1962–76, *Mon. Wea. Rev.* **113,** 1970–1996.

Lau, N. C. and Oort, A. H., 1984. Response of a GFDL general circulation model to SST fluctuations observed in the tropical Pacific Ocean during the period 1962–1976, in *Coupled Atmosphere–Ocean Models*, Elsevier, New York.

Malone, R. C., Pitcher, E. J., Blackmon, M. L., Puri, K., and Bourke, W., 1984. The simulation of stationary and transient geopotential height eddies in January and July with a spectral general circulation model, *J. Atmos. Sci.* **41,** 1394–1419.

Manabe, S. and Hahn, D. G., 1981. Simulation of atmospheric variability, *Mon. Wea. Rev.* **109**, 2260–2286.

Manabe, S. and Smagorinsky, J., 1967. Simulated climatology of a general circulation model with a hydrologic cycle. II. Analysis of the tropical atmosphere, *Mon. Wea. Rev.* **95**, 155–169.

Manabe, S., Hahn, D. G., and Holloway, J. L., 1974. The seasonal variation of the tropical circulation as simulated by a global model of the atmosphere, *J. Atmos. Sci.* **31**, 43–83.

Manabe, S., Hahn, D. G., and Holloway, J. L., 1979. Climate simulations with GFDL spectral models of the atmosphere: Effect of spectral truncation, in *GARP Publication Series No. 22*, World Meteorological Organization, Geneva, Switzerland.

Manabe, S., Holloway, J. L., and Stone, H. M., 1970. Tropical circulation in a time-integration of a global model of the atmosphere, *J. Atmos. Sci.* **27**, 580–613.

Mansfield, D. A., 1981. The incidence of blocking in the Meteorological Office's 5-level model, *Met. 0.13 Branch Memorandum No. 99*, Meteorological Office, Bracknell, England.

Mintz, Y., 1984. The sensitivity of numerically simulated climates to land-surface boundary conditions, in John T. Houghton, Ed. *The Global Climate*, Cambridge University Press, London.

Mintz, Y. and Dean, G., 1952. The observed mean field of motion of the atmosphere, *Geophys. Res. Papers* **17**, 1–65.

Moura, A. and Shukla, J. 1981, On the dynamics of droughts in northeast Brazil, observation, theory, and numerical experiments with a general circulation model, *J. Atmos. Sci.*, **38**, 2653–2675.

Philander, S. G. H. and Seigel, A., 1985. Simulation of the El Niño of 1982–1983, Proceedings of the 16th International Liège Colloquium on Hydrodynamics, in *Coupled Atmosphere–Ocean Models*, Elsevier, New York.

Pitcher, E. J., Malone, R. C., Ramanathan, V., Blackmon, M. L., Puri, K., and Bourke, W., 1983. January and July simulations with a spectral general circulation model, *J. Atmos. Sci.* **40**, 580–604.

Sadler, J. C., 1975. *The Upper Tropospheric Circulation over the Global Tropics*, Department of Meteorology, University of Hawaii, Report No. UHMET 75-05, pp. 1–35.

Shukla, J., 1981a. Dynamical predictability of monthly means, *J. Atmos. Sci.* **38**, 2547–2572.

Shukla, J., 1981b. Predictability of the tropical atmosphere, *NASA Technical Memo. No. 83829*, Goddard Space Flight Center, Greenbelt, MD, pp. 1–51.

Shukla, J. and Mo, K. C., 1983. Seasonal and geographical variation of blocking, *Mon. Wea. Rev.* **111**, 388–402.

Shukla, J. and Mintz, Y., 1982. Influence of land-surface evapotranspiration on the earth's climate, *Science* **215**, 1498–1501.

Shukla, J. and Wallace, J. M., 1983. Numerical simulation of the atmospheric response to equatorial Pacific sea surface temperature anomalies, *J. Atmos. Sci.* **40**, 1613–1630.

Shukla, J., Straus, D., Randall, D., Sud, Y., and Marx, L., 1981a. Winter and summer simulations with the GLAS climate model, *NASA Technical Memo. 83866* (NTIS N821880), Goddard Space Flight Center, Greenbelt, MD.

Shukla, J., Mo, K. C., and Eaton, M., 1981b. Climatology of blocking in the GLAS climate model, *NASA Technical Memo. No. 83907*, Goddard Space Flight Center, Greenbelt, MD, pp. 207–216.

Tung, K. K. and Lindzen, R. S., 1979. A theory of stationary longwaves. Part I. A simple theory of blocking, *Mon. Wea. Rev.* **107**, 714–734.

---

# ☐ COMMENTS ON "GENERAL CIRCULATION MODELING AND THE TROPICS"

**James E. Hansen**

Shukla has done a good job of describing numerical results obtained with a typical general circulation model. I therefore confine my comments to (1) several remarks about GCM studies that have been used to analyze physical processes in the tropics and (2) some questions concerning the reliability of GCM simulations of climate change in the tropics.

Early GCM studies were focused mainly on middle latitudes, but useful insight regarding tropical circulation has been provided in the past decade by certain GCM experiments. These experiments illustrate that a good deal can be learned from GCM experiments provided that the user focuses on general conclusions that are independent of model details and imperfections.

Charney et al. (1975) examined the effect of a regional-scale increase in surface albedo, such as may occur with defoliation or deforestation of vegetated land. They found that the increase of surface albedo leads to increased radiative cooling by the atmosphere, increased local subsidence, and thus a suppression of cumulus convection and its associated rainfall. Since reduced rainfall would tend to further reduce vegetation cover, the process represents a positive-feedback mechanism. The process is most likely to be important in arid or semiarid regions where large-scale subsidence already occurs, where most of the rainfall is from cumulus clouds, and where transports by the winds are weak and inefficient at counteracting temperature changes due to the albedo change. Reduced vegetation cover also reduces the potential for local evapotranspiration, and this too tends to contribute to the positive feedback. Therefore, at least in areas of marginal precipitation, there appears to be a real possibility that anthropogenic desertification may tend to feed on itself, creating a chronic problem of inadequate rainfall. Although the natural variability of rainfall in the tropics is so large that wet years and dry years will always occur, the GCM experiments suggest that it is important to better understand the relation between anthropogenic effects on vegetation cover and regional climate. Obtaining such understanding will require more realistic modeling of the biosphere in GCMs than that done to date.

GCM experiments have also revealed information on the mechanisms that drive the large-scale longitudinal (Walker) and meridional (Hadley) circulation in the tropics. Manabe and Terpstra (1974) did an experiment in which they removed all mountains on the globe. They found that the mountains cause a great deal of long-wave stationary eddy energy in the atmosphere but have little effect on the total eddy energy, which is dominated by smaller-scale transient eddy energy in the no-mountain case. Topography was also found to cause cyclogenesis on the lee side of major mountain ranges and to affect the global distribution of precipitation by altering the three-dimensional advection of moisture. However, the large changes were all at middle and high latitudes; the tropical circulation and hydrological cycle were found to be much less dependent on topography.

A series of GCM experiments were made by Stone and Chervin (1984) and Chervin and Druyan (1984) in which they investigated systematically the roles of continentality, sea surface temperature gradients, and topography in maintaining the tropical Walker circulation. They found that the primary factor affecting the Walker circulation in the model is the global distribution of continents and oceans; ocean surface temperature gradients were found to also be important, but topography was relatively unimportant, the latter conclusion being consistent with the experiment of Manabe and Terpstra (1974). The Stone and Chervin (1984) experiments show that both continentality and ocean surface temperature gradients force the model atmosphere by modifying the surface heat balance. Where the atmosphere is heated, rising motions are generated, causing convergence of moisture and condensation, the resulting heating of the atmosphere reinforcing the rising motion. The vertical motions were found to be highly correlated with the surface heating and precipitation, and the precipitation was correlated more with moisture convergence than with evaporation. One very interesting conclusion from these experiments was that the forcing by ocean surface temperature gradients contains a large nonlocal component; that is, the changes in the local heat balance and forcing of the atmosphere can, to a large extent, depend on nonlocal changes in ocean surface temperatures. Indeed, in the south tropical Pacific, the model response was greatly enhanced by the continentality and was controlled more by distant ocean surface temperature gradients than by local ocean surface temperature gradients.

A series of experiments was made by Rind and Rossow (1984) to investigate the effects of different physical processes on the Hadley circulation. These experiments included changes such as "turning the sun off," eliminating sea surface temperature gradients, eliminating evaporation, eliminating surface friction, and eliminating mixing of momentum by convection. The results indicate that the Hadley circulation responds to both thermal and momentum forcing, but the response tends to be complicated, with adjustments among the several processes that force the Hadley circulation taking place in response to changes of a single process. The occurrence of these adjustments suggests that prediction of the effects of anthropogenic surface perturbations on the Hadley circulation will depend on the availability of models with realistic representation of complex atmospheric processes and their interactions.

The above studies are examples of cases in which useful insights about tropical circulation and climate have been derived from GCM studies. But are GCMs capable of reliable simulation of the effects of changes, anthropogenic or otherwise, of vegetation or other surface conditions? It will be relatively easy to incorporate into the GCMs representations of the biosphere and surface that are as detailed as the biologists care to contribute. This will undoubtedly permit some interesting sensitivity studies and general conclusions of the type obtained in the studies discussed above. However, it should not be assumed that GCMs will be ready for reliable assessment of the climatic impact of regional surface perturbations. Quite apart from the possibility that such assessments may require much higher spatial resolution than that employed in current GCMs, there are serious questions about how well present models represent first-order atmospheric processes.

One area of particular concern is the parameterization of moist convection for GCMs. Baker et al. (1978) tried two different parameterizations of moist convection, a convective adjustment scheme and a more elaborate convective parameterization of Kuo (1974), finding a strong sensitivity to the convective parameterization in 10-day forecasts, probably resulting from differences in the release of latent heat. We also note that forecasts made with the model of the European Centre for Medium Range Weather Forecasts (ECMWF), which has been shown to be more accurate than other current operational forecast models, are very much less accurate in the tropics than at higher latitudes (Bengtsson and Simmons, 1983). Assessments of the model forecasts by the ECMWF group lead them to suggest that there are serious deficiencies in their parameterizations of convection. Bengtsson and Simmons (1983) conclude that tropical forecasts respond more quickly and acutely to defects in the model than do forecasts at middle and high latitudes.

The need for a better understanding of the GCMs in tropical regions and for improvements in the representations of physical processes apparently is not limited to short-range forecasts. The GCM experiments with doubled $CO_2$ by Manabe and Stouffer (1980) and Hansen et al. (1984) yield relatively similar climate sensitivities at high latitudes but differences of more than a factor of 2 at low latitudes. Differences in clouds and convection in the models are a likely explanation for the difference in sensitivity, but whether either model has a realistic tropical climate sensitivity is open to question.

In this short comment, it is not practical to discuss satisfactorily how well current GCMs simulate tropical climate, and I have omitted major topics such as modeling of the El Niño, which, however, is included in Shukla's review. I only note that although GCMs have been used to infer valuable information on certain weather and climate processes in the tropics, there is still a great need for improvement in our understanding of current models and for improvement of the models. It is not at all clear that the modeling tools are yet in hand for reliable assessment of the interactions between man, the biosphere, and climate in the tropics.

## ACKNOWLEDGMENTS

I am particularly indebted to my colleagues Drs. Peter Stone and David Rind for their suggestions and comments.

## REFERENCES

Baker, W. E., Kung, E. C., and Somerville, R. C. J., 1978. An energetics analysis of forecast experiments with the NCAR general circulation model, *Mon. Wea. Rev.* **106**, 311–323.

Bengtsson, L. and Simmons, A. J., 1983. Medium-range weather prediction—operational experience at ECMWF, in B. Hoskins and R. Pearce, Eds., *Large-Scale Dynamical Processes in the Atmosphere*, Academic, New York.

Charney, J., Stone, P. H., and Quirk, W. J., 1975. Drought in the Sahara: A biogeophysical feedback mechanism, *Science* **187**, 434–435.

Chervin, R. M. and Druyan, L. M., 1984. The influence of ocean surface temperature gradient and continentality on the Walker circulation. Part I: Prescribed tropical changes, *Mon. Wea. Rev.* **112**, 1510–1523.

Hansen, J., Lacis, A., Rind, D., Russell, G., Stone, P., Fung, I., Ruedy, R., and Lerner, J., 1984. Climate sensitivity: Analysis of feedback mechanisms, in J. Hansen and T. Takahashi, Eds., *Climate Processes and Climate Sensitivity*, American Geophysical Union, Washington, DC.

Kuo, H. L., 1974. Further studies of the parameterization of the influence of cumulus convection in large-scale flow, *J. Atmos. Sci.* **31**, 1232–1240.

Manabe, S. and Stouffer, R. J., 1980. Sensitivity of a global climate model to an increase of $CO_2$ concentration in the atmosphere, *J. Geophys. Res.* **85**, 5529–5554.

Manabe, S. and Terpstra, T. B., 1974. The effects of mountains on the general circulation of the atmosphere as identified by numerical experiments, *J. Atmos. Sci.* **31**, 3–42.

Rind, D. and Rossow, W. B., 1984. The effects of physical processes on the Hadley circulation, *J. Atmos. Sci.* **41**, 479–507.

Stone, P. H. and Chervin, R. M., 1984. The influence of ocean surface temperature gradient and continentality on the Walker circulation. Part II: Prescribed global changes, *Mon. Wea. Rev.* **112**, 1524–1534.

# Chapter 20

# Effects of Change in Land Use on Climate in the Humid Tropics

**Ann Henderson-Sellers**

Tropical deforestation is known to be an important ecological feature of the present-day environment (Gomez-Pompa et al., 1972; Myers, 1983), and there have been suggestions that deforestation is detrimental to the climate of regions distant from the perturbed area (Newell, 1971). Modelers study tropical land use change partly for these reasons but also because the model changes required to simulate forest removal are large. Hence, although the assumed changes may be totally unrealistic, a resulting large response would be relatively easy to distinguish from the inherent model "noise." Such climate model sensitivity studies are all too easily but wrongly interpreted as climatic predictions.

In this essay, I shall discuss why it is now nearly impossible to make a realistic estimate of the probable effects of land use change on climate in the humid tropics. The data pertaining to land use change are difficult to obtain and exceedingly difficult to verify (e.g., Myers, 1980a,b; Lanly and Clement, 1981; Lanly and Rao, 1981; Fearnside, 1982). Furthermore, the global climate models that have been applied to this problem are, in this particular instance of specific locational change, extremely blunt instruments (Schneider, 1984). At best they are inappropriate, and at worst their results are unusable.

Additional secondary difficulties that thwart understanding of the possible impact of land use change on climate in the tropics include the inadequacy of the statistical methodology for interpretation of both land use change information and the results of climatic simulations, selective quotation of both observational and simulation results, and a general lack of statement of caveats in both cases. These secondary aspects combine with the two primary difficulties making model-based studies of the possible impact of land use change on the large-scale climate in tropical environments extremely difficult.

## ONLY A FEW MODELING STUDIES

Only two studies using global climate models have been undertaken to study the climatic effects of land use change encompassing the whole of the humid tropics. Potter et al. (1975) used the Lawrence Livermore Laboratory two-dimensional statistical dynamic model to assess the impact of changing surface albedo from 0.07 to 0.25 in a fraction of the tropical zone. This experiment was first done with no prescribed change in surface hydrology (wet case) and then repeated with a prescribed reduction in evaporation (dry case) in an attempt to incorporate the effects of increased runoff and reduced effective rooting depth. They calculated that globally averaged surface temperature would decrease by 0.2 and 0.3 K, respectively, in the dry and wet cases. The experiment was essentially a global-scale assessment, and precipitation changes were given for all latitude zones. In the deforested zone (5°N–5°S), precipitation decreased in both the wet and dry simulations. The decreases were 0.24 and 0.22 m $y^{-1}$, respectively.

An analysis of the sensitivity of the U.K. Meteorological Office (UKMO) global climate model to land use changes throughout the humid tropics has recently been undertaken by Wilson (1984). She studied the results from a series of global climate model experiments* designed to permit identification of the individual effects of perturbations made to radiative and hydrological properties. In her deforestation experiment, both moisture capacity and surface albedo were changed from values appropriate for forest conditions to those appropriate for a grassland vegetation cover. Wilson (1984) found the UKMO model to be sensitive to the prescribed changes at a regional scale. The response was initially dominated by surface albedo modification, but as the nine-month integration progressed, the soil moisture availability, which was affected by both soil moisture capacity changes and changes in rainfall distribution, became increasingly more influential in determining the partitioning of the latent and sensible heat flux terms. She found that in Amazonia there was a decrease in precipitation of between 1.0 and 5.0 mm $day^{-1}$ during the wet season and less than 2 mm $day^{-1}$ in the dry season and a decrease in evaporation of between 0.5 and 5.0 mm $day^{-1}$ which was greatest in the center and west of the basin. Similar, but weaker, responses were noted in the Zaire basin. The temperature change was variable, with no systematic response in any of the deforested regions. The global response was negligible in all fields, and no regional changes that differed from the control simulation by greater than $2\sigma$ were discovered.

---

* Global climate model is used in this essay synonymously with general circulation model (GCM) used for climate studies.

There have been two other climate "predictions" pertaining to land use change in the tropics that focused on one region: Amazonia. Lettau et al. (1979) used a simple climatonomic approach based on hydrological data from 28 stations in Amazonia (Molion, 1975) and mean regional wind information to assess the possible impact of tropical deforestation on the regional-scale climate. These authors predicted increases in both local temperature and rainfall.

In the simulation described by Henderson-Sellers and Gornitz (1984), an attempt was made to maximize the possible impact of tropical deforestation by concentrating in the Amazon, the deforestation appropriate to the whole globe. The magnitude of the change imposed is approximately the equivalent of 35–50 y of global deforestation at the current rate. In this simulation, using the Goddard Institute for Space Studies (GISS) global climate model (Hansen et al., 1983), a total area of $4.95 \times 10^6$ km$^2$ of tropical moist forest was replaced by grass. The surface roughness length, the effective rooting depth, moisture-holding capacity of the two soil layers, and surface albedo were all modified. Although the surface albedo increased from 0.11 to 0.17, the change of the local surface temperature was negligible. However, other climatic parameters were altered locally (Fig. 1). Rainfall decreased by 0.5–0.7 mm day$^{-1}$ and evapotranspiration and total cloud cover also decreased. There was no local temperature change in spite of the increased surface albedo because the reduction in evapotranspiration and the decrease in cloud cover counteracted the increase in the surface albedo. Likewise, temperature changes could not be identified by Henderson-Sellers and Gornitz (1984) at the hemispheric or global scale, nor could changes in the planetary albedo or precipitation, and there was no important response in the Hadley or Walker (see Julian and Chervin, 1978, 1980) circulation regimes (Fig. 2).

Table 1 compares results from these four different climate model experiments. Potter et al. (1975) predict a decrease in precipitation of about 0.23 m y$^{-1}$ and a decrease in temperature of about 0.5 K, while Lettau et al. (1979) predict (somewhat surprisingly) a precipitation increase of 0.075 m y$^{-1}$ and a temperature increase of about 0.5 K. Henderson-Sellers and Gornitz's (1984) results are somewhat similar to those of Potter et al. (1975) for the region of Amazonia in that they predict a decreased precipitation of about 0.20 m y$^{-1}$ but no significant temperature change. Wilson's (1984) results seem to suggest a larger hydrological response than these earlier experiments, with rainfall decreasing by between 0.1 and 0.8 m y$^{-1}$ although she too reported no systematic change in local temperature and could detect no significant response outside the region of perturbation.

The results of these few simulation experiments suggest some common themes: first, that changes in the surface hydrology are at least as important as changes in the surface albedo; second, that the results are sensitive to the parameterizations inherent in the model and to the input land surface information; and third, that while the local meteorological disturbance may

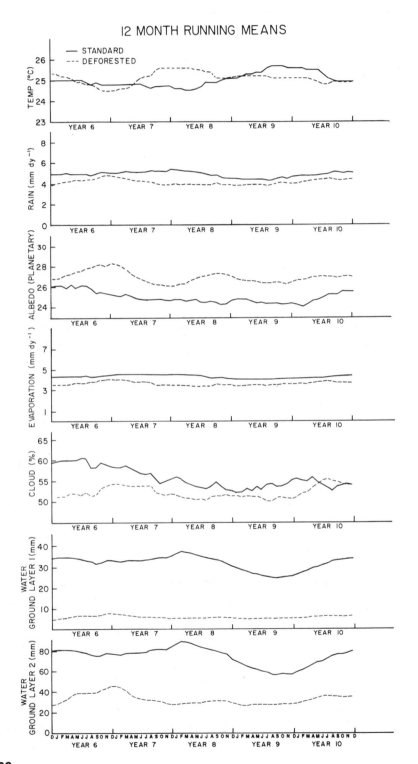

## 12 MONTH RUNNING MEANS

— STANDARD
--- DEFORESTED

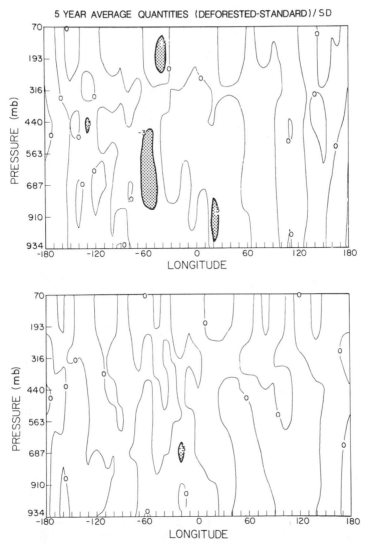

VERTICAL VELOCITY

5 YEAR AVERAGE QUANTITIES (DEFORESTED-STANDARD)/SD

**FIGURE 2.** Five-year average of climate change test statistic given by the ratio (perturbation − control)/(control standard deviation). Values greater than ±3 occur in regions where the perturbation vertical velocity differs significantly (99% confidence) from the control field. The fields shown are derived from the vertical velocities in the latitude band 8°N to 15°S for January (*upper*) and July (*lower*). [After Henderson-Sellers and Gornitz (1984).]

---

**FIGURE 1.** Twelve-month running means of various climatic parameters for the last 5 y of the control and Amazonian deforestation simulations. The region for which the values were averaged is shown in Fig. 4*b* as the GISS GCM Amazonian region. [From Henderson-Sellers and Gornitz (1984).] Figures 1–3 reproduced with permission of D. Reidel, Copyright ©, 1984.

**TABLE 1. Comparison of Model Simulations of Tropical Deforestation**

| Model Attributes | Throughout Humid Tropics | | Amazonia Only | |
|---|---|---|---|---|
| | Potter et al., 1975 | Wilson, 1984 | Lettau et al., 1979 | Henderson-Sellers and Gornitz, 1984 |
| **Features** | | | | |
| Areal coverage | Global two-dimensional statistical dynamic model (tropical deforestation) | Global climate model (tropical land-type change) | Amazon Basin | Global climate model (deforestation in Amazonia) |
| Spatial resolution | 10° latitude | 2.5° latitude × 3.75° longitude | 5° longitude | 8° latitude × 10° longitude |
| **Perturbation** | | | | |
| Albedo increase | 0.18 | 0.08 | 0.03 | 0.06 |
| Hydrology change | Dry case had increased runoff and evaporation | Soil moisture capacity reduced by 32, 20, and 12 cm for fine, medium, and coarse textured soils | Evaporative flux from soil increased | Soil moisture capacity reduced from 200 to 30 cm and from 450 to 200 cm in upper and lower ground layers |

| Other changes | None | None | Infrared emissivity changed | Roughness length decreased |
| --- | --- | --- | --- | --- |
| **Results** | | | | |
| Atmospheric circulation | Weakened Hadley cell | No significant (>2σ) change detected | Assumed regional trade winds unchanged | Walker circulation showed no significant (>1%) disturbance; no Hadley cell circulation change |
| Precipitation | Decrease 230 mm y$^{-1}$ in 5°N–5°S zone | Decrease Amazonia 100–800 mm y$^{-1}$; Congo 200–600 mm y$^{-1}$ | Increase 75 mm y$^{-1}$ (Amazonia) | Decrease 220 mm y$^{-1}$ (Amazonia) |
| Surface temperature | Decrease 0.4°C in 5°N–5°S zone | No systematic change | Increase 0.55°C | No significant change |

be very large, there is dispute about whether to expect detectable climatic change in any areas separate from the region of perturbation.

## LAND USE CHANGE: A DEARTH OF DATA

Tropical forests are being perturbed in a number of different ways, all of which result in at least partial clearance and may lead to a rapid degeneration of the underlying soil (e.g., Myers, 1980a,b; Jordan, 1982). The traditional shifting cultivation is being overtaken by wholesale removal of vast tracts, often prompted by highway development and economic incentives for large cattle ranches and small-scale farming colonization (Fearnside, 1982, and Chapter 4).

Estimates of loss of tropical forest to shifting cultivation and new permanent agriculture range between 10 and 20 million hectares per year (Myers, 1980a,b) and 3.5 and 8.3 million hectares per year (Seiler and Crutzen, 1980). Deforestation by forest clearing for cattle grazing has been estimated at 1.35–2.0 million hectares per year (Myers, 1980a) and 4.8–6.0 million hectares per year (Seiler and Crutzen, 1980). Logging could account for 1.8–2.9 million hectares per year, and the demand for fuelwood could consume up to 2.5 million hectares per year (Myers, 1980a). Taken together, these various processes could remove up to 9–15 million hectares per year (Seiler and Crutzen, 1980), or even 24.5 million hectares per year of tropical moist forest (Myers, 1980a). Lanly (1982) finds a deforestation rate of around 7.3 million hectares per year of all closed forests and 3.8 million hectares per year of open forest, or a total of 11.1 million hectares per year (0.6% per year), falling within the range of Seiler and Crutzen (1980). Myers's (1980a,b) higher figure (Table 2) applies to the total area of degraded forests and therefore covers a larger area than that of Lanly (1982), who considers deforestation in a more restricted sense of a complete (and permanent) removal of the tree cover. Degradation includes partial destruction of forests or selective tree removals. Even when focusing on a specific area, data are difficult to establish. As is illustrated in Table 2, many of the difficulties in assessing the rate of land use change have to do with definitions of current land use. For example, in one of the earliest attempts at a global forest survey, Zon and Sparhawk (1923) define forest land as (p. xi) "land covered with wooded growth of economic importance." This definition makes comparison of these early figures with more recent surveys such as those listed in Table 2 very difficult and hence inhibits long-term assessment of tropical deforestation.

Recent years have seen greater efforts to assess the current rate of tropical forest removal as well as the extent of present tropical forests. For example, in 1978, a collaborative project between the Brazilian Institute for Forest Development (IBDF) and the National Institute for Space Research (INPE)

**TABLE 2.   Extent of Tropical Forests (1000 km²)[a]**

| Authors | Forest type | Asia and Pacific | Latin America | Africa | Total |
|---|---|---|---|---|---|
| Myers, 1980b | Tropical moist forest | 2,713.96 | 6,415.80 | 1,513.90 | 10,643.66 |
| Sommer, 1976 | Moist forest | 2,540.00 | 5,060.00 | 1,750.00 | 9,350.00 |
| | Total forest | 4,170.00 | 9,640.00 | 3,340.00 | 17,150.00 |
| Persson, 1974[b] | Closed forests | 2,940.05 | 5,768.22 | 1,959.47 | 10,667.74 |
| | Total forest | 4,059.83 | 7,340.65 | 7,549.60 | 18,950.08 |
| FAO, 1980[b] (data for 1979) | All | 3,570.54 | 9,430.57 | 6,692.13 | 19,693.24 |
| Lanly, 1982 | Closed forests | 3,055.10 | 6,786.55 | 2,166.34 | 12,007.99 |
| | All forest land | 3,364.58 | 8,956.52 | 7,030.79 | 19,351.89 |

Mean (total forest) $18,790 \pm 1130 \times 10^3$ km²
Mean (closed forest) $10,670 \pm 1330 \times 10^3$ km²

[a] After Henderson-Sellers and Gornitz (1984).
[b] Data for same 16 countries (Asia), 23 countries (Latin America), and 37 countries (Africa) as in Lanly (1982).

was launched with the objective of verifying to what extent Legal Amazonia[a] [area ~4,975,527 km²; Fearnside (1982)] has been deforested. After an initial pilot study, the project was extended to cover the whole of Legal Amazonia and deforestation was calculated for two periods, 1975–1976 and 1976–1978, using Landsat images (Tardin et al., 1979). The results presented in Table 3 show that during the period 1975–1978, deforestation of Legal Amazonia reached 77,172 km², or 1.55% of the total area (Parada et al., 1981). The largest deforested area was in Mato Grosso (28,255 km²) followed by Pará (22,445 km²) and Goiás (10,288 km²). As do many such statistical analyses, Table 3 refers to the Legal Amazon or essentially double the rain forest area (Lovejoy and Salati, 1983), which Fearnside (1982) gives as $2.6 \times 10^6$ km². Hence assessments of deforestation from such data are underestimates.

Further confusion can arise when deforestation rates are discussed. For example, the last two columns in Table 3 show deforestation rates calculated using two different methods: assuming an exponential increase in clearing and assuming a linear increase in clearing. While in both cases the federal territory of Rondônia has the highest deforestation rate, with Goiás and Matto Grosso taking second and third places, the percentage rates are very different. Fearnside (1982) discusses these different methods of measuring deforestation rates and proposes that clearing rates be expressed in terms

[a] The partitioning of the Amazon Basin (Moran, 1983b) is Brazil ~65.9%; Peru ~14.5%; Bolivia ~9.4%; Colombia ~5.7%; Ecuador ~2.6% and Venezuela ~1.9%. The Legal Amazon is an area of Brazil which encompasses the Brazilian part of the basin.

**TABLE 3. Observed Cumulative Cleared Areas for Brazilian Amazon[a]**

| States and Federal Territories | Area (km²) | Observed Cumulative Cleared Areas (km²) | | Percentage of Deforestation of State or Territory | Clearing Rate for Exponential Increase[b] (% per year) | Clearing Rate for Linear Increase[c] (% per year) |
|---|---|---|---|---|---|---|
| | | 1975 | 1978 | | | |
| Amapá | 139,068 | 152.50 | 170.50 | 0.122 | 3.719 | 0.0043 |
| Pará | 1,227,530 | 8,654.00 | 22,445.25 | 1.828 | 31.769 | 0.37 |
| Roraima | 243,004 | 55.00 | 143.75 | 0.059 | 32.025 | 0.012 |
| Maranhão[d] | 257,451 | 2,904.75 | 7,334.00 | 2.848 | 30.462 | 0.57 |
| Goiás[d] | 285,793 | 3,307.25 | 10,288.50 | 3.600 | 35.873 | 0.81 |
| Acre | 152,589 | 1,165.50 | 2,464.50 | 1.615 | 24.961 | 0.28 |
| Rondônia | 230,104 | 1,216.50 | 4,184.50 | 1.818 | 41.180 | 0.43 |
| Mato Grosso | 881,001 | 10,124.25 | 28,255.00 | 3.218 | 34.211 | 0.69 |
| Amazonas | 1,558,987 | 779.50 | 1,785.75 | 0.114 | 27.631 | 0.022 |
| Legal Amazon | 4,975,527 | 28,595.25 | 77,171.75 | 1.551 | 33.093 | 0.33 |

[a] After Parada et al. (1981) except as noted.
[b] From Fearnside (1982); increase is expressed in terms of the exponential rate coefficient $r$ given in equation (2).
[c] Calculated linear rate of deforestation of total area.
[d] The area of the state is not totally included in the Legal Amazon.

of an exponential increase in the amount of cleared land. The area cleared after $t$ years, $A_t$, is related to the initial value $A_0$ by

$$A_t = A_0 \exp(rt) \tag{1}$$

where $r$ is the exponential rate coefficient. From the observations of cleared areas at the beginning and end of the 3-y period, $r$ can be calculated using

$$r = \tfrac{1}{3}\ln(A_{1978}/A_{1975}) \tag{2}$$

Not only are the computed deforestation rates different but the extrapolated date of complete clearing also differs significantly depending on the evaluation method employed.

These and other difficulties surround any attempt to assess the magnitude of current rates of deforestation. As Myers (1980b) points out, much of the data base is unreliable, while definitional differences add to the difficulty of comparing estimates. Myers (1980b), for example, defines tropical moist forest (p. 11) as "evergreen or partly evergreen forests, in areas receiving not less than 100 mm of precipitation in any month for 2 out of 3 years, with mean annual temperature of greater than 24°C and essentially frostfree," and he defines conversion as (p. 7–8) ranging from marginal modification to fundamental transformation. Modification, in general, means that the original forest ecosystem maintains some continuity, while transformation refers to complete forest removal. Thus Myers (1980b) is concerned mostly with alteration to primary forests, whereas Parada et al. (1981) make no distinction between primary and secondary forest.

Even within an individual country, the nature of anthropogenic changes differs according to location, need, and incentive. According to Parada et al. (1981), there are four major critical areas of deforestation in Brazil: the first localized in Mato Grosso, the second in Rondônia (transition area between open forest and cerrado), the third along the Belém–Brasília road, and the fourth situated in an area of dense forest in the triangle Belém–Altamira–Santarém. All the different types of deforestation, the confusion over definition, and the selectivity involved in numerical evaluation makes estimation of rates and comparison of evaluations very difficult. To underline this point, Table 4 lists some of the wide range of currently available estimates of the rate of forest clearing in the Brazilian Amazon.

The INPE/IBDF finding reported in Parada et al. (1981) that only 1.55% of Brazil's Legal Amazon had been deforested by the time of the 1978 images is probably an underestimate. Several problems hamper successful interpretation of Landsat imagery (Myers, 1980b), such as the inability to identify very small areas (Fearnside, 1982), and most of these lead to an underestimate of deforestation. Brown (1979) has estimated that approximately 8% of the Amazon Basin is in secondary forests; distinguishing this secondary growth from primary growth is difficult. There are many other inconsist-

**TABLE 4.  Rates of Forest Clearing in Brazilian Amazon**[a]

| Rate of Clearance ($km^2 y^{-1}$) | Dates | Source[b] | Reference | Note |
|---|---|---|---|---|
| 100,000 | 1978 | O. Bittencourt, RADAMBRASIL in 1978 | Sioli, 1980 | Legal Amazon |
| 100,000 | 1975 | "Satellite photos" | *Jornal do Brasil*, 26-7-77, cited in Mahar, 1979 | Legal Amazon |
| 10,000 | 1960–1975 average | FAO/IBDF study, 1975 | Muthoo, 1977, cited in Reis, 1978 | "Brazilian Amazon Forest" |
| 10,427 | 1966–1977 average | IBDF officials in 1979 | Myers, 1980b | Rain forest area |
| 12,777 | 1966–1975 average | SUDAM officials in 1979 | Myers, 1980b | Rain forest area |
| 16,192 | 1975–1978 average | Table 3 (this work) | Fearnside, 1982 | Legal Amazon |
| 23,000 | ? | Programa de Monitoramento da Cobertura Florestal do Brasil, Brasília, 1982 | Salati and Vose, 1984 | Brazilian Amazon |

[a] After Fearnside (1982) and (last entry) Salati and Vose (1984).
[b] IBDF, Brazilian Institute for Forestry Development; SUDAM, Superintendency for Development of the Amazon; RADAMBRASIL, Radar in Amazonia—Brazil Project; FAO, Food and Agriculture Organization of the United Nations.

encies. For example, the Zona Bragantina, an area of Pará of approximately 30,000 $km^2$ near the town of Bragança, has been settled since the late-nineteenth century and has been virtually cleared for many years (Penteado 1967; Sioli, 1973). As Fearnside (1982) notes, the extent of this zone alone is greater than the 28,595 $km^2$, indicated by the INPE/IBDF study as being cleared by 1975 in the entire Legal Amazon, and is almost four times the 8654 $km^2$ area indicated as cleared by 1975 in Pará.

Clearly the question of how much of the tropical forests has been cleared is very difficult to resolve. The interpretation of satellite imagery, often offered as a panacea, is unlikely to provide a complete answer (Otterman, 1977, 1981). Careful definition of terminology and dates encompassed by surveys, as well as areas and types of vegetation included, are essential prerequisites for any land use change assessment.

## GLOBAL CLIMATE MODEL "PREDICTIONS": STILL AN INAPPROPRIATE TOOL

Global climate models seem, on first inspection, to offer the best way of determining the probable effects of changing land surface boundary conditions since they include interactive thermodynamic and hydrodynamic processes. However, land surface parameterization schemes in existing global climate models are highly simplistic, and global-scale information for present-day conditions and likely perturbations are not agreed upon (Rowntree, in press). A number of experiments pertaining to the land surface boundary conditions have been undertaken using global climate models. Mintz (1984) groups these under three headings: (i) experiments in which different noninteractive soil moistures or albedos are prescribed as time-invariant boundary conditions; (ii) experiments in which either different soil moistures or different albedos are prescribed initially and the soil moisture is allowed to vary with time; and (iii) hybrid experiments in which the effects of interactive and noninteractive soil moistures are compared. For the hybrid experiments, Mintz (1984, p. 81) states, "To the extent that the calculation with interactive soil moisture simulates the observed rainfall, temperature and circulation of the Earth's atmosphere, the comparison will show how the Earth's climate may be affected by such imposed changes in the land surface evapotranspiration as might be brought about by large-scale deforestation. . . ."

Two points follow: first, the importance of correct simulation of the present-day environment as a prerequisite and, second, that the conclusions drawn are about the sensitivity of the Earth's large-scale climate rather than any immediate environmental changes. In particular, global climate models, which have spatial resolutions ranging between about 2° and 10°, are not designed to permit focused analyses at local to regional scales. It is for this reason that a series of scaled experiments including observation and numerical modeling has been proposed as a major component of the International Satellite Land Surface Climatology Project (ISLSCP, 1983). While the type of global climate model experiments undertaken to date (e.g., Mintz, 1984) can reveal a great deal about the sensitivity of the particular model to changes in its land surface boundary, they are probably not yet suited to climatic predictions for the reasons given below and may never provide information at a resolution appropriate to environmental monitoring and management unless mesoscale submodels can be "embedded" within the global climate models.

## Differing Input and Land Surface Parameterization Schemes

The land surface types and parameterization schemes used in the global climate models employed, or likely to be employed, in land use change studies differ considerably. Development of land surface parameterization and examination of the possible impact of man on climate through surface modification are important and currently active fields of research within the World Climate Research Programme. To apply land surface parameterization schemes, the global distribution of climatically important parameters must be prescribed as input data for the models.

An early attempt was made by Posey and Clapp (1964) to provide information about global vegetation for use in albedo studies, but these data were produced only in map form. The only global land surface information known to the author to be available currently in digital format are the land classifications of Hummel and Reck (1979), that of Matthews (1983), and the recently described soils and land cover data archives of Wilson and Henderson-Sellers (1985). The latter two were designed specifically for incorporation into general circulation climate models. Both have been compiled at a 1° × 1° resolution. Despite the common aim of the authors and the similarity of the intended implementation, these data sets differ in format and content. The Matthews (1983) data base contains a preagricultural vegetation description based on 32 possible classes. These data must be used in association with her "cultivation intensity" data set defining the percentage areal extent of presently cultivated land in the 1° × 1° cells. The land cover data archive of Wilson (1984) described in Wilson and Henderson-Sellers (1985), on the other hand, contains both vegetation and soil information. The soil file includes descriptions of drainage, color, and texture, while the vegetation file contains the primary ($\geq 50\%$) and secondary ($\geq 25\%$ but $<50\%$) vegetation types, which can be one of 53 possible classes. Existing data should be documented and compared in order to improve and agree on the basic data to be incorporated into climate models and thus to facilitate intercomparison between models.

Not only do the input land surface information data sets differ from model to model but also there are significant differences between the land surface parameterization schemes implemented in various global climate models (Eagleson, 1982; Rowntree, in press). Global circulation models have used extremely simple parameterizations of surface radiative and hydrological interactions (Carson, 1982). Rainfall is generally assumed to "fill the soil" with water, with any excess effectively disappearing from the computational scheme in a "runoff" term. This simplistic scheme is termed a bucket hydrological model. Many global climate models [e.g., the UKMO model described in Wilson (1984)] still retain a single soil layer in the surface parameterization scheme. The lack of lower soil layers, which can retain moisture and heat, and the bucket hydrological model are acceptable only in global climate models that still use diurnally averaged solar heating, since surface energy exchanges, which are in reality strongly controlled by the diurnal cycle of solar heating, could not in any case be modeled correctly.

Recently, attempts have been made to improve the sophistication of the land surface parameterization schemes. For example, Hansen et al. (1983) describe a two-layer soil model with moisture and heat storage and transfer taking place between soil layers. More recently, Dickinson (1984) has discussed a land surface parameterization scheme developed specifically for global climate models that includes a surface layer within a deeper active soil layer and distinguishes between evaporation from the ground and evapotranspiration from plant foliage. This scheme was developed by comparison with a more complex 100-layer soil model. Clearly, successful implementation of improved parameterization schemes such as that of Dickinson (1984) depends on adequate and accepted vegetation and soil data appropriate both for the present and for the land surface state following the hypothesized perturbation.

The sensitivity of global climate models to the data prescription and to the parameterization schemes used is illustrated by the experiment of Wilson (1984), which was aimed at improving the existing hydrological regime in tropical forest regions. In this experiment, an *effective rooting depth* of 1.5 m was assumed in an attempt to allow the moisture reservoir to incorporate the influence of root depth and intercepted moisture within the framework of the existing model formulation. This rooting depth was used in conjunction with the texture and drainage soil categories described in Wilson and Henderson-Sellers (1985) to assign values of soil moisture capacity in areas of tropical woodland and forest. The major responses were (i) a buildup of a moisture store in the wet season to values that locally exceeded the 15 cm maximum currently used in the UKMO model by up to 20 cm; (ii) a rise in evaporation rates of between 0.5 and 5.0 mm day$^{-1}$ where evaporation had been limited by moisture availability in the control integration; (iii) repartitioning of energy between sensible and latent heat flux including decreases in sensible heat flux typically on the order of 10–50 W m$^{-2}$ but locally exceeding 100 W m$^{-2}$ where evaporation increases were large; and (iv) small increases, mostly less than 10 W m$^{-2}$, in total heat flux, which were coincident with surface cooling of between 0.5 and 5.0 K. In general, the increase in evaporation was compensated for by decreases in sensible heat flux and upward long-wave radiation.

Thus, a relatively small change in one aspect of the surface parameterization scheme of a global climate model gave rise to significant changes in a number of fields locally. While it is unlikely that these changes would disturb the general atmospheric circulation significantly, the "prediction" of local climatic sensitivity would certainly be modified.

## How Well Do Climate Models Perform before Perturbation?

General circulation climate models have been designed to reproduce the large-scale attributes of the atmospheric circulation around the globe. The

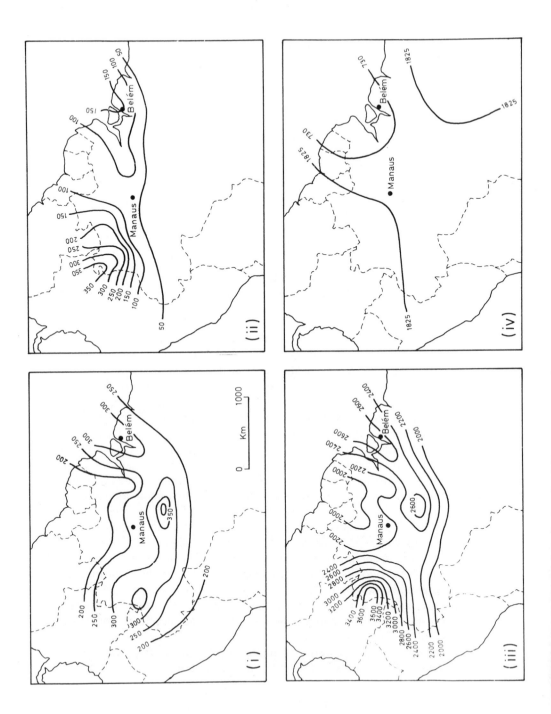

fundamental aim of climate modelers is to reproduce the global-scale distribution of pressure, temperature, precipitation, and so on. It is as unreasonable to expect a coarse spatial resolution global climate model to model surface parameters accurately for one or a few grid elements as to expect that local-scale rainfall will be well predicted by weather forecast models whose results are broadcast routinely by the media. Despite this, if specific anthropogenic land use changes are to be considered, it is important to try to establish whether the global climate model with which the sensitivity experiment will be undertaken is performing well in the specific location of the perturbation.

One of the most difficult parameters to predict is precipitation. Comparison of Fig. 3(iii) and Fig. 3(iv) suggests that the GISS global climate model [which Henderson-Sellers and Gornitz (1984) used for their Amazonian deforestation simulation] is underestimating rainfall over the whole of the Amazon Basin. Annual values are only ~50% of the values observed by Salati et al. (1978). This difficulty is not specific to the GISS global climate model, and while modelers recognize deficiencies in their models, they attempt to overcome these problems by considering differences between control and perturbation experiments rather than absolute values.

The seasonal distribution of precipitation in equatorial latitudes is not well simulated in the current version of the UKMO 11-layer model (used by Wilson, 1984). The predicted southern boundary of the intertropical convergence zone (ITCZ) and the associated rainfall migrate too far north with respect to the observed (Jaeger, 1976) climatology. Rainfall totals associated with the ITCZ are generally smaller than the observed values. For example, in February, in the observational data set, rainfall rates >5 mm day$^{-1}$ and often >10 mm day$^{-1}$ extend from the equator to 15°S, west of 60°W, and from the equator to ~25°S, east of 60°W. However, in the first February of an annual cycle integration of the UKMO global climate model, rainfall rates are 5 mm day$^{-1}$ south of the equator and 1 mm day$^{-1}$ in the south of the Amazon Basin. Wilson (1984) showed that the incorporation of a geographical distribution of albedo derived from the distribution of land cover and soil color classes (Wilson and Henderson-Sellers, 1985) alleviated this problem to some extent by increasing precipitation in December–January–February and March–April–May. However, throughout much of the tropical forest regions (especially southwest Amazonia, south Congo-Zaire basin, Sumatra, and Borneo), the simulated climate remained too dry, particularly in the June–July–August season.

Figure 4a shows the results from the last 5 y of long-integration control runs of the Goddard Institute for Space Studies (GISS) and Canadian Climate

---

**FIGURE 3.**   Precipitation over the Amazon Basin (mm). Observations for (i) January, (ii) July, and (iii) annual (from Salati et al., 1978) and (iv) annual precipitation as a 5-y average from the GISS global climate model. (From Henderson-Sellers and Gornitz, 1984).

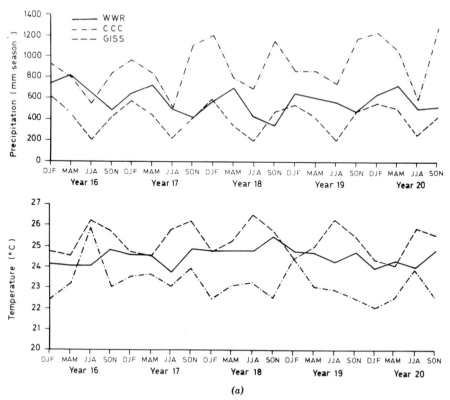

**FIGURE 4.** (a) Seasonal precipitation (mm per season) (*upper*) and average seasonal surface temperature (°C) (*lower*) as computed in the CCC and GISS global climate models for the Amazonian regions shown in (b). The observational results have been computed from data in the World Weather Record for the years 1951–1960. Values are averages for three stations [Manaus (03,08S; 60,00W); Uaupes (00,08S; 67,05W); Santa Elena (04,36N; 61,07W)] within the Amazonian areas of the two models. (b) Two grid areas from which the simulation results shown in (a) were drawn. The CCC global climate models area is composed of nine 5° × 5° grid elements, whereas the GISS global climate model area is composed of four 8° × 10° grid elements. The spatial resolution and the areal coverage of these Amazonian regions differ.

Centre (CCC) global climate models. The plots are of cumulative seasonal precipitation and seasonally averaged temperature for the "Amazonian" regions of the two models. These regions differ somewhat as is shown in Fig. 4b. The CCC global climate model (Boer and McFarlane, 1979; Boer et al., 1984) is a spectral model having a spatial resolution of about 5°, and the Amazonian results are drawn from nine grid elements that cover the upper part of the Amazon Basin. The GISS global climate model (Hansen et al., 1983) is a coarse-resolution grid model (grid elements have dimensions 8° × 10°). In this model, the Amazonian region is represented by four grid elements spanning most of the region of Legal Amazonia (Fig. 4b). Also

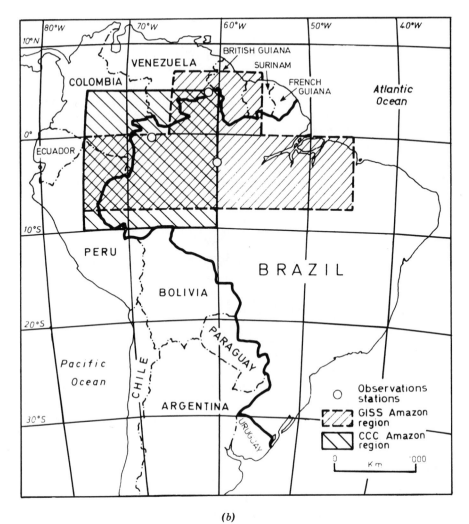

(*b*)

**FIGURE 4.** (*continued*)

shown in Fig. 4*a* are plots of observed temperature and rainfall averaged from data for three stations selected from the World Weather Record and lying within both global climate model Amazonian regions.

For both global climate models, equilibrium has presumably been achieved, since the results shown are for the last 5 y of a 20-y simulation. I do not wish to draw any conclusions about the verity of the climatic simulations with these two models, particularly as it must be noted in the context of Fig. 4*a* that the observational data are at least as suspect as the results of the global climate models (cf. Salati et al., 1978). Rather I wish to draw attention to the difficulties inherent in evaluating the performance of global climate models in specific locations.

The seasonality in the precipitation regime is stronger in both global climate models than in the composite observational data. Rainfall data do show seasonality that is strong but out of phase between the northern and southern Amazon. The fact that both models exhibit the seasonality of the southern Amazon suggests that modeled rain belts may be displaced northward, especially in the CCC global climate model. Figure 3 suggests that the GISS global climate model was significantly underestimating total precipitation in the Amazon Basin, while Fig. 4a indicates a more reasonable simulation. The CCC global climate model seems to be overestimating precipitation in the Amazon region, but the data in Fig. 3 (from Salati et al., 1978) suggest that the CCC precipitation rates are satisfactory.

In the case of surface temperature, the composite observational data fall between the two model simulations. It is possible that the three-station composite underestimates the Amazonian temperature because one of the stations, Santa Elena, is ~800 m higher than much of the region. Its temperatures are ~4°C cooler than those of Manaus and Uaupes. Perhaps the CCC global climate model Amazonian region, which is further to the west than that of the GISS global climate model, might be expected to be influenced by similar effects due to the Andes. It is certainly very much more difficult to untangle the effects of altitude and the ITCZ from coarse-resolution global climate model results than from observational data.

The conclusion that one is forced to draw from Figs. 3 and 4 is that global climate models are not particularly easy to use for specific locational analysis. Certainly, results drawn from one global climate model may differ from those drawn from other, differently formulated models. The lack of precision in simulations is seen to be particularly disturbing when observations suggest that deforestation could lead to a change in the nature of precipitation events, a particularly difficult feature to simulate. For example, long-term observations of rainfall in rubber plantations in Malaysia (UNESCO, 1978) suggest that large-scale forest clearing left rainfall totals unaffected but that the number of rainfall incidents decreased and the intensity of rainfall in each incident increased.

## STATISTICS, SELECTIVE QUOTATION, AND OTHER UNACKNOWLEDGED CAVEATS

It is extremely difficult to include all the caveats that are strictly necessary in any discussion of environmental hazards. In this section, I have chosen to illustrate the confusion that can all too easily be caused by inadvertent or incomplete understanding or discussion. The difficulties considered range from inadequate statistical methodologies through incomplete quotation of results to a lack of understanding of human motivation. That no specific criticism is intended should be clear since I reassess my own findings and methodologies as well as those of others.

## How Good Are Statistical Procedures?

Statistics lend weight to arguments. I use two recent examples to illustrate some of the difficulties that must be guarded against. Climate change experiments can be examined by identifying areas where the difference between the control and perturbation simulations exceeds $2\sigma$, drawing on the fact that a normally distributed variable will fall within $\pm 1.96\sigma$ of the mean 95% of the time. For example, Wilson (1984) examines the climatic response to tropical deforestation in terms of the standard deviation $\sigma$ of an 8-y control simulation in this way. The variance, $\sigma'^2$, of the difference variable is $2\sigma^2$ if it is assumed that both control and perturbation are distributed normally with variances equal to $\sigma^2$. The probability that this difference is less than $2\sigma$ is then given by the probability that this difference is less than $\sqrt{2}\sigma' = 0.84$. Thus, there is a 16% probability of a single grid point exhibiting a $\pm 2\sigma$ difference by chance. Conversely, to identify a 95% significant local difference, a value of $1.96\sigma' = 1.96 \sqrt{2}\sigma = 2.77\sigma$ is required.

Moreover, the identification of a number of areas where a $2.77\sigma$ threshold is achieved does not necessarily imply a global change because points within each area are likely to be spatially correlated. For example, Livesey and Chen (1983), in analyzing the results of Chen (1981), demonstrate that the number of degrees of freedom may be relatively small. Chen's (1981) 936 values are shown to have only approximately 52 degrees of freedom. Using Livesey and Chen's (1983) evaluation of the number of degrees of freedom, it can be shown that to demonstrate a globally significant change at a 95% significance level, 11.4% of the model grid points must show a difference (between control and perturbation) of $\geq \pm 2.77\sigma$ significant at the 95% level, as discussed above.

In their discussions of the importance of their results, Henderson-Sellers and Gornitz (1984) take a significance level of 1% in order to make the rejection of the null hypothesis (no climatic change) more difficult (see Fig. 2). What they fail to discuss is that in doing so, the type II error (the chance of accepting the null hypothesis when it is indeed false) has been increased. Theirs is a reasonable course of action *only* if the risk of environmental change is viewed in economic terms. Henderson-Sellers and Gornitz (1984) have followed the arguments of Chervin (1981) regarding type I and type II errors. He proposed to reduce his type I error (which necessarily increases the type II error) in exercises designed to test the performance of global climate models. He defends this proposition by pointing out that a conclusive rejection of the null hypothesis (of, in his case, no difference between global climate model simulation and observations—that is, a good simulation) would automatically entail considerable cost in further model development. He wished, quite reasonably, to retain the model *status quo* (a cheaper course of action) until it could be shown to be performing badly at a very high ($\geq 99\%$) significance level. It is, however, highly debatable whether such good grounds exist for the similar decision by Henderson-Sellers and Gornitz (1984) to minimize the type I error. If the only argument is that "proof" of climatic change would incur very large costs to reduce the cause (in their case, tropical deforestation), then minimizing the type I error is justifiable. However, if a more environmentally oriented attitude had been taken, it could have been argued that the type II error should be reduced (i.e., the chance of incorrectly accepting the null hypothesis of no change when it is false), thus requiring a larger type I error, that is, a lower significance level. Thus, in using a significance level of 99%, Henderson-Sellers and Gornitz (1984) reduce the risk that they will be responsibe for "crying wolf." They may, however, have incorrectly "proved" that tropical deforestation is an unimportant climatic agent by their neglect of type II errors.

### How Much Care Is Taken in Quoting Results?

Confusion can be caused when results are quoted out of context and without adequate caveats. Misquotation usually arises from a desire to substantiate a point being argued by the author. I present two specific examples. In "Deforestation and Climatic Modification," Schneider (1984) describes previous attempts to evaluate the possible climatic effect of tropical deforestation; he cites the work by Newell (1971), Potter et al. (1975), and Shukla and Mintz (1982). Schneider states (p. 227): "These authors concluded that the normal atmospheric circulation in the tropical regions, for example, could be substantially disturbed by large scale deforestation. Not only might local rainfall rates be substantially reduced but circulation patterns could be disrupted elsewhere." However, the Shukla and Mintz (1982) experiment is difficult to interpret as one of tropical deforestation. They undertook two 60-day integrations for the month of July starting from identical conditions on June 15 with two different constraints placed on the land surface evapotranspiration. In one case, the evapotranspiration was always set equal to the evapotranspiration that would occur were the soil completely wet and covered by vegetation and in the other case no evapotranspiration was allowed.

This experiment, which has been nicknamed the "global irrigation experiment," is a fascinating examination of the potentially important role of land surface hydrology in global climate models. It is *not*, however, a tropical deforestation simulation. The land surface was modified globally, and there were no changes in the albedo, roughness length, or any other surface properties. In their concluding paragraph, Shukla and Mintz (1982, p. 1500) ask whether altering vegetation cover can have a significant influence on the climate. They suggest that this is a possibility if the area of change is "of large magnitude and large horizontal extent. But the exact response will vary from region to region depending on how the large-scale circulation is modified." Thus, the experiment of Shukla and Mintz (1982) cannot tell us anything directly about tropical deforestation.

Salati and Vose (1984), primarily concerned with the detrimental effects of deforestation on the Amazon environment, review the few climatic modeling experiments pertaining to Amazonian deforestation (notably Potter et al., 1975, and Lettau et al., 1979) and, in addition, consider the results of the first 2 y of the experiment described in full in Henderson-Sellers and Gornitz (1984). They choose to quote the preliminary results of Henderson-Sellers (1981), which showed the immediate (and large) response to catastrophic vegetation change rather than the final description of the experiment contained in Henderson-Sellers and Gornitz (1984). They state (p. 163), "we are not experts in climatic modeling, but from the considerations outlined above in particular, recycling of precipitation, the real loss of water from the soil system, and the scale effect of clearing unprecedented large areas of forest, we believe that Henderson-Sellers's (1981) estimate of a decrease in Amazon rainfall of about 600 mm y$^{-1}$ is, to date, the most reasonable interpretation of the situation." While Salati and Vose (1984) may well have genuinely believed this, they should have been aware of the fact that Henderson-Sellers did not, since they had the equilibrium results of the deforestation experiment (as described by Henderson-Sellers and Gornitz, 1984), which give a final precipitation decrease of only about 200 mm y$^{-1}$ (Table 1).

Such apparent selective quotation of results pervades the scientific literature. In any new subject for which data are very scarce and results only tentative, for example the climate effects of tropical deforestation, greater care than normal must be exercised and inadequate quotation must be guarded against.

## The Human Factor

The characteristics of the humid tropics (endemic disease, inaccessibility, and alternative resources exploitable at less cost and less hazard) restricted development until very recently. Prior to the 1950s, it was difficult to identify any coherent development policy in many countries. Colonial exploitation was characterized by an extractive sector directed primarily toward the gathering of food products. More recently, the tropical forests have become a major focus of governmental attention (Goodland, 1980; Lovejoy and Salati, 1983). The factors that initiate and modify human response to the "opening up" of the humid tropics are highly complex.

In Brazil, for example, the construction of the federal capital of Brasília, together with frontier military colonies, was an important step toward Amazonian development (Tambs, 1974; Alvim, 1978; Moran, 1981). The Third National Development Plan contains in principle the guidelines for Amazonian development policy in the first half of the 1980s. It calls for the gradual occupation and integration of the region based on the nonpredatory exploitation of its natural resources (Moran, 1983a). However, no details are given as to how these objectives are to be attained, and the role of the Brazilian government in both active and passive encouragement of Amazonian development and colonization seems to be contrary to these aims. In particular, government agencies encourage development in the tropical rain forest regions of Amazonia in a number of ways, ranging from direct fiscal and tax incentives to the provision of social and economic infrastructures associated with colonization schemes (e.g., Fearnside and Rankin, 1982). At one extreme, spontaneous colonization tends to be prompted by such government action as road building (Fearnside, 1979). The occupation of the lands along the Belém–Brasília highway is a classic case of spontaneous settlement with over two million people settling on the margin of this highway in less than a decade (Moran, 1983a).

The present system of land tenure in Amazonia encourages deforestation, since it is the act of forest removal, according to tradition, that gives the person right of possession. The extremely low price of land in Amazonia also encourages deforestation. For example, land sold by the National Institute for Colonisation and Agrarian Reform (INCRA) for cattle ranches in the area of Altamira is priced ($\sim$U.S. \$1.8 per hectare) at 2% of the minimum monthly wage, and financing terms are highly favorable to the buyer (Hecht, 1981). Cattle ranching projects enjoy substantial financial incentives including interest-free loans and preferential duty terms for importation of machinery. Hecht (1983) estimates that of the 16,000 $km^2$ of forest cleared each year, 95% is for cattle ranching.

There seems to be some genuine misunderstanding about the detrimental nature of land clearance (Dudal, 1980). Central to the confusion is the widely cited EMBRAPA study prepared by Falesi (1976) and expanded by Serrão et al. (1979). These reports suggested that there were beneficial effects to soil fertility caused by conversion to pasture. Studies by Fearnside (1980) and Hecht (1983) failed to reveal any such beneficial effects apart from possible transient increases in nutrient levels from the initial burning. Despite scientific evidence to the contrary (Salati and Vose, 1984), the widespread belief that land clearance can result in productive alternative agriculture persists (e.g., Sanchez, 1976; Nicholaides, 1979; Cochrane and Sanchez, 1982).

Inadequate research or understanding of research and a complete lack of education of local farmers characterize much of the development in tropical regions (e.g., Toledo and Serrão, 1981). In addition, the very real economic gains to be made from logging plus explicit governmental incentives and land ownership laws combine to make the chances of controlled and intensive land development negligibly small in many areas of the humid tropics (Clark, 1973, 1976; Fearnside, 1982).

## REQUIREMENTS FOR IMPROVING MODELING OF CLIMATE EFFECTS OF TROPICAL DEFORESTATION

Tropical deforestation is one of the major causes of land surface change at the present time (Sagan et al., 1979). Currently, it is estimated as occurring at the rate of about 11 million hectares per year, that is, about 0.6% per year, much of it in the Amazonian region. Such land clearance results in the removal of original forest and the intensification and modification of agricultural practices (Pires and Prance, 1977). Both these effects can have significant detrimental environmental impact through the destruction of ecological niches (Gomez-Pompa et al., 1972; Carvalho, 1981), depletion of genetic resources (Richards, 1973), and enhanced erosion of the fertile top soil. Furthermore, deforestation probably has an important effect on the local climate and may possibly cause larger-scale climatic perturbation. The features of tropical deforestation believed to be of significance for the climate are (a) changes in local hydrology and the water balance, especially an increase in runoff and a decrease in evapotranspiration (Salati and Vose, 1984); (b) an increase in surface albedo (and possibly infrared emissivity) (Otterman, 1974; Pinker et al., 1980); (c) perturbation of turbulence characteristics in areas where tall and diverse forest stands are replaced by low crops or grazing land (Dickinson, 1980); (d) perturbation of the carbon cycle, probably imposing a further burden on the already increasing level of atmospheric $CO_2$ (Bolin, 1977; Hansen et al., 1981); and (e) addition of particulates to the troposphere both directly from combustion and from increased windblown dust from exposed and drier soil surfaces (UN, 1977).

To date, attempts have been made to incorporate features (b) and (c) and, much less satisfactorily, feature (a) in some global climate model sensitivity experiments (Rind, 1982; Mintz, 1984). It must be understood, however, that these experiments are designed to answer questions about large-scale atmospheric circulation, not mesoscale climatology. It seems likely that the coarse spatial resolution of global climate models will always inhibit prediction of likely environmental changes at a scale useful to those concerned with ecological management (e.g., Eckholm, 1979; Smith, 1981) even if the present inadequacies in local-scale simulation were to be satisfactorily resolved. The only productive way forward seems to be to use the output of such improved global climate models to drive more appropriate mesoscale climatological models.

In this essay, I have reviewed some of the difficulties in assessing the results of climate modeling experiments and establishing the degree and type of land use change. Many of the statements have related directly to my own work since I am one of the few people unwise enough to have ventured into specific detail for a specific area. It seems to me that only through interchange of information and detailed discussion of assumptions and results can the complexities of anthropogenic disturbance of land use in the humid tropics ever be more fully understood.

## ACKNOWLEDGMENTS

I am particularly grateful to M. F. Wilson, whose work on the sensitivity of the UKMO global climate model was drawn upon here; to G. Thomas, who undertook some of the research into land use changes in Brazil; and to A. Pitman and J. G. Cogley, who analyzed the CCC global climate model results.

## REFERENCES

Alvim, P. T., 1978. Perspectives de Produção Agrícola na Região Amazônica, *Interciência* **3**, 243–249.

Boer, G. J. and McFarlane, N. A., 1979. The AES atmospheric general circulation model, Report of the JOC Study Conference on Climate Models, *GARP No. 22, I*, World Meteorological Organization, Geneva, Switzerland, pp. 409–460.

Boer, G. J., McFarlane, N. A., Laprise, R., Henderson, J. D., and Blanchet, J.-P., 1984. The Canadian Climate Centre spectral atmospheric general circulation model, *Atmos.-Ocean* **22**, 397–429.

Bolin, B., 1977. Changes of land biota and their importance for the carbon cycle, *Science* **196**, 613–621.

Brown, K. S., 1979. Ecologia Geografia e Evolucão nas Florestas Neotropicais, Ph.D. Dissertation, University of Campinas, Brazil.

Carson, D. J., 1982. Current parameterizations of land-surface processes in atmospheric general circulation models, in P.S. Eagleson, Ed., *Land Surface Processes in Atmospheric General Circulation Models*, Cambridge University Press, Cambridge, England.

Carvalho, J. C. de M., 1981. The conservation of nature and national resources in the Brazilian Amazon, *Revista Companhia Vale do Rio Doce* **2**, 1–48.

Chen, W. Y., 1981. Fluctuations in Northern Hemisphere 700 mb height field associated with the Southern Oscillation, *Mon. Wea. Rev.* **110**, 808–823.

Chervin, R. M., 1981. On the comparison of observed and GCM simulated climate ensembles, *J. Atmos. Sci.* **38**, 885–901.

Clark, C. W., 1973. The economics of overexploitation, *Science* **181**, 630–634.

Clark, C. W., 1976. *Mathematical Bioeconomics: The Optimal Management of Renewable Resources*, Wiley Interscience, New York.

Cochrane, T. T. and Sanchez, P. A., 1982. Land resources, soil properties and their management in the Amazon region: A state of knowledge report, in S. B. Hecht, Ed., *Amazonia: Agriculture and Land Use Research*, Centro Internacional de Agricultura Tropical (CIAT), Cali, Colombia.

Dickinson, R. E., 1980. Effects of tropical deforestation on climate, from "Blowing in the wind: Deforestation and long-range implications," No. 14, *Studies in Third World Societies*, Department of Anthropology, College of William and Mary, Williamsburg, VA.

Dickinson, R. E., 1984. Modeling evapotranspiration for three-dimensional global climate models, in J. E. Hansen and T. Takahashi, Eds., *Climate Processes and Climate Sensitivity*, Geophysical Monograph 29, American Geophysical Union, Washington, DC.

Dudal, R., 1980. Soil-related constraints to agricultural development in the tropics, in *Priorities for Alleviating Soil Related Constraints to Food Production in the Tropics*, International Rice Research Institute (IRRI), Los Bânos, Laguna, Philippines.

Eagleson, P. S., Ed., 1982. *Land Surface Processes in Atmospheric General Circulation Models*, Cambridge University Press, Cambridge, England.

Eckholm, E., 1979, *Planting for the Future: Forestry for Human Needs*, Worldwatch Paper 26, Worldwatch Institute, Washington, DC.

Falesi, I., 1976, Ecosistema de pastagen cultivada na Amazônia Brasileira boletim técnico 1. do Centro de Pesquisa Agropecuária do Trópico Úmido (CPATU) Belém, Emprêsa Brasileira de Pesquisa Agropecuária (*EMBRAPA*) Belém, Brazil.

FAO, 1980. *FAO Production Yearbook*, FAO, Rome.

Fearnside, P. M., 1979. The development of the Amazon rain forest: Priority problems for the formulation of guidelines, *Interciência* **4**, 338–342.

Fearnside, P. M., 1980. The effects of cattle pasture on soil fertility in the Brazilian Amazon: Consequences for beef production sustainability, *Trop. Ecol.* **21**, 125–137.

Fearnside, P. M., 1982. Deforestation in the Brazilian Amazon: How fast is it occurring? *Interciência* **7**, 82–88.

Fearnside, P. M. and Rankin, J. M., 1982. The new Jari: Risks and prospects of a major Amazonian development, *Interciência, 7*, 329–339.

Gomez-Pompa, A., Vazquez-Yanes, C., and Guevara, S., 1972. The tropical rain forest: A non-renewable resource, *Science* **177**, 762–765.

Goodland, R. J. A., 1980. Environmental ranking of development projects in Brazil, *Environ. Conserv.* **1**, 9–25.

Hansen, J., Johnson, D., Lacis, A., Lebedeff, S., Lee, P., Rind, D., and Russell, G., 1981. Climate impact of increasing atmospheric carbon dioxide, *Science* **213**, 957–966.

Hansen, J., Russell, G., Rind, D., Stone, P., Lacis, A., Lebedeff, S., Ruedy, R., and Travis, L., 1983. Efficient three-dimensional global models for climate studies: Models I and II, *Mon. Wea. Rev.* **111**, 609–622.

Hecht, S. B., 1981. Agroforestry in the Amazon Basin, in S. Hecht and G. Nores, Eds., *Land Use and Agricultural Research in the Amazon Basin*, Centro Internacional de Agricultura Tropical (CIAT), Cali, Colombia.

Hecht, S. B., 1983. Cattle ranching in the eastern Amazon: Environmental and social implications, in E. F. Moran, Ed., *The Dilemma of Amazonian Development*, Westview, Boulder, CO.

Henderson-Sellers, A., 1981. Climatic sensitivity to variations in vegetated land surface albedoes, presented at 6th Annual Climate Diagnostics Workshop, Lamont Doherty Observatory, October 14–16.

Henderson-Sellers, A. and Gornitz, V., 1984. Possible climatic impacts of land cover transformations, with particular emphasis on tropical deforestation, *Climatic Change* **6,** 231–258.

Hummel, J. R. and Reck, R. A., 1979. A global surface albedo model, *J. Appl. Meteor.* **18,** 239–253.

ISLSCP, 1983. Development of the Implementation Plan for the International Satellite Land-Surface Climatology Project, UNEP Project Report PP/1303-83-03, UNEP, Nairobi, Kenya.

Jaeger, L., 1976. Monatskarten des Niederschlags für die ganze Erde, *Berichte des Deutschen Wetterdienstes,* Vol 18, No 139, Offenbach, FRG.

Jordan, C. F., 1982. Amazon rain forests. *Amer. Sci.* **70,** 394–401.

Julian, P. R. and Chervin, R. M., 1978. A study of the Southern Oscillation and Walker circulation phenomenon, *Mon. Wea. Rev.* **106,** 1433–1451.

Julian, P. R. and Chervin, R. M., 1980. Reply to comment of J. C. Sadler on "A study of the Southern Oscillation and Walker circulation phenomenon," *Mon. Wea. Rev.* **108,** 828–829.

Lanly, J. P., 1982. *Tropical Forest Resources*, FAO Forestry Paper 30, FAO, Rome.

Lanly, J. P. and Clement, J., 1981. *Forest Resources of Tropical Africa, Part I: Regional Synthesis*, FAO, Rome.

Lanly, J. P. and Rao, Y. S., 1981. *Forest Resources of Tropical Asia*, FAO, Rome.

Lettau, H., Lettau, K., and Molion, L. C. B., 1979. Amazonia's hydrologic cycle and the role of atmospheric recycling in assessing deforestation effects, *Mon. Wea. Rev.* **107,** 227–238.

Livesey, R. E. and Chen, W. Y., 1983. Statistical field significance and its determination by Monte Carlo techniques, *Mon. Wea. Rev.* **111,** 46–59.

Lovejoy, T. E. and Salati, E., 1983. Precipitating change in Amazonia, in E. F. Moran, Ed., *The Dilemma of Amazonian Development*, Westview, Boulder, CO.

Mahar, D. J., 1979. *Frontier Development Policy in Brazil: A Study of Amazonia*, Praiger, New York.

Matthews, E., 1983. Global vegetation and land use: New high-resolution data bases for climate studies, *J. Clim. Appl. Meteor.* **22,** 474–487.

Mintz, Y., 1984. The sensitivity of numerically simulated climates to land-surface boundary conditions, in J. T. Houghton, Ed., *The Global Climate*, Cambridge University Press, Cambridge, England.

Molion, L. C. B., 1975. A climatonomic study of the energy and moisture fluxes of the Amazonas Basin with consideration of deforestation effects, Ph.D. Thesis, University of Wisconsin, Madison, WI.

Moran, E. F., 1981. *Developing the Amazon*, Indiana University Press, Bloomington, IN.

Moran, E. F., Ed., 1983a. *The Dilemma of Amazonian Development*, Westview, Boulder, CO.

Moran, E. F., 1983b. Growth without development: Past and present development efforts in Amazonia, in E. F. Moran, Ed., *The Dilemma of Amazonian Development*, Westview, Boulder, CO.

Myers, N., 1980a. The present status and future prospects of tropical moist forests, *Environ. Conserv.* **7,** 101–114.

Myers, N., 1980b. *Conversion of Tropical Moist Forests*, National Academy of Sciences, National Academy Press, Washington, DC.

Myers, N., 1983. Tropical moist forests: Over-exploited and under-utilized. *For. Ecol. Manag.* **6**, 59–79.

Newell, R. E., 1971. The Amazon forest and atmospheric general circulation, in W. H. Matthews, W. W. Kellogg, and G. D. Robinson, Eds., *Man's Impact on the Climate*, MIT, Cambridge, MA.

Nicholaides, J. J., III, 1979. Crop production systems on acid soils in humid tropical America, in D. W. Thorne and M. D. Thorne, Eds., *Soil, Water and Crop Production*, AVI, Westport, CT.

Otterman, J., 1974. Baring high albedo soils by overgrazing; a hypothesized desertification mechanism, *Science* **186**, 531–533.

Otterman, J., 1977. Monitoring surface albedo change with Landsat, *Geophys. Res. Lett.* **4**, 441–444.

Otterman, J., 1981. Satellite and field studies of man's impact on the surface in arid regions, *Tellus* **33**, 68–77.

Parada, N. de Jesus, Tardin, A. T., dos Santos, A. P., Filho, P. H., and Shimabukaro, Y. E., 1981, *Remote Sensing in Forestry: Application to the Amazon Region*, INPE-2035-PRE/292, São José dos Campos, Brazil.

Penteado, A. R., 1967. *Problemas de Colonizacão e de Uso da Terra no Região Bragantina do Estado do Pará*, Universidade Federal do Pará, Belém.

Persson, R., 1974. *World Forest Resources*, No. 17, Royal College Forestry, Stockholm.

Pinker, R. T., Thompson, D. E., and Eck, T. F., 1980. The albedo of a tropical evergreen forest, *Quart. J. Roy. Meteor. Soc.* **106**, 551–558.

Pires, J. M. and Prance, G. T., 1977. The Amazon forest: A natural heritage to be preserved, in G. T. Prance and T. Elias, Eds., *Extinction is Forever*, New York Botanical Gardens, New York.

Posey, J. W. and Clapp, P. F., 1964. Global distribution of normal surface albedo, *Geofis. Int.* **4**, 33–48.

Potter, G. L., Ellsaesser, H. W., MacCracken, M. C., and Luther, F. M., 1975. Possible climatic impact of tropical deforestation, *Nature* **258**, 697–698.

Reis, M. S., 1978. Una definicâo tecnicopolitica para o aproveitamento racional dos recursos florestais da Amazônia brasileira. Conferência proferida durante o 3 Congresso Florestal Brasileiro, Manaus, Amazonas, 04–07 de dezembro de 1978, Brasília, Projeto de Desenvolvimento e Pesquisa Florestal (PRODEPEF)/ Instituto Brasileiro de Desenvolvimento Florestal (IBDF), Manaus, Brazil.

Richards, P. W., 1973. The tropical rain forest, *Sci. Amer.* **229**, 58–67.

Rind, D., 1982. The influence of ground moisture conditions in North America on summer climate as modelled in the GISS GCM, *Mon. Wea. Rev.* **110**, 1487–1494.

Rowntree, P. R., in press. Review of general circulation models as a basis for predicting the effects of vegetation change on climate, in *Proceedings of the United Nations University Workshop on Forests, Climate and Hydrology: Regional Impacts.*

Sagan, C., Toon, O. B., and Pollack, J. B., 1979. Anthropogenic albedo changes and the earth's climate, *Science* **206**, 1363–1368.

Salati, E. and Vose, P. B., 1984. Amazon basin: A system in equilibrium, *Science* **225**, 129–138.

Salati, E., Marques, J., and Molion, L. C. B., 1978. Origen e distribuição das chuvas na Amazonia, *Interciência* **3**, 200–205.

Sanchez, P. A., 1976. *Properties and Management of Soils in the Tropics*, Wiley-Interscience, New York.

Schneider, S. H., 1984. Deforestation and climatic modification: An editorial, *Clim. Change* **6**, 227–230.

Seiler, W. and Crutzen, P. J., 1980. Estimates of gross and net fluxes of carbon between the biosphere and the atmosphere from biomass burning, *Clim. Change* **2**, 207–247.

Serrão, A., Falesi, I., Vega, J. B., and Teixeira, J. F., 1979. Productivity of cultivated pastures on low fertility soils of the Brazilian Amazon, in P. A. Sanchez and L. E. Tergos, Eds., *Pasture Production in Acid Soils of the Tropics*, Centro Internacional de Agricultura Tropical (CIAT), Cali, Colombia.

Shukla, J. and Mintz, Y., 1982. Influence of land-surface evapotranspiration on the earth's climate, *Science* **215**, 1498–1501.

Sioli, H., 1973. Recent human activities in the Brazilian Amazon region and their ecological effects, in B. J. Meggers, E. S. Ayensu, and W. D. Duckworth, Eds., *Tropical Forest Ecosystems in Africa and South America: A Comparative Review*, Smithsonian Institution Press, Washington, DC .

Sioli, H., 1980. Foreseeable consequences of actual development schemes and alternative ideas, in F. Barbira-Scazzacchio, Ed., *Land, People and Planning in Contemporary Amazonia*, Centre of Latin American Studies Occ. Publ. No. 3., Cambridge, England.

Smith, N. J. H., 1981. Colonization lessons from a tropical forest, *Science* **214**, 755–761.

Sommer, A., 1976. Attempt at an assessment of the world's tropical moist forests, *Unasylva* **28**, 5–25.

Tambs, L., 1974. Geopolitics of the Amazon, in C. Wagley, *Man in the Amazon*, University of Florida Press, Gainesville, FL.

Tardin, A. T., dos Santos, A. P., Lee, D. C. L., Maia, F. C. S., Mendoca, J. J., Assuncão, C. V., Rodrigues, J. E., de Moura Abdon, M., Novaes, R. A., Chen, S. C., Duarte, V., and Shimabukuro, Y. E., 1979. Levantamento de Areas de Desmatamento na Amazônia Legal Através de Imagens de Satélite Landsat, INPE-COM3/NTE, C.D.U., 621.385R, Instituto Nacional de Pesquisas Especiais, São José dos Campos, São Paulo.

Toledo, J. and Serrão, A., 1981. Pasture and animal production in Amazonia, in S. B. Hecht and G. A. Nores, Eds., *Land Use and Agricultural Research in the Amazon Basin*, Centro Internacional de Agricultura Tropical (CIAT), Cali, Colombia.

UN Conference on Desertification, 1977. *Desertification: Its Causes and Consequences*, Pergamon, Oxford, England.

UNESCO, 1978. *Tropical Forest Ecosystems*, UNESCO/UNEP/FAO, Paris.

Wilson, M. F., 1984. Construction and use of land surface information in a general circulation climate model, Ph.D. Thesis, University of Liverpool, Liverpool, England.

Wilson, M. F. and Henderson-Sellers, A., 1985. Land cover and soils data sets for climate modelling: a new global archive, *J. Clim.* **5,** 119–143.

Zon, R. and Sparhawk, W. N., 1923. *Forest Resources of the World*, vols. I and II, McGraw-Hill, New York.

# ☐ COMMENTS ON "EFFECTS OF CHANGE IN LAND USE ON CLIMATE IN THE HUMID TROPICS"

## John S. Perry

In recent years, the influence of the land surface on climate has received steadily increasing attention on the part of climate analysts and modelers. A troposphere but a few kilometers thick overlies continental land masses thousands of kilometers in extent, forming but a thin onionskin on the surface of the globe. Energy, moisture, gases, and particles cycle between surface and atmosphere in a manner powerfully influenced by the character of the surface and the physical, chemical, and biological processes occurring on and near the surface. In turn, the nature of the surface—be it barren desert or multicanopied forest—is shaped by that complex and dynamic statistical abstraction we call climate.

This essay focuses on the probable effects that changes in land use in the humid tropics will have on climate in these regions. The topic may well, however, have much broader significance for the globe as a whole. Most of the solar energy that drives global circulation systems is deposited in the tropics, and changes in surface characteristics therefore seem to offer a powerful lever for modifying global climate. Moreover, tropical forests contain massive stocks of carbon, and changes in their extent must be accompanied by movements of carbon to other reservoirs in the atmosphere and ocean. The carbon held in the atmosphere as carbon dioxide is thought to be an important control on global climate, with the polar regions and mid-latitude agricultural zones being particularly sensitive (NAS, 1983b). Hence, there are strong linkages between the tropical regions addressed by the author and the climatic concerns of the temperate latitudes.

The essay, however, surveys in a notably comprehensive fashion what insights we have obtained about a narrower question: tropical land use changes and their influence on climate in the tropical regions themselves. The author finds this knowledge to be woefully limited and unreliable. The major land use change considered is the clearing of forest and its conversion to other uses. Estimates of the areas currently being converted each year vary by factors of 2 or more and are complicated by severe definitional problems. Satellite observations can tell us that something is going on but give little quantitative information. Thus, even if armed with a perfect predictive model of climate, we could hardly specify the climatic changes associated with tropical deforestation with any degree of precision.

However, as the author observes, climate models are far from perfect in their treatment of land surface processes. The richly variegated land surface is specified by a handful of parameters on an unrealistically coarse scale of resolution. The exchanges of energy and moisture between atmosphere and land surface are approximated crudely at best. Yet, as the author cites, a few numerical experiments relevant to the moist tropics have shown suggestive evidence that changes in land surface can produce at least local changes in climate. Considerable work on the effects of surface albedo changes in desert regions might also be cited (e.g., Charney, 1975). Evidence for more distant influences can at present be discerned only for the larger changes in surface energy inputs produced by anomalies in tropical sea surface temperatures. Here, the global implications of the El Niño phenomenon have been widely studied, and large-scale international research programs are being developed within the World Climate Research Program (WCRP) of the World Meteorological Organization (WMO) and the International Council of Scientific Unions (ICSU) (WMO, 1984).

The incorporation of land surface effects in climatic models has long been recognized as a major problem by the planners of the WCRP. An international scientific working group was established in the late 1970s, a major international conference was organized in 1981 (Eagleson, 1982; WMO, 1981), and an International Land Surface Climatology Program is being developed (WMO, 1984) to include regional field data-gathering and research projects. One may hope that these programs will slowly fill in the gaps in basic data and scientific understanding noted in this essay.

Man-made changes on the earth have broader implications, however, than those considered in this consciously specialized essay. The world we live in has in large measure been shaped by biological processes: by life. The character of our atmosphere, ocean, and the very soil beneath our feet is not the product of physical and chemical processes alone but rather reflects a complex synergism between living and inorganic matter. For the most part, this work has been done by species other than ourselves. But today, as recognized by Vernadsky (1945), man, uniquely and powerfully armed with the terrible tool of human thought, has become "a large-scale geological force." The biological and geological processes that entombed vast resources of fossil carbon over millenia are being reversed by man over the course of a few centuries. Changes from forest to grassland or desert analogous to those accompanying the advance and retreat of the great ice sheets are being accomplished in but a few decades. Thus, we are "in a unique epoch when one species, the human race, has achieved the ability to alter its environment on a global scale" (Goody, 1982).

This rapid pace of change, change paced not by the slow rhythms of nature but by the quicksilver thrust of the human, poses new challenges for science. If the earth were a static system, it could be studied with a leisurely reductionist approach by the individual scientific disciplines. A meteorologist, for example, could deal with the atmosphere by treating the ocean and land surface as static boundary conditions or at worst by assuming equilibrium on some reasonable time scale. If, however, all components of the system, and their interactions with each other, are changing in important ways, then a synoptic, interdisciplinary methodology is indispensable. Moreover, if human influences are important, then the study of human society—its economics, demographics, sociology, history, and future—is surely as important as research on the physical/biological system with which it interacts.

The need for such a holistic approach is suggested even in this narrowly focused paper. Current and future changes in the land surface can only be measured by improving our data base on the functioning of human society. Where are people moving? How much land are they clearing for what ends? How can data be obtained through the existing network of human institutions? To assess the future development of the land surface, we need to project the future development of human society itself. Thus, a rational attack on this single question of interest to atmospheric scientists inherently requires the participation of demographers, sociologists, geographers, and economists. Similarly, the treatment of a changing land surface in climate models inescapably involves questions of plant physiology, hydrology, ecology, and ocean dynamics. The implications of global change paced by human actions have been increasingly perceived by the world's scientific community. Some 25 years ago, scientists from virtually all branches of the earth sciences mounted an International Geophysical Year (IGY), in which for the first time the resources of space were utilized to acquire a synoptic view of the earth as a whole. The Global Atmospheric Research program (GARP) of WMO and ICSU sought more detailed understanding of the atmosphere and ocean through carefully planned field studies. More recently, proposals were made for concerted efforts to assess the "habitability" of the planet. Now, efforts are under way within ICSU and various national groups (NAS, 1983a) to mount an international program for the remainder of this century that would deal with the whole question of global change.

The scope and central focus of such a program are as yet incompletely defined. In principle, changes in our terrestrial environment are influenced by everything from the center of the sun to the center of the earth. However, it is clear that the type of interactions between human activities, the large-scale biology of the planet, and the physical elements of the system that are the focus of the present essay will be major objects of attention. One objective of this emerging program will undoubtedly be to deal with the description and understanding of the interactive physical, chemical, and biological processes that regulate the earth's unique environment for life, the changes that are occurring in this system, and the manner in which they are influenced by human actions.

This effort will place great stresses on the disciplinary, institutional, and political structures of science and society. It cannot prosper by allocation of resources on the basis of intellectual interest and historical entitlement. It cannot be organized and managed within the discipline-oriented institutional structures of today's international science, and it does not fit easily within the parallel disciplinary structures of national scientific establishments. Progress will not be achieved if the exchange of talent, resources, data, and knowledge is impeded by political barriers. The problems are problems of the whole planet and of all its inhabitants; they must be addressed by us all together.

We may thus view the issues raised by Henderson-Sellers as harbingers of a larger and broader endeavor that will increasingly enlist the energies and talents of the world's scientists over the years to come.

## REFERENCES

Charney, J. G., 1975. Dynamics of desert and drought in the Sahel, *Quart. J. Roy. Meteor. Soc.* **101,** 193–202.

Eagleson, P. S., 1982. *Land Surface Processes in Atmospheric General Circulation Models*, Cambridge University Press, Cambridge, England.

Goody, R., 1982. *Global Change: Impacts on Habitability*, California Institute of Technology, Pasadena, CA, JPL D-95.

NAS, 1983a. *Toward an International Geosphere–Biosphere Program*, National Academy of Sciences, National Academy Press, Washington, DC.

NAS, 1983b. *Changing Climate*, National Academy of Sciences, National Academy Press, Washington, DC.

Vernadsky, W. I., 1945. The biosphere and the noosphere, *Amer. Scie.* **33**(1), 1–12.

World Meteorological Organization (WMO), 1981. *Report of the JSC Study Conference on Land Surface Processes in Atmospheric General Circulation Models*, WCP-46, World Meteorological Organization, Geneva, Switzerland.

World Meteorological Organization (WMO), 1984. *Report of the Fifth Session of the Joint Scientific Committee*, WMO/TD-1, World Meteorological Organization, Geneva.

# PART V

## CONFERENCE DISCUSSIONS AND FUTURE DEVELOPMENT: SCENARIO WORKSHOP

# Foreword to the Conference

Nelson de Jesus Parada[a]

It was a great honor and pleasure for us to host the International Conference on Climatic, Biotic and Human Interactions in the Humid Tropics with Emphasis on the Vegetation and Climate Interactions in Amazonia. We are quite aware of the importance of this event for the preservation of life and the natural environment of our planet. For five days some of the leading scientists discussed scientific studies concerning topics crucial for the maintenance of our ecosystems and the interactions between man and his surroundings. The papers and the conference discussions mainly referred to scientific areas such as tropical climatology and meteorology, tropical biology and ecology, biogeochemical cycles, hydrology, soil science, modeling, and systems analysis, among others.

Most Brazilians know that Amazonia is the biggest resource of our country, and for this same reason, at the same time, we are all worried about inadvertent changes in our tropical forests. Brazil is a blessed land in terms of its natural resources, but we know that they will not last forever if these resources are not well managed according to scientific guidelines.

Unfortunately, commercial, political, and even personal interests are causing serious damage to our tropical forests, which should be preserved for the interests of human life as a whole. On the other hand, many people, even some of those who are really worried about tropical forest preservation, present speculative studies with no solid scientific evidence and analysis, resulting in only confusion and ineffective discussion.

[a] Former Director General of Instituto de Pesquisas Espaciais.

By bringing to light at least some of the most important aspects concerning the vegetation and climate interactions in Amazonia, we hope that this conference and book will help us reach a better understanding of our land. Solid scientific arguments will certainly help us fight for the preservation of all that is important for life on earth.

# The Conference

The conference was opened on Monday, February 25, 1985, by Dr. Walter Shearer of United Nations University (UNU) with about 70 people in attendance. The director of the host institution, N. Parada of the Instituto de Pesquisas Espacias (INPE), welcomed the participants, pointed out the importance of the questions they were asking, and summarized INPE's research activities. INPE is Brazil's equivalent to the U.S. NASA and carries out a wide research program on space science and applications, including meteorology and remote sensing.

All the material in this book except that prepared by the editor was presented and discussed at the conference. In discussions of the conference papers, many stimulating ideas and questions were raised that are not contained in the chapters of this book. An attempt is made to summarize some of them here.

## DISCUSSION OF PAPERS

In commenting on the overview paper by J. Marden dos Santos, S. Mori pointed out that because many of the plants and animals of the humid tropics, and especially of the Amazon region, are still unknown or incompletely known, there is a continuing need for exploration and classification of tropical diversity; also, we need better coordination of research efforts on Amazonian botany and ecology and standardization of the units in which data are gathered and presented for the data to be of much use to nonbotanists. It is especially important that species identification be based on botanical collections rather than on common names, and this correct identification requires considerable care.

The paper by E. Salati on the Amazon water budget emphasized the large fraction of rainfall that is returned locally to the atmosphere by evapotranspiration from the forest. However, there was no general agreement among the participants as to the implications of this finding for possible climatic effects of deforestation. Only detailed mathematical models of the role of the forests in climate processes could potentially answer such questions.

L. C. B. Molion reviewed the first field results from an Anglo-Brazilian micrometeorological study. Subsequent discussion emphasized the need to extend such studies to regions of other land cover besides primary forest and to regions of different rainfall in order to obtain an observational basis for inferring effects of deforestation on the hydrological cycle. Molion replied that the equipment was portable and that he would like to study other sites.

In his oral presentation, J. Paegle emphasized the possibility that a yet-undetected low-level jet over the Amazon forest could be important for the Amazon water budget. This suggestion provoked considerable discussion. Brazilian scientists doubted that they would not yet have noticed such a jet if it were there but concluded that they should look more carefully for it because of its potential importance.

In reviewing the application of general circulation models (GCMs) to tropical climate, J. Shukla suggested that such models up to now have not been adequate to study climate change from changing surface characteristics in the tropics. W. E. Reifsnyder asked him what would be the use of numerical experiments with large, unrealistic alteration of surface conditions. Shukla suggested that such studies were intended to understand the sensitivity of the climate system to changed surface conditions, not to make detailed assessments of deforestation. He has not attempted to make any such assessments with his model because of its unsatisfactory treatment of soil hydrology and other processes.

The subsequent paper by P. Sellers suggested parameterizations for the surface energy budget and evapotranspiration over forested areas that could be used in GCMs and may be realistic enough for studying the effects of tropical deforestation. This presentation provoked an extended reaction from the audience. Several participants expressed surprise that such a complex and detailed treatment of vegetation would be required with models that have spatial scales of 500 km or so. Others pointed out that the model was immensely oversimplified compared to real vegetation. E. G. Bonkoungou was not satisfied with an average-stomatal-response approach, since stomatal behavior is very much species-dependent and tropical forests have many species, indeed. Sellers responded that most species would respond similarly to radiation because of their development in the same environment.

A. Henderson-Sellers reviewed past studies that attempted to ascertain the climate change resulting from tropical deforestation. R. Lal pointed out that deforestation is accompanied by changes in water-holding capacity and pore size distribution of the soil and that these changes should be included in climate change studies. J. Shukla questioned the suitability of the GCM that Henderson-Sellers used for her deforestation study. W. J. Shuttleworth said that although GCM modeling of land properties will improve in the next few years, he thought that little progress would be made unless the parameterizations are calibrated and validated against observational data.

Many conference participants expressed the opinion that GCMs linked to land surface models might be the only potentially satisfactory tool for studying the climatic effects of tropical deforestation. However, how soon adequate models could be developed is controversial, with suggestions ranging from three years to a time well after tropical forests would have disappeared.

Assessing the impact of deforestation, W. E. Reifsnyder emphasized the need to know what happens to the land after all or some of the trees are removed. Is the land abandoned or converted to temporary or permanent agriculture or pasture? Is it burned frequently? The treatment of the land subsequent to tree removal would determine the vegetation cover and what course ecological succession would take.

In reviewing the biological processess important for maintaining soil fertility in the tropics, P. Lavelle gave the participants an appreciation of the many environmental roles of earthworms. A point he made, that shifting cultivation degrades soil fertility, raised considerable controversy. P. de T. Alvim commented that the harm comes after population density increases to the point that shifting cultivation is no longer sustainable. He remarked that, in any case, shifting cultivation is a subsistence type of agriculture, supporting only the farmer and his family at a very low standard of living. He added that improvements in living conditions in the tropics require finding alternatives to shifting cultivation. R. Herrera commented that shifting cultivation systems as developed by indigenous people contain a wealth of information on crop adaptability and agronomic systems, which can be used as a basis for improved and presumably more efficient and sustainable systems.

# Scenario Workshop and Recommendations

To stimulate further scientific exchange and discussion, the Conference Steering Committee devised three scenarios for the Amazon 50 years from now. These scenarios were not intended as either likely or desirable plans for regional development. Such plans are not available. Almost no consideration has yet been given by the Amazonian countries to the implications of the processes discussed in this book for whatever future development plans they may have. Thus, the scenarios were designed to explore what kinds of environmental disruptions might be associated with alternative paths of future development and therefore should be accounted for in future development planning. An understanding of such disruptions would help planners to find alternative, less destructive uses of their environmental resources. The workshop participants were not asked to focus on socioeconomic and political questions raised by the scenarios. Such questions are, of course, important, but they have been addressed by others. The special expertise of this conference was in the relatively unexplored areas of basic science and its multidisciplinary synthesis. The participants were given the following instructions.

Each group will consider a *what if* extreme-change scenario. These are like general circulation model sensitivity studies. That is, we try to learn how the total system will respond to a large, but simple change. Such information suggests what we might expect if the actual future changes proceed in various directions. We have no way of knowing what the Amazon will actually look like 50 years from now. To put the scenarios in a more concrete framework, assume that they represent a development plan of the Amazonian countries. You are asked not whether these should be done, but rather what could be the consequences if they are done and what could be strategies to minimize the negative consequences. All of the scenarios are assumed to occur 50 years from now or over the next 50 years. None of these scenarios may be desirable for future development. They all should be compared with a scenario of no change.

## THE SCENARIOS

Although the scenarios were not intended to be plausible or desirable futures for the Amazon, they were inferred by extreme extrapolation of various current trends and supported by at least some current thinking about the future.

### Industrialization and Urbanization Scenario

This scenario was inspired in part by Brazil's current Grande Carajás development program (Mahar, 1983), which includes a large iron mine at Serra dos Carajás, the aluminum mines at Trombetas and refining complex at São Luís, and electric power from the world's fourth largest hydroelectric complex at Tucuruí on the Tocantins River (Stone, 1985) and several more dams under construction (Barham and Caufield, 1984). It was also inspired by the growth of Manaus and Belém into large cities.

According to this scenario:

> Many dams are built on the Amazon and tributaries to provide vast amounts of cheap electricity, hundreds of thousands of megawatts. For example, the Tocantins River Basin Hydroelectric Project in Brazil converts the river into an almost continuous chain of lakes 1200 miles long, from Tucuruí to within 75 miles of Brasília. This power, many tens of times greater than previously available to all of Brazil, and cheap labor from northeast Brazil attracts many heavy industries, and many large mining enterprises are developed. The population reaches 50–100 million people in Amazonia. About 25% of the forest has been converted to industrial and urban use, 50% has been converted to agriculture or secondary forest, and 25% primary forest is maintained.

### Savannization Scenario

This scenario was suggested by the large area of forest converted to pasture over the past decade and by the beliefs among some agronomists that such land usage, generally recognized as having been very wasteful up to now, could be made productive and sustainable, for example, by use of suitable grasses and fertilizer supplements (e.g., Toledo and Serrão, 1982). Many ecologists and agronomists, however, believe that successful and sustainable cattle ranching in the Amazon is extremely unlikely. Fearnside suggested it would require more than the world's supply of phosphate fertilizer.

This scenario envisages that:

Fifty years from now, 75% of the Amazon has been converted to savannalike conditions. The region is covered by large cattle ranches with low but economic stocking capacities. Grasslands are maintained by seasonal burning of secondary forest biomass with the assistance of herbicides; populations have increased only slightly from twentieth-century levels. Most of the population growth of the Amazonian countries has occurred outside the Amazon.

## Agriculture Scenario

This scenario was inspired by the optimism for the Amazonian agriculture conveyed by the agronomists connected with the Yurimaguas field experiment in Peru at the western end of the Amazon Basin (e.g., Nicholaides et al., 1983; Valverde and Bandy, 1982), which has shown high agriculture productivity with careful supplementation of limiting nutrients. There is considerable doubt as to whether such high-technology agriculture could be successfully applied in more remote regions by uneducated farmers. Values of about 10% are usually suggested as upper limits to the potentially arable land in the Amazon. However, we have assumed for the sake of the scenario a value of 50%, corresponding to the suggestion of R. Revelle in his comments on Chapter 4 as an ultimate limit to Amazonian agriculture. Presumably, devoting a large fraction of the Amazon Basin to agriculture would make sense, if at all, only after the lands more suitable for agriculture outside Amazonia were fully utilized, a criterion not close to being satisfied in the countries with Amazon territories. For example, a number of studies in recent years have indicated that about 30% of Brazil as a whole could be used for agriculture rather than the 5% used today. However, the inhospitable climate, poor soils, and small population of the Amazon make it unsuitable for anything but tree crops (Callis and Kirk, 1982).

According to this scenario:

About half of the Amazon has been converted to intensive agriculture, including extensive paddies and irrigated systems. These systems are economic and sustainable, the result of research findings in the late-twentieth century as to how to fertilize and maintain favorable soil properties. Valuable information in this regard was gained by careful studies of the Amazonian Indian populations.

## Little Change Scenario

A fourth scenario that all the groups considered in examining the implications of their drastic-change scenarios was the possibility of only small departures from current conditions; such a future would be motivated by the recognition that any drastic change in the Amazon would not be justified because of economic and environmental costs. Such a scenario would still imply considerable development of, and wealth extraction from, the Amazon, but of a nondestructive or less destructive nature. For example, there could be considerable exploitation of the wild biological reserves for medicines and other uses, and a limited amount of sustainable timber harvesting, agroforestry, and agriculture to maintain populations at present levels with improved standards of living. Some participants suggested that the Amazon could easily become one of the most popular spots in the world for international tourists and bring to the Amazonian countries tens of billions of U.S. dollars.

## QUESTIONS FOR THE WORKING GROUPS

The following questions were asked of the scenario groups.

a. What are the functions of the humid tropical system that might be seriously affected by the scenario? In particular, what thresholds might be involved in those impacts?

*Functions* should be described for the local (less than 200-km on edge), regional (200–2000-km), and global (more than 2000-km) scales.

Functions might include (i) basic biogeophysical properties of the system such as a heat source for the global circulation, a refuge for species diversity, a cleaner of the atmosphere; and (ii) socioeconomic functions related to the maintenance and improvement of human well-being, for example, provision of sustainable food and fiber, provision of water for hydropower, provision of a disease-free living environment, and so on.

b. What guidelines can present knowledge give to help manage the development scenarios in ways that minimally damage important functions of the humid tropics system? These guidelines should include (i) information on alternative land use strategies, the size of deforested and preserved regions, and the like, and (ii) information on the restorative (regenerative) activities that might be used to repair functions already damaged.

c. What research is most important to produce more usable guidelines for management? The research agendas should focus on monitoring and data collection activities; modeling and synthesis efforts, experimental tests, and perturbations. What research strategies would be most useful to produce usable management guidelines, about 5 years from now? What additional research would be most useful to produce guidelines 20 years from now? The discussion of research priorities should make an effort to identify the approximate cost and resource requirements, as well as what could be obtained, under various research agendas.

## WORKSHOP DISCUSSION

Because of the short time available, the lack of prior preparation, and the great difficulty of the questions posed, the workshop participants were not able to even identify all important areas of inquiry, let alone provide definitive answers. However, some important concepts evolved from the working group discussions.

### Industrialization Scenario

The group examining this scenario suggested that without proper guidelines massive air pollution in previously clean environments was one possible consequence of the scenario. There could be large emissions of oxides of nitrogen that would react with the natural hydrocarbons to produce photo-oxidant (ozone) pollution (e.g., Crutzen in Chapter 8). There could also be considerable aerosol pollution.

The large population envisioned in this scenario would have to be supported by sustainable agriculture and forestry, and these activities in turn would be a hazard for the environment because of the intense industrialization. There would be potential for considerable acid rain damage (acid rain from natural sources has already been reported in the Amazon; e.g., Haines et al., 1983) and considerable pressures for further forest cutting for industrial wood, fuel and charcoal, household land use, and timber harvesting. An extensive scientific research establishment would be required to help avoid the worst damage possible from the industrialization by providing a detailed understanding of the required meteorology, ecology, plant nutrient cycles, and plant physiology. To define the changing composition of the atmosphere, atmospheric chemists would have to make detailed studies, including sampling from airplanes and meteorological towers.

Hydroelectric power could be crucial to the success of heavy industrialization and, although nonpolluting, could introduce or exacerbate other serious problems, such as water-borne disease. Larger numbers of smaller dams might be preferable to fewer, larger dams (e.g., Bunyard, Chapter 5).

Extensive hydropower development and the concomitant urbanization of the Amazon Basin would make major changes in river hydrology. The presence of numerous dams along tributaries operated for power generation could reduce seasonal fluctuations in river flow. On the other hand, extensive urbanization and forest removal would modify runoff, thereby increasing peak flows on affected tributaries [as Gentry and Lopez-Parodi (1980, 1982) suggested might have happened for the upper Amazon]. Such urbanization and attendant agricultural activities and forest degradation could also increase surface erosion and river sediment loads and greatly shorten the lifetimes of dams by excessive siltation.

Much information on changing river hydrology, derived from extensive temperate-zone studies and some tropical studies, is available for immediate application. However, long-term studies on Amazon hydrology and hydrometeorology are needed in order to develop more relevant information. The Amazon River system is much larger than any other river system in the world, and so the whole-basin hydrology of the Amazon could differ significantly from that of the more well-understood rivers.

Among the important observations and studies that should be continued, enhanced, or initiated are

   **a.** baseline river flow measurements on major tributaries, especially those projected for hydropower development;

   **b.** an expanded network of climatological stations measuring rainfall and temperature;

   **c.** several benchmark meteorological observation stations in areas to be maintained in a "pristine" condition (i.e., unaffected by urbanization, major land use change, etc.). Such observations should include solar and long-wave radiation, soil temperatures, evaporation, and soil moisture as well as standard class A meteorological observations; and

   **d.** specific studies of evapotranspiration in several areas of diverse land use, such as secondary forest and grassland as well as important mature forest types. These observations could well be combined with small-watershed studies.

An important focal point for research could be the concept of human carrying capacity, the size and consumption of the population, and the requirements of sustainable food production within the region or the importation of agriculture products from elsewhere. The energy systems required by the scenario should be studied to maximize their output and efficiencies while minimizing their environmental damage.

## Savannization Scenario

The group examining savannization suggested several integrating themes. Fundamental processes should be studied, both in the natural and the changed systems, for example, in wet and seasonal forest, grassland, and various stages of secondary succession. Past failures in utilization of environmental resources should be considered (e.g., Hecht, 1983). Studies and data could be organized by watershed as the natural minimum area to consider. About three to six carefully selected watersheds would allow extrapolation to the rest of the region. The biology of secondary succession is now almost unknown, and studies of this topic could be quite valuable. Other important processes were identified: for example, nutrient cycles, soil biology, basic hydrology, the meteorology and micrometeorology of the region, and the sources and distribution of important trace gases. Remote sensing would be required to identify change over large areas.

The fundamental physiology of plants should be studied, for example, root and stomatal functioning and plant water budgets. In view of the anticipated drastic change, it would be important now to accelerate the classification of plants and the search for species of economic value and to identify, set aside, and protect reserves for preserving biological and tribal knowledge. The savannization scenario implies loss of considerable economic value of the natural forest, for example, the Brazil nuts. The wet environment would promote many infections of the cattle. There would have to be considerable infrastructure, for example, fertilizer plants, fences, packing houses, and plants for freezing and canning of the meat. The savannas would burn much more readily than the forest, which would introduce aerosols and other forms of pollution.

The frequency of convective rainfall could change considerably as a result of the forest removal, leading to increased seasonality, and climatic stresses on the remaining primary forest. Much more flooding might be expected, depending on the degree of soil compaction. The forests in the foothills of the Andes are especially important for flood control.

## Agriculturization Scenario

The group examining agriculturization suggested that to analyze the future requires considering activities and impacts on various scales (i.e., local, regional, and global) as well as the cultural dimension that cuts across scales. On the local scale, agricultural development should be made as ecologically conservative and as independent of external inputs as possible, consistent with maintaining high yields. Agricultural–ecological potential maps should be developed for the regions to be farmed in order to define long-term, minimum inputs for sustainable production and regional carrying capacity along lines explored in recent FAO studies (FAO et al., 1983). We should establish how these maps might change with other changes brought on by development or by global climate change (e.g., Parry et al., 1984). It would be important to evaluate historical experience, both in terms of successes and failures, and the impacts of continuous versus planned colonization.

To elaborate on the scenario, this group suggested that the following crops might be grown: annuals—rice, corn, sugarcane, beans, cassava, sweet potatoes, jute, and adapted horticulture; perennials—rubber trees, oil palm, cocoa, black-pepper, Brazil nuts, tropical fruit trees, forest, and pasture. The jute and rice would be grown in flood-prone soils and accompanied by water buffalo. Many of the flood crops would require supplemental irrigation. The managed land might be divided into 25% each of perennial crops, annual crops, pasture, and forest.

Research would be required to develop nitrogen-fixing legumes and perennial shrubs that can be grown in association with cereals; develop mulch farming, no-till agriculture, and native sources of fertilizers; integrate live-

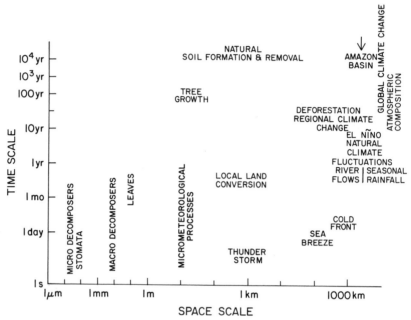

**FIGURE 1.** Range of space and time scales over which various components of the geophysiology of Amazonia occur.

stock and perennial crops with annuals; adapt crops to soil conditions; and identify the local constraints of soil moisture and nutrient availability.

### All Groups

A wide range of observational and modeling studies applied at the different spatial scales would be needed. Figure 1 illustrates the range of spatial scales of concern. Meteorological models would be required for local, regional, and global processes, and these should be suitably linked. Studies at the latter two scales would involve mesoscale and general circulation three-dimensional models. Such models should be related to chemical process models to study the sources, numbers, and transformations of atmospheric trace constituents.

Models would also be needed for soil and river hydrology and biogeochemistry. The water chemistry of the streams could be measured using various tracers to assess loss of soil and nutrients from agricultural sites.

All groups also suggested the need for research on human interactions in the Amazon. In particular,

**a.** the protection of Indians in the region and the conservation of Indian knowledge about the complex natural relationships in the forest and the utility of particular species to humans and

b. the assessment of the social impacts of development on Amazonian settlements (towns, cities) and especially of impacts generated if such settlements exceed the carrying capacity of the area.

## WORKSHOP RECOMMENDATIONS

Other tropical forest regions besides the Amazon can be expected to undergo considerable development in the future. Recognizing the need for a scientific basis for evaluating possibilities such as discussed in the scenarios, the workshop participants adopted the following statement.

### Conference Statement

We met in response to concerns about interactions between humankind and the environment in the humid tropics in general and the Amazon in particular—concerns about the conservation of biological and local traditional knowledge in the face of the inevitable development pressures expected over the next several decades and concerns about the need to understand much better the natural systems and how they interact in order to provide a scientific basis for sustainable development and management of the region. We are impressed by the need for programs of organized data collection and disturbed by our very limited knowledge regarding the atmospheric chemistry, soil systems, the hydrological cycle, and the chemistry of surface waters in the humid tropics. We are impressed by the importance of climate for the tropical systems and of the tropics in the global climate system.

To understand the humid tropics better, both the tropical and the temperate countries need to strengthen their research programs in the disciplinary aspects of the relevant questions. We have been especially struck by the great potential for a cross-disciplinary research approach to the tropics, which would emphasize change and synthesis. To date, this approach is almost lacking. Such an approach would have strong components of modeling and monitoring, which should proceed in parallel.

We have identified three areas that could benefit especially from a cross-disciplinary approach.

#### Climate, the Hydrological Cycle, and Regional Development

Research would be directed to evaluating how the suitability of lands for sustainable production of food, fiber, and energy is affected by linkages with climate and the hydrological cycle. What are the ecosystem impacts of different land use options as defined by climate observation and modeling studies, by local field studies, and by soil land capacity and agroclimatic mapping?

### Biogeochemical Cycles in the Humid Tropics
Study is needed of the natural systems and the systems that have been perturbed by human activities, with a focus on soil and river nutrient cycles, sources, sinks, and transformations of atmospheric trace constituents and impacts of pollution. What is the natural state and its variability, what are the kinds of changes that major developments would entail, and what is the best approach for monitoring the atmosphere and rivers to establish the system function and paths of change?

### Biological Systems and Environmental Interaction
Research is needed to understand the components and functioning of the present biological systems, their sensitivity and response to environmental change. We need to improve our classifications of tropical diversity and our understanding of the connections of climate change to the functioning and interaction of tropical biological systems. How much disturbance can be inflicted upon tropical environments before their individual species populations and ecosystems would undergo drastic change? What are the impacts of new environments (such as those brought on by land conversion and dams) on disease ecology and on airborne and waterborne pollutants?

### Recommendations
a. Within the next year, establish International Interdisciplinary Steering Committees to organize the above research programs.
b. Develop training programs, help establish or strengthen centers and networks, and promote research funding to encourage the fullest possible involvement of scientists from countries within the humid tropics in observational and modeling programs related to the above areas.
c. The required local field studies should be conducted in representative areas of the most important ecosystems, where possible making the fullest use of existing research centers.

## REFERENCES

Barham, J. and Caufield, C., 1984. The problems that plague a Brazilian dam, *New Sci.* **11**, 10.

Callis, S. and Kirk, R., 1982. *Agroclimatic Handbook*, Vol. 2, *Brazil*, NOAA/NESDIS CIAD Models Branch, Columbia, MO.

FAO/UNFPA, IIASA, 1983. *Potential Population Supporting Capacities of Lands in the Developing World*, Technical Report FPA/INT/513, FAO, Rome.

Gentry, A. H. and Lopez-Parodi, J., 1980. Deforestation and increased flooding of the upper Amazon, *Science*, **210**, 1356–1359.

Gentry, A. H. and Lopez-Parodi, J., 1982. Response to comments by C. F. Nordin and R. H. Meade, **215**, 426–427.

Haines, B., Jordan, C., Clark, H., and Clark, K. E., 1983. Acid rain in an Amazon rainforest, *Tellus*, **35B**, 77–80.

Hecht, S., 1983. Cattle ranching in the eastern Amazon: Environmental and social implications, in E. F. Moran, Ed. *The Dilemma of Amazonian Development*, Westview, Boulder, CO.

Mahar, D. J., 1983. Development of the Brazilian Amazon: prospects for the 1980s, In E. F. Moran, Ed., *The Dilemma of Amazonian Development*, Westview, Boulder, CO.

Nicholaides, J. J., III, Sanchez, P. A., Bandy, D. E., Villachica, J. H., Coutu, A. J., and Valverde, C. S., 1983. Crop production systems in the Amazon basin, in E. F. Moran, Ed. *The Dilemma of Amazonian Development*, Westview, Boulder, CO.

Parry, M. L., Carter, T. R., and Konjin, N. T., 1984. Climate impact analysis in cold regions, *Nordia* **18**, 67–79.

Stone, R.D., 1985. *Dreams of Amazonia*, Viking Penguin, New York, NY.

Toledo, J. M. and Serrão, E. E. S., 1982. Pasture and animal production in Amazonia. in S. B. Hecht, Ed., *Amazonia: Agriculture and Land Use Research*, Centro Internacional de Agricultura Tropical, Cali, Colombia.

Valverde, C. S. and Bandy, D. E., 1982. Production of annual food crops in the Amazon, in S. B. Hecht, Ed., *Amazonia: Agriculture and Land Use Research*, Centro Internacional de Agricultura Tropical, Cali, Colombia.

# Appendix

## LIST OF CHAPTER COMMENTATORS: Amazon Conference

RALPH J. CICERONE, National Center for Atmospheric Research, Boulder, Colorado

JAMES E. HANSEN, Goddard Institute for Space Studies, New York, New York

KEITH G. MCNAUGHTON, Department of Scientific and Industrial Research, Palmerston, New Zealand

JOHN S. PERRY, National Academy of Sciences, Washington, District of Columbia

WILLIAM E. REIFSNYDER, School of Forest and Environmental Studies, Yale University, New Haven, Connecticut

ROGER REVELLE, University of California, San Diego, La Jolla, California

JOHN C. RODDA, Institute of Hydrology, Wallingford, United Kingdom

JOHN M. WALLACE, University of Washington, Seattle, Washington

STEVEN G. WOFSY, Harvard University, Cambridge, Massachusetts

## LIST OF OTHER PARTICIPANTS: Amazon Conference

PAUL DE T. ALVIM, Center for Research on Cacao (CEPLAC), Itabuna, Brazil

THEREZINHA XAVIER BASTOS, Center for Research on Tropical Agriculture, Embrapa—CPATU, Belém, Brazil

EDOUARD G. BONKOUNGOU, Institut de Recherche en Biologie et Ecologie Tropicale, Ouagadougou, Burkina Faso

GERARDO BUDOWSKI, Center for Tropical Agronomy (CATIE), Turrialba, Costa Rica

WILLIAM C. CLARK, International Institute for Applied Systems Analysis, Laxenburg, Austria

PEDRO LEITE DA SILVA DIAS, Department of Meteorology, University of São Paulo, São Paulo, Brazil

ALCEU JONES FARIA, Forestry Institute of São Paulo, São Paulo, Brazil

THOMAS R. FISHER, The University of Maryland, Horn Point Laboratories, Cambridge, Maryland

ENRIQUE FORERO, Instituto de Ciencias Naturales, Universidad Nacional, Bogota, Colombia

PEDRO FRAZAO, Estrada Rio Comprido, São Paulo, Brazil

JOHN E. GEISLER, Department of Meteorology, University of Utah, Salt Lake City, Utah

JOAO REGIS GUILLAUMON, Forestry Institute of São Paulo, São Paulo, Brazil

RAFAEL HERRERA, Instituto Venezoelano de Investigaciones Cientificas, Caracas, Venezuela

VOLKER W. J. H. KIRCHHOFF, Institute for Space Research (INPE), São José dos Campos, Brazil

WALTER MANSHARD, University of Freiburg, Freiburg, Federal Republic of Germany

ANDRES MINO, Quito, Ecuador

ANTONIO DIVINO MOURA, Institute for Space Research (INPE), São José dos Campos, Brazil

CARLOS A. NOBRE, Institute for Space Research (INPE), São José dos Campos, Brazil

LYCIA M. MOREIRA NORDEMANN, Institute for Space Research (INPE), São José dos Campos, Brazil

MARTIN PARRY, International Institute for Applied Systems Analysis, Laxenburg, Austria

FRANCISCA MARIA ALVES PINHEIRO, Department of Meteorology, Federal University of Pará, Belem, Brazil

MIEN A. RIFAI, National Biological Institute, Bogor, Indonesia

JENNIFER ROBINSON, National Center for Atmospheric Research, Boulder, Colorado

LEONARDO D. DE A. SA, Institute for Space Research (INPE), São José dos Campos, Brazil

ROGERIO VASCONCELLOS DE SA, Departamento de Recursos Naturais e Meio Ambiente, Rio de Janeiro, Brazil

RICARDO HENRIQUE SAMPAIO SANTIAGO, Setor de Edificios Publicus Norte, Brazilía, Brazil

WALTER SHEARER, United Nations University, Tokyo, Japan

W. JAMES SHUTTLEWORTH, Institute of Hydrology, Wallingford, United Kingdom

G. THOMAS, Department of Geography, University of Liverpool, Liverpool, United Kingdom

S. UNNINAYAR, World Climate Programme, World Meteorological Organization, Geneva, Switzerland

VANGU-LUTETE, Institut Facultaire des Sciences Agronomiques du Zaire, Kinshasa, Zaire

MAURO VICTOR, CONSEMA, São Paulo, Brazil

JIM WEBER, National Aeronautics and Space Administration, Washington, District of Columbia

EDITH BROWN-WEISS, Georgetown University Law Center, Washington, District of Columbia

# Index

Acid rain, 8
Acid river water, 66–67
Acre, 39, 472
Aerodynamic resistances, 310–312, 317–322
Aerosol, 164–168, 170–171
  biogenic, 164
  composition, 165, 170–171
Agoutis, 83, 84, 85
Agriculture, 7, 37, 54–57, 87, 107, 120,
    199–201, 204–206, 221–222, 244, 271,
    273, 291, 292, 486, 507, 511–512. *See
    also individual crops*
Agroforestry, 6, 54, 57, 60, 200–202, 222, 244
    293, 511
Air pollution, 509
Albedo, 258–260, 297–298, 299, 303, 307,
    315–317, 334, 347, 454, 458, 464, 465,
    468, 479, 487, 499
Aluminum, 7, 49, 177, 506
Amapa, 278, 471–472
Amazonas, 472
Amerindians, 36, 50, 65, 507, 512
Angiosperms, 69
Anoxic (anaerobic) ecosystems, 21, 133
  lakes and river sediments, 66–67
  soils, 136–139

Bacteria:
  acetogenic, 137
  cyano–, 145
    dentitrifying, 139
    hydrogen, 90
    methanogenic, 137, 143
    nitrifying, 141, 143
    sulfate reducing, 137
    *See also* Microorganisms
Bahia, 70, 71
Bats, 76, 83, 85
Bees, 76–81, 85
Bertholletia (Brazil nut tree), 73, 77, 79, 80, 82
Bignoniaceae, 69
Biogeochemical cycling, river basin, 245–249,
    274, 512–514
Biomass, 19, 56, 58, 133, 147, 177, 182
  burning, 107, 111, 114, 122–123, 131, 139,
    142–151, 163, 221, 507
  invertebrates, 184
Blocking, 403, 432–434. *See also* Jet stream
Bolivia, 54
Boundary layer, *see* Planetary boundary layer
Bowen ratio, 261–262, 299, 301
Brazil, 54–55, 64, 335, 349, 373, 473, 485–486
Brazil nut (family), Lecythidaceae, 69–84
Brazil nut tree, *see* Bertholletia

Cacao, 44, 55, 200, 511
CAMREX, 248
Capital, 41, 48, 58
Carbon dioxide ($CO_2$), 9, 17–21, 56, 92–94, 97,
    306, 309, 410, 487

Carbon monoxide (CO), 103, 107, 108,
    110–111, 114, 117–119, 123–124,
    131–132, 133–137, 141–143, 145–146,
    147, 149–150, 164, 168–169
    deposition velocity, 142
*Cariniana,* 72, 77, 84
Carrying capacity, 50
Cassava, 201, 511
Catena effect, 191–192
Cattle:
    pasture, 7, 43, 47, 56, 176, 193, 197,
        201–203, 244, 506–507
    population, 121–122, 146, 148
    ranching, 7, 43, 50, 201, 205, 486, 506–507
Charcoal, 48–49, 56, 59, 96
Chlorine compounds, 126, 131–132
Circulation, *see* General circulation
Clearing (methods), 198–199, 244
Climate, 6, 9, 26, 32–33, 91, 126, 182,
    391–405, 410–427
    change, 70, 84, 91–97, 298, 347, 484
    effects of deforestation, 268, 284, 291–293,
        364–367, 404–405, 455, 463–487,
        502–503, 513
    micro–, *see* Microclimate
    paleoclimate, 91–98
    trace gases, *see* Greenhouse gases
Climate regulation, 17–20
Climatic, Biotic and Human Interactions in the
    Humid Tropics, conference, project, 4, 499
Clouds, 20, 25, 166–169, 277, 293, 301, 350,
    351, 363, 375, 396–398, 410
Coal, 119, 148. *See also* Charcoal
Coevolution, 69
Colombia, 54, 73, 278
Colonists, 39, 40, 45, 198, 486
Computer use, 8, 307, 409, 464
Conservation, *see* Preservation
Convection, moist, 348, 361, 364, 372–377,
    387–390, 400–401, 460. *See also* Rainfall
*Couratari,* 72, 77, 80, 84
*Couroupita,* 77, 81, 82
Cretaceous, 92

Daisyworld, 15–19
Dams, 7, 29, 36, 49, 63–67, 105. *See also*
    Tucuruí
Decomposition, 133, 163, 175, 179, 182, 192
Deforestation, 9, 37–50, 85, 180, 193–194,
    197–198, 205–206, 225–244, 268, 271,
    291–293, 346, 404–405, 409, 463–465,
    468–475, 487, 502

causes, 42–49
control, 37, 48–50
method of clearing, 198–199, 244
Degradation of soil, 59, 56, 175, 203, 205, 214,
    216
Denitrification, 136, 139
Development (future alternatives), 7, 9, 21, 35,
    85, 205–206, 225, 485
    scenarios, 505–513
Dimethyl sulfide, 134, 170
Diurnal cycle, 33, 229–235, 256–267, 331–333,
    348, 361–364
Diversity, biological, 27, 31, 69–70, 84–85,
    191–192, 197, 204, 206, 501
    centers of, 94
Drainage basins, 245
Drought, 347, 355, 454, 458
    stress in plants, 26, 31, 218, 220
Dry season, *see* Seasonality
Ducke Reserve, 256

Earthworms, 104, 184–190, 219, 239–241, 503
Ecology, planetary, 21
Ecuador, 54
Eletronorte, 63, 67
El Niño-southern oscillation (ENSO), 345, 347,
    355, 359, 373, 403, 494
EMBRAPA, 59, 274
Erosion, 5, 56, 67, 96, 176, 195–198, 203,
    206, 216, 219–220, 293, 487
*Eschweilera,* 72, 77, 79, 80
Euglossine bees, *see* Bees
Evaporation, 236, 267, 360. *See also*
    Evapotranspiration; Interception of rainfall
Evaporation fraction, 261–262
Evapotranspiration, 9, 20–21, 25, 33, 181, 252,
    255, 260–263, 267–268, 274, 284,
    286–288, 292, 298–302, 303–306, 308,
    310–312, 321–322, 325–326, 329–331,
    359, 361, 365–366, 477, 484, 501
Extinction, 54, 84–85, 487
Extratropical response to tropical convection,
    373, 375–377, 381, 389–390, 465. *See
    also* General circulation

FAO, 55, 58, 193, 194
Farmers, 37, 39, 42, 44, 46, 48, 206, 507
Fertilizers, 54, 201, 205, 214, 220, 291
Fires, 5, 9, 73, 96–97, 180, 198, 220. *See also*
    Biomass, burning
Flooded soils, *see* Anoxic; Várzea
Flooding, 96, 283, 454, 509

Fluxes of energy, *see* Evapotranspiration; Longwave (thermal IR) radiation; Sensible heat flux; Solar radiation

Forests, 7, 9, 21, 26–31, 37–61, 94–98, 114, 115, 118, 193, 194, 236–237, 256, 271, 273, 285, 290–293, 404–405
  as chemical sources, 134–135

Formaldehyde ($CH_2O$), 111–114

Fossil fuel, 48, 56, 119, 148

French Guiana, 54, 70, 71, 74

Fresh water systems, 145–146

Fronts, 349–351, 401–403

Fuelwood, 196, 470

Gaia hypothesis, 13, 17, 19

General circulation, 377–381, 391–400, 410–420
  models (GCMs), 297–299, 344, 367, 371, 409–461, 463–470, 475–482, 502
  tropics as a heat source, 25, 255, 268, 292–293, 375–377, 464, 475–482
  *See also* Winds

Geophysiology, 6, 11–15

Geopotential height variability, *see* Variability, of geopotential height

Glaciation, *see* Ice age

Global Change Program, 5, 495

Global climate models, *see* General circulation, models

Global Weather Experiment (GWE), 357–358

Goiás, 39, 472

Grande Carajas Project, 49

Greenhouse gases, 9, 20, 92, 126, 134

*Grias*, 77, 81

*Gustavia*, 74, 75, 77, 78, 81

Guyana, 54, 165–166, 289

Hadley circulation, 353–354, 372, 377–381, 449–450, 469

Heterogeneous reactions, 112, 127

Homeostasis, 17, 21

Humidity, 233–236, 264–267, 281–283

Humus, 141, 177–179, 183, 190, 195, 214, 221

Hurricanes, 352–353

Hydraulic conductivity of soil, 180

Hydroelectric power, *see* Dams

Hydrogen, molecular, 133, 134, 136, 139–141, 149–159
  deposition velocity, 140

Hydrogenase, 140–141

Hydrogen sulfide ($H_2S$), 66, 170

Hydrological cycle, 9, 25, 50, 274, 283–293, 296, 366, 405. *See also* Evapotranspiration; Rainfall; Runoff

Hydroxyl (OH), 103, 107–114, 116–117, 123–127, 134, 140, 164

Ice age, 19, 91, 93–95

Immigration, 40–41

*Imperata*, 200

Industrialization, 7, 506, 509–510

Infiltration, 180, 190, 199, 204, 216, 240, 242–243, 325

Inflation, effect on deforestation, 42, 45

Infrared cooling, *see* Longwave (thermal IR) radiation

INPA, 256, 274, 285, 294

INPE, 39, 274, 294, 470, 473, 501

Instability:
  barotropic and baroclinic, 380, 449
  lines, *see* Squall lines

Interannual variability, 403–404, 409, 434–441, 449–451

Interception of rainfall, 226, 255, 262–263, 285, 298, 327–329, 405

International Satellite Land Surface Climatology Project (ISLSCP), 475, 494

Intertropical convergence zone (ITCZ), 26, 142, 166, 348, 353, 388, 398, 403, 420

Invertebrates, 183–191, 204, 219–220

Isoprene ($C_5H_8$), 119, 169

Isotopes, 274, 289–291
  carbon, 248

Jet stream, 373–376, 379–381, 427. *See also* Low-level jet

Kudzu, 201

Lakes, 93–96, 145–146

LANDSAT, 39–40, 54, 202

Land speculation, 42–43

Land surface parameterization, 297–334, 455, 476–477, 502

Latent heat flux, *see* Evapotranspiration

Leaf area index, 315, 319–320

Leaf drag coefficient, 318

Lecythidaceae, *see* Brazil nut family

*Lecythis*, 72, 74, 77, 80, 82, 83

Legumes, 140, 200, 221, 511

Lightning, 111

Lignin, 248–249. *See also* Humus

Linkages between tropical forests and climate, 7–9, 19–22, 84–85, 97–98, 268, 291–293, 464–470, 511
Litter, leaf, 179, 182, 186–187, 236–237
Loans, 44, 486
Longwave (thermal IR) radiation, 257, 300, 354
Low-level jet, 364, 367–369, 502

Malaria, 66
Maranhão, 39–40, 472
Mato Grosso, 39–40, 202, 471–473
Methane (CH$_4$), 8, 103–104, 107, 108, 111–117, 121–127, 133–134, 136–138, 143–144, 145–149, 151, 160–161, 164
   sources, 119–123, 137–138, 143, 147–148
Methanogenesis, 136, 137, 146
Methylchloroform (CH$_3$CCl$_3$), 116, 117, 126, 131–132
Microclimate, 9, 84–85, 180–183, 220, 225–236, 244, 251–268, 292
Micrometeorological measurements, 255–267, 274, 333–334, 510
Microorganisms, 183, 186. *See also* Bacteria
Milankovich effect, 19, 93, 97
Mineral extraction, 7, 49
Mineralization, 176, 182, 183, 187, 219
Modeling, 21, 293, 297–344, 347, 367–371, 409–461
Momentum transfer:
   at surface, 32, 297–300, 307, 308, 317–322, 334, 463–470, 475–482, 487, 494. *See also* Roughness, aerodynamic
   troposphere, 378–381
Mycorrhizae, 27, 182

National parks, 85
Natural gas, 119
Net radiation, *see* radiation, net at surface
Nigeria, 226
Nitrates, 138, 247–249
Nitric oxide, 107–108, 110–112, 114–116, 119, 123–126, 134
   lifetime, 115
Nitrification, 119
Nitrogenase, 140
Nitrogen dioxide (NO$_2$), 110–111, 116, 133
Nitrogen fixation, 140–141, 205
*Nitrosomonas,* 141
Nitrous oxide (N$_2$O), 8, 104, 119, 134, 144–146, 149
Nocturnal jet, *see* Low-level jet
Nutrients, 7, 27, 104, 171, 175, 177, 182, 186–187, 190, 193, 195, 198–203, 205, 214, 216–217, 246, 291, 486, 510

Obidos, 246, 247
Ocean surface temperature, effects on circulation, 346, 359–360, 404, 433–434, 445–452, 459
Odd hydrogen, *see* Hydroxyl
Odd nitrogen, *see* Nitric oxide; Nitrogen dioxide
Orbit, effects on climate, 19, 93, 97
Orographic influences, *see* Topographic influences
Oxic:
   ecosystems, 133
   soils, 139–145
Oxygen:
   budget, 21, 92
   molecules, 109, 136
Ozone, 8, 104, 107, 109–115, 123–126, 165, 168–169

Para, 39–40, 202, 471–472, 474
Pasture, cattle, 7, 43, 47, 56, 176, 193, 197, 201–203, 244, 271, 273, 291, 470, 510–511
Peru, 54, 58, 278
Phenology, 30–31, 74–75
Phosphate, 58, 177, 178, 203, 214, 506
Photochemistry, 108–115, 126
Photorespiration, 134
Photosynthesis, 55
Planetary boundary layer, 142, 164–166, 299, 367–371
Planetary ecology, are forests vital, 21
Planetary waves, 428–431. *See also* Blocking; Jet stream
Plant diseases and pests, 200
Plant water transfer, 325–326
Pleistocene, 70–71
Pollen cores, 94, 95
Pollination, 7, 69, 75–81
Population, 5–7, 45, 50, 55, 107, 122, 149, 196–197
Precipitable water, 281–282
Precipitation:
   scavenging, 112, 127
   *See also* Rainfall
Predictability of tropical circulation, 449–451
Preservation, 9, 21, 36, 50, 60, 85, 204, 497, 507–508, 513
Pressure, sea level, 350, 411–413, 442, 448
Primary productivity, 177, 204

Radiation, net at surface, 256–260, 292, 304–305, 311, 326, 333. *See also* Longwave (thermal IR) radiation; Solar radiation

Radiative transfer in plant canopy, 314–316, 323

Rainfall (precipitation), 8–9, 20, 25, 32–33, 74, 93–98, 195–196, 220, 226, 228, 256, 278–280, 284–287, 292, 299, 345, 348, 354–355, 357, 359, 361–363, 365, 372–377, 389, 397, 399, 401, 425–426, 443–445, 464–466, 478–480

Refuges, 95

Reserves, 85, 197

Rhizosphere, 137, 182, 187

Rice fields (paddies), 107, 120–123, 126, 137, 147–148, 511

Rivers, 7–8, 21, 94, 104, 245–249, 510
  discharge, see Runoff

Roads, 40–41, 274, 486

Rondônia, 39–40, 471–473

Root exudates, 182, 187

Roots, 27, 182–183, 219
  depth, 479
  resistance, 313, 324–325

Roraima, 472

Roughness, aerodynamic, 263, 267, 297–300, 304–305

Ruminants, 119, 146, 147

Runoff, 195, 244, 245, 284–288, 292, 302, 306, 405, 468. See also Erosion

Satellite remote sensing, 39–40, 54, 165, 350, 375–376, 388, 396, 398–400, 402, 471, 474

Savanna, 72, 114, 118, 135, 143, 147, 180, 182

Savannization, 9, 85, 506–507, 510–511

Scales of change, 512

Scavenging, by precipitation, 112, 127

Scenarios for future Amazonia, 505–513

Schistosomiasis, 66

Sea breeze, 32–33, 363, 400–401

Seasonality, 9, 27, 30–31, 70, 71, 74–75, 84, 94, 96–98, 373, 389, 396, 405, 479, 482, 511

Sea surface temperature (SST), see Ocean surface temperature

Seed dispersal, 7, 69, 81–84

Sensible heat flux, 260–262, 297–301, 307, 310–312, 329–331, 477

Shifting cultivation, 193–194, 199–200, 204, 291, 470, 503

Silviculture, see Agroforestry

Soils, 8, 27, 54, 57, 104, 135, 176–181, 185–198, 215–220, 225–227, 239–243, 293, 313
  acidity, 177, 214

cation exchange capacity, 177
density, 239–242
desert, 142
enzymes, 139, 144
fauna, see Invertebrates
field capacity, 180, 214, 217–218, 220
gas fluxes from, 136–145
hydraulic conductivity, 324–326
impacts on weather, 364–367, 369–370, 454
infiltration, see Infiltration
management, 176, 186, 193, 195, 197, 205, 214, 219, 221–222, 293
model, 329
moisture, 9, 134, 140, 142, 180–181, 204, 302–303, 306, 309, 311, 313, 468, 476–477
organic matter, see Humus
porosity, 180, 190, 199, 203, 214, 219
respiration and decomposition, 133, 163
savanna, 142, 180
structure, 115, 176, 180, 204, 219
temperature, 179–180, 204, 215–219, 230–233, 309, 331
texture, 177, 215, 220, 239, 477

Solar radiation, 25–26, 95, 220, 226, 228, 229, 255–259, 275–278, 284, 292, 297–300, 308, 310–312, 314–317, 322–323, 354, 477

Soybeans, 42, 55, 201

Squall lines, 26, 32, 348–349, 401

Statistics, 482–484

Stemflow, 285

Stomata, 134
  resistance, 322–326, 332–333, 511

Storms, tropical, 352–353, 372–377

Stratosphere, 124, 125, 148–149

Streams, 286

Subsistence production, 47, 48

Sugar cane, 42, 44, 55, 511

Sulfate reduction, 137

Surface drag, see Momentum transfer

Surinam, 54, 66, 79

Sustainable land use, 46, 204–206, 221–222, 244
  lack of, 50

Tax incentives and penalties, 43

Teleconnections, see Extratropical response to tropical convection

Temperature, 20, 25, 32, 228–233, 264–266, 309–311, 331, 350, 416–417, 480–482. See also Ocean surface temperature; Soils temperature

Termites, 104, 120, 146–147, 160–161, 184–186, 190, 219, 237–238
Timber production (lumber companies), 5, 48–49, 196, 197, 205, 470
Tocantins River, hydroelectric project, 49, 64, 66, 506
Topographic influences, 32, 351, 361, 369, 370, 372, 391, 434, 459
Tourism, 508
Trace gases, 8, 107–171. *See also* Greenhouse gases
Transamazon highway, 26, 37, 59, 203
Transfer of energy, *see* Evapotranspiration; Longwave (thermal IR) radiation; Sensible heat flux; Solar radiation
Tropical Ocean Global Atmosphere (TOGA) Program, 360
Tucuruí Dam, 29, 36, 48, 49, 66–67, 506

Ultraviolet radiation, 108
United Nations University, 4

Vargem Grande, 247–248
Variability, of geopotential heights, 428–431, 435–438, 454
Várzea, 28, 70, 131
Vegetation index, 335
Venezuela, 54

Vortices, 352–353

Walker Circulation, 345, 354–359, 396, 403, 449–450, 469
Water balance or cycle, *see* Hydrological cycle
Water deficit, *see* Drought, stress in plants
Water hyacinth, 66
Water recycling, 33, 289–291, 366–367
Water vapor:
  convergence, 284, 292
  flux, 281–283, 293
  *See also* Humidity
Waves, weather, 352–353, 357, 359, 373
Weathering of rocks, 19, 21, 176, 219
Weather patterns, 347–405
Weeds, 199
Wetlands (swamps and marshes), 119, 121, 122, 135–139, 147, 161
Winds, 33, 356–358, 391–396, 413, 416, 420–424
  in forest, 263–264, 267
  *See also* Low-level jet
World Bank, 64

Zaire, 464
Zero plane displacement, 263, 267, 319–320
Zona Bragantina, 39, 474